Eduardo J. Echeverria

POPE FRANCIS

The Legacy of Vatican II

Revised and Expanded
Second Edition

lectio

Lectio Publishing, LLC
Hobe Sound, Florida, USA

www.lectiopublishing.com

Cover photo of Pope Francis provided by the Government of the Philippines under Creative Commons Attribution-Share Alike license.

The diagram in Chapter Four, courtesy of Branislav Kuljovsky, is a reproduction of the original in Branislav Kuljovsky, "The Law of Gradualness or the Gradualness of Law? A Critical Analysis of *Amoris Laetitia*," p. 57.

Design by Linda Wolf
Edited by Eric Wolf
ISBN 978-1-943901-11-1
Library of Congress Control Number: 2019941758
Published by Lectio Publishing, LLC
on 15 May 2019.
Hobe Sound, Florida 33455
www.lectiopublishing.com

It is urgent to rediscover and to set forth once more the authentic reality of the Christian faith, which is not simply a set of propositions to be accepted with intellectual assent. Rather, faith is a lived knowledge of Christ, a living remembrance of his commandments, and a truth to be lived out. Faith is a decision involving one's whole existence. Faith also possesses a moral content. It gives rise to and calls for a consistent life commitment; it entails and brings to perfection the acceptance and observance of God's commandments. (*Veritatis Splendor §88*)

I dedicate this book to the following servants of the Lord and His Church who are deeply committed to the rediscovery that St. John Paul II expressed in this passage from his 1993 landmark encyclical, *Veritatis Splendor*.

Gerhard Cardinal Müller

Robert Cardinal Sarah

Archbishop Charles J. Chaput, O.F.M. Cap.

Archbishop Carlo Maria Viganò

Endorsements

Since the beginning of his pontificate on March 13, 2013, Pope Francis has been a controversial leader of the Roman Catholic Church. From his comments about the possible salvation of atheists to his handling of the sexual scandal within the Church, Francis has both invigorated and exasperated Roman Catholics and Protestants alike. Indeed, some (many?) wonder to what extent this pope faithfully adheres to and promotes traditional Catholic theology and practice. Hence, we have need for a second edition of Eduardo Echeverria's *Pope Francis: The Legacy of Vatican II*. With deep respect for and adherence to the Church's Tradition and Magisterium, Echeverria contends that "the faith of the Church and the concomitant unity of faith and communion is endangered by the confusion generated by Pope Francis in specific teachings." This book is a must-read for those who are concerned by such endangerment.

— ***Gregg R. Allison***, *Professor of Christian Theology,*
The Southern Baptist Theological Seminary, Louisville, Ky.
Pastor, Sojourn East Community Church, Louisville, Ky.
Secretary, the Evangelical Theological Society

A responsible evaluation of the sometimes controversial statements on doctrinal matters made by Pope Francis requires deep knowledge of Catholic theology and of the pope's own thought, respect for the person and office of the Holy Father, and the intellectual honesty seriously to grapple with the difficult questions raised by some of the statements in question. Few scholars meet all of these conditions, but Eduardo Echeverria certainly does. This revised version of his important study of Pope Francis is most welcome and urgently needed.

— ***Edward Feser***, *Associate Professor of Philosophy,*
Pasadena City College, CA

Eduardo Echeverria provides a needed critical assessment of Pope Francis's pontificate to this date, one that is balanced and rooted in a lively faith and deep knowledge of the documents of Vatican II.
— ***Patrick Lee****, John N. and Jamie D. McAleer Professor of Bioethics, Franciscan University of Steubenville*

If Christianity is not a revealed religion, it is a false religion. That is why Christians must always "contend for the faith which was once for all delivered to the saints," a task at which Eduardo Echeverria excels. Here he offers a penetrating analysis of the contending interpretations of the II Vatican Council that is faithful to what has been believed always, everywhere, and by all orthodox Catholics but also employs the best of contemporary theological insight to assist the reader in understanding all that the Church believes and teaches to be revealed by God.
— ***Fr. Jay Scott Newman****, President, Center for Evangelical Catholicism, Pastor, St Mary's Catholic Church, Greenville, SC*

Echeverria takes on the hard task of offering a 'filial correction' of Pope Francis' approach to the immutability of Church dogma, yet he does it in a spirit of faithfulness and with a hermeneutics of charity. His arguments are saturated with the wisdom of tradition, deeply set in scripture, and enriched by ecumenical receptivity.
— ***Dr. Adonis Vidu****, Professor of Theology, Gordon-Conwell Theological Seminary, South Hamilton, MA*

More than five years after his election, the person and the pontificate of Pope Francis remains for many an enigma. What is one to make of his many varied writings, addresses, and the like, on a vast array of topics? Answering this question requires that one be extremely well-read in the ever-growing body of writings and commentaries on Pope Francis. But it also requires a vast and penetrating knowledge of the history of Christian doctrine, philosophical and theological acuity, serene objectivity, and intellectual honesty. The reader will find all of this in Eduardo Echeverria's *Pope Francis, The Legacy of Vatican II*. As he takes the reader through the most crucial topics of this pontificate, such as the permanence and meaning of truth, mercy and justice, marriage, ecumenism, and interreligious dialogue, Echeverria takes up the Christian tradition in a Catholic and ecumenical perspective. He discusses, in a bold but compelling and fact-based manner, Pope Francis's contribution to the current doctrinal confusion regarding the claims of the Catholic faith. By offering such a clear analysis of the philosophical and theological foundations of the current pontificate, Echeverria has done an immense service for the Church and the Christian faith, a service which few theologians are able to do. The book should serve as the "state of the question" for this most important matter confronting any Christian community.

—***Jörgen Vijgen***, *Tilburg School of Catholic Theology, Tilburg University (Netherlands)*

For the last fifty years, the interpretation of the Second Vatican Council has been at the center of Catholic intellectual life. In recent years, the enigmatic papacy of Pope Francis has been the object of similar hermeneutical debates. In this book, Eduardo Echeverria provides important keys for understanding the pontificate of Francis and its relationship to the legacy of Vatican II. Echeverria penetratingly unearths the philosophical presuppositions of the Pope's thought. In this substantially revised second edition, he convincingly argues that the Council's legacy is essentially contested in Francis's papacy.

— ***Dr. Mats Wahlberg***, *Associate Professor of Systematic Theology, Department of Historical, Philosophical and Religious Studies, Umeå University*

ENDORSEMENTS OF THE FIRST EDITION

Eduardo Echeverria, one of the liveliest and most insightful thinkers practicing the ancient craft of theology in the United States today, sheds new light on the Catholic Church and Pope Francis at this challenging moment in history.

—***George Weigel***, *Distinguished Senior Fellow, Ethics and Public Policy Center*

This greatly needed book frankly admits that at times the man Jorge Mario Bergoglio, who is now Pope Francis, shoots from the hip, expressing himself in ways which discourage faithful Catholics even while attempting to encourage them. I hope the Pope is listening, because he does not seem to recognize that he has this problem. Yet he could not have had a more careful, honest, or sympathetic expositor than Eduardo Echeverria, whose appreciative discussion deepens, strengthens, and enlarges our understanding not only of Pope Francis, but of the papal magisterium as a whole and the manner in which it develops. The author demonstrates beyond a shadow of a doubt that contrary to the fears of some critics and the hopes of some admirers, the Pope is not trying to "change Catholic doctrine," but to find new ways to explain it to the world. Profoundly committed to the deposit of faith that he is charged to uphold, he is in continuity with his recent predecessors and the Second Vatican Council, zealous to promote the New Evangelism, and alive to the reality of spiritual warfare. A special strength of the book is the respect with which it treats Protestants, even while clear about the difficulties and delicacies of bridge-building.

—***J. Budziszewski,*** *University of Texas, author of "Commentary on Thomas Aquinas's Treatise on Law"*

This is a very timely and much-needed book. Informed by a careful study of the Pope's speeches and writings, Professor Echeverria presents a Francis who no doubt differs in many ways from his two remarkable predecessors, but nonetheless fully shares their mission. Like John Paul II and Benedict XVI, he hears the call of the Second Vatican Council to offer the Catholic faith, whole and entire, to a needy but often hostile world. Whatever their view of Pope Francis, readers of this book will learn much about him that they will want to know.

—***Bruce D. Marshall,*** *Lehman Professor of Christian Doctrine, Perkins School of Theology, Southern Methodist University*

Both Catholics and Protestants are asking what direction Pope Francis's papacy will go, and what it means for Catholicism's working out of Vatican II. Is the Church moving away from the directions in which the last two popes have steered it? Is Francis pointing toward a different interpretation of the Council? There are few theologians better equipped to answer these pressing questions. Professor Echeverria is a master of the Council documents, their recent interpreters, and the last three popes. He is also impressively informed by important Protestant theologians. This is a must-read for those wanting to learn about the future of Christianity.

—***Gerald R. McDermott,*** *Jordan-Trexler Professor of Religion, Roanoke College*

This important study is a gift to so many who have been puzzled by the diverse assessments--often driven by selective citations and ideologically biased depictions--of Pope Francis's leadership. Eduardo Echeverria carefully explores the complex record of what Francis has actually said and done thus far, in the context of a concise narrative of post-Vatican II developments. Echeverria's concluding account of the Pope's commitment to "spiritual warfare" offers profound counsel for all of us who want to contend for the faith without resorting to partisan engagement in "culture wars."

—***Richard J. Mouw, PhD,*** *President Emeritus, Professor of Faith and Public Life, Fuller Theological Seminary*

CONTENTS

Endorsements v

Foreword to Second Edition xv

Foreword to First Edition xix

Acknowledgement 1

Preface 3

Abbreviations 15

1

A Contested Lérinian Legacy 17
- The Legacy of the Second Vatican Council 17
- The Lérinian Legacy of Vatican II 21
- The *Nouvelle Théologie* and Modernism 26
- Is Faith in Propositions or in God? 33
- Absolute Truth? 40
- A Theologico-Pastoral Epistemology 44
- Language, Truth, and Reality 46
- Pastoral Oriented Doctrine 48
- Realist View of Truth 54
- Lérinian Interpretations 56
- The Nature of Revelation 57
- Authentication of Truth 58

2

Mercy and Justice Meet at the Cross 69
- Liberal Christianity 70
- What is Mercy? 71
- Divine Acceptance versus Divine Redemption 78
- Moralistic Therapeutic Deism 80
- God's Two Feet 83
- Jesus' Disfigurement 84

Justice and Mercy as Aspects of God's Love. 84
Once Again, Mercy and Justice. 88
The Merciful Father and Prodigal Son 92
Justice and Mercy Meet at the Cross 93
We Will Be Judged by Our Love 93
Inclusion, Yes; Relativism, No. 97

3

Christ is the Fulfillment of the Law 109
Legalism and Antinomianism. 111
What is the Clash between Jesus and the Pharisees?. . . 119
Is Righteousness Increasing Rigor in Obeying the Law? 129
Legalism, Again 132
What is the Chief Enemy of the Christian Life?. 135
Christ is the Fulfillment of the Law 138
The Central Commandment of Love 139
Freedom in Christ. 140
Ethical Maximalism 146

4

The Controverted Chapter 8 of 'Amoris Laetitia' 155
Marriage in the Light of Creation, Fall, and Redemption 158
Nature and Grace 160
Sin and Grace 166
The Two-in-One-Flesh *Bodily* Unity 167
Sacramental Union Presupposes Sexual Differentiation 173
Various Proposals Swirling Around about *Amoris Laetitia* 174
The Logic of Pastoral Reasoning and Discernment 176
Mercy and Truth 180
Objective and Subjective Morality 182
Culpability for Rejecting Moral Rules. 185
The Law of Gradualness vs the Gradualness of the Law 189
Judgments of Conscience in Conflict with Moral Law . . 191
Aquinas, Natural Law, and Concrete Action 193
Appendix. 199

5

An Integral Hermeneutics of Life 217
Believing in Joy 217
What is Man? 218
Christianity is Life-Affirming 219
The Key to Joy 221
Christian Joy—A Gift of the Holy Spirit 222
Mission and Vocation 223
The Hierarchy of Truths 224
A More Balanced Perspective 228
Once Again, Hierarchy of Truths 230
Evangelium Vitae 232
The Moral Life in Christ 237

6

The One Church, the Many Churches 245
Receptive Ecumenism 247
Ecumenical Dialogue 249
Credo in unam ecclesiam 252
Unicity and Inner Unity of the Church 257
Kuyperian Ecclesiastical Epistemology:
Truth and Its Formulations 261
Vatican II and Lérinian Hermeneutics 265
"Subsistit in": The Church as *concretum universale* 270
Proselytism, Evangelization, "Ecumenism of Return" . . 273
Unity, Catholicity, and Fullness 277
Hierarchy of Truths, Encore 280

7

The Dialogue of Religions
and the Question of Truth 299
Leaving Behind Absolutism and Relativism? 300
The Full Meaning of the Assisi Meeting 309
A Genuinely Dialogical but Also Critical Encounter . . . 314
Once Again, Beyond Absolutism and Relativism—
This Time, Schillebeeckx 321
The Necessity of Interreligious Apologetics 326

8

The Crisis of the Church 341
Ressourcement and *Aggiornamento* 343
History, Unchanging Truth, and Vatican II. 346
Christian Anthropology and Sexual Ethics 352
How Do We Love Responsibly? 362
Four Foundational Presuppositions to Sexual Ethics . . . 367
Returning to the Love-Ethic 370
The Learning Church and the Teaching Church 376

Works Cited 393

Index 429

Foreword to Second Edition

Scholars rarely revisit previous publications in such a way that they not only adjust their evaluation of their subject but reverse it. Eduardo Echeverria is doing that in his revised and expanded version of Pope Francis, The Legacy of Vatican II.

The arrival of Pope Francis on the world stage with his freewheeling style, one not wedded to the scholarly approach characteristic of most of his predecessors and especially his immediate predecessors, was a challenge for those who are accustomed to engaging systematic scholarly thought. Moreover, that freewheeling style from the start caused uneasiness among those who believe that the Church is incapable of changing settled teaching in any substantial way. Faithful Catholic thinkers, such as Echeverria, rightly act upon the principle that what a pope says must by default be considered to be in continuity with the tradition. In the first edition, Echeverria maintained that Pope Francis' thought could be interpreted to be in continuity with the tradition. But in subsequent years, Francis has spoken in a way that has caused Echeverria to reassess his initial evaluation and to be more wary of Francis' "theological pluralism." In this text, Echeverria attempts to answer this question: "How does Francis account for legitimate theological pluralism and authentic diversity within a fundamental permanence of meaning and truth?"

For much of his scholarly career, Echeverria has been interested in the status of propositional truth—truth stated as propositions—as opposed to such other possibilities of truth as a person or event, concept, experience, or feeling. To many thinkers, propositional truth seems incapable of capturing the fullness and richness of truth as well as being too confined to language bound to a certain time, culture or philosophical system. Echeverria has defended the legitimacy of propositional truth while at the same time, he is fully open to the possibility that because of various reasons, such as deeper understanding of truth, or the need to use more accessible language, that the way in which truths are expressed may develop. Following the practice of Saint Vincent of Lérins, a practice affirmed by Vatican I and reaffirmed by Vatican II, he insists that, nonetheless, the meaning and truth of the original proposition remains even when its formulation changes as long as that formulation mediates the same meaning and judgment of truth.

Pope Francis also claims Lérins' approach as legitimizing his own, and in the first edition of his book Echeverria agreed. But Echeverria contests that in this second edition. He has come to think, "[Francis] has a difficult time affirming dogma's permanence given his dismissal of abstract truth, reluctance to speak of absolute truth, and his theologico-pastoral epistemology with its attending principle that "realities are greater than ideas." This "flexibility" in respect to truth combined with Francis' focus on pastoral approaches to issues has resulted in Echeverria's view that "because of the lack of clarity, ambiguity of [Francis'] words and actions, one-sidedness in formulating issues, and a tendency for demeaning Christian doctrine and the moral law… a pervasive presence of doctrinal confusion exists in the Church."

Echeverria's revised assessment is, clearly, a very serious criticism of the Holy Father, a criticism that is clearly in tension with Echeverria's proper filial piety towards the Holy Father. He adamantly and rightly denies that his critique in any way qualifies him as a dissenter and indeed, in his preface, makes the case that he is not so much challenging Pope Francis' thought but showing how it is difficult to reconcile some of his positions with the tradition of the Church (I would have liked to have seen the pope's teaching on capital punishment included among those issues). Echeverria provides a defense of his critical approach to Pope Francis' thought by reviewing what obligations Catholics have to believe various kinds of Church teaching. There is more liberty for a Catholic to register concern about what a Holy Father teaches than may be customarily thought, especially for a learned theologian.

Echeverria's shift of evaluation, shared by many, was provoked largely by chapter 8 of Amoris Laetitia, wherein the Holy Father suggests that those who have divorced and remarried without benefit of annulment may worthily receive the Eucharist, a claim that seems to conflict with the understanding that marriage is indissoluble. This suggestion is just one example of proposals by Francis that reflect an uncomfortableness with the understanding that there are immutable truths to which we must conform our behavior no matter how difficult the conformity is.

Throughout the book, Echeverria shows that, with some regularity, Francis makes statements that cannot easily be reconciled with each other—if one is true, it is hard to determine how the other could be true—for instance, Francis' rejection of both absolutism and relativism. The confusion that this lack of clarity—indeed, this inconsistency—creates can be unsettling, to say the least. Moreover, it also has some disturbing implications and consequences. Echeverria's new chapter 7—one of several new chapters in this second edition—on the dialogue of religions and the question of truth shows that Francis' desire for Christian unity and even unity with other religions has led him to make statements that call into question the universality of the truth of Christianity. In this chapter, as elsewhere, Echeverria compares and contrasts Francis' views with those of his immediate predecessors and of other scholars to highlight how his views break with previous understandings of the purpose and methods of ecumenism and interreligious dialogue. A useful pedagogical tool that Echeverria employs in chapter 7 is a list of various approaches to interreligious dialogue that permits him to identify what approach Francis uses, which unfortunately does not yield a sharp description of Francis' approach since it swings between contradictory principles.

The concluding chapter draws together many of the insights developed in previous chapters to explain why the worldwide Church seems incapable of explaining the causes of the current sexual abuse crisis and of finding any suitable response to the crisis itself. Echeverria shows that doctrinal confusion is very much behind this incapacity and that until we return to a proper understanding of the status of Church teaching and of the role of the sensus fidelium in shaping Church teaching, we will continue to wallow in confusion and indeed, continue to be ineffective if not immobilized in dealing with one of the greatest crises the Church has ever faced.

In this book, Echeverria performs a tremendous service for Catholics who have struggled hard to maintain their implicit, default trust in the wisdom of our Holy Father. Echeverria shows us the deep reasons why our increasing lack of confidence in the approach of Francis has more justification than any of us would like.

Prof Janet E. Smith
Father Michael J. McGivney Chair of Life Ethics
Sacred Heart Major Seminary, Detroit, MI

Foreword to First Edition

Of the making of books there is no end, as was already evident millennia ago and is even more so today. Given the sheer tidal wave of texts of all sorts amid which we live today, most current books need to offer some justification—if not an outright apology—for why they were written. This very valuable volume is not one of them. Shortly after the worldwide enthusiasm that met the election of Jorge Mario Bergoglio to the papacy, with the name Pope Francis, there followed what can only be called an equally global confusion about various things that he has said and done. Non-Catholics and even many Catholics believe he is a pope of "rupture," one about to jettison the demanding Catholic moral tradition, especially on sexual matters. Others see him as a figure of mercy and compassion who is perhaps artless, at times, in his spontaneous, off-the-cuff remarks, but deeply committed to the traditional doctrines. Papa Bergoglio himself has expressed surprise on several occasions that people are confused by what he's said, done, and written—pointing to what he thinks is a clear record. But people are confused.

So Professor Echeverria's careful study of the pope's record and his insights into how this first pontiff from the Americas comes out of and is guiding the post-Vatican II Church could not be more welcome. Other important books for the understanding of this singular pope have already appeared, most notably Austen Ivereigh's *The Great Reformer*, whose primary value lies in the way it situates Jorge Mario Bergoglio in his Argentinian context—one little known to most people outside of that country—and in recent Latin American history more generally. Ivereigh touches on how those experiences shaped the future pope's *theological* understanding of the Church and the world: Bergoglio steered a course between what he regarded as a stiff traditionalism and a utopian liberation theology, both far distant from the true aspirations of the poor and the folk Catholicism of his preferred touchstone: the *pueblo fiel*.

No previous study, however, has gone very much into situating Pope Francis in the larger sweep of recent Catholic history and especially the defining event of the past half century in the Church: the Second Vatican Council. Professor Echeverria not only notes Jorge Mario Bergoglio's personal relationship to the Council, he has developed a sophisticated *theological* reading of the pope's life and thought.

There has been a fair amount of general acknowledgement that Francis, as the first pope to have been ordained (in 1969) after the Council, needs to be understood from a different perspective than his immediate predecessors. But there are many ways of understanding the Council and its effects, and Professor Echeverria wisely spends a good bit of time at the outset of this book carefully parsing out how the Council ought to be regarded. That establishes a clear baseline from which everything else may be examined.

The Church cannot expect much accurate understanding from the world—or, sadly, even from many uninformed Catholics these days. But the cultural meme that Francis somehow has exploded earlier notions like spiritual combat and moral teaching in favor of compromise and dialogue with the world seriously distorts what he is all about. He is quite clear that much of the world is a kind of "anti-Kingdom" that denies God, Jesus, the Word, and its own best interest. A real Christian must be a discerner of spirits, to use the traditional term (which Francis does). And through careful reading of the pope's earlier writings, Professor Echeverria has even discovered in them correctives to misimpressions such as his most notorious—and most misunderstood—remark: "Who am I to judge?"

> My attitude toward the world should be fundamentally the same as toward my own sins, toward the disordered and sinful roots in myself: keen awareness and aversion! From this attitude alone springs the desire for conversion. [This], in turn, over time, forges in us the faculty that is so solidly Christian: *the capacity to judge.* The "yes, yes . . . no, no" [Matt 5:37] that Jesus teaches us implies a spiritual maturity that rescues us from the superficiality of the foolish heart. A Christian needs to know what can be accepted and what must be condemned [1 Thess 5:21-22]. We cannot sit down and "dialogue" with the enemy of our salvation: we need to meet him head on, ready to combat his every intention. [Emphasis added.]

That "spiritual maturity" is a far cry from the cultural shibboleths that have been foisted on to casual remarks by the pope in informal press conferences.

In a similar vein, while Pope Francis, in line with his Argentine experience with the poor and marginalized, has called for the Church to go out and meet people in the "peripheries"—and has demonstrated a generous manner himself in dealing with those outside the Faith—this should not at all be understood to mean that the Church should abandon its fidelity to truth and its historic development of doctrine in favor of some democratic outreach or indiscriminate inclusiveness. The *pueblo fiel* that Jorge Bergoglio opposed to the Marxist-inspired liberationist currents as well as the legalistic stance of some in the Church has to be understood by paying attention to both words: both "people" and "faithful." Again, Professor

Echeverria has discovered a key text: "of course, we must be very careful not to think that this *infallibilitas* of all the faithful I am talking about in the light of Vatican II is a form of populism. No; it is the experience of 'holy mother the hierarchical church,' as St. Ignatius called it, the church as the people of God, pastors and people together."

A whole world remains to be discovered in texts such as these and Professor Echeverria is owed a debt of gratitude for having already brought a good deal of it to light. It's only when we have these fundamental things clear that we can hope to understand the theory and practice of the Bergoglio papacy, in real terms, rather than those concocted by the media. The pope seems to believe that his track record is already clear and that by acquainting ourselves with it we will appreciate his ongoing efforts.

So this book is essential. Without what it offers us, we might miss the firmness along with the tenderness in a text like the pope's closing remarks after the highly controverted 2013 Synod on the Family:

> [T]his is the Church, the vineyard of the Lord, the fertile Mother and the caring Teacher, who is not afraid to roll up her sleeves to pour oil and wine on people's wound; who doesn't see humanity as a house of glass to judge or categorize people. This is the Church, One, Holy, Catholic, Apostolic and composed of sinners, needful of God's mercy. This is the Church, the true bride of Christ, who seeks to be faithful to her spouse and to her doctrine. It is the Church that is not afraid to eat and drink with prostitutes and publicans. The Church that has the doors wide open to receive the needy, the penitent, and not only the just or those who believe they are perfect! The Church that is not ashamed of the fallen brother and pretends not to see him, but on the contrary feels involved and almost obliged to lift him up and to encourage him to take up the journey again and accompany him toward a definitive encounter with her Spouse, in the heavenly Jerusalem.

Dr. Robert Royal
Washington, DC
March 17, 2015

Acknowledgement

As always, I am immensely grateful for the ongoing support of the administrators and staff of Sacred Heart Major Seminary, Detroit, Michigan, and for my many friends and colleagues, especially for their deep commitment to the Catholic faith and the teachings of the Church. To them all who provide me with a sanctuary, indeed, a home for teaching and writing, I owe a debt of gratitude. I am grateful to the following colleagues who commented on chapters of this book: Thomas Berg, Philip Blosser, Thomas Guarino, Robert Imbelli, Daniel Keating, Richard Spinello, Daniel Trapp, Thomas Weinandy, and Marsha Williamson. I am also grateful to the endorsers of my book: Gregg Allison, Edward Feser, Patrick Lee, Fr. Jay Scott Newman, Adonis Vidu, Jörgen Vijgen, Mats Wahlberg, and George Weigel. I give a special word of thanks to Janet Smith for writing the Foreword. I dedicate this book to all my colleagues at Sacred Heart Major Seminary for their deep commitment to carrying out the legacy of the Second Vatican Council in their teaching and scholarship, indeed in their lives. I also want to thank Fr. Thomas Guarino of Seton Hall University for his ongoing spiritual and intellectual support throughout the years. I wish finally to thank Eric and Linda Wolf of Lectio Publishing for their support in publishing a second edition of my 2015 book and for their work in preparing the manuscript for publication.

> May God grant that I speak with judgment and have thoughts worthy of what I have received, for he is the guide even of wisdom and the corrector of the wise. For both we and our words are in his hand, with all our understanding, too (Wis 7:15-16).

Preface

> Peter has no need of our lies or flattery. Those who blindly and indiscriminately defend every decision of the Supreme Pontiff are the very ones who do most to undermine the authority of the Holy See—they destroy instead of strengthening its foundations.[1] –Fr. Melchior Cano OP[2]

This second edition of my 2015 book, *Pope Francis, The Legacy of Vatican II*, is a revised and expanded version of the first edition.[3] Almost four years have elapsed since the first edition was published. Since then much has been written by Pope Francis and about him that I examine in this second edition. This edition is necessary because in that time the Church has moved through a period of uncertainty about the direction to which Pope Francis would take her to a deep crisis of doctrinal, moral, and ecclesial proportions. Like the first edition, it is a study not only in the theological thought of Pope Francis on the same issues, particularly with respect to the legacy of Vatican II, but also one that addresses those issues systematically within the normative tradition of confessional Catholicism, the documents of Vatican II, and the thought of John Paul II and Benedict XVI.

This study is also an ecumenical work, indeed, a work in receptive ecumenism, and hence I listen attentively to the writings of fellow Christian theologians from other traditions of reflection and argument. Receptive Ecumenism means, "Dialogue is not simply an exchange of ideas. In some way it is always an 'exchange of gifts.'... Dialogue does not extend exclusively to matters of doctrine but engages the whole person; it is also a dialogue of love" (UUS §§28, 47).[4]

This new edition is still especially interested in understanding the legacy of Vatican II, and, in particular, Francis' stance toward that legacy and its effects in his theology of ecumenism, the dialogue of religions, and others. I have now corrected my earlier interpretation of that stance *per se* because it has become clearer to me, which I will argue particularly in Chapter 1, that the legacy of Vatican II is essentially contested in Francis' papacy. He proposes a hermeneutics of creative retrieval and renewal of the faith in order to move faithfully forward in the contemporary context. In Francis's own words,

> The Church is herself a missionary disciple; she needs to grow in her interpretation of the revealed word and in her understanding of truth. It is the task of exegetes and theologians to help 'the judgments of the Church to mature' [DV §12]. The other sciences also help to accomplish this, each in its own way. ... Different currents of thought in philosophy, theology, and pastoral practice, if open to being reconciled by the Spirit in respect and love, can enable the Church to grow, since of all of them help to express more clearly the immense riches of God's word. For those who long for a monolithic body of doctrine guarded by all and leaving no room for nuance, this might appear as undesirable and leading to confusion. But in fact such variety serves to bring out and develop difference facets of the inexhaustible riches of the Gospel. (EG §40)

However, this hermeneutics is, as Francis understands it, unclear. The question is whether dogmas themselves require change as dogmas, and not just in their formulations and expressions, in order to mediate more deeply the core of the Christian kerygma, the substance of the deposit of the faith, the "eternal Gospel" that "will always be the same: the God who revealed his immense love in the crucified and risen Christ" (EG §11). This approach raises the question regarding the truth-status of dogmatic formulations, such as Nicaea, Trent, Chalcedon, Vatican I and II, and so forth. In other words, what is the relationship between the dogmas that mediate God's actual revelation? Does Francis separate "doctrine" from the "cognitive and propositional content" of revelation? Francis' answer is a pragmatic one. "We should not think, however, that the Gospel message must always be communicated by fixed formulations learned by heart or by specific words which express an absolutely invariable content. This communication takes place in so many different ways that it would be impossible to describe or catalogue them all, and God's people, with all their many gestures and signs, are its collective subject" (EG §129). But the question here is not whether there are in practice many ways to communicate the Gospel. Rather, the question is whether there are permanent dogmatic truths that the Church regards as "first-level doctrines" such that the truth-status of these formulations of revealed biblical truth is such that that the whole Church must consider them authoritative?[5] Alternatively, do new doctrinal formulations mediate the universality and material identity—a dogmatic conceptual hard core (to borrow a phrase from Oliver Crisp[6]—of the truths of Christian dogmas in and of themselves, such as that of the Trinity, Incarnation, and Atonement, according to the same meaning and same judgment (*eodem sensu eademque sententia*)? If the latter, the new linguistic formulation or expression can vary, as long as they mediate the same meaning and same judgment of truth.

My thesis is that Vatican II's legacy is Lérinian in inspiration precisely on the question reconciling the historicity of human thought, in particular, the historically conditioned formulations of dogma, with their possible correction, modification, and complementation, with the permanence of its meaning and truth.[7] This inspiration is found in John XXIII's opening address to Vatican II, *Gaudet Mater Ecclesia*: "The deposit or the truths of faith, contained in our sacred teaching, are one thing, while the mode in which they are enunciated, keeping the same meaning and the same judgment [*'eodem sensu eademque sententia'*], is another thing." Briefly here, the pope's statement raised the question of the continuity or material identity of Christian truth over the course of time. The subordinate clause in this passage is part of a larger passage from Vatican I, *Dei Filius* (Denzinger §3020), and this passage is itself from the *Commonitorium primum* 23.3 of Vincent of Lérins (died c. 450), a Gaelic monk and chief theologian of the Abbey of Lérins:[8] "Therefore, let there be growth and abundant progress in understanding, knowledge, and wisdom, in each and all, in individuals and in the whole Church, at all times and in the progress of ages, but only with the proper limits, i.e., *within the same dogma, the same meaning, the same judgment*" (*in eodem scilicet dogmate, eodem sensu eademque sententia*). In my view, because of the connection between meaning and truth such that what is meant is judged to be true to reality, the most fitting translation is "according to the same meaning and the same judgment."[9]

Significantly, normative Catholicism has been Lérinian on this very point since Vatican I, through Vatican II and post-conciliar interpretations of dogmas/doctrine—and hence anti-historicist. Vincent already saw this clearly in the early fifth century—dogmas can develop, but cannot change their fundamental meaning, i.e., the meaning and truth-content embedded in the creeds themselves. Bernard Lonergan, S.J., wrote clearly and decisively about this in his magisterial work, *The Way to Nicaea*. In short, the Lérinian legacy of Vatican II is that of commensurable pluralism—allowing for legitimate pluralism and authentic diversity within a fundamental unity of truth.[10] Commensurable pluralism is, arguably, presupposed, even if not fully worked out, in post-conciliar interpretations of dogma/doctrine. Commensurable pluralism can (a) account for the need for new dogmatic formulations; (b) explain why propositions of dogmas/doctrines are unchangeable, irreformable, or definitive; and (c) justify the distinction between content/context, form/content, propositions and sentences, message and the medium.

How does Francis account for legitimate theological pluralism and authentic diversity within a fundamental permanence of meaning and truth? Francis, it appears, chooses one of two very different answers, answers which depend on how one understands the Lérinian legacy of Pope John XXIII. One answer is that of commensurable pluralism: the hermeneutics of renewal operates only "the proper limits, i.e., *within the same dogma, the same meaning, the same judgment*" (*in eodem scilicet dogmate, eodem sensu eademque sententia*). Indeed, this is the principle governing St. Vincent of Lérins' claim in his *Commonitorium Primum* 23: "*ut annis scilicet consolidetur, dilatetur tempore, sublimetur aetate* [*consolidated with years, expanded with time, grow loftier with age*]." However, it is precisely these limits that Francis overlooks in his frequent citation of this statement of Vincent. Does that mean that he does not affirm the permanence of meaning and truth of dogmas? In the first edition of this book, I thought he did, but I now see more clearly that he has a difficult time affirming dogma's permanence given his dismissal of abstract truth—that is, propositional truth—his reluctance to speak of absolute truth, and his theologico-pastoral epistemology with its attending principle that realities are greater than ideas. The second answer to this question is the approach that is called the "pastorality of doctrine,"[11] which arguably bears a tenuous link to the Lérinian legacy, and that promotes a perpetual hermeneutics, an ongoing recontextualization and reinterpretation of the substance of the faith. The "pastorality of doctrine" principle is historicist in character. I have now come to see that Pope Francis' hermeneutics of renewal bears some affinity to the pastorality principle. I will examine the various reasons for this claim in the revised Chapter 1.

Now, Chapters 2 (mercy, justice, and the cross), 3 (the Gospel and the law), 5 (an integral hermeneutics of life), and 6 (ecumenism) have been revised to a greater or lesser degree. Chapter 7 deals with the dialogue of religions and the question of truth. In all these revisions, where I formerly raised questions and gently criticized Francis, always giving him the benefit of the doubt in light of the Ignatian principle of charity,[12] I have now come to accept that Francis has contributed to the current crisis in the Church—doctrinal, moral, and ecclesial—due to the lack of clarity, ambiguity of his words and actions, one-sidedness in formulating issues, and a tendency for demeaning Christian doctrine and the moral law. There is a pervasive presence of doctrinal confusion and uncertainty in the Church and this is due in no small measure to the push for synodality—a listening and dialogical Church—as an end in itself rather than as a consultative instrument in the service of the Church's life.[13] This runs the risk of turning the Church's whole life into a series of discussions about the content of Christianity and of ways of realizing it. Intentionally or not, this is the way that some have understood Francis' push for a synodal Church, and Francis has not intervened to stop that push. Furthermore, I show that Francis' dismissal of abstract truth, his reluctance to speak of absolute truth, and his theologico-pastoral epistemology with its attendant principle that realities are greater than ideas, has also contributed to this confusion. More below on the justification of filial correction of a Pope.

While Chapter 5 is still on *Evangelii Gaudium*, I have brought into clearer focus the chapter from the first edition by dealing with the relationship between Christian anthropology, life in Christ, and Christian morality. This chapter required fewer revisions since the first edition. There are two new chapters. Chapter 4 is on *Amoris Laetitia* and the controverted nature of its Chapter 8, particularly the moral logic of pastoral reasoning and discernment and its doctrinal implications. Chapter 6 is a substantially revised chapter on ecumenism and the question regarding ecclesial unity and diversity within the one Church, the Catholic Church. Chapter 7 is on the dialogue of religions, truth, and evangelization. Like his predecessors, John Paul II and Benedict XVI, dialogue is an essential dimension of interreligious relationships, but unlike them, the question of truth and evangelization is muted, left in the shadows, not to say ignored.

I conclude, in a final Chapter 8, with an account of the current crisis in the Church. My thesis is that this crisis is doctrinal, moral, and ecclesial—in particular, the epistemological significance of the *sensus fidei fidelium* in the life of the Church. Furthermore, I have dropped two chapters from the first edition. The chapter that dealt with spiritual warfare and the evangelization of culture was dropped since it seemed less relevant to understanding the Francis papacy than the chapters I added. The portions of the chapter that outlined the temptations that Francis warned us to resist have been integrated into Chapter 1 of the second edition. I conclude this second edition with an outline of the task of renewal and reform that is necessary to work towards resolving the crisis that is doctrinal, moral, and ecclesial.

Some Catholics may find what amounts to a filial public correction of the theological reflections of Pope Francis beyond the boundary of what is permissible for a faithful Catholic.[14] They may even refer to me as a dissenter.[15] The latter reference pertains to opposition to definitive teaching that is infallible and hence irreformable, deserving of acceptance either on divine faith or firmly accepted and held (*sententia definitive tenenda*). I categorically deny my opposition to any such teaching. Even with respect to non-definitive teaching, however, I generally respond to the call to accept that teaching with "a religious submission of will and mind" (LG §25; CCC §892). Still, there is a distinction to be made here since expressing difficulties with, and raising critical questions of, magisterial teaching is not the same as the act of dissenting. In his apostolic exhortation *Paterna cum benevolentia*, Paul VI distinguishes "public opposition to the Magisterium of the Church, also called 'dissent'... from the situation of personal difficulties." In the document *Donum Veritatis*, the CDF concurs with Paul VI, making it clear that with respect to situations of that sort, "It can happen, however, that a theologian may [with respect to matters *per se* not irreformable], according to the case, raise questions regarding the timeliness, the form, or even the contents of magisterial interventions... When it comes to the question of interventions in the prudential order, it could happen that some Magisterial documents might not be free from all deficiencies. Bishops and their advisors have not always taken into immediate consideration every aspect or the entire complexity of a question" (DV §24).

Of course, I heartily agree that my primary stance towards the ordinary exercise of the Church's magisterium regarding doctrine authoritatively but non-definitively taught must be to accept it because, as the CDF states in *Donum Veritatis*, "[I]t would be contrary to the truth, if, proceeding from some particular cases, one were to conclude that the Church's Magisterium can be habitually mistaken in its prudential judgments, or that it does not enjoy divine assistance in the integral exercise of its mission." However, since non-definitive teaching is neither infallible nor irreformable, there remains a possibility that it might be proved wrong, that the supporting arguments of this teaching are flawed. In particular, one may show that the teaching's pastoral application is inconsistent, a rupture, with the Church's constant and universal practice, and hence not in continuity with the Church, even as a matter of development. Throughout this study what I am seeking is clarity regarding the continuity of the pope's teaching not only in *Amoris Laetitia*, but also regarding other teachings (e.g., Gospel, law, morality, and dialogue of religions) with the rest of tradition. Francis himself stipulated this hermeneutical principle as a prerequisite for properly understanding *Amoris Laetitia*, but to be consistent it applies to all his teaching. It should be "treated with a hermeneutic of the Church, always in continuity (without ruptures), yet always maturing."[16]

However, even with respect to non-definitive teaching, the CDF states, "Even if the doctrine of the faith is not in question, the theologian will not present his own opinions or divergent hypotheses as though they were non-arguable conclusions. Respect for the truth as well as for the People of God requires this discretion [cf. Rom 14:1-15; 1 Cor 8; 10:23-33]. For the same reasons, the theologian will refrain from giving *untimely* public expression to them." (DV §27, emphasis added). This concluding sentence raises the question whether there could be timely public expression of grave concern, urging clarification, and the like? In other words, may there be "*licit* public expression of grave concerns made by theologians regarding problems in magisterial statements."[17] Regarding criticism of non-definitive magisterial teaching, Ratzinger replies in the affirmative. "We have not excluded all kinds of publication, nor have we closed him up in [silent] suffering. The Vatican insists, however, that theologians must choose the proper place to expound their ideas." He explains:

> Taken out of context, in fact, they [namely, articles 29 through 31 of *Donum Veritatis*] can give rise to the impression that the Instruction allows the theologian the sole option of submitting divergent opinions to the magisterial authorities in secret .... It is quite obvious that the Instruction is not proposing "secret" communications but dialogue which remains on an ecclesial and scientific plane and avoids distortions at the hand of the mass media.... In actuality, the point is precisely to use arguments instead of pressure as a means of persuasion.[18]

Although I cannot fully argue the case here in this Preface, I will argue briefly that my position meets the fiducial criteria—hermeneutics of trust and not suspicion vis-à-vis the papacy—established by the Church's tradition as well as the canonical directives and theological positions of faithful theologians, such as Thomas Aquinas, regarding reformable, or non-definitive, magisterial teaching. I will make it clear that my filial public corrections pertain to that teaching, particularly in Chapter 8 of Amoris Laetitia, by using charitable and reasonable arguments. Indeed, my assessments throughout are motivated by love for Christ, the Church, the faithful, and the pope.

The *Catechism of the Catholic Church* clearly expresses a conviction regarding the hermeneutics of trust—which I deeply share—in the Church's authority to teach.

> The apostles entrusted the "Sacred deposit" of the faith (the depositum fidei) [[19]], contained in Sacred Scripture and Tradition, to the whole of the Church. "By adhering to [this heritage] the entire holy people, united to its pastors, remains always faithful to the teaching of the apostles, to the brotherhood, to the breaking of bread and the prayers. So, in maintaining, practicing and professing the faith that has been handed on, there should be a remarkable harmony between the bishops and the faithful." ... Mindful of Christ's words to his apostles: "He who hears you, hears me" [Lk 10:16; cf. LG 20]. The faithful receive with docility the teachings and directives that their pastors give them in different forms. ... By this appreciation of the faith, aroused and sustained by the Spirit of truth, the People of God, guided by the sacred teaching authority (Magisterium) ... receives ... the faith, once for all delivered to the saints ... the People unfailingly adheres to this faith, penetrates it more deeply with right judgment, and applies it more fully in daily life. (CCC §§85, 87, 93)[20]

Canonically speaking, Canon 212 §1 also expresses a hermeneutics of trust: "Conscious of their own responsibility, the Christian faithful are bound to follow with Christian obedience those things which the sacred pastors, inasmuch as they represent Christ, declare as teachers of the faith or establish as rulers of the Church." For my purpose here, the variety of theological notes regarding magisterial authority and their corresponding fiducial response to dogmas and doctrines are as follows:[21]

(1) *De fide*: dogmas of the faith. These are divinely revealed truths contained in the Word of God, written or handed down, either (a) formally defined by a pope or Council; or (b) taught by the ordinary and universal magisterium. They constitute basic truths of faith, dogmas per se, definitive teaching that must be believed by Catholics on divine faith, since they concern matters of faith. They are called primary objects of infallibility.

(2) *Fides ecclesiastica*: doctrines that are infallibly and irreformably taught to be truths; they are not revealed *per se* but they materially belong to Catholic faith. They are, in other words, inseparably connected with

revealed truths concerning matters required to support the faith; that to deny these truths entails the denial of revealed truths. These truths are called secondary objects of infallibility; they are necessarily connected with revelation by virtue of either an *historical relationship*, or a *logical connection*, expressing a stage in the development of the understanding of revelation. They are (a) formally defined by a pope or Council; or (b) taught infallibly by the ordinary and universal magisterium of the Church as a *sententia definitive tenenda*, meaning thereby that this second class of truths must be firmly accepted and held. This is why they are called the "faith of the Church." Both primary and secondary objects of infallibility are such that they are at one and the same time not only fundamentally irreversible, or irreformable, and hence can never be contradicted, but also may need to be gradually clarified over time in order to discern what truly pertains to the *depositum fidei*.[22]

(3) *Sententia fidei proxima*: doctrine authoritatively but non-definitively taught by the ordinary and universal magisterium. "When the Magisterium, not intending to act 'definitively', teaches a doctrine [1] to aid a better understanding of Revelation and make explicit its contents, or [2] to recall how some teaching is in conformity with the truths of faith, or [3] finally to guard against ideas that are incompatible with these truths, *the response called for is that of the religious submission of will and intellect*."[23] This judgment is proximate to the faith.

(4) *Sententia ad fidem pertinens*, or *theologice certa*: pertains to "theological conclusions logically deduced from a proposition of faith and taught by the magisterium, which have a high degree of certainty."

(5) *Sententia probabilis*: denotes "probable opinion, although in theological discussion there are many other levels operating: well founded, pious, and tolerated opinions (with the least authority)."[24]

The crux of the dispute regarding Chapter 8 of *Amoris Laetitia* pertains to the stance of a faithful Catholic with respect to non-definitive teachings—which above is the teaching having the theological note of *sententia fidei proxima*. My concern is one of contributing "to the clarification of doctrinal issues and render service to the truth" (DV §30).

Canonically speaking, filial concerns and corrections expressed publicly of Pope Francis are justified, not just as a right but as a duty, under certain conditions, namely, when the good of the Church is at stake. The current code of Canon Law recognizes this duty and identifies its criteria: "According to the knowledge, competence, and prestige which they possess, they have the right and *even at times the duty* to manifest to the sacred pastors their opinion *on matters which pertain to the good of the Church* and *to make their opinion known to the rest of the Christian faithful*, without prejudice to the integrity of faith and morals, *with reverence toward their pastors, and attentive to common advantage and the dignity of persons*."[25] Thus, there are four criteria that I will meet throughout my book. They are:

1. Competent, knowledgeable persons;
2. matters pertaining to the good of the Church;

3. maintaining reverence towards their pastors and especially the Holy Father; and
4. attentive to the common good and the dignity of persons.[26]

One last point, I stand with St. Thomas Aquinas, who "drawing from the rich tradition of the Church's history, specifically from St. Paul's account of rebuking St. Peter in Galatians 2 as commented upon by St. Augustine, shows quite clearly that not only is it permissible for a subordinate to correct fraternally his prelate, but that it is also necessary for him to do so publicly in certain circumstances."[27] Furthermore, St Thomas holds that a believer "can and even must resist, by virtue of the *sensus fidei*, his or her bishop if the latter preaches heterodoxy."[28] Aquinas elaborates, "In such a case, the believer does not treat himself or herself as the ultimate criterion of the truth of faith, but rather, faced with materially 'authorized' preaching which he or she finds troubling, without being able to explain exactly why, defers assent and appeals interiorly to the superior authority of the universal Church."[29] In particular, then, it may even prove necessary to correct one's superiors in the Church. However, though he must criticize, says Aquinas, he must do so not with "impudence and harshness, but with gentleness and respect." And such criticism may even be given publicly to a prelate. Aquinas argues, "It must be observed, however, that if the faith were endangered, a subject ought to rebuke his prelate even publicly. Hence, Paul, who was Peter's subject, rebuked him in public, on account of the imminent danger of scandal concerning faith, and, as the gloss of Augustine says on Gal 2:11, 'Peter gave an example to superiors, that if at any time they should happen to stray from the straight path, they should not disdain to be reproved by their subjects.'"[30]

Moreover, Aquinas says, "To correct the wrongdoer is a spiritual alms deed. But alms deeds are works of charity, as stated above (ST II-II, 32,1). Therefore fraternal correction is an act of charity." Aquinas argues that, in general, "fraternal correction" is a spiritual work of mercy, correcting the sinner, accordingly then, being an act of love. In other words, "The correction of the wrongdoer is a remedy which should be employed against a man's sin. Now a man's sin may be considered in two ways, first as being harmful to the sinner, secondly as conducing to the harm of others, by hurting or scandalizing them, or by being detrimental to the common good, the justice of which is disturbed by that man's sin."

It is my contention that the faith of the Church and the concomitant unity of faith and communion is endangered by the confusion generated by Pope Francis in specific teachings, and the general methodological and philosophical weaknesses mentioned above.[31] Yes, Francis has given us beneficial teachings on the centrality of the poor in the Christian's relationship with Christ, on the circumscribed but actual temptations of evil spirits, and also beautiful, insightful, and deeply biblical and practical teachings on marriage preparation, moral formation of children, and moral ecology. Still, he has contributed to the rise of polarization and partisan mentalities. Admittedly, this polarization has also been exacerbated by some of his critics—neo-traditionalists—who see Francis as the embodiment of everything that is wrong with Vatican II and its documents; hence, their fight with Francis is in reality a fight with Vatican II to which they attribute the source of conflicting interpretations. I do not share that view of Vatican II with neo-traditionalism. This is abundantly clear from this work before the reader, but also from my recent work.[32] Furthermore, in Francis's papacy, "The light of faith, hope, and love is not absent,"[33] of course, and I show that, too, in this work. Yet, "too often it is obscured by the ambiguity of [his] words and actions."[34] Moreover, it is not only ambiguity, but also flawed arguments, overlooking important distinctions, disdain for doctrine and the moral law, that obscures that light. That is exactly what I hope to show in the second edition of this work. I do so acting uprightly for the good of the Church, for the integrity of the papal Magisterium,[35] and the honor of Christ, Lord and Savior.

NOTES

1. Those who have a false devotion to the papacy are, in a nutshell, committed to "papalotry." Its apotheosis is expressed recently by Fr. Thomas Rosica, "Pope Francis breaks Catholic traditions whenever he wants because he is 'free from disordered attachments.' Our Church has indeed entered a new phase: with the advent of this first Jesuit pope, it is openly ruled by an individual rather than by the authority of Scripture alone or even its own dictates of tradition plus Scripture" (Rosica, "The Ignatian Qualities of the Petrine Ministry of Pope Francis").

2. "Nunc illud breviter dici potest, qui summi Pontificis omne de re quacumque iudicium temere ac sine delectu defendunt, hos sedis apostolicæ auctoritatem labefactare, non fovere; evertere, non firmare. Nam ut ea prætereamus, quæ paulo ante in hoc capite explicata sunt, quid tandem adversum hæreticos disputando ille proficiet, quem viderint non iudicio, sed affectu patrocinium auctoritatis pontificiæ suscipere, nec id agere, ut dispositionis suæ vi lucem ac veritatem eliciat, sed ut se ad alterius sensum voluntatemque convertat? Non eget Petrus mendacio nostro, nostra adulatione non eget." — *De locis theologicis*, lib. V, cap. 5. My gratitude to Chad Pecknold for the reference.

3. The first English edition was translated into Spanish, *El Papa Francisco: El Legado del Vaticano II* (Bilbao, Spain: Descleee De Brouwer, 2017).

4. See also, International Theological Commission, *Theology Today, Perspectives, Principles, and Criteria*, §49: "Ecumenical dialogue and research provides a uniquely privileged and potentially productive field for collaboration between Catholic theologians and those of other Christian traditions. *In such work, issues of faith, meaning and language are deeply pondered.* As they work to promote mutual understanding on issues that have been contentious between their traditions, perhaps for many centuries, theologians act as ambassadors for their communities in the holy task of seeking the reconciliation and unity of Christians, so that the world may believe (cf. John 17:21). That ambassadorial task requires particular adherence to the criteria outlined here on the part of Catholic participants, so that the manifold gifts that the Catholic tradition contains can truly be offered in the '*exchange of gift*' that ecumenical dialogue and collaboration more widely always in some sense is" [emphasis added].

5. I address this question at length in Chapter 2 of my recent book, *Revelation, History, and Truth, A Hermeneutics of Dogma*, 47-92.

6. I borrow this phrase from the British philosophical theologian Oliver Crisp who defends a version of essentialism in his article, "*Ad* Hector," at 138.
7. Bernard J.F. Lonergan, SJ, *Method in Theology*, 284, 324.
8. *Catholic Encyclopedia*, entry on St. Vincent of Lérins, http://www.newadvent.org/cathen/15439b.htm.
9. I follow Joseph Komonchak's translation of the official Latin text, which also happens to be the translation in Denzinger §3020.
10. I owe this phrase to Thomas Guarino.
11. This phrase was coined to my knowledge by Christoph Theobald, S.J., "The Principle of Pastorality at Vatican II." See also, Richard R. Gaillardetz, *An Unfinished Council*. I discuss their views in Chapter 1.
12. *Spiritual Exercises of St. Ignatius of Loyola*, Presupposition, "[L]et it be presupposed that every good Christian is to be more ready to save his neighbor's proposition than to condemn it. If he cannot save it, let him inquire how he means it; and if he means it badly, let him correct him with charity. If that is not enough, let him seek all the suitable means to bring him to mean it well, and save himself." http://jesuit.org/jesuits/wp-content/uploads/The-Spiritual-Exercises-.pdf.
13. See Joseph Cardinal Ratzinger, *Principles of Catholic Theology*, 374.
14. For the reflections that follow on the matter of publicly correcting the pope, I am grateful to Michael Sirilla's two articles, "On the Moral Liceity of Publicly Correcting the Pope"; "Superstition, Dissent, and Scandal? A Brief Defense of Fr. Thomas Weinandy."
15. Stephen Walford, "The Amoris Laetitia Dissenters, The Murky World of Distorting Facts, Creating False Arguments and Sowing Confusion."
16. One of three principles in Pope Francis' Preface to Stephen Walford, *Pope Francis, The Family and Divorce*, xi-xii. This second hermeneutical principle obviously involves a reference to the significant address of Pope Benedict XVI, in his now famous 2005 Christmas address to the Roman Curia, where he called the hermeneutics of Vatican II "the 'hermeneutic of reform,' of renewal in the continuity of the one subject-Church which the Lord has given to us. She is a subject which increases in time and develops, yet always remaining the same, the one subject of the journeying People of God."
17. Sirilla, "On the Moral Liceity of Publicly Correcting the Pope."
18. Cited in the 5 July 1990 issue of the USCCB publication Origins and in Ratzinger, "On the 'Instruction concerning the Ecclesial Vocation of the Theologian'" in *The Nature and Mission of Theology*, 101-20, and at 117.
19. *Dei Verbum* §10.1; see 1 Tim 6:20; 2 Tim 1:12-14.
20. See also, *Catechism of the Catholic Church* on the Church's teaching office, §§888-92.
21. See Congregation for the Doctrine of the Faith, Instruction, *Donum Veritatis*, §IV.
22. *Catechism of the Catholic Church* §88: "The Church's Magisterium exercises the authority it holds from Christ to the fullest extent when it defines dogmas, that is, when it proposes truths contained in divine Revelation or also when it proposes in a definitive way truths having a necessary connection with them." Walter Cardinal Kasper makes the same point in commenting on *Lumen Gentium* §25, "And this infallibility with which the Divine Redeemer willed His Church to be endowed in defining doctrine of faith and morals, extends as far as the deposit of Revelation extends, which must be religiously guarded and faithfully expounded" (emphasis added). Says Kasper, "The wording 'must be' is intended to leave open the possibility of presenting infallible truths which are not directly contained in revelation but which, however, are historically or logically necessarily entailed in truths of faith" (*The Catholic Church: Nature, Reality, and Mission*, 423n309).
23. *Donum Veritatis* §23; emphasis added. See *Lumen Gentium* §25.

24. D'Costa, *Vatican II*, 14–15, with some adaptation. Similarly, Ludwig Ott, *Fundamentals of Dogma*, Introduction, §8: The Theological Grades of Certainty, 9–10. Dulles, *Magisterium, Teacher and Guardian of the Faith*, 83–84. Helpful here is Joseph Ratzinger, the 1998 CDF document, "Doctrinal Commentary on the Concluding Formula of the *Professio fidei*," and Harold E. Ernst, "The Theological Notes and the Interpretation of Doctrine."

25. *CIC*, can. 212, §3; emphasis added.

26. See *Gaudium et Spes* §62, "In order that they [the laity] may fulfill their function [of developing and deepening the doctrine of the Church concerning God, man and the world], let it be recognized that all the faithful, whether clerics or laity, possess a lawful freedom of inquiry, freedom of thought and of expressing their mind with humility and fortitude in those matters on which they enjoy competence."

27. Sirilla, "On the Moral Liceity of Publicly Correcting the Pope."

28. Cited by the International Theological Commission, *Sensus Fidei in the Life of the Church*, §63n78, "Thomas Aquinas, Scriptum, III, d.25, q.2, a.1, qla 4, ad 3: '[The believer] must not give assent to a prelate who preaches against the faith.... The subordinate is not totally excused by his ignorance. In fact, the habitus of faith inclines him against such preaching because that habitus necessarily teaches whatever leads to salvation. Also, because one must not give credence too easily to every spirit, one should not give assent to strange preaching but should seek further information or simply entrust oneself to God without seeking to venture into the secrets of God beyond one's capacities.'"

29. Cited by the International Theological Commission, *Sensus Fidei in the Life of the Church*, §63n79, See Thomas Aquinas, *Scriptum*, III, d.25, q.2, a.1, qla 2, ad 3; *Quaestiones disputatae de veritate*, q.14, a.11, ad 2.

30. Aquinas, *Summa Theologiae*, II-II, q. 33, a. 4, ad 2.

31. Pace Massimo Borghesi, *The Mind of Pope Francis, Jorge Mario Bergoglio's Intellectual Journey*. Regarding the issues I examine in this book, for example, Gospel and law, dogma and life, the nature of truth and its reception, morality, mercy, justice, and truth, the dialogue of religions, ecumenism, I see no evidence that Francis is a dialectical thinker à la Romano Guardini or Johan Adam Möhler, as Borghesis claims, one who thinks in terms of polarities, contrasts, oppositions, rather than contradictions, in accounting for unity and diversity. I employ the distinction that Yves Congar draws between contrast (*Gegensatz*) and contradiction (*Widerspruch*) in accounting for the difference between difference and division in an ecumenical context in Chapter 6. See Congar, *True and False Reform in the Church*, 205-8; The distinction originates with Johann Adam Möhler (1796-1938), and "Cardinal [Charles] Journet has felicitously rendered [these distinctions] by the words contrast and contradiction" (as cited in Congar, *True and False Reform in the Church*, 205).

32. *Revelation, History, and Truth: A Hermeneutics of Dogma.*

33. For example, see Francis, "Pope Francis Message for World Mission Day 2018."

34. Thomas Weinandy "Letter to Pope Francis."

35. The *Catechism of the Catholic Church* §890: "The mission of the Magisterium is linked to the definitive nature of the covenant established by God with his people in Christ. It is this Magisterium's task to preserve God's people from deviations and defections and to guarantee them the objective possibility of professing the true faith without error. Thus, the pastoral duty of the Magisterium is aimed at seeing to it that the People of God abides in the truth that liberates. To fulfill this service, Christ endowed the Church's shepherds with the charism of infallibility in matters of faith and morals."

Abbreviations

AA	Vatican II, *Apostolicam Actuositatem.*
AL	Francis, *Amoris Laetitia* (*On Love in the Family*). Apostolic Exhortation, 2016.
CA	John Paul II, *Centesimus Annus*, Encyclical, 1991.
CCC	USCCB, *Catechism of the Catholic Church.*
CDF	Congregation for the Doctrine of the Faith.
CRV	Francis, *Christus Vivit*. Apostolic Exhortation, 2019.
CV	Benedict XVI, *Caritas in Veritate* (*On Integral Human Development in Charity and Truth*). Encyclical, 2009.
DCE	Benedict XVI, *Deus Caritas Est* (*On Christian Love*). Encyclical, 2005.
DF	Vatican I, *Dei Filius*, 1870.
DH	Vatican II, *Dignitatis Humanae*. Declaration on Religious Freedom, 1965.
DI	CDF, *Dominus Iesus*, 2000.
DM	John Paul II, *Dives in Misericordia* (*Rich in Mercy*), Encyclical, 1980.
DV	Joseph Cardinal Ratzinger, *Donum Veritatis* (*On the Ecclesial Vocation of the Theologian*), 1990.
EG	Francis, *Evangelii Gaudium* (*The Joy of the Gospel*) Apostolic Exhortation, 2013.
ET	English translation (of a work).
EV	John Paul II, *Evangelium Vitae* (*On the Value and Inviolability of Human Life*). Encyclical, 1995.
EN	Paul VI. *Evangelii Nuntiandi*, Apostolic Exhortation, 1975
ES	Paul VI. *Ecclesiam Suam*, Encyclical, 1964.
FC	John Paul II, *Familiaris Consortio* (*On the Role of the Christian Family in the Modern World*) Apostolic Exhortation, 1981.
FR	John Paul II, *Fides et Ratio* (*On Faith and Reason*), Encyclical, 1998.
GD	Pope Paul VI. *Gaudete in Domino* ("On Christian Joy"), Apostolic Exhortation, 1975.

GE	Francis, *Gaudete et Exsultate* (*On the Call to Holiness in Today's World*), 2018.
GS	Vatican Council II, *Gaudium et Spes*, Pastoral Constitution on the Church in the Modern World, 1965.
HV	Paul VI, *Humanae Vitae*. Encyclical, 1968.
LF	Francis (with Benedict XVI), *Lumen Fidei* (*The Light of Faith*), Encyclical, 2013.
LG	Vatican II, *Lumen Gentium*. Dogmatic Constitution on the Church. 1964.
LR	Karol Wojtyla (future Pope St. John Paul II), *Love and Responsibility*, 1960.
LS	Francis, *Laudato Si'* (*On Care for Our Common Home*), Encyclical, 2015.
MA	Pius XI, *Mortalium Animos*, Encyclical, 1928.
ME	Congregation for the Doctrine of the Faith, *Mysterium ecclesiae*, 1973.
MV	Francis, *Misericordiae Vultus* (*The Face of Mercy*), 2015.
NGM	Francis, *The Name of God is Mercy*, 2016.
NMI	John Paul II, *Novo Millennio Ineunte*, Apostolic Letter, 2001.
PCB	Paul VI, *Paterna Cum Benevolentia*, Apostolic Exhortation, 1974
PDG	Pius X, *Pascendi Dominici Gregis*, Encyclical, 1907.
RP	John Paul II, *Reconciliatio et Paenitentia* (*On Reconciliation and Penance in the Mission of the Church Today*), 1984.
RM	John Paul II, *Redemptoris Missio*. Encyclical, 1990.
SD	International Peace Institute, *Salzburg Declaration*, 2015.
SF	International Theological Commission, *Sensus Fidei in the Life of the Church*. 2014.
ST	St. Thomas Aquinas, *Summa Theologica*.
TBN	Leo XIII, *Testem Benevolentiae Nostrae*, Encyclical, 1899.
UR	Vatican II, *Unitatis Redintegratio*, Decree on Ecumenism. 1964.
UUS	John Paul II, *Ut Unum Sint* (*On Commitment to Ecumenism*), Encyclical, 1995.
VG	Francis, *Veritatis Gaudium*, Apostolic Constitution, 2017.
VS	John Paul II, *Veritatis Splendor* (*The Splendor of Truth*) Encyclical, 1993.

1

A Contested Lérinian Legacy

> The tradition which comes from the apostles develops in the Church with the help of the Holy Spirit. For there is a growth in the understanding of the realities and the words which have been handed down.... For, as the centuries succeed one another, the Church constantly moves forward toward the fullness of divine truth until the words of God reach their complete fulfillment in her. (DV §8)

The Legacy of the Second Vatican Council

What is the legacy of Vatican II? This question has been an intensely debated one for the last half century. Thus, I cannot hope to settle it in this chapter.[1] Rather, my main concern is to expound the crucial features of that legacy as a hermeneutics of creative renewal with its corresponding notion of doctrinal development, having its roots in the thought of the fifth century monk St. Vincent of Lérins (d. c. 445). Vatican II's legacy is Lérinian in inspiration precisely on the question reconciling the historicity of human thought, in particular, the historically conditioned formulations of dogma, with their possible correction, modification, and complementation, with the permanence of its meaning and truth.[2] I begin by considering Pope Francis' understanding of that hermeneutics. I also consider its reception by his illustrious predecessor, John Paul II. My aim is to illuminate the issues dividing John Paul's understanding of that hermeneutics, which is indebted to Vatican II's *Lérinian* hermeneutics, in the realm of morality with that of proponents of a "new paradigm," the so-called "principle of pastorality." I refer here to proponents such as Richard Gaillardetz, Professor of Systematic Theology at Boston College, and Christoph Theobald, SJ, Professor of Fundamental Theology at the Jesuit Faculties of Paris. In the following, therefore, examined are the crucial matters of the permanence of meaning and truth, the historicity of dogmatic formulations, the nature of divine revelation, language, truth, and reality, propositional truth and how truth is authenticated, as well as the normative and comprehensive dynamics of the moral life. These matters are fundamental to the hermeneutics of creative renewal and the corresponding notion of doctrinal and moral development.

In his "God Lives in the City" address on 25 August 2011, the then Cardinal Bergoglio raises the question regarding the hermeneutics of Vatican II.[3] Is it a matter either of "rupture or, as Pope Benedict XVI has said when speaking of the interpretations of the Second Vatican Council" or "renewal in the continuity of the one subject-Church which the Lord has given to us[?]"[4] Bergoglio acknowledges in a note, appealing to the then Angelo Scola,[5] that Benedict does not oppose "'discontinuity-continuity' or 'rupture-continuity,' but speaks of discontinuity and rupture versus a hermeneutic of reform or renewal in the continuity of the subject-Church, specified as 'the journey People of God.'"[6]

Some two years later, the now Pope Francis, in the interview book, *A Big Heart Open to God*, responds very briefly to the question, "What did the Second Vatican Council accomplish?"

> "Vatican II was a rereading of the Gospels in light of contemporary culture,"[7] says the pope. "Vatican II produced a renewal movement that simply comes from the same gospel. Its fruits are enormous. Just recall the liturgy. The work of liturgical reform has been a service to the people as a rereading of the Gospels from a concrete historical situation. Yes, there are hermeneutics of continuity and discontinuity, but one thing is clear: the dynamic of reading the Gospels,[8] actualizing its message for today—which was typical of Vatican II—is absolutely irreversible."[9]

Francis's short response suggests that he did not want to get bogged down in the conflict of interpretations—continuity vs. discontinuity—regarding Vatican II. He alludes to the conflict of hermeneutics, of which he expressed his awareness two years earlier. "Vatican II was a rereading of the Gospels in light of contemporary culture." This statement is obviously a reflection of *Gaudium et Spes* §4: "To carry out such a task [to carry forward the work of Christ], the Church has always had the duty of scrutinizing the signs of the times and of interpreting them in the light of the Gospel." It is also reflected in latter passages of the same Vatican II document and referred to as the "law of evangelization."

> For, from the beginning of her history she [the Church] has learned to express the message of Christ with the help of the ideas and terminology of various philosophers, and and has tried to clarify it with their wisdom, too. Her purpose has been to adapt the Gospel to the grasp of all as well as to the needs of the learned, insofar as such was appropriate. Indeed this accommodated preaching of the revealed word ought to remain the law of all evangeli-

> zation. For thus the ability to express Christ's message in its own way is developed in each nation, and at the same time there is fostered a living exchange between the Church and the diverse cultures of people.... With the help of the Holy Spirit, it is the task of the entire People of God, especially pastors and theologians, to hear, distinguish and interpret the many voices of our age, and to judge them in the light of the divine word, so that revealed truth can always be more deeply penetrated, better understood and set forth to greater advantage (GS, §44).

This "law of evangelization," which is about recontextualizing and reinterpreting the Gospel, by- passes the crux of the conflict of hermeneutics of Vatican II, but it leaves unanswered the questions raised by that conflict. Pressing on, however, Francis gives us a further glimpse into his view of Vatican II in his Letter to the Special Envoy, Walter Cardinal Brandmüller, on the 450th anniversary of the close of the Council of Trent.[10] He aligns himself with Pope Benedict XVI over the conflict of the hermeneutics of Vatican II. In Benedict's 2005 Christmas address before the Roman Curia, he distinguishes between "a hermeneutic of discontinuity and rupture" versus a "hermeneutic of reform and renewal." Francis refers to these competing hermeneutical approaches and continues by explaining the latter hermeneutic with the words of Benedict. A hermeneutic of reform means "of renewal in the continuity of the one-subject-Church which the Lord has given to us. She is a subject that increases in time and develops, yet always remains the same, the one subject of the journeying People of God."[11] This hermeneutics of renewal is the one Francis writes about in his Letter, and refers us once again to Benedict XVI:

> Graciously hearing the very same Holy Ghost, the Holy Church of our age, even now, continues to restore and meditate upon the most abundant doctrine of Trent. As a matter of fact, the "hermeneutic of renewal" (interpretation *renovationis*) which Our Predecessor Benedict XVI explained in 2005 before the Roman Curia, refers not only to the Tridentine Council but also to the Vatican Council. The mode of interpretation, certainly, places one honorable characteristic of the Church in a brighter light that is given by the Same Lord (Benedict XVI): "She is a subject which increases in time and develops, yet always remaining the same, the one subject of the journeying People of God."[12]

In another letter commenting on Vatican II, this time to Archbishop Agostino Marchetto, who wrote the 2009 polemical work: *The Second Vatican Ecumenical Council: A Counterpoint for the History of the Council.* Marchetto argues against the "Bologna School" (Giuseppe Alberigo), which he argues considers Vatican II to represent a "hermeneutic of rupture or discontinuity" between the pre- and post-conciliar periods, and he falls in line with Benedict XVI, Vatican II represents a "hermeneutic of reform, of renewal in continuity" with the tradition of the Church.[13] Pope Francis states in his letter:

> Dear Monsignor Marchetto,
>
> With these lines I wish to make myself close to you and to join the ceremony of the presentation of the book "Papal Primacy and the Episcopate: From the First Millennium to the Second Ecumenical Vatican Council." I ask you to feel me spiritually present. The theme of the book is a tribute to the love you have for the Church, a loyal and at the same time poetic love. Loyalty and poetry are not objects of commerce: they are not bought or sold, they are simply virtues rooted in the heart of a son who feels the Church as Mother, or to be more precise, and to say it with an Ignatian family "air," as "the hierarchic Holy Mother Church." You have manifested this love in many ways, including correcting an error or imprecision on my part—and for this I thank you from my heart—but above all it has been manifested in all its purity in the studies made on Vatican Council II. Once I said to you, dear Monsignor Marchetto, and today I wish to repeat it, that I consider you the best interpreter of Vatican Council II. I know that it is a gift of God, but I also know that you have made it fructify.[14]

Although these letters do not tell us everything about Francis' understanding of Vatican II's hermeneutics of renewal, nonetheless taken at face value they say something important, namely, that Francis views himself in continuity with that hermeneutics. He repeats this very point most recently in a letter that appears as a preface to a book on *Amoris Laetitia* as well as in a book of interviews.[15] The second hermeneutical principle for properly reading *Amoris Laetitia* is, according to Francis, that it should be "treated with a hermeneutic of the Church, always in continuity (without ruptures), yet always maturing."[16] In that recent book of interviews, he repeats this very point, "Pope Benedict said something very clear: the changes in the Church must be carried out with the hermeneutic of continuity. A lovely phrase.... [S]ome things change, but there is always continuity. It doesn't betray its roots, it clarifies them, making them easier to understand."[17] However, there is more to say.

We find textual cues in his prepapal and papal writings that will contribute to our getting a grasp of his position vis-à-vis Vatican II's hermeneutics. One of the key questions I now pose is this: What does he understand by that hermeneutics? My second question arises from my understanding that Vatican II's hermeneutical legacy is Lérinian in inspiration precisely on the question reconciling the historicity of human thought, in particular, the historically conditioned formulations of dogma, with their possible correction, modification, and complementation, with the permanence of its meaning and truth.[18] How does Francis then account for legitimate theological pluralism and authentic diversity within a fundamental permanence of meaning and truth? The question here has received two very different answers. One is the the Lérinian legacy of Pope John XXIII. The other is the approach that is called the "pastorality of doctrine,"[19] which some theologians have proposed as a "new paradigm," of which I have now come to see that for various reasons Pope Francis's hermeneutics of renewal bears some affinity.

The Lérinian Legacy of Vatican II

Throughout his pontificate, Francis has often criticized what he calls a "hostile inflexibility" regarding doctrine.[20] This term reflects his objection to a tendency to ideologize faith.[21] It shows itself, according to Francis, in those who manifest a "doctrinal rigidity,"[22] who are Pharisaic stone-throwers who embody a merciless rigorism,[23] an "ahistorical fundamentalism" (EG §231), as Francis also puts it, or an immobilism at the level of theological formulation or expression, because it may lead to petrifaction of the understanding of faith. How is authentic doctrine transformed into ideology?

In answering this question, Francis does not refer us to 1 Cor 1:10, "I appeal to you, brothers, by the nature of our Lord Jesus Christ, that all of you agree, and that there be no divisions among you, but that you be united in the same mind and the same judgment." But he should have because it is precisely this spirit of divisiveness that drives ideology, according to Francis. The Church is therefore entrusted with the responsibility to "clarify doctrine," meaning thereby "what the Church has always taught and continues to teach us," and it has taken up that responsibility throughout the centuries in councils. "In fact, the pope affirms, 'it is a duty of the Church to clarify doctrine so that what Jesus said in the Gospels... can be understood well." Still, there have always been those who stand athwart the work of the Holy Spirit in the Church's authentic magisterium, of the pope and the bishops, and of the councils. "They had an ideology which closed their heart to the work of the Holy Spirit." This work, mediated through the magisterium, is about clarifying doctrine. Doctrine unites; ideology divides. "For them ideology is more important than doctrine: they leave the Holy Spirit to the side." Francis concludes:

> "Today I am inspired to ask for the grace of mature obedience to the Magisterium of the Church," Pope Francis said, "the obedience to what the Church has always taught and continues to teach us." With this obedience,

> one "develops the Gospel; explains it better each time, in fidelity to Peter, to the bishops and, ultimately, to the Holy Spirit who guides and sustains this process." To this end, the Pope invited the faithful "to also pray for those who transform doctrine into ideology, so that the Lord may give them the grace of conversion to the unity of the Church, to the Holy Spirit, and to true doctrine."[24]

So arguably, this conflict between the ideologue and the faithful adherent of Catholic doctrine is a veiled reference to the critics of Chapter 8 of Francis's Apostolic Exhortation, *Amoris Laetitia*. I devote Chapter 4 to a critical discussion of this controverted chapter, so I defer from discussing it here.

Francis claims in the above account of ideologizing doctrine that the ideologue, unlike Francis, is not interested in the material continuity of doctrinal teaching over time; rather, he is just interested in his own views and hence is not open to the work of the Holy Spirit. Francis, then, calls us to the mature obedience to the Magisterium of the Church, to the Church's unity, to the Holy Spirit, and hence to "true doctrine."

How do we know that it is true doctrine, in continuity with the Church's teaching and not a reversal of that historic teaching? Francis' claim may be formulated in the following way: "What the Catholic Church teaches with the assistance of the Holy Spirit must be true; but the Catholic Church teaches X. Therefore X must be true."[25] This is an *a priori* argument that purports to be the basis for trusting in the promise of Christ that the Spirit of truth will guide the Church into the fullness of truth (John 16:13). I think this argument runs the risk of collapsing all distinction between the magisterium, on the one hand, and its normative sources, such as Holy Scripture, ecumenical councils, the consensus of holy and learned doctors, and the *sensus fidei fidelium*, on the other. As Ratzinger argues, this argument "threatens the primacy of the sources which (were one to continue logically in this direction) would ultimately destroy the serving character of the teaching office."[26] In short, the problem with this *a priori* argument is that it confuses the difference between two statements: one, we should accept the Church's teaching because it is true in accordance with the Holy Scripture and other authoritative sources of faith, and two, we should accept the Church's teaching simply because the Church's teaching is illuminated by the work of the Holy Spirit. The former statement is true, but not the latter because it leads to the position of solum magisterium. Furthermore, this position regards the magisterium as the supreme rule of faith, and hence to magisterial positivism. "Whatever the current magisterium says is always what is 'orthodox.'"[27]

Thus, in this connection of transforming doctrine into ideology, the greatest danger, according to Francis, is that even "with the holy intent of communicating the truth about God and humanity" we may "hold fast to a *formulation* while failing to convey its substance" (EG §41, emphasis added). Francis makes a plea for a creative retrieval of the Gospel in order to mediate its content faithfully as the Church goes forth in the context of contemporary culture. (EG §20). What is not clear about this project of creative retrieval and renewal, as Francis understands it, is whether the phrases new formulations or expressions refer to the dogmas themselves as such, having then the status of secondary formulae,[28] as it were, which then mediate the core of the Christian kerygma, the substance of the deposit of the faith, that "will always be the same: the God who revealed his immense love in the crucified and risen Christ." (EG §11). Francis does not seem particularly concerned with the hermeneutics of reinterpreting the *unchanging affirmations* of faith, and the issues of meaning and truth and theological epistemology raised by this hermeneutics. In other words, he does not seem concerned with the permanence of the meaning and truth of dogmas. For him, it seems hermeneutical retrieval seems all about church doctrines which, as secondary formulae and in varying degrees, mediate the content of divine revelation. That content is, says Francis, about "Christ [who] is the 'eternal Gospel' [Rev 14:6]; he 'is the same yesterday and today and forever' [Heb 13:8], yet his riches and beauty are inexhaustible. He is forever young and a constant source of newness. The Church never fails to be amazed at 'the depth of the riches and wisdom and knowledge of God' [Rom 11:33]" (EG §11). But Francis's distinction between an "eternal Gospel" and its inadequate expressions does not get to the crux of the issue before us, namely, whether God has revealed enduring propositional truths about himself, man, and the world, in history and in sentences.

Alternatively, do new doctrinal formulations mediate the universality and material identity—a dogmatic conceptual hard core—of the permanent meanings and truths of Christian dogmas, such as that of the Trinity, Incarnation, and Atonement, according to the same meaning and same judgment (*eodem sensu eademque sententia*). If the latter, the new linguistic formulation or expression can vary, as long as they mediate the same meaning and same judgment of truth. As Lonergan puts it, "The meaning of the dogma is not apart from a verbal formulation, for it is a meaning declared by the church. However, the permanence attaches to the meaning and not to the formula. To retain the same formula and give it a new meaning is precisely what the third canon [of Vatican I] excludes [Denzinger §3043]."[29] I will return to this question of reconciling the historicity of dogmatic formulations with the permanence of meaning and truth of dogmas below.

For now, it is clear that Francis holds that this project is two-sided: interpreting doctrine in relation to the "eternal Gospel" and in light of the new pastoral context. "Whenever we make the effort to return to the source [of faith] and to recover the original freshness of the Gospel, new avenues arise, new paths of creativity open up, with different forms of expression, more eloquent signs and words with new meaning for today's world. Every form of authentic evangelization is always 'new'" (EG §11).

Now, consider in this connection the then Archbishop Jorge Bergoglio's (the future Pope Francis) response to the question as to how we can allow for legitimate pluralism and authentic diversity within a fundamental doctrinal permanence.

In a work co-authored with Rabbi Skorka, *On Heaven and Earth*, Bergoglio responds to this question. "In the third and fourth centuries[[30]] the revealed truths of faith were theologically formulated and transmitted as our nonnegotiable inheritance."[31] He is quick to add, however:

> That does not mean that throughout history, through study and investigation, other insights were not discovered about these truths: such as what Christ is like, or how to configure the Church, or how and what should be true Christian conduct, or what are the commandments. All of these are enriched by these new explanations. There are things that are debatable, but—I repeat—this inheritance is not negotiable. The content of a religious faith [*fides quae creditur*] is capable of being deepened through human thought, but when that deepening is at odds with the inheritance, it is a heresy.

In this passage, Bergoglio affirms the non-negotiable inheritance of revealed truths that have been handed down and developed by our understanding. In the interview book, *A Big Heart Open to God*, he rejects a largely static, ahistorical understanding of doctrinal formulations or expressions. "The view of the church's teaching as a monolith to defend without nuance or different understandings [of that teaching] is wrong."[32] It isn't clear whether Bergoglio is referring here to the dogmas or to their dogmatic formulations. In *Evangelii Gaudium*, it becomes clearer that he is relativizing dogmas and not just their formulations. "The Church ... needs to grow in her interpretation of the revealed word and in her understanding of the truth.... Within the Church, countless issues are being studied and reflected upon with great freedom. Differing currents of thought in philosophy, theology and pastoral practice, if open to being reconciled by the Spirit in respect and love, can enable the Church to grow, *since all of them help to express more clearly the immense riches of God's word*. For those who long for a *monolithic body of doctrine* guarded by all and leaving no room for nuance [in expression], this might appear as undesirable and leading to confusion. But such variety [of expression] serves to bring out and develop different facets of the inexhaustible riches of the Gospel" (EG §40, emphasis added).[33] He adds, "We need to listen to and complement one another in our partial reception of reality and the Gospel" (EG §40n44). Otherwise, we run the risk of ideologizing faith, meaning thereby the stifling of intellectual investigation "by the imposition of rigid and sterile patterns [of thought] (one thinks of certain areas of philosophical and theological research)."[34] In his recent Apostolic Exhortation, *Gaudete et Exsultate*, he reiterates this point:

> It is not easy to grasp the truth that we have received from the Lord. And it is even more difficult to express it. So we cannot claim that our way of understanding this truth authorizes us to exercise a strict supervision over others' lives. Here I would note that in the Church there legitimately coexist different ways of interpreting many aspects of doctrine and Christian life. (GE §43)

These legitimately different ways of understanding the truth must be complementary—Francis does say—rather than conflicting. Still, harping on the risk of ideologizing faith, it leaves unconsidered the question of the permanence of the meaning and truth of dogma. I will return to this matter below. For now, we should note that his point is not relativism about revealed truth; rather, it suggests an epistemic perspectivalism, not just about dogmatic formulations, but also dogmas themselves, because our view of the truth is always imperfect and inadequate. Francis makes clear that "today's vast and rapid cultural changes demand that we constantly seek ways of *expressing* unchanging truths in a language which brings out their abiding newness." These "unchanging truths" do not refer to the Church's dogmas, but rather to the "authentic Gospel of Jesus Christ," and the 'Gospel message in its unchanging meaning'" (EG §41). He substantiates his position by citing from John XXIII's opening address at Vatican II, *Gaudet Mater Ecclesia*, precisely where John distinguishes between truths and its formulations.[35] "'The deposit of the faith is one thing... the way it is expressed is another.'" However, he cites the Italian version of John XXIII's statement—not the official Latin publication—of the hermeneutics of creative retrieval, distinguishing between the substance of the deposit of the faith, and the way it is expressed,[36] but without the subordinate clause, namely, "according to the same meaning and the same judgment [*eodem sensu eademque sententia*]."[37] The subordinate clause in this passage is part of a larger passage from the constitution of Vatican Council I, *Dei Filius*,[38] which is earlier invoked by Pius IX in the bull of 1854, *Ineffabilis Deus*, also cited by Leo XIII in his 1899 Encyclical, *Testem benevolentiae Nostrae*, and this passage is itself from the *Commonitórium primum* 23 of Vincent of Lérins: "Therefore, let there be growth and abundant progress in understanding, knowledge, and wisdom, in each and all, in individuals and in the whole Church, at all times and in the progress of ages, but only within the proper limits, i.e., within the same dogma, the same meaning, the same judgment" (*in eodem scilicet dogmate, eodem sensu eademque sententia*).[39] The permanence of meaning and truth is taught in the constitution: "... is sensus perpetuo est retinendus... nec umquam ab eo sensu, altior intelligentiae specie et nomine, recedendum... in eodem scilicet dogmate, eodem sensu, eademque sententia" (Denzinger §3020). "... ne sensus tribuendus sit alius" (Denzinger §2043).[40]

The Lérinian hermeneutics of creative renewal is, arguably, based on the distinction between truth and its historically conditioned formulations, between form and content, truth-content and context, in sum, propositions and sentences. Yves Congar,[41] for one, has argued that this distinction between the permanence of meaning and truth of dogmas, on the one hand, and their historically conditioned formulations, with the possibility of the latter's correction, modification, and complementation summarizes the meaning of the entire council. But it is also the crucial difference between the *nouvelle théologie* and modernism. How so?

The *Nouvelle Théologie* and Modernism

Yves Congar answers this question about the difference between the *nouvelle théologie* and modernism in his description of modernism: "The conception of the relation between dogmatic pronouncements and religious realities (is taken to be) a relation of symbol to reality, not as an expression *proper* (however inadequate) to reality."[42] In other words, adds Congar, "The dogmatic formulas which come to light in the course of centuries are only a useful expression of that which we are led to think conforms to the spirit of Christ. Between them and the primitive, revealed fact, the relation is not that of a formula to an objective and intellectually definite datum, but that of a formula born of the needs of a given time, and adapted to them, and to a spirit that is the Christian spirit which dwells in each believer and animates the entire Church."[43] Hence, there is a disjunction between faith and a determinable content of truth, propositions whose truth-status bear a relation to reality; rather, for the modernist, the content of faith is always derived from faith's experience of God, and hence is only a product of theological reflection upon this faith, with doctrines mediating that experience in their secondary formulae.

Berkouwer rightly argues, along with Congar, against identifying the *nouvelle théologie* as a "new" modernism.[44] Still, he adds, "They do touch each other in a number of questions and problems that both throw on the table for discussion, problems that according to the new theology cannot be avoided simply because of their association with modernism."[45] As Aidan Nichols says succinctly, "though modernism had been a false answer it had set a real question."[46] What is the real question that it raised? Congar replies: Modernism raised the problem of "the variations in the representations and the intellectual construction of the affirmations of faith." How, then, did the *nouvelle théologie* address this problem?

Congar responds: The *nouveaux théologiens* "solved the problem by distinguishing between an invariant of affirmations, and the variable usage of technical notions to translate essential truth in historic contexts differing culturally and philosophically." Adds Congar:

> "For them, first of all, the invariant was a set of affirmations that have a real content of truth. And secondly, in the differing notional translations which the theologians had given, there existed an analogy of relations, or a func-

> tional equivalence, between the notions used to express that truth. In this way they escaped the accusation of ruinous anti-intellectualism, and dogmatic relativism justly brought against the Modernists."[47]

It was then the question regarding the relationship between unchangeable truth, and the human expression of that truth, in the variety of historically conditioned forms of thoughts, inclusive of different philosophical concepts that have played a role in explicating the content of revelation. Succinctly put, the real question is, according to Catholic theologian Thomas G. Guarino, how to explain "the material identity of Christian truth over the course of time."

In fact, Berkouwer himself is persuaded that "Modernism has definitely seen a very real problem—despite its untenable solutions—that has not been seen by anti-modernistic reaction in upholding the '*semper eadem*,' namely the absolutizing of continuity in a way that had no appreciation for the historical nature of human expression. In more recent times, this compelling problem naturally resurfaced and the distinction between form and content returned."[48] Thus, the distinction between abiding truth and its historically conditioned formulation resurfaced with the *nouveaux théologiens*, and with that came the problem regarding the relation between history and truth, context, and content, propositions and sentences.

Berkouwer is right that the distinction itself cannot "be used as a magician's wand to clear up every burning question."[49] The problem was that the presupposition of the hermeneutics of continuity no longer seemed self-evident, given that truth's expressions are historically conditioned, and that these expressions are in some sense never absolute, wholly adequate, and irreplaceable. Thus, the "problem of truth was placed on a slippery slope," as Edward Schillebeeckx was to refer to historicity, because no attempt was made "to show how truth, in this historicity, is more than a historical expression that changes in each period."[50] Berkouwer elaborates, "That harmony had always been presumed, virtually self-evidently, to be an implication of the mystery of the truth "*eodem sensu eademque sententia*."[51] He adds, "Now, however, attention is captivated primarily by the historical-factual process that does not transcend the times, but is entangled with them in all sorts of ways. It cannot be denied that one encounters the undeniable fact of the situated setting of the various pronouncements made by the Church in any given era." How, then, exactly, is a single and unitary revelation homogeneously expressed, according to the same meaning and the same judgment, given the undeniable fact "of time-conditioning, one can even say: of historicity."[52] Berkouwer insightfully states, "All the problems of more recent interpretation of dogma are connected very closely to this search for continuity.... Thus, the question of the nature of continuity has to be faced."[53]

In considering this question of continuity, Ratzinger also attends to the essentials of the faith, in particular, their "nucleus," as it were, their "dogmatic conceptual hard core,"[54] which, he says, "seemed to be unambiguously defined, at least in its essential core, by the Creeds, conciliar decisions and dogmas. Today, even this nucleus is called into discussion." He explains:

> Though it is not general practice to contest dogma formally, it is usual to point out that all human speech is culturally conditioned. It is said to be impossible to hand on the faith in definitive formulae. Precisely in order to transmit the identical content, it is supposedly necessary to find constantly new ways of expressing it.

But there is a problem.

> And just who would be these illuminated spirits able to intuit the *enduring content* behind all speech despite the absence of any continuity whatsoever in speech itself? Are there really two classes of Christians—the initiated few whose gaze penetrates behind speech and the mass of naïve believers who cling to speech and passively accept whatever new linguistic clothing is served to them without any interest in its connection with the previous one, since this connection is beyond their understanding? [55]

One may answer this question by referring to the *nouveaux théologiens* solution, which I discussed above, distinguishing between an invariant of affirmations, and the variable formulations to translate essential truth in historic contexts differing culturally and philosophically.

One may add here that there is a crucial difference for Lérinians between change and development (progress). For the latter must occur within the "proper limits, i.e., within the same dogma, the same meaning, the same judgment [*in eodem scilicet dogmate, eodem sensu eademque sententia*]." Although the truths of the faith may be expressed differently, we must always determine whether those new re-formulations are preserving the same meaning and judgment (*eodem sensu eademque sententia*), and hence the material continuity, identity, and universality of those truths.

The absence—unintentional?—of this clause in Francis's citation is significant for understanding his views of doctrinal truth, especially given Francis's apparent rejection of the notion of abstract truth (propositional truth), skepticism regarding the language of absolute truth, and his theologico-pastoral epistemology and its prioritizing of realities over ideas.[56] I shall return to these matters below by asking about Francis's understanding of the nature of truth.

For now, I want to underscore that Francis distinguishes between truth and its formulations throughout his writings. But I have been arguing that truth here refers to the "authentic Gospel of Jesus Christ," and the 'Gospel message in its unchanging meaning'" (EG §41) rather than the meaning and truth of dogmas. It is the received revelation that is being recontextualized and reinterpreted in new formulations reflecting a deepened understanding of the Gospel. He explains: "At any rate, religions refine certain *expressions* [of the truth] with time, even though it is a slow process because of the sacred bond that we have with the received inheritance... the *received revelation*."[57] Again, referring to the Gospel, Francis states, "The *revealed message* is not identified with any of its [formulations]; its content is transcultural" (EG §117, emphasis added). He adds, "The faith cannot be constricted to the limits of understanding and expression of any one culture. It is an indisputable fact that no single culture can exhaust the *mystery of our redemption in Christ*" (EG §118, emphasis added). Bergoglio is affirming here a growth of human understanding, its refinement, maturation, and development of the *dogmas* of the Christian religion. Clearly, the emphasis of Vincent of Lérins is other than the development in our understanding of the Gospel, of the revealed message; rather, although inclusive of revelation because dogmatic development and understanding must be homogeneous with that revelation, Vincent is concerned with development within the proper limits of the same dogma, according to the same meaning, the same judgment. In short, it is a hermeneutics of dogma.

Francis's references to formulations mean the dogmas and doctrine of the Church as such. They mediate the substance of the deposit of the faith, the revealed truth of the Gospel. If we note carefully, I think it is fair to say that the Gospel message is transcultural, according to Francis, but dogmas and doctrines, which are its manifestation, are actually subject to variation, given their historically conditioned character. Thus, their dogmatic formulations are subject to correction, modification, and complementation.[58]

Still, in that early interview, *A Big Heart Open to God*, Bergoglio cites a passage from the *Commonitórium primum* of Vincent of Lérins: "Thus even the dogma of the Christian religion must proceed from these laws. It progresses, solidifying with years, growing over time, deepening with age."[59] He continues in this interview:

> St. Vincent of Lérins makes a comparison between the biological development of man and the transmission from one era to another of the deposit of faith, which grows and is strengthened with time. Here, human self-understanding changes with time and so also human consciousness deepens.... *So we grow in the understanding of the truth*. Exegetes and theologians help the church to mature in her own judgments. Even the other sciences and their development help the church in its growth in understanding.... Even the *forms for expressing truth* can be multiform, and this is indeed necessary for the transmission of the Gospel in its timeless meaning.[60]

Notice that Francis does not hold the truth itself to be variable with time and place, but only the formulations, namely, "the forms for expressing truth... in order to develop and deepen the Church's teaching."[61] Indeed, he aligns himself with John Paul II making clear that it is the expression *not* the truth that changes: "Let us never forget that 'the expression of truth can take different forms. The renewal of these forms of expression becomes necessary for the sake of transmitting to the people of today the Gospel message in its unchanging meaning'" (EG §42).[62] Elsewhere he adds, "It [the task of evangelization] constantly seeks to communicate more effectively the truth of the Gospel in a specific context, *without renouncing the truth,* the goodness and the light which it [the Gospel] can bring" (EG §45, emphasis added). Again, the reference here is to the truth of the Gospel, not the permanence of meaning and truth of dogma.

Furthermore, of particular relevance to understanding the hermeneutics of creative renewal is Vincent's distinction between *progress* and *change*, the import of which is not lost on Francis who, like Vincent, compares the transmission of faith with biological development of man. Hence, development must be organic and homogeneous. Vincent writes: "But it [progress of religion] must be such as may be truly a *progress* of the faith, not a *change*; for when each several thing is improved in itself, that is *progress*; but when a thing is turned out of one thing into another, that is *change*." In other words, the import here of this distinction is that (as Guarino notes) "'development' can never mean a substantial transformation, a change in the very essence of a church teaching. The theologian of Lérins very carefully balances growth and preservation."[63] This distinction means that he understands the development of faith as progress that is organic and homogeneous and occurring within the boundaries of the dogma. In other words, the faith remains identical with itself in its progress. He distinguishes this idea of development from another in which an understanding of faith's development involves "a thing [being] turned out of one thing into another, that is, of *change*." The point here is made clear by Vincent: progress in understanding may result in new modes of expression, but such expressions are authentic and legitimate only if they keep the same meaning and the same judgment [*eodem sensu eademque sententia*]. In other words, the same datum of faith is said in different ways. In short, truth is unchangeable, development of dogma is not a development of truth, or a change in Church teaching, but a development in the Church's *understanding* of the truth.

Furthermore, in his encyclical, *Laudato Si'*, Francis explicitly appeals to Vincent after the following statement: "Christianity, in fidelity, to its own identity and the rich deposit of truth which it has received from Jesus Christ, continues to reflect on [contemporary] issues in fruitful dialogue with changing historical situations. In doing so, it reveals its eternal newness."[64] This is Francis's call to return to the sources, that is, *ressourcement*, in order to revitalize the present. However, *aggiornamento* is a corollary of *ressourcement*. Accordingly, Francis rejects an opposition between doctrine and pastoral practice as a false approach. He says in his address to the International Theological Congress: "We not infrequently identify doctrine with conservatism and antiquity; and on the contrary, we tend to think of pastoral ministry in terms of adaptation, reduction, accommodation. As if they had nothing to do with each other. A false opposition is generated between theology and pastoral ministry, between Christian reflection and Christian life.... The attempt to overcome this divorce between theology and pastoral ministry, between faith and life, was indeed one of the main contributions of Vatican II." Briefly, the way to avoid this dilemma "is through reflection, through discernment, taking very serious both the Church's Tradition and today's reality, bringing both into dialogue."[65] Otherwise, adds Francis, "to break the relationship between Tradition handed down and practical reality would be to endanger the faith of the People of God. To consider either of these two instances as insignificant is to throw ourselves into a labyrinth that will not lead to life for our people. To break this communication [between the Church's Tradition and today's reality] will easily lead us to construct an ideology out of our point of view, out of our theology."[66]

Furthermore, Francis resists the implication that this dialogical strategy means adapting or accommodating the Tradition to today's standards; the pastoral context is not an isolated motive for renewal. As Francis put it succinctly in a recent homily: "[T]here is no need to negotiate with 'novelties'; there is no need to 'water down the proclamation of the Gospel.'"[67] Renewal is rather about transmitting the Tradition today in its eternal newness. Yes, the deposit of faith given in the Church's teaching is greater than its dogmatic formulations, but its new formulations must be developed in harmony with the "eternal Gospel" (EG §11). Still, given the "law of evangelization," a mere repetition of previous doctrinal formulations is unacceptable; rather, what this "law" requires is a penetration of church doctrine in view of the pressing realities and questions of our social and cultural context. In fact, we shall see below, according to Francis, this "law" is informed by the first principle that "realities are greater than ideas" (EG §§231-33). This principle contributes to Francis' repeated warnings about the temptation of Gnosticism in which the openness of dogmas to being reformulated, and hence subject to change, is denied. Francis says, "The attraction of Gnosticism, a purely subjective faith whose only interest is a certain experience or set of ideas and bits of information which are meant to console and enlighten, but which ultimately keep one imprisoned in his or her own thoughts and feelings" (EG §94).[68] More about Gnosticism below.

Moreover, in his address to the International Theological Congress, Pope Francis looks again to Vincent.[69] As in the encyclical *Laudato Si'*, in his address to the International Congress, Pope Francis cites from Vincent's work in Latin, but I will give the English translation of the clauses he selects (emphasis added) setting them within the context:

> Thus it behooves the dogma of the Christian religion, too, to observe these laws of progress; it [Christian religion] may be *consolidated with years, expanded with time, grow loftier with age*; yet must remain incorrupt and undefiled: it may attain to fullness and perfection in all the

> proportions of its parts, and as it were in all its proper members and senses, but can admit nothing more in the way of change, can suffer no loss of any property, no variation in its definition.

Francis explains, in this connection, the task of the theologian, referring once again to a favorite passage of his from Vincent: "The theologian who is satisfied with his complete and conclusive thought is mediocre. The good theologian and philosopher has an open, that is, an incomplete, thought, always open to the *maius* of God and of the truth, always in development, according to the law that Vincent describes as: '*annis consolidetur, dilatetur tempore, sublimetur aetate*' (*Commonitorium primum*, 23: PL 50, 668): it is strengthened over the years, it expands over time, it deepens with age. This is the theologian who has an open mind."[70] Indeed, according to Francis, this theologian is not only mediocre, but also he is a "contemporary gnostic," an enemy of the Christian faith, because, first, "he judges others based on their ability to understand the complexity of certain doctrines;" second, he traffics in an "encyclopedia of abstractions,"[71] which purport to explain the "entirety of the faith," claiming to make "the Gospel perfectly comprehensible," and, lastly, he "absolutizes [his] own theories and forces others to submit to [his] way of thinking." In short, this mediocre theologian "seeks to domesticate the mystery," possessing a "doctrine without mystery," by "reducing Jesus' teaching to a cold and harsh logic that seeks to dominate everything," including "God's transcendence," and hence are not open to the fresh movement of the Spirit, the God who is full of surprises. (GE §§37-42)[72]

By contrast with this neo-gnostic position, Francis says that divinely revealed truth is "not easy to grasp." Furthermore, he adds, "it is even more difficult to express it." Moreover, the then Cardinal Bergoglio wrote, "In order to open ourselves up to the whole mystery of Christ, we need to overcome the widespread *positivism* that often abounds in theology."[73] How is the term positivism being used here? It refers to what Karl Rahner once called *Denzingertheologie*,[74] and others called "Christian positivism."[75] The latter, says Lonergan, "conceives the function of the theologian to be that of a propagandist for church doctrines. He did his duty when he repeated, explained, defended just what had been said in church documents." On this view, which is, adds Lonergan, a "static, deductivist style—which admits no conclusions that are not implicit in premises," doctrines are abstract formulations or irrefutable syllogisms. *Contra* this rationalist paradigm, as Francis sees it, he continues by drawing out the implications of our stammering God-talk:

> So we cannot claim that our way of understanding this truth authorizes us to exercise a strict supervision over others' lives. Here I would note that in the Church there legitimately coexist different ways of interpreting many aspects of doctrine and Christian life; in their variety, they "help to express more clearly the immense riches

> of God's word." It is true that "for those who long for a monolithic body of doctrine guarded by all and leaving no room for nuance, this might appear as undesirable and leading to confusion."... In effect, doctrine, or better, our understanding and expression of it, "is not a closed system, devoid of the dynamic capacity to pose questions, doubts, inquiries... The questions of our people, their suffering, their struggles, their dreams, their trials and their worries, all possess an interpretational value that we cannot ignore if we want to take the principle of the incarnation seriously. Their wondering helps us to wonder, their questions question us." (GE §43)

These claims of Francis raise many questions. Is he suggesting that doctrinally correct formulations or expressions of revealed truth do not completely or adequately express such truth without however denying that—in the words of John Paul II—"human language is capable of expressing divine and transcendent reality in a universal way—analogically, it is true, but no less meaningfully for that[?]" (FR §84). Alternatively, is he suggesting that inadequacy of expression means that divine truth itself is inexpressible? Furthermore, are these different ways of expressing doctrinal truth commensurable or incommensurable? If the latter, in what sense do such doctrinal formulations have a truth-conveying status, meaning thereby that what is asserted in them is objectively true. For dogmatic formulations "must bear some determinative relationship to truth itself... unless one has a view that language has no proper referencing function to reality."[76] Reminding ourselves that Francis is neither a systematic theologian nor a philosopher, I will tease out the implications from Francis's denial of truth as abstract and absolute for his understanding of the hermeneutics of creative retrieval. Following those reflections, I will examine what I will call Francis's praxis-oriented theology, a theologico-pastoral epistemology, as Gustavo Gutiérrez called it,[77] in light one of Francis's first principles: "realities are more important than ideas."

Is Faith in Propositions or in God?

I started reading Pope Francis's recent Apostolic Constitution, *Veritatis Gaudium*, and, honestly, I was stuck on the first part of the second sentence, "For truth is not an abstract idea, but is Jesus himself." In a recent homily that raised eyebrows, Francis urged us to "be careful not to fall into the temptation of making idols of certain abstract truths."[78] Now, we might think that Francis is rightly insisting that truth itself must be authenticated existentially—that is, lived out, practiced, carried out—and hence cannot be reduced to propositional truth—to being merely believed, asserted, and claimed. Perhaps he is merely saying, as John Paul II once said, "No, we shall not be saved by a formula but by a Person, and the assurance which he gives us: *I am with you!*" (NMI §29). But the contrast in this first sentence is between abstract truth and reality rather than between two complementary ways of understanding truth, propositional truth and existential truth.

Indeed, Francis's opening statement on truth vs abstract ideas reminds me of the great theologian and philosopher, and Doctor of the Church, St. Thomas Aquinas's consideration of the question whether the object of faith is a proposition or God. Francis seems implicitly to be putting us before a similar choice. Nevertheless, Aquinas argues that this choice is a specious one. Our faith is in both propositions and in the reality of the divine Word, Jesus Christ.

What is, then, an abstract idea? Francis does not say so, but I think we must say that abstract ideas are propositions that we assert to be true, and the context does not determine the truth-status of the proposition. So, abstract ideas are abstract truths. For example, "The Word was made flesh and dwelt among us" (John 1:14). "Christ is risen from the dead" (1 Cor 15:20). Other examples of abstract truths that are asserted may be taken from the Pastoral Letter of First Timothy: "Christ Jesus came into the world to save sinners" (1:15). "God our Savior... desires all men to be saved and to come to the knowledge of the truth" (2:3-4). "For there is one God, and there is one mediator between God and men, the man Christ Jesus" (2:5). "For everything created by God is good, and nothing is to be rejected if it is received with thanksgiving" (4:4).

On this view, the truth-status of these propositions are, if true, such that they will be true always and everywhere. It is not the context that determines the truth-status of their conceptual content. A doctrinal proposition is true if and only if what that proposition asserts is in fact the case about objective reality; otherwise, the proposition is false. It is not the context that determines the truth of the proposition that is judged to be the case about objective reality; rather, reality itself determines the truth or falsity of a proposition. Abstract truths, such as the ones from First Timothy, are part of the content of faith. Isn't our faith, then, in both propositions and in the objective reality of the Person of Christ?

In what sense then is faith a way of knowing divine reality, and how, as Romanus Cessario, OP, asks, "can propositions serve as true objects of faith, even though the act of faith finds its ultimate term in the divine reality?" Cessario adds, "For Catholic theology, the act of faith reaches beyond the formal content of doctrines and attains the very referent—'*res ipsa*'—of theological faith."[79] In Aquinas's account of faith, he argues, "the object of faith may be considered in two ways. First, as regards the thing itself which is believed, and thus the object of faith is something simple, namely, the thing itself about which we have faith; secondly, on the part of the believer, and in this respect the object of faith is something complex, such as a proposition." Aquinas understood this matter well. Yes, realities are in the knower according to the mode of the knower—according to Aquinas—but in the knower knowledge of the truth in man is propositional.

Still, Aquinas does say, "*Actus autem credentis non terminatur ad enuntiabile sed ad rem*" [The believer's act (of faith) does not terminate in the propositions, but in the realities [which they express].[80] While it is true to say that the *ultimate term of faith* is not a set of theological formulas that we confess, but rather God himself, it is also the case that for Aquinas articles of faith are necessary for knowing God. Aquinas explains: "We do not form statements except so that we may have apprehension of things through them. As it is in knowledge, so also in faith."[81] In other words, one primarily knows God himself only to the extent as mediated in and through determinate propositions.

Propositions are, then, an authentic mediation of God's self-revelation because faith involves belief, and to have a belief means that one is intellectually committed, or has mentally assented, to the truth of some proposition or other. Faith involves belief, continues Aquinas, and "belief is called assent, and it can only be about a proposition, in which truth or falsity is found."[82] In short, propositions of faith are true because they correspond to reality; they are as true judgments an "*adaequatio intellectus et rei*," corresponding to what is, and hence "a claim to the possession in knowledge of what is."[83] To be clear, what does it mean to say that truth is propositional? A proposition is true if and only if the state of affairs to which it refers is the case; otherwise, it is false.[84] "On the third day Jesus of Nazareth was raised from the dead" is true if and only if on the third day Jesus of Nazareth was raised from the dead.

Francis's statement dismissal of abstract truth misses out the indissoluble link of faith, beliefs, truth, and the relationship of the latter to objective reality. However, note the *Catechism of the Catholic Church*: "We do not believe in formulae, but in those realities they express, which faith allows us to touch. 'The believer's act [of faith] does not terminate in the propositions, but in the realities [which they express]'. All the same, we do approach these realities with the help of formulations of the faith which permit us to express the faith and to hand it on, to celebrate it in community, to assimilate and live on it more and more. (§170)" If we are to understand the nature of the Christian faith, we need to do so in light of the teaching of the Apostle Paul who calls us to believe with one's heart and to confess what one believes (Rom 10:9). The then Lutheran theologian, the late Jaroslav Pelikan, informs us of a twofold Christian imperative—the creedal and confessional imperative—that is at the root of creeds and confessions of faith. Faith involves both the *fides qua creditur*—the faith *with which* one believes—and the *fides quae creditur*—the faith *which* one believes.[85] Maximally, a biblical account of faith involves knowledge (*notitia*), assent (*assensus*), and trust (*fiducia*). Indeed, normatively speaking, these are three elements of a single act of faith involving the whole person who commits himself to God in Christ and through the power of the Holy Spirit. Minimally, however, faith involves belief, and to have a belief means that one is intellectually committed to the whole truth that God has revealed.[86]

Furthermore, faith involves holding certain beliefs to be true, explains Aquinas, because "belief is called assent, and it can only be about a proposition, in which truth or falsity is found."[87] Moreover, the *fides quae creditur* is the objective content of truth that has been unpacked and developed in the creeds and confessions of the Church, dogmas, doctrinal definitions, and canons. Therefore, let us ask again, "Is faith in propositions or in God?" The answer is that it is in both.

There is another aspect to this question of abstract truth, and it pertains to the distinction I drew above between both the *fides qua creditur*—the faith *with which* one believes, and the *fides quae creditur*—the faith *which* one believes.

In his 2017 book, *The Cardinal Müller Report*, Gerhard Cardinal Müller, until recently the Prefect of the Congregation for the Doctrine of the Faith, offers many insights on the state of the Church and a corresponding set of theological, doctrinal, moral, and philosophical questions. One of his insights is expressed in response to a question regarding the relationship between doctrine and personal encounter with Jesus Christ. This is a particularly important question since we often hear nowadays that the Gospel is about a person, an event, not doctrine. The interviewer, Fr. Carlos Granados, asks: "Is there such a thing as a doctrine that does not relate to a personal encounter, to a life? And, on the other hand, is there such a thing as a personal encounter or a life that does not involve or encompass doctrine? Is it conceivable in Christianity that there should be a scheme that begins with the personal encounter and then, as a further, secondary matter, ends with doctrine?"

On the one hand Granados is asking whether there is such a thing as a doctrine that does not relate to a personal encounter, to a life. In other words, how truth is authenticated—that is, lived out, practiced, carried out—cannot be reduced to being merely believed, asserted, and claimed because "what is communicated in catechesis is not [merely] a body of conceptual truths, but the mystery of the living God" (FR §99). In the jointly authored encyclical *Lumen Fidei*, Benedict XVI makes this point clear: "The creed does not only involve giving one's assent to a body of abstract truths; rather, when it is recited the whole of life is drawn into a journey towards full communion with the living God. We can say that in the creed believers are invited to enter into the mystery which they profess and to be transformed by it."[88] Now, although Francis signed on to this encyclical with his own contribution, it is clear to me that—unlike Benedict—his view sets up an opposition between the truth that is to be lived out, practiced, and carried out, on the one hand, and the truth that is to be believed, asserted, and claimed on the other. For instance, the then Cardinal Bergoglio says, "Christ's truth does not revolve primarily around intellectual [propositional] 'revelation', which is more like the Greek way of thinking. This revelation will be complete when 'we shall see him as he is' (1 John 3:2), because now 'we see in a mirror dimly' (1 Cor 13:12)." Yes, Ratzinger appreciates Francis's allusion to the qualification of an eschatological element such that "All knowledge in the time of the Church remains knowledge seen in a mirror—and hence fragmentary." He adds, "The direct relation to reality, to the face of God itself, is kept for the *eschaton* [cf. 1 Cor 13:12]."[89] Still, given an eschatological perspective of our knowledge, such that our dogmatic formulations cannot exhaustively grasp the content of revealed truth, there is no need to withdraw the claim that one can express truth determinately. We can know something truly without knowing it exhaustively.

On the other hand, we must give "priority to the person over ideas." Bergoglio understands this point well, "Christ's truth revolves around adherence in faith, an adherence that involves our whole being—heart, mind, and soul. This adherence is an adherence to the person of Jesus Christ, 'the Amen, the faithful and true witness' [Rev 3:14], whom we can trust and whom we can support because he gives us his Spirit, who guides us 'into all the truth' and allows us to discern between good and evil."[90] This description pertains to the *fides qua creditur*, which is the faith *with which* one believes by adhering to God the Father in Christ by the power of the Holy Spirit. But what about the *fides quae creditur*, which is the faith *which* one believes, the conceptual content, the beliefs which one holds to be true, affirms, and asserts?

The same question arises in Francis' concluding homily of the Synod of Bishops dedicated to young people. He states that faith is concerned with neither purely doctrinal formulae nor mere moralizing and social work. "Faith, instead, is life. It is living in the love of God who has changed our lives. We cannot choose between doctrine and activism." Rather, "faith has to do with encounter, not theory. In encounter, Jesus passes by; in encounter, the heart of the Church beats."[91] Indeed, Francis regularly cites Benedict XVI's *Deus Caritas Est* in support of this point: "Being Christian is not the result of an ethical choice or a lofty idea, but the encounter with an event, a person, which gives life a new horizon and a decisive direction" (DCE §1). In the same vein, Francis also regularly cites Benedict's statement that "the church does not grow through proselytism but through attraction." In short, Francis adds, "Being a Christian is not adhering to a doctrine.... Being Christian is about an encounter."[92] Respectfully, Francis misunderstands Benedict's point.

Francis insists that becoming a Christian happens through the "attraction" of the gospel rather than doctrine or moral teaching. By contrast, Benedict means by "attraction" the power of truth. As Vatican II's *Dignitatis Humanae* states, "The truth cannot impose itself except by virtue of its own truth, as it makes its entrance into the mind at once quietly and with power" (§1). In *Caritas in Veritate*, Benedict explains the inextricable connection between charity and truth such that charity without truth "degenerates into sentimentality." In other words, "Love becomes an empty shell, to be filled in an arbitrary way. In a culture without truth, this is the fatal risk facing love. It falls prey to contingent subjective emotions and opinions, the word "love" is abused and distorted, to the point where it comes to mean the opposite." On the one hand, then, "Truth frees charity from the constraints of an emotionalism that deprives it of relational and social content, and of a fideism that deprives it of human and universal breathing-space. In the truth, charity reflects the personal yet public dimension of faith in the God of the Bible, who is both *Agápe* and *Lógos*: Charity and Truth, Love and Word" (§3). On the other hand, Benedict explains, "Because it is filled with truth, charity can be understood in the abundance of its values, it can be shared and communicated. *Truth*, in fact, is *lógos* which creates *diá-logos*, and hence communication and communion. Truth, by enabling men and women to let go of their subjective opinions and impressions, allows them to move beyond cultural and historical limitations and to come together in the assessment of the value and substance of things. Truth opens and unites our minds in the *lógos* of love: this is the Christian proclamation and testimony of charity" (§4). Clearly, Francis's reduction of "attraction" to encounter empties the latter of truth-content.

If I understand Francis correctly, his emphasis is on the object of faith as it is experienced, encountered, and lived. Of course, this emphasis is necessary and important. Still, Francis leaves unanswered—and he does so consistently, hence suggesting an opposition—the question how both asserted truth and lived truth, the *fides quae creditur*, which is the faith *which* one believes, the conceptual content, the beliefs which one holds to be true, affirms, and asserts, and the *fides qua creditur* belong to faith as a whole. In short, he leaves in the dark the Church's teaching that faith is both a personal and cognitive-propositional encounter with the divine revelation of Christ.[93]

His recent Post-Synodal Apostolic Exhortation, *Christus Vivit*, bears out once again very clearly that he does not give an integral place to the fides quae creditur in his understanding of the life of faith. Francis says, "In the words of a saint, 'Christianity is not a collection of truths to be believed, rules to be followed, or prohibitions. Seen that way, it puts us off. Christianity is a person who loved me immensely, who demands and asks for my love. Christianity is Christ'" (CRV §156).[94] However, Francis's view is inconsistent with the *Catechism of the Catholic Church*: "Faith is first of all a personal adherence of man to God. At the same time, and inseparably, it is a *free assent to the whole truth that God has revealed*" (§150). Again, the *Catechism* teaches, "There is an *organic* connection between our spiritual life and the dogmas. Dogmas are lights along the path of faith; they illuminate it and make it secure. Conversely, if our life is upright, our intellect and heart will be open to welcome the light shed by the dogmas of faith" (§89, emphasis added). Finally yet importantly, the *Catechism* clearly teaches that faith involves both the *fides qua creditur*—the faith *with which* one believes—and the *fides quae creditur*—the faith *which* one believes.[95] "Faith is the theological virtue by which we believe in God and believe all that he has said and revealed to us, and that Holy Church proposes for our belief, because he is truth itself. By faith 'man freely commits his entire self to God'" (§1814). Unfortunately, this rich account of faith is missing in Francis's thought.

However, it is not missing in the thought of Cardinal Müller. Almost as if he directing himself critically against Francis's view, Müller states, "when speaking of God, one must be careful not to let this prioritization of living out, practicing, and carrying out Christ's truth drain doctrine of all its value." Müller adds, "An encounter with God involves doctrine in an inseparable way." That is, "an encounter with Jesus is not empty and content-free. Instead, it is an encounter with the Person of the Son of God, which implies that in the encounter I am confessing my faith in Jesus as the Son of God. In fact, the content of faith is already present in the encounter and makes it possible, so it does not appear afterward."[96]

John Paul II understood this matter admirably well, *fides qua creditur* and *fides quae creditur* exist in a mutual correlation in which neither can exist without the other; neither is basic to the other because neither is the source of the other.

> "I have already drawn your attention to the difference between the catechism formula, 'accepting as true all that God reveals', and surrender to God. In the first definition, faith is primary intellectual, in so far as it is the welcoming and assimilation of revealed fact. On the hand, when the constitution *Dei verbum* tells us that man entrust himself to God 'by the obedience of faith', we are confronted with the whole ontological and existential dimension and, so to speak, the drama of existence proper to man."[97]

Not surprisingly, Francis makes no reference to *Veritatis Splendor* and John Paul II's account of the fundamental question of how truth is authenticated as existential truth, including moral truth, John Paul correctly notes, that it is not merely about propositional truth, but rather how truth is borne out in life.

> It is urgent to rediscover and to set forth once more the authentic reality of the Christian faith, which is not simply a set of propositions to be accepted with intellectual assent. Rather, faith is a lived knowledge of Christ, a living remembrance of his commandments, and a *truth to be lived out*. A word, in any event, is not truly received until it passes into action, until it is put into practice. Faith is a decision involving one's whole existence. It is an encounter, a dialogue, a communion of love and of life between the believer and Jesus Christ, the Way, and the Truth, and the Life [cf. John 14:6]. It entails an act of trusting abandonment to Christ, which enables us to live as he lived [cf. Gal 2:20], in profound love of God and of our brothers and sisters. Faith also possesses a moral content. It gives rise to and calls for a consistent life commitment; it entails and brings to perfection the acceptance and observance of God's commandments. (VS §88)

There is one other factor to consider regarding the nature of truth and that is Francis's skepticism about "absolute" truth.

Absolute Truth?

In his letter of 4 September 2013 to a non-believer, Francis responds to the questions of Eugenio Scalfari, a journalist of the Italian newspaper, *La Repubblica*. One of his questions asks whether there is "no absolute, and therefore no absolute truth, but only a series of relative and subjective truths."[98] Francis does not define "subjective truth," but *Lumen Fidei* §25, which was coauthored with Benedict XVI, we read: "subjective truths of the individual... consist in fidelity to his or her deepest convictions, which are truths valid only for that individual and not capable of being proposed to others." This understanding of truth could also be called "personal truth." Wilfred Cantwell Smith claims that religious truth should be understood as "personal truth" rather than propositional truth. Describing Smith's view, Harold Netland explains, "Personal truth is a property not of propositions or statements but rather of persons and is a function of one's inner life.... In other words, personal truth does not signify objective correspondence with reality but rather personal integrity, sincerity, faithfulness, and the existential appropriation of particular beliefs in the believer's conduct."[99] By contrast, a true belief is simply *true* and therefore valid even for those who do not hold it, in short, it is true for everyone, as the way things are. This is propositional truth, as I defined it above.

Is this what Francis says in his answer to Scalfari? Not quite.

> To begin with, I would not speak about "absolute" truths, even for believers, in the sense that absolute is that which is disconnected and bereft of all relationship. Truth, according to the Christian faith, is the love of God for us in Jesus Christ. Therefore, truth is a relationship. As such each one of us receives the truth and expresses it from within, that is to say, according to one's own circumstances, culture and situation in life, etc. This does not mean that truth is variable and subjective, quite the contrary. But it does signify that it comes to us always and only as a way and a life. Did not Jesus himself say: "I am the way, the truth, and the life?" In other words, truth, being completely one with love, demands humility and an openness to be sought, received and expressed.[100]

This is a crucial passage and it requires much unpacking. Of course, Francis is not a "relativist" about truth, but he is skeptical about speaking of "absolute" truth. Does he seek to leave behind both absolutism and relativism in matters of religion? I will return to this crucial question in Chapter 7 when I address the question of the dialogue of religions and the question of truth. For now, let us note that Francis is skeptical of speaking of "absolute" truth because, for Christians, he claims, truth is not only mediated through a relationship with a divine person, Christ, but also known under the conditions of history. Thus, in his skepticism about absolute truth, he implies that he objects to the idea of a truth-in-itself, without a knowing subject. In my judgment, Francis confuses the conditions under which I know that something is true and the conditions that make something true.[101] In other words, he confuses the "question of whether one knows that the statement is true or is justified in believing it" with the question of "whether the statement is in fact true."[102] *Pace* Francis, affirming the existence of absolute truth and the conditions that make *p* true—which is objective reality—does not mean that one ignores the separate matter regarding the conditions under which I come to know that *p* is true. Those conditions may include—as Francis rightly says—acknowledging that this claim is made *from* a social, cultural/historical, and ecclesial location in life. Furthermore, the epistemic conditions under which one comes to know the truth involves the right dispositions, moral and religious character, of the inquirer, as Francis correctly suggests. However, Francis also confuses the matter in question. Truth itself is not a relationship; rather, the *knowledge* of truth consists of a relationship—personal encounter, trust, obedience, and love—between the knower and the known. Furthermore, personal knowledge is indissolubly linked with conceptual content, with believing and hence affirming certain things to be true, claims regarding "what" God says to us. It is no wonder that the *Catechism of the Catholic Church* teaches, "Faith is first of all a personal adherence of man to God. *At the same time, and inseparably* [emphasis added], it is a *free assent to the whole truth that God has revealed*" (CCC §150). This teaching is missing in Francis. John Paul II rightly sees what Francis overlooks.

> With regard to the *intellectus fidei*, a prime consideration must be that divine Truth "proposed to us in the Sacred Scriptures and rightly interpreted by the Church's teaching" [Saint Thomas Aquinas, ST, II-II, 5, 3 ad 2] enjoys an innate intelligibility, so logically consistent that it stands as an authentic body of knowledge. The *intellectus fidei* expounds this truth, not only in grasping the logical and conceptual structure of the propositions in which the Church's teaching is framed, but also, indeed primarily, *in bringing to light the salvific meaning of these propositions for the individual and for humanity*. From the sum of these propositions, the believer comes to know the history of salvation, which culminates in the person of Jesus Christ and in his Paschal Mystery. *Believers then share in this mystery by their assent of faith.* (FR §65, emphasis added)

Yes, the judgments that we make about truth may vary, in other words, their epistemic status, but truth itself does not change because it transcends the limits of a cultural context. In his own words, as John Paul II rightly states, "Truth can never be confined to time and culture; in history it is known, but it also reaches beyond history" (FR §95).

Francis must agree here with John Paul because he denies that truth is variable, subjective, or personal. But—unlike John Paul—he overlooks the epistemic conditions under which I know that something is true and conditions that make it true. Presupposing that distinction, allows one to see that there is no opposition here between asserting that *p* is true *simpliciter*—what *p* says is the case, actually is the case, valid for everyone—and acknowledging the conditions under which I know that *p*. Consider propositions such as that "God created the world," that "Jesus Christ our Lord was conceived by the Holy Spirit, Born of the Virgin Mary, Suffered under Pontius Pilate, Was crucified, dead and buried," and that "Jesus Christ was raised from the dead"—all these assertions are true since what they say is the case, actually is the case. Now, if we focus on the content of what is asserted here in these statements, its theological truth-content, rather than the conditions under which they were asserted, we surely may say of such assertions that they are objectively true, in other words, "once true always true, permanently true." The latter means that the truth or falsity of our beliefs and assertions is objective in virtue of certain facts about reality, which holds for all men—absolutely. In short, the source of truth is reality. We can know absolute truth, because to believe, assert, or claim that *p* is absolutely true is identical with asserting that it is true *simpliciter*.

Moreover, the then Cardinal Bergoglio affirms that "Truth, beauty, and goodness exist. The absolute exists. It can, or rather, it should be known and perceived."[103] Yet, sometimes Bergoglio does not seem to understand the idea of logically exclusive beliefs and what is entailed by that idea. For instance, he stresses, "Let us not compromise our ideas, utopias, possessions, and rights; *let us give up only the pretension that they are unique and absolute*" (emphasis added).[104] Does he realize that this sounds like "subjective truth" or "personal truth?" Is Bergoglio suggesting that Christianity is not absolute? Does he realize that giving up this so-called pretension means renouncing the finality, fullness, and superiority of God's revelation in Christ? Elsewhere, but similarly, he writes, "To dialogue [with other religions] means to believe that the 'other' has something worthwhile to say, and to entertain his or her point of view and perspective. Engaging in dialogue does not mean renouncing our own ideas and traditions, *but the [renouncing of the] claim that they alone are valid or absolute.*"[105] His disclaimer withdrawing the validity or absoluteness of Christian beliefs sounds like relativism. Is Francis a relativist about truth?[106]

Elsewhere Francis says in a similar vein,

> The truth of God is inexhaustible, it is an ocean from which we barely see the shore. It is something that we are beginning to discover in these times: not to enslave ourselves to an almost paranoid defense of *our truth* (if I *have* it, he doesn't *have* it; if he can *have* it, then I don't *have* it). *The truth is a gift that remains* large, and precisely for this reason it *enlarges us, it amplifies us, it elevates us*. And it makes us servants of such a gift, which does not entail relativisms, but rather that the truth requires a continual path of deepening comprehension.[107]

Yes, knowledge of the truth requires such a path, involving then new linguistic formulations in the deepening comprehension that may result in doctrinal development. However, Francis doesn't make clear here that these linguistic formulations do not logically entail discontinuity of doctrine. On the *Lérinian* interpretation new formulations must keep the same meaning and the same judgment (*eodem sensu eademque sententia*). Again, he says, "To dialogue means to believe that the 'other' has something worthwhile to say, and to entertain his or her point of view and perspective. Engaging in dialogue does not mean renouncing our own ideas and traditions, *but the [renouncing of the] claim that they alone are valid or absolute.*"[108] What does Francis mean?

What does Francis mean when urging us to renounce the claim that the central truth claims of Christianity are alone valid or absolute? As it stands, this claim is confusing. If *p* is true, then –*p* must be false, and hence anyone who holds –*p* must be wrong. We live in a culture where people claim that there are no true propositions; yet if there are no true propositions, then there are no false ones either. There are just differences and no one is wrong. This is relativism about truth. Now, given Francis's critique of practical relativism,[109] he cannot be asking us to withdraw our truth claims, because that *p* is only true for me, or to hold them hypothetically or conditionally. In the first place, if we give up the idea that our beliefs are unique such that they are absolutely true, then aren't we giving up holding them as true? Surely, Jeffrey Stout is right when he says that we do not necessarily "lack humility when we conclude that our beliefs are true, and, by implication, that those who disagree with us hold false beliefs." Again, Stout rightly says, "To hold our beliefs is precisely to accept them as true." Therefore, he adds, "It would be inconsistent, not a sign of humility, to say that people who disagree with beliefs that we hold true are not themselves holding false beliefs."[110]

In the second place, of course, given that truth is inexhaustible, it does "require a continual path of deepening comprehension," as Bergoglio puts it—but properly understood in the Lérinian sense, as I have explained, "according to the same meaning and the same judgment [*eodem sensu eademque sententia*]." As the then Cardinal Bergoglio put it: "One characteristic of solid [reliable, trustworthy] truth is that it is always open to more truth, it is always open more widely and deeply to transcendent truth."[111] And surely Bergoglio holds that one can express truth determinatively—inadequacy of expression does not mean inexpressibility of truth. For if the latter were the case, there would be no revealed truth, and no reliable access to these sets of truth (FR §81). The belief-content of faith (*fides quae creditur*) expresses truth determinatively, and not merely approximately, because "the dogmatic expression must bear some relationship to truth for it to be considered *de fide*, unless one has a view that language has no proper referencing function to reality."[112] In sum, faith of its very nature involves belief, and to have a belief means that I am intellectually committed to the truth of that belief. Now, truth is such that if a proposition is true, then what that proposition states is in fact the case about objective reality. Propositionally being the case about objective reality means that it is absolutely, objectively and universally true. A proposition is absolutely and objectively true when it is true for not only those who believe it—that's relativism—but equally true even when it is rejected. This means that a proposition is true regardless of whatever anyone thinks about it. Truth in itself is, therefore, universal in that "if something is true then it must be true for all people and at all times" (FR §27).

A Theologico-Pastoral Epistemology

One of the first principles guiding Francis's reflections of the theological task is that theologians must attend, personally and vitally, to the historical realities of specific times and places. This is because those realities are more important than ideas; according to Francis, "Reality is greater than ideas" (EG §231). This is one of Francis' first principles. Robert Royal is right, however. "But *this idea,* taken seriously, is self-refuting. It's only through ideas, concepts, words that we can apprehend the meaning of reality at all or know that it's greater than ideas."[113] Still, why is there this priority, according to Francis? If I understand him correctly, there are three reasons for this priority. First, Francis wants to avoid the fallacy of misplaced concreteness, which is the error of treating an abstract truth, idea, doctrinal formulation, as if it were the real concrete thing. This is Francis's critique of reification. Rather, he emphasizes, "There... exists a constant tension between ideas and realities. Realities simply are, whereas ideas are worked out. There has to be continuous dialogue between the two, lest ideas become detached from realities" (EG §231). Otherwise, he adds, we tend to mistake abstract concepts or ideas for accurate descriptions of reality, and we run the risk of "masking reality" by means of "angelic forms of purity, dictatorships of relativism, empty rhetoric, objectives more ideal than real, brands of ahistorical fundamentalism, ethical systems bereft of kindness, intellectual discourse bereft of wisdom" (EG §231).

This first point raises one question in particular that Francis does not address, but which is crucial to understanding the truth-status of dogmatic formulations. Are the truths of faith expressed in the creedal statements of Nicaea and Chalcedon, more particularly, orthodoxy, just "ideas," mere theory, mere thoughts or mere sets of words, altogether separate from God, or do they convey or grasp divine reality itself, the truth about that reality, fulfilling the truth-attaining capacity of the human mind to lay hold of divine reality? Cardinal Müller rightly says, "Christian doctrine is not a theory, a system of the sort that idealism or even ideology offers—that is, a formulation of human ideas. If a man falls in love with a woman, he does not see that person as an example of a sociological theory of human relations! Christianity, for its part, has always given priority to the person over ideas, but when speaking of God, one must be careful not to let this prioritization drain doctrine of all its value. God is truth, and the events in the story of salvation are a realization, under the conditions of concrete human history, of that truth which is God." Therefore, he adds,

"Redemption is conditioned on orthodoxy, as is the correct conception of eternal life: orthodoxy is not just a theory about God, but a matter of God's personal relationship with me."[114] Unfortunately, Francis misses all these important points, which results in leaving doctrines in the shadows or on the back burner, a position that is further complicated by his theologico-pastoral epistemology, and its attendant emphasis on the "listening" Church to the neglect of the "teaching Church."

Second, Francis's theologico-pastoral epistemology, in moving against "ineffectual forms of idealism and nominalism" (EG §232), affirms the interrelationship of thought and action, is praxis-oriented, meaning thereby that it is theoretically reflective action, with conceptual elaboration being an inherent aspect of action. He explains. "Ideas—conceptual elaborations—are at the service of communication, understanding, and praxis." Disconnecting ideas from realities results in a categorical system—classifying and defining realities—says Francis, in a failure to communicate, understand, and "certainly not calling to action." Actions here are "realities illuminated by reason"—theoretically reflective actions.

Third, Francis's reflections align him with the proponents of a praxis-oriented theological epistemology, such as the one famously proposed by Gustavo Gutiérrez. "Theology [is] a critical reflection on Christian praxis in the light of the Word." Reality is greater than ideas, says Francis, because the Word that has been made flesh is "constantly striving to take flesh anew," and that "is essential to evangelization." This is the "law of evangelization" of which I spoke at the start of this chapter when Francis stated, "Vatican II was a rereading of the Gospels in light of contemporary culture." Hence, his support for a hermeneutics of creative retrieval and renewal of the Word that normatively precedes us. This is Francis's version of the continuation of the Incarnation, an ongoing recontextualization and reinterpretation of the Gospel in a new context—"without pretending to come up with a system of thought detached from the treasury [deposit of faith], as if we wanted to reinvent the Gospel." Reinventing the Gospel renders the Gospel an ideology. Ideology is a perennial temptation, he says, "to interpret the Gospel apart from the Gospel itself and apart from the Church." What does Francis mean by this?

The Church's life of faith is, according to Francis, an indispensable epistemic and hermeneutical context for properly interpreting the Gospel. Furthermore, the Gospel is not to be reduced to interpretations of faith, but rather the Gospel itself provides its own meaningful content, its own message, which is a transcultural substance of faith that is the normative basis of our non-ideological interpretations (EG §§40-41, 45, 116-117, 129). Any approach that succumbs to the above described temptation would be epistemically and hermeneutically defective because it measures the Gospel by an *external* standard that is foreign to the revelatory narrative. Furthermore, Pope Francis is self-consciously aware that there can be no interpretation of the Gospel without presuppositions. He explicitly rejects a "neutral" (his own word is "antiseptic") hermeneutics—in other words, a presuppositionless hermeneutics, that is, "detached and unengaged, which is impossible." He adds, "The way we 'see' is always affected by the way we direct our gaze.... The question [is], rather: How are we going to look at reality in order to see it?" He replies: "With the eyes of discipleship."[115] In other words, with the eyes of the supernatural gift of faith we see reality, make judgments, and then act as missionary disciples. Moreover, adds Francis, given the pre-existing Word, "At the same time, this principle [of reality's priority] impels us to put the word into practice, to perform works of justice and charity which makes that word fruitful. Not to put the word into practice, not to make it reality, is to build on sand, to remain in the reality of pure ideas and to end up in a lifeless and unfruitful self-centeredness and gnosticism" (EG §233).[116]

Given Francis's dismissal of the idea of abstract truth—that is, propositional truth—his reluctance to speak of absolute truth, and his theologico-pastoral epistemology, with its attendant principle of realities being greater than ideas, there is some serious justification for the claim that Francis has shifted to a new paradigm, the so-called pastorality of doctrine. This shift is evident to me now since the first edition of my Francis book. In the next section, I examine this alleged shift in the context of John Paul II's appropriation and development of the *Lérinian* legacy of Vatican II.

Language, Truth, and Reality

According to John Paul II, moral actions are situated in the normative and comprehensive dynamics of the moral life, which are fourfold. "These are: [1] the *subordination of man and his activity to God,* the One who 'alone is good'; [2] the *relationship between the moral good* of human acts *and eternal life;* [3] *Christian discipleship,* which opens us before the perspective of perfect love; and finally [4] the *gift of the Holy Spirit,* source and means of the moral life of the 'new creation' [cf. 2 Cor 5:17]" (VS §28).

Briefly, God, the "Supreme Good" (FR §83), is not only the chief end of man's whole moral life (VS §29)—the source and ground of all goodness—but also Truth itself (*prima veritas*).[117] Good moral actions must be virtuous, conforming to the moral law, and the good of the person himself, and only then are they consistent with that end and hence integrally good. Furthermore, the truths of the moral life must be lived out, practiced, carried out, as integral to Christian discipleship, and hence cannot be reduced to being merely believed, asserted, and claimed. Last but not least, to be a "new creation" in Christ means that the moral life in Christ is about the renewal of man's fallen nature from within the order of creation by God's redemptive grace in Christ, properly ordering man to his chief end. In short, our Adamic humanity, with its darkened understanding, alienation from God, and blindness of heart, is transformed in Christ, putting on the new man, "created according to God in true righteousness and holiness" (Eph 4:22-24). God who created all things in and through Christ (Col 1:16), has restored his fallen creation, which was savagely wounded by sin, by re-creating it in Christ.

In this normative setting, says John Paul, "Sacred Scripture remains the living and fruitful source of the Church's moral doctrine; as the Second Vatican Council recalled, the Gospel is 'the source of all saving truth and moral teaching' [DV §7]." In particular, he holds "that there exists, in Divine Revelation, a specific and determined moral content, universally valid and permanent" (VS §37). In general, John Paul claims, "The Bible, and the New Testament in particular, contains texts and statements which have a genuinely ontological content. The inspired authors intended to formulate true statements, capable, that is, of expressing objective reality." In addition, says John Paul, "This applies equally to the judgments of moral conscience, which Sacred Scripture considers capable of being objectively true." (FR §82). The pope develops this very claim in *Veritatis Splendor* §60: "The dignity of this rational forum (conscience) and the authority of its voice and judgments derive from the *truth* about moral good and evil, which it is called to listen to and express. This truth is indicated by the 'divine law', *the universal and objective norm of morality*."[118]

These moral truths are grounded in the eternal law of God, and that law gives moral propositions something to be true of without which moral objectivity would be groundless. Underscoring the universal and permanent validity of moral propositions is foundational for understanding why there are intrinsically evil acts. These moral truths belong to the deposit of faith. Assisted by the Holy Spirit, the Church has attained a doctrinal development about morality that is "analogous to that which has taken place in the realm of the truths of faith" (VS §28).

Development here is by way of clarification, that is, "'looking for a *more appropriate way of communicating* doctrine to the people of their time; since there is a difference between the deposit or the truths of faith and the manner in which they are expressed, keeping the same meaning and the same judgment [*eodem sensu eademque sententia*]' [GS §62]" (VS §29). Thus, in line with the thought of Vincent of Lérins as discussed above, John Paul follows Vatican II by distinguishing between truth and its historically conditioned formulations, truth-content and context; in sum, propositions and sentences.[119] John XXIII alluded to these distinctions in his opening address at Vatican II, *Gaudet Mater Ecclesia*: "For the deposit of faith [2 Tim 1:14], the truths contained in our sacred teaching, are one thing; the mode in which they are expressed, but with the same meaning and the same judgment [*eodem sensu eademque sententia*], is another thing."

As I have stated above, the subordinate clause here—*eodem sensu eademque sententia*—is part of a larger passage from Vatican I's *Dei Filius* (§4.14), and this passage is, in turn, from Vincent's *Commonitórium primum* (23.3): "Therefore, let there be growth and abundant progress in understanding, knowledge, and wisdom, in each and all, in individuals and in the whole Church, at all times and in the progress of ages, but only with the proper limits, i.e., within the same dogma, the same meaning, the same judgment." We must always determine whether those new re-formulations are preserving the same meaning and judgment (*eodem sensu eademque sententia*), and hence the material continuity, identity, and universality of those truths. Furthermore, given Francis's dismissal of abstract truths, indeed propositional truths, and his reluctance to speak of absolute truths, as well as his theologico-pastoral epistemology, it should by now be clear that Francis does not appropriate the *Lérinian* legacy of Vatican II. I turn now to refute the claims that Vatican II's legacy is a pastoral orientation of doctrine.

Pastoral Oriented Doctrine

Richard Gaillardetz claims that "Vatican II offered a new way of thinking about doctrine," meaning thereby that "it presented doctrine as something that always needed to be interpreted and appropriated in a *pastoral key*."[120] What does "pastoral" mean? Pared down for my purpose here, the word "pastoral" may mean three things.

First, looking back to the then Joseph Ratzinger who wrote during Vatican II: "'Pastoral' should not mean nebulous, without substance, merely 'edifying'—meanings sometimes given to it. Rather what was meant was positive care for the man of today who is not helped by condemnations and who has been told for too long what is false and what he may not do. Modern man really wishes to hear what is true. He has, indeed, not heard enough truth, enough of the positive message of faith for our time, enough of what the faith has to say to our age."[121] In sum, "pastoral" means presenting the life-affirming truth of the Christian faith.

Second, "pastoral" may also mean to affirm that the preaching of the Word of God should come before doctrine, and hence pastoral is not about the application of doctrine. Pastoral then has priority such that the "church has to mediate to the world not just a doctrine but the living Christ." As Lonergan puts it, "The task of the church is the kerygma, announcing the good news, preaching the gospel. That preaching is pastoral. It is the concrete reality. From it one may abstract doctrines, and theologians may work the doctrines into conceptual systems. But the doctrines and systems, however valuable and true, are but the skeleton of the original message."[122] In sum, the kerygma is pastoral—"living speech that from the start... [is] at once concrete and alive, interpersonal and communal, historical and ecumenical."[123] Let me suggest here that the Lérinian perspective may integrate these two meanings of pastoral within its purview. But that is not the case with the third meaning of pastoral that is nowadays being promoted as a "new paradigm" in some Catholic circles.

There is a third meaning of "pastoral," and it is historicist in character. This is precisely how Christoph Theobald, SJ, defines the "principle of pastorality." He claims that the Latin version of John XXIII's opening speech at Vatican II, which Theobald claims John rejected, distinguishes between "the deposit of faith itself, *that is the truths contained in our ancient doctrine*" and "the form in which these truths [plural] are proclaimed."[124] This version, too, overlooks the subordinate clause cited by Vatican I and derived from Vincent of Lérins, namely, that new formulations and expressions of the truths contained in the deposit of the faith must keep the same meaning and the same judgment (*eodem sensu eademque sententia*). However, the original version, presumably Theobald means the Italian version, of John's intervention, "simply underlines the fundamental difference between the deposit of faith, taken here as a *whole*—without reference to an internal plurality inherent in the expression—and the historical form it takes at one time or another."[125] If I understand Theobald correctly, he prefers the Italian version, which is the original version, because there is no correction by the curia of the pope's speech. This version does not refer to an internal plurality of truths in the substance of the deposit of faith, which are then expressed in alternative formulations.[126] This principle collapses the distinction between the substance of the deposit of faith and their formulations into a historical context, without attending to the subordinate clause—*eodem sensu eademque sententia*—but also dismissing the notion of propositional truths and sentences, truth-content and context, and the like, that may be distinguished within the deposit of faith. This means, as Theobald puts it, that the substance of the deposit of faith as a whole is "subject to continual reinterpretation [and re-contextualization] according to the situation of those to whom it is transmitted." This is a plea for a perpetual hermeneutics.[127] On this principle, doctrines are not absolute truths, or objectively true affirmations, because what they assert is in fact the case about objective reality. (FR §82).

We find a similar line of reasoning in Theobald's reflections on the "law of evangelization" expressed in Vatican II's *Gaudium et Spes* §44, and *Ad Gentes* §22. The core idea of this law is, "*accommodated preaching of the revealed word ought to remain the law of all evangelization.*" As Theobald understands this "law," ongoing accommodation of the Gospel—and hence a perpetual hermeneutics—is necessary given the cultural and historical diversity of the context in which the Gospel is preached. This means that the principle of pastorality, according to Theobald, presupposes a double hermeneutic, that is, a mutually critical correlation between a "hermeneutic of the Gospel and a hermeneutic of languages and cultures open to receive the Good News of Christ." Theobald rejects the "absolutizing" and "identification" of the Gospel "with the various doctrinal truths contained in the tradition, as found collected in the *Catechism of the Catholic Church* and, in the life of a believer, in a uniform liturgy and, as regards Church procedures, in the *Code of Canon Law*." He assures us that the principle of pastorality does not set up an opposition between doctrine, on the one hand, and pastoral ministry of those to whom doctrine is addressed in the historical and cultural plurality of contexts, on the other. Yes, "'pastorality'... must *include* doctrine, but also leaves us with the hermeneutical task of isolating its authoritative element, *not in itself* [emphasis added], *but in relation with those who whom it is addressed today.*"[128] This approach relativizes the authority of doctrinal truths to the addressees. It is hard to see how it does not imply a subjectification of doctrinal truths that only *become* true, and hence authoritative, through acknowledgment. There is also a failure to recognize the distinction between the conditions that make something true and the conditions under which I know something to be true. More on this distinction below. In sum, *pace* Theobald, the principle of pastorality is inconsistent with the Lérinian hermeneutics of Vatican II. Furthermore, this hermeneutics is not inconsistent with the law of evangelization because historical context, on the one hand, and unchanging and absolute truth on the other, are not mutually exclusive in Lérinian hermeneutics.

Richard Gaillardetz draws on Theobald's principle of pastorality in his interpretation of Pope John XXIII's hermeneutics of creative retrieval and renewal.[129] Furthermore, he thinks that Francis fits this key. In other words, Francis is amenable to a so-called "pastoral orientation of doctrine," as Gaillardetz calls it. On Francis's view, says Gaillardetz, "doctrine is always at the service of the fundamental Christian message." Francis warns against putting "doctrine at several degrees of abstraction from the Gospel as it is experienced concretely in the life of [Christian] discipleship."[130] What this means here is that the Church seeks to mediate to the world not just doctrines but, chiefly, the living Word of God. Francis says, "In reality, doctrine has the sole purpose of serving the life of the People of God and it seeks to assure our faith of a sure foundation."[131] Put differently, Francis underscores the "eternal newness" of the Gospel. "The heart of its message will always be the same: the God who revealed his immense love in the crucified and risen Christ. God constantly renews his faithful ones, whatever their age.... Christ is the 'eternal Gospel' [Rev 14:6]; he 'is the same yesterday and today and forever' [Heb 13:8], yet his riches and beauty are inexhaustible" (EG §11).

Now, since the first edition of this book where I interpreted Francis's appropriation of John XXIII's *Lérinian* distinction between the truths of faith and their formulations, I have come to appreciate that I was wrong about Francis's understanding of that distinction. Recall that I wrote above that Francis distinguished between the substance of the deposit of the faith, and the way it is expressed, but without the subordinate clause, namely, "according to the same meaning and the same judgment [*eodem sensu eademque sententia*]." I am no longer surprised that this clause is missing. In light of his dismissal of abstract truth, skepticism about absolute truth, and his theologico-pastoral epistemology and the attending first principle that realties are greater than ideas, it makes sense that he would not be a full-fledged *Lérinian*.

Furthermore, Gaillardetz cites fellow theologian John O'Brien to explain this historicist view that underpins the claim that doctrine has a pastoral orientation:

> [The] pastoral had regained [with Pope John XXIII] its proper standing as something far more than mere application of doctrine but as the very context from which doctrines emerge, the very condition of the possibility of doctrine, the touchstone for the validity of doctrine and the always prior and posterior praxis which doctrine at most, attempts to sum up, safeguard, and transmit.[132]

Now, the above statement of O'Brien is saying much more than "the specific formulation of doctrine represents an acknowledgment that doctrine is always historically conditioned." It is also saying much more than "the interpretation of church doctrine requires knowledge of the specific historical contexts in which it was first formulated and in which it is being appropriated."[133] These two points are correct, but particularly relevant only in respect of the conditions under which we come to know that something is true. Yet those conditions are distinct from the conditions under which something *is* true. In sum, conditions of *truth* must be distinguished from conditions of *justification*. Yet the above passage seems to blur the distinction between the conditions under which I come to know that a doctrine is true with the conditions that make it true. Gaillardetz is a modernist on Christian doctrine because he doesn't understand the truth-status of the doctrinal formulation in its relation to reality. A doctrinal proposition is true if and only if what that proposition asserts is in fact the case about objective reality; otherwise, the proposition is false. It isn't the context that determines the truth of the proposition that is judged to be the case about objective reality; rather, reality itself determines the truth or falsity of a proposition. In sum, the historical context does not determine the validity—the truth-status—of the doctrine.

Furthermore, doctrinal essentialism is correct. Characteristic of essentialism is the claim that there is a "dogmatic conceptual hard-core"[134] of Catholic dogmas, such as the Trinity and the Incarnation, whose meaning does not change precisely because it is true to reality. The content of the concepts informing the propositions that God is Triune, and that the Second Person of the Trinity is God Incarnate, has invariant meaning, is fixed and hence determinate. Therefore, as Ratzinger rightly states, "faith establishes specifiable dogmatic reference points."[135] Essentialism as such is, however, not incompatible with the claim, as Thomas Guarino notes, "that every statement requires further thought and elucidation, that every assertion is open to reconceptualization and reformulation, and that no statement comprehensively exhausts truth, much less divine truth."[136] But the linguistic formulation or expression can vary, as long as they mediate the same judgment. This, too, is the view of David Tracy.[137] His view is more faithful to John XXIII's Lérinian conception than are those of Gaillardetz, Theobald, *et al.* Tracy says, "Fidelity to orthodox judgment intrinsic to the particular meaning expressed in propositions is what counts, not the language itself." Again, "The judgments endure but always need new cultural and therefore linguistic formulations." And again, "A purely classicist understanding of language believes that a static unchanging, unchangeable, normative language is alone capable of expressing (*semper idem*) the community's *ortho-dox* beliefs."[138] The import of these distinctions totally elude those who support a historicist approach to doctrinal development/change.

Furthermore, *pace* Gaillardetz, there is no reason to think that the acceptance of truth as propositional leads to the claim that doctrinally correct formulations or expressions of revealed truth completely express such truth.[139] We need to be careful here; it is one thing to say that our doctrinal formulations exhaustively grasp the content of revealed truth, and it is another to say—which I would argue we must say—that dogmatic formulations "must bear some determinative relationship to truth itself... unless one has a view that language has no proper referencing function to reality."[140] Consider briefly Karl Rahner's claim that the truth of revelation is expressed incompletely, inadequately, given the profound effects on our knowledge of being historically conditioned. The one crucial factor in Rahner's view is that the truth of revelation may be expressed incompletely and inadequately—and here is what's crucial and often missed—*but not falsely*. In short, Rahner holds a realist's view of truth—*adaequatio rei et intellectus*. For a realist, the meaning of truth is such that a proposition is true if (and only if), what that proposition asserts is in fact the case about objective reality. Whether a proposition is true or not depends on whether reality is as the proposition says that it is. Rahner's point is this: If what a dogmatic formula asserts about reality is entirely truthful, then that means that its description of reality is *adequatio intellectus et rei*, in so far as dogmatic formula states absolutely nothing that is false. As Rahner puts it:

> All human statements, even those in which faith expresses God's saving truths, are finite. By this we mean that they never declare the *whole* of reality.... This is even truer of spiritual and divine realities. The statements which we make about them, relying on the Word of God which itself became 'flesh' in human words, can never express them once and for all in an entirely adequate form. *But they are not for this reason false.* They are an "adequatio intellectus et rei," in so far as they state absolutely nothing which is false. Anyone who wants to call them 'half false' because they do not state everything about the whole of the truth of the matter in question would eventually abolish the distinction between truth and falsehood. On the other hand, anyone who proposes to regard these propositions of faith, because they are wholly true, as in themselves *adequate* to the matter in question, i.e., as exhaustive statements, would be falsely elevating human truth to God's simple and exhaustive knowledge of himself and of all that takes its origin from him.[141]

Consider, for example, the creeds of Nicaea and Chalcedon. Is what they assert and hence make judgments about the Trinity and the person and natures of Christ true to reality? In other words, do they have a truth-conveying status, meaning thereby that what is asserted in them is ontologically true? And what about linguistically articulated doctrine, judgments expressive of propositional truth, supporting the conclusive and abiding assertions of revelation and doctrine, and logically sustaining the affirmations of Christian belief, their universality, continuity, and material identity? As Avery Dulles once put it, "If we are to worship, speak, and behave as though the Son of God were himself God..., is it not because the Son really and ontologically is God, whether anyone believes it or not? By inserting the *homoousion* in the creed, the Council of Nicaea was indeed laying down a linguistic stipulation; but more importantly, it was declaring an objective truth."[142] Truth here is understood in a realist sense: *adaequatio speculativa rei et intellectus* as John Paul II holds in *Fides et Ratio* §82. It is not understood as the *adaequatio realis mentis et vitae* (the real correspondence between life and mind). Here the choice is between different accounts of truth—"does truth depend on its conformity with the measure of human knowledge in a given day" or "on its conformity to the reality of things as they are"? The former is a relativist view of truth; the latter is a realist view of truth, also known as a correspondence view.

Yes, G.C. Berkouwer is right that it is surely simplistic to ignore the historical context in understanding "the various terms, concepts, images, and propositions that the Church has used to confess its faith." He is also surely right that the meaning of dogmas is not always immediately transparent. For example, there exists unclear terms "in the Christological and Trinitarian controversies, such words as consubstantial, hypostasis, person, nature, and many others. The terms often evoked misunderstandings, and different interpretations of them created conflict of opinion."[143] Berkouwer's insistence here is, then, that to grasp the meaning of a dogma we must understand its historical context. If this is all that Gaillardetz means, then of course he is right. Still, Grisez is also right that "if the propositions signified by certain expressions were true," say, the Chalcedonian formula of faith regarding the relationship between the two natures in the unity of the divine person, "subsequent variations in the meaning of the expressions do not affect the truth of the propositions, but only the ability of the expressions to communicate truth without interpretation." In short, adds Grisez, "If this proposition is true, it will be true always and everywhere."[144] Therefore, the question at hand is, arguably, a matter of judging whether or not what is meant is true to reality. Bernard Lonergan is right that "meaning of its nature is related to what is meant, and what is meant may or may not correspond to what is in fact so [is the case]." "If it corresponds," Lonergan adds, "the meaning is true. If it does not correspond, the meaning is false."[145] Lonergan then correctly notes the implication of denying the correspondence view of truth, namely, that a proposition is true if what it says corresponds to what is in fact the case; otherwise, it is false.

> To deny correspondence is to deny a relation between meaning and meant. To deny the correspondence view of truth is to deny that, when the meaning is true, the meant is what is so [is the case]. Either denial is destructive of the dogmas.... If one denies that, when the meaning is true, then the meant is what is so, one rejects propositional truth. If the rejection is universal, then it is the self-destructive proposition that there are no true propositions. If the rejection is limited to the dogmas,

> then it is just a roundabout way of saying that all the dogmas are false.[146]

Put differently, a dogma's meaning is unchangeable because that meaning is true.[147] "If one denies that, when the meaning is true, then the meant is what is so, one rejects propositional truth."[148] The truths of faith are, if true, always and everywhere true; the different way of expressing these truths may vary in our attempts to more clearly and accurately communicate revealed truths, but these various linguistic expressions do not affect the truth of the propositions. The distinction between the propositional truths of faith and their expressions is of utmost importance because it provides us with "the criterion for distinguishing between form and content, representation and affirmation."[149]

Contra Gaillardetz, the Council and John XXIII referred to the truths contained in our sacred teaching as propositional truths—absolute truths—meaning thereby truths that are unchangeable, permanent, and universal. This presupposes a realist view of truth in which a proposition is true if—and only if—what it asserts is in fact the case about objective reality; otherwise, it is false. The crucial difference here between Vatican II, John Paul II, on the one hand, and Gaillardetz and Theobald on the other, pertain to the relation between language, truth, and reality in respect of doctrine. Unfortunately, since Francis dismisses abstract truth, is reluctant to speak of absolute truth, and works with a theologico-pastoral epistemology with its attending principle that realities are greater than ideas, his views fall on the same side as the "pastorality of doctrine" approach, and hence suffers from the same problems.

Realist View of Truth

For Gaillardetz, "pastoral" means that "the *central values* [emphasis added] embedded in doctrine" or in "particular doctrinal formulations [are] mediated by the saving message of God's transforming love."[150] According to him, the affirmations of faith do *not* have a determinable content of propositional truth in respect of their correspondence to reality. Rather, he subscribes to an instrumentalist or functionalist view of doctrine reminiscent of the late nineteenth and early twentieth century modernist rather than a realist view with its corresponding notion of propositional truth.[151] These "truths" are understood in a purely functional way.[152] Dogma bears no determinative relation to truth itself because the truth-status of doctrinal formulations have as such no proper referencing function to reality. Rather, they are historically determined[153] which means that Gaillardetz historicizes the meaning and truth of dogma by expanding the meaning of pastoral. "Pastoral" here has a historicist meaning, explicitly or implicitly denying the enduring validity of propositional truth: truth itself and not just its formulations are subject to reform and perpetual reinterpretation.

However, Gaillardetz is mistaken. For example, if the assertions of the Apostles' Creed, as the late British theologian Colin Gunton correctly notes, "were once true, they are always true." In other words, these statements never stopped being true, even after Jesus stopped suffering, and so on, and hence are now forever true. Consider, for example, the assertion expressing the proposition that Jesus came into the world to save sinners (1 Tim 1:15). Yes, we are focusing here on propositional truth, on the truth of what St. Paul asserted, the theological truth-content, rather than on the fact that he asserted it in a particular context, and so forth. Indeed, this is the case "even though we may need to explain, gloss and expand them in all kinds of ways." In other words, the claim that once something is true it is always true, forever true, and unchangeably true, is not inconsistent with finding new ways of expressing the truth of dogmas when the need arises. Therefore, the question at hand is, arguably, a matter of judging whether or not what is meant is true to objective reality, and not, *contra* O'Brien and hence Gaillardetz, the historical circumstances in which the dogmatic assertion was made. In other words, those circumstances are not "the touchstone for the validity of doctrine."

Thus, although O'Brien, cited above by Gaillardetz, is correct that historical conditions are particularly relevant as the conditions under which we come to know that something is true, those conditions are distinct from the conditions under which something is true. In sum, conditions of truth must be distinguished from conditions of justification. However, the above passage seems to blur the distinction between the conditions under which I come to know that a doctrine is true with the conditions that make it true. In that blurring, it is clear that Gaillardetz is both a historicist about doctrine and hence an anti-realist about language, truth, and reality. Says Gaillardetz, "Doctrine changes when pastoral contexts shift and new insights emerge such that particular doctrinal formulations no longer mediate the saving message of God's transforming love. Doctrine changes when the church has leaders and teachers who are not afraid to take note of new contexts and emerging insights."[154]

Contra Gaillardetz, however, Vatican II's *Lérinian* hermeneutics is realist in orientation because a doctrinal proposition is true if and only if what that proposition asserts is in fact the case about objective reality; otherwise, the proposition is false. It is not the historical context that determines the truth of the proposition that is judged to be the case about objective reality; rather, reality itself determines the truth or falsity of a proposition. In sum, the historical context does not determine the validity—the truth-status—of the doctrine.

Hence, Gaillardetz is a historicist regarding the truth-status of dogmatic formulations and an instrumentalist or pragmatist because he rejects propositional truth and the corresponding idea, as John Paul II states, that "dogmatic statements, while reflecting at times the culture of the period in which they were defined, formulate an unchanging and ultimate truth" (FR §95). John Paul adds, "Human language may be conditioned by history and constricted in other ways, but the human being can still express truths which surpass the phenomenon of language. Truth can never be confined to time and culture; in history it is known, but it also reaches beyond history" (FR §95). Put differently, abandoning the content/context, propositions and sentences, distinction threatens us with historicism, which denies the enduring validity of truth. "For," as Aidan Nichols rightly notes, "if the content/context distinction is irredeemably naïve, then with a change of context—so imperious logic demands—a change in content necessarily follows."[155]

Lérinian Interpretations

In this light, we can understand that John Paul did *Lérinian* interpretations when he successfully synthesized into a coherent whole personalism, existential/hermeneutic phenomenology, and Thomism in his philosophical and theological work. This synthesis shows itself in his works on Christian anthropology, metaphysics, and sexual ethics.[156] In a *Lérinian* manner he acknowledged a "need to seek out and to discover the *most adequate formulation* for universal and permanent moral norms in the light of different cultural contexts, a formulation most capable of ceaselessly expressing their historical relevance, of making them understood and of authentically interpreting their truth." He explains, "This truth of the moral law—like that of the 'deposit of faith'—unfolds down the centuries: the norms expressing that truth remain valid in their substance, but must be specified and determined '*eodem sensu eademque sententia*' [according to the same meaning and the same judgment] in the light of historical circumstances by the Church's Magisterium, whose decision is preceded and accompanied by the work of interpretation and formulation characteristic of the reason of individual believers and of theological reflection" (VS §53).

The understanding of the truth of the moral law has unfolded in the interpretation and application of that law down the centuries. Drawing on the distinction between truth and its formulations, between moral propositions and their linguistic expressions, John Paul explains that the moral norms expressive of moral truths, although taking account of various conditions of life according to places, times, and circumstance, "remain valid in their substance" and hence "must be specified and determined '*eodem sensu eademque sententia*' [according to the same meaning and the same judgment]" about that moral truth. So, there is growth in the understanding of moral truth, seeking out and discovering "the *most adequate formulation* for universal and permanent moral norms" without changing the substantive and determinate truth of morality.

Now, Gaillardetz would probably respond to John Paul II's idea of propositional revelation and the corresponding notion of dogmatic truth by charging that it forgets "almost entirely the ancient conviction that divine revelation has come to us first and primarily as an offer to saving communion in the person of Jesus Christ."[157] Yet God revealing himself as well as revealing truths about himself, man, and the world are two compatible descriptions of revelation; similarly, dialogical and propositional views of revelation are compatible.

The Nature of Revelation

Revelation is personal because in a fundamental sense, God reveals *himself*, and so we may say that the content of revelation is God's own proper reality, his self-revelation, the gift of himself, in the words of the late Germain Grisez, "as a communion of persons inviting human persons to enter into communion." God is then the *who* of divine revelation.

Revelation is Christological and pneumatological because "His will was that men should have access to the Father, through Christ, the Word made flesh, in the Holy Spirit, and thus become sharers in the divine nature [cf. Eph 2:18; 2 Pet 1:4]. By this revelation, then, the invisible God [cf. Col 1:15; 1 Tim 1:17], from the fullness of his love, addresses men as his friends [cf. Exod 33:11; John 15:14-15], and moves among them [cf. Bar 3:38], in order to invite and receive them into his own company" (DV §2). This is the *to whom* of divine revelation. Indeed, *Dei Verbum* discloses that the soteriological purpose of God's self-revelation is coming to know him. This is the *why* of divine revelation. "Now this is life eternal: that they may know you, the only true God, and Jesus Christ, whom you have sent" (John 17:3). We are invited, therefore, to Trinitarian communion with the Father, through the Son, Jesus Christ, the Word made flesh, in the power of the Holy Spirit. Revelation is, then, not the *mere* communication of truths but rather "the life-bestowing self-communication of the Trinitarian God, in which he addresses humans as friends," as *Dei Verbum* states. Thus, the notions of revelation as life-transforming and as information-providing are not incompatible.

Indeed, there is the necessity of a cognitive and propositional understanding of revelation. It seems to me that *Dei Verbum* §2 recognizes that we need to be taught by God in its affirmation that "the plan of revelation is realized by deeds and *words* having an inner unity." In other words, *Dei Verbum* states that there are two distinct but intrinsically united modes of revelation, and hence it speaks of the deed-word revelation. In the words of George Eldon Ladd, "Christ *died* is the deed; Christ died *for our sins* is the [divinely given] word of interpretation that makes the act revelatory."[158]

Thus, jointly constitutive of God's special revelation are its inseparably connected words (verbal revelation) and deeds, intrinsically bound to each other because neither is complete without the other; the historical realities of redemption are inseparably connected to God's verbal communication of truth in order that we may, as Catholic theologian Francis Martin puts it, "participate more fully in the *realities* mediated by the words." In other words, a core presupposition of the concept of revelation in *Dei Verbum* §2 is that "without God's acts the words would be empty, without His word the acts would be blind," as was admirably stated by Reformed theologian Geerhardus Vos.[159]

Furthermore, the idea that God's self-revelation is a *word*-revelation, forming an essential element of God's self-revelation, entails the idea of propositional revelation, of revealed *truth*, namely, that assertions expressing propositions are part of the way that God reveals himself. *Contra* Gaillardetz, *Dei Verbum* also affirms the centrality of "assertions," or propositions, by the Holy Spirit in God's verbal revelation: "Therefore, since everything asserted by the inspired authors or sacred writers must be held to be asserted by the Holy Spirit, it follows that the books of Scripture must be acknowledged as teaching solidly, faithfully and without error that truth which God wanted put into sacred writings for the sake of salvation" (DV §11). Aidan Nichols is correct. "Whatever else doctrines are, they are propositions, and no account of revelation which would exclude propositions wholly from its purview could do justice to the role of doctrines in Catholic Christianity."[160] Given Gaillardetz's instrumentalist and functionalist view of doctrine, and his corresponding anti-realism, his pastoral-oriented "new paradigm" cannot do justice to the role of doctrines in Catholicism because there is no intrinsic link between language, truth, and reality regarding the truth-status of dogmatic formulations. Unfortunately, Pope Francis's views suffer from the same problem.

One wonders whether Francis's understanding of revelation has room for propositional revelation given his claim that "God has revealed himself as history, not as a compendium of abstract truths."[161] Who thinks that divine revelation is a "compendium of abstract truths?" Is this a straw man? What, then, is an abstract truth? Earlier in this chapter, I argued that abstract truths are propositions that we assert to be true to reality, and the context does not determine the truth-status of the proposition. Therefore, abstract truths are propositional truths; for example, "The Word was made flesh and dwelt among us" (John 1:14). "Christ is risen from the dead" (1 Cor 15:20). Other examples of abstract truths that are asserted may be taken from the pastoral letter of First Timothy: "Christ Jesus came into the world to save sinners" (1:15). "God our Savior... desires all men to be saved and to come to the knowledge of the truth" (2:3-4). "For there is one God, and there is one mediator between God and men, the man Christ Jesus" (2:5). "For everything created by God is good, and nothing is to be rejected if it is received with thanksgiving" (4:4). The truth-status of these propositions is such that they will be true always and everywhere. A doctrinal proposition is true if—and only if—what that proposition asserts is in fact the case about objective reality; otherwise, the proposition is false. It is not the *context* that determines the truth of the proposition that is judged to be the case about objective reality; rather, *reality itself* determines the truth or falsity of a proposition.

Authentication of Truth

In conclusion, although propositional truth is an indispensable dimension of truth itself, how truth is authenticated existentially—that is, lived out, practiced, carried out—cannot be reduced to it—to being merely believed, asserted, and claimed because "what is communicated in catechesis is not [merely] a body of conceptual truths, but the mystery of the living God" (FR §99).[162] In other words, says John Paul,

> "The *intellectus fidei* expounds [these] truth[s], not only

> in grasping the logical and conceptual structure of the propositions in which the Church's teaching is framed, but also, indeed primarily, in bringing to light the salvific meaning of these propositions for the individual and for humanity. From the sum of these propositions, the believer comes to know the history of salvation, which culminates in the person of Jesus Christ and in his Paschal Mystery. Believers thus share in this mystery by their assent of faith." (FR §66)

Regarding, then, the fundamental question of how truth is authenticated as existential truth, including moral truth, John Paul correctly notes, that it is not merely about propositional truth, but rather how truth is borne out in life. He writes:

> It is urgent to rediscover and to set forth once more the authentic reality of the Christian faith, which is not simply a set of propositions to be accepted with intellectual assent. Rather, faith is a lived knowledge of Christ, a living remembrance of his commandments, and a *truth to be lived out*. A word, in any event, is not truly received until it passes into action, until it is put into practice. Faith is a decision involving one's whole existence. It is an encounter, a dialogue, a communion of love and of life between the believer and Jesus Christ, the Way, and the Truth, and the Life [cf. John 14:6]. It entails an act of trusting abandonment to Christ, which enables us to live as he lived [cf. Gal 2:20], in profound love of God and of our brothers and sisters. Faith also possesses a moral content. It gives rise to and calls for a consistent life commitment; it entails and brings to perfection the acceptance and observance of God's commandments. (VS §88)[163]

On this twentieth-fifth anniversary of St. John Paul II's great encyclical *Veritatis Splendor*, it is time to engage in a creative retrieval of this authentically *Lérinian* work in order to revitalize the present theological culture and life of the Church from its drift—in view of the "new paradigm"—which is nothing other than a drift toward a new modernism.

NOTES

1. I give a book-length treatment of Vatican II's legacy, particularly with respect to a hermeneutics of dogma, in my 2018 book, *Revelation, History, and Truth: A Hermeneutics of Dogma*. I draw on portions of this book in the section on "Pastoral Oriented Doctrine."
2. Bernard J.F. Lonergan, SJ, *Method in Theology*, 284, 324.
3. *Contra* Massimo Faggioli who claims that Francis "carefully avoid[s] interacting directly with the problematic teaching of Ratzinger on the [hermeneutics of] the council" *Pope Francis: Tradition in Transition*, 35.

4. Pope Francis, *Only Love Can Save Us*, 33-48, and at 42.

5. "Credo Ecclesiam," *Communio*, ed. Argentina, No. 1, Fall 2011, 5; as cited in Pope Francis, *Only Love Can Save Us*, 152. See original, "Credo Ecclesiam," http://angeloscola.it/espanol/2010/06/04/credo-ecclesiam-seminario-de-eclesiologia-propuesto-por-la-revista-communio/.

6. Francis, *Only Love Can Save Us*, 151n5.

7. Of course, Francis's biblical hermeneutics is such that it includes the principle, "to understand the meaning of the central message of a text we need to relate it to the teaching of the entire Bible as handed on by the Church. This is an important principle of biblical interpretation [that] recognizes that the Holy Spirit has inspired not just a part of the Bible, but the Bible as a whole.... It also prevents erroneous or partial interpretations which would contradict other teachings of the same Scriptures" (EG §148).

8. What is the "truth-content" of the Gospels, and how is it mediated through the living tradition of the Church, its creeds, confessions, dogmas, liturgy, sacraments, and the like?

9. Francis, *A Big Heart Open to God*, 43, emphasis added.

10. Francis, "Letter to Cardinal Brandmüller."

11. Pope Benedict XVI, "Address of his Holiness Benedict XVI to the Roman Curia offering them his Christmas greetings."

12. Francis, "Letter to Cardinal Brandmüller."

13. I discuss Alberigo's hermeneutical position on Vatican II, along with others, in chapter 1 of my book, *Revelation, History, and Truth*, 1-45.

14. Francis, "Pope Supports 'Hermeneutic of Continuity' Approach to Vatican II in Letter."

15. Pope Francis, "Preface," to Stephen Walford, *Pope Francis, The Family and Divorce*, xi-xii, and 224.

16. This second hermeneutical principle obviously involves a reference to the significant address of Pope Benedict XVI, in his now famous 2005 Christmas address to the Roman Curia, where he called the hermeneutics of Vatican II "the 'hermeneutic of reform', of renewal in the continuity of the one subject-Church which the Lord has given to us. She is a subject which increases in time and develops, yet always remaining the same, the one subject of the journeying People of God."

17. Pope Francis, with Dominique Wolton, *A Future of Faith*, 224.

18. Lonergan, *Method in Theology*, 284, 324.

19. This phrase was coined to my knowledge from Christoph Theobald, S.J., "The Principle of Pastorality at Vatican II." See also, Richard R. Gaillardetz, *An Unfinished Council, Vatican II, Pope Francis, and the Renewal of Catholicism*.

20. Francis, "Pope Francis's Address to the Synod Fathers."

21. Francis, "Doctrine and Ideology." For a general discussion of this tendency, see Rocco D'Ambrosio, *Will Pope Francis Pull it Off?*, 26-36.

22. In an address of 18 February 2009, "The Importance of Academic Formation," *Only Love Can Save Us*, 139-49, and at 145. In a recent book of interviews, *God is Young*, Francis says, "A person who turns to extremes and tends toward rigidity is a fearful person. He hides behind rigidity as a defense. Behind and under every rigidity there is always an unresolved problem and also, perhaps, an illness" (59-60). This criticism that "rigidity" is a sickness or illness is fairly typical for Pope Francis. See Edward Pentin, "Pope Francis: Rigid People Are Sick."

23. There is a steady drumbeat of this charge throughout Francis' pontificate. I cite only a couple of instances here. Francis, *Amoris Laetitia* §37, which is citing from "Concluding Address of the Fourteenth Ordinary General Assembly of the Synod of Bishops." See also, *Amoris Laetitia* §305 where he repeats the charge of Pharisaic stone-thrower but

adds, "This would bespeak the closed heart of one used to hiding behind the Church's teachings, 'sitting on the chair of Moses and judging at times with superiority and superficiality difficult cases and wounded families.'"

24. Francis, "Address of His Holiness Pope Francis to Participants in the Meeting Promoted by the Pontifical Council for Promoting the New Evangelization": "Doctrine cannot be preserved without allowing it to develop, nor can it be tied to an interpretation that is rigid and immutable without demeaning the working of the Holy Spirit."

25. Aidan Nichols, O.P., *From Newman to Congar*, 38.

26. Ratzinger, "Commentary on Dogmatic Constitution on Divine Revelation." *Commentary on the Documents of Vatican II*, 167–98, 262–72, and at 269. See also José Antonio Ureta, *Pope Francis's "Paradigm Shift": Continuity or Rupture in the Mission of the Church?*, 151-63.

27. Ureta, *Pope Francis's "Paradigm Shift"*, 151-52.

28. I am retrieving here a phrase that is used by Pius X in his 1907 encyclical on modernism, *Pascendi Dominici Gregis* §12. Pius X's objection to modernism is that it denies that the affirmations of faith have a determinable content of unchanging truth. How so? I explain in the text.

29. Lonergan, *Method in Theology*, 323.

30. Although Bergoglio is correct here in the point he is making about the dogmatic development of creeds, he is not accurate by only referring to the third and fourth centuries. Actually, there are seven ecumenical councils in the first eight centuries of the Church's history: The First Council of Nicaea, 325; the First Council of Constantinople, 381; The First Council of Ephesus, 431; The Council of Chalcedon, 451; the Second Council of Constantinople, 553; the Third Council of Constantinople, 680-681; and the Second Council of Nicaea, 787.

31. Jorge Mario Bergoglio and Abraham Skorka, *On Heaven and Earth*, 25.

32. Francis, *A Big Heart Open to God*, 62.

33. In the same vein, Pope Francis argues, "cultural diversity is not a threat to Church unity. The Holy Spirit, sent by the Father and the Son, transforms our hearts and enables us to enter into the perfect communion of the blessed Trinity, where all things find their unity.... It is he who brings forth a rich variety of gifts, while at the same time creating a unity which is never uniformity but a multifaceted and inviting harmony.... We would not do justice to the logic of the Incarnation if we thought of Christianity as monocultural and monotonous. While it is true that some cultures have been closely associated with the preaching of the Gospel and the development of Christian thought, the revealed message is not identified with any of them; its [truth-] content is transcultural" (§117; see also, §131).

34. D'Ambrosio, *Will Pope Francis Pull it Off?*, 29.

35. Francis, *Evangelii Gaudium*, n. 45: "Est enim aliud ipsum depositum fidei, seu veritates, quae veneranda doctrina nostra continentur, aliud modus, quo eaedem enuntiantur." Francis' note gives AAS (*Acta Apostolicae Sedis*) 54 (1962), 792, as the source for this quotation from John XXIII's Opening Address. Nevertheless, John XXIII's full statement includes the phrase, "eodem tamen sensu eademque sententia." Some writers, such as Peter Hebblethwaite, and Christoph Theobald, SJ, claim that this phrase was later added (see *Pope John XXIII, Shepherd of the Modern World*, 432; "The Theological Options of Vatican II: Seeking an 'Internal' Principle of Interpretation," 107n31). Fr. Marcel Chappin, S.J., has refuted Hebblethwaite's claim decisively in a critical review of the latter's book, "Pope and Journalist, On a Recent Biography of Pope John XXIII," and at 528: "'Oportet ut haec doctrina *certa et immutabilis, cui fidele obsequium est praestandum*, ea ratione pervestigetur et exponatur, quam tempora postulant nostra. Est enim aliud ipsum depositum Fidei, *seu veritates, quae veneranda doctrina nostra continentur*, aliud modus, quo eadem enuntiantur, *eodem tamen sensu eademque sententia*'. [What is needed is that this certain and unchangeable doctrine, to which loyal submission is due, be investigated and presented in the way demanded by our times. For the deposit of faith, the truths con-

tained in our venerable doctrine, are one thing; the fashion in which they are expressed, but with the same meaning and the same judgement, is another thing.] In italics are the words that did not appear in the draft by the Pope, neither in the Italian text published, *without censure*, by the *Osservatore Romano*, on 12 October 1962. The Latin text with its additions (quoted not without inaccuracies by Mr. Hebblethwaite on 432) is the text that the Pope had in front of him while reading the speech; the official publication in the *Acta Apostolicae Sedis* and the *Acta Synodalia Concilii Vaticani II* is thus *not censoring*. Did the Pope disagree with the additions put into the Latin version of his speech? If he during its public reading did omit these words, then we have a strong indication; Mr. Hebblethwaite says the Pope did and invites us to check the Archives of Vatican Radio. Well, I found out that the Pope did *not* omit these words.... [Note 26: Information given by Rev. Pasquale Borgomeo, General Director of Vatican Radio (Letter of 3 April 1986, accompanied by a tape!) to whom I express my gratitude]. Why is Mr. Hebblethwaite stating something that is not true?" Furthermore, this phrase, "according to the same meaning and the same judgment" ("eodem tamen sensu eademque sententia.") is not omitted in the Dutch and German translations of the opening speech. Besides the English translation, it is omitted in the Spanish. It is also missing in *Gaudium et Spes* (§62).

36. According to Chappin, this "famous distinction ([was] already used by Leo XIII and put into the speech because of a letter from five cardinals to the Pope)." Edward Schillebeeckx, OP, "Towards a Catholic Use of Hermeneutics," "A traditional distinction has always been made between the 'essential dogmatic affirmation' (the *id quod*) and its 'mode of expression' (the *modus cum quo*). The first pointed to the 'unchangeable essence', the second to the changeable, varying elements" (11).

37. In his book, *Pope Francis, The Family and Divorce*, Walford refers to the subordinate clause, "*eodem sensu eademque sententia*" (115), but does not acknowledge that Francis leaves it out. When that subordinate clause has been translated it has usually been inadequately translated as "provided their sense and meaning are retained," with the same sense and the same meaning," "with their meaning preserved intact" or "retaining the same meaning and message." These last two translations are used by Gavin D'Costa, *Vatican II: Catholic Doctrines on Jews & Muslims*, 30, 45. Walford uses the second possible translation. The Flannery translation renders it: "For the deposit of faith or revealed truths is one thing; the manner in which they are formulated without violence to their meaning and significance is another." In my view, because of the connection between meaning and truth such that what is meant is judged to be true to objective reality, the most fitting translation is "according to the same meaning and the same judgment"— "*eodem sensu eademque sententia.*" I follow Joseph Komonchak's translation of the official Latin text (https://jakomonchak.files.wordpress.com/2012/10/john-xxiii-opening-speech.pdf). This is also the translation in Heinrich Denzinger, *Compendium of Creeds*, §3020.

38. Denzinger, §3020.

39. *The Commonitory of Vincent of Lérins*, Chapter 23, §28. On the importance of Vincent for doctrinal development, see Yves Congar, *The Meaning of Tradition*, 119-20. See also, the magisterial study of Thomas G. Guarino, *Vincent of Lérins and the Development of Christian Doctrine; The Disputed Teachings of Vatican II: Continuity and Reversal in Catholic Doctrine.*

40. Vatican I, *Dei Filius*, Chapter 4, Faith and Reason, "Hence also that meaning of the sacred dogma is perpetually to be retained which our Holy Mother Church has once declared, and there must never be a deviation from that meaning on the specious ground and title of a more profound understanding.... Therefore, let there be growth and abundant progress in understanding, knowledge, and wisdom, in each and all, in individuals and in the whole Church, at all times and in the progress of ages, but only within the proper limits, i.e., *within the same dogma, the same meaning, the same judgment*" [Vincent of Lérins]. Canon 3: "If anyone says that, as science progresses, at times a sense is to be given to dogmas proposed by the Church *different from the one* that the Church has understood and understands, let him be anathema." The italicized words are the ones cited in the text.

41. Yves Congar, *A History of Theology*, 18-19. So, too, Benedict XVI, "Address of His Holiness Benedict XVI to the Roman Curia Offering Them His Christmas Greetings." In the following several paragraphs, I am drawing on Chapter 1 of my book, *Berkouwer and*

Catholicism.

42. Congar, *A History of Theology*, 10.
43. Ibid.
44. Berkouwer, *Vatikaans Concilie en de Nieuwe Theologie*, 62.
45. Ibid., 82 [72].
46. Aidan Nichols, O.P., "Thomism and the Nouvelle Theologie," at 5.
47. Congar, *A History of Theology*, 10.
48. Berkouwer, *Nabretrachting op het Concilie*, 72.
49. Berkouwer, *Vatikaans Concilie en de Nieuwe Theologie*, 99 [84].
50. E. Schillebeeckx, "Towards a Catholic Use of Hermeneutics," 10.
51. Berkouwer, *Nabetrachting op het Concilie*, 52.
52. Ibid., 52–53.
53. G. C. Berkouwer, *De Kerk*, I, *Eenheid en Katholiciteit*, 236–37. This is Volume I of a two volume work on ecclesiology, both of which were translated in one complete volume by James E. Davidson and published in 1976 as *The Church*, 190–91.
54. I borrow this phrase from the British Evangelical philosophical theologian Oliver Crisp who defends a version of essentialism in his article, "*Ad* Hector," 138.
55. Ratzinger, "Pluralism as a Problem for Church and Theology," in *The Nature and Mission of Theology*, 73-98, and at 90-91, emphasis added.
56. Prioritizing reality over ideas means, in a fundamental sense, that theological reflection must contend consistently with the historical and cultural realities, and the corresponding questions derived from the world and history (EG §231).
57. Bergoglio and Skorka, *On Heaven and Earth*, 26-27, emphasis added.
58. Lonergan, *Method in Theology*, 284.
59. This passage seems to be a favorite of Bergoglio/Francis because it is also cited in other works, e.g., *Laudato Si'* and in his co-authored work, *On Heaven and Earth*, 26; as well as, "Address of His Holiness Pope Francis to Participants in the Meeting Promoted by the Pontifical Council for Promoting the New Evangelization." It was recently cited again in his Francis' March 31 in-flight press conference from Rabat to Rome. Thomas G. Guarino develops the import of Vincent of Lérins for Francis's thought in "Pope Francis Looks to St. Vincent of Lérins."
60. Francis, *A Big Heart Open to God*, 62-63.
61. Ibid., 63.
62. The quote within the quote is from John Paul II, *Ut unum sint*, §19. The immediate context within which this quote occurs is: "Because by its nature the content of faith is meant for all humanity, it must be translated into all cultures. Indeed, the element which determines communion in truth is *the meaning of truth*."
63. Guarino, "Pope Francis Looks to St. Vincent of Lérins," *First Things*.
64. Pope Francis, *Laudato Si'*, §121. Endnote 98 explicitly refers to the *Commonitorium Primum*, 23, §29, of Vincent of Lérins.
65. Francis, "Video Message of His Holiness Pope Francis to Participants in an International Theological Congress Held at the Pontifical Catholic University of Argentina."
66. Ibid.
67. Francis, "Pope at Mass: Gospel newness does not permit a double life."
68. Idem, "Address of the Holy Father, Meeting with the Participants in the Fifth Convention of the Italian Church."

69. Idem, "Video Message of His Holiness Pope Francis... International Theological Congress."

70. Idem, "Address of Pope Francis to the Community of the Pontifical Gregorian University, together with Members of the Pontifical Biblical Institute and the Pontifical Oriental Institute."

71. In an address of 18 February 2009, "The Importance of Academic Formation," the then-Cardinal Bergoglio said, "Thus if someone thinks of abstract formulations or irrefutable syllogisms when he hears someone talking about solid doctrine, he is thinking within a rationalist paradigm that is different from the soundness of Christ's truth, which is that of mercy and faithfulness of salvation" (*Only Love Can Save Us*, 144).

72. John Waters writes, "According to papal confidant Antonio Spadaro, discernment entails eschewing 'a definitive or complete word on every question which affects the Church and the world'" ("Theological Deplorables").

73. Francis, "The Importance of Academic Formation" in *Only Love Can Save Us*, 149.

74. This term refers to Heinrich Joseph Dominicus Denzinger (1819-1883), a leading German Catholic theologian and author of the Enchiridion Symbolorum et Definitionum commonly referred to simply as "Denzinger." This work is now in its 43rd ed. *Compendium of Creeds, Definitions, and Declarations on Matters of Faith and Morals.*

75. Lonergan, *Method in Theology*, 330-31.

76. Gavin D'Costa, *Vatican II, Catholic Doctrines on Jews & Muslims*, 35.

77. Gustavo Gutiérrez, *A Theology of Liberation*, 3-12.

78. Francis, "Homily at Holy Chrism Mass."

79. Romanus Cessario, O. P., *Christian Faith & the Theological Life*, 71.

80. Aquinas, *Summa Theologiae*, II-II, q. 1, a. 2, ad. 2.

81. Ibid.

82. Idem, *Disputed Questions on Truth*, q. 14, art. 8, ad. 12.

83. Guy F. Mansini, "Dogma," in *Dictionary of Fundamental Theology*, 242. See also, John Paul II, *Fides et Ratio*, §82.

84. See William P. Alston, *A Realist Conception of Truth*, 5.

85. Jaroslav Pelikan, *Credo, Historical and Theological Guide*, 35.

86. *Catechism of the Catholic Church* §150: "Faith is first of all a personal adherence of man to God. At the same time, and inseparably, it is a *free assent to the whole truth that God has revealed.*"

87. Aquinas, *Summa Theologiae* II-II, q. 1, a.2, ad. 2.

88. Francis with Benedict XVI, *Lumen Fidei* §45. Francis acknowledges that Benedict mostly wrote this encyclical. "These considerations on faith—in continuity with all that the Church's magisterium has pronounced on this theological virtue—are meant to supplement what Benedict XVI had written in his encyclical letters on charity and hope. He himself had almost completed a first draft of an encyclical on faith. For this I am deeply grateful to him, and as his brother in Christ I have taken up his fine work and added a few contributions of my own" (§7).

89. Francis, "The Importance of Academic Formation" in *Only Love Can Save Us*, 143.

90. Ibid., 144-45.

91. Francis, "Homily at the Final Mass of the Synod."

92. Gerald O'Connell, "In Morocco Pope Francis explains what it means to be Christian in a majority Muslim Land."

93. Matthew Levering, *An Introduction to Vatican II as an Ongoing Theological Event*, 6; and Chapter 1, "Persons and Propositions."

94. The saint referred to here by Francis in CRV 156n82 is Oscar Romero.

95. Jaroslav Pelikan, *Credo, Historical and Theological Guide to Creeds and Confessions of Faith*, 35.

96. Gerhard Cardinal Müller, *The Cardinal Müller Report*, 99. In reply to Fr. Granados's question as to whether doctrine is a secondary matter, Cardinal Müller says, "Doctrine and confession of faith, in themselves, are not that later reflection [a better understanding of the faith and a more complete synthesis]; instead, they are the actual context of the encounter."

97. André Frossard and John Paul II, *Be Not Afraid*, 66.

98. Francis, "Letter to a Non-Believer."

99. Harold A. Netland, "Can All Religions be True?", 147. Like me, Netland holds to propositional truth.

100. Francis, "Letter to a Non-Believer."

101. Raeburne S. Heinbeck rightly explains this distinction, "If we admit, therefore, that it is one thing for something *to be the case* (or not be the case) and another for us *to know or have reason for believing* that it is the case (or not the case), and if we admit that it is one thing for a statement *to be true* (or false) and quite another thing for us *to know or have reason for believing* that it is true (or false), then we have *ipso facto* acknowledge the validity of the distinction between criteria and evidence. For the gist of that distinction, to repeat, is simply the difference between the conditions which would have to be fulfilled for a statement to be true (or false) and the conditions which would have to be fulfilled for us to know or have reason for believing it to be true (or false)' (*Theology and Meaning, Critique of Metatheological Scepticism*, 48).

102. Netland, "Can All Religions be True?" 147.

103. Francis, *The People Wish to See Jesus*, 72.

104. Ibid., 68.

105. Francis, "Message of Pope Francis for the 48th World Communications Day," emphasis added.

106. I return to these questions and others in Chapter 7, "The Dialogue of Religions and the Question of Truth."

107. Bergoglio, *Education for Choosing Life*, 56-57.

108. "Message of Pope Francis for the 48th World Communications Day," emphasis added.

109. See Chapter 2 of this book.

110. Stout, *Ethics After Babel*, 24-25.

111. Bergoglio, "The Importance of Academic Formation," 145.

112. Gavin D'Costa, *Vatican II*, 35.

113. Robert Royal, "First Reports—Part II," *The Catholic Thing*.

114. Müller, *The Cardinal Müller Report*, 97.

115. Francis, "Address to the Leadership of the Episcopal Conferences of Latin America." See also, "Pope's Morning Homily: While True Doctrine Unites, Ideology Divides."

116. See my discussion earlier in this chapter, on Francis' critique of contemporary gnosticism, which is an enemy of the Christian faith. Another concern that Francis shares with Gutiérrez is amply reflected here in Francis' theologico-pastoral epistemology. "A theology which has its points of reference in only 'truths' which have been established once and for all—and not the Truth which is also the Way—can only be static and, in the long run, sterile. In this sense the often-quoted and misinterpreted words of Bouillard take on a new validity: 'A theology which is not up-to-date is a false theology'" (*A Theology of Liberation*, 10).

117. John Paul II, *Veritatis Splendor* §§9, 35, 40; *Fides et Ratio* §22.

118. See the whole context, *Veritatis Splendor* §§57-61, 51-53. I draw in this section on portions of my article, "The Splendor of Truth in *Fides et Ratio*."

119. *Contra* Thomas Knieps-Port Le Roi, "Preserving and Perpetuating the Heritage of Pope John Paul II," at 512, who claims that in applying dogmatic and moral truths, John Paul II does not attend to "hermeneutical standards," but only to "indoctrination." The *Lérinian* hermeneutics of John Paul II stands in contradiction to Knieps-Port Le Roi's claim.

120. Richard Gaillardetz, "Francis wishes to release Vatican II's bold vision from Captivity."

121. Joseph Ratzinger, *Theological Highlights of Vatican II*, 23.

122. Lonergan, "Pope John's Intention," 227. Lonergan is here describing the view of M.D. Chenu on the meaning of pastoral.

123. Ibid., 228.

124. Christoph Theobald, S.J., "The Theological Options of Vatican II" 107n31.

125. Ibid.

126. See note 31 of this chapter where I refute Theobald's interpretation.

127. Christoph Theobald, S.J., "The Principle of Pastorality at Vatican II".

128. Idem, "The Courage to Anticipate the Future of the Church," 15.

129. Gaillardetz, *An Unfinished Council*, 36-38, 52-53, 133-35.

130. Ibid., 130-31.

131. Francis, "Address to the Plenary Session of the Congregation for the Doctrine of the Faith."

132. Cited in Gaillardetz, *An Unfinished Council*, 38.

133. Gaillardetz, *An Unfinished Council*, 52.

134. I borrow this phrase from the British Evangelical philosophical theologian Oliver Crisp who defends a version of essentialism in his article, "*Ad* Hector," 138.

135. Ratzinger, "Pluralism as a Problem for Church and Theology," in *The Nature and Mission of Theology*, 92.

136. Guarino, *Foundations of Systematic Theology*, 139n59; see also, 100n20. Crisp also argues that essentialism is compatible with the view "that our *understanding* of the concept might develop, becoming conceptually richer, being developed along the lines of a particular model of the Trinity, and so on" ("*Ad* Hector," 138).

137. David Tracy, "A Hermeneutics of Orthodoxy".

138. Ibid., 74, 75.

139. Gaillardetz, *An Unfinished Council*, 5.

140. D'Costa, *Vatican II*, 35.

141. Rahner, "The Development of Dogma," 43–44.

142. Avery Cardinal Dulles, "Postmodernist Ecumenism."

143. Berkouwer, *Vatikaans Concilie en Nieuwe Theologie*, 85 [74].

144. Grisez, *The Way of the Lord Jesus*, Vol. I, 172.

145. Lonergan, "The Dehellenization of Dogma," 11–32, and at 14-15, 16, respectively.

146. Ibid., 14.

147. Idem, *Doctrinal Pluralism*, 53–56.

148. Idem, "The Dehellenization of Dogma," 16.

149. Berkouwer, *Vatikaans Concilie en de Nieuwe Théologie*, 73 [65].

150. Gaillardetz, *An Unfinished Council*, 134-35.

151. See Pius X, *Pascendi Dominici Gregis* §§11-13. See also, International Theological Commission, *Interpretation of Dogma* (1989), Section II.2, "At the beginning of this [20th] century, Modernism addressed itself to the question [of making dogma intelligible to a new culture]. It was a poor solution: revelation was improperly conceived and dogmas were given a pragmatic slant."

152. See John Paul II, *Fides et Ratio* §97.

153. Gaillardetz, *An Unfinished Council*, 52.

154. Ibid., 134.

155. Aidan Nichols, O.P., "Relaunching Christian Philosophy," 58.

156. For example, *Love and Responsibility, Man and Woman He Created Them: A Theology of the Body, The Acting Person*, and the collection of essays, *Person and Community*.

157. Gaillardetz, *An Unfinished Council*, 7.

158. George Eldon Ladd, *A Theology of the New Testament*, 31.

159. As Geerhardus Vos says in his address, "The Idea of Biblical Theology as a Science and as a Theological Discipline," Inaugural address as Professor of Biblical Theology, Princeton Theological Seminary, delivered at the First Presbyterian Church, Princeton on 8 May 1894. Reprinted in Richard B. Gaffin Jr. *Redemptive History and Biblical Interpretation*, 3–24. I draw in this section on portions of my article, "*Dei Verbum* and the Nature of Revelation."

160. Nichols, *From Newman to Congar*, 175.

161. Francis, *A Big Heart Open to God*, 59; similarly, 46.

162. Although Massimo Borghesi claims that this, too, is Francis's view—"*essential* truth must be found in the *existential* truth"—I see no evidence in Francis's writings that he holds that view (*The Mind of Pope Francis*, 256). The absence of that view is not surprising given Francis's dismissal of abstract truth, his skepticism about absolute truth, and his theologico-practical epistemology with its attendant principle that realities are greater than ideas.

163. Some ten years earlier in an interview book with André Frossard, "*Be Not Afraid*," John Paul drew a similar distinction, "I have already drawn your attention to the difference between the catechism formula, 'accepting as true all that God reveals', and surrender to God. In the first definition, faith is primarily intellectual, in so far as it is the welcoming and assimilation of revealed fact. On the hand, when the constitution *Dei verbum* tells us that man entrust himself to God 'by the obedience of faith', we are confronted with the whole ontological and existential dimension and, so to speak, the drama of existence proper to man" (66).

2

Mercy and Justice Meet at the Cross

> A God without wrath brought men without sin into a kingdom without judgment through the ministrations of a Christ without a cross.[1]

> Christian tradition has not failed to observe... [an] open conflict between justice and mercy, and depicted it as the two arms or hands of God, or as his two daughters. This same tradition has been concerned to show that justice and mercy are not divorced in the works of God. In fact, their necessary co-existence should never be forgotten. Spiritual life should certainly be based on an intense conviction of God's mercy, but it is equally certain that this should not serve as a pretext for taking an easy line with regard to the demands made by his justice.[2]

> There can be no doubt that Scripture, in its entirety, is very clear when it comes to this matter of God and man's sin. God only threatens his judgment against the mutilation of his gifts. The words of grace in Scripture do not tone down the seriousness of God's wrath. As a matter of fact, it is only in connection with the reality of wrath that the miracle of God's grace is fully understood.[3]

One of the most often cited statements of John XXIII from his opening address at the Second Vatican Council is his saying that in dealing with errors, the "Church has [frequently] condemned them with the greatest severity." He adds, "Nowadays, however, the Spouse of Christ prefers to make use of the *medicine of mercy* rather than that of severity." What does Pope John mean by mercy? Briefly, the Church has a divine calling to be an instrument of Christ, to bring his merciful love into the world. Furthermore, he quickly explains that the Church must "consider that she meets the needs of the present day by demonstrating the validity of her teaching rather than by condemnations."[4] In this contrast between showing validity versus issuing condemnations lies the meaning of the word pastoral. The Council is called to be pastoral.

The clearest explanation of this concept is given by the then Joseph Ratzinger. He explains, "'Pastoral' should not mean nebulous, without substance, merely 'edifying'—meanings sometimes given to it. Rather what was meant was positive care for the man of today who is not helped by condemnations and who has been told for too long what is false and what he may not do. Modern man really wishes to hear what is true. He has, indeed, not heard enough truth, enough of the positive message of faith for our time, enough of what the faith has to say to our age."[5] In this connection, we can easily appreciate why John states that the "greatest concern of the Ecumenical Council" is "that the sacred deposit of Christian doctrine should be guarded and proclaimed more efficaciously."[6] To that end, this chapter addresses the fundamental question of how God is both just and merciful in the light of some insights of Pope Francis derived chiefly, although not exclusively, from his book entitled, *The Church of Mercy*, Walter Cardinal Kasper's book, *Mercy*, and St. John Paul II's 1980 Encyclical, *Dives et misericordia*. The chapter concludes by expounding Francis's view on the proper response to God's merciful love in Christ that he has shown to us.

Walter Cardinal Kasper has recently written that since the sixteenth century the "relation of justice and mercy [is] the fateful question of Western theology."[7] Although this is an exaggeration, in my judgment, the question regarding the relation of justice and mercy is certainly one of the perennial questions that we need to face in order to avoid the following dilemma: how do we avoid both despair when confronted with the gravity of our sins, on the one hand, and a sentimental view of God and of his love, on the other?[8] Despair because the meaning of Jesus' death is reduced to uncompromising justice; sentimentality because its meaning is reduced to unconditional mercy. As Kevin Vanhoozer rightly insists, however: "On the cross neither mercy nor justice loses out; the cross is rather their mutual fulfillment."[9] Indeed, Pope Francis at his clearest says similarly, "[T]hese [justice and mercy] are not two contradictory realities, but two dimensions of a single reality that unfolds progressively until it culminates in the fullness of love" (MV §20). God's love is the single reality that unfolds dynamically throughout salvation history in the dimensions of justice and mercy with these two harmoniously coming together supremely in the cross. Unfortunately, Francis is not always at his clearest, and so his insistence that the cross is the mutual fulfillment of justice and mercy requires some explanation. Therefore, I shall discuss the weaknesses in Pope Francis's account of the atonement in his book, *The Name of God is Mercy*. I judge there to be three weaknesses: his doctrine of God, the muted character, not to say, absence of the justice of God and its satisfaction by Christ's cross, and, consequently, the essential place of the law in the redemptive efficacy of the cross.[10]

Liberal Christianity

Kasper is critical of the view of liberal Christianity, which is famously described by Niebuhr in the epigraph to this chapter. Sin, judgment, wrath, and cross—muting or suppressing these has given rise to a sentimental view of God and his love.[11] Says Kasper, "Mercy becomes pseudomercy when it no longer has a trace of trembling before God, who is holy, and trembling before his justice and his judgment." Indeed, he adds, "It becomes pseudomercy when 'yes' is no longer a 'yes' and 'no' is no longer a 'no'; when it does not exceed, but rather undercuts the demand for justice." Reaching the core point he seeks to make, Kasper continues: "the gospel teaches the justification of the sinner, but not the justification of the sin. For this reason, we should love the sinner, but hate the sin."[12] Turning to Pope Francis, he is quick to state in response to the question, "Who is Jorge Mario Bergoglio?": "I am a sinner, but I trust in the infinite mercy and patience of our Lord Jesus Christ, and I accept in a spirit of penance."[13] In other words, sorrow for our sins must be tempered with the reality of God's mercy so as to avoid despair. He asks, "Are we often weary, disheartened, and sad? Do we feel weighed down by our sins?... Let us not close our hearts, let us not lose confidence, let us never give up. There are no situations that God cannot change; there is no sin that he cannot forgive if only we open ourselves to him."[14] Summarily stated, "God always thinks with mercy: do not forget this. God always thinks mercifully."[15] Indeed, he adds elsewhere, "Trust in the power of Christ's cross! Welcome its reconciling grace into your own hearts and share that grace with others!"[16] What does it mean to say that God is merciful?

What is Mercy?

God is rich in mercy (Eph 2:4). But what is mercy? Mercy is the face of God's love turned toward sinners, searching them out, and offering them pardon and salvation (MV §§7-8). Says Pope Francis, "Etymologically, 'mercy' derives from *misericordi[a]*, which means opening one's heart to wretchedness.... Mercy is the divine attitude which embraces, it is God's giving himself to us, accepting us, and bowing to forgive" (NGM §8). He adds elsewhere, "When faced with the gravity of sin, God responds with the fullness of mercy" (MV §3). Again, "Mercy: the word reveals the very mystery of the Most Holy Trinity. Mercy: the ultimate and supreme act by which God comes to meet us" (MV §2). One should add here that mercy is not only identified with forgiveness but also compassion. In the Old Testament, the Hebrew word for compassion is *rahamīn*. This word "expresses the instinctive attachment of one being for another." That is,

> This feeling, according to Semitic thought, has its seat in the maternal bosom (*raham*: 1 Kings 3:26), in the bowels (*rahamīn*)—we would say: the heart—of a father (Jer 31:20; Ps 103:13) or of a brother (Gen 43:30); it is tenderness; it readily translates itself into action: it is compassion on the occasion of a tragic event (Ps 106: 45) or pardon of offenses (Dan 9:9).

> *Hesed* is a second Hebrew word that is usually translated by a Greek word meaning mercy, namely, *eleos*. English translations of *rahamīn, hesed,* and *eleos* "oscillate between *mercy* and *love*." In fact, these words reflect a variety of meanings: "tenderness, pity, compassion, clemency, goodness, and even grace (Hebrew *hēn*) which, however, has a much broader sense. Despite this variety, it is not impossible to discern the biblical meaning of mercy. From beginning to end the manifestation of God's tenderness is occasioned by human misery; and man, in his turn, ought therefore to show mercy to his neighbor in imitation of his Creator."[17]

These statements by Francis and also the summation in the concluding sentence of the previous paragraph suggest that God's mercy is related to his acts *ad extra*. This means that mercy is, as Daniel Maloney puts it, only the mirror of the Trinity, that is, "only 'the mirror' of God's love among the Trinity, that the love between the Father and the Son which proceeds the Holy Spirit *has a counterpart* in God's merciful love for creation."[18] Rightly seen by Francis, mercy is indeed related to God's acts *ad extra*. He says, "[M]ercy is a key word that indicates God actions toward us." Furthermore, mercy is manifesting God's love towards the sinner. "He does not limit himself merely to affirming his love, but makes it visible and tangible.... The mercy of God is his loving concern for each one of us" (MV §9).

Although Francis shares this perspective of mercy, there are other times when he relates mercy to God's inner nature.[19] Francis then suggests that mercy is God's defining attribute. "I will say this: mercy is real; it is the *first* attribute of God" (NGM §62, emphasis added). He adds, in response to the question, "Why does God never tire of forgiving us?" "Because he is God, because he is mercy, and because mercy is the *first* attribute of God. The name of God is mercy" (NGM §85, emphasis added). "Mercy is God's identity card. God of mercy, merciful God. For me, this really is the Lord's identity" (NGM §9). But here because Francis sees mercy as the first attribute of God, such that mercy is essential to God, he seems to blur the distinction between God's inner nature and attributes, such as the mercy that is related to God's acts *ad extra*.[20] Maloney summarily states the problem with this view:

> There is a distinction in theology between the divine attributes in general, which includes all things correctly said of God, and "pure perfections," those divine attributes which admit no imperfection into the concept. Only the pure perfections can be essential to God.... Mercy cannot be a pure perfection because mercy always needs someone in need of mercy, who has some sort of sin or imperfection or fallenness. If mercy were essential to God, then God would not be able to exist without some creature

> who needed mercy. But before creation, there was only God, and it would be "absurd" (in the sense of *reductio ad absurdum*) to claim that God shows mercy to himself.[21]

Thus, does God's mercy refer to an attribute of God himself or to the mercy that he reckons *ad extra* to believers? Francis suggests that it is an attribute of God himself. The implication that follows from the view that divine mercy is essential to God—indeed, Francis claims, his *first* attribute—is that divine justice takes a back seat to mercy, mostly ignored, with Francis sometimes saying, without any explanation, that "God's justice is his mercy" (MV §20), or "justice is mercy and mercy is justice,"[22] that mercy goes beyond or surpasses justice (NGM §78; MV §21), or even that it is the fullness of justice (AL §311).[23] Francis assures us that the supremacy of mercy "does not mean that justice should be devalued or rendered superfluous" (MV §21). But he is concerned that we not "focus exclusively on justice," because "mere justice is not enough" (MV §21).[24] Yes, Francis says, justice is the first necessary and indispensable step in God's work of salvation (MV §10). How so? What is the role of divine justice in Christ's atoning work? Francis never says because he pushes justice too far into the background. He does urge that overvaluing justice and the corresponding notion of the law leads us to legalism because we think that salvation comes through the observance of the law rather than through faith in Jesus Christ. With St. Paul, Francis urges us to reject the Pelagian heresy (GE §§52-56): "We have believed in Christ Jesus, in order to be justified by faith in Christ, and not by the works of the law, because by works of the law shall no one be justified" (Phil 2:16). "I do not nullify the grace of God, for if righteousness were through the law, then Christ died for no purpose" (Gal 2:21). Yes, Francis is right that the gospel is the ground of our salvation, and not the law. But, says Francis, "Jesus... "goes *beyond* the law" (MV §20, emphasis added). Beyond? In what sense?[25] Here, too, Francis doesn't say, and hence he leaves the impression of pushing the law too far into the background as well. Francis is unclear, not to say confused and confusing, on the believer's relationship to God's law.

Michael Horton is right that "the gospel assures us of God's favor, and the law indicates how we are to walk in the light of our blessings in Christ."[26] In emphasizing the grace and mercy of God—and correspondingly, unrelentingly criticizing legalism as he understands it—Francis leaves us with the impression that he pits gospel and law over against each other, and that to be truly righteous and holy involves the *abrogation* of the law, of its contents and demands.

Indeed, a prominent Italian Rabbi, Giuseppe Laras, criticized Pope Francis's homilies for their "resumption of the old polarization between the morality and theology of the Hebrew Bible and of pharisaism, and Jesus of Nazareth and the Gospels."[27] In 1998, Joseph Ratzinger wrote a chapter titled, "Israel, the Church, and the World," in his short study, *Many Religions—One Covenant*. He argued there: "Jesus did not act as a liberal reformer recommending and presenting a more understanding interpretation of the Law. In Jesus' exchange with the Jewish authorities of his time, we are not dealing with a confrontation between a liberal reformer and an ossified traditionalist hierarchy. Such a view, though common, fundamentally misunderstands the conflict of the New Testament and does justice neither to Jesus nor to Israel."[28] This view of the relationship between the Gospel and the Law of Israel sounds familiar because Rabbi Laras is right: it is a steady drumbeat in Pope Francis's homilies.

Of course the message conveyed by the drumbeats is, whether intentionally or not, that of antinomianism—literally, anti-law-ism, or lawlessness—which abolishes the normative status of the law for the believer, which is in turn the third use of the law, "guiding believers" as the magisterial Reformers called it.[29] Indeed, by way of reminder, the law's normative status for the Christian life is affirmed in the Catholic faith: the *Catechism of the Catholic Church*'s section on the Ten Commandments has 500 paragraphs (§§2052-2557) about God's law and its inner connection for the sanctification of lives. Whatever must be said about the moral law and salvation, at the very least it must be clearly stated that we are deceived if we think that we can inherit God's kingdom, which is man's chief end, without keeping the divine commandments (1 Cor 5:9-11; Gal 5:16-26).

I am not saying that Francis is an antinomian. Still, he has on multiple occasions, unfortunately, obscured the vital point that the law is, as St. Paul teaches, holy, just, and good (Rom 7:12), bearing an inherent connection to salvation. Moreover, Francis never actually addresses the question: if the moral law is good—which he surely believes it is—then what is its place in living the Christian life? Moreover, we read in Matthew that Jesus Christ came not "to abolish the law but to fulfill it" (Matt 5:17). Indeed, we shall need to understand the teaching that "Jesus did not abolish the Law but fulfilled it by giving its ultimate interpretation in a divine way" (CCC §581). But what exactly is Jesus' relation to the law? Says Ratzinger:

> Jesus opened up the Law quite theologically conscious of, and claiming to be, acting as Son, with the authority of God himself, in innermost unity with God the Father. Only God himself could fundamentally reinterpret the Law and manifest that its broadening transformation and conservation is its actually intended meaning. Jesus' interpretation of the Law makes sense only if it is interpretation with divine authority, if God interprets himself. The quarrel between Jesus and the Jewish authorities of his time is finally not a matter of this or that particular infringement of the Law but rather of Jesus' claim to act *ex auctoritate divina*, to be this *auctoritas* himself. "I and the Father are one" (John 10:30).[30]

The relation between Jesus and the law will be discussed in further detail in the next chapter.

One central aspect though of Jesus' fulfillment of the law—it is overlooked by Francis—is its essential place in the redemptive efficacy of the cross such that the law is thereby satisfied by Jesus. In Rom 7:4-6 we read that those who live in Christ have "died to the law" and are "released from its demands. "So... we serve not under the old written code but in the new life of the Spirit." In 1 John 3:4 we read that "Everyone who commits sin is guilty of lawlessness; sin is lawlessness." The lawbreaker cannot be treated with impunity, and hence, according to St. Paul, they are "cursed" (see Deut. 27:15-26; 30:15-20). What is the curse of the law? Briefly, the curse brings with it the sentence of death. Jesus' perfect fulfillment of the Law includes his taking upon himself the "'curse of the Law' incurred by those who do not 'abide by the things written in the book of the Law, and do them'" (Gal 3:11). "Christ redeemed us from the curse of the law by becoming a curse for us" (Gal 3:10, 13). In this light, we can understand why the *Catechism of the Catholic Church* states that Jesus brings about "the perfect fulfillment of the Law by being the only Righteous One in place of all sinners" (CCC §580). Herman Ridderbos rightly says, "At issue here is satisfaction of violated justice, as is evident from the phrase: *from the curse of the law*."[31] He explains:

> It is from this sentence of death that Christ has redeemed them by Himself "becoming a curse" for them—that is to say, a cursed one. This refers to the way in which He gave Himself to death. What we have here, in other words, as is evident from the phrase "for us," is the thought of *substitution*. The curse to which Christ yielded Himself victim, is not an independently operative principle, but the personal judgment of God, in which He had Christ undergo the sentence instead of the condemned one (cf. Rom 8:3 and 2 Cor 5:21). How Christ ransomed his own in this way is not more specifically set forth. The thought is that God in His grace made the punishment accomplished in Christ valid for His own, and so brought reconciliation through Christ's death. Such a redemption (ransoming, redeeming) has not, therefore, the character of a transaction, a nice balance of the active and passive, but is a mystery of salvation in which is manifested the integrity of God's justice and His grace, and the deep bonds of unity between Christ and His own.[32]

In sum, Jesus' cross is a satisfaction of God's law. Hence, I am not *under the law* (Gal 5:18), because that would suggest that I have not been freed from its curse, from its condemnation, from its bondage, impotence, and spiritual death. Ridderbos elaborates, "In this verse [Gal 5:18] the emphasis is on the spiritual inability in which man lives, if he has only the law. He is defenseless against the flesh. In this lies the connection with the preceding verse. If one is to offer resistance in the struggle between Spirit and flesh, one must be in the service of the Spirit and not in that of the law. *That the demand of the law remains* (verse 14) *is not denied, of course* [emphasis added]. The issue, in short, is the strength, the power, that is necessary for the fulfillment of the law."[33] I return in the next chapter to a discussion of the sense in which the law retains its obliging force in the believer's life after he has been set free in Christ (Gal 5:1, 13).

For now, looking back at Francis's statements about the relation between mercy and justice, I think it is fair to say that statements like those above remain mostly assertions that are never developed. Furthermore, in Francis's reflections, divine righteousness, holiness, and wrath are overlooked. There is absolutely no mention of these divine attributes and their concretization in the cross in Francis's reflection. Maloney correctly remarks, however, that "divine justice must be more fundamental than divine mercy, because justice is essential to God and mercy is not. But God's justice is not more fundamental than his love, since both are essential—God is Love (and loving), and God is Justice (and just). This suggests that there must be some way of talking about love and justice... such that they are at least not contraries."[34] Of course Francis agrees, as I said above, that justice and mercy are not contradictory realities, opposed to each other.

Yet to understand properly the reality of God's merciful pardon and how it is that mercy triumphs over judgment (Jas 2:13), we cannot minimize the wrath of God. God's wrath is His response to the sins of men (Eph 2:4)—His holy displeasure against their sin (NGM §32) that entails the breaking of communion with Him (MV §2)—as the expression of His fundamental justice, righteousness, and holiness, and in turn, his wrath. The truth of what these concepts refer cannot exist with sin. As Evangelical Anglican theologian, John R. W. Stott, puts it, "God's holiness exposes sin; his wrath opposes it."[35] Still, unfortunately, Francis does not explicitly link God's displeasure at our sin with his holiness and wrath.

When we reflect on mercy the question naturally arises about the relationship of mercy to God's justice, righteousness, and holiness. This relationship is muted and certainly undeveloped in Francis's account. In his Wednesday Audience talk of 3 February 2016, he addressed the question of the relationship of mercy to justice. "Sacred Scripture presents us with God as infinite mercy," he stated, "but also as perfect justice. How are these two things reconciled? How can the reality of mercy be articulated with the need for justice?" Yes, he says, God is not merciful *at the expense of his justice*. Mercy does not exclude His justice, nor is it opposed to it (MV §21). How could it? "God's justice is his mercy given to everyone [oppressed by slavery to sin and its consequences] as a grace that flows from the death and resurrection of Jesus Christ" (MV §21).[36] God's justice entails His taking sin seriously, indeed, "of all the injustice we have committed before God" (NGM §58), by virtue of taking away and atoning for our guilt in history. In the reality of the atoning work of Jesus Christ there is a turning from real wrath to real grace.

This "turning" is not clear in Francis because he never clearly explains that the demands of divine justice were satisfied by Christ's cross. This is the view of the atonement called objective redemption, or the satisfaction theory. In Francis's reflection there is no mention of the satisfactory character of Christ's death, and that is because the justice of God is muted even if not altogether ignored. According to the Spanish theologians,

"The notion of satisfaction is an integral part of doctrine on the mystery of the Redemption and should never be set aside."[37] In particular, the Council of Trent uses the term satisfaction when referring to Christ as the meritorious cause of our justification. "The meritorious cause is the most beloved only begotten Son of God, our Lord Jesus Christ, who, 'while we were enemies' [Rom 5:10], merited for us justification by his most holy Passion on the wood of the Cross and made satisfaction for us to God the Father."[38] The papal magisteria of Leo XIII, Pius XII, John Paul II, and the *Catechism of the Catholic Church* §§615-616, for example, refer to satisfaction when explaining the manner in which Christ redeems us from sin.[39]

Francis seems to have more of an Abelardian view of subjective redemption, or the moral influence theory, in that the "subjective influence of the cross... leads sinners to repentance and so enables God to forgive them."[40] Still, in Francis objective redemption theory is muted even if not altogether ignored. In one of the only references to divine judgment, Francis says, "Thus the Cross of Christ is God's judgment on all of us and on the whole world, because through it he offers us the certitude of love and new life" (MV §21). Moreover, we probably should think of Francis's view of the atonement as the *Christus victor* (Christ the Victor) view of redemption in which Christ's death defeated the powers of evil, sin, and death.[41] On this view, "[Christ] disarmed the rulers and authorities and put them to open shame, triumphing over them in [the cross]" (Col 2:15). Says Francis, "Jesus takes upon himself the evil, the filth, the sin of the world, including the sin of all us, and he cleanses it; he cleanses it with his blood, with the mercy and the love of God. Let us look around: how many wounds are inflicted upon humanity by evil? ... Jesus on the cross feels the whole weight of the evil, and with the force of God's love he conquers it; he defeats it with his resurrection. This is the good that Jesus does for us on the throne of the cross."[42]

In sum, given objective redemption, the cross takes our sins away, achieving reconciliation with God, because it is the act of God's gracious judgment on Christ for our benefit: "For our sake he made him to be sin who knew no sin, so that in him we might become the righteousness of God" (2 Cor 5:21). The basis of this act is divine love: "In this is love, not that we loved God but that he loved us and sent his Son as an atoning sacrifice for our sins" (1 John 4:10). "For God so loved the world that he gave his one and only Son, that whoever believes in him shall not perish but have eternal life" (John 3:16). "But God demonstrates his own love for us in this: While we were still sinners, Christ died for us" (Rom 5:8). "But because of his great love for us, God, who is rich in mercy, made us alive with Christ even when we were dead in transgressions—it is by grace you have been saved" (Eph 2:4-5).

Pope Francis echoes St. John Paul II who teaches that God has shown us his justice and mercy "in the cross of Christ, on which the Son, consubstantial with the Father, *renders full justice to God*." His death on the cross, adds John Paul, "is also *a radical revelation of mercy*, or rather of *the love* that goes against what constitutes the very root of evil in the history of man:

against sin and death" (DM §8, emphasis added).

Furthermore, Francis affirms that "humanity is wounded" (NGM §6) and that is why "sin is more than a stain. Sin is a wound; it needs to be treated, healed" (NGM §39). The first step towards this healing is being "conscious of our sins, of the evil we have done, of our wretchedness, and of our need for forgiveness and mercy."[43] The way that the believer receives the grace of Christ's atoning work, his gift of infinite mercy, is by faith (Rom 3:21-25; Eph 2:8-9). Thus, Pope Francis identifies the need "to recognize our emptiness, our wretchedness" (NGM §43), "of our need for forgiveness and mercy," in short, to confess "our miseries, our sins" in order to obtain mercy by faith in Jesus Christ (NGM §32). Approaching the Lord of mercy with confidence requires, adds Francis, a shattered heart" (NGM §32), and of course even this recognition of oneself as a sinner and the corresponding act of repentance stems from an act of grace that is the Lord's gift to us. We hear in Francis an echo of the promise in 1 John 1:9: "If we confess our sins, He is faithful and just to forgive us our sins and to cleanse us from all unrighteousness." And yet, adds Kasper, sensing the incompleteness of the Pope's thought, we must temper God's mercy with his judgment and holiness, so as to avoid "falling victim to the banal and trivializing image of a saccharine 'dear God', which turns God into a good-spirited pal and no longer takes seriously [his] holiness." Yes, God is merciful, indeed, rich in mercy (Eph 2:4), as Francis rightfully urges, but, Kasper rightly insists, "Our merciful God is not simply the saccharine 'dear God', who lets our negligence and malice pass."[44] Alternatively put, "Let us ask for the grace not to take sin lightly [cf. Rom 6:1]."[45] Rather, in the Sacred Scriptures it is unmistakably clear that "the sin of man touches on God himself, since every transgression is," as G.C. Berkouwer rightly insists, "a forsaking and rejecting of him [cf. Jer 2:13] and a choosing of man's autonomy instead of his [God's] good and beneficent rule."[46]

Divine Acceptance versus Divine Redemption

Muting or suppressing sin, judgment, wrath, and the cross—has given rise to a theology of divine *acceptance* rather than a theology of divine *redemption*, and hence to a sentimental view of God and his love.[47] Many of us can relate to Philip Turner's account of listening to a pastor's sermon—in Turner's example it is listening to a seminarian's sermon—on the question, "What is the Christian Gospel?" The student's entire sermon answered this most important question with the mere statement: "God is love. God loves us. We, therefore, ought to love one another." Turner adds, "I waited in vain for some word about the saving power of Christ's cross or the declaration of God's victory in Christ's resurrection. I waited in vain for a promise of the Holy Spirit. I waited in vain also for an admonition to wait patiently and faithfully for the Lord's return. I waited in vain for a call to repentance and amendment of life in accord with the pattern of Christ's life."[48] The upshot of all this is that the "incarnation is to be understood as merely a manifestation of divine love." Divine love here is understood as a doctrine of radical inclusion. "From this starting point," Turner continues, "several conclusions are drawn." It is easy to see that this position is a contemporary representation of Niebuhr's description of liberal Christianity: "A God without wrath brought men without sin into a kingdom without judgment through the ministrations of a Christ without a cross."[49] Permit me to sketch two arguments here that purportedly support this version of liberalism:

ARGUMENT 1	
Premise:	God is love pure and simply.
Premise:	One is to see in Christ's death no judgment upon the human condition. Rather, one is to see an affirmation of creation and the persons we are.
Conclusion:	Therefore, the life and death of Jesus reveal the fact that God accepts and affirms us.

From this conclusion another argument is sketched, beginning with the alleged implication of the conclusion of the first argument.

ARGUMENT 2	
Premise:	God wants us to love one another.
Premise:	Such love requires of us both acceptance and affirmation of the other.
Premise:	Accepting love requires a form of justice that is inclusive of all people, particularly those who in some way have been marginalized by oppressive social practice.
Conclusion:	Therefore, the mission of the Church is to see that those who have been rejected are included.
Conclusion:	God has already included everybody, and now we ought to do the same.
Conclusion:	The equation of the Gospel and social justice constitutes a primary expression of Christian truth.

Turner then concludes that we find here a "theological chasm—one that separates those who hold a theology of divine *acceptance* from those who hold a theology of divine *redemption*."[50] Evidence for this chasm is most recently manifested within the Episcopal Church's allowance of "open communion for the non-baptized." What we have here is a doctrine of radical inclusion. "Once we have reduced the significance of Christ's resurrection and downplayed holiness of life as a fundamental marker of Christian identity, the notion of radical inclusion produces the view that one need not come to the Father through the Son. Christ is *a* way, but not *the* way. The Holy Eucharist is a sign of acceptance on the part of God and [His] people, and so should be open to all—the invitation unaccompanied by a call to repentance and amendment of life."[51] This doctrine of radical inclusion has had far-reaching effects both in respect to our understanding of God and our relationship to human beings. With respect to God, Turner argues, we have a "quasi-deistic theology." What does he mean? He means a "benevolent God who favors love and justice as inclusion" in the sense defined above. But God, however, "acts neither to save us from our sins nor to raise us to new life after the pattern of Christ." This last point supports the description of this theology being in some sense deistic because God's involvement with the world is reduced to the "inner sphere of one's own private world."[52] Furthermore, adds Turner, "in respect to human beings, it produces an ethic of tolerant affirmation that carries with it no call to conversion and radical holiness."[53] We may fill out this picture with what Christian Smith has called "moralistic therapeutic deism."[54]

Moralistic Therapeutic Deism

Briefly, Moralistic Therapeutic Deism is a creed with the following points:

> 1. A God exists who created and orders the world and watches over human life on earth.
>
> 2. God wants people to be good, nice, and fair to each other, as taught in the Bible and by most world religions.
>
> 3. The central goal of life is to be happy and to feel good about oneself.
>
> 4. God does not need to be particularly involved in one's life except when he is needed to resolve a problem.
>
> 5. Good people go to heaven when they die.[55]

This creed is moralistic—one might add, Pelagian—because it believes that "central to living a good and happy life is being a good, moral person."[56] Furthermore, it is "also about providing therapeutic benefits to its adherents," that is, "about feeling good, happy, secure, at peace. It is about attaining subjective well-being, being able to resolve problems, and getting along amiably with other people." Significantly, Jorge Bergoglio has also written about this manifestation of the religious in postmodernity. He observes that "postmodernity does not bring an aversion to the religious; however, it does force it into the private sphere." A corollary of this privatization of religion is a "diluted deism... which tends to reduce faith and religion to the sphere of the 'spiritualistic' and the subjective."[57] Clearly, Bergoglio shares this analysis with Smith.

Furthermore, Pope Francis identifies this as one of the errors that some in the Church have embraced and that threatens to make the Gospel message an ideology.[58] He calls it the temptation of "psychologizing." Others have called it the triumph of the therapeutic mentality. "Here we have to do with an elitist hermeneutics which ultimately reduces the 'encounter with Jesus Christ' and its development to a process of growing self-awareness. It is ordinarily to be found in spirituality courses, spiritual retreats, etc. It ends up being an immanent, self-centered approach. It has nothing to do with transcendence and consequently, with missionary spirit."[59] Although one finds this view today among American Catholics,[60] there is nothing new here. Adds Francis, "[I]t can take the form of a spiritual consumerism tailored to one's unhealthy individualism" (EG §89).

Early in the first quarter of the twentieth century, Roman Guardini (1885-1968) also noted that in the modern period "religion was considered as something which belonged to the subjective sphere—it was simply something within a man, a condition of his soul."[61] In addition, says Guardini, "there was no genuine belief in the existence of objective religious realities. This subjectivism dominated religious life all through the second half of the nineteenth century and during the beginning of the twentieth. Man felt imprisoned within himself."[62] In short, human subjectivity became the basis and center of all meaning, value and reality, and with man's experience assuming the role of determining what will be acceptable as valid, as true.[63] "This attitude was also making its influence felt in the religious sphere.... The individual was sure only of that which he personally experienced, perceived, and yearned for, and on the other hand of the concepts, ideas, and postulates of his own thought."[64] That this attitude—the logic of modern subjectivism: "Only accept what rings true to your own inner Self"[65]—is still making its influence felt in a very practical way more than ninety years later is evident from what Joseph Komonchak has written:

> I think what Charles Taylor[[66]] describes as the "new individualism" is very widespread in our culture and even among Catholics. This is the tendency to reduce religion to one's own very personal, even private, spirituality ("following your bliss," "be true to your own inner Self"), which then becomes the criterion by which to decide what tradition, if any, to follow, what community, if any, to enter, what beliefs to hold, if any. As Taylor argues, this is an almost perfect exemplification of William James's definition of religion as "the feelings, acts and experiences of individual men in their solitude, so far as they apprehend"... "theologies, philosophies and ecclesiastical organizations may secondarily grow." This seems to me different from the often deplored "cafeteria Catholicism" (although it may be one if its inspirations), that is, picking and choosing among church teachings; that at least allowed that there were church teachings. For those

> whom I am describing it is nearly incomprehensible that one's spirituality might need itself to be tested against any external reality or authority. If this phenomenon is as widespread as Taylor thinks it is, then it may be that many of the disputes about doctrines or worship or morality that so often occupy Catholics are rather missing the point: there are many people claiming to be Catholic who couldn't care less.[67]

What Bergoglio refers to as a "diluted deism," but only in a passing observation about the religions in postmodernity, is filled out by Smith. Last then, this creed holds a "deistic" concept of God, of "one who exists, created the world, and defines our general moral order, but not one who is particularly personally involved in our affairs—especially affairs in which we would prefer not to have God involved. Most of the time, the God of this faith keeps a safe distance." God is an absentee landlord who has nothing to do with our lives. Like Turner's doctrine of radical inclusion that has no place for faith, forgiveness, judgment, repentance, and amendment of life, God is simply depicted as an "accepting presence—not unlike that of a therapist."[68]

Not surprisingly, however, this theology of divine acceptance with its doctrine of radical inclusion doesn't have concepts such as "'faith', 'justification', 'repentance', and 'holiness of life'." Also gone is "the notion that the Church is a community elected by God for the particular purpose of bearing witness to the saving event of Christ's life, death, and resurrection." Rather, having obliterated sin, judgment, wrath, and cross at the heart of God's redemptive love in Christ, this theology leaves us with "inclusion *without qualification*."[69] Ratzinger hits the nail right on the head in his description of deism, which has made headway even among Christians, both Catholic and Protestant.

> I am convinced that deism today—the notion that God may well exist but that, ultimately, he has nothing to do with our lives—is present not only in the so-called secularized world but it is also decisive and to a dangerous degree I would say within the Churches and within our lives as Christians. We have no longer dared to talk of eternal life and judgments. For us, God has becomes a distant God, an abstract God. We no longer have the courage to believe that this created being, man, is so important in the eyes of God that God cares, is concerned with us and for us.[70]

Later in this chapter, I will lay out Bergoglio/Francis's account of inclusion that rejects not only the relativistic implication of this doctrine of radical inclusion. But also we shall see that Francis's idea of inclusion is, arguably, grounded in a theology of divine redemption.

God's Two Feet

Following Francis's emphasis, it is deeply biblical to affirm that God is merciful, indeed, rich in mercy (Eph 2:4). But Kasper rightly insists, as I argued above, "Our merciful God is not simply the saccharine 'dear God', who lets our negligence and malice pass." John Paul II puts Kasper's point differently, a point completely missing in Francis's reflection, "*forgiveness does not cancel out* the objective *requirements of justice*." Indeed, Bernard of Clairvaux makes clear that mercy and judgment are the two feet of God, warning us not to neglect either foot. Neglecting the latter leaves us with "cheap grace," says Kasper, "and not authentic mercy." Authentic mercy must be at the service of justice. Neglecting the former leaves us with despair, hopelessness, and a sense of being abandoned. Yet the Bible teaches that "mercy triumphs over judgment" (Jas 2:13). Kasper echoes this biblical thought. "Mercy is victorious over justice in God." Elsewhere he writes, "God's mercy is, so to speak, superproportional. It exceeds every measure." Still, though mercy exceeds the demand for justice, surpassing it, justice is not undercut, but rather is fulfilled. Francis says, "God does not deny justice. He rather envelopes it and surpasses it with an even greater event in which we experience love as the foundation of true justice"(MV §21). What, then, is the relation of divine mercy and divine justice, and regarding the latter of making satisfaction to God for man's sin?

Kasper responds, "Mercy is insolubly bound up with God's holiness and gives expression to it." Given his holiness, then, God's response to sin and evil is resistance, revulsion, his holy displeasure to all that opposes him; this response the Sacred Scriptures call—says Kasper rightly—"the wrath of God" (Eph 2:3).[71] He adds: "But God's wrath does not mean an emotionally surging rage or an angry intervention, but rather [his] resistance to sin and injustice. Wrath is, so to speak, the active and dynamic expression of his holy essence. For this reason, the message of judgment cannot be expunged from the message of the Old or New Testament or be harmlessly interpreted away. God's holiness conforms to his justice." In sum, muting or suppressing God's wrath, judgment, and holiness, in short, the justice of God, turns "the message of God's mercy," Kasper concludes, into "a message of cheap grace," and hence we will not know the greatness of mercy. As Pope Francis has recently described that mercy:

> "But without forgetting that we were estranged from Him because of original sin, which separated us from our Father: our filial relationship was profoundly wounded. Therefore, God sent his Son to rescue us at the price of His blood. And if there is a rescue, it is because there is a slavery. We were children, but we became slaves, following the voice of the Evil One. No one else rescues us from that essential slavery except Jesus, who assumed our flesh from the Virgin Mary and died on the cross to free us from the slavery of sin and to restore us to our lost filial condition."[72]

Jesus' Disfigurement

In this connection, the then Joseph Cardinal Ratzinger wrote of Jesus' disfigurement, of reducing the Jesus in the Gospels "to that of a bland philanthropist." "Today in broad circles, even among believers, an image has prevailed of a Jesus who demands nothing, never scolds, who accepts everyone and everything, who no longer does anything but affirm us." Adds Ratzinger, "The Jesus of the Gospels is quite different, demanding, bold. The Jesus who makes everything okay for everyone is a phantom, a dream, not a real figure. The Jesus of the Gospels is certainly not convenient for us.... We must again set out on the way to this real Jesus."[73]

In light of this distortion of Jesus, which sets aside God's word of judgment by muting or suppressing it, we will never understand the seriousness of sin, and hence the need for the atoning work of Christ for it to be overcome. The latter manifests the immense grace of God, which Francis refers to as the logic of God, that is, "the logic of the cross, which is not primarily that of suffering and death, but rather that of love and of the gift of self that brings life."[74] He describes the greatness of mercy, echoing Pope Benedict, saying "True revolution, the revolution that radically transforms life, was brought about by Jesus Christ through his resurrection." He adds, "He changes your heart, from that of a sinner—a sinner: we are all sinners—he transforms you into a saint. Is there any one of us who is not a sinner? If so, raise your hand! We are all sinners, each and every one. We are all sinners! But the grace of Jesus Christ saves us from sin: it saves us! [It is] this immense grace that changes our heart.... To become saints only one thing is necessary: to accept the grace that the Father gives us in Jesus Christ."[75] The Gospel, then, is the message of immense grace that has its origin in the redemptive work of Christ, and the Church, which is holy, but does not reject sinners, "calls everyone to allow themselves [by God's saving grace fully revealed in the cross] to be enfolded by the mercy [of the cross], the tenderness, and the forgiveness of the Father, who offers everyone the possibility of meeting him, of journeying toward sanctity."[76]

Justice and Mercy as Aspects of God's Love

God's love is inseparably connected with his holiness and his justice, and hence God therefore must manifest his wrath when confronted with sin and evil. Yes, of course the gospel is an expression of the love of God, indeed, the supreme example: "This is how God showed his love among us: He sent his one and only Son into the world that we might live through him. This is love: not that we loved God, but that he loved us and sent his Son as an atoning sacrifice for our sins" (1 John 4:9-10). But God's love is never expressed at the expense of any other attribute of his character, such as his holiness and wrath, the latter being God's holy reaction to evil and sin. "It would be offensive to speak of God's wrath if we did not also know of His holiness and love. But, just as man must repent his sins to enter into God's grace, so the believer must approach the mystery of God's anger if he will rightly approach God's love. To wish to reduce the mystery of divine wrath to a mythical expression of human experience is to mistake the seriousness of sin and to forget the tragic side of God's love. There is a fundamental incompatibility between holiness and sin."[77] In sum, the wrath of God is the real and effective opposition to sin of the all-holy God, that is, "the revelation of the *absolute distance* and the radical and clear antithesis between God and man's sin."[78]

The crucial issue before us is to give an interpretation of the relation between God's love (mercy) and his wrath (holiness and justice) that avoid the polarization of his holiness and love, justice and mercy. God is not merciful *at the expense of* his justice as if these divine attributes are pulling in mutually opposing directions in a tug-of-war. Nor must we oppose the reality of God's wrath to the revelation of Christ as the Son of God who was sent by the Father's love (see 1 John 4:9; John 3:16).[79] The doctrine of the atonement affirms the equal ultimacy of God's love (mercy) and his justice (holiness and wrath) as central to the gospel. God has shown us his justice and mercy in, says John Paul II, "the cross of Christ, on which the Son, consubstantial with the Father, *renders full justice to God*" (DM §8). His death on the cross, adds John Paul, "is also *a radical revelation of mercy*" (ibid.) God's wrath, which is his response to the sins of men, is altogether an expression of his righteousness and holiness, and indeed of his love. The demands of divine justice need to be satisfied in order to remove the guilt for sin that on the part of God is a barrier to his fellowship with sinners. This point is made by Sacred Scripture:

> God was reconciling the world to himself in Christ, not counting men's sins against them. And he has committed to us the message of reconciliation. We are therefore Christ's ambassadors, as though God were making his appeal through us. We implore you on Christ's behalf: Be reconciled to God. God made him who had no sin to be sin for us, so that in him we might become the righteousness of God (2 Cor 5:19-21).

Furthermore, in the words of the *Catechism of the Catholic Church*, "By his obedience unto death, Jesus accomplished the substitution of the suffering Servant, who 'makes himself an *offering for sin*,' when 'he bore the sin of many,' and who 'shall make many to be accounted righteous,' for 'he shall bear their iniquities.' Jesus atoned for our faults and made satisfaction for our sins to the Father" (CCC §615). In other words, Christ has made substitutionary satisfaction for our sins by his sacrifice on the cross. St. Paul writes, "Since we have now been justified by his blood, how much more shall we be saved from God's wrath through him. For if, when we were God's enemies, we were reconciled to him through the death of his Son, how much more, having been reconciled, shall we be saved through his life" (Rom 5:9-10). For St. Paul, what God effects in Christ's death has reference especially to his justice. God's justice is manifested in being the justifier of the one who has faith in Jesus Christ. "But now the righteousness of God has been manifested... through faith in Jesus Christ for all who believe. For there is no distinction: for all have sinned and fall short of the glory of God, and are justified by his grace as a gift, through the redemption that is in Christ Jesus" (Rom 3:21-24). In short, the redemption accomplished in Christ Jesus shows the righteousness of God "so that he might be just and the justifier of the one who has faith in Jesus" (Rom 3:26). Therefore, in addition to satisfying justice and the law, Christ has also merited new life for us as the efficient cause of that life.[80] In the words of the Council of Trent, the *Decree on Justification*, "The efficient cause [of justification] is the merciful God who gratuitously washes and sanctifies [cf. 1 Cor 6:11], sealing and anointing [cf. 2 Cor 1:21f.] 'with the promised Holy Spirit, who is the guarantee of our inheritance' [Eph 1:12f.]."[81]

Nevertheless, it is not an angry and remote God that sinners need to placate before he can love and forgive on the other hand; the gospel is an expression of the love (mercy) of God, prior to any merit on our part. As Joseph Ratzinger puts it in his classic study, *Introduction to Christianity*,

> It is not man who goes to God with a compensatory gift, but God who comes to man, in order to give to him. He restores disturbed right on the initiative of his own power to love, by making unjust man just again, the dead living again, through his own creative mercy. His righteousness is grace; it is active righteousness, which sets crooked man right, that is, bends him straight, makes him correct.... God does not wait until the guilty come to be reconciled; he goes to meet them and reconciles them. Here we can see the true direction of the Incarnation, of the Cross.[82]

This point is so important that it is worth repeating.[83] In the words of John Murray, "It is one thing to say that the wrathful God is made loving. *That would be entirely false*. It is another thing to say the wrathful God is loving. That is profoundly true. But it is also true that the wrath by which he is wrathful is propitiated through the cross. This propitiation is the fruit of divine love that provided it.... The propitiation is the ground upon which the divine love operates and the channel through which it flows in achieving its end."[84] In sum, the cross proceeds from the initiative of God's universal redeeming love. "In this is love, not that we loved God but that he loved us and sent his Son as an atoning sacrifice for our sins" (1 John 4:10). "For God so loved the world that he gave his own and only Son, that whoever believes in him shall not perish but have eternal life" (John 3:16). "But God demonstrates his own love for us in this: While we were still sinners, Christ died for us" (Rom 5:8). "But because of his great love for us, God, who is rich in mercy, made us alive with Christ even when we were dead in transgressions—it is by grace you have been saved" (Eph 2:4-5). And again: "In this the love of God was manifested toward us, that God has sent His only begotten Son into the world, that we might live through Him" (1 John 4:9).

To deal with this issue of the relation of mercy and justice, then, we need to turn to the atonement because it is in the cross of Christ that God's justice, mercy, and love are *simultaneously* revealed.[85] Space does not permit any further elaboration of the doctrine of the atonement. I conclude my brief discussion of the atoning work of Christ—its absolute value as redemption and reparation, as propitiation and satisfaction—with a long passage from John Paul II's *Dives et Misericordia* and some commentary.

> Christ, as the man who suffers really and in a terrible way in the Garden of Olives and on Calvary, addresses himself to the Father—that Father whose love he has preached to people, to whose mercy he has borne witness through all his activity. But he is not spared—not even he—the terrible suffering of death on the cross. "For our sake God made him to be sin who knew no sin" [2 Cor 5:21]. St. Paul will write, summing up in a few words the whole depth of the cross and at the same time the divine dimension of the reality of the Redemption. Indeed this Redemption is the ultimate and definitive revelation of the holiness of God, who is the absolute fullness of perfection: fullness of justice and of love, since justice is based on love, flows from it and tends toward it. In the passion and death of Christ—in the fact that the Father did not spare his own Son, but "for our sake made him sin"—absolute justice is expressed, for Christ undergoes the passion and cross because of the sins of humanity. This constitutes even a "superabundance" of justice, for the sins of man are "compensated for" by the sacrifice of the Man-God. Nevertheless, this justice, which is properly justice "to God's measure," springs completely from love: from the love of the Father and of the Son, and completely bears fruit in love. Precisely for this reason the divine justice revealed in the cross of Christ is"to God's measure," because it springs from love and is accomplished in love, producing fruits of salvation. The divine dimension of redemption is put into effect not only by bringing justice to bear upon sin, but also by restoring to love that creative power in man thanks to which he once more has access to the fullness of life and holiness that come from God. In this way, redemption involves the revelation of mercy in its fullness.
>
> The Paschal Mystery is the culmination of this revealing and effecting of mercy, which is able to justify man, to restore justice in the sense of that salvific order which God willed from the beginning in man and, through man, in the world. (DM §7)[86]

That God is holy is foundational to John Paul's account of the reality of redemption in this passage. This is not surprising since it is foundational to biblical religion and his thought is steeped in that religion. Equally important in his thought is the corollary that sin is incompatible with God's holiness and justice. God is holy, and therefore punishes sin and expresses his wrath against it. God's wrath is closely related to his holiness, indeed it is his holy reaction to sin and evil. Someone may object that the pope here does not speak of the "wrath of God."[87] True, but the reality of sin to which God's wrath refers is fully present: "God's holiness exposes sin; his wrath opposes it."[88] In the words of the then Joseph Ratzinger on the matter of God's wrath: "From this [the reality of sin] one can understand what the 'wrath of God' and the anger of the LORD are all about: necessary expressions of his love that is always identical with the truth. A Jesus who is in agreement with everybody and anybody, a Jesus without his holy wrath, without the toughness of the truth and of true love, is not the true Jesus as Scripture shows him but a miserable caricature. A presentation of the 'gospel' in which the seriousness of God's wrath no longer exists has nothing to do with the biblical gospel.... A Jesus who approves of everything is a Jesus without the cross, because the tribulation of the cross would not then be needed to bring men and women salvation."[89] In short, God cannot simply overlook sins; his justice must be satisfied in some way. The cross is a satisfaction, indeed, a superabundant satisfaction. "[It] constitutes even a 'superabundance' of justice," says John Paul, "for the sins of man are 'compensated for' by the sacrifice of the Man-God."

The reference to the "superabundance" of justice and hence satisfaction is an allusion to its perfection, its excess, indeed, its infinite value: past, present and future sins are fully satisfied by Christ's death on the cross. But it means more than this allusion. Chiefly, I think, it refers to the "excessive" character of God's reconciling act in the death of Christ. This saving act is "excessive" in that God gives himself in the self-sacrificial love of Jesus' death on the cross *for his enemies*. The cross is an act of merciful justice, and the mercy is a just mercy. "When we were God's enemies we were reconciled to him through the death of his Son" (Rom 5:10). In this light, we might also speak of the "superabundance of mercy."[90]

Looking back to Francis's claims about "God's justice is his mercy" (MV §20), that mercy goes beyond or surpasses justice (NGM §78; MV §21), or even that it is the fullness of justice (AL §311),[91] I'd like to say something in support of these claims, with respect to the views of Aquinas and John Paul II.

Once Again, Mercy and Justice

In describing mercy, St. Thomas uses the phrase "fullness of justice" in the following paragraph:

> God acts mercifully, not indeed by going against His justice, but by doing something more than justice; thus a

> man who pays another two hundred pieces of money, though owing him only one hundred, does nothing against justice, buts acts liberally or mercifully. The case is the same with one who pardons an offense committed against him, for in remitting it he may be said to bestow a gift. Hence the Apostle calls remission a forgiving; *Forgive one another, as Christ has forgiven you* [Eph 4:31]. Hence it is clear that mercy does not destroy justice, but in a sense is the fullness thereof. And thus it is said: Mercy exalteth [triumphs] itself about judgment [Jas 2:13]. (ST I, q. 21, a. 3)

Thomas makes several important points here in response to the question of the relationship of mercy to justice. First, God is not merciful at the expense of His justice. Mercy does not exclude His justice, nor is it opposed to it. We have already seen that Francis shares this conviction: "Mercy is not opposed to justice but rather expresses God's way of reaching out to the sinner, offering him a new chance to look at himself, convert, and believe" (MV §21). Second, Jesus atones for our sins by paying our debt, as it were, to God for sinning against his holiness and justice. In other words, Jesus makes perfect satisfaction for our sins. God's justice cannot be understood without the righteous wrath of God, and His wrath, which is God's holy displeasure, is motivated by the sins of men. Since man has sinned against God and is therefore guilty, God takes sin seriously and hence man's guilt against God, holding man responsible for it. Third, the reality of God's mercy does not undermine the reality of His wrath against man's sin. In and through the atoning work of Christ, God the Father not only forgives us our sins, wiping away our guilt, having Christ compensate for them by his sacrificial death on the Cross. But also God the Father acts liberally or mercifully such that mercy realizes fully the aim of justice, which is to restore our relationship with God, and in that sense is the fullness of justice. Therefore, God's justice and mercy (the latter being an expression of love) are, in that sense, but one, simultaneously revealed in the reality of the Cross. In that sense, mercy triumphs over judgment (Jas 2:13). Fourth, God acts liberally, or mercifully, because He is love (1 John 4:16). Indeed, the love of God sets mercy in motion—mercy is the face of God's love turned toward sinners, searching them out, and offering them pardon and salvation through Christ's atoning work, a redemption that reveals the fullness of justice. As John Paul II puts it, "love is 'greater' than justice: greater in the sense that it is primary and fundamental. Love, so to speak, conditions justice and, in the final analysis, justice serves love." He adds, "The primacy and superiority of love vis-à-vis justice—this is a mark of the whole of revelation—are revealed precisely through mercy" (DM §4). Of course this is a constant theme—albeit undeveloped—throughout Pope Francis's proclamation of the Gospel.

In sum, the cross takes our sins away because it is the act of God's gracious judgment on Christ for our benefit: "For our sake he made him to be sin who knew no sin, so that in him we might become the righteousness of God" (2 Cor 5:21). Furthermore, the basis of this act is divine love: "In this is love, not that we loved God but that he loved us and sent his Son as an atoning sacrifice for our sins" (1 John 4:10). "For God so loved the world that he gave his one and only Son, that whoever believes in him shall not perish but have eternal life" (John 3:16). "But God demonstrates his own love for us in this: While we were still sinners, Christ died for us" (Rom 5:8). "But because of his great love for us, God, who is rich in mercy, made us alive with Christ even when we were dead in transgressions—it is by grace you have been saved" (Eph 2:4-5). Again, in that sense God's merciful love brings the aim of justice to fulfillment, because God was in Christ reconciling us to himself, and hence mercy is the fullness of justice's aim, and is, therefore, its perfection as well as its profound source.

Now, John Paul II refers to mercy with the phrases I used in the conclusion of the last sentence, namely, "perfection of justice" (DM §8), "most profound source of justice," and the "fulfillment of justice" (DM §14). Insightfully, John Paul says that the relationship between mercy and justice is such that "love is transformed into mercy when it is necessary to go beyond the precise norm of justice—precise and often too narrow" (DM §5). Too precise? Because the standards of justice would only give us what we truly deserve for breaking them. Too narrow? Because if it was only about justice—of course, it is certainly about divine justice—Christ would only pay satisfaction for our sins. But rather, as we saw above, justice serves divine love, which is a love that is revealed through mercy. Indeed, as John Paul says, "Redemption is the ultimate and definitive revelation of the holiness of God, who is the absolute fullness of perfection: fullness of justice and of love, since justice is based on love, flows from it and tends toward it....[T]his justice, which is properly justice 'to God's measure,' springs completely from love: from the love of the Father and of the Son, and completely bears fruit in love [through the power of the Holy Spirit]" (DM §7).

So both justice and mercy have their origin in God's holy love. Pope Francis rightly states—without explanation—that "these [justice and mercy] are not two contradictory realities, but two dimensions of a single reality that unfolds progressively until it culminates in the fullness of love" (MV §20). God's love is the single reality that unfolds dynamically throughout salvation history in the dimensions of justice and mercy with these two harmoniously and simultaneously coming together supremely in the cross. In this way, mercy is the fullness of justice—the perfection of justice, the most profound source of justice, and the fulfillment of justice—because mercy triumphs over judgment, granting man "access to the fullness of life and holiness that come from God" (DM §7). Thus, by restoring man to God, the loving mercy of God also restores man to himself and to his relationship with his fellow man (DM §14). So, Pope Francis is right that mercy is the fullness of justice.

Moreover, in loving his enemies, God makes us just, righteous, by grace. John Paul underscores God's excessive nature of this justifying act in Christ: "how much more" (Rom 5:9). For the redemptive sacrifice of the Man-God did not merely compensate for the sins of man as if to say that he simply made up for sin's deficit. Rather, as St. Paul states, "Therefore, since we have been justified through faith, we have peace with God through our Lord Jesus Christ, through whom we have gained access by faith into this grace in which we now stand" (Rom 5:1-2). Yes, through the death of Jesus, God is both just and a justifier. He is just in that he justifies the one who has faith in Jesus Christ, and being the justifier means that he makes all who are in Christ just, righteous. Being justified, as the Council of Trent teaches, "consists not only in the remission of sins [can. 11], but also in the sanctification and renewal of the interior man through the voluntary acceptance of grace and of the gifts, whereby from unjust man becomes just, and from enemy a friend, that he may be 'an heir in hope of eternal life'" [Titus 3:7].[92] Most important, the cross is the power of God's love to salvation; for through Jesus' passion and death, his self-giving and forgiving and mercy on behalf of sinners is taken "to the end" (John 13:1). "In this way the cross of Christ, on which the Son, consubstantial with the Father, renders full justice to God," says John Paul, "is also a radical revelation of mercy" (DM §8). He adds, "True mercy is, so to speak, the most profound source of justice" (DM §14). John Paul elaborates on the excessive nature of this mercy, "Mercy in itself, as a perfection of the infinite God, is also infinite.... Infinite are the readiness and power of forgiveness which flow continually from the marvelous value of the sacrifice of the Son. No human sin can prevail over this power or even limit it. On the part of man only a lack of goodwill can limit it, a lack of readiness to be converted and to repent, in other words, persistence in obstinacy, opposing grace and truth, especially in the face of the witness of the cross and resurrection of Christ" (DM §13).

Thus far we've been talking about justice—judgment, wrath and holiness—and mercy, not making clear that both originate from the one loving God. In sum, both mercy and justice (wrath) are aspects of the love of God. Recall that John Paul II says, "[L]ove is 'greater' than justice: greater in the sense that it is primary and fundamental. Love, so to speak, conditions justice and, in the final analysis, justice serves love." Alternatively put, God's love itself, given his essentially holy nature, implies his justice, and hence God's judgment and wrath are aspects of his love. How so?

On the one hand, there is no true divine love without God's responding to human evil, which is an offense against him, his holiness, with divine wrath, judgment; the former without the latter degenerates into a sentimental view of God and of his love. British Evangelical historical theologian Anthony Lane rightly notes the basic indisputable point here, namely, "that lack of wrath against wickedness is a lack of caring, which is a lack of love." This is evident to us from the following example that Lane gives: "A husband who did not respond to his wife's infidelity with a jealous anger would thereby demonstrate his lack of care for her." His jealous anger is a consequence of his spousal love. How much more than human spousal love does the infinite love of God—a love that is perfect, absolutely pure and holy—respond to sin and evil with a righteous wrath. As Lane adds, "Failure to hate evil implies a deficiency in love."[93]

On the other hand, says John Paul, "The primacy and superiority of love vis-à-vis justice—this is a mark of the whole of revelation—is *revealed precisely through mercy*." This is a particularly important point because it makes clear that God does not begin to love us until the demand of justice is met. Indeed, the New Testament teaches that it is precisely because God loved the world, even while we were still sinners, in fact, enemies of God (Rom 5:8-10), that "he gave up his only-begotten Son, so that those who believe in him may not perish, but have eternal life" (John 3:16). Therefore, adds John Paul, "[L]ove is transformed into mercy when it is necessary to go beyond the precise norm of justice." That mercy and justice are aspects of the love of God is brought out most clearly in the parable of the prodigal son, also sometimes referred to as the parable of the merciful father.

The Merciful Father and Prodigal Son

Referring to this parable solely as being about the merciful father—as Pope Francis does—underscores the possibility of avoiding the despair that may come with sorrow for our sins. But referring to it as the parable of the prodigal son, as it has traditionally been called, and as St. John Paul II calls it, brings out most clearly the humiliation and shame that the prodigal son is ready to suffer, the dimension of judgment and justice that the prodigal son deserves. It also shows us that mercy—which, as John Paul puts it, "has *the interior form of the love* that in the New Testament is called *agápe*"—is God's own justice, and, furthermore, makes possible the fullest realization of mercy in and through the call to conversion, which restores man in an integrally existential way to God the Father, in Christ, through the power of the Holy Spirit. Both aspects of mercy and justice then are needed if we are to understand God's love.

Says John Paul, "The prodigal son, having wasted the property he received from his father, deserves—after his return—to earn his living by working in his father's house as a hired servant.... This would be demanded by the order of justice, especially as the son had not only squandered the part of the inheritance belonging to him but *had also hurt and offended his father* by his whole conduct." Still, adds John Paul, "The father of the prodigal son *is faithful to his fatherhood, faithful to the love* that he has always lavished on his son.... We read, in fact, that when the father saw the prodigal son returning home 'he had *compassion*, ran to meet him, threw his arms around his neck, and kissed him.'" In this action of the merciful father, mercy triumphs over judgment, and the former is an expression of the father's love. "The relationship between justice and love, which is manifested as mercy, is inscribed with great exactness in the content of the Gospel parable." In sum, love, particularly in light of judgment, is transformed into mercy.

Justice and Mercy Meet at the Cross

God's mercy and justice, whose origin is the love of God, is manifested above all in the saving work of the cross. God "sending His own Son in the likeness of sinful flesh and for sin, ... condemned sin in the flesh" (Rom 8:3). Put differently, mercy and justice meet at the cross of Jesus Christ, decisively condemn man's sin within the cross, and the latter is the way to God's grace and reconciliation.[94] This is the view of Cardinal Kasper. "God's mercy, which is decisively revealed on the cross, allows us, who have deserved judgment and death, to revive and to live anew, without having earned it. It bestows on us a hope against all hope (Rom 4:18)." Still, there remains to ask how God's mercy comports with his justice, his wrath with his love? In the letters of St. Paul, we read that even when we were dead in our sins, indeed, enemies of God, and therefore under his wrath, we were reconciled to God through the death of his Son—in this way God showed his own love toward us (Rom 5:8-9). In this biblical light, we can easily understand why the cross of Jesus Christ is then the ultimate and definitive revelation of not only the holiness of God but also the "fullness of justice and of love," says John Paul, "since justice is based on love." He adds, "In the passion and death of Christ—in the fact that the Father did not spare his own Son, but 'for our sake made him sin'—absolute justice is expressed, for Christ undergoes the passion and cross because of the sins of humanity. This constitutes even a 'superabundance' of justice, for the sins of man are 'compensated for' by the sacrifice of the Man-God." Yes, God's justice is superabundant, or superproportional, as Kasper also puts it, because justice is in service to mercy, and God's mercy is beyond measure, which is another way of referring to the wideness of God's grace.

Moreover, continues John Paul, the redemptive work of Christ not only brings justice to bear upon sin, but also "restores to love that creative power in man thanks to which he once more has access to the fullness of life and holiness that come from God. In this way, redemption involves the revelation of mercy in its fullness." Most simply, then, the cross of Christ not only renders full justice to God but also is a revelation of mercy. Indeed, it is also the revelation of "the love that goes against what constitutes the very root of evil in the history of man: against sin and death." Praise God! He is rich in mercy and because of his great love with which he loved us in Christ, while we were still sinners, he made us alive together with Christ, and so by grace we have been saved (Eph 2:4-5).

We Will Be Judged by Our Love

In the remainder of this chapter, I turn to expound Francis's view on the proper response to God's merciful love in Christ that he has shown to us. Two points in particular I here consider. One, in Jesus' parable of the Good Samaritan (Luke 10:25-37) and in his discourse about the final judgment (Matt 25:31-46), we are told that we will be judged by love. Francis concludes his book on mercy by urging us to remember the words of St. John of the Cross: "In the evening of life, we will be judged on love alone" (NGM §99). What does that mean? What is the "logic of love," that is, as Balthasar puts it in *Love Alone is Credible,* "the presuppositions or consequences implied in our encounter with our neighbor when illuminated by the light of judgment?"[95] Two, the theological virtue of charity, *agápe,* says Bergoglio, "saves us from having to relativize truth in order to be inclusive."[96] The question is how can the Christian faith be inclusive, yet not relativistic, as we found in the doctrine of radical inclusion that was entailed by the theology of divine acceptance?

I will show how Bergoglio's understanding of inclusion is grounded in a theology of divine redemption rather than a theology of divine acceptance. I will start by laying out his account of neighborly love and consider the sense in which we will be judged by our love. By way of preface to this account, I shall say something briefly about future judgment according to works in order to distinguish it from works righteousness, meaning thereby that our salvation is based on works because it is earned through our works. Consider the following verses that our future judgment is according to our works:

2 Cor 5:10 — For we must all appear before the judgment seat of Christ, so that each one may receive what is due for what he has done in the body, whether good or evil.

Matt 16:27 — For the Son of Man is going to come with his angels in the glory of his Father, and then he will repay each person according to what he has done.

John 5:28-29 — Do not marvel at this, for an hour is coming when all who are in the tombs will hear his voice and come out, those who have done good to the resurrection of life, and those who have done evil to the resurrection of judgment.

Rom 2:6-8 — God will render to every man according to his works: to those who by patience in well-doing seek for glory and honor and immortality, he will give eternal life; but for those who are factious and do not obey the truth, but obey wickedness, there will be wrath and fury.

Gal 6:7-9 — Do not be deceived: God is not mocked, for whatever one sows, that will he also reap. For the one who sows to his own flesh will from the flesh reap corruption, but the one who sows to the Spirit will from the Spirit reap eternal life. And let us not grow weary of doing good, for in due season we will reap, if we do not give up.

Rev 20:13; 22:12 — And the sea gave up the dead who were in it, Death and Hades gave up the dead who were in them, and they were judged, each one of them, according to what they had done. Behold, I am coming soon, bringing my recompense with me, to repay each one for what he has done.

St. Paul informs us that we "were dead in trespasses and sins," and hence and "were by nature children of wrath, like the rest of mankind." Still, he adds, "God, being rich in mercy, because of the great love with which he loved us, even when we were dead in our trespasses, made us alive together with Christ—by grace you have been saved—and raised us up with him and seated us with him in the heavenly places in Christ Jesus, so that in the coming ages he might show the immeasurable riches of his grace in kindness toward us in Christ Jesus." And if we didn't hear it the first time St. Paul repeats this great truth regarding our salvation: "For by grace you have been saved through faith. And this is not your own doing; it is the gift of God, not a result of works, so that no one may boast. For we are his workmanship, created in Christ Jesus for good works, which God prepared beforehand, that we should walk in them" (Eph 2:1-10). In this light, we must understand the distinction between salvation being based on works and our being judged according to our works. The last verse makes clear that good works are a fruit of God's grace in our lives such that they will be the fruits of the Spirit (Gal 5:22), and the manifestation of the light of faith (Matt 5:16); in short, corroborating evidence of our faith. As John Piper puts it, "The place of our works at the judgment is to serve as corroborating evidence that we did indeed put our trust in Christ. Therefore when we are acquitted and welcomed into the kingdom it will not be *earned by works* but it will be *according to works*. There will be an 'accord' or an agreement between our salvation and our works."[97]

First then, what are the presuppositions or consequences of loving our neighbor, of being, as Bergoglio puts it, "artisans of charity, of love, and of reconciliation?"[98] We are enjoined by the teaching of the New Testament: "Let us not love in word or speech, but in deed and in truth" (1 John 3:18). Yes, adds St. John, "all who know the truth, because of the truth that abides in us and will be with us forever," are called to "love in truth" (2 John 1-2). Love and truth go hand-in-hand; otherwise, love degenerates into "being sheer sentimentality or mere impulse."[99] Bergoglio here alludes to Benedict XVI's Encyclical Letter *Caritas in Veritate* on the interdependency of truth and love. According to Benedict, "*Only in truth does charity shine forth*, only in truth can charity be authentically lived. Truth is the light that gives meaning and value to charity." Otherwise, Benedict continues:

> Without truth, charity degenerates into sentimentality. Love becomes an empty shell, to be filled in an arbitrary way. In a culture without truth, this is the fatal risk facing love. It falls prey to contingent subjective emotions and opinions, the word "love" is abused and distorted, to the point where it comes to mean the opposite. Truth frees charity from the constraints of an emotionalism that deprives it of relational and social content, and of a fideism that deprives it of human and universal breathing-space. In the truth, charity reflects the personal yet public dimension of faith in the God of the Bible, who is both *Agápe* and *Lógos*: Charity and Truth, Love and Word. (CV §3)

Bergoglio clearly agrees. In his 2013 Encyclical Letter, *Lumen Fidei*, Pope Francis writes on the inseparability of truth and love:

> Love cannot be reduced to an ephemeral emotion. True, it engages our affectivity, but in order to open it to the beloved and thus to blaze a trail leading away from self-centeredness and towards another person, in order to build a lasting relationship; love aims at union with the beloved. Here we begin to see how love requires truth. Only to the extent that love is grounded in truth can it endure over time, can it transcend the passing moment and be sufficiently solid to sustain a shared journey. If love is not tied to truth, it falls prey to fickle emotions and cannot stand the test of time. True love, on the other hand, unifies all the elements of our person and becomes a new light pointing the way to a great and fulfilled life. Without truth, love is incapable of establishing a firm bond; it cannot liberate our isolated ego or redeem it from the fleeting moment in order to create life and bear fruit. If love needs truth, truth also needs love. Love and truth are inseparable. (LF §27)

Returning now to *Only Love Can Save Us*, Bergoglio then adds, "Love is a sublime, irreplaceable, and fundamental task that we need to propose in this day and age to a dehumanized society."[100] More precisely, love is a supernatural virtue, one of the three theological virtues (faith and hope being the others), which animates and inspires what Bergoglio calls above the fundamental task of loving our neighbor. Let me say a few words about this theological virtue called charity, *agápe*.

The *Catechism of the Catholic Church* teaches that charity is a theological virtue that is supernatural in origin, a gift of God's grace, "by which we love God above all things for his own sake, and our neighbor as ourselves for the love of God" (CCC §1822). Let's call this the central commandment of love.[101] "In all its simplicity," says Bergoglio, this commandment—"steady, humble, unassuming but firm in conviction and in commitment to others—can save us."[102] But it is also something by which we will be judged. How so?

Charity, then, rooted in faith in Christ, is the love that comes from him, proceeds from the Holy Spirit, and takes root in my interior life, my heart (Rom 5:5). Only that divine love that is charity, a love coming from God who first loves us by pouring himself out for us in the cross of Christ, can open the heart to the love of *all* men, desiring for all men the same divine good, the same eternal life. Thus, given that my actions toward my neighbor is animated and inspired by love and is ordered to love, we can understand why "the love of Christ compels us [to love our neighbor], because we have concluded this: that one has died for all, therefore all have died; and he died for all, that those who live might no longer live for themselves but for him who for their sake died and was raised" (2 Cor 5:14-15).

The theological virtue of charity is the fundamental principle of all Christian ethics because it is the *form of the virtues*, such as, "compassion, kindness, humility, meekness, patience, and forgiveness." Divine charity—continues St. Paul—"binds everything together in perfect harmony [Col 3:14]... ; it articulates and orders them among themselves; it is the source and the goal of their Christian practice" (CCC §1827). We are now in a position to answer the question implied in Bergoglio's claim that we will be judged by love. What does that mean to him?

Briefly, it means that in any encounter with one's fellow man we shall be judged by God by the measure of absolute love that he has made known in Christ. As Bergoglio rightly sees, in light of the "immeasurable gift of the Redemption," realizing "that everything has been given to us by the free initiative of God," then this gift "cannot fail to lead us to thanksgiving and then to passing on its fruits in love."[103] That gift is God's absolute love and it is the measure by which we shall be judged. In other words, as Balthasar puts it, "if we live in loving faith, our ethical standard is in the end taken from our hands and placed in the [absolute] love of God."[104] Since Christian action towards my neighbor is, Balthasar adds, "above all a secondary reaction to the primary action of God [in Christ] toward man," our standard of judgment is absolute love rather than the mere fact that we have our humanity in common, which we live in community and hence are mutually responsible for each other, and so forth.[105]

No, the measure of God's absolute love is his immeasurable forgiveness and therefore "there are no limits to human kindness." Explains Balthasar: "All the boundaries are erased: For since God forgave me when I was still his enemy (Rom 5:10), I must forgive my fellow creatures, when they are still my enemies; and since God's gifts to me—extending to the point of losing himself (Matt 27:46)—were 'uncalculated', I must now forgo reckoning the balance between giving and a tangible reward (Matt 6:1-4; 6:19-34)."[106] Most important, therefore, is that "God's measure must become my measure, according to which I shall be judged—this is not 'mere justice', but [rather] the logic of absolute love; once again, it is the absolute nature of what has been done to us [in Christ], and what we must do in return [to my neighbor], that is 'fearful.'"[107] Fearful here surely alludes to St. Paul who enjoins us to "work out your own salvation with fear and trembling" (Phil 2:12). Fearful, in a word, because we are sinners. And yet, because we are partakers of God's grace, adds St. Paul, "We are sure of this, that he who began a good work in you will bring it to completion at the day of Jesus Christ" (Phil 1:6). Indeed, the *First Letter of John* reveals that when God's love takes root in us, transforming us, we shall have "confidence in the day of judgment." This love-engendering confidence rids us of fear, "There is no fear in love; but perfect love casts out fear. And he who fears is not perfected in love. Let us therefore love, because God first loved us" (1 John 4:17-19).

Inclusion, Yes; Relativism, No.

The second insight of Bergoglio is found in his distinguishing the concept of inclusion from that of relativism; in short, he is *not* talking of inclusion without qualification. Bergoglio says that relativism means "anything goes." Relativism operates under the presupposition of respect for differences, respect for all; in short, that diversity and hence all differences should be celebrated. This raises the question of what limits there might be to celebrating differences. Should all differences be celebrated and hence should anything be allowed regardless of the content of the beliefs? Bergoglio is critical of relativism because it "wishes to avoid being burdened by all the inconveniences required of a mature courage to uphold values and principles." In other words, relativism "is immature, complacent, and cowardly." How so? Well, it is the sign of an immature mind that lacks the intellectual virtue characteristic of the one who is pursuant of the truth to ask critical questions in order to judge truly. Indeed, in Easter 2005 the then Cardinal Bergoglio urged his teachers in his home archdiocese of Buenos Aires to "develop the capacity of critical judgment in order to escape the 'dictatorship of opinion.'"

> Let us not tire of asking ourselves over and over if we are not simply transmitting information instead of reeducating for liberty, which requires the ability to understand and critique situations and discourses. If we live ever more in an *information society* that saturates us with indiscriminate data, all at the same level, school ought to protect its role of teaching to think, and to think critically. To do this, we teachers have to be able to show the reasons that underlie the differing options for reading reality as well as promote the practice of listening to all voices before issuing judgments.[108]

Most importantly, as Christians we are called to "test everything; hold fast to what is good. Abstain from every form of evil" (1 Thess 5:21-22).

In this connection, we must note another reason why Bergoglio rejects relativism, indeed, following Benedict XVI, what he too calls the "dictatorship of relativism." Francis says, "But there is another form of poverty! It is the spiritual poverty of our time, which afflicts the so-called richer countries particularly seriously. It is what my much-loved predecessor, Benedict XVI, called the 'tyranny of relativism', which makes everyone his own criterion and endangers the coexistence of peoples." Why does relativism endanger the coexistence of peoples? He answers: "Relativism is the possibility of fantasizing about reality, thinking of it as if it could be dominated by an order carried out in a game. This leads to valuing and judging solely by subjective impression: it does not depend on practical, concrete, objective norms."[109] Bergoglio continues: "This subjectivist withdrawal from [objective] values leads us to 'progress through situational consensus'. Here we are entering into debasement: 'leveling toward the bottom' by means of negotiated consensus. Agreements keep on being made."

In other words, what Bergoglio is calling here a "leveling down" through consensus means a process, which is driven by agnosticism and skeptical relativism, where truth is determined by consensus and hence is unable to take seriously the fundamental convictions, the life-orienting beliefs, of an individual's tradition and community, integral to his identity and life. "But in undertaking the path of dialogue with individuals and cultures, what should be our point of departure and our fundamental point of reference, which guides us to our destination? Surely it is our own identity, our identity as Christians. We cannot engage in real dialogue unless we are conscious of our own identity. We can't dialogue, we can't start dialoguing from nothing, from zero, from a foggy sense of who we are."[110] Relativism asks us to withdraw our truth claims that are constitutive of our identity, of our Christian worldview. It holds that neutrality—a naked public square, in the words of the late Richard John Neuhaus[111]—is necessary for dialogue.

> Constructive dialogue between persons of different religious traditions helps also to overcome another fear, which we unfortunately increasingly see in strongly secularized societies: fear directed toward the various religious traditions and toward the religious dimension as such. Religion is looked upon as something useless or even dangerous; Christians are even required at times to act in the exercise of their profession with no reference to their religious and moral convictions (cf. Benedict XVI, *Address to the Diplomatic Corps*, 10 January 2011). It is widely thought that coexistence is only possible by hiding one's own religious affiliation, by meeting in a kind of neutral space, devoid of references to transcendence. But here, too: how would it be possible to create true relationships, to build a society that is a common home, by imposing that each person set aside what he considers to be an intimate part of his very being? It is impossible to think of fraternity being "born in a laboratory." Of course it is necessary that all things be done while respecting the convictions of others, and of unbelievers, but we must have the courage and patience to come together as we are. The future lies in the respectful coexistence of diversity, not in homologation to a single theoretically neutral way of thought.[112]

The demand for neutrality creates an artificial division in an individual's life between his faith and life, denying the integral role that his Christian commitment plays in the life of a committed Christian. In his address on the Feast of St. Stephen, 26 December 2014, Pope Francis said: "To truly welcome Jesus in our existence, and to prolong the joy of the Holy Night, the path is precisely the one indicated in this Gospel: that is, to bear witness in humility, in silent service, without fear of going against the current, able to pay in person. And if not all are called, as Saint Stephen was, to shed their own blood, nonetheless, *every Christian is called in every circumstance to be to live a life that is coherent with the faith he or she professes.*[113]

With this point, Francis echoes the teaching of Vatican II's *Gaudium et spes*: "This split between the faith which many profess and their daily lives deserves to be counted among the more serious errors of our age" (GS §43).

There is another point of criticism to consider: since no ultimate truth exists to guide and direct the process of dialogue, Bergoglio here echoes a claim of John Paul II who wrote that without ultimate truth, "then ideas and convictions can easily be manipulated for reasons of power." John Paul adds, "As history demonstrates, a democracy without values easily turns into open or thinly disguised totalitarianism" (CA §46). So, too, Bergoglio says regarding relativism, "In the end, the logic of force triumphs."[114] Exit truth, enter tyranny. In this light, we can understand why Bergoglio rejects "the deceptive light of relativism, which obscures the splendor of truth and, shaking the earth beneath our feet, pulls us toward the shifting sands of confusion and despair. It is a temptation which nowadays also affects Christian communities, causing people to forget that in a world of rapid and disorienting change, 'there is much that is unchanging, much that has its ultimate foundation in Christ, who is the same yesterday, and today, and forever' (GS, §10; cf. Heb 13:8). Here I am not speaking about relativism merely as a system of thought, but about that everyday practical relativism which almost imperceptibly saps our sense of identity."[115]

The claim that relativism ends up with the logic of force triumphing brings me to another reason why Bergoglio rejects relativism. He says, "Relativism is, curiously, absolutist and totalitarian." It may start out with the adage of respect for all, promoting the value of diversity, but it soon ends up "not allowing for any differing opinion." Thus, adds Bergoglio, "In no way does it differ from an attitude of 'shut up' or 'don't get involved.'" Anyone who has followed the advance of homosexualism in the culture on the legal and cultural grounds that difference, sexual diversity in this case, should be celebrated cannot have failed to notice that it does not allow for any differing view of homosexual practice and same-sex marriage. People have lost their jobs, their businesses, and the freedom to exercise religious liberty by putting into practice their convictions when holding to a judgment that homosexual practice and hence same-sex marriage is morally wrong. Thus, says Bergoglio, "relativism, under the guise of respect for differences, is homogenized into transgression and demagoguery."[116]

In particular, I would add, relativism is the view that all beliefs are equally valid and that all truth is relative to individuals, and has nothing to do with objective reality. The concept of inclusion is sometimes used to suggest that truth of its very nature is inclusive of all viewpoints. Suppose, then, that we hold that all beliefs are not inclusive. What does it mean to hold exclusive beliefs? Says English philosopher Roger Trigg, "Exclusive beliefs are normally seen as those which assert truth in such a way that those who do not share them must be regarded as mistaken." Now, Bergoglio doesn't engage in a philosophical defense of exclusive or absolute beliefs. He clearly holds to the notion of exclusive beliefs—"In the Saving Power of Christ's Cross Alone is our Hope!"[117]—but he is more interested in the question of relating to people rather than merely judging their beliefs. Helpful here in understanding his approach is the distinction drawn in *Gaudium et spes* "between error, which always merits repudiation, and the person in error, who never loses the dignity of being a person, even when he is flawed by false or inadequate religious notions" (GS §28). Working with this distinction between judging beliefs and relating to persons, we can see why Bergoglio argues for a concept of inclusion that pertains to relating to persons via constructive dialogue[118] rather than attending to philosophical criticisms of relativism. Therefore, he says, "including people, each with their own face and name, does not imply that we need to relativize values or justify anti-values." The Christian stance toward his neighbor can then be inclusive in three ways.

Bergoglio underscores the claim that love neither discriminates nor relativizes because it is (1) merciful, (2) open to friendship, and (3) creative. It not only relates to a person qua person, and hence it doesn't discriminate, but it also doesn't succumb to the temptation that we need to relativize truth in order to be inclusive. A brief word about each of these is due.

God is rich in mercy (Eph 2:4). He forgave me of my sins out of love for me in Christ even while I was dead through my trespasses (Eph 2:5), even while I was still his enemy (Rom 5:10). Thus, in light of God's prior and inconceivable forgiveness, that is, says Balthasar, as I noted above, "because God has given to me without counting the costs, to the point of wholly losing himself (Matt 27:46), the standard that God lays down becomes the standard by which I myself am measured, according to which I shall be judged. This is not a principle of 'mere justice', but the logic of absolute love." In this light, we can easily understand the wideness of God's mercy, why mercy is inclusive, grounded in divine redemption, and hence neither discriminating nor relativizing—all men are sinners and are under the power of sin (see Rom 3:9-18). But "God so loved the world that He gave His only begotten Son, that whoever believes in Him should not perish but have eternal life" (John 3:16).

In this light, says Bergoglio, "Mercy creates even greater closeness—the closeness that comes from seeing faces—and, since it truly wishes to help, *it seeks the truth that hurts the most—that of sin*—but with the aim of finding its proper remedy [emphasis added]." The proper remedy of sin, according to Bergoglio, is "to recognize that we are sinners." "We need to open our hearts [to the saving power of Christ's cross] so that [the Father] can enter with his mercy and forgiveness [cf. 1 John 1:9]." In short, mercy without truth—the truth that we are sinners and under the judgment of God—is empty because it does not lead the person "ever closer to God," adds Bergoglio, (EG §172) "in whom we attain true freedom." Yes, we love sinners by extending to them the mercy of God, not so that they would stay as they are but rather so they would change for the better.

But how shall they know that they are called by the Gospel to repentance and amendment of life, if they have not heard that call (see Rom 10:14-17)? Thus, when proclaiming the Father's mercy in Christ and in the power of the Holy Spirit towards others it must be clear to them that our action is rooted in God's prior act of mercy shown to us in and through the finished work of Christ. In this connection, says Bergoglio, "we correct others and help them to grow [in true freedom] on the basis of a recognition of the objective evil of their actions (Matt 18:15)." Of course, as St. Paul writes, we must "not rejoice at wrongdoing, but rejoice with truth" (1 Cor 13:6). *The truth being that we in the Church are all sinners who are saved by grace*: "For all have sinned and fall short of the glory of God, and are justified by his grace as a gift, through the redemption that is in Christ Jesus, whom God put forward as a propitiation by his blood, to be received in faith" (Rom 3:23-25). We hate the sin while loving the sinner.

Moreover, "Love neither discriminates nor relativizes because it is *open to friendship*." Here, too, in the friendship of charity there is acceptance of each other as we are. But there is also that aspect of friendship in which we "tell each other the truth." Being social in nature, we accompany others and align ourselves with them, working next to them, respecting our similarities and differences. Last, love is *creative* and hence neither discriminates nor relativizes. It is creative in that "Gratuitous love is a leaven that stimulates and enhances everything that is good, transforming evil into good, problems into opportunities." In sum, the grace of God's love is creative because it transforms fallen reality from within properly ordering it to its divinely appointed ends so that human beings may flourish by being made new in Christ. "To re-establish all things in Christ, both those in the heavens and those on the earth" (Eph 1:10).

In keeping with the major theme of this chapter, we conclude this chapter by beseeching the Lord for His mercy:

> Lamb of God, you take away the sins of the world,
> have mercy on us.
>
> Lamb of God, you take away the sins of the world,
> have mercy on us.
>
> Lamb of God, you take away the sins of the world,
> grant us peace.[119]

NOTES

1. Niebuhr, *The Kingdom of God in America*, 193.
2. Congar, "Mercy: God's Supreme Attribute," 61.
3. Berkouwer, *Sin*, 40.
4. John XXIII, "Pope John's Opening Speech to the Council."
5. Joseph Ratzinger, *Theological Highlights of Vatican II*, 23. Ratzinger continues: "'Pastoral' should not mean something vague and imprecise, but rather something free from wrangling, and free also from entanglement in questions that concern scholars alone. It should imply openness to the possibility of discussion in a time which calls for new re-

sponses and new obligations. 'Pastoral' should mean, finally, speaking in the language of Scripture, of the early Church Fathers, and of contemporary man. Technical theological language has its purpose and is indeed necessary, but it does not belong in the kerygma and in our confession of faith" (23-24).

6. John XXIII, "Pope John's Opening Speech to the Council," 713. The original Latin is: "Quod Concilii Oecumenici maxime interest, hoc est, ut sacrum christianae doctrinae depositum efficaciore ratione custodiatur atque proponatur," in Ioannes XXIII, "Allocutio habita d. 11 oct. 1962, in initio Concilii," 54 *Acta Apostolicae Sedis* (1962).

7. Kasper, *Mercy*, 12.

8. During the process of preparing this manuscript for publication of the First Edition, Pope Francis announced on 13 March 2015, an "Extraordinary Jubilee that has the mercy of God at its center. It will be a Holy Year of Mercy." See Elise Harris, "Pope Francis declares Holy Year for Mercy." Given this emphasis on mercy, it is all the more important to be clear on the relation between mercy and justice and the Cross of Jesus Christ.

9. Kevin J. Vanhoozer, "The Atonement in Postmodernity," at 403.

10. Pope Francis's lack of an essential place for the law in the redemptive efficacy of the cross is also reflected in his understanding of the law in the moral life and, consequently, in the call to holiness. More on this matter later in this chapter and more fully in the next chapter on the relationship of Jesus and the law.

11. The themes of sin, judgment, wrath, and cross are muted or suppressed in an address of Oscar Andres Cardinal Rodriguez Maradiaga, "The Meaning of Mercy": "The Church is not here to judge, to condemn, to reproach or to reject anybody, but to embrace as in a home where love reigns for everyone who needs it." In this connection, the then Joseph Cardinal Ratzinger understands what must be said about God in order to avoid "cheap grace" and a sentimental view of God and of his love. "Nor should we forget that the God of reason and of love is also the judge of the world and of human beings, the *one who guarantees justice*, because everyone must give account to him. In view of the temptations [e.g.,] to misuse power, it is fundamentally important for us not to forget the truth of judgment: everyone must give account of himself. There is a justice that is not simply abolished by love" ("Searching for Peace," 113).

12. Kasper, *Mercy*, 10.

13. Francis, *A Big Heart Open to God*, 7-8.

14. Francis, *Church of Mercy*, 10.

15. Ibid., 73.

16. Francis, "Homily at Holy Mass for Peace and Reconciliation."

17. "Mercy," entry in Léon-Dufour, *Dictionary of Biblical Theology*, 351-54, and for these passages, 351.

18. Daniel P. Maloney is describing the view of Cardinal Kasper's book, *Mercy*. See the review article, "What Mercy is: A Review of *Mercy*." Cardinal Kasper responds to Maloney and, in turn, Maloney responds to Kasper in a subsequent article: "Cardinal Kasper Responds to First Things Review of *Mercy*." See also, "Love," entry in Léon-Dufour, *Dictionary of Biblical Theology*, 322-27, and at 325: "Of all human words, with their richness and their limitations, it is this word 'love' that gives the best idea of the mystery of God the Trinity, the eternal and reciprocal gift of the Father, Son and Spirit."

19. Pope Francis is under the influence of Cardinal Kasper's book, *Mercy*, on this matter.

20. NGM, 7: "Mercy is in reality the core of the Gospel message; it is the name of God himself, the face with which he revealed himself in the Old Testament and fully in Jesus Christ, incarnation of Creative and Redemptive Love." It is clear in this passage that mercy that is related to God's acts *ad extra*. But I will show in the text that this understanding is in tension with Francis's speaking of mercy as the "first attribute of God" (62).

21. Maloney, "Cardinal Kasper Responds to First Things Review of *Mercy*." Kasper claims that this view is wrongly ascribed to him by Maloney. "I cannot understand how Moloney's [*sic*] critique could suppose the contrary and then end up with a *reductio ad absurdum*. Sure, if mercy would be the inner nature of God, the Father would have mercy with the Son and the Son with the Spirit. But I don't know whether there is one Catholic theologian who teaches such nonsense." Maloney responds: "Cardinal Kasper complains that I attribute to him the view that there is mercy within the Trinity, that for example, the Father shows mercy to the Holy Spirit. He points out that in the section of his book regarding the Trinity, the section entitled "Mercy as Mirror of the Trinity," he makes no such assertion. And he doesn't. But my argument was with the previous section, "Mercy as God's Defining Attribute," pointing out that the view *there* leads to the implication that there would be mercy within the Trinity, an implication we both find absurd. The two sections are obviously related: Since all three persons of the Trinity share the one divine nature, what is true of the divine nature will be true of each of the persons."

22. Francis, "On divorce/remarriage, Pope says keep justice and mercy together."

23. Similarly, Francis,"When there is mercy, justice is more just, and it fulfills its true essence" (NGM §80). I return later in this chapter to give an account of these claims that is "consistent with the traditional view that only pure perfections pertain to God's essence" (Maloney, "Cardinal Kasper Responds to First Things Review of *Mercy*").

24. Similarly, in "Message of His Holiness Pope Francis for the Thirty First World Youth Day 2016," Francis repeats this point, "Justice is necessary, very much so, but by itself it is not enough. Justice and mercy must go together."

25. In what sense are believers no longer under the law? In the next chapter, I shall reflect on the importance of the phrase "under law" in St. Paul, a phrase that occurs eleven times in his letters, Rom 6:14, 15; 1 Cor 9:20 [4 times]; Gal 3:23; 4:4-5, 21; 5:18). On this matter, see Thomas R. Schreiner, *40 Questions about Christians and Biblical Law*, 73-76.

26. Michael Horton, *Christian Faith, A Systematic Theology for Pilgrims on the Way*, 395.

27. Sandro Magister, "Catholic and Papal Anti-Judaism."

28. Joseph Cardinal Ratzinger, *Many Religions—One Covenant*, 38-39.

29. Horton, *Christian Faith*, 678.

30. Ratzinger, *Many Religions—One Covenant*, 39. For more on this relation of Jesus and the Law, see Pope Benedict XVI, *Jesus of Nazareth*, Vol. 1, 99-127.

31. Herman N. Ridderbos, *The Epistle of Paul to the Churches of Galatia*, 126-27.

32. Ibid., 127.

33. Ibid., 204-205.

34. Maloney, "Cardinal Kasper Responds to First Things Review of *Mercy*."

35. Stott, *The Cross of Christ*, 107.

36. This conviction is often repeated but remains undeveloped. Most recently, Pope Francis, "Mercy does not exclude justice and truth" (GE §105).

37. F. Ocáriz, L.F. Mateo Seco, and J.A. Riestra, *The Mystery of Jesus Christ*, 276.

38. Heinrich Denzinger, *Compendium of Creeds*, §1529.

39. Leo XIII, *Tametsi Futura Prospicientibus*, §3; Pius XII, *Haurietis Aquas* (On Devotion to the Sacred Heart), §37; John Paul II, *Dives in Misericordia* §9.

40. Stott, The Cross of Christ, 122.

41. For a discussion of these three theories of the atonement, see Ocáriz, et al. *The Mystery of Jesus Christ*, 271-91. See also, William Lane Craig, *The Atonement*, 28-53.

42. Francis, *The Church of Mercy*, 78-79; idem, *Misericordiae Vultus* §22: "In the death and resurrection of Jesus Christ, God makes even more evident his love and its power to destroy all human sin."

43. Francis, *The Name of God is Mercy*, 32, and also 34, 43, 67.
44. Kasper, *Mercy*, 52; see also, 13.
45. Jorge Mario Bergoglio, "The Challenge of Sin," in *Open Mind, Faithful Heart*, 74.
46. Berkouwer, *Sin*, 38-39.
47. Philip Turner, "An Unworkable Theology."
48. Ibid., 10.
49. Niebuhr, *The Kingdom of God in America*, 193.
50. Turner, "An Unworkable Theology," 11.
51. Ibid.
52. Michael Horton, *Christless Christianity*, 41.
53. Turner, "An Unworkable Theology," 11.
54. Christian Smith et al., *Soul Searching: The Religious and Spiritual Lives of American Teenagers*, 162-71, 258, 262.
55. Ibid., 162-63.
56. The focus on being a "good person" takes the "focus off doctrines altogether and places it upon the moral commitments derived from the church's teachings." "When queried about what best defines a good Catholic, parishioners almost unfailingly equate this with simply trying to be a 'good person.'" Evidence of this among Catholics in the parishes is provided by Jerome P. Baggett, "Another Legacy of Vatican II, at 50. Baggett adds, "Data for this is easy to come by. One recent national survey, for instance, presented Catholics with the statement 'How a person lives is more important than whether he or she is Catholic' and discovered that the vast majority either strongly (55 percent) or somewhat (31 percent) agreed" (50). This national survey is found in William V. D'Antonio, et al., *American Catholics in Transition*, 167.
57. Francis, *The People Wish to See Jesus*, 65.
58. I discuss Francis's notion of ideology in Chapter 1.
59. Pope Francis's address to the Leadership of CELAM.
60. Evidence of this among Catholics in the parishes is provided by Jerome P. Baggett, "Another legacy of Vatican II," at 44-47.
61. Romano Guardini, *Vom Sinn der Kirche*, 2 [12].
62. Ibid., 2 [13].
63. Kenneth L. Schmitz is very helpful in describing the development of this view in "St. Thomas and the Appeal to Experience."
64. Guardini, *Vom Sinn der Kirche*, 4 [14].
65. Charles Taylor, *Varieties of Religion Today*, 101. Similarly, see Walter Cardinal Kasper, "The Timeliness of Speaking of God": "In any case, the so-called return of religion does not simply lead back to Christian faith in God, and it does not on any account fill the empty church pews.... Sometimes what is termed a return to religion is a religiosity without God, a religion-like atheism (J.B. Metz). It can lead to a vague, diffuse, free-floating religiosity, a syncretistic do-it-yourself, what-you-will religiosity which narcissistically seeks the divine not above us but in us" (297). Evidence of this among Catholics in the parishes is also provided by Jerome P. Baggett, "Another Legacy of Vatican II: Cultural Dilemmas among American Catholics": "*Do you think the Catholic faith is better or truer than other religious faith?* To put it simply, I'd say Catholicism is the best religion for me. *Hmm. What do you mean by that exactly?* I think that if you have a relationship with God, it doesn't make any difference what you are.... *Interesting. But, if that's the case, then why be specifically Catholic?* Because this is what works for me. It's the path that I think is working to make me closer to God. Besides, this is the Tradition I know and feel comfortable with" (48). See also, a recent survey studying the state of American Evangelical Theology, examin-

ing 34 beliefs, released by Ligonier Ministries and LifeWay Research, in Jeremy Weber, "Christian, What Do You Believe? Probably a Heresy About Jesus, Says Survey."

66. Charles Taylor, *Varieties of Religion Today*, 101.

67. Fr. Joseph A. Komonchak, "Dealing with Diversity and Disagreement, Vatican II and Beyond."

68. Turner, "An Unworkable Theology," 12.

69. Ibid.

70. Joseph Cardinal Ratzinger, "Dialogue on the Papacy and Ecumenism between the Prefect of the Congregation for the Doctrine of the Faith and Rome's Waldensian Community."

71. Reformed theologian G.C. Berkouwer correctly notes, "Certainly, in both the Old and New Testament we read of God's wrath—against His own people as well as against His enemies—but it is nowhere detached from the perfect holiness which reacts against guilt. That explains that His wrath may attain tremendous proportions, and yet altogether lacks the traits of the demonic, so that in repentance and faith there is always a way to turn from wrath to grace.... In this turning from wrath to grace God's sovereignty is recognized. This turning is never a matter of course, but is experienced and acknowledged as mercy, precisely because of its freedom. That is why the preaching of God's wrath—no matter what proportions it assumes—never affects the basis of one's trust whenever this trust rediscovers the way to God's heart in experiencing His judgment and its righteousness" (*Divine Election*, 91).

72. Francis, "Pope's Homily at Vespers on Eve of New Year [2015]."

73. Joseph Cardinal Ratzinger, *On the Way to Jesus Christ*, 7.

74. Pope Francis, "General Audience, Wednesday of Holy Week," at 17.

75. Francis, *Church of Mercy*, 13-14.

76. Ibid., 12.

77. "Wrath," entry in Léon-Dufour, *Dictionary of Biblical Theology*, 683-88, and for this quotation, 683. See also, Berkouwer, *Sin*, Chapter 11, "Sin, Wrath, and Forgiveness," 354-423.

78. Berkouwer, *Sin*, 39.

79. Ibid., 362.

80. F. Ocáriz et al., *Mystery of Jesus Christ*, 270.

81. Denzinger, §1529.

82. Joseph Ratzinger, *Introduction to Christianity*, 282-83.

83. Kasper, *Mercy*, 75: "With the idea of substitutionary atonement, it is not... a matter of a vengeful God needing a victim so that his wrath can be assuaged. On the contrary, by willing the death of his Son on account of his mercy, God takes back his wrath and provides space for his mercy and thereby also for life. By taking our place in and through his son, he takes the life-destroying effects of sin upon himself in order to bestow upon us life-anew. 'So if anyone is in Christ, there is a new creation; everything old has passed away; see, everything has become new!' (2 Cor 5:17). It is not we who can reconcile God with us. He is the one who has reconciled himself with us (2 Cor 5:18)."

84. J. Murray, *Redemption*, 37-38. *Pace* Edward Schillebeeckx, *Mensen als Verhaal van God*, 144; ET: 125, "God is said to call for a bloody sacrifice which stills or calms his sense of justice. First sin must be avenged and only then is reconciliation possible. The rejection of Jesus by God is said then to reconcile us with God." This is a caricature of the Anselmian theory of the atonement.

85. Fundamental to my thinking on this question is John Paul II, *Dives in Misericordia*. See also, G. C. Berkouwer, *The Work of Christ*, 277. *Pace* Schillebeeckx, *Mensen als Verhaal van God*, 145; ET: 125, "To attempt to reconcile mercy and justice is to attempt to harmonize

the irreconcilable."

86. See also, §§4, 8, 13, and 14.

87. John R.W. Stott writes, "God's wrath in the words of Dr. Leon Morris is his 'personal divine revulsion to evil' and his 'personal vigorous opposition' to it. To speak thus of God's anger is a legitimate anthropomorphism, provided that we recognize it as no more than a rough and ready parallel, since God's anger is absolutely pure and uncontaminated by those elements that render human anger sinful. Human anger is usually arbitrary and uninhibited; divine anger is always principled and controlled. Our anger tends to be a spasmodic outburst, aroused by pique and seeking revenge; God's is a continuous, settled antagonism, aroused only by evil and expressed in its condemnation. God is entirely free from personal animosity or vindictiveness; indeed, he is sustained simultaneously with undiminished love for the offender" (*The Cross of Christ*, 107).

88. Stott, *The Cross of Christ*, 107.

89. Joseph Ratzinger, *The Yes of Jesus Christ*, 94-95.

90. "Mercy," entry in *Dictionary of Biblical Theology*, 354.

91. Similarly, Francis, "When there is mercy, justice is more just, and it fulfills its true essence" (NGM §80).

92. Denzinger, §1528.

93. Anthony Lane, "The Wrath of God as an Aspect of the Love of God," at 160.

94. Berkouwer, *Sin*, 48.

95. Hans Urs von Balthasar, *Love Alone is Credible*, 111.

96. Francis, *Only Love Can Save Us*, 44.

97. John Piper, "Final Judgment According to Works."

98. Francis, *Only Love Can Save Us*, 31.

99. Ibid., 90.

100. Ibid.

101. I discuss the nature of the central commandment of love in Chapter 3.

102. Francis, *Only Love Can Save Us*, 90.

103. Francis, *Encountering Christ*, 53.

104. Balthasar, *Love Alone is Credible*, 111.

105. Ibid., 112.

106. Ibid., 113.

107. Ibid., 122.

108. Jorge Mario Bergoglio, *Education for Choosing Life*, 113.

109. Francis, *The People Wish to See Jesus*, 63.

110. Francis, "Address in Meetings with the Bishops of Asia, Shrine of Haemi."

111. Richard John Neuhaus, *The Naked Public Square*.

112. Francis, "Address to the Participants in the Plenary Assembly of the Pontifical Council for Interreligious Dialogue."

113. Francis, "Address On the Feast of St. Stephen." See also, Pope Francis, *Church of Mercy*, "Dear brothers and sisters, we need to let ourselves be bathed in the light of the Holy Spirit so that he may lead us into the Truth of God, who is the one Lord of our life. In this Year of Faith let us ask ourselves whether we really have taken some steps to know Christ and the truth of faith better by reading and meditating on Sacred Scripture, by studying the *Catechism*, and by receiving the sacraments regularly. However, let us ask ourselves at the same time what steps we are taking to ensure that faith governs the

whole of our existence. We are not Christian 'part-time', only at certain moments, in certain circumstances, in certain decisions; no one can be Christian in this way. We are Christian all the time! Totally! May Christ's truth, which the Holy Spirit teaches us and gives to us, always and totally affect our daily life" (45).

114. Francis, *The People Wish to See Jesus*, 64.

115. Francis, "Address in Meetings with the Bishops of Asia."

116. Francis, *The People Wish to See Jesus*, 64.

117. Bergoglio, *In Him Alone is Our Hope*, 67.

118. Bergoglio writes, "The exercise of constructive dialogue is the most human way of communicating. In all areas, space for serious, constructive, and not merely formal dialogue should be established. Exchange that breaks down prejudices and, on the basis of a common search, builds up sharing, but that seeks the interaction of wills to promote common work and shared projects.... Dialogue requires patience, clarity, and a good disposition toward the other. This does not exclude the confrontation of various points of view, but with ideas serving as light rather than as weapons' (*The People Wish to See Jesus*, 68).

119. *Daily Roman Missal* (Woodbridge, Ill., 2011), The Order of Mass, The Liturgy of the Eucharist, Communion Rite, Breaking of the Bread, 813.

3

Christ is the Fulfillment of the Law

Saint Paul is the greatest Doctor of freedom.... He knows that freedom, in which we are established by faith, is only achieved and fulfilled—thanks to the Cross—by the Spirit and by love. To say that "charity is the bond of perfection" [Col. 3:14] is to say that it is the soul of freedom. A freedom without charity is a corpse of freedom; it disintegrates in the misery of created things; it rots away. The law, which is a tutor, educates us for freedom. As we follow the narrow paths of the moral law, so long as it is the love and Spirit of God which keeps us to them, we little by little learn to be free; free of evil and sin—and at last free of the law itself, since then we fulfill the precepts not through fear but through love, and as though willing them of ourselves and from what is deepest in us, our will having been transformed into the will of Him we love.[1]

Christian freedom is as far removed from legalism as it is from libertinism [antinomianism].[2]

We confess together that persons are justified by faith in the gospel "apart from works prescribed by the law" (Rom 3:28). Christ has fulfilled the law and by his death and resurrection has overcome it as a way to salvation. We also confess that God's commandments retain their validity for the justified and that Christ has by his teaching and example expressed God's will that is a standard for the conduct of the justified also.[3]

Christ does not renounce any point in the Decalogue (what is called... the "Law"). There is not a single commandment which "gives way" to love. On the contrary, all the commandments *find their accomplishment in love*—and this accomplishment does not involve the renunciation of any of them: not an *iota* will pass away until all is accomplished.[4]

During the years of his pontificate some of Pope Francis's homilies have prompted me to ask the following question: In what sense does the moral law remain God's will for the life of the Christian when he has been called to freedom in Christ? (Gal 5:1, 13). I gave my reasons for raising this question in the last chapter. Throughout his pontificate thus far, characteristic of Francis's criticism of the legalist, as he understands him, are such statements as this: "Their hearts, closed to God's truth, clutch only at the truth of the Law, taking it by 'the letter.'"[5] Early on in his pontificate we find such criticisms of the legalist. Francis says:

> This is the path that Jesus teaches us, totally opposite to that of the doctors of law. And it's this path from love and justice that leads to God. Instead, the other path, of being attached only to the laws, to the letter of the laws, leads to closure, leads to egoism [self-righteousness].The path that leads from love to knowledge and discernment, to total fulfillment, leads to holiness, salvation and the encounter with Jesus. Instead, the other path leads to egoism [self-righteousness], the arrogance of considering oneself to be in the right, to that so-called holiness of appearances, right?[6]

He adds, "Do not ensnare salvation in the constrictions of legalism."[7] Again, Francis lambasts the legalist, as he understands him, with such statements as this: "Their hearts, closed to God's truth, clutch only at the truth of the Law, taking it by 'the letter.'" He adds, "The path that Jesus teaches us [is] totally opposite to that of the doctors of law. And it's [the] path from love and justice that leads to God. Instead, the other path, of being attached only to the laws, to the letter of the laws, leads to closure, leads to egoism [self-righteousness]. The path that leads from love to knowledge and discernment, to total fulfillment, leads to holiness, salvation and the encounter with Jesus."

For the moment, I shall just note that the problem with statements like these is that they seem to set up an opposition between the gospel and the moral law. Their lack of clarity leave us wondering what the relationship of believers to the moral law is.[8] Surely, the pope knows that God's moral law proposes what is good for us for living life in Christ. Yes, although he says the Ten Commandments "represent the core of God's will,"[9] indicating "the boundary of life, the limit beyond which man destroys himself and his neighbor, spoiling his relationship with God,"[10] Chapter Three of his Apostolic Exhortation, *Gaudete et Exsultate* focuses exclusively on the Beatitudes to the exclusion of the commandments. Similarly, although Francis clearly states in *Amoris Laetitia* that "the law is itself a gift of God which points out the way, gift for everyone without exception" (§295),[11] Chapter Seven of this apostolic exhortation (§§259-90) focuses exclusively on virtue ethics and moral formation again to the exclusion of the Ten Commandments and the natural (creational) law (see AL §§265-67).

Furthermore, although Francis rightly recognizes that the law as such, in and of itself, cannot change human hearts, he never makes clear that the moral law is always normatively binding upon us, that we have a duty to obey it. This is a big gap in Francis's reflections given that Part III of the *Catechism of the Catholic Church*, Life in Christ, spends 500 paragraphs (§§2052-2557) on the Ten Commandments. Of course the *Catechism* puts the moral life in Christ in the context of man's chief end (§§1716-24) and the moral and theological virtues (§§1803-45). These, too, are integral to the life in Christ. Still, the Ten Commandments are singularly unique in this life because they "embody an abiding law of human life."[12] "The moral law is the work of divine Wisdom," states the *Catechism of the Catholic Church* (§1950), echoing St. Paul, for whom, too "the Law reveals God's will."[13] And in the *Catechism of the Catholic Church*, Chapter 3, Article 3, The Church, Mother and Teacher, "The *Magisterium of the Pastors of the Church* in moral matters hands down "the deposit of Christian moral teaching... [is] a deposit composed of a characteristic body of rules, commandments and virtues proceeding from faith in Christ and animated by charity." In addition, the basis for this [moral] catechesis has traditionally been the Decalogue which sets out the principles of moral life valid for all men" (CCC §2033). Such a statement is missing in Francis. As St. John Paul II decisively states: "Law must therefore be considered an expression of divine wisdom: by submitting to the law, freedom submits to the truth of creation" (VS §41). Furthermore, as John Paul also clearly sees, the moral Law protects the "*good* of the person, the image of God, by protecting his *goods*," that is, "human life, the communion of persons in marriage, private property, truthfulness and people's good name" (VS §13). Therefore, whatever must be said about the moral law and salvation, man's chief end and the virtues, both moral and theological, Pope Francis unfortunately has obscured, unintentionally, the vital point that the law is, as St. Paul teaches, holy, just, and good (Rom 7:12).[14]

Furthermore, the pope's overall emphasis on the error of legalism is such that he never addresses the antithesis of legalism,[15] namely, antinomianism (from Greek, *anti*, against + *nomos*, law)[16]—and we surely live in age of antinomianism, moral subjectivism, relativism.[17] Moreover, he never actually addresses the question: if the moral law is good, which Francis surely believes it is (AL §295), then, what is its place in the Christian life?

Legalism and Antinomianism

Still, in response to this question, there are times when Francis points us in the right direction. The core teaching in his homily of 13 October 2014, is summarized in the following conclusion:

> "Do I believe in Jesus Christ—in Jesus, in what he did: He died, rose again and the story ended there—Do I think that the journey continues towards maturity, toward the manifestation of the glory of the Lord? Am I able to understand the signs of the times and be faithful to the

> voice of the Lord that is manifested in them? We should ask ourselves these questions today and ask the Lord for a *heart that loves the law—because the law belongs to God—but which also loves God's surprises and the ability to understand that this holy law is not an end in itself*."[18]

In what sense is the law not an end in itself? Francis doesn't say. Is this an allusion to Rom 10:4, "For Christ is the end [*telos*] of the law for righteousness to everyone who believes." Is St. Paul making the law void? Although the "law" is imperfect, and the Gospel is "perfect," the law is a "shadow," the Gospel "reality," the law is "old," the gospel is "new," those contrasts do not mean the abolition of the law.[19] Clearly not, since earlier in Rom 3:31 he states: "Do we then make void the law through faith? Certainly not! On the contrary, we establish the law." Rather than making the law void, St. Paul is saying that the objective or goal of the law, its aim or purpose, is the mind of Jesus Christ (Gal 4:19; Phil 2:5). Thus, Christ is the "end" of the law not only by being its completion, its fulfillment—its *finis*—but also *telos*. John Paul II is helpful here. "Commenting on Paul's statement that 'Christ is the end of the law' (Rom 10:4), Saint Ambrose writes: 'end not in the sense of a deficiency, but in the sense of the fullness of the Law: a fullness which is achieved in Christ (*plenitudo legis in Christo est*), since he came not to abolish the Law but to bring it to fulfillment [Matt 5:17]" (VS §15). In what sense Jesus Christ brings God's commandments to fulfillment will be discussed below.

For now, I turn to another Sunday homily of Francis. He returns to the theme of the place of the law in Jesus' proclamation of the central commandment of love—what Francis calls "the one commandment that is the basis of all others—which is love: love God and love your neighbor"[20]—in other words, unrestricted love for God, firstly, and then, secondly, to love one's neighbor as one loves oneself. The Ten Commandments simply stipulate the entailments of the central commandment of love. "Now, in the light of the words of Jesus [about the central commandments of love], love is the measure of faith, and faith is the soul of love." Francis is correct here that the summary of the whole law is the love of God and neighbor (Matt 22:36-40). This summary is already given by Moses in Deut 6:5 and Lev 19:18 as the heart and soul of the commandments.

Unfortunately, statements like these from Francis's homilies are far and few between the steady drumbeat in his homilies of criticizing legalism with its, as he puts it, "dense forest of rules and regulations." He says that Jesus did not come to bring rules and precepts that bar us from encountering God and neighbor. Rather, he made it possible for us to encounter the face of God and the face of neighbor. "No! Not precepts or rules, He gives us two faces! Actually, it is one face: that of God that is reflected in the faces of so many, because in the face of every brother and sister, especially the smallest, the fragile, the helpless and the needy, the very image of God is present. We should ask ourselves when we meet one of these brothers or sisters: Are we able to recognize in them the face of God? Are we capable of doing this?"[21]

As is usually the case, Francis's reflections leave us with unanswered questions. He regularly objects to views that he perceives as dogmatic or rigid, and—he claims—expressive of legalism, self-righteousness, or hypocrisy. For instance, in his concluding address at the 2015 Ordinary Synod on the Family, he said, "The Synod experience also made us better realize that the true defenders of doctrine are not those who uphold its letter, but its spirit; not ideas but people; not [doctrinal] formulae but the gratuitousness of God's love and forgiveness." Here we find a set of contrasts: letter vs. spirit, ideas vs. people, and formulae vs. love and forgiveness. What does he mean by these contrasts? He doesn't say.

Consider the Pauline principle of 2 Cor 3:6, "for the letter kills, but the Spirit produces life." Is this what Francis is alluding to in his contrast of letter vs. spirit? He doesn't say. Briefly, the Pauline principle contrasts letter and Spirit. Significantly, as Herman Ridderbos correctly states, "The antithesis between the law and the Spirit is... not situated in the fact that the Spirit places himself over against *the content and demands of the law*."[22] Of course the Christian's moral life, and the responsibility to make choices that are worthy of the calling that we have received in Christ, is situated within the context of the overarching salvation historical narrative of creation, fall into sin, redemption, and eschatological fulfillment. Therefore, yes, this authoritative biblical narrative is central for understanding the meaning and purpose of the moral life. Still, since the historic Christian faith teaches the Scriptures to be divinely authoritative for morals, then, we must still come to terms with the moral authority of specific moral directives, commandments, and rules. "There exists in Divine Revelation," John Paul II correctly states, "a specific and determined moral content, universally valid and permanent" (VS §37). There are moral norms formulated in Scripture not only having the status of fundamental revealed moral truth but also are in themselves relevant for salvation. The New Testament moral teaching affirms not only the continuing validity of the Decalogue but also its perfection and superabundant fulfillment. As Grisez correctly emphasizes, "In the Sermon on the Mount, Jesus broadens and deepens several of the commandments and demands their interiorization (see Matt 5:21-37). All the synoptics, moreover, present Jesus as affirming the commandments as a necessary condition for entering eternal life (see Matt 19:16-20; Mark 10:17-19; Luke 18:18-21)."[23] St. Paul, too, adds Grisez "assumes the truth of the Decalogue and its permanent ethical relevance."[24]

Now someone might object to this view that the Bible is full of specific commands that are often, say, culturally conditioned. Well, yes, concrete commands, such as, "Anyone who curses his father or mother must be put to death" (Exod 21:17), are culturally conditioned. But this concrete command is a contingent *application* of a primary commandment that is absolute and universal: "Honor your father and your mother" (Exod 20:12).[25] Helpful here in distinguishing between commandments that are still valid from those that are not, is Lewis Smedes' distinction between "primary commandments" and "concrete commandments." The former cover specific areas of life, such as human existence, property, communication, marriage, family. The latter demand or prohibit a specific act. At the root of each and every command is the "foundational commandment" that covers all of life, namely, the central commandment of Love: We are called to love God completely and to love our neighbor as we love ourselves.[26] Does any Christian who confesses the moral authority of the Bible think that all the biblical commands are culturally conditioned such that there are no universally valid and permanent moral precepts?[27] Aren't the biblical commandments against incest, bestiality (Exod 22:19), adultery (Exod 20:14), child sacrifice, prostitution (Lev 19:29; Deut 23:17-18), and rape (Deut 22:25-29), absolute and universally valid? Is it ever morally acceptable to oppress the poor? Commit idolatry (Exod 20:4; Deut 13:6-11)?[28] Bribery (Exod 23:8; 2 Chr 19:7)? Bearing false witness against one's neighbor (Exod 23:1-2)? Surely not.[29] Scriptural moral norms are the Creator's norms, that is, expressions of his design for human life.

Of course, deriving moral norms from Sacred Scripture raises hermeneutical questions. Briefly:

> 1) Moral guidelines (norms) can and must be *deduced* from the Bible as the revealed Word of God:
>
> a. Variant (a): they can be deduced directly because Revelation=Word=Scripture=text;
>
> b. Variant (b): they can be deduced directly but not without taking account of the *historical distance* between the biblical writers and our time. This is done by factoring the difference in situation into the formation of a judgment;
>
> c. Variant (c): they can be deduced *indirectly* by way of an appeal to central biblical motifs (covenant, view of man, view of the body, the love-command), etc.
>
> 2) One can indeed deduce guidelines for action from the Bible, not primarily because their moral validity is rooted in the fact that they are laid down in Scripture, but because, from an ethical viewpoint, they are good for people. Consequently we find them also in the Bible. To "deduce" means one can also trace them to Scripture. In the Bible, though morality often turns out to be crucial in the end, it is not the central issue. God's design is to continue to teach us even through a fallen nature, culture, and history.
>
> 3) Central to our agenda must be the doing of God's will. That does not consist in following rules but is discovered in seeing what God is concretely doing in history. The church has found that God's action is liberating. The

> Bible is the story of liberation from oppression. For that reason we must not automatically do the same today as what God's people did in earlier times. The church must understand the Bible in light of its concrete experience with liberation and oppression.[30]

As I see it, model (1), in all its variants, has been consistently used by Christians throughout the centuries in appealing to the authority of Scripture—but only as long as the unity of Scripture and its reliability as the Word of God was accepted as a first principle of the moral life as well as in doctrinal matters, indispensable and decisive.[31] Model (2), which is compatible with (1), should be understood in terms of natural law, or orders of creation, which purports to defend the universal claims for biblical morality. On model (2), Scriptural moral norms are the Creator's norms, and they are expressions of his design for human life. In order to work out the relation between Models (1) and (2) we need to discuss the larger question of how Christ relates creation and the will of God. "Is Christ in continuity with creation? Or is Christ in disjunction with creation?" In other words, what is the relation between redemption and creation?

Lewis Smedes summarizes the point admirably well that the law of God is the order that God has placed in the cosmos and Christ is in continuity with that law:

> Christ is continuous with creation, the restorer of creation's original intent. It comes to a universal claim for the morality taught by Jesus: it is the way *all* persons should live. The morality of the Bible is not an esoteric way of life for a relatively few disciples; it is the *human* way of life. But is it a way of life which ordinary people can be persuaded to accept? The continuity between Christ's law and God's original purpose with his creatures does not entail an ability of sinful people either to tune into it or live by it. Jesus' moral teachings assume that a conversion is necessary in the hearts of those who hear them, a personal conversion that includes both a new vision of God and new power to will to do his will. So, even though the special morality of the Gospel is—in the deepest sense—valid for all people, it is—in terms of its feasibility—applicable only to those who are prepared by the Spirit to accept it. Still, it is important that when one does accept Jesus' moral law, he is accepting, not an odd, esoteric, enclave morality, but the morality of the truly human existence.[32]

We find models (1) and (2) at work in Part III of the *Catechism of the Catholic Church*, the Moral Life in Christ. As to model (3), its popularity arose with the surrender of the unity and reliability of Scripture under the influence of historical critical methodologies, but also with the denial that there exists in Holy Scripture, as a special revelational act of God, fundamental revealed moral truth. With this denial came the acceptance of the claim that "the revelation of the will of God is not given in the form of immutable and universally valid ethical norms."[33] What encouraged this acceptance was the rejection of revealed truth, that is, propositional revelation.[34] "It is for this reason that there is among scholars, across the Christian traditions, a movement away from what we might call a 'biblical rules' approach to theology. 'Realizing the impossibility of transposing rules from biblical times to our own, interpreters look for larger themes, values, or ideals which can inform moral reflection without determining specific practices in advance.'"[35] So on this model (3) biblical authority can be ascribed to themes like love, justice, freedom even though their concrete applications in the present brings one into open conflict with biblical commandments. This is not the view of the Catholic Church, or for that matter of any orthodox Christian rooted in the historic moral teaching of Christianity.

Furthermore, following the pattern of Christ, St. Paul urges us to avoid self-deception regarding the inseparability of the moral choices we make that are worthy of the calling we have received in Christ and eternal life. Thus, he links fundamental moral decisions with admission to, as well as exclusion from, the Kingdom of God (see 1 Cor 6:9-11).[36] John Paul II reminds us of this inseparability: "In point of fact, man does not suffer perdition only by being unfaithful to that fundamental option whereby he has made 'a free self-commitment to God.' With every freely committed mortal sin, he offends God as the giver of the law and as a result becomes guilty with regard to the entire law (see Jas 2:8-11); even if he perseveres in faith, he loses 'sanctifying grace', 'charity' and 'eternal happiness.' As the Council of Trent teaches, 'the grace of justification once received is lost not only by apostasy, by which faith itself is lost, but also by any other mortal sin'" (VS §68). Yes, the law does not save man, but it is, according to the New Testament, a necessary condition for the moral guidance of Christ's disciples, existing to correct, instruct, and lead to maturity. In fact, St. Paul exhibits his commitment to the authority of the Old Testament law, for example, "Beloved, never avenge yourselves, but leave it to the wrath of God; for it is written, 'Vengeance is mine, I will repay, says the Lord'" (Rom 12:19; see Lev 19:18; Deut 32:35. See also 1 Cor 9:9; 10:1; 14:34; also 2 Cor 8:15; 9:9). In sum, the Mosaic Law is positive and constructive in the New Testament. "Freedom from the law as the road to salvation is simultaneously freedom for the law as a commandment with a specific content."[37] Of course, the Decalogue is not the only normative source of biblical ethics, but it is a fundamental source. Indeed, as Grisez incisively says, "no reasonable reading of the Decalogue can deny it's the status of fundamental revealed moral truth—a status always recognized by common Christian practice in moral instruction."[38]

Unfortunately, the interpretation that places the Spirit over against the content and demands of the law is precisely what is suggested by the contrast that Pope Francis draws between "letter and spirit." And who can be blamed for thinking this since Francis draws this contrast in the context of claiming that the "true defenders of doctrine are not those who uphold its letter, but its spirit." What does that contrast mean? He doesn't say.

Furthermore, the main point of this Pauline principle is that the letter of the law kills because man in his sinfulness lacks power to keep the precepts of the law and that law itself is unable to effect the obedience of vital faith in sinners, which is something that only the Spirit can work in a man. In other words, the law is unable to give life; it fails to vanquish the power of sin, freeing man from his enslavement, and hence man is left with his inability to keep the law. Moreover, the letter kills "because it enslaves one to the presumption that righteousness inheres in one's doing of the law, when it is actually the case that true righteousness comes only as a gift from God."[39] Perhaps this, too, is what Francis has in mind with the other contrast he draws, "formulae vs. righteousness." For St. Paul, as Ernest Käsemann writes, "everything which forces us back on our own strength, ability and piety kills because it snatches the creature out of his creatureliness and this away from the almighty power of grace, of which we are in constant need."[40] Thus, the grace of the Holy Spirit is the effective agent who "gives life" by changing the human heart, which is given through faith in Christ, enabling us to keep the law out of an interior freedom that is expressed in the obedience of faith. Yes, for St. Paul, the law declares God's will. The moral law retains its meaning as, in St. Paul's words, "holy law" and as "holy and just and good" (Rom 7:12), and hence no disparagement of the moral law is intended.

Consider here another example of this criticism in Francis's Santa Marta homily of 24 February 2017.[41] He reflects on the question posed by the teachers of the Law to Jesus in that day's Gospel reading: "Is it lawful for a man to divorce his wife?" (Mark 10:1-12). Francis responds:

> *Jesus does not answer whether it is permitted or not.* He does not enter into their [the Pharisees'] classic casuistry. Because they [the Pharisees] thought of faith merely in the framework of "one may not" or "one may"—up to which point one may, up to which point one may not. Thus the logic of casuistry: Jesus does not enter into it. And He Himself poses a question: "Now, what did Moses command you? What is written in your law?" And they explain the permission which Moses gave to write a divorce certificate and to dismiss a woman from marriage; and it is they who went into a trap, yes. Because Jesus calls them "hard hearted": "only because you are so hard hearted, he has given you this law," and He spoke the truth. Without casuistry, without permissions. The truth.

Now, what is casuistry? Francis doesn't say except to say that it is moral reasoning about dos and don'ts, suggesting that morality is pure casuistry resulting in a casuistic pastoral approach. This approach must be avoided.[42] Helpfully, Simon Blackburn defines "casuistry": "The approach to ethical problems in which the circumstances of cases affect the application of general rules; a casuist is one who distinguishes and marshals the relevance of different cases and rules."[43] This is the mode of reasoning in casuistry. Francis states that Jesus "puts aside casuistry." Well, that's true insofar as Jesus doesn't engage in casuistic reasoning in response to this question, but, *contra* Francis, that is not the same thing as saying that Jesus doesn't answer the question regarding the lawfulness of divorce. Of course he does. His answer logically excludes as "lawful" a state of affairs in which a man and a woman divorce each other and then remarry another because in doing so they commit adultery (Mark 10:11-12; Matt 19:9).[44] So, Jesus does say what is permitted, indeed, obligatory. Why doesn't Francis see this point?[45]

Briefly, he conflates casuistry and legalism. Francis rejects a legalistic mentality that drives some uses of casuistry: "The term [casuistry] is often used pejoratively, implying the multiplication of doubtful distinctions, and their use to defend apparently self-serving and conflicting moral verdicts." For the legalist, and the pope has him in mind when speaking of the casuist, he is "attached only to the laws, to the letter of the laws, [which] leads to closure, [and] leads to egoism [self-righteousness]."[46] Furthermore, the legalist is someone who has "excessive respect for the letter of the law... at the expense of wider moral and social considerations."[47]

Most recently, in a book of interviews, Francis continues his lambasting of the legalist.[48] He says, "The temptation is always towards a *uniformity of rules*[[49]]... Take for example the apostolic exhortation *Amoris Laetitia*. When I talk about families in difficulty, I say, 'We must welcome them, accompany them, discern with them and integrate them into the Church...' and then everyone will see the open doors. What happens, in fact, is that you hear people saying, 'They can't take communion,' 'They can't do this or that.' There you have the temptation of the Church. No, no, no! That type of prohibition is what you find in the clash between Jesus and the Pharisees. The same thing!"[50] Thus, Francis doesn't see a single legitimate question raised here regarding Chapter 8 of *Amoris Laetitia* that is not a reflection of a legalist or rigid mentality.[51] I shall return to this matter in Chapter 4.

For now, we can see that given his reluctance to talk about absolute boundaries, exceptionless moral norms, and what you can and cannot do, no wonder Francis sees too many of us to be suggesting a loosening of the Moral Law's sexual commands. Significantly, he thinks that support for this loosening is found in Jesus' clash with the Pharisees. John Paul II disagrees with such a view of Jesus.

> To return to [the] question, in my opinion, if the Church has to fear not 'imitating' Christ sufficiently, it is certainly not in the sense of being 'strict' where he was 'indulgent.' No, Christ was demanding. But he had such power to penetrate consciences that the very people who came to know his demands felt touched by love. In this the Church can never imitate Christ enough. But she will

never cease to imitate him; she will never cease striving to do so.[52]

Therefore, if Francis thinks that Christ is loosening the Moral Law, as he often seems to suggest, then it is obvious that Francis is wrong because in Jesus' discussion on divorce, remarriage, and adultery with the Pharisees (Mark 10:2-12; Matt 19:3-12), it is they who were intent on keeping remaining loopholes for the possibility of divorce; Jesus closed them in the Law's sexual commands by, as John Paul II says, further "interiorizing their demands and by bringing out their fullest meaning" (VS §15). Fewer loopholes rather than greater license in Jesus' teaching leave us with his stress on adultery of desire, the indissolubility of marriage, and hence living in public sin judged to be a situation of permanent adultery.

The priorities of those raising such questions about divorce and remarriage are turned around, according to Francis; rather than focusing on the more important matters of pastoral mercy and discernment in situations that do not conform fully with the objective demands of the moral law, these legalists, or cold bureaucratic moralist (AL §312), engage in the approach of casuistic reasoning to interpreting God's will. "The logic of black and white can lead to casuistic abstraction. Instead, discernment means going beyond the grey areas of life according to God's will. And you look for God's will by following the true doctrine of the Gospel and not in the fixity of an abstract doctrine."[53]

What is the Clash between Jesus and the Pharisees?

In the previous chapter, I considered what seemed to be Francis's oppositional interpretation of the Gospel and the Law. I referred to the then Joseph Ratzinger's critique of this type of interpretation. He argued: "Jesus did not act as a liberal reformer recommending and presenting a more understanding interpretation of the Law. In Jesus' exchange with the Jewish authorities of his time, we are not dealing with a confrontation between a liberal reformer and an ossified traditionalist hierarchy. Such a view, though common, fundamentally misunderstands the conflict of the New Testament and does justice neither to Jesus nor to Israel."[54] Unfortunately, *I think there are echoes of this interpretation in Francis's thought*. I now want to discuss Cardinal Ratzinger's reasons for rejecting such a "crass contrast" between the Gospel and the Law. With respect to the Catechism of the Catholic Church, he says, "Instead of interpreting his [Jesus'] way superficially in the sense of an ostensibly prophetic attack on hardened legalism, it strives to fathom its real theological depth."[55]

Ratzinger characterizes this contrast between the Gospel and the Law as a "cliché in modern and liberal descriptions where Pharisees and priests are portrayed as the representatives of a hardened legalism, as representatives of the eternal law of the establishment presided over by religious and political authorities who hinder freedom and live from the oppression of others.... In light of these interpretations, one sides with Jesus, fights his fight, by coming out against the power of priests in the Church." Why does Ratzinger hold that this contrast fundamentally misconstrues the New Testament understanding of the relationship between the Gospel and the Law, and hence fails to do justice to Jesus and Israel?

The key biblical principle that helps Ratzinger plumb the theological depth of the relationship between the Gospel and the Law is expressed in the words of Jesus: "Do not think that I have come to abolish the Law or the Prophets; I have not come to abolish them but to fulfill them" (Matt 5:17). The *Catechism of the Catholic Church* §§577-82 functions as the interpretive lens through which Ratzinger understands the words of Jesus. That the Law is fulfilled in Christ does not mean that the Gospel has no further relation to the Law. The moral Law remains God's will for the life of the Christian. How so?

Jesus fulfills the Law by bringing out its fullest and complete meaning. He also fulfills it by bringing the finishing or capstone revelation. He radicalizes the Law's demands by going to its heart and center. Jesus says, "On these two commandments hang all the Law and the Prophets" (Matt 22:40). Jesus neither replaces nor adds to the moral teachings of the Law, but rather he exposes its true and positive, indeed, fullest meaning in light of the twofold yet single, central Commandment: that we love God completely and love our neighbor as ourselves (Matt 7:12; 22:34-40; Mark 12:38-43; Luke 10:25-28; John 13:34; Rom 13:8-10).

In that sense, Jesus interiorizes the demands of the Law because fulfillment of the Law must be measured by that central commandment to love. Because love of God and neighbor is the heart of the Law, Jesus shows that the commandments prohibiting murder and adultery mean more than the letter of the Law states. Jesus is not an ethical minimalist, a view that associates the Law with mere formality and externalism in morals, but rather an ethical maximalist. A maximalist—and Christ was a maximalist—refers to the dimension of interiority (see Matthew 5). Christ appeals to the inner man because "the Law is led to its fullness through the renewal of the heart" (CCC §1964).[56]

Indeed, the *Catechism* teaches that the central Commandment of love expresses the "fundamental and innate vocation of every human being" (CCC §604). Ratzinger explains: "By saying Yes to the double commandment, man lives up to the call of his nature to be the image of God that was willed by the Creator and is realized as such in loving with the love of God."[57] The moral laws, whose core is the Ten Commandments, retain their direct and unchanging validity. Moreover, even these Commandments receive a new foundation in the Gospel. In short, "The Law of the Gospel 'fulfills,' refines, surpasses, and leads the Old Law to its perfection" (CCC §1967).

Furthermore, as I argued in the previous chapter, Jesus' perfect fulfillment of the Law includes his taking upon himself the "'curse of the Law' incurred by those who do not 'abide by the things written in the book of the Law, and do them'" (Gal 3:11). In this light, we can understand why

Catechism of the Catholic Church §579 states that Jesus brings about "the perfect fulfillment of the Law by being the only Righteous One in place of all sinners." Christ's atonement is vicarious, that is, it is a substitutionary atonement. He was a substitute for others, taking their place by paying the penalty for their sins—sins that involved breaking the Law of God. When a law is broken, a punishment is incurred. That is, Jesus was made sin on our behalf so that he would satisfy God's righteousness and hence we might become righteous (see 2 Cor 5:21). "He who was delivered up because of our transgressions, and was raised because of our justification" [Rom 4:25]. So, "Jesus did not abolish the Law of Sinai, but rather fulfilled it [cf. Matt 5:17-19] with such perfection [cf. John 8:46] that he revealed its ultimate meaning [cf. Matt 5:33] and redeemed the transgressions against it [cf. Heb 9:15]" (CCC §592). Mercy and justice meet at the Cross.

Now, according to Francis, Jesus undercuts the concern with casuistic reasoning and goes straight to the heart of the issue posed by the Pharisees regarding divorce. He tells them the truth, and hence Jesus explains that Moses permitted divorce because of the hardness of their hearts. Says Francis, "Jesus always speaks the truth," that is, "he explains how things were created." In his homily of 24 February 2017, Francis merely alludes to the seminal creation texts that Jesus appeals to in his response to the question of divorce and remarriage. That is, Jesus says, "But from the beginning of creation, 'God made them male and female.' [Gen 1:27] 'Therefore a man shall leave his father and mother and hold fast to his wife, and the two shall become one flesh.' [Gen 2:24] So they are no longer two but one flesh. What therefore God has joined together, let not man separate" (Mark 10:6-9).

Similarly, in Matt 19:3-8, the words of Jesus Christ refer back to the Genesis texts of 1:27 and 2:24. "Back-to-creation" is the leitmotif in Jesus' teaching. In his own teaching regarding marital monogamy and indissolubility (Mark 10:6-9; Matt 19:4-6), creation texts in Genesis 1-2 have foundational importance, in particular Gen 1:27 and 2:24: "Male and female he created them" and "for this reason... a man will be joined to his wife and the two will become one flesh." These texts are absolutely normative for marriage, indeed, for sexual ethics. Jesus unites into an inextricable nexus the concepts of permanence, twoness, and sexual complementarity. Yes, Gen 2:24 is about the permanence of marriage; it is also about the exclusivity of the relationship: "twoness"; but it also is about the fundamental prerequisite of complementary sexual differentiation for effecting the "two-in-one-flesh" union of man and woman: "So then they are no longer two but one flesh. What therefore God has joined together, let not man put asunder" (Mark 10:8-9). In this last verse we have Jesus' insistence "on the original intention of the Creator who willed that marriage be indissoluble." The divorce and civilly "remarried spouse is then in a situation of public and permanent adultery" (CCC §§2382, 2384).

This perspective—call it theological realism[58]—raises the question: Is marriage a two-in-one-flesh union between a man and a woman because the Church says so, positing or postulating its existence and nature according to its own judgment, that is, Church law? If so, then, one accepts ecclesial "positivism," the view that these are basically mere conventions. Indeed, Catholics, such as Johan Bonny, the Bishop of Antwerp, may be regarded as an ecclesial positivist because he gives as the only reason for rejecting same-sex marriage the fact that "Church law" says otherwise.[59] This positivism is similar to one thinking that human beings have rights because the state or society says so.

Alternatively, does the Church judge that marriage is a two-in-one-flesh union between a man and woman because that judgment is true to an objective reality, according to the order of creation? If so, then one is a Christian realist: marriage is grounded in the order of creation, of an independently existing reality, and therefore has an objective structure judged by the Church to be the case, or the way things really are.

On this view, the fact that the Church teaches that marriage is a two-in-one-flesh union between a man and a woman adds nothing to the truth-status of this dogma. This realism about the truth-status of dogmatic propositions is similar to one holding that human beings have rights by virtue of their nature as human beings, and that the state simply secures, rather than confers, those rights by writing them down in a constitution.

I contend that the Church holds to Christian realism. Vatican II's *Gaudium et Spes* states, "The intimate partnership of married life and love has been established by the Creator and qualified by His laws"(GS §48). The *Catechism of the Catholic Church* adds, "The vocation to marriage is written in the very nature of man and woman as they came from the hand of the Creator" (CCC §§1603; 1614-1615). As Francis said in his homily, "Jesus always speaks the truth," that is, "he explains how things were created."

Now, Francis of course recognizes that Jesus judged adultery to be a grave sin. Yet, he then suggests that Jesus refrains from judging the adulterous woman: "I do not condemn you. Sin no more." Yes, Jesus leaves aside the matter of making judgments in light of the logic of casuistry, and opposes this logic to the logic of truth and mercy. But Francis, then, misleads by suggesting that the mere setting of boundaries and limits—"You can; you cannot"—is a "deception of casuistry."[60] How can that be if Jesus tells us that adultery is a grave sin? That's a moral boundary judging that one should not commit adultery. Indeed, it is the sixth commandment: "Thou shalt not commit adultery." Does Jesus call us to be nonjudgmental about the morality of actions?[61] How can that be? Yes, Christ meets people where they are, but he calls them to rise from that condition to new life, calling them to *metanoiete* (convert, turn their life around). Francis himself recognizes this point, as he says, "The Gospel tells us to correct others and to help them to grow [ever closer to God] on the basis of a recognition of the objective evil of their actions [cf. Matt 18:15]" (EG §172). Inexplicably, how can we correct others "without making judgments about their responsibility and culpability," as Francis also suggests, for behaving and believing as they do? In fact, in Chapter 8 of *Amoris Laetitia* (§§301-303), the key to the moral logic of pastoral discernment is the issue of culpability, the imputation of guilt, mitigating factors, in order to open a way under certain conditions to the reception of the Eucharist. Of course, that way cannot be had without "making judgments about responsibility and culpability." Furthermore, to avoid "therapeutic self-absorption" (EG §170), which is a condition closed to God, a person must be corrected, informed of the objective evil of his actions. There is an equivocation here regarding the meaning of judgment.

On the one hand, we must refrain from judging a person's eternal standing before the Lord. Francis righty says in this sense, "The Lord asks us above all *not to judge* and *not to condemn*" (MV §14). Of course—and Francis overlooks this second point—refraining from this kind of judgment does not mean, on the other hand, that we must not warn someone that a man's unrighteous actions are such that they may prevent him from entering the Kingdom, especially if they are not redeemed by repentance and God's forgiveness (1 Cor 6:9-11). Thus, the *Catechism* teaches, "Mortal sin is a radical possibility of human freedom, as is love itself. It results in the loss of charity and the privation of sanctifying grace, that is, of the state of grace. If it is not redeemed by repentance and God's forgiveness, it causes exclusion from Christ's kingdom and the eternal death of hell, for our freedom has the power to make choices for ever, with no turning back" (CCC §1861). But even here the first sense of judgment is left in God's hands: "However, although we can judge that an act is in itself a grave offense, we must entrust [the eternal] judgment of persons to the justice and mercy of God" (CCC §1861). On the other hand, to correct others is not possible "without making judgments about their responsibility and culpability" for behaving and believing as they do. Even Francis recognizes this to be so.

Of course it is in principle possible to judge that an action is objectively evil without imputing blame for practicing it, but we must be able to judge whether they are responsible or culpable. Indeed, in chapter 8 of *Amoris Laetitia* the lynchpin of Francis's logic of pastoral reasoning is the distinction between objective morality and subjective morality.[62] Francis insists that his approach in *Amoris Laetitia* is Thomistic[63], and insofar as Aquinas sought "to uphold the subjective factor [in moral evaluation] while also recognizing the determinative place of the objective truth of the act" then Francis is correct.[64] Does *Amoris Laetitita* keep a balanced synthesis between the objective aspect and the subjective factors in the moral evaluation of situation-specific actions of a person?[65] I shall return to answer that question in Chapter 4.

For now, I just want to define the difference between these two aspects. The former pertains to what is morally wrong in itself, objectively speaking; the latter to the judgment whether the moral agent is subjectively responsible, blameworthy, and guilty for having done the wrong thing, or whether there are factors that "mitigate moral responsibility" (AL §§301-303).[66] In Chapter 8 of *Amoris Laetitia,* Francis is primarily focusing on determining culpability—in itself entirely legitimate from a Thomistic view—because he thinks that the logic of mercy and pastoral discernment requires that approach. Furthermore, he also thinks that mercy requires making exceptions to the moral law; otherwise, we fall prey to legalism. I will argue in a later chapter that it isn't clear whether Francis affirms exceptionless moral norms, that is, moral absolutes. This question arises in *Amoris Laetitia* because Francis fails in his appeal to Aquinas, unlike Aquinas himself, to distinguish between "moral absolutes" (exceptionless moral norms, or negative moral norms that hold *semper et ad semper*) and "prima facie obligations" (affirmative, positive norms).[67]

It is important at this point to see that Francis cannot avoid the role of judgments in determining moral responsibility, in light of the distinction between objective morality and subjective morality. He explains, "For this reason, a negative judgment about an objective situation does not imply a judgment about the imputability or culpability of the person involved" (AL §302). But Francis is not urging us to avoid making judgments in this sense altogether (AL §296). How could he? Rather, he is simply urging us to "take into account the complexity of various situations" (AL §296) so as to determine the degree of responsibility imputable to a person since "responsibility with respect to certain actions or decisions is not the same in all cases" (AL §302).

Now, returning to Francis's homily on marriage and divorce in Jesus' dispute with the Pharisees casuistic reasoning, it is actually the legalistic mentality driving some uses of casuistry that he is primarily lambasting. This mentality is that of a cold orthodoxy unaccompanied by mercy and in which, therefore, one applies "moral laws to those living in 'irregular' situations, as if they were stones to throw at people's lives" (AL §305). "Rather than offering the healing power of grace and the light of the Gospel message, some would 'indoctrinate' that message, turning it into 'dead stones to be hurled at others'" (AL §49). Francis adds, "This would bespeak the closed heart of one used to hiding behind the Church's teachings, 'sitting on the chair of Moses and judging at times with superiority and superficiality difficult cases and wounded families'" (AL §305).[68] Yes, the pope warns against reducing doctrines "to a set of abstract and static theories," "desk-bound theology," (EG §133) "rigidity,"[69] and in that sense urges the pastoral purpose of doctrine. Still, he doesn't set up an opposition between doctrine and pastoral care: "Theology and pastoral care go together. A theological doctrine that cannot be guiding and shaping the evangelizing purpose and pastoral care of the church is just as unthinkable as a pastoral care that does not know the treasure of revelation and tradition with a view to better understanding and transmission of the faith."[70] Yet, Francis's rhetoric about doctrines raises question about whether he is at worst anti-doctrinal, or at best a doctrinal minimalist.[71] A representative example of such rhetoric is found in *Amoris Letitia*.

He claims there that "at times we [the Church] have also proposed a far too abstract and almost artificial theological ideal of marriage, far removed from the concrete situations and practical possibilities of real families." He speaks of an "excessive idealization, especially when we have failed to inspire trust in God's grace" (AL §36). Francis adds, "[This] has not helped to make marriage more desirable and attractive, but quite the opposite." Speaking of situations common in our culture that contradict the Church's teaching on marriage, the pope says, the Church must refrain from "imposing straightaway a set of rules that only lead people to feel judged and abandoned by the very Mother [Church] called to show them God's mercy. Rather than offering the healing power of grace and the light of the Gospel message, some would 'indoctrinate' that message, turning it into 'dead stones to be hurled at others'" (AL §49).

What does indoctrinating the Gospel message mean for Francis? It means imposing from the outset moral rules upon a person, resulting in his feeling judged and abandoned by Mother Church whose calling is to offer him God's mercy. Of course Francis is correct, "The Church's pastors, in proposing to the faithful the full ideal of the Gospel and the Church's teaching, must also help them to treat the weak with compassion, avoiding aggravation or unduly harsh or hasty judgments." But we meet again with the equivocation that I discussed earlier when he adds, "The Gospel itself tells us not to judge or condemn" (AL §308). There is an equivocation here again regarding the meaning of judgment. Yes, no judgments about a man's eternal standing. Yet, missing in Francis's perspective is that we can warn someone, as St. Paul consistently does throughout his New Testament Letters, that a man's unrighteous actions are such that they may prevent him from entering the Kingdom, especially if they are not redeemed by repentance and God's forgiveness (1 Cor 6:9-11). Most to the point: how can we correct others, which Francis insists we must, without making judgments about their responsibility and culpability for behaving and believing as they do? (EG §172).

Francis's equivocation and lack of clarity about the status of doctrinal (propositional) truth[72] in the Christian life, yet most of all because he emphasizes the aspect of mitigated responsibility in his moral theory, with a corresponding emphasis on the "law of gradualness" in his logic of pastoral reasoning (as I shall show later in Chapter 4), which despite Francis's disclaimers to the contrary—namely that "gradualness is not in the law itself" (AL §§295, 302)—arguably slips into the "gradualness of the law."[73] This slippage occurs because he seeks to create a moral space to justify the choices that a person makes in certain problematic situations which do not objectively embody the moral law. He uses the language of moral *ideals*[74] rather than a matter of rule-following, which suggests, as John Paul II argues, a regard of the moral law "as merely an ideal to be achieved in the future," rather than a consideration of it "as a command of Christ the Lord to overcome difficulties with constancy."[75] In Francis's attempt to justify a person's situation-specific choices in morally problematic situations, his logic of discernment teeters in the direction of situation ethics. This is because Francis not only searches for exceptions to the moral law, but also, as Flannery and Berg correctly state, "the moral life is not, in the end, about conformity to moral rules, but about ever-closer approximations to the Gospel 'ideal.'"[76] They add that *Amoris Laetitia* "implies that, in lieu of attaining the ideal, there can be degrees of disorder that an individual knowingly, deliberately, and indeed, with *moral rectitude*, allows into his life, since this is the 'most generous response' he can make in pursuit of that ideal."[77]

In my judgment, Francis here runs the risk of setting up an opposition, not to say separation, between the Church as *Mother*—a field hospital administering mercy—and as *Teacher*, between mercy and truth; and if not an opposition, certainly giving a subdued or muted role for the Church as Teacher. This is mainly because Francis does not want to begin relating to individuals in morally problematic relationships by presenting the moral law straightaway, which to Francis runs the risk of being experienced by individuals as synonymous with judgment and condemnation. However, this is a straw man. Besides, how do we avoid watering down the Gospel if when proclaiming the Gospel of mercy we exclude from the outset its foundation in God's justice and truth? Isn't mercy emptied of its concrete meaning and real significance without the condition of knowing the objective evil of one's action as well as the degree of culpability? Yes, it is, and Francis recognizes that point.

In Chapter 2, I showed that Francis affirms that "humanity is wounded" (NGM §6) and that is why "sin is more than a stain. Sin is a wound; it needs to be treated, healed" (NGM §39, §26). Francis regarded the first step towards this healing to involve being "conscious of our sins, of the evil we have done, of our wretchedness, and of our need for forgiveness and mercy" (NGM §32, also 34, 43, 67). The way that the believer receives the grace of Christ's atoning work, his gift of infinite mercy, is by faith (Rom 3:21-25; Eph 2:8-9). Thus, Pope Francis identifies the need "to recognize our emptiness, our wretchedness" (NGM §43), "of our need for forgiveness and mercy," in short, to confess "our miseries, our sins" in order to obtain mercy by faith in Jesus Christ (NGM §32). "Approaching the Lord of mercy with confidence requires," adds Francis, "a shattered heart" (NGM §32), and of course even this recognition of oneself as a sinner and the corresponding act of repentance stems from an act of grace that is the Lord's gift to us. The knowledge of all these conditions is attached to the reception of mercy.

Hence, without the co-existence and mutual influence of mercy, justice, and truth, we are left with the watering down of the Gospel. John Paul II stresses that "'genuine understanding and compassion must mean love for the person, for his true good, without concealing its demands of radicalness and perfection' [FC §33]." He adds, "And this does not result, certainly, from concealing or weakening moral truth, but rather from proposing it in its most profound meaning as an outpouring of God's eternal Wisdom, which we have received in Christ, and as a service to man, to the growth of his freedom and to the attainment of his happiness." Perhaps what contributes to Francis's separation—even if not dualism—between Church as Mother and Church as Teacher is a "clear and forceful presentation of moral truth [that] can never be separated from a profound and heartfelt respect, born of that patient and trusting love which man always needs along his moral journey, a journey frequently wearisome on account of difficulties, weakness and painful situations" (VS §95). Completely absent here in John Paul's emphasis on the interdependence of truth and mercy is the *ad hominem* frequently made by Francis that those who seek to "apply moral laws to those living in 'irregular' situations" take up the stance of those who "were throw[ing] stones at people's lives." I return to this matter in Chapter 4.

For now, I want to stress that John Paul II avoided this opposition in his 1981 Post-synodal Apostolic Exhortation, *Familiaris Consortio*. He understands the moral norm as a liberating truth and that is something missing from Francis's perspective.

> As *Teacher*, she never tires of proclaiming the moral norm that must guide the responsible transmission of life. The Church is in no way the author or the arbiter of this norm. In obedience to the truth which is Christ, whose image is reflected in the nature and dignity of the human person, the Church interprets the moral norm and proposes it to all people of good will, without concealing its demands of radicalness and perfection.
>
> As *Mother*, the Church is close to the many married couples who find themselves in difficulty over this important point of the moral life: she knows well their situation, which is often very arduous and at times truly tormented by difficulties of every kind, not only individual difficulties but social ones as well; she knows that many couples encounter difficulties not only in the concrete fulfillment of the moral norm but even in understanding its inherent values.
>
> *But it is one and the same Church that is both Teacher and Mother.* And so the Church never ceases to exhort and encourage all to resolve whatever conjugal difficulties may arise *without ever falsifying or compromising the truth*: she is convinced that there can be no true contradiction between the divine law on transmitting life and that on fostering authentic married love. Accordingly, the concrete pedagogy of the Church must always remain linked with her doctrine and never be separated from it. With the same conviction as my predecessor, I therefore repeat: "To diminish in no way the saving teaching of Christ constitutes an eminent form of charity for souls."
>
> On the other hand, authentic ecclesial pedagogy displays its realism and wisdom only by making a tenacious and courageous effort to create and uphold all the human conditions-psychological, moral and spiritual-indispensable *for understanding and living the moral value and norm* (FC §33).

It isn't that Francis doesn't see that one and the same Church is both Teacher and Mother. Yes, he does insist that pastoral discernment in complex situations must always remain linked with her doctrine and never be separated from it. He says, "Unity of teaching and practice is certainly necessary in the Church, but this does not preclude various ways of interpreting some aspects of that teaching or drawing consequences from it" (AL §3). Again, Francis says, "Discernment can never prescind from the Gospel demands of truth and charity, as proposed by the Church" (AL §300).[78] Nevertheless, regarding the various ways of interpretation that Francis alludes to above, pastoral discernment begins, then, not with presenting the moral law straightaway, which to Francis runs the risk of being experienced as synonymous with judgment and condemnation, but positively with the acceptance of the good in every person and his particularly complex situation, so-called "irregular situations," such as cohabiting, only civilly married, or divorced and civilly remarried. "Some forms of union radically contradict this ideal [conjugal union between a man and a woman who give themselves to each other in a free, faithful, and exclusive love, who belong to each other until death and are open to the transmission of life], while others realize it in at least a partial and analogous way. The Synod Fathers stated that the Church does not disregard the constructive elements in those situations which do not yet or no longer correspond to her teaching on marriage" (MV §14; AL §§292, 78).[79]

How does Francis theologically justify, for example, the good or constructive elements in these situations? He employs the concept of the "*semina Verbi*," or "seeds of the Word," in order to find goodness or positive elements in these relationships, suggesting that these relationships qua relationships are imperfect forms, partial and analogous, and hence incomplete realizations of conjugal marriage, ordered to the good of an exclusive and permanent relationship (AL §§76-79, 292-93).[80] But this is a misinterpretation and hence misapplication of this concept, which is typically applied in the context of appreciating the elements of goodness and truth found in other cultures and religions as a preparation for the reception of the gospel (*praeparatio evangelica*). But Vatican II does not move from recognizing those elements to concluding that those religions qua religions are themselves vehicles of salvation, imperfectly bringing us into a saving relationship with God.

No wonder Vatican II's *Ad Gentes* §9 takes the Church's missionary activity to involve a "purg[ing] of evil associations [of] every element of truth and grace which is found among peoples." No wonder that *Lumen Gentium* §16-17 speaks of "deceptions by the Evil One" at work in a man's resistance to God's prevenient grace as well as that the gospel "snatches them [non-Christians] from the slavery of error and of idols" and the "confusion of the devil." Indeed, *Ad Gentes* §9 speaks of the fragments of truth and grace to be found among the nations that the gospel "frees from all taint of evil and restores [the truth] to Christ its maker, who overthrows the devil's domain and wards off the manifold malice of vice." In short, the Church's missionary practice is a transformative one of bringing "every thought captive" to Christ (2 Cor 10:5) by treating whatever truth or goodness is found in those cultures and religions as steppingstones that are brought into the service of the gospel and its reception.

Similarly, consider the use of this concept with respect to cohabitation. Let us suppose that a cohabiting couple with children possesses certain stability for the raising of children (AL §78). This is good, and let us say that it is even a sign of God's common grace. But that doesn't mean that a cohabiting relationship *qua* relationship is itself good, and that it is an imperfect form and incomplete realization of marriage.[81] No more than the presence of truth and goodness in non-Christian religions by virtue of God's common grace turns those religions into imperfect vehicles of salvation.

What is distinctive about cohabitation is that the couples are having sexual intercourse—fornication is morally wrong according to the definitive teaching of the Church—without having made a lifetime commitment to each other (and as the divorce rates show is a bad preparation for marriage). This relationship is incompatible with marriage, but is also not a suitable preparation or precursor to marriage. Simply stated, it is a sinful relationship, alienating the couple from God (1 Cor 6:9-10, 15-19), and hence it is not an incomplete or imperfect relationship that is as such ordered to the good of marriage but rather is a violation of marriage, of two people living in sin.

Is Righteousness Increasing Rigor in Obeying the Law?

Benedict XVI says, "The intention is not to abolish, but to fulfill [the law], and this fulfillment demands a surplus, not a deficit of righteousness, as Jesus immediately goes on to say: 'Unless your righteousness exceeds that of the scribes and Pharisees, you will never enter the kingdom of heaven' (Matt 5:20). Is the point, then, merely increased rigor in obeying the Law? What else is this greater righteousness if not that?"[82] Here, too, Benedict rejects the interpretation of the clash between Jesus and the Pharisees that he "broke open a narrow-minded, legalistic practice and replaced it with a more generous, more liberal view."[83] But rather than merely increasing the moralistic rigor in obeying the Law, Benedict argues that Matt 5:20 is "a highly theological text, or, to put it more precisely, a Christological one."[84] This theological perspective is, unfortunately, missing completely in Francis's reflections on Jesus and the Law.

Benedict argues that the Torah itself is an integral whole and so "the worship of God is completely inseparable from morals, cult [ritual and juridical observances], and ethos [a spiritual environment or atmosphere]." Thus, given that it is something integral, adds Benedict, "one cannot simply separate out universally valid moral principles and transitory ritual and legal norms without destroying the Torah itself... which owes its existence to God's address to Israel. The idea that, on the one hand, there are pure morals that are reasonable and universal and, on the other, that there are rites that are conditioned by time and ultimately dispensable mistakes entirely the inner structure of the five books of Moses."[85] Benedict's point here is not about whether Scripture contains universally valid and permanent moral precepts. Of course he thinks it does. Rather, his point is about the *indivisible unity* of love of God and neighbor, that is, the inner structure of the Law being integrally related to the central commandment of Love, the worship of the one God of all men. "Hear, O Israel: The Lord our God, the Lord is one. Love the Lord your God with all your heart and with all your soul and with all your strength. These commandments that I give you today are to be upon your hearts" (Deut 6:4-6). There is more: The faith of Israel is, says Benedict, directed universally to all men, from all nations, because the God of Israel is the one God of all men, and Israel is called to proclaim the glory of God among the nations (see Is 66:19). Israel is called by the Lord to be a light to the nations. Benedict suggestively traces the universalistic promises of Scripture, through Genesis and Exodus, through the Psalms and into the Prophets (especially Isaiah). God's promises encompass the nations of the entire world. Arguably, the so-called Servant Songs in Isaiah refer to Israel. Of the Servant it is said, "I will keep you and will make you to be a covenant for the people, a light to the nations, to open eyes that are blind, to free captives from prison and to release from the dungeon those who sit in darkness" (Is 42:6-7). In short, Israel is called to be a light to the nations.[86] Benedict XVI elaborates:

> The history of Israel should become the history of all. Abraham's sonship is to be extended to the "many." This course of events has two aspects to it: the nations can enter into the community of the promises of Israel in entering into the community of the one God, who now becomes and must become the way of all because there is only one God and because his will is therefore truth for all. Conversely, this means that all nations, without the abolishment of the special mission of Israel, become brothers and receivers of the promises of the Chosen People; they become People of God with Israel through adherence to the will of God and through acceptance of the Davidic kingdom.[87]

On the one hand, then, we have the faith of Israel that bears within itself the universalist promise of becoming the faith of all nations. On the other hand, we have the Law, says Benedict, in whom the faith of Israel in the one God of all men is expressed and his will, as expressed in the Law, is therefore truth for all. But this Law is particular because "concretely directed to Israel and its history." "It could not be universalized in this form," adds Benedict.[88] It will take Jesus Christ to fulfill the universalist promises of Scripture and hence the universality of the Law by putting it on an entirely new basis and bringing it to its fullness of meaning. In other words, as I said above, "Jesus exposed the true and positive meaning of the old commandments."[89] Jesus, unlike Moses who was merely a transmitter of the Law, had the authority to interpret the Law. "It was said to them of old... but I say to you..." Says Benedict, "Jesus' 'I' is accorded a status that no teacher of the Law can legitimately allow himself." Why? Because of "the open claim that he himself [Jesus] is on the same exalted level as the Lawgiver—as God."[90] In other words, says Benedict,

> Jesus opened up the Law quite theologically conscious of, and claiming to be, acting as Son, with the authority of God himself, in innermost unity with God the Father. Only God himself could fundamentally reinterpret the Law and manifest that its broadening transformation and conservation is its actually intended meaning. Jesus' interpretation of the Law makes sense only if it is interpretation with divine authority, if God interprets himself. The quarrel between Jesus and the Jewish authorities of his time is finally not a matter of this or that particular infringement of the Law but rather of Jesus' claim to act *ex auctoritate divina*, indeed, to be this *auctoritas* himself. 'I and the Father are one' (John 10:30).[91]

We don't have the full picture yet, however. "Salvation is from the Jews" (John 4:22). God's salvific mission is a theme indivisibly binding the Old and New Testaments, Jesus and Israel, together. What this means, says Benedict, is "that there is no access to Jesus, and thereby there can be no entrance of the nations into the People of God, without the acceptance in faith of the revelation of God who speaks in the Sacred Scripture that Christians term the Old Testament."[92] Furthermore, Benedict argues, given the interrelation of both Testaments, that an inner continuity and coherence exists between the Gospel of Jesus Christ and the Law. "The whole Law, including the Prophets, depends on the twofold yet one commandment of love of God and love of neighbor (CCC §1970; Matt 7:12; 22:34-40; Mark 12:28-43; Luke 10:25-28; John 12:34; Rom 13: 8-10). For the nations, being assumed into the children of Abraham is concretely realized in entering into the will of God in which moral commandments and profession of the oneness of God are indivisible, as this becomes clear especially in Saint Mark's version [Mark 12:29-31] of this tradition, in which the double commandment [of love of God and love of neighbor] is expressly linked to the 'Shema Israel' [of Deut 6:4: "Hear, O Israel, the Lord our God, the Lord is one"], to the Yes to the one and only God. Man's way is prescribed for him."[93]

Moreover, Jesus came to fulfill rather than to abolish the Law. Jesus said, "Do not think that I have come to abolish the Law or the Prophets; I have come not to abolish but to fulfill" (Matt 5:17). Thus, Jesus opened up the Law "not as a liberal reformer, not out of a lesser loyalty to the Law, but in strictest obedience to its fulfillment, out of his being one with the Father in whom alone Law and promise are one and in whom Israel could become blessing and salvation for the nations."[94] And the ground of that fulfillment is the life, passion, death, resurrection, and ascension of Jesus Christ. In sum:

> That means then that all cultic ordinances of the Old Testament are seen to be taken up into his death and brought to their deepest meaning. All sacrifices are acts of representation, which, from symbols, in this great act of real representation become reality, so that the symbols can be dropped without one iota being lost. The universalizing of the Torah by Jesus, as the New Testament understands it, is not the extraction of some universal moral prescriptions from the living whole of God's revelation. It preserves the unity of cult and ethos. The ethos remains grounded and anchored in the cult, in the worship of God, in such a way that the entire cult is bound together in the Cross, indeed, for the first time has become fully real. According to Christian faith, on the Cross Jesus opens up and fulfills the wholeness of the law and gives it thus to the pagans, who can now accept it as their own in this its wholeness, thereby becoming children of Abraham.[95]

So Jesus Christ is the mediator of the universality of God: of the one God of all men and of his Law, which is expressive of his will, and which is the truth for all men.

Legalism, Again

There is another sense of legalism that is, arguably, particularly important in this context. A legalist is an ethical minimalist, that is, someone who considers righteousness to be achieved by actions that conform to what the law requires. The minimalist confuses the distinction between what is necessary and what is sufficient.[96] Although conformity with the moral law is necessary for righteousness and hence faithfulness to God, such conformity is not sufficient. Consider the conversation between Jesus and the rich young man,

Now behold, one came and said to Him, 'Good Teacher, what good thing shall I do that I may have eternal life?' So He said to him... If you want to enter into life, keep the commandments." The rich young man said in response, "Which ones?" "Jesus said, 'You shall not murder,' You shall not commit adultery,' 'You shall not steal,' 'You shall not bear false witness,' 'Honor your father and mother,' and 'You shall love your neighbor as yourself.' The young man said to Him, 'All these things I have kept from my youth. What do I still lack?' Jesus said to him, 'If you want to be perfect, go, sell what you have and give to the poor, and you will have treasure in heaven; and come, follow me.' But when the young man heard that saying, he went away sorrowful, for he had great possessions' (Matt 19:16-22).

The point I want to concentrate on here has to do with Jesus not merely demanding an "increased rigor in obeying the law" in order to attain perfection. The rich young man had kept the commandments, but something was missing. Elsewhere, in Matt 5:20, Jesus was demanding a "surplus, not a deficit, of righteousness."[97] What else is, then, this greater righteousness if not merely an increased rigor in obeying the law?

On the one hand, to avoid ethical minimalism, or legalism, we must understand that, as John Paul II says, "*Following Christ is thus the essential and primordial foundation of Christian morality.*" In other words, Christian morality, he adds, "is not a matter only of disposing oneself to hear a teaching and obediently accepting a commandment. More radically, it involves *holding fast to the very person of Jesus*, partaking of his life and his destiny, sharing in his free and loving obedience to the will of the Father. By responding in faith and following the one who is Incarnate Wisdom, the disciple of Jesus truly becomes a *disciple of God* [cf. John 6:45]" (VS §19).

On the other hand, John Paul II gives us the answer to this question. He wrote: "*Jesus brings God's commandments to fulfillment*, particularly the commandment of love of neighbor, *by* interiorizing *their demands and by bringing out their fullest meaning.*" In other words, "Jesus shows that the commandments must not be understood as a minimum limit not to be gone beyond, but rather as a path involving a moral and spiritual journey towards perfection, at the heart of which is love [cf. Col 3:14]" (VS §15). He then goes on to give us examples from Matt 5:21-22, 27-28, which illustrates the interiorization of the law through the central commandment of love. Interiorizing the law gives us the sense in which Jesus is an ethical maximalist.

> Thus the commandment, "You shall not murder" becomes a call to an attentive love which protects and promotes the life of one's neighbor. The precept prohibiting adultery becomes an invitation to a pure way of looking at others, capable of respecting the spousal meaning of the body: "You have heard that it was said to the men of old, "*You shall not kill*; and whoever kills shall be liable to judgment." *But I say to you* that everyone who angry with his brother shall be liable to judgment.... You have heard that it was said, "You shall not commit adultery." But I say to you that everyone who looks at a woman lustfully has already committed adultery with her in his heart" (Matt 5:21-22, 27-28). *Jesus himself is the living "fulfillment" of the Law* inasmuch as he fulfills its authentic meaning by the total gift of himself: *he himself becomes a living and personal law*, who invites people to follow; through the Spirit, he gives the grace to share his own life and love and provides the love and the strength to bear witness to that love in personal choices and actions [cf. John 13:34-35]. (VS §15)

Because love of God and neighbor is the heart of the law, Jesus shows that the commandments prohibiting murder and adultery mean more than the letter of the law states. Jesus is not an ethical minimalist, a view which associates righteousness with the mere keeping of the law in morals, but rather an ethical maximalist.[98] A maximalist, and Christ was a maximalist, refers to the dimension of interiority. Christ appeals to the inner man (see Mark 7:21-23). As I argued above, Jesus neither replaces nor adds to the moral teachings of the Law, but rather he exposes its true and positive, indeed, fullest meaning in light of the central Love commandment: that we love God completely and love our neighbor as ourselves. In that sense Jesus interiorizes the demands of the law because fulfillment of the law must be measured by that central commandment.

John Paul II in the *Theology of the Body*[99] makes precisely the claim we are supporting here; that Christ does not abandon the Old Law, but introduces another element of the law, the interior perspective that opens up and fulfills the whole meaning of the law. He states, "The casuistry of the books of the Old Testament, which was preoccupied with investigating what, according to external criteria, constituted such an 'act of the body,' and was at the same time oriented toward fighting adultery, opened various legal 'loopholes' for adultery. In this way, on the basis of many compromises 'because of hardness of... heart' (Matt 19:8), the meaning of the commandment willed by the Legislator [Creator] suffered deformation. One was concerned with the legalistic observation of the formula, which did not 'superabound' in the inner righteousness of hearts. *Christ shifts the essence of the problem into another dimension* when he says, 'Whoever looks at a woman to desire her has already committed adultery with her in his heart.'" So Christ calls us, at one and the same time, to enter "into the depth *of the norm itself and descend into the interior of man, the subject of morality.*"[100] Interiority is important because the standard of the Christian life is an interior state: holiness, or sanctification, and "we are sanctified by God to God."[101] Obedience to the commandments is then both a moral and spiritual journey, in Christ and through the grace of the Holy Spirit, toward perfection, shown in faith working through love (see Col. 3:14). In this light, John Paul adds,

> [T]he commandment 'You shall not murder' becomes a call to an attentive love that protects and promotes the life of one's neighbor. The precept prohibiting adultery becomes an invitation to a pure way of looking at others.... 'You have heard that it was said to men of old, You shall not murder, and whoever murders will be liable to judgment. But I say to you that whoever is angry with his brother shall be liable to judgment... You have heard that it was said, You shall not commit adultery. But I say to you that whoever looks at a woman lustfully has already committed adultery with her in his heart' [Matt 5:21-22]. (VS §15)

Thus, Jesus does not merely call for an increased rigor in obeying the Law. If it were merely the latter, then our righteousness would not exceed that of the scribes and Pharisees, and we would be trapped in legalism, in fact, works-righteousness. Rather, John Paul's stress on the Christological fulfillment of the law as being the precondition for the reign of God's Kingdom in temporal existence is made possible by Jesus' life, death, resurrection, and ascension. The saving grace of God precedes and makes possible the demand for righteousness that God has willed. In other words, the moral and spiritual journey of obedience to the commandments, that is, righteous living in God's Kingdom, is built on the foundation of fulfillment in Christ.[102]

Now, although propositional truth is an indispensable dimension of truth itself, including moral truth, how truth is authenticated—that is, lived out, practiced, carried out—cannot be reduced to it—to being merely believed, asserted, and claimed because "what is communicated in catechesis is not [merely] a body of conceptual truths, but the mystery of the living God" (FR §99). Regarding, then, the fundamental question of how moral truth is authenticated, John Paul correctly notes,

> It is urgent to rediscover and to set forth once more the authentic reality of the Christian faith, which is not simply a set of propositions to be accepted with intellectual assent. Rather, faith is a lived knowledge of Christ, a living remembrance of his commandments, and a *truth to be lived out*. A word, in any event, is not truly received until it passes into action, until it is put into practice. Faith is a decision involving one's whole existence. It is an encounter, a dialogue, a communion of love and of life between the believer and Jesus Christ, the Way, and the Truth, and the Life [cf. John 14:6]. It entails an act of trusting abandonment to Christ, which enables us to live as he lived [cf. Gal 2:20], in profound love of God and of our brothers and sisters. (VS §88)

What is the Chief Enemy of the Christian Life?

I want now to consider briefly the question whether is it really true that the chief enemy of the Christian life is legalism. Isn't the flip-side to legalism, antinomianism? And isn't our culture deeply antinomian such that people consider themselves to be above the moral law? If I had the opportunity to add an error to Pope Francis's two enemies of holiness, I would add to legalism the error of antinomianism (GE §§35-62). Both are present in our culture; indeed, both were present in St. Paul's time, as we find in his *Letter to the Galatians* where he rejects the view that when we live in Christ we are wholly separated now from a requirement to obey the moral law (Gal 5). The proponents of the antinomian position "maintain that the Apostle had... completely rejected the ancient *Nomos*, namely, the Mosaic law, and law of any sort. They say, correspondingly, that he never sought to impose any 'binding precept' on his Christians but was satisfied to propose some suggestions to them, leaving them free to assent or to dissent."[103] In other words, an antinomian is one who believes that "faith alone," or, as is sometimes also put, love alone, "not moral law, is necessary for salvation."[104] But the separation of moral choices from salvation is unbiblical. St. Paul states:

> Or do you not know that the unrighteous will not inherit the kingdom of God? Do not be deceived; neither fornicators, nor idolaters, nor adulterers, nor homosexuals,[[105]] nor thieves, nor the covetous, nor drunkards, nor revilers, nor swindlers, will inherit the kingdom of God. Such were some of you; but you were washed, but you were sanctified, but you were justified in the name of the Lord Jesus Christ and in the Spirit of our God. (1 Cor 6:9–11)
>
> But we know that the Law is good, if one uses it lawfully, realizing the fact that law is not made for a righteous person, but for those who are lawless and rebellious, for the ungodly and sinners, for the unholy and profane, for those who kill their fathers or mothers, for murderers and immoral men and homosexuals and kidnappers and liars and perjurers, and whatever else is contrary to sound teaching, according to the glorious gospel of the blessed God, with which I have been entrusted. (1 Tim 1:8–11)

In light of this dilemma between legalism and antinomianism, there is one question in particular that I would like to address in the following reflections in light of the pope's claim that the "holy law is not an end in itself." That question is in what sense, then, does the moral law remain God's will for the Christian when he has been called to freedom in Christ? (Gal 5:1, 13). Properly understood, Francis's claim that the "holy law is not an end in itself" is biblically true. Actually, in one of his first homilies,[106] Pope Francis well understands the relationship between commandments and love. He says, "Jesus asks all of us to remain in his love. It is from this very love that the observance of his commandments is born." This, Francis reiterates, is "the Christian community that says yes." "This love," says the pope, "leads us to be faithful to the Lord." This amounts to saying that "I will not do this or that because I love the Lord." "A community of 'yes' and 'no' are a result of this 'yes' [to the Lord]." We ask the Lord that the Holy Spirit helps us always to become a community of love, of love for Jesus who loved us so much. [This is] a community of this "yes." And from this "yes," Francis adds, "the commandments are fulfilled." In short, adds Kasper insightfully, "Because Jesus asks us first for love, love for Him, and to remain in His love, the obligation of fidelity to observe the commandments" flows from and is embedded in this love. As Kasper succinctly puts it, "love is the inner law of freedom."[107] So, those who love in this sense will not commit adultery, murder, steal, dishonor their parents, or covet (see Rom 2:21-22; 7:7-8; Eph 6:2). These moral norms are still valid.[108]

In Francis's brief sketch of the relationship between love and the commandments, in sum, the law, the latter is not a constraining imperative imposed upon us from without. "The commandments," he said, "are the path towards freedom, [to authentic human fulfillment] because they are the Father's word, which makes us free to walk this path... with the heart of sons and daughters."[109] Therefore, the law has been interiorized through love, indeed, the central commandment of love: the love of God above all things, in the first place, and, secondly, the love of neighbor as one loves oneself. Interiorizing the law through love brings with it a kind of freedom to obey the commandments.[110] This why Francis says above, "It is from this very love that the observance of his commandments is born." And what Francis is teaching here finds its source in the Fourth Gospel: "If you love Me [Jesus says], keep my commandments" (John 14:15). Elsewhere Jesus says in the same vein: "As the Father loved Me, I also have loved you; abide in My love. If you keep My commandments, you will abide in My love, just as I have kept My Father's commandments and abide in His love" (John 15:9-10).

This interior law is the law of the Gospel, and it is the "New Law," not by differing from or adding new precepts to the ones that Jesus already refers to in his dialogue with the rich young man. In this perspective, we should understand why Pope Francis says that Christ didn't bring more precepts or rules. It is about the New Law of the Gospel (VS §24). The reference here to "New Law" is a way of making clear that the "law of the New Testament" is an interior law that "is instilled in our hearts." Thomas Aquinas cites the *Letter to the Hebrews* 8:10, in which is a reference to Jeremiah 31:31, 33 as biblical support for the use of this term, New Law of the Gospel: "Behold the days are coming, declares the Lord, when I will make a new covenant with the house of Israel and the house of Judah.... I will put my law within them, and I will write it on their hearts, and I will be their God, and they shall be my people." "Therefore," Thomas concludes, "The New Law is instilled in our hearts" (ST, I-II, q. 106, sed contra).

Furthermore, as Thomas Aquinas rightly says, "the New Law is in the first place a law that is inscribed on our hearts, but that secondarily it is a written law." Indeed, he adds, "The New Law is the law of the New Testament. But the law of the New Testament is instilled in our hearts." In short, "Now that which is preponderant in the law of the New Testament, and whereon all its efficacy is based in the grace of the Holy Spirit, which is given through faith in Christ. Consequently the New Law is chiefly the grace itself of the Holy Spirit, which is given to those who believe in Christ." Thomas adds importantly, "In this way the New Law is instilled into man, not only by indicating to him what he should do, but also by helping him to accomplish it."[111] Jacques Maritain put it just right: "Perfectly interiorized through love, the law has become connatural with him. He is no longer *under* the law, says St. Paul, he is doing what he loves. This is the privilege of those whom St. Paul calls the 'sons of God'; they have come to be not above the law but above the constraining imperative that it imposes."[112] This is Pauline freedom. "But if you are led by the Spirit," St. Paul writes, "you are not under the Law" (Gal 5:18). "Now the Lord is the Spirit; and where the Spirit of the Lord is, there is freedom" (2 Cor

3:17). In what sense, then, does the moral law remain God's will for the Christian when he has been called to freedom in Christ (Gal 5:1, 13)?

Christ is the Fulfillment of the Law

I have been arguing in this chapter that St. Paul teaches that the law's fulfillment is in Christ. In other words, the revelation of Christ is the "goal" of the law. He is not the law's termination, but rather that toward which it moves (Rom 10:4), neither absorbing nor superseding it; rather, Christ has perfected the law. In this light, I think we can understand what Francis is getting at: Christ is the interpretive key to unlocking the meaning (*telos*) of the law.[113] This is the view of John Paul II:

> Jesus brings about a *fundamental revision of the way of understanding and carrying out the moral law of the Old Covenant....* Especially significant are the words... Jesus declares, "Do not think that I have come to abolish the Law or the Prophets; I have not come to abolish but to fulfill" [Matt 5:17]. In the sentences that follow, Jesus explains the meaning of this antithesis and the necessity of the "fulfillment" of the law for the sake of realizing the kingdom of God.... *The fulfillment of the law is the* underlying *condition* for [the] reign [of God's Kingdom] in the temporal dimension of human existence. It is a question, however, of a fulfillment that fully corresponds to the meaning of the law, of the Decalogue, of the single commandment. Only such a fulfillment *builds the righteousness that God, the Legislator, has willed.* Christ, the Teacher, urges us not to give the kind of human interpretation of the whole law, and of the single commandments contained in it, that does not build the righteousness willed by God, the Legislator. "Unless your righteousness exceeds that of scribes and Pharisees, you will never enter the kingdom of heaven" [Matt 5:20].[114]

John Paul II is making several important points here. First, Jesus neither replaces nor adds to the moral teachings of the Law, but rather he exposes its true and positive, indeed, fullest meaning in light of the central Love commandment: that we love God completely and love our neighbor as ourselves. In that sense Jesus interiorizes the demands of the law because fulfillment of the law must be measured by that central commandment to love. Indeed, the *Catechism* teaches that the central commandment of love expresses the "fundamental and innate vocation of every human being." (CCC §1604). In this connection, David Yeago's insight may be applied: "What is at stake here is clearly more than a sum of rules for behavior, a list of dos and don'ts. God's law bears not only on our actions, not only on our thoughts and words, but even on our *nature*. It calls for a certain way of *being*, a disposition of the self as its deepest roots. God wants us to *exist* in this way; otherwise, His purpose is not fulfilled in us and God is not satisfied with us. Divine law thus understood cries out for explication in terms of the doctrine of creation."[115] In short, as I argued earlier in this chapter, the Bible's moral norms are the Creator's norms, that is, expressions of God's designs for human life, the morality of truly human existence.[116]

The Central Commandment of Love

Second, Jesus does not merely call for an increased rigor in obeying the Law, as I noted earlier.

Third, against this background, we can appreciate the correct conclusion of Dutch Reformed theologian Joachim Douma: "When we take into account this *fulfillment in Christ*, it is impossible to view the Mosaic legal code in its totality as still being the guide for today. Moreover, the unity of Holy Scripture presupposes that in our moral reflection we will always use the *entire canon* of Scripture."[117] Indeed, this is the first hermeneutical imperative of *Dei Verbum* §12: to attend to the canonical sense of the Scripture, which is arrived at by interpreting the literal sense in the context of the whole Bible. In light of this imperative, in short, attending to the unity of Scripture, we can develop the notion of the law's fulfillment in Christ.

The Gospel of Christ is, according to the Catechism, "a law of freedom, because it sets us free from the ritual and juridical observances of the Old Law" (CCC §1972). Civil, criminal, and cultic (ritual) Old Testament Laws are no longer binding for us. Laws regarding temple sacrifices, ritual cleanliness, and diet, like forbidding unclean meats, whose point is holiness and forgiveness of sins, have been fulfilled by the sacrificial death of Jesus on the cross. His atoning death both perfected and transformed the OT sacrificial system, because He makes a full and perfect sacrifice for sin on our behalf. "We have been sanctified through the offering of the body of Jesus Christ once for all... For by one offering He has perfected forever those who are being sanctified" (Heb 10:10, 14). Again, we read in the *Letter to the Hebrews*:

> But Christ came *as* High Priest of the good things to come, with the greater and more perfect tabernacle not made with hands, that is, not of this creation. Not with the blood of goats and calves, but with His own blood He entered the Most Holy Place once for all, having obtained eternal redemption. For if the blood of bulls and goats and the ashes of a heifer, sprinkling the unclean, sanctifies for the purifying of the flesh, how much more shall the blood of Christ, who through the eternal Spirit offered Himself without spot to God, cleanse your conscience from dead works to serve the living God? And for this reason He is the Mediator of the new covenant, by means of death, for the redemption of the transgressions

> under the first covenant, that those who are called may receive the promise of eternal inheritance (Heb 9:11-15).

Indeed, the key to understanding what happens to the whole law (cultic, civil and moral) of the Old Testament is Jesus Christ. Jesus said, "Do not think that I have come to abolish the Law or the Prophets; I have come not to abolish but to fulfill" (Matt 5:17). As the *Catechism* rightly states: "The Law of the Gospel 'fulfills', refines, surpasses, and leads the Old Law to its perfection" (CCC §1967).

On the one hand, Christ's fulfillment of the law means that we are free from the law as a means of salvation. Because of sin, which the law cannot remove, sins remain a form of bondage from which Christ sets us free. Thus, we are justified through the saving work of Jesus Christ. We are no longer under God's law, then, but under His grace.

On the other hand, that the law is fulfilled in Christ does not mean that the gospel has no further relation to the law. Although we are freed from bondage to the law as a way of salvation, the moral law remains God's will for the life of the Christian.

Freedom in Christ

In what sense does the moral law remain God's will for the Christian when he has been called to freedom in Christ? To answer this important question, Aquinas's distinction between the *obliging* and *compelling* forces of the moral law is helpful here.[118] I am particularly interested in how Aquinas moves us beyond the problems involved in autonomy and heteronomy.[119]

The Obliging Force of the Law

Some key texts are found in St. Paul, who says, "Now the Lord is the Spirit, and where the Spirit of the Lord is, there is freedom" (2 Cor 3:17). Elsewhere he writes: "But if you are led by the Spirit, you are not under the law" (Gal 5:18). Again, he says, "For you are not under law, but under grace" (Rom 6:14). St. Paul here is talking of the interior freedom of those who are moved by the Spirit. But those who are moved by the Spirit would not be against the moral laws expressed in the second table of the Decalogue for these laws have an *obliging* force. St. Paul tells us that "the law is holy and the commandment holy and just and good" (Rom 7:12). "We know," says St. Paul, "that the law is spiritual" (Rom 7:14), and, again, "I agree with the law that it is good" (Rom 7:16). Furthermore, in this connection it is important to underscore one of the uses of the law in the New Testament, namely, that the law illumines human sinfulness. St. Paul writes, "I would not have known sin except through the law. For I would not have known covetousness unless the law had said, '*You shall not covet*' [Exod 20:17; Deut 5:21]" (Rom 7:7). Indeed, as a Jesuit, Pope Francis is deeply familiar with the Ignatian *Spiritual Exercises*,[120] especially the Law/

Gospel dynamic belonging to these exercises.[121] For our purpose here, let me give another Jesuit's summary of this dynamic in the Christian life. The *Spiritual Exercises*, explains Jared Wicks:

> [B]egin by having the person meditate as a sinner confronted by the destructive inroads of sin in human history and personally in himself.... Early in a retreat according to the *Exercises*, the 'light' one asks for is a sense of 'shame and confusion', because Scripture shows how sin brings lives to disaster and I know that I have deserved condemnation for my own sins. One prays before Jesus Christ on his Cross, marveling that he came into the world to die for our sins—there I will reflect on myself (no. 53). The sinner extols the mercy of God for granting life and forgiveness. Then as the *Exercises* further unfold, the retreatant meditates on gospel passages, gradually focusing on his response to Jesus Christ—the Lord and Savior, incarnate, suffering, and gloriously risen—who addresses followers, who know they are forgiven sinners, but find themselves grace with Christ's personal call to dedicated and costly discipleship in service for the good of the human family.[122]

In short, this is the first use of the law, as St. Augustine writes, "The law orders, that we, after attempting to do what is ordered, and so feeling our weakness under the law, may learn to implore the help of grace."[123] I won't say anything more here about the topic of sin, God's wrath/justice, and mercy since I already discussed it at length in Chapter 2.

I turn now to consider St. Paul's response to the question that he poses in his *Letter to the Romans* whether he means, in his teaching, to "make void the law through faith." Briefly, his answer is, "Certainly not! On the contrary, we [mean to] establish the law" (Rom 3:31). VanHoye explains St. Paul's meaning: "How true this is can be verified in Romans 8:4 when Saint Paul states the purpose of the Incarnation and the death of Christ in these terms: 'so that the just precept [righteous requirement] of the law might be fulfilled in us [who do not walk according to the flesh but according to the Spirit]' (8:4). The purpose of God, when he 'sent his Son in the likeness of sinful flesh' (8:3), was to give us the ability to fulfill the just decisions of the law. This affirmation of Saint Paul attributes a high position to the law."[124]

Indeed, Aquinas himself, in an allusion to Jesus' own words (Matt 5:17), sets the Pauline touchstone on the relationship between the law and the Gospel: "All the faithful are under the Law, because it was given to all—hence it is said: 'I have not come to abolish the law but to fulfill it.'"[125] *Pace* antinomians, moral laws do tell us what one is allowed or not allowed to do, permitted or forbidden. Indeed, this use of the law is most important because it reveals what is pleasing to God. Yes, "For freedom Christ has set us free" (Gal 5:1). But our freedom in Christ does not mean that we are no longer obliged to be faithful to "binding precepts"[126] in marriage (and not commit adultery), to protect human life (and not commit murder), to honor our parents, keep our promises, tell the truth (and not bear false witness against our neighbor), and the like. Being free in Christ does not mean that we're *above* or *beyond* the law. Christians are not antinomians. The moral law revealed in Scripture is always binding upon us.

This is evident from St. Paul's description of those persons who "walk by the Spirit." We are called to make choices that are worthy of the calling we have received in Christ. "Walk by the Spirit and you will certainly not carry out [the] desires of the flesh.... If you are being led by the Spirit you are not under [the jurisdiction] of the law. Now the works of the flesh are evident: sexual immorality [*porneia*], [sexual] impurity [*akatharsia*; a term used of same-sex intercourse in Rom 1:24-27], [sexual] licentiousness [*aselgeia*]... I warn you, just as I warned you beforehand, that those who do such things will not inherit the kingdom of God.... And those who belong to Christ [Jesus] [have] crucified the flesh with its passions and its desires. If we live by the Spirit, let us also walk by the Spirit" (Gal 5:16-25). Against this background, we can surely understand that the New Testament teaches that the moral law is inherently related to life in Christ because by obeying the law we are loving God.[127] Indeed, these precepts of the law are presented "as requirements absolutely necessary to "inherit the kingdom of God."[128] As the Council of Trent teaches,

> The grace of justification, once received, is lost not only by unbelief [can. 27], which causes the loss of faith itself, but also by any other mortal sin, even though faith is not lost [can. 28]. Thus is defended the teaching of divine law that excludes from the kingdom of God not only unbelievers, sodomites, thieves, greedy, drunkards, revilers, robbers [cf. 1 Cor 6:9],[[129]] and all others who commit mortal sins that they can avoid with the help of divine grace and that separate them from the grace of Christ [can. 27].[130]

The Compelling Force of the Law

So those who are moved by the Spirit are not under the law—and thus are not constrained or compelled by it—means that they have the interior freedom to choose the good out of love for God, with the dynamism of the Holy Spirit in them being their inspiration. Thus, we do not obey the law because we are compelled to do so. "If you love me, you will keep my commandments," says Jesus (John 14:15). This is a "*participated theonomy*," as John Paul II calls this authentic freedom, "since man's free obedience to God's law effectively implies that human reason and human will participate in God's wisdom and providence" (VS §41). Both the truth and the good of the moral law is interiorized by affirming that these moral norms are related to man's good and to his dignity. *Contra* those who think that obedience to God's laws is a heteronomy of morality, "as if the moral life were subject to the will of something all-powerful, absolute, extraneous to man and intolerant of his freedom." John Paul adds, "Such a heteronomy would be nothing but a form of alienation, contrary to divine wisdom and to the dignity of the human person." Yes, there is a law that is not of man's own making, and in this sense there is a heteronomous morality, which by submitting to this law man submits to the truth of creation. In that sense, however, a heteronomy of morality does not mean "a denial of man's self-determination or the imposition of norms unrelated to his good." Rather, what John Paul calls a *participated theonomy* involves the interiorization of the law, of God's wisdom and providence, as true and as good for man.

Thus, to love Christ entails keeping his commandments. "For charity inclines to the very things that the Law prescribes. Therefore, because the just have an inward law, they willingly do what the Law commands and are not constrained by it."[131] Elsewhere Thomas gives an explanation of human action that flows from an inward law. He writes: "One must bear in mind that the sons of God are moved by the Spirit of God not as though they were slaves, but as being free. For, since to be free is to be the cause of one's own actions, we are to do freely what we do of ourselves." Thomas then contrasts doing something willingly, as a matter of agent causality, with doing it unwillingly, that is, "as slaves, not as free persons, either because we act under absolute compulsion, or because compulsion is mixed with voluntary decision, as when a man is willing to do or suffer that which is less opposed to his will, in order to avoid that which is more opposed to it." Different from both these examples of doing something unwillingly, in particular, acting under absolute compulsion, is the one where I am the cause of my own actions inwardly disposed to do the right thing "because the love of God has been poured out in our hearts by the Holy Spirit who was given to us" (Rom 5:5). Thomas Aquinas explains:

> Well, by the very fact that He infused in us the love of God, it in making us act according to the very motion of our will that the Spirit of sanctity inclines us to act. (For it is proper to friendship that the friend be at one with the loved one in the things which the latter wishes.) Hence the sons of God are moved by the Spirit of God to act freely and for love, not slavishly and for fear: "Now you have not received a spirit of bondage so as to be again in fear, but you have received a spirit of adoption as sons, by virtue of which we cry, Abba! Father!"[132]

Therefore he who would do evil but is held back by a sense of shame or by fear of the law is constrained to keep the law, acts slavishly, not freely, because he is acting under some extraneous principle, and thus experiences the moral law as a form of bondage, imposing moral precepts unrelated to his good. This man is still *under* the law, and hence not free in a Pauline sense.

On true freedom, then, Aquinas writes:

> A person is free when he belongs to himself; a slave, on the contrary, belongs to his master. In the same way, he acts freely who acts spontaneously, while he who receives his impulse from another does not act freely. Therefore, he who avoids evil not because it is evil but because of a commandment of God is not free. But he who avoids evil because it is evil is free. Now it is precisely this that the Holy Spirit brings about, for he perfects our spirit interiorly, giving it a new dynamism, and thus the person refrains from evil out of love, as if the divine law commanded it of him. He is free, therefore, not in the sense that the divine law no longer holds for him, but in the sense that his interior dynamism moves him to do what the divine law prescribes.[133]

Thus, it is not that, in Christ, the law no longer has an obliging force, holding for him, as Aquinas puts it, but rather it is that those who belong to Christ in the Spirit are inclined, interiorly disposed to do the true good by love (see AL §267). Adds Thomas,

> [B]y love it [the Spirit of God] causes the will entirely to lean, here and now, toward that indeed which is in line with its deepest wish. The Holy Spirit, therefore, removes both that servitude whereby a man, the slave of passion and sin, acts against the natural inclination of his will [to what is truly good], and that servitude whereby a man, the slave and not the friend of the law, acts in obedience to the law against the present movement of his will: "Where the Spirit of the Lord is, says the Apostle Paul, there is freedom; and: If you are led by the Spirit, you are not under the law."[134]

Yet the Apostle reminds us elsewhere that "the law is good, if one uses it lawfully." The lawful use of the law is a use that flows from the interior disposition to the true good by love. Otherwise, we fall prey to legalism. To avoid legalism, St. Paul reminds that

> [T]he law is not laid down for the just but for the lawless and disobedient, for the ungodly and sinners, for the unholy and profane, for those who strike their fathers and mothers, for murderers, the sexually immoral, men who practice homosexuality, enslavers, liars, perjurers, and whatever else is contrary to sound doctrine, in accordance with the glorious gospel of the blessed God with which I have been entrusted. (1 Tim 1:8-11)

Once Again, Christ is the Fulfillment of the Law

Aquinas's concluding point that the divine law still holds for the man of

Pauline freedom is clear because both Jesus and the Apostles appeal to the Ten Commandments (Matt 19:18; Rom 13:9; Eph 6:2; Jas 2:11). The moral law retains its meaning as, in St. Paul's words, 'holy law' and as "holy and just and good" (Rom 7:12). As Maritain puts it: "The Law is holy because it is the created expression of the wisdom of God."[135]

Thus, on the one hand, that Jesus fulfills the law cannot mean that Christians can break with the moral law. On the other hand, as Ratzinger correctly explains, "universalizing of the Torah by Jesus, as the New Testament understands it, is not the extraction of some universal moral prescriptions from the living whole of God's revelation. It preserves the unity of cult and ethos. The ethos remains grounded and anchored in the cult, in the worship of God, in such a way that the entire cult is bound together in the Cross, indeed, for the first time has become fully real."[136]

So, as the law's fulfiller, Jesus takes up the Law into His death and brings it to its deepest meaning by perfecting and transforming it (see Matt 5:17-20). The *Catechism* clearly articulates the relation of the Old Law to the New Law:

> The Law of the Gospel *fulfills the commandments* of the Law. The Lord's Sermon on the Mount, far from abolishing or devaluing the moral prescriptions of the Old Law, releases their hidden potential and has new demands arise from them: it reveals their entire divine and human truth. It does not add new external precepts, but proceeds to reform the heart, the root of human acts, where man chooses between the pure and the impure, where faith, hope, and charity are formed and with them the other virtues. The Gospel thus brings the Law to its fullness through imitation of the perfection of the heavenly Father, through forgiveness of enemies and prayer for persecutors, in emulation of the divine generosity. (CCC §1968)

Jesus fulfills the law by bringing out its fullest and complete meaning. He fulfills it also by bringing the finishing or capstone revelation—He radicalizes the law's demands by going to its heart and center, which is that we love God above all and our neighbors as ourselves. In Matt 22:40, Jesus says, "On these two commandments hang all the Law and the Prophets." That is, as God's expressed will, love of God and love of neighbor is the root of the Ten Commandments.

As John Paul II explains, "Jesus brings God's commandments to fulfillment... by interiorizing their demands and by bringing out their fullest meaning. Love of neighbor springs from a loving heart." Because the love of God has been poured out in our hearts by the grace of the Holy Spirit, given to us through faith in Christ (Rom 5:5), not only does His love now indwell in, and act through, us, but God's law is placed within our hearts (Jer 31:33f.; Heb 10:16).

Ethical Maximalism

Because love of God and neighbor is the heart of the law, Jesus shows that the commandments prohibiting murder and adultery mean more than the letter of the law states. Jesus is not an ethical minimalist, one who considers a law to be satisfied by an act that conforms to what the law requires without looking more deeply at the intention of the law and the intention of the person, but rather an ethical maximalist.[137] A maximalist, and Christ was a maximalist, refers to the dimension of interiority. Christ appeals to the inner man and the standard is holiness, the sanctification of a man's whole life, making choices that are worthy of the calling that he has received in Christ. As I argued above, Jesus neither replaces nor adds to the moral teachings of the Law, but rather he exposes its true and positive, indeed, fullest meaning in light of the central Love commandment: that we love God completely and love our neighbor as ourselves. This is the law of love, the supreme law (Deut 6:5; Matt 22:23-40; Luke 10:25-28). Benedict Ashley rightly says, this "is the law of the Holy Spirit dwelling in the heart of the Christian in grace."[138] For the law of the spirit of life in Christ Jesus has freed you from the law of sin and death (Rom 8:2)." "Love," adds Ashley, "is the law that orders all that we are and have to God in response to his love for us (1 Cor 13)."[139] In that sense, Jesus interiorizes the demands of the law because fulfillment of the law must be measured by that central commandment. Pope Francis is, then, right: "Now, in the light of the words of Jesus, love is the measure of faith, and faith is the soul of love."[140]

NOTES

1. Jacques Maritain, *The Living Thoughts of Saint Paul*, 5-6.
2. Walter Kasper, *The Christian Understanding of Freedom and the History of Freedom in the Modern Era*, 9.
3. Lutheran World Federation and the Catholic Church, *Joint Declaration on the Doctrine of Justification*, 4.5 Law and Gospel, §31.
4. John Paul II book of interviews with André Frossard, *"Be Not Afraid!"* 130.
5. Francis, "Pope Francis warns against those who judge [according to the Law] with closed hearts."
6. Francis, "Pope at Mass: Love and Justice are more important than attachment to laws."
7. Francis, "Pope Tells Tribunal: Do not Ensnare Salvation in the constrictions of Legalism."
8. See Philip F. Lawler, "Reverence for the Law," 187-89, "In his written statements and public appearances, Francis has often spoken with warmth and obvious love about the beauties of the Catholic Faith. But he has rarely, if ever, spoken about the love for God's Law that rings throughout the Old Testament. Psalm 119 offers only one of many examples" (187).
9. Francis, *Our Father: Reflections on the Lord's Prayer*, 64.
10. Francis, "Pope Continues Teachings on Ten Commandments." More than five years into

his pontificate, Pope Francis began recently (June 2018) a series of Wednesday Audience talks on the Ten Commandments

11. *Contra* Stephen Walford, "The Amoris Laetitia Dissenters," who cites this statement of Francis suggesting that Francis ascribes a significant and clear place to the moral law in the Christian life.

12. Lewis Smedes, *Mere Morality*, 18.

13. Karl Rahner, Herbert Vorgrimler, *Theological Dictionary*, entry on Law, 256-57.

14. Yeago, "Grace and the Good Life," 83.

15. Notwithstanding Massimo Borghesi's insistence that "dialectical polarity" is at the core of Bergoglio/Pope Francis's thought, meaning thereby that he thinks in terms of the opposition of contraries, not contradictions, there is no evidence in his thought of dialectical thinking on this question of legalism and antinomianism (see *The Mind of Pope Francis*, Chapters 1, 6, 9, 12-13, 19, and Chapters 2 and 3).

16. Rahner, Vorgrimler, *Theological Dictionary*, entry on Antinomianism, 29, "An attitude which denies the justice and validity of all law. In particular it represents the assertion that once the Gospel was promulgated the moral law is not binding on Christians as such."

17. Francis does mention in passing an alleged autonomous freedom that nowadays confuses "genuine freedom with the idea that each individual can act arbitrarily, as if there were no truths, values, and principles to provide guidance, and everything were possible and permissible" (AL §34). He also comments, again in passing, on the mistaken reading of the primacy of conscience as an autonomous conscience for deciding good and evil: "The contemporary world risks confusing the primacy of conscience, which must always be respected, with the exclusive autonomy of an individual with respect to his or her relations" Indeed, Francis rejects an understanding of conscience that reflects "a worship of the self, on whose altar everything is sacrificed." (Nicole Winfield, "Pope Francis reaffirms primacy of conscience amid criticism of 'Amoris Laetitia.'").

18. Pope Francis, "The God of Surprises," italics added. Of course, referring to the God of the Bible as the "God Surprises"—as Francis consistently does—is not a biblical way to speak of God. Throughout the Bible, God is referred to as faithful, trustworthy, and truthful, but nowhere as the "God of surprises."

19. Robert Knudsen, "May we use the Term 'Theonomy'?" at 81.

20. Francis, "An Infinite Horizon."

21. Slightly different translation of this paragraph is found in the Apostolic Exhortation of Francis, *Gaudete et Exsultate*, §61.

22. Ridderbos, *Paul: An Outline of His Theology*, 216; emphasis added.

23. Grisez, *The Way of the Lord Jesus*, Vol. 1, 838.

24. Ibid.

25. On these distinctions, see Lewis Smedes' *Mere Morality*, especially chapter 1. Smedes develops these distinctions more fully in the conference paper, "The Bible and Ethics." Portions of this paper have been published in the first and last chapter of Smedes' *Mere Morality*.

26. Smedes, *Mere Morality*, 11-29. Helpful in understanding the central commandment of Love is David E. Holwerda, "Jesus and the Law: A Question of Fulfillment."

27. Robert A.J. Gagnon, "Are There Universally Valid Sex Precepts?"

28. Of course here, too, we have an instance of a concrete command ("Whoever sacrifices to any god other than the LORD must be destroyed" [Exod 22:20]) which is an application of a primary commandment from the Decalogue (Exod 20:1-6). The concrete command is contextually conditioned, but not the primary command on which it is based.

29. Of course, I am not suggesting that Francis denies the ongoing validity and permanence

of these commandments. However, he does leave in the shadows this matter of universally valid, exceptionless, and permanent moral precepts. This is one of the "dubia" (§2) that the so-called "dubia cardinals" were seeking clarification: "existence of absolute moral norms that prohibit intrinsically evil acts and that are binding without exceptions." Pentin, "Full Text and Explanatory Notes of Cardinals' Questions on 'Amoris Laetitia.'" I discuss this matter in Chapter 4.

30. On these models, see Pim Pronk, *Against Nature? Types of Moral Argumentation regarding Homosexuality*, 283-84.

31. See *Dei Verbum* §12: "But, since Holy Scripture must be read and interpreted in the sacred spirit in which it was written, no less serious attention must be given to the content and unity of the whole of Scripture if the meaning of the sacred texts is to be correctly worked out. The living tradition of the whole Church must be taken into account along with the harmony which exists between elements of the faith."

32. Smedes, "The Bible and Ethics."

33. Typical of this acceptance is a statement adopted by the Reformed Ecumenical Council, Athens 1992, *Hermeneutics and Ethics*.

34. I address this matter of propositional revelation in Chapter 2 of my book, *Revelation, History, and Truth: A Hermeneutics of Dogma*, 47-92.

35. Michael G. Lawler, *What Is and What Ought to Be*, 84. The quote within the quote is from Lisa Sowle Cahill, "Is Catholic Ethics Biblical?", 5-6. For a similar view that rejects propositional revelation and hence claims "the futility of attempting to derive specific moral solutions from particular biblical texts or even combination of texts," see Sandra Schneiders, *The Revelatory Text*, 63n35; see also 54, 58-59.

36. Ratzinger, "The Church's Teaching Authority—Faith—Morals."

37. George Wolfgang Forell, *History of Christian Ethics*, Vol. I, 24-25. See also, John Paul II, *Veritatis Splendor* §§41-42. I address the question of how the law and freedom are related more explicitly later in this chapter.

38. Grisez, *The Way of the Lord Jesus*, Vol. 1, 838.

39. Victor Paul Furnish, *II Corinthians*, 201. See also, Ridderbos, *Paul*, 214-18.

40. As cited in Furnish, *II Corinthians*, 201.

41. In German translation, the full homily is here: Pope Francis, "Gerechtigkeit und Barmherzigkeit - wider die kranke Kasuistik," http://www.kath.net/news/58626. For a partial English translation of this homily see, "On divorce/remarriage, Pope says keep justice and mercy together."

42. Iacopo Scaramuzzi, "The Pope on Amoris Laetitia's Comments: Respectable but Wrong."

43. Simon Blackburn, *The Oxford Dictionary of Philosophy*, 56.

44. In *Amoris Laetitia*, Francis acknowledges that "Christ's teaching on marriage (cf. Matt 19:3-9) is inserted within a dispute about divorce" (§19), but overlooks Jesus' teaching, both in Mark 10:11-12 and Matt 19:9 about the sin of adultery committed by men and women who divorce and remarry.

45. Francis does not distinguish between method and content. We should heed the words of the Dominican theologian Servais Pinckaers that "the teaching of the manuals should [not] be discarded as old-fashioned or outmoded. We need to distinguish here between the container and the contents, between a systematization of moral theology that is a period piece and its contents, which include positions and concrete moral laws belonging to revelation and the tradition of the Church. These latter have permanent value. Certain parts of moral theology at the rational level, such as the teaching on natural law, also have lasting value and may be endorsed by us, even though they require reinterpretation in order to be fully useful. The critic should endeavor to remain always in the service of the upholding and renewal of Christian moral theology" (*The Sources of Christian Ethics*, 293).

46. Francis,"Pope at Mass: Love and Justice are more important than attachment to the laws."

47. Blackburn, *Oxford Dictionary of Philosophy*, 215.

48. Pope Francis can be harsh, not to say judgmental, at times in his obvious contempt for the legalist, as he understands him. The personification of the legalist is the Pharisee. Francis says, "Doctors of the law, the pope noted, "have an attitude that only hypocrites often use: they are scandalized": "But look at this scandal! We cannot live like this! We lost values... now everyone has the right to enter a church, divorced too, everyone. Where are we? " It is "the scandal of hypocrites... it is the hypocrisy of the 'righteous', the 'pure', of those who believe themselves saved by their own external merits," continued Pope Francis: they are "unable to meet love because they have a closed heart." And "the Church, when she walks in history, is persecuted by the hypocrites," "from the inside and the outside," observed the Pope: "The devil has nothing to do with sinners repented, because they look at God and say, 'Lord, I am a sinner, help me.' And the devil is powerless. But he is strong with the hypocrites. He is strong and uses them to destroy, destroy people, destroy society, [and] destroy the Church. The devil's workhorse is hypocrisy, because he is a liar: he shows himself to be a mighty prince, very handsome, and behind he is a murderer" ("Santa Marta: Love with Small Gestures"). This lambasting of the doctors of the law continues, most recently, 16 October 2018: "Pope at Mass: Be careful around rigid Christians."

49. Fr. Antonio Spadaro, SJ, one of Pope Francis's prominent spokesmen interprets this claim as a rejection of moral absolutes, exceptionless moral norms, namely, "a rule that is absolutely general and valid in every instance" ("Discernment as the Landscape, Notes on the Italian Reception of *Amoris Laetitia,*" in *Amoris Laetitia, A New Momentum for Moral Formation and Pastoral Practice*, 115-21, and at 119). Spadaro's claim seems to cohere with Francis's own assessment that there are general moral principles but they do not suffice for governing actions. In AL §303, Francis states, "It is true that general rules set forth a good which can never be disregarded or neglected." Still, he adds, "But in their formulations they cannot provide absolutely for all particular situations." *Pace* Robert Fastiggi ("Responding to the Five Dubia from Amoris Laetitia Itself," *La Stampa* 3/12/2018), and Stephen Walford, *Pope Francis, The Family and Divorce*, 60, 92, there is a difference between general rules and moral absolutes, exceptionless moral norms, and Francis is clearly talking here about the former not the latter. So, Fastiggi fails to persuade that *Amoris Laetitia* has already responded to the second of the five dubia (doubts or questions) submitted to Pope Francis by four Cardinals on 19 September 2016, regarding the existence of absolute moral norms that prohibit intrinsically evil acts and that are binding without exceptions. He says in a 2016 meeting with the Jesuits in Rome, "In the field of morality, we must advance without falling into situationalism.... St. Thomas and St. Bonaventure affirm that the general principle holds for all but—they say it explicitly—as one moves to the particular, the question becomes diversified and many nuances arise without changing the principle" ("'Amoris Laetitia' is built on traditional Thomist morality, pope says").

50. Pope Francis, with Dominique Wolton, *A Future of Faith, The Path of Change in Politics and Society*, 60, emphasis added. In his talk with the Polish Jesuits at World Youth Day 2016, he made a similar point but then with reference to priestly formation programs. "[They] run the risk of educating in the light of overly clear and distinct ideas, and therefore to act within limits and criteria that are rigidly defined a priori, and that set aside concrete situations: 'you must do this, you must not do this.' And then the seminarians, when they become priests, find themselves in difficulty in accompanying the life of so many people and adults" ("Pope Francis says priests must be taught to see shades of gray"). Similarly, in a question/answer session with Jesuits gathered for their General Chapter, Rome, October 2016, Pope Francis warned that in the formation of priests "We run the risk of getting used to 'white or black,' to that which is legal.... One thing is clear: today, in a certain number of seminaries, a rigidity that is far from a discernment of situations has been introduced. And that is dangerous, because it can lead us to a conception of morality that has a casuistic sense.... [and] I am afraid of this" (as quoted by Flannery and Berg, "*Amoris Laetitia,* Pastoral Discernment, and Thomas Aquinas," at 82). I return

to a discussion of the controverted chapter 8 of *Amoris Laetitia* in chapter 4.

51. This, too, is the stance of Stephen Walford reflected in the series of articles he has written defending Chapter 8 of *Amoris Laetitia*.

52. Andre Frossard and Pope John Paul II, *"Be Not Afraid!"* 130.

53. Pope Francis with Antonio Spadaro, SJ, *Open to God, Open to the World*, 118.

54. Ratzinger, *Many Religions—One Covenant*, 38-39. See also, Pope Benedict XVI, *Jesus of Nazareth*, Vol. 1, 99-127.

55. Ratzinger, *Many Religions—One Covenant*, 31.

56. Ross Douthat is right, "The moral law, the Ten Commandments and their corollaries, Jesus never qualifies or relativizes. He never suggests that there exists some shades-of-grey world in which apostasy or adultery (or fraud or murder or theft or gluttony or any other sin) are actually part of God's complicated plan. Instead he heightens moral demands—urging purity of heart as well as purity of actions, proposing a more sweeping rule of charity toward the poor, a more sweeping warning against the temptations of great wealth, and a more exalted view of sex and marriage" (*To Change the Church*, 176).

57. Ratzinger, *Many Religions—One Covenant*, 34.

58. A theological realist, such as John Paul II, affirms the ordering of everything that exists within creation, and this order is an expression of the ordered wisdom of the divine plan for creation. So, we can speak here of a creation revelation in and through the created order, in which man and all things have been given their structure in the cosmos. See, too, Oliver O'Donovan, *Resurrection and Moral Order*, "The *created order*... is the structure of the world in its objectivity, which includes... its authority to evoke our actions" (191).

59. See my article review of his book, co-authored with Belgian moral theologian Roger Burggraeve, *Mag ik? Sorry, Dank je, Vrijmoedige dialoog over relaties, huwelijk en gezin* [*May I? Sorry, Thank you, Open Dialogue about relationships, marriage and family*], "Belgium bishop co-authors book in support of pre-marital sex, same-sex relations."

60. This suggestion caused Philip F. Lawler mistakenly to conclude that Pope Francis "was engaged in a deliberate effort to change what the Church teaches [about marriage]" (*Lost Shepherd*, 2018), x.

61. Yes, says Bishop Robert McElroy, being nonjudgmental is one of the key elements of Pope Francis's pastoral theology, and it derives from Jesus. "There is no sin which Jesus mentions more frequently in the gospels than the sin of judgmentalism." In: "Pastoral Theology for a Post-Modern World (The Pastoral Theology of Pope Francis)," https://www.scribd.com/document/382719025/Robert-McElroy-AUSCP-Presentation-June-26-2018. McElroy provides no biblical or theological justification for this extravagant claim in light of, for example, Matthew 23 and Jesus' judgment of the Pharisees as hypocrites, blind guides, and the like. He makes no effort to give an exegesis of Matt 7:1-5, and parallel passages in Luke 6:37-42, and John 8:1-8, regarding Jesus' call that we should refrain from judging others.

62. *Amoris Laetitia* and its controverted claims, particularly Chapter 8, employs this distinction between objective and subjective morality. In Chapter 4 of this book, I will show how Francis develops this distinction and its implications in the moral logic of pastoral reasoning.

63. Representative of this claim is the following: "To those who maintain that the morality underlying the document is not 'a Catholic morality' or a morality that can be certain or sure, 'I want to repeat clearly that the morality of *Amoris Laetitia* is Thomist', that is, built on the moral philosophy of St. Thomas Aquinas, he said" ("'Amoris Laetitia' is built on traditional Thomist morality, pope says"). Francis does not tell us how it is Thomistic. But we'll return to this claim later in Chapter 4.

64. Serge-Thomas Bonino, O.P., "Saint Thomas Aquinas in the Apostolic Exhortation *Amoris Laetitia*," at 509.

65. Rocco Buttiglione charges critics of *Amoris Laetitia* with "ethical objectivism." Says

Buttiglione, "Just as subjectivism (the ethics of the situation) sees only the subjective side of action, that is, the intention of the subject, so objectivism sees only the objective side of action, that is, the mora or less grave matter. Catholic ethics is realistic. Realism sees both the subjective and objective side of the action, and therefore assesses both the grave matter and the full knowledge and deliberate consent" (Buttiglione, "Here is the deviation in which Amoris Laetitia's critics fall"). I think that this is a straw man. The critics agree that there is an objective and subjective aspect to the moral evaluations of action, but press on to ask whether *Amoris Laetitia* keep a balanced synthesis between these two factors in the moral evaluation of situation-specific actions of a person. I return to this question in Chapter 4.

66. Francis is drawing here on the *Catechism of the Catholic Church* §§1735-36, but he could have referred to other sources pre-dating the Catechism, such as *Persona Humana*, 1975 Declaration on Certain Questions Concerning Sexual Ethics, Sections IX-X; *Homosexualitatis problema*, 1986, §11; and *Moral Norm of Humanae Vitae and Pastoral Duty*, 1989, §3. I will return to a discussion of this matter later in Chapter 4.

67. This distinction is central to the teaching of John Paul II, *Veritatis Splendor*, on intrinsically evil acts, §§52, 67. The truth is that *Amoris Laetitia* does not refer to *Veritatis Splendor* in any of its 391 footnotes. And one wonders why, since this encyclical treats some of the same issues raised by Francis in *Amoris Laetitia*.

68. The quote within the quote here is from Francis's Address for the Conclusion of the Fourteenth Ordinary General Assembly of the Synod of Bishops, 24 October 2015, §13.

69. It is not surprising that Francis holds this view since he holds, "There is no white or black; there is white, black, gray, and then all the many shades of gray.... Life itself is gray; it is a journey in search of something toward which we cannot be rigid but, as society, proudly multicolored" (*God is Young*, 58).

70. Francis, "Discorso del Santo Padre Francesco Alla Comunità Accademica del Pontificio Istituto 'Giovanni Paolo II' Per Studi su Matrimonio E Famiglia."

71. It also raises the question whether Francis has a pastoral approach to doctrine, meaning thereby an instrumentalist or functionalist view of doctrine. I addressed this question in Chapter 1 on the theme of Vatican II's legacy.

72. See Chapter 1 to this book.

73. John Paul II, FC §34, "And so what is known as "the law of gradualness" or step-by-step [moral] advance cannot be identified with "gradualness of the law," as if there were different degrees or forms of precept in God's law for different individuals and situations." For Francis's disclaimers, see, AL §§295, 300.

74. Francis uses the language of "ideal," or "objective ideal," when referring to the moral norm of marriage, marital permanence or indissolubility. "Ideal" is how the Latin term "exemplar" has been translated. This suggests something to be aspired after rather than an obligation. Some have also suggested that the norm is rarely attained or even unattainable. But that "exemplar" does not have that connotation has been argued by Robert Fastiggi and Dawn Eden Goldstein, "Does Amoris Laetitia 303 Really Undermine Catholic Moral Teaching?" Still, suppose, as blogger P.J. Smith asks, "we acknowledge that *exemplum* more precisely means 'pattern, model, exemplar, original, an example' (per the standard reference Lewis & Short dictionary). Fine. But what is the difference between *a pattern* or *a model* and *an ideal*? They [Fastiggi and Goldstein] never say. It is enough for them to suggest that, well, the Latin original says *exemplum*." In particular, how does it make a difference to the logic of pastoral reasoning and discernment in evaluating morally problematic situations? Does Francis not think of "ideal" as more like something to be aspired after rather than an obligation?

75. John Paul II, "Married people too are called upon to progress unceasingly in their moral life, with the support of a sincere and active desire to gain ever better knowledge of the values enshrined in and fostered by the law of God. They must also be supported by an upright and generous willingness to embody these values in their concrete decisions. They cannot however look on the law as merely an ideal to be achieved in the future:

they must consider it as a command of Christ the Lord to overcome difficulties with constancy. 'And so what is known as "the law of gradualness" or step-by-step [moral] advance cannot be identified with "gradualness of the law," as if there were different degrees or forms of precept in God's law for different individuals and situations." The quote within the quote is from John Paul II, "Los padres sinodales, dirigiéndose a los que ejercen el ministerio pastoral en favor de los esposos y de las familias, han rechazado toda separación o dicotomía entre la pedagogía, que propone un cierto progreso en la realización del plan de Dios, y la doctrina propuesta por la Iglesia con todas sus consecuencias, en las cuales está contenido el precepto de vivir según la misma doctrina. No se trata del deseo de observar la ley como un mero 'ideal', como se dice vulgarmente, que se podrá conseguir en el futuro, sino como un mandamiento de Cristo Señor a superar constantemente las dificultades. En realidad no se puede aceptar un 'proceso de gradualidad,' como se dice hoy, si uno no observa la ley divina con ánimo sincero y busca aquellos bienes custodiados y promovidos por la misma ley. Pues la llamada 'ley de gradualidad' o camino gradual no puede ser una 'gradualidad de la ley,' como sí hubiera varios grados o formas de precepto en la ley divina, para los diversos hombres y las distintas situaciones" (§8). ("Homily at the Close of the Fifth Synod of Bishops." The homily is not available in English.)

76. The term "ideal" suggests something one aspires after rather than an obligation. The moral law has an obliging force rather than merely an aspiring one. I treat Aquinas's view of the law's obliging force later in this chapter.

77. Flannery and Berg, "*Amoris Laetitia*, Pastoral Discernment, and Thomas Aquinas," 94-95. I develop these claims in Chapter 4, *Amoris Laetitia*, The Controverted Apostolic Exhortation.

78. Similarly, Francis, *Amoris Laetitia* §§38, 303, 307, 311.

79. How does one present the moral law as a liberating truth? I return to this question in a later chapter on *Amoris Laetitia*.

80. Francis is influenced here by the reports of the Extraordinary and Ordinary Synods on the Family, 2014-2015. For my analysis and critique of the Interim Report of 2014 where this approach is evident see my article, "The Synod's Interim Report: Ambiguity and Misinterpretation."

81. Similarly, Gerhard Cardinal Müller correctly writes, "Even when some constitutive elements of marriage are found in cohabitations that resemble marriage, however, the sinful transgression against other constitutive elements of marriage and against marriage as a whole, is not good. Contradiction with goodness can never become part of it, or the beginning of a journey towards the fulfillment of God's holy and sanctifying will" ("Communion to the remarried, 'There can be mitigating factors in guilt'"). Inexplicably, Müller overlooks that this point is precisely what Francis affirms.

82. Benedict XVI, *Jesus of Nazareth*, Vol. 1, 102.

83. Ibid.

84. Ibid., 110.

85. Ratzinger, *Many Religions—One Covenant*, 37-38.

86. On Israel's calling, see Walter C. Kaiser, Jr., *Mission in the Old Testament: Israel as a Light to the Nations*. See also, Andreas J. Köstenberger & Peter T. O'Brien, *Salvation to the Ends of the Earth, A Biblical Theology of Mission*, particularly chapter 2 on mission in the Old Testament. Their conclusion on mission in the OT is that the "final paragraph of Isaiah (66:18-24) [presents] an eschatological 'vision of staggering proportions,' in which God's gracious plan for the world is marvelously presented. The Lord himself is the missionary who gathers and rescues, not simply the dispersed of Israel, but also people from 'all nations,' in order that they may see his glory. The goal of mission is the glory of God, that he may be known and honored for who he really is" (52).

87. Ratzinger, *Many Religions—One Covenant*, 27-28.

88. Ibid., 38.

89. Lewis Smedes, *Mere Morality*, 258, note 19.
90. Benedict XVI, *Jesus of Nazareth*, Vol. 1, 102.
91. Ratzinger, *Many Religions—One Covenant*, 39.
92. Ibid., 28.
93. Ibid., 33-34.
94. Ibid., 39.
95. Ibid., 41.
96. See Finnis and Grisez, "The Misuse of *Amoris Laetitia* to Support Errors Against the Catholic Faith," 8.
97. Benedict XVI, *Jesus of Nazareth*, Vol. 1, 102.
98. Aidan Nichols, O.P., *Epiphany: A Theological Introduction to Catholicism*, at 392.
99. John Paul II, *Man and Woman He Created Them: A Theology of the Body*.
100. Ibid., 24.4, 24.3.
101. Webster, *Holiness*, 90.
102. David E. Holwerda, "Jesus and the Law: A Question of Fulfillment," 115-17.
103. Rev. Albert VanHoye, S.J., "The Apostle Paul as Moral Teacher and Guide," at 22.
104. Peter Angeles, "antinomian," in *The Harpers Collins Dictionary of Philosophy*, Second Edition (New York: HarperCollins, 1992), 15-16.
105. Two Greek words are rendered by this term: μαλακός (Malakos), and αρσενοκοίτης (Arsenokoites).
106. Pope Francis, "A Church of 'yes.'"
107. Kasper, *Christian Understanding of Freedom*, 11.
108. Schreiner, *40 Questions about Christians and Biblical Law*, 93.
109. Francis, "Commandments are paths to freedom."
110. *Contra* Michael Horton, who criticizes the Catholic tradition for allegedly replacing law with love (*Christian Faith*, 665).
111. ST, I-II., a. 1 conclusion and ad 2m.
112. Jacques Maritain, *Moral Philosophy*, 105.
113. I am drawing here on my book, Chapter 2, *"In the Beginning..." A Theology of the Body*.
114. John Paul II, *Man and Woman He Created Them*, 24.1.
115. David Yeago, "Grace and the Good Life:," at 80.
116. There is a certain kind of continuity between Christ's law and God's original purpose for creation that may be explained in terms of the natural law, or the structures of creation. The limitations of this chapter prohibit me from explaining that relationship here in this chapter. I have done so elsewhere: *"In the Beginning . . ." A Theology of the Body*, 109-14. I return to this matter in Chapter 4 of this book.
117. Jochem Douma, "Appendix: The Use of Scripture in Ethics," in *The Ten Commandments: Manual for the Christian Life*, at 389.
118. St. Thomas Aquinas, *Commentary on Saint Paul's Epistle to the Galatians*, Chapter 5, 172.
119. On this, see St. John Paul II, *Veritatis Splendor* §§40-41.
120. His deep knowledge of the *Spiritual Exercises* may be seen in his work on practical ecclesiology, *In Him Alone is Our Hope*. I discussed this work in the Conclusion to the first edition (2015) of this book.
121. St. Ignatius of Loyola, *The Spiritual Exercises of St. Ignatius Loyola*, no. 48.

122. Wicks, "A Catholic Theology Teacher Drawing on the Lutheran Legacy," at 56.

123. St. Augustine, de Corrept. et Gratia. Ambros. Lib. 1 de Jac. et cap. 6 de Vita Beat., as cited by John Calvin, Institutes of the Christian Religion, Book II, 7.7.

124. VanHoye, "The Apostle Paul as Moral Teacher and Guide," 25.

125. Aquinas, *Commentary on Saint Paul's Epistle to the Galatians*, 172.

126. VanHoye, "The Apostle Paul as Moral Teacher and Guide," 31-33. VanHoye uses the phrase "binding precepts," and Aquinas is getting at the same by speaking of the "obliging force" of the law.

127. John Paul II, "No damage must be done to the *harmony between faith and life*: the unity of the Church is damaged not only by Christians who reject or distort the truths of faith but also by those disregard the moral obligations to which they are called by the Gospel [cf. 1 Cor 5:9-13]" (VS §26).

128. The same moral teaching is presented in 1 Cor 6:9-10 and again in Eph 5:5 with the same warning: "Do you not know that the unrighteous will not inherit the kingdom of God? [1 Cor 6:9]"

129. St Paul writes in 1 Cor 6:9-11: "Or do you not realize that unrighteous people will not inherit God's kingdom? Stop deceiving yourselves. Neither the sexually immoral (the *pornoi*), nor idolaters, nor adulterers, nor soft men (*malakoi*, i.e., effeminate males who play the sexual role of females), nor men who lie with males (*arsenokoitai*)... will inherit the kingdom of God. And these things some of you used to be. But you washed yourselves off, you were made holy (or sanctified), you were made righteous (or justified) in the name of the Lord Jesus Christ and in the Spirit of our God" (as translated by Robert A. J. Gagnon, in a book he co-authored with Dan O. Via, *Homosexuality and the Bible*, 81). It seems that Trent's use of the word "sodomite" is doing double-duty for malakoi and arsenokoitai.

130. Denzinger, §1544. John Paul II refers to the significance of Trent's teaching for seeing the inherent connection between faith and the moral choices we make (see VS, §68). See also, Canon 19: "If anyone says that nothing is commanded in the Gospels except faith and that everything else is indifferent, neither prescribed nor prohibited, but free; or that the Ten Commandments in no way concerns Christians, let him be anathema" (Denzinger, §1569).

131. St. Thomas Aquinas, *Commentary on Saint Paul's Epistle to the Galatians*, Chapter 5, 172.

132. St. Thomas Aquinas, *Summa Contra Gentiles*, Book IV, 22.

133. Idem, *Commentary on St. Paul's Second Epistle to the Corinthians*, Chapter 3, Lesson 3.

134. Aquinas, *Summa Contra Gentiles*, Book IV, 22,

135. Maritain, *The Living Thoughts of Saint Paul*, 59.

136. Joseph Ratzinger, *Many Religions—One Covenant*, 41.

137. Nichols, *Epiphany*, 392.

138. Ashley, *Living the Truth in Love*, 456.

139. Ibid.

140. Francis, "An Infinite Horizon."

4

The Controverted Chapter 8 of 'Amoris Laetitia'

The good of the person lies in being in the Truth and doing the Truth.—John Paul II[1]

The pastoral policy of truth can hurt and be uncomfortable. But it is the way to healing, peace, and interior freedom. A pastoral policy that truly seeks to help people must always be based on the truth; only what is true can ultimately be pastoral. Then you will know the truth, and the truth will set you free (John 8:32).—Benedict XVI[2]

Truth has such a clear and calm power. My aim in pastoral work is this: to help by the power of the truth. —Romano Guardini[3]

The whole notion of marriage is so confused in our time, not just among the laity and ecclesial culture at large, but also even among Catholic bishops, that there is a desperate need to recover some basic and foundational truths. For example, there is a confusion regarding the ontological basis of marriage. Is marriage a two-in-one-flesh union between a man and a woman because the Church says so, positing or postulating its existence and nature according to its own judgment, that is, Church law? If so then, one accepts ecclesial or doctrinal "positivism," the view that these are mere conventions, official Church teaching. For example, two Belgians, Johan Bonny, the Bishop of Antwerp,[4] and Josef Cardinal de Kesel, Archbishop of Brussels-Malines,[5] are ecclesial positivists because they give as the only reason for rejecting same-sex marriage the fact that "Church law" says so. This positivism is similar to one thinking that human beings have rights because the state or society says so. Alternatively, does the Church judge that marriage is a two-in-one-flesh union between a man and woman because that judgment is true to an objective reality, according to the order of creation? If so, then one is a Christian realist: marriage is grounded in the order of creation, of an independently existing reality, and therefore has an objective structure judged by the Church to be the case—the way things really are. Ecclesial positivism vs. Christian realism is one of the points of confusion.

Pope Francis is helpful, in this connection, by upholding the objectivity of God's "primordial divine plan" (see Gen 1:27, 2:24) of the deepest reality of marriage, grounded in the order of creation.[6] In a recent book of interviews, he insists on marriage's ontological nature. "'Marriage' is a historical word. Forever, throughout humanity, and not only in the Church, it is between a man and a woman. You can't change it just like that. It's the nature of things."[7] Indeed, his reflections in *Amoris Laetitia* §§8-30, which draw on the Church's living tradition, on marriage and family life are beautiful, insightful, and, yes, deeply biblical (AL §§9-10).[8] Furthermore, his reflections on the tradition of magisterial teaching regarding marriage and family life in light of creation, fall into sin, and redemption, (see AL §§61-75, 80-88) provide a catechesis that is foundational to our thinking as Christians. On these matters, he is in continuity with the Church's tradition on marriage and family life.

In fact, in this theological and anthropological context, Francis also affirms the core doctrine of Paul VI's 1968 encyclical *Humanae Vitae*, "The Church, nevertheless, in urging men to the observance of the precepts of the natural law, which it interprets by its constant doctrine, teaches that each and every marital act must of necessity retain its intrinsic relationship to the procreation of human life" (§11, and also §12). Similarly, Francis says, "From the outset, love refuses every impulse to close in on itself; it is open to a fruitfulness that draws it beyond itself. Hence no genital act of husband and wife can refuse this meaning, even when for various reasons it may not always in fact beget a new life" (AL §80). He says writing with appreciation of *Humanae Vitae* §10, Paul VI "brought out the intrinsic bond between conjugal love and the generation of life." This bond was broken by contraception and hence changed the sex act itself by separating sex and babies. Furthermore, we live in a culture, argues Francis, where "marriage, with its [essential] characteristics of exclusivity, indissolubility, and openness to life, comes to appear as an old-fashioned and outdated option. Many countries are witnessing a legal deconstruction of the family [and its basis in conjugal marriage], tending to adopt models based almost exclusively on the autonomy of the individual will" (AL §53). Francis counters the "autonomous will, particularly in respect of "an ideology of gender 'that denies the difference and reciprocity in nature of a man and a woman and envisages a society without sexual differences, thereby eliminating the anthropological basis of the family', by stressing that "We are creatures, and not omnipotent. Creation is prior to us and must be received as a gift" (AL §56). He adds, "Learning to accept our body, to care for it and to respect its fullest meaning, is an essential element of any genuine human ecology. Also, valuing one's own body in its femininity or masculinity is necessary if I am going to be able to recognize myself in an encounter with someone who is different.... It is not a healthy attitude which would seek 'to cancel out sexual difference because it no longer knows how to confront it'" (LS §155). Francis and his predecessors, John Paul II[9] and Benedict XVI,[10] affirm the importance of an integral human ecology, meaning thereby an ecology protecting marriage and family and the divinely given orientation of human sexuality towards unity and procreation.[11]

In response to gender ideology, Francis rightly encourages us: "As Christians, we can hardly stop advocating marriage simply to avoid countering contemporary sensibilities, or out of a desire to be fashionable or a sense of helplessness in the face of human and moral failings. We would be depriving the world of values that we can and must offer" (AL §35). Therefore, according to Francis, "What we need is a more responsible and generous effort to present the reasons and motivations for choosing marriage and the family, and in this way to help men and women better to respond to the grace that God offers them" (AL §35).

Accordingly, this chapter begins with an account of conjugal marriage, drawing not only on *Amoris Laetitia,* but also Vatican II's *Gaudium et Spes* §§47-52, John Paul II's Theology of the Body[12] as well as the *Catechism of the Catholic Church* (§§1601-1617). This account is followed by considering in depth the logic of pastoral reasoning and discernment in *Amoris Laetitia,* particularly about individuals in morally problematic relationships, such as the divorced and civilly remarried, and cohabitation, whether hetero- or homosexuals.[13] I pay special attention to the distinction between objective morality and subjective morality, the law of gradualness, and whether this logic inserts gradualness into the law. Also treated by me is the hermeneutical value of sin in the moral evaluation of actions, invincible and vincible ignorance, and the nature of conscience. I conclude with addressing Francis's claim regarding the Thomistic roots of that logic, and his insistence that *Amoris Laetitia* is Thomistic.

In a recent letter, Francis stipulates the hermeneutical principles for properly reading *Amoris Laetitia.*[14] First, we should treat *Amoris Laetitia* as a unity such that "in order to understand its message, it must be read in its entirety and from the beginning.... If the Exhortation is not read in its entirety and in the order it is written, it will either not be understood or it will be distorted."[15] Yes, a necessary condition for understanding fairly the claims Francis makes in *Amoris Laetitia* is to read the whole work. However, it is not a sufficient condition for agreeing with Francis's claims. I may read the book in its entirety, understand Francis's claims, but still disagree with them. Understanding him does not entail agreement because I find some of his claims troubling, not to say wrong. It is sheer arrogance to suggest otherwise.[16]

The second hermeneutical principle is that *Amoris Laetitia* should be "treated with a hermeneutic of the Church, always in continuity (without ruptures), yet always maturing."[17] Yes, absolutely, this hermeneutic requires presenting a convincing case that the moral logic of pastoral reasoning and its concomitant "presentation of the faith is in itself coherent and in continuity with the rest of Tradition."[18] However, this criterion also means that it is also possible to show that *Amoris Laetitia* "would validate pastoral applications that are inconsistent with the Church's constant and universal practice, founded on the Word of God, of not admitting the divorced and remarried to Holy Communion—a practice that the Church has long held to be binding and not subject to modifications because of diverse circumstances or situations."[19] To show his rootedness in the Church's tradition, Francis cites his favorite statement of St. Vincent of Lérins in his *Commonitorium Primum* 23: "*ut annis scilicet consolidetur, dilatetur tempore, sublimetur aetate* [*solidified over the years, expanded with time, and refined with age*]."[20] Francis says most recently in a book of interviews. "Pope Benedict said something very clear: the changes in the Church must be carried out with the hermeneutic of continuity. A lovely phrase. Hermeneutic means growth[21]: some things change, but there is always continuity. It doesn't betray its roots, it clarifies them, making them easier to understand."[22] I have already argued in Chapter 1, that overall, Francis falls short of properly understanding Vincent of Lérins, and so I will not repeat my arguments in this chapter. Third, Francis concludes, "With respect to the problems that involve ethical situations, the Exhortation follows the classical doctrine of St. Thomas Aquinas."[23] We shall need to consider whether *Amoris Laetitia* correctly appeals to Aquinas in attempting to justify its positions. Be that as it may, Francis has helpfully stated three hermeneutical principles by which *Amoris Laetitia* must be measured.

Marriage in the Light of Creation, Fall, and Redemption

The *Catechism* states that marriage belongs to the sacramental order of redemption, is under the regime of sin, but is first and foremost grounded in the order of creation.[24] Regarding the creation, it states:

> "The intimate community of life and love which constitutes the married state has been established by the Creator and endowed by him with its own proper laws.... God himself is the author of marriage" [Gaudium et Spes §48]. The vocation to marriage is written in the very nature of man and woman as they came from the hand of the Creator. Marriage is not a purely human institution despite the many variations it may have undergone through the centuries in different cultures, social structures, and spiritual attitudes. These differences should not cause us to forget its common and permanent characteristics. Although the dignity of this institution is not transparent everywhere with the same clarity, some sense of the greatness of the matrimonial union exists in all cultures. (CCC §1603, see also GS §48).

This creational perspective is fundamental to a Catholic understanding of marriage. As I argued in Chapter 3, and identified at the start of this chapter as one of the current confusions about marriage even in the Church, the Church judges that marriage is a two-in-one-flesh union between a man and woman because that judgment is true to an objective reality, according to the order of creation. On this view, the fact that the

Church teaches that marriage is a two-in-one-flesh union between a man and a woman adds nothing to the truth-status of this dogma. Says Francis, "The result of this union is that the two 'become one flesh,'' both physically and in the union of their hearts and lives, and, eventually, in a child, who will share not only genetically but also spiritually in the 'flesh' of both parents" (AL §13). This realism about the truth-status of dogmatic propositions is similar to one holding that human beings have rights by virtue of their nature as human beings, and the state simply secures, rather than confers, those rights by writing them down in a constitution. I contend that the Church holds to theological realism.

For one, John Paul II, a theological realist, wrote regarding marriage: "Willed by God in the very act of creation, marriage and the family are interiorly ordained to fulfillment in Christ and have need of His graces in order to be healed from the wounds of sin and restored to their 'beginning' [back to creation], that is, to full understanding and the full realization of God's plan" (FC §3). This major claim regarding Jesus' restoring and fulfilling God's plan for marriage, along with its undergirding theology of nature and grace, is adumbrated in *Amoris Laetitia* §§61-63, but developed throughout John Paul II's *Man and Woman He Created Them*. John Paul states that Genesis 1-2 and 3 theologically gives us an "account that is a description of events" that makes clear "the essential difference *between the state of man's sinfulness and that of his original innocence*." That is, there are "two different states of human nature, '*status naturae integrae*' (state of integral nature) and '*status naturae lapse*' (state of fallen nature).[25] Yet John Paul argues that the order of creation is the essential continuity between creation, fall into sin, and grace in Christ. He writes, "*Christ's words* [in Matt 19:3-8], which appeal to the 'beginning,' *allow us to find an essential continuity in man and a link* between these two different states or dimensions of the human being ['*status naturae integrae*' and '*status naturae lapsae*,' that is, the state of integral nature and the state of fallen nature]."[26] Redemption, then, is about the restoration of the fallen creation. In short, grace restores or renews nature, meaning thereby that God's grace in Christ restores all life to its fullness, penetrating and perfecting and transforming the fallen creation from within its own order, bringing creation into conformity with His will and purpose. This holds also for marriage, as Francis clearly sees.

Furthermore, the Word of God teaches that the redemptive work of Christ reaffirms and simultaneously renews the goodness of creation—and hence of marriage, of the human body sharing in the dignity of the image of God, of the complementary sexual differentiation of man and woman, and of a faithful, reciprocal, and fruitful love. Yes, in light of the redemptive work of Christ, the Catholic sacramental tradition teaches that the sacrament of marriage renews and restores the reality of marriage—given that it is savagely wounded by the fall and our own personal sin—from within its order (see AL §61). As Francis explains, "The sacrament of marriage is not a social convention, an empty ritual or merely the outward sign of a commitment. The sacrament is a gift given for the sanctification and salvation of the spouses, since 'their mutual belonging is a real representation, through the sacramental sign, of the same relationship between Christ and the Church'" (AL §72).

Marriage is under the fall into sin and hence marital "union has always been threatened by discord, a spirit of domination, infidelity, jealousy, and conflicts that can escalate into hatred and separation." This brokenness "does not stem from the nature of man and woman, nor from the *nature* of their relations, but from *sin*.... Nevertheless, the order of creation persists, though seriously disturbed" (CCC §1606-1607). The redemptive work of Christ is, however, continuous with the order of creation, with God's original intent for marriage, because he came "to restore the original order of creation disturbed by sin." Furthermore, Christ himself "gives the strength and grace to live marriage in the new dimension of the Reign of God. It is by following Christ, renouncing themselves, and taking up their crosses that spouses will be able to 'receive' the original meaning of marriage and live it with the help of Christ. This grace of Christian marriage is a fruit of Christ's cross, the source of all Christian life." (CCC §1615). In short, redemption restores the creation to its true identity, illuminating and fulfilling that creation (see AL §77).

As the *Catechism of the Catholic Church* puts it: "Jesus came to restore creation to the purity of its origins" (CCC §2336). Elsewhere in the *Catechism* we read: "In his preaching Jesus unequivocally taught the original meaning of the union of man and woman as the Creator willed it from the beginning.... *By coming to restore the original order of creation disturbed by sin*, [Jesus] himself gives the strength and grace to live marriage in the new dimension of the Reign of God" (CCC §§1614-15, emphasis added). This question is raised against the background of a fallen creation. Given the fallen creation, does new life in Christ oppose creation? Put differently: does grace replace fallen nature? "Nature" here has the chief meaning of ontological rather than merely physical or biological. So when we ask about the relation between nature, sin and grace, we are asking in what manner and to what extent sin and grace affect the essence or structure of reality. On the one hand, are the structures of creation so corrupted that grace, no longer able to transform them, merely replaces them altogether by adding the spiritual realm over and above creation, a *donum superadditum*? On the other hand, does grace leave nature untouched, merely completing or supplementing it, with nature taken to be unaffected by the Fall or, in turn, by Redemption internally, which effectively limits the scope of sin and redemption to the supernatural realm and results in naturalism on the level of nature.[27]

Nature and Grace

In the early twentieth century, the great French Catholic thinker, Jacques Maritain, wisely noted that it is erroneous to ignore that there is a distinction between nature and grace as well as a union.[28] How then should we understand the union-in-distinctness of nature and grace? In particular, how do we understand the Thomistic dictum that grace does not abolish nature but presupposes it? The brief answer to this question must be that *grace restores or renews nature*, meaning thereby that God's grace in Christ *restores all life to its fullness, penetrating and perfecting and transforming the fallen creation from within its own order*, bringing creation into conformity with His will and purpose.[29] In the words of Henri de Lubac, "The supernatural does not merely *elevate* (this traditional term is correct, but it is inadequate by itself)... [Rather] it *transforms it*... 'Behold, I make all things new!' (Rev 21:5). Christianity is 'a doctrine of transformation' because the Spirit of Christ comes to permeate the first creation and make of it a 'new creature'. What is true of the final great transformation, on the occasion of the 'Parousia' at which there will arise 'new heavens and a new earth' (Rev 21:1), is already true now, according to St. Paul, of each one of us."[30] Thus, the key idea here is that *grace restores nature*. "Faith in redemption cannot be separated from faith in the Creator." Redemption, adds Joseph Ratzinger, "is an act of new creation, the restoration of creation to its true identity."[31]

Now, as I understand John Paul II's theology of nature and grace, the redemption accomplished through Jesus Christ's saving work—His life, passion, death, resurrection, and ascension, in short, the Christ event—does not (a) stand opposed to, and hence replace altogether, created reality, as if to say that the structures of reality need to be by-passed or suppressed because they are hopelessly corrupt as a consequence of the fall into sin, meaning thereby the replacement of one nature by another. But nor does his redemptive work merely (b) supplement or (c) parallel that reality, which would leave nature untouched by grace, and thus nature and grace would have only an *extrinsic* relation to each other. Furthermore, nor does his redemptive work merely involve (d) acceptance of created reality, of humanity, *as it is*, for that would deny created reality's structures' fallen state, which would, as Thomas Guarino puts it, "overlook God's judgment on the world rendered dramatically in the cross of Christ."[32] Rather, the structures of reality—in short, nature—stand in need of being reconsecrated to its Maker, and hence Christ's redemption (e) seeks to penetrate, restore, and renew *from within* the fallen order of creation.[33] These various possibilities of conceiving the relation of nature, sin and grace require some explanation. There are five types of ways in which that relation has been understood.[34]

The first type understands grace and nature to be opposed to each other. Nature has been rendered a corrupt vessel by the fall into sin, needing to be replaced altogether with something new by grace. One influential account of this relation sees human nature to be completely closed to God and hence as capable of nothing but sin, with the accompanying loss or destruction of the natural power of the will. The will itself, as a consequence of the fall and man's fallen state, is "capable of nothing except... malicious, empty self-seeking... possessing an insuperable bent toward evil."[35] The fall eliminates all natural inclination to goodness in man's will, on this view, and also tempts us to disparage natural virtue as well as our natural capacity for contrary moral choice between good and evil—that is, the will's power to choose good over evil, or vice-versa. In short, on this view of the relation between nature and grace, the very nature of the will as God created it is disparaged in order to magnify grace. In this sense, nature would be the very opposite of grace, and hence cannot be united with grace; rather nature has to struggle against grace and be replaced altogether with something new by grace, meaning thereby a supernatural life of faith and a consequent supernaturalized freedom. Thus, supernatural freedom is to be construed as a "superstructure" added to natural freedom, rather than as determining and elevating our whole being, including our natural, but fallen, will. In short, on this view the Christian withdraws from the corrupt vessel that is human nature and seeks a salvation that is separate from it because human nature in its fallen condition is, essentially, *irreclaimable*. Against this view, John Henry Newman put it just right. He writes,

> [The Church] does not teach that human nature is irreclaimable, else wherefore should she be sent? [N]ot that it [human nature] is to be shattered and reversed, but to be extricated, purified, and restored; not that it is a mere mass of evil, but that it has the promise of great things, and even now has a virtue and a praise proper to itself. But in the next place she knows and she preaches that such a restoration, as she aims at effecting in it, must be brought about, not simply through any outward provision of preaching and teaching, even though it be her own, but from a certain inward spiritual power or grace imparted directly from above, and which is in her keeping.[36]

The second and third types understand the relation between nature and grace to be such that grace is a "plus factor," a mere "add on" to the natural level. Consider, say, the relationship between the natural virtues and the supernatural virtues of faith, hope and charity in light of these types. The *Catechism* teaches that "The theological virtues are the foundation of Christian moral activity; they animate it and give it its special character. They inform and give life to all the moral virtues" (CCC §1813). Now, I want to show that neither of these types can make sense of what the *Catechism* claims here, namely, that the grace of the supernatural virtues directs and orders nature from *within* rather than alongside of or above nature as if those virtues merely add on to the excellencies of virtuous man.[37] The Anglican neo-Thomist Eric L. Mascall critically remarks on what it means to think that grace is simply alongside of or above nature—a mere superstructure erected on top of nature. "The Thomist maxim 'Grace does not destroy nature but perfects it' has been interpreted as if it means simply that it is better for man to enjoy grace *in addition* to nature, although nature would be perfectly complete without it."[38] Mascall correctly rejects this interpretation of the Thomist maxim, giving us a right reading of two complementary principles in Aquinas' thought. He adds,

"'Grace does not destroy nature but perfects it,' because nature always lies open to God," and "'Grace presupposes nature,' not in the sense that grace is a mere superstructure erected on top of nature and needing nature only to prevent it from falling through the floor, *but that nature is the very material in which grace works and for whole ultimate perfection grace itself exists.*"[39] Therefore, the reason why neither type can make sense of the Thomist maxim, and hence of the *Catechism*'s teaching regarding the relation between the natural and supernatural virtues is because they view the relationship between the natural and supernatural virtues in a dualistic and hence extrinsic fashion. In short, thinking in terms of "two-tiers," we can say that, on these types, the upper-level of grace was lost because of original sin, leaving the lower-level relatively intact and integrally unaffected by sin. Thus, both types view the redemption accomplished through the saving work of Christ as something that merely *supplements* or *parallels* our created nature. On this "two-tier" relationship between nature and grace, the latter is merely added (*donum superadditum*) to a nature that has not been integrally affected by sin, and hence human nature requires little or no internal healing and restoration.

The chief problem with these types is that by limiting the scope of man's fallen condition, they in turn limit the scope of Christ's redemptive work. The dualism between faith and life is, for example, one of the practical implications of this limitation and it is well expressed by Vatican II. "This split between the faith which many profess and their daily lives deserves to be counted among the more serious errors of our age." In critical response to this bifurcation, the council Fathers teach, "Since they have an active role to play in the whole life of the Church, laymen are not only bound to penetrate the world with a Christian spirit, but are also called to be witnesses to Christ in all things in the midst of human society" (GS §43). The Fathers add to this, "The good news of Christ continually renews the life and culture of fallen man" (GS §58). Years later the newly established Pontifical Council for Culture states in the same vein, "[This view] gives Christ, the redeemer of man, center of the universe and of history, the scope of completely renewing the lives of men 'by opening the vast fields of culture to His saving power.'"[40] Rather than those vast fields which make up the whole human cultural enterprise—the sciences, arts, such as music, literature, the work of civilization, as in pursuing a culture of life—being bypassed or suppressed by grace as in the first type; and rather than that grace being just a "plus factor," or mere "add on" to that enterprise; the Pontifical Council has correctly understood the two complementary principles of "grace does not destroy nature but perfects it" and "grace presupposes nature."[41] In sum, (to quote Mascall again) the whole human cultural enterprise—nature, as it were—"is the very material in which grace works and for whose ultimate perfection grace itself exists."[42]

The fourth type I mentioned above understands the relation between nature and grace in such a way that it conflates human nature and divine grace, threatening, as Romanus Cessario puts it, "to confuse God's creative presence to the human creature with the realization of the same person's call to beatitude."[43] This statement requires explanation. God's creative presence refers to man having been created *by* God and *for* God. Man is a creature of God such that he is "totally dependent for his existence on the incessant creative activity of the self-existent God."[44] And the importance of this is that, having been created for God, the meaning of man's existence is such that his relation to God is constitutive of his existence. The *Compendium of the Social Doctrine of the Church* expresses well this first principle of Christian anthropology. "This is a relationship that exists in itself, it is therefore not something that comes afterwards and is not added from the outside.... The human being is a personal being created by God to be in relationship with him; man finds life and self-expression only in [that] relationship, and tends naturally to God."[45] The *Compendium*'s formulation here avoids the dualistic and hence extrinsic construal of the relation of nature and grace (in which grace is a "plus factor" or an "add-on") discussed above.

We come now to the fifth way of thinking of the relation between nature, sin, and grace. By "nature" here this type understands the deepest foundations of human nature that remain in place after the fall, a nature that has been savagely wounded by the fall, but still remains what God originally made them to be. These foundations are not totally corrupted, destroyed. Rather, sin corrupts God's good creation yet the order of creation persists. The good news is that God's salvation in Christ restores the whole fallen creation from *within*. Consider, for example, the *Catechism*'s teaching on marriage in light of creation, fall into sin, and redemption. Marriage is grounded in the order of creation: "'The intimate community of life and love which constitutes the married state has been established by the Creator and endowed by him with its own proper laws.... God himself is the author of marriage.'" Yet marriage as it actually functions in its fallen state is under the regime of sin and hence no longer properly functioning. Significantly, the *Catechism* applies an Augustinian principle, namely, "the natures in which evil exists, in so far as they are natures, are good. And evil is removed, not by removing any nature, or part of a nature... but by healing and correcting that which had been vitiated and depraved."[46]

In this light, we can easily understand the teaching of the *Catechism* on the relation between sin and nature: "According to faith the disorder we notice so painfully does not stem from the *nature* of man and woman, nor from the nature of their relations, but from *sin*.... Nevertheless, the order of creation persists, though seriously disturbed.... In his mercy God has not forsaken sinful man.... After the fall, marriage helps to overcome self-absorption, egoism, pursuit of one's own pleasure, to open oneself to the other, to mutual aid and to self-giving." Furthermore, "In his preaching Jesus unequivocally taught the original [i.e., creational] meaning of the union of man and woman as the Creator willed it from the beginning.... By coming to restore the original order of creation disturbed by sin, [Jesus] himself gives the strength and grace to live marriage in the new dimension of the Reign of God."[47]

On this view, then, of the relation between nature and grace, the relation is such that grace penetrates and transforms and perfects fallen nature from within, and thus nature is redeemed in its own domain. In this connection, let me cite several key passages on the relation between nature and grace from a remarkable book by Etienne Gilson, *Christianity and Philosophy*, written in 1931. "The true Catholic position consists in maintaining that nature was created good, that it has been wounded, but that it can be at least partially healed by grace [here and now] if God so wishes. This *instauratio*, that is to say, this renewal, this re-establishment, this restoration of nature to its primitive goodness, is on this point the program of authentic Catholicism." As Gilson also rightly says elsewhere, "To say that grace is necessary to restore nature is quite other than to suppress that nature to the profit of grace: it is to confirm it by grace. Grace presupposes nature, whether to restore or to enrich it. When grace restores nature, it does not substitute itself for it, but re-establishes it; when nature, thus re-established by grace, accomplishes its proper operations, they are indeed natural operations [now transformed] which it performs." Finally, as Gilson also says later in this book, "Catholicism teaches that before everything the restoration of wounded nature by the grace of Jesus Christ. The restoration of nature: so there must be a nature, and of what value, since it is the work of God, Who created it and re-created it by repurchasing it at the price of His own Blood! Thus grace presupposes nature, and the excellence of nature which it comes to heal and transfigure."[48] Thus, grace restores and transforms nature from within its own domain. Indeed, this is how the late philosopher-pope John Paul II describes the Church's mission of evangelization and, in fact, "the purpose of the Gospel," namely, "'to transform humanity from within and to make it new'. Like the yeast which leavens the whole measure of dough (cf. Matt 13:33), the Gospel is meant to permeate all cultures and give them life from within, so that they may express the full truth about the human person and about human life" (EV §95).[49] In sum, grace restores or renews nature, meaning thereby that God's grace in Christ restores all life to its fullness, penetrating and perfecting and transforming the fallen creation from within its own order, bringing creation into conformity with His will and purpose.

As John Paul II himself states, "*Redemption* means, in fact, a '*new creation*', as it were, it means *taking up all that is created* to express in creation the fullness of righteousness, equity, and holiness planned for it by God and to express the fullness above all in man, created male and female 'in the image of God.'"[50] "New creation" does not, however, mean that grace is a plus-factor, a superadded gift, to the order of creation. Rather, nature and grace, creation and re-creation, the sacrament of creation and redemption are united such that God's grace affirms and simultaneously renews the fallen creation from within its own internal order. As the *Catechism* puts it, "Jesus came to restore creation to the purity of its origins" (CCC §2336). Elsewhere, the *Catechism* explains, "In his preaching Jesus unequivocally taught the original meaning of the union of man and woman as the Creator willed it from the beginning.... By coming to restore the original order of creation disturbed by sin, [Jesus] himself gives the strength and grace to live marriage in the new dimension of the Reign of God" (CCC §§1614-15). Grace penetrating fallen nature and renewing it from within ("*gratia intra naturam*") means there is an essential continuity in man and a link between creation and redemption. "Endowment with grace is in some sense a 'new creation,'" says John Paul.

God, who created all things in and through Christ (Col 1:16), has restored his fallen creation, which was savagely wounded by sin, by re-creating it in Christ. "Therefore, if anyone is in Christ, he is a new creation; the old has passed away, behold the new has come" (2 Cor 5:17). How does the pope understand the "*living forms of the 'new man'*" to which Christ calls man? He replies: "In the ethos of the redemption of the body, the original ethos of creation was to be taken up anew.... In this way a connection is formed, even a continuity, between the 'beginning' and the perspective of redemption."[51] What is the import of this latter understanding of nature and grace for understanding the sacrament of marriage in the order of redemption?

Sin and Grace

Thus, the grace of marriage communicated by the sacrament has two main ends: first, that of healing, i.e., of repairing the consequences of sin in the individual and in society; and second—and above all—that of perfecting and raising persons and the conjugal institution. "According to faith the disorder we notice so painfully does not stem from the nature of man and woman, nor from the nature of their relations, but from sin. As a break with God, the first sin had for its first consequence the rupture of the original communion between man and woman" (CCC §§1607). This sacrament not only recovers the order of creation but also, while reaffirming this ordinance of creation, it simultaneously deepens, indeed, fulfills the reality of marriage in a reciprocal self-giving, a joining of two in a one-flesh union that is a visible sign of the mystery of the union of Christ with the Church (Eph 5:31-32). Vatican II summarizes all of this: "This [marital] love God has judged worthy of special gifts, healing, perfecting and exalting gifts of grace and of charity" (GS §49).

This two-fold effect means that the grace of the "marital sacrament is not a 'thing' added to the reality of the couple from the outside; rather, the couple itself is and must become the living sign of an invisible reality of grace," as Canadian Cardinal Marc Ouellet puts it. There is an intrinsic relationship between the natural order and the order of Christ's grace such that grace renews the fallen order of marriage from within, orienting it to its proper ends.

The unity attained in becoming "two-in-one-flesh" (Gen 2:24) in marriage is grounded in the order of creation, and it is affirmed and simultaneously renewed and restored in redemption. Since continuity exists between creation and redemption, we can understand why John Paul II sees marriage as "the primordial sacrament."

When we look at the visible sign of marriage ("the two shall be one flesh") in the order of creation from the perspective of the visible sign of Christ and the Church, which is defined in Ephesians as the fulfillment and realization of God's eternal plan of salvation, we can see John Paul's point. He says, "In this way, the sacrament of redemption clothes itself, so to speak, in the figure and form of the primordial sacrament.... Man's new supernatural endowment with the gift of grace in the 'sacrament of redemption' is also a new realization of the Mystery hidden from eternity in God, new in comparison with the sacrament of creation. At this moment, endowment with grace is in some sense a 'new creation.'"

Let's be clear that he calls it a "new creation" in the specific sense that "Redemption means... taking up all that is created [in order] to express in creation the fullness of justice, equity, and holiness planned for it by God and to express that fullness above all in man, created male and female 'in the image of God.'" Thus, nature and grace, creation and re-creation, the sacrament of creation and redemption are united such that God's grace affirms and simultaneously renews the fallen creation from within its own internal order. For JPII and the main Catholic tradition: "Marriage is organically inscribed in this new sacrament of redemption, just as it was inscribed in the original sacrament of creation."

The Two-in-One-Flesh *Bodily* Unity

St. John Paul II, Benedict XVI, and, most recently Pope Francis—every one of these popes—affirms the moral and sacramental significance of the two-in-one-flesh *bodily* unity as foundational to the marital form of love.[52] Francis says, "In the Church's Latin tradition, the ministers of the sacrament of marriage are the man and the woman who marry; by manifesting their consent and expressing it physically, they receive a great gift. Their consent and their bodily union are the divinely appointed means whereby they become 'one flesh'" (AL §75). However, it is precisely the embodiment of human persons, as man and woman, which has been lost in our culture, even among Catholics, for a proper understanding of marriage.

The starting point of John Paul II's theology of the body, too, is that sexual difference is grounded in an ontology of creation. In other words, the sexual difference between male and female is a creational given such that all mankind is bound to the structures of creation. It is also a creational given that, at one and the same time, mankind is one and a bi-unity: male and female. John Paul explains:

> Let us enter into the setting of the biblical "beginning." In it the revealed truth concerning man as "the image and likeness" of God constitutes the *immutable basis of all Chris-*

> *tian anthropology*. "God created man in his own image, in the image of God he created him; male and female he created them" (Gen 1:27). This concise passage contains the fundamental anthropological truths: man is the high point of the whole order of creation in the visible world; the human race, which takes its origin from the calling into existence of man and woman, crowns the whole work of creation; *both man and woman are human beings to an equal degree*, both are created *in God's image*.

Indeed, the pope imitates Christ (see Matt 19:3-9; Mark 10:1-10) by appealing to the "beginning," to the creational structure for marriage, drawing on Genesis 1 and 2 for his understanding of the normative intent of a biblical ontology of creation, the objective structures of creation, as they pertain to a bi-unity of husband and wife, united as complementary, bodily persons, in a two-in-one-flesh communion.

John Paul's treatment of these foundational texts is ultimately theological, because it is grounded in an historical-redemptive dialectic of creation, fall (sin), redemption, and fulfillment. But it is also philosophical—it articulates a philosophical anthropology of the body-person, which in its broadest sense is man himself in the temporal form of existence of human life. Most significantly, the pope is arguing that, in the totality of the personal structure of man, his body is a basis, a substructure forming part of the unity of man and thus of the person. Indeed, the meaning of the human body is an integral part of the structure of the personal subject, rather than being "extrinsic to the person, the subject and the human act."

The pope does not deny that the inner structures and regularities of the human organism, *per se*, require scientific analysis and explanation. But he distinguishes the body as a "physiological unit" and the "bodiliness" of the human person. John Paul then argues, "the human body is not only the field of reactions of a sexual character, but [rather] it is at the same time the means of the expression of man as an integral whole, of the person, which reveals itself through the 'language of the body.'"

"This 'language' has an important interpersonal meaning," he adds, "especially in the area of the reciprocal relations between man and woman." As I have argued here, this shows that the "'language of the body' should *express*, at a determinate level, *the truth of the sacrament*," namely, a one-flesh union. "So then they are no longer two but one flesh" (Mark 10:8).

The unity attained in becoming "two-in-one-flesh" in marriage is grounded in the order of creation (Gen 1:27; 2:24), persists through the regime of sin, and it is affirmed and simultaneously renewed through the redemptive sacrament of marriage. Let me underscore that real bodily oneness, a one-flesh union between a man and a woman, *actualizes* marital unity. Francis explains: "In the Church's Latin tradition, the ministers of the sacrament of marriage are the man and the woman who marry; by manifesting their consent and expressing it physically, they receive a great gift. Their consent and their bodily union are the divinely appointed means whereby they become "one flesh'" (AL §75, and §74).

Now, a key to understanding Catholic sexual ethics is the truth that the human person is bodily.[53] This view rejects a dualistic view of the human person—"dualistic in the sense of viewing the self as something which *has* or *inhabits* a body, rather than being a living, bodily entity."[54] But if the "human person is essentially a bodily being, a unity of body and soul, and that therefore the masculinity or femininity of the human being is internal to his or her personhood (rather than just interesting external 'equipment')," as John Paul II has argued, then it seems likely that this view does not do justice to the embodiment of human persons as man and woman and hence to sexual differences between them. By assuming the insignificance of sexual difference for making a sexual act morally right, this view fails to grasp the unified totality that is the body-person and hence the human meaning of the body, especially but not only for sexual acts (VS §50). Says John Paul, "The body can never be reduced to mere matter: it is a *spiritualized body*, just as man's spirit is so closely united to the body that he can be described as *an embodied spirit*."[55]

Underscoring the anthropological unity of body and soul, Karol Wojtyla explains, "The human person is not just a consciousness prolific in experiences of various content, but is basically a highly organized being, an individual of a spiritual nature composed into a single whole with the body (hence, a *suppositum humanum* [that is a person]."[56] Indeed, "The human body shares in the dignity of the image of God" (CCC §364). John Paul's theology of the body is central to understanding the basic issues in sexual ethics, in my judgment, because that theology emphasizes the bodily nature of the human person, meaning thereby that the body is intrinsic to human beings as bodily persons. Given that my body is intrinsic to myself, there is a unitary activity such that, as the pope says, "[t]*he person, including the body, is completely entrusted to himself, and it is in the unity of body and soul that the person is the subject of his own moral acts*" (VS §48). In short, since the human person is bodily, then sexual moral choices are exercised in and through an act in which my bodily "activity is as much the constitutive subject of what one does as one's act of choice is."[57] In short, our bodies can be the subject of virtues, in particular, love of the person in the ethical sense, and therefore as a virtue, that is, "as a concretization (and also, of course, a realization) of the personalistic norm... in light of the commandment of love."[58]

Wojtyla's anthropology regarding the structural whole that is the body-person is really a contemporary expression of Aquinas' anthropology, namely, the soul is the form of the body (*anima forma corporis*), and of the Church's teaching on the unity of the human person as body and soul.[59] The then Joseph Cardinal Ratzinger explains, "the material elements from out of which human physiology is constructed receive their character of being 'body' only in virtue of being organized and formed by the expressive power of soul. Distinguishing between 'physiological unit' and 'bodiliness' now becomes possible.... The individual atoms and molecules do not as such add up to the human being.... The physiology becomes truly 'body' through the heart of the personality. Bodiliness is something other than a summation of corpuscles."[60] That is, in light of considering the human person as a unity of body and soul, we can understand why the *body is personal*. Rather than bodily existence being a mere instrument or extrinsic tool of man's personal self-realization, the body is the indispensable medium, argues Wojtyla, in and through which I reveal myself. In other words, Wojtyla's basic point is that the body and bodily action is in some sense communicative activity that reveals the person as a whole. As John Paul II says in *The Acting Person*, "For us action *reveals* the person, and we look at the person through his action."[61] Later he says, "man manifests himself... through his body.... It is generally recognized that the human body is in its visible dynamism the territory where, or in a way even the medium whereby, the person expresses himself."[62] And in the theology of the body, we find a sample of statements expressing the same point. "The body reveals man," "the body is an expression of man's personhood," and "the body *manifests* man and, in manifesting him, acts as an intermediary that allows man and woman, from the beginning, to 'communicate' with each other according to that *communio personarum* willed for them in particular by the Creator."[63] In sum, "In this sense, the body is the territory and in a way the means for the performance of action and consequently for the fulfillment of the person."[64]

Dutch neo-Calvinist philosopher, Herman Dooyeweerd succinctly puts this point, "The human body is man himself in the structural whole of his temporal appearance."[65] Budziszewski explains Dooyeweerd's seminal anthropological insight and its importance for sexual ethics. This means, Budziszewski argues, that "we say things to each other by what our bodies do. Indeed, the body is the visible sign by which the invisible self is actually made present and communicates. But if this is true, then the union of the spouses has more-than-a-bodily significance: the body emblematizes the person, and the joining of bodies emblematizes the joining of persons. It is a symbol which participates in, and duplicates the pattern of, the very thing that it symbolizes; one-flesh-unity is the body's language for one-life unity."[66]

Furthermore, human bodily existence has the character of a subject. In other words, given man's anthropological unity of body and soul, he exercises the capacity for ethical self-determination as a whole man, meaning thereby in and through his body.[67] John Paul II writes, "*The structure of this body is such that it permits him to be the author of genuinely human activity.* In this activity, the body expresses the person."[68] Elsewhere the pope develops the moral significance that the human person is bodily, namely, that his body is not extrinsic to who he really is, and hence to his moral acts. "*The person, including the body, is completely entrusted to himself, and it is in the unity of body and soul that the person is the subject of his own actions*" (VS §48). This implies, as Schockenhoff rightly argues, that "the body is freedom's boundary." That is, he explains, "We can respect each other as subjects capable of moral action only when we respect each other in the expressive form of our bodily existence. Only so do we make it possible for each other to unfold a personal existence which is a goal in itself."[69] Respecting another person's bodily life unconditionally is to respect that person himself because the "representation of his person... is accessible to us... only in the medium of its unity as body and soul."[70]

A human person's body is not a mere extrinsic tool, an instrument, to be used for providing him with subjective states of consciousness, such as giving and obtaining pleasure. Rather, the body is intrinsic to one's self as a unified bodily person; in other words, as a unified whole the one and ontically unique person. This implies that the subject of one's own moral actions is the unified bodily person so that "bodily activity... is," as John Finnis says, "as much the constitutive subject of what one does as one's act of choice is."[71] This emphasis on the body being intrinsic to one's own self is rooted in the Church's teaching on the unity of the human person. As John Paul says, "In fact, *body and soul are inseparable*: in the willing agent and in the deliberate act *they stand or fall together*" (VS §49). Therefore, he adds, we can easily understand why separating "the moral act from the bodily dimensions of its exercise is contrary to the teaching of Scripture and Tradition" (VS §49).

Such a separation occurs when the biological dimension of the human person is reduced to a "raw datum, devoid of any [intrinsic] meaning and moral values until freedom has shaped it in accordance with its design" (VS §48). That freely chosen design confers on sexual union the personal meaning of causal fun, of spousal commitment, or of procreative openness, and so forth. Significantly, any one of these meanings may be conferred by persons, as well as revoked by them. For sexual union as such does not by its very nature have any definite personal meaning.[72] "Consequently," John Paul adds, "human nature and the body appear as [mere] *presuppositions or preambles*, materially *necessary*, for freedom to make its choice, yet extrinsic to the person, the subject and the human act" (VS §48). On this view, given that sexual union is devoid of any intrinsic meaning, not having by its very nature any definite personal meaning, and because we can in freedom confer on it an instrumental meaning that is more than merely physiological, sexual union is, therefore, an extrinsic sign or symbol of personal communion, fostering marital love and friendship by signifying it. But on John Paul's view, the sexual act is much more than a natural bodily symbol; indeed, it embodies marital union, becoming bodily, or organically complete, and thus one, expresses total self-giving and makes it bodily present in the sense that, as Lee says, "this expression is not extrinsic to what it expresses, but is the visible and tangible embodiment of it."[73]

In other words, given man's anthropological unity of body and soul, he exercises the capacity for ethical self-determination as a whole man, meaning thereby in and through his body.[74] This implies, as Schockenhoff rightly argues, that "the body can be called the concrete limit of freedom." That is, he explains, "the body and physical life are not 'goods' external to human personal realization, standing in a purely instrumental relation to the person's authentic determination as a subject. The body is rather the irreducible means of expression in which human persons in all their acts... are represented."[75] Respecting another person's bodily life unconditionally is to respect that person himself because a person shows himself only in and through his own body. So, "respect for the personal worth of persons relates not only to their inner convictions or moral values but must also include the inviolability of their bodily existence."[76] If the body is, then, freedom's boundary, such that respecting one's own body as well as others' bodies is both to respect our own person and other persons, this raises the question regarding the conditions under which a sexual act is the morally right way that my body *embodies* me."[77]

Wojtyla, in an effort to explain the "special way" in which man has his body, cites Dutch phenomenologist Wilhelmus Luijpen.[78] He says that Luijpen "criticizes views that treat the body as an object of having (he is of course speaking of 'having' in the literal sense of the word)." Says Luijpen, "My Body is not the Object of 'Having'.... I 'have' a car, a pen, a book. In this 'having' the object of the 'having' reveals itself as an exteriority. There is a distance between me and what I 'have'. What I 'have' is to a certain extent independent of me." Thus, if my body is not the object of having, then I may not conceive of either sperm or eggs, either penis or vagina, in impersonal terms. For thinking of my body in impersonal terms is to think of it as a mere instrument or extrinsic tool of man's personal reality. Therefore, Luijpen continues, "My body is not something external to me [because] I cannot dispose of my body or give it away as I dispose of money.... All this stems from the fact that my body is not 'a' body, but *my* body... in such a way that my body *embodies* me."[79] In short, the lived body is myself ("I") in my many activities; my subjectivity. Any concrete act of man, the pope seems to be arguing, is a bodily expression of the person given the unity of the person as body and soul. Thus, the body grounds human subjectivity, so that all knowledge and thought has bodily roots. It is impossible to pause here to give an account of the sense in which all knowledge and thought has bodily roots.

Furthermore, the body is then as such an expression or disclosure of the person, particularly in conscious human acts such as the sincere gift of self, which is the fullest unfolding of the "spousal meaning of the body."[80] Says John Paul, "Here we mean freedom above all as *self-mastery* (self-dominion). Under this aspect, self-mastery is indispensable *in order for man to be able to 'give himself,'* in order for him to become a gift, in order for him (referring to the words of the Council) to be able to 'find himself fully' through 'a sincere gift of self' [GS, 24:3]."[81]

Agreeing with Pope Francis's critique of "gender ideology," Gerhard Cardinal Müller, former head of the Congregation of the Doctrine of the Faith, recently stated that gender ideology claims, "that man's identity does not depend on nature, with a body that is limited to a masculine or feminine sexuality." He adds, "There is an evident dualism behind all this: the body loses its significance vis-à-vis its own identity."[82]

Contrary to this anthropological dualism, the Catholic tradition affirms that the body is intrinsic to selfhood, the human person *is*, bodily. This affirmation is rooted in the Church's teaching on the soul/body unity of the human person (CCC §§362-68). As John Paul says, "In fact, *body and soul are inseparable*: in the willing agent and in the deliberate act *they stand or fall together*" (VS §49). Therefore, we can easily understand why separating "the moral act from the bodily dimensions of its exercise is contrary to the teaching of Scripture and Tradition" (VS §49).[83]

Elsewhere, John Paul explains that the body is intrinsic to self-identity: "Man is a subject not only by his self-consciousness and by self-determination, but also based on his own body. *The structure of this body is such that it permits him to be the author of genuinely human activity.* In this activity, the body expresses the person."[84] The body is intrinsic to one's own self. Not surprisingly, since the "human body shares in the dignity of the image of God" (CCC §364).

Sacramental Union Presupposes Sexual Differentiation

Anthropological dualism has also led to the denial that the foundation of the form of love that is marriage is a bodily sexual union of man and woman as *one flesh*. But since the body is intrinsic to personhood, the nature of marriage is such that it requires sexual difference, the bodily-sexual act, as a foundational prerequisite, indeed, as also *intrinsic* to a one-flesh sacramental union.

In his Theology of the Body, John Paul II develops the sacramental importance of the bodily-sexual act as intrinsic to a one-flesh union. The *sacramental sign* of marriage is constituted by the couple, by the "word" they exchange—"I take you as my wife/as my husband, and I promise to be faithful to you always, in joy and in sorrow, in sickness and in health, and to love you and honor you all the days of my life." And in their reciprocal "fidelity," they commit themselves to "living" a reality of grace. John Paul comments, "This reality (the *copula conjugale*), moreover, has been defined from the very beginning by institution of the Creator. 'A man will leave his father and his mother and unite with his wife, and the two will be one flesh'" (Gen 2:24).

Why the sacrament of marriage presupposes sexual differentiation is made clear in the realization of what is meant by the "sacramental sign": "The words [*form*] spoken by them would not of themselves constitute the sacramental sign if the human subjectivity of the engaged man and woman and at the same time the consciousness of the body linked with the masculinity and the femininity of the bride and the bridegroom did not correspond to them [*matter*]."

John Paul explains: "What determines it [the sacramental sign of marriage] is *in some sense 'the language of the body,'* inasmuch as the man and the woman, who are to become one flesh by marriage, express in this sign the reciprocal gift of masculinity and femininity as the [creational] foundation of the conjugal union of the persons. The sign of the sacrament of Marriage is constituted by the fact that the words spoken by the new spouses take up again the same 'language of the body' as at the 'beginning' [from creation] and, at any rate, give it a concrete and unrepeatable expression.... In this way the perennial and ever new 'language of the body' *is not only the 'substratum'*, but *in some sense also the constitutive content of the communion of persons.*"[85]

The *reality* that corresponds to these words and which the sacramental sign signifies and produces specifies the content of this sacramental grace: "The spouses participate in it as spouses, together, as a couple, so that the first and immediate effect of marriage (*res et sacramentum*) is not supernatural grace itself, but the Christian conjugal bond, a typically Christian communion of two persons because it represents the mystery of Christ's incarnation and the mystery of His covenant" (FC §13).

Hence, this one-flesh union is not just posited by ecclesiastical law. Rather, Jesus calls us back to the law of creation (Mark 10:6-7) that grounds an inextricable nexus of permanence, twoness, and sexual differentiation for marriage. In particular, marriage is such that it requires sexual difference, the bodily-sexual act, as a foundational prerequisite, indeed, as *intrinsic* to a one flesh union of man and woman: "So then they are no longer two but one flesh" (Mark 10:8).

In this context, a rehabilitation of the "culture of the person" is necessary because the objective good of the person constitutes the essential core of all human culture. To promote that culture requires a whole nexus of fundamental goods that together determine marriage and family life. Marriage is grounded in God's purpose for creation. It is the two-in-one-flesh union of a man and a woman, with conjugal love being the integrating principle of the whole communion of marriage and family life. Vatican II stated it this way: "Marriage and conjugal love are by their nature ordained toward the begetting and educating of children. Children are really the supreme gift of marriage" (GS §50). Given the proper ends of our sexual powers and their relationship to the nature of marriage, giving oneself in sexual intercourse to the other is fully justified only in marriage. "[Marriage corresponds to the truth of love and mutually safeguards the dignity of person, only if both a man and a woman perform it [sexual intercourse] as spouses, as husband and wife."[86]

Various Proposals Swirling Around about *Amoris Laetitia*

I turn now to examine the controverted Chapter 8 of *Amoris Laetitia*. The single most troubling aspect of this chapter is that it raises questions regarding the normativity of doctrine and its anchor for life in an objective state of affairs, for example, pastoral practice of the civilly remarried divorcees, and the impact that changing that practice might have on the doctrine. Some have insisted that such a change will not mean a change in doctrine; others have argued that one cannot compartmentalize doctrine and pastoral life, and hence allowing the divorce and civilly remarried to receive the Eucharist would undermine the Church's teaching—indeed, the teaching of Jesus Christ!—on the permanence of marriage.[87] Still others insist that there is no change in doctrine when pastoral practice is changed, but rather a development of doctrine.

In this connection, consider the claim by Christoph Cardinal Schönborn who suggests that there is true innovation in pastoral directives in Pope Francis's *Amoris Laetitia* but "there is no change [in doctrine]." To make his point, the Cardinal draws a comparison between John Paul II referring "explicitly to a married couple, man and woman together, as an 'image of God.'"[88] One might add here the reference in the *Catechism* where it states: "The human body shares in the dignity of the image of God" (CCC §364). Both these examples, arguably, reflect an *organic* development of doctrine, yes, innovation *and* continuity, regarding Christian anthropology. However, critics of the Cardinal's claim insist that allowing the divorced and civilly remarried, or a cohabiting couple, to receive the sacrament of communion is not an *organic* development. Rather, it is an innovation, but there is a *rupture* with dogma about marriage. As one astute observer noted, "admitting the divorced and civilly remarried to Communion was the first step in accommodating Catholic teaching to the sexual revolution. If sex could be separated from marriage without sin, then the unraveling of the teaching on contraception, any sexual activity outside of marriage and homosexual acts could follow."[89]

By contrast, still others propose that a pastorally-oriented approach to doctrine gives an account of exactly how doctrine changes. Richard Gaillardetz describes this approach.

> Vatican II offered a new way of thinking about doctrine; it presented doctrine as something that always needed to be interpreted and appropriated in a *pastoral key*.... This is why he [Francis] doesn't think he is compromising on doctrine when he suggests we may need a more compassionate pastoral response to the divorced and [civilly] remarried. Being pastoral, in short, is not a matter of overlooking doctrine; it is how pastoral "style" makes doctrinal "substance" meaningful and transformative.... Doctrine changes when pastoral contexts shift and new insights emerge such that particular doctrinal formulations no longer mediate the saving message of God's transforming love. Doctrine changes when the church has leaders and teachers who are not afraid to take note of new contexts and emerging insights.[90]

I won't repeat my objections to this pastoral approach to doctrine. I have already critically examined it in Chapter 1 and found it wanting, not only because it is inconsistent with the Lérinian hermeneutics of Vatican II, but also because it is both a historicist and instrumentalist view of doctrine. In sum, this approach denies that doctrines are absolute truths, or objectively true affirmations, because what they assert is in fact the case about objective reality. (FR §82)

With all the different proposals swirling around out there, one can understand why one's head is spinning and hence many faithful are crying out for clarity in order to regain one's balance. It is precisely that cry that

I attempt to answer in the next section.

The Logic of Pastoral Reasoning and Discernment

Pope Francis underwrites, in *Amoris Laetitia*, the normativity of this ontology of conjugal marriage grounded in the order of creation, namely, the inextricable nexus of permanence, twoness, and sexual differentiation in a two-in-one-flesh unity of man and woman. Anyone who denies this is irresponsible and unfair to him.[91] Nonetheless, as I will argue in the remainder of this chapter, Francis's logic of pastoral reasoning and discernment is theologically problematic. This problematic is not about a footnote in *Amoris Laetitia* (§351).[92] Rather, it is about the logic and implications of his model of pastoral reasoning and discernment. Nothing more and nothing less. This is precisely because it implies, as Ross Douthat incisively states, "that the ontological reality of a marriage didn't matter under specific extenuating circumstances (like a stable second marriage with kids) and teaches that what the church and Jesus Christ considered adultery was also, somehow and in some cases, not."[93] Furthermore, the troubling character of Francis's pastoral strategy also shows itself in its potential application to other morally problematic relationships, so-called "irregular situations" (AL §297). What exacerbates the concern I have here regarding the extension of this strategy to a whole range of morally problematic relationships is this strategy's presupposition that fails to see the interdependency, co-existence, and mutual influence of mercy and truth. More about all these points below.

Still, this normative view of conjugal marriage is nevertheless explicitly inherent to the logic of pastoral reasoning and discerning in morally problematic situations. "Accompanying" individuals in those morally problematic situations, discerning and helping to bring about an integration of them into the life of the Church requires transformation, namely, "those [individuals in] situations that fall short of what the Lord demands of us" must heed the "call to perfection... a fuller response to God" (AL §7, §291). Says Francis, "Along these lines, Saint John Paul II proposed the so-called 'law of gradualness' in the knowledge that the human being 'knows, loves, and accomplishes moral good by different stages of growth" (FC §34). In other words, Francis affirms that "the [moral] law is itself a gift of God which points out the way, a gift for everyone without exception; it can be followed with the help of grace, even though each human being *advances gradually*" (AL §295, emphasis added). However, this statement only means to support Francis's claim that "discernment is dynamic" and that "it must ever remain open to new stages of growth and to new decisions which can enable the ideal to be more fully realized" (VS §303). Later in this chapter, I will show that this dynamic, according to Francis, et al., doesn't exclude a circumstance in which a person is said to be incapable of keeping the moral law, and, moreover, is allegedly justified in doing less than what the moral law objectively demands, that is, doing something less good than adherence to the moral law, but also that doing something less is right for that person in that circumstance. Following this line of thought, Cardinal Cupich claims,

> It's a lot easier to tell people what they are doing in black and white. The important thing in all of this as we move forward is to recognize that people's lives are very complicated. There are mitigating circumstances, psychological, their own personal history, maybe even biological. It's not a matter of detracting from what the ideal is.[94]

Therefore, he adds, homosexual couples may be led "through a period of discernment, to understand what God is calling them to *at that point*."[95] We have a situation-ethic at work here. Under certain circumstances, acting contrary to the moral law, is good, but not the highest good of attaining the ideal. Given this line of thought, I will need to ask whether gradualness is inserted in the law itself—despite Francis's denial to the contrary (AL §§295, 300).[96] For now, I simply mean to show that, in light of this law of gradualness, which Francis embraces, we should understand the following passages from *Amoris Laetitia* expressing that calling to give a fuller response to God.

> For the Church's pastors are not only responsible for promoting Christian marriage, but also the "pastoral discernment of the situations of a great many who no longer live this reality. Entering into pastoral dialogue with these persons is needed to distinguish elements in their lives that can lead to a greater openness to the Gospel of marriage in its fullness." In this pastoral discernment, there is a need "to identify elements that can foster evangelization and human and spiritual growth" (AL §293).
>
> It is a matter of reaching out to everyone, of needing to help each person find his or her proper way of participating in the ecclesial community and thus to experience being touched by an "unmerited, unconditional and gratuitous" mercy. No one can be condemned forever, because that is not the logic of the Gospel![[97]] Here I am not speaking only of the divorced and remarried, but of everyone, in whatever situation they find themselves. Naturally, if someone flaunts an objective sin as if it were part of the Christian ideal, or wants to impose something other than what the Church teaches, he or she can in no way presume to teach or preach to others; this is a case of something which separates from the community (cf. Matt 18:17). Such a person needs to listen once more to the Gospel message and its call to conversion.... As for the way of dealing with different "irregular" situations, the Synod Fathers reached a general consensus, which I support: "In considering a pastoral approach towards people

> who have contracted a civil marriage, who are divorced and remarried, or simply living together, the Church has the responsibility of helping them understand the divine pedagogy of grace in their lives and offering them assistance so they can reach the fullness of God's plan for them," something which is always possible by the power of the Holy Spirit. (AL §297)
>
> Naturally, every effort should be made to encourage the development of an enlightened conscience, formed and guided by the responsible and serious discernment of one's pastor, and to encourage an ever greater trust in God's grace.... Let us recall that this discernment is dynamic; it must remain ever open to new stages of growth and to new decisions which can enable the ideal to be more fully realized.... In every situation, when dealing with those who have difficulties in living God's law to the full, the invitation to pursue the *via caritatis* must be clearly heard. (AL §§303, 306)
>
> In order to avoid all misunderstanding, I would point out that in no way must the Church desist from proposing the full ideal of marriage, God's plan in all its grandeur.... A lukewarm attitude, any kind of relativism, or an undue reticence in proposing that ideal, would be a lack of fidelity to the Gospel and also of love on the part of the Church for young people themselves. To show understanding in the face of exceptional situations never implies dimming the light of the fuller ideal, or proposing less than what Jesus offers to the human being. (AL §307)

Several aspects are in play in this process of dynamic discernment. First, discernment is situation- and person-specific, and hence "the discernment of pastors must always take place "by adequately distinguishing," with an approach which "carefully discerns situations" that are morally problematic, typically described infelicitously, in my judgment, as "irregular situations" (AL §298).[98] This discernment was also called for by John Paul II in *Familiaris Consortio* §84, and Francis is following his lead here. "Pastors must know that, for the sake of truth, they are obliged to exercise careful discernment of situations."[99] As I noted in Chapter 3, pastoral discernment begins, according to Francis, however, not with presenting the moral law—the truth—straightway, which to Francis runs the risk of the individual experiencing this presentation as synonymous with judgment and condemnation, burdening them with laws and precepts, alienating them.[100] In fact, Francis is so intensely concerned about the priority of mercy over against truth that he warns of "making idols of certain abstract truths."[101] This "truth idolatry," he claims, "distances ordinary people from the healing closeness of the word and of the sacraments of Jesus."[102]

The then Cardinal Bergoglio sets up an opposition between Hebrew and Greek ways of thinking about truth, the latter regarding truth as abstract truth and the former as "'*émeth*', which means to be solid, reliable, trustworthy, and worthy of faith."[103] Francis continues in this fashion by stating, "Truth is also fidelity (*émeth*)." Truth is something that can be relied upon, faithful, trustworthy, and constant. He then jumps to the conclusion: "It [*émeth*] makes you name people with their real name, as the Lord names them, before categorizing them or defining 'their situation.' There is a distasteful habit, is there not, of following a 'culture of the adjective': this is so, this is such and such, this is like... No! This is a child of God. [[104]] Then come the virtues or defects, but [first] the faithful truth of the person and not the adjective regarded as the substance."[105]

It is unclear why truth in this sense (*émeth*) leads to Francis's conclusion. In *Lumen Fidei* §28, co-authored with Benedict XVI, we read, not that truth itself is fidelity, such as Francis claims, but rather "[I]n the Bible, truth and fidelity go together: the true God is the God of fidelity who keeps his promises and makes possible, in time, a deeper understanding of his plan." In other words, truth in the Bible overwhelmingly means constancy, certainty, and trustworthiness, or reliability. Therefore, truth matters because it pertains to the trustworthiness or fidelity of God himself. The biblical view of things frees us from the lack of confidence in the truth-attaining powers of man because we know that our cognitive power, indeed, the very fact that we are truth-seekers is underwritten by the truthfulness or trustworthiness (*émeth*) of God. Our truth-seeking desire fits the world and life is not fundamentally deaf to its aspiration all because, as Os Guinness admirably puts it, "truth is that which is ultimately, finally, and absolutely real, or the 'way it is', and therefore is utterly trustworthy and dependable, [and is] grounded and anchored in God's own reality and truthfulness."[106]

Nevertheless, surely Francis's substantive conclusion is lopsided. It is only a half-truth to affirm the dignity of an individual in a sinful condition. It misses the *whole truth* about human nature: the tension in human existence itself between being created good and our actual fallen state, between our human greatness and wretchedness, as Pascal said. In sum, it is precisely the humanity of man in his relation to God that makes the seriousness of his sin fully evident.

Put differently, using traditional theological distinctions, Francis distinguishes here the order of creation and the order of fall into sin—except he does not say anything about the order of the fall into sin and the impact of sin upon human nature. St. John Paul II, in his 1991 encyclical *Centesimus Annus*, wrote that "man, who was created for freedom, bears within himself the wound of original sin, which constantly draws him towards evil and puts him in need of redemption. Not only is *this doctrine an integral part of Christian revelation*; it also has great hermeneutical value insofar as it helps one to understand human reality. Man tends towards good, but he is also capable of evil" (CA §25). It is precisely this integral part of Christian revelation that is central to Christian anthropology, and that has hermeneutical value in understanding human reality, which is missing in Francis's account. Rather than the order of the fall and the truth of moral norms, Francis's pastoral strategy begins positively with the acceptance of good elements in a particularly complex situation, morally problematic relationships, so-called "irregular situations," such as cohabiting (hetero- or homosexual), those married only civilly, or divorced and civilly remarried.[107]

In Chapter 3, I criticized not only the theological justification of this approach but also its assumption. Let us suppose that a cohabiting couple with children possesses a certain stability for the raising of children (AL §78). This is evidence that there is a good aspect to this relationship, and let us say that it is even a sign of God's common grace. However, that does not mean, as some have concluded, that a cohabiting relationship *qua* relationship is itself good, and that it is an imperfect form and incomplete realization of marriage, and hence ordered to the good of marriage.[108]

Mercy and Truth

There is another problem with Francis's starting point. It runs the risk of *separating* mercy and truth because he claims that the former comes before the latter and hence fails to see that the truth itself is merciful. Says Francis, "The proclamation of the saving love of God comes before moral and religious imperatives. Today sometimes, it seems that the opposite order is prevailing.... The message of the gospel, therefore, is not to be reduced to some aspects that, although relevant, on their own do not show the heart of the message of Jesus Christ."[109] However, surely the moral norms expressing the normative truth, say, of conjugal marriage grounded in the order of creation is constitutive of the saving love of God for those cohabiting individuals. We read in the *Catechism*: "In his preaching Jesus unequivocally taught the original meaning of the union of man and woman as the Creator willed it from the beginning.... *By coming to restore the original order of creation disturbed by sin,* [Jesus] himself gives the strength and grace to live marriage in the new dimension of the Reign of God" (CCC §§1614-15). This truth about marriage is liberating, is itself merciful, and hence is integral to the message of Jesus Christ about marriage; but Francis sees moral norms as merciless laws, imposed from without on those living in "irregular" situations, "as if they were stones to throw at people's lives" (AL §305).

Furthermore, emphasizing the indivisible unity of mercy and truth, their coexistence and mutual influence, suggests to Francis "that we put so many conditions on mercy that we empty it of its concrete meaning and real significance" (AL §311). But only truth is the light that sets us free from the blindness of sin. Francis fails in *Amoris Laetitia*[110] to appreciate the hermeneutical value of sin in explaining human reality.[111] The individual's "natural mind" is none other than what the Sacred Scriptures call the vanity of the "carnal mind" (Col 2:18), the "futility of one's thinking," a "darkened understanding" (Eph 4:17-18), indeed, a "gnoseological concupiscence,"[112] in which the intellect is apostate from Christ by declaring itself sovereign "due to the hardening of one's heart." In his approach, Francis deviates —it's a rupture and not a development—from John Paul II's pastoral strategy[113] found in the 1993 Encyclical Letter, *Veritatis Splendor* §§95-105, but even earlier in his 1984 post-synodal Apostolic Exhortation, *Reconciliatio et Paenitentia* §34 where there is an emphasis on the "coexistence and mutual influence of two equally important [complementary] principles." Coexistence and mutual influence: these are the two key terms crucial to grasping the relationship between mercy and truth, and what is distinctive about John Paul's pastoral strategy in contrast with Francis's approach. John Paul explains:

> The first principle is that of compassion and mercy, whereby the church, as the continuer in history of Christ's presence and work, not wishing the death of the sinner but that the sinner should be converted and live [Ezek 18:23], and careful not to break the bruised reed or to quench the dimly burning wick [Cf. Is 42:3; Matt 12:20], ever seeks to offer, as far as possible, the path of return to God and of reconciliation with him. The other principle is that of truth and consistency, whereby the church does not agree to call good evil and evil good. Basing herself on these two complementary principles, the church can only invite her children who find themselves in these painful situations to approach the divine mercy by other ways, not however through the sacraments of penance and the Eucharist until such time as they have attained the required dispositions. On this matter, which also deeply torments our pastoral hearts, it seemed my precise duty to say clear words in the apostolic exhortation *Familiaris Consortio*, as regards the case of the divorced and remarried [§84], and likewise the case of Christians living together in an irregular union.

Of course, Francis insists that ongoing pastoral discernment of morally problematic relationships must show "concern for the integrity of the Church's moral teaching" (AL §311).[114] For instance, concern for the teaching of the Church is shown in limiting those who can teach or preach to others who do not "flaunt an objective sin as if it were part of the Christian ideal, or wants to impose something other than what the Church teaches." Here, says Francis, there "is a case of something which separates from the community [cf. Matt 18:17]. Such a person needs to listen once more to the Gospel message and its call to conversion" (AL §297). But no sooner does Francis say this about the individual who is living in a state of objective sin,[115] that he continues to welcome that very person in the life of the Church who is flaunting being in that state: "Yet even for that person there can be some way of taking part in the life of community, whether in social service, prayer meetings, or another way that his or her own initiative, together with the discernment of the parish priest, may suggest" (AL §297).[116] Would the Church be a caring community without explaining the harm of sin to the sinner, reinforcing that explanation without sanctions, understanding that genuine care must be based on truth not on making people welcomed?

However, as I have been arguing, Francis's expressed concern for the integrity of the Church's moral teaching is undermined because his pastoral approach runs the risk of *separating*, according to John Paul II, "genuine understanding and compassion... for the person, for his true good, for his authentic freedom... [from] a clear and forceful presentation of moral truth." He adds, "The Church can never renounce 'the principle of truth and consistency, whereby she does not agree to call good evil and evil good'; she must always be careful not to break the bruised reed or to quench the dimly burning wick [cf. Is 42:3]" (VS §95).[117] Furthermore, John Paul II was not unfamiliar with claims, like those of Francis' and others, that the Church runs the risk of demeaning people in morally problematic relationships by its firmness in defending the universal and unchanging moral norms. He rejects this claim as baseless. "[The Church's] only purpose is to serve man's true freedom. Because there can be no freedom apart from or in opposition to the truth, the categorical—unyielding and uncompromising—defense of the absolutely essential demands of man's personal dignity must be considered the way and the condition for the very existence of freedom" (VS §96). Francis does not recognize the merciful nature of moral truth.

Objective and Subjective Morality

Second, in light of the distinction between objective morality and subjective morality, between objective truth and subjective evaluation of mitigating factors and situations, Francis's emphasis is on the latter—rather than on an individual's awareness of the gap between his morally problematic situation and the objective moral norm—to discern the matter of responsibility, blameworthiness, or guilt for believing and behaving as an individual does. In order to avoid thinking that "the demands of the Gospel are in any way being compromised," says Francis, he draws on a solid body of reflection of the Church's teaching on mitigating factors regarding imputability and responsibility. For example: "Imputability and responsibility for an action can be diminished or even nullified by ignorance, inadvertence, duress, fear, habit, inordinate attachments, and other psychological or social factors." Again, "To form an equitable judgment about the subjects' moral responsibility and to guide pastoral action, one must take into account the affective immaturity, force of acquired habit, conditions of anxiety, or other psychological or social factors that lessen or even extenuate moral culpability" (CCC §1735, §2352). These mitigating factors help to discern a person's responsibility and blameworthiness such that an individual might be blameless, subjectively speaking, even though he is doing something that involves objective wrongdoing and hence a sin.

Furthermore, there are other factors enlisted in such subjective evaluations of an individual's act, namely, whether certain acts are committed freely with "full knowledge and deliberate consent" (CCC §1857).

Third, Francis claims that "mitigating factors" are sufficient in certain cases to conclude that the individuals in those cases are not in a state of mortal sin or deprived of sanctifying grace, because they are blameless, lacking culpability, for doing the wrong thing, objectively speaking (AL §301). Unlike John Paul II, Francis is not here speaking of couples who have decided to live "as brother and sister."[118] Francis rules out this interpretation. He does not explicitly endorse John Paul's position, although he could have. In fact, *he avoids citing it*, although he refers to the very paragraph §84 of *Familiaris Consortio* where John Paul's position is found. He explicitly refers only to the statement in that paragraph that it is crucial to the logic of pastoral care "'to exercise careful discernment of situation.'" Furthermore, in *Amoris Laetitia* footnote 329 he contradicts John Paul's position. He says, "In such situations ['where for serious reasons, such as the children's upbringing, a man and woman cannot satisfy the obligation to separate' (§298)], many people, knowing and accepting the possibility of living 'as brothers and sisters' which the Church offers them, point out that if certain expressions of intimacy are lacking, 'it often happens that faithfulness is endangered and the good of the children suffers' [GS §51]."[119] This is the concrete situation in which a couple, knowing full well the rule prohibiting fornication or adultery, cannot, as Francis says, "act differently and decide otherwise without further sin" (AL §301). Does he, then, hold that a cohabiting couple or a divorced and civilly remarried couple may be free from sin, not committing adultery, subjectively speaking, although they do not live as brother and sister—and hence, objectively speaking do fornicate or commit adultery—because of mitigating factors that render them inculpable?

Yes, he does. Hence, according to Francis the changes in the Church must be carried out with the hermeneutic of continuity, but then how can his position be considered a homogeneous development of John Paul II's *Familiaris Consortio* §84—which teaches that the divorced and civilly remarried must resolve to live as brother and sister in Christ, or else refrain from approaching the sacraments? As Cardinal Müller incisively states, "There are only two options. One could explicitly deny the validity of *Familiaris Consortio* §84.... Or one could attempt to show that *Familiaris Consortio* §84 *implicitly* anticipated the reversal of the discipline that it *explicitly* set out to teach. On any honest reading of John Paul II's text, however, such a procedure would have to violate the basic rules of logic, such as the principle of non-contradiction."[120]

Recall that Francis says, "Here I am not speaking only of the divorced and remarried, but of everyone, in whatever [irregular] situation they find themselves" (AL §297). Douthat suggests, for example, "If the obligations involved in a second marriage need to be accommodated by the church, why not the obligations of a polygamous marriage—where promises are made, similar entanglements are present, and children are just as (if not more) likely to be involved?"[121] Thus, there is no reason why Francis's logic of pastoral reasoning cannot be applied to a variety of morally problematic relationships. I think that is the implication of his logic of pastoral reasoning, namely, the morally permissible choice is made under a lesser-of-two-evils calculus.[122] That is certainly what several of Francis's interpreters closest to him have suggested, such as Fr. Antonio Spadaro, the Editor of *La Civilità Cattolica*;[123] Cardinal Francesco Coccopalmerio, late President of the Pontifical Council for the Interpretation of Legal Texts;[124] Archbishop Victor Manuel Fernàndez, Rector of the Catholic University, Buenos Aires;[125] Walter Cardinal Kasper,[126] and last but not least, Blaise Cardinal Cupich.[127] If Pope Francis rejects their interpretation of *Amoris Laetitia* §303 as a distortion and misreading of it, then why doesn't he say so? Let me suggest that the pope does not say so because he does not hold there to be a "yes" or "no" answer to that question in the logic of pastoral mercy (AL §305).

By contrast, in Aquinas's view, this is a situation of "perplexity," indeed, a moral dilemma, and not a case of ignorance. Hence, Dominican theologian, Bonino, correctly sees that this is not a question "of a factor that limits the voluntary or the subjective capacity to decide (which we ordinarily understand as a mitigating circumstance) but of a situation that limits the 'objective' choice and that forces the person to choose, between two (moral evils), the evil that seems to him to be the lesser." He elaborates:

> A person is placed in conditions such that it seems—no matter what he does or abstains from doing—that he cannot avoid sin. Now, on this point, St. Thomas seems rather to judge that there cannot exist such a "true" (*simpliciter*) moral dilemma that would oblige a person to do an objective evil act or, as the saying goes, to choose the lesser evil. Or rather, the dilemma exists, but it is caused by an earlier framework of sin that the person can and ought to renounce.[128]

In other words, Thomas denies that this individual is perplexed or in a moral dilemma "because he can lay aside his error, since his ignorance is vincible and voluntary."[129] This, too, is the approach of John Paul II and of Benedict XVI, but not Francis. Therefore, Francis differs with Thomas not only in his analysis of the morally problematic situation but also in his solution.

Cardinal Francesco Coccopalmerio has grappled with what I have called a perplexity, or moral dilemma, but he does not describe it as a situation where a person is forced to choose between two moral evils.[130] He says, "There is another element... here... and it is crucial for understanding this delicate problem correctly." Coccopalmerio claims that this divorced and remarried couple are conscious of this union's "irregularity and of the great difficulty of going back without feeling in conscience that one would fall into new sins."[131] Given their Christian commitment, he claims that the people in question are conscious of the sinful condition of their irregular situation. Significantly, in an effort to avoid the moral dilemma, as I described it above, Coccopalmerio claims that these "persons intend to change their irregular status." Of course, he readily acknowledges, that this intention is implicit but not stated explicitly. But he insists that they "have considered the problem of changing and thus they intend to, or at least desire to, change their situation... but cannot act on their desire."[132]

Is Coccopalmerio suggesting that their intention or desire to change, even if they cannot now change, renders morally justified their choice to stay in this union for the time being for the sake of the family such that they are acting with moral rectitude?[133] He implies this conclusion. However, he is mistaken—in light of the sources of morality in the Catholic tradition (CCC §§1749-61, see also VS §§79-83). "The object, the intention, and the circumstances make up the 'sources' or constitutive elements, of the morality of human acts" (CCC §1750). Consider, first, the circumstances, which also includes the consequences, as described above. These "are secondary elements of a moral act" which might increase or diminish the moral goodness or evil of certain moral acts, such as, choosing to stay in a union for the sake of the children. "Circumstances of themselves cannot change the moral quality of acts themselves; they can make neither good nor right an action that is in itself evil" (CCC §1754). Intending or desiring to change does not alter the moral evil of adultery. Of course, their intention to preserve the well-being of their family is good. However, the end does not justify the means. Thus, neither the circumstances nor the intentions are in themselves sufficient to make an action morally good. Since this circumstance involves committing adultery, and this act is the moral object, the latter act is a mortal sin, and hence the individuals involved cannot be acting with moral rectitude.

Culpability for Rejecting Moral Rules

Fourth, Francis considers another situation where the issue is not merely about the ignorance of a rule, such as, the rule prohibiting fornication or adultery as a sin (CCC §2353), but rather of someone who does not accept the moral rule. "A subject may know full well the rule, yet have great difficulty in understanding 'its inherent values' [FC §33]" (AL §301).[134] Francis's emphasis in pastoral ministry is on the mitigating factors that may render an individual blameless. He sees this as a matter of mercy. Here, clearly, Francis leaves behind John Paul II, because Francis creates a moral space in which an individual is blameless, and hence without sin, for doing something not in harmony with the relevant objective moral norm.[135] John Paul's emphasis is other, I argued earlier, because he insists on the interdependency and mutual influence of truth and mercy such that, in pastoral ministry, there can be no mercy without truth.[136] "Pues es la verdad la que libera; la verdad es la que pone orden y la verdad es la que abre el camino a la santidad y a la justicia" [It is the truth that liberates; the truth that restores order and the truth that opens the path to holiness and justice].[137] He adds, "And so the Church never ceases to exhort and encourage all to resolve whatever conjugal difficulties may arise without ever falsifying or compromising the truth." Indeed, John Paul praises men and women in so-called "irregular unions" who nonetheless "testify to the indissolubility of marriage" by promising to live fully continently [continencia total], that is, abstaining from acts that are proper only to married couples."[138]

Furthermore, we may ask whether the individual actually knows the moral rule regarding the reception of communion by the divorced and civilly remarried. Since he "does not accept it, he does not *believe* that the norm is good and true, and a person who does not believe a moral truth can be said not to know that truth. He is, at least in that sense, ignorant of the corresponding norm." The question is whether he is culpable for his ignorance. Similarly, Coccopalmerio says, "that this inability to recognize that the rule is good, is in fact equivalent to lack of knowledge of the rule.[139] And, therefore, lack of culpability in the case of the infringement of that rule." Now, although both sources attribute ignorance to the individual, Flannery & Berg probe more deeply than Coccopalmerio because they go on to consider whether the alleged ignorance is voluntary or not, invincible or vincible.

Well, since the case here is about an individual's difficulty in understanding a moral rule rather than ignorance of it, according to Francis, it is not a question of invincible ignorance but of vincible ignorance, which, as such, does not excuse from culpability. John Paul II explains the difference:

> [Saint] Paul's admonition [1 Tim 1:5; Rom 12:2] urges us to be watchful, warning us that in the judgments of our conscience the possibility of error is always present. Conscience *is not an infallible judge*; it can make mistakes. However, error of conscience can be the result of an *invincible ignorance*, an ignorance of which the subject is not aware and which he is unable to overcome by himself. The [Second Vatican] Council reminds us that in cases where such invincible ignorance is not culpable, conscience does not lose its dignity, because even when it directs us to act in a way not in conformity with the objective moral order, it continues to speak in the name of that truth about the good which the subject is called to seek sincerely.... Conscience, as the ultimate concrete judgment, compromises its dignity when it is *culpably erroneous*, that is to say, "when man shows little concern for seeking what is true and good, and conscience gradually becomes almost blind from being accustomed to sin [GS §16]" (VS §§62-63).

Looking to Thomas for assistance here, he distinguishes two situations: one in which an individual voluntarily commits an objectively evil act itself, but does so without knowing, say, that adultery or fornication is a sin; the other in which his ignorance is voluntary, occurs before the action, and the latter is a sin. In the former case, a person "voluntarily performs an act of fornication but does not voluntarily commit a sin." In the latter case, says Thomas, "When therefore a person directly wills to be ignorant so as not to be pulled back from sin by the knowledge, such ignorance does not excuse sin either wholly or in part but rather increases it, for it appears that, out of great love of sinning, the person wills to suffer the loss of knowledge so that he might freely cling to the sin."[140] Now, is a couple's difficulty in understanding the inherent values of a moral rule sufficient in specific cases to claim that individuals are not culpable for living in a state of mortal sin or deprived of sanctifying grace, as Francis, Coccopalmerio, and others claim?

Regarding the claim of diminished culpability that allegedly follows from having great difficulty in understanding the inherent truth or good regarding the morality of fornication or adultery, it is clear that rejecting these precepts does not as such diminish culpability. Why? Well, an individual may "'take little trouble to find out what is true and good, or when [his] conscience is by degrees almost blinded through the habit of committing sin' [GS §16]. In such cases, the person is culpable for the evil he commits'" (CCC §1791). There is a certain optimism in Francis's readiness to hold individuals blameless without considering the reasons why they are unwilling to address the difficulty. Karl Rahner rightly explains, "[Conscience] can easily make mistakes and it is very difficult to distinguish its voice—the real voice of conscience—from the voice of precipitation, passion, convenience or self-will, or of moral primitiveness which cannot see the finer distinctions or the more remote consequences of the act." Francis overlooks all this and hence softens the responsibility an individual has "to conform his conscience to the objective moral law [here and now], to inform himself and let himself be taught and make himself prepared to accept (how difficult this often is!) instruction from the Word of God, the magisterium of the Church and every just authority in its own sphere."[141]

In light of Rahner's remarks, we must consider the possibility that perhaps these individuals are deliberately avoiding being informed on the issue, which would increase the likelihood that they are "living in a state of mortal sin and are deprived of sanctifying grace." The *Catechism* insightfully teaches, "An action can be indirectly voluntary when it results from negligence regarding something one should have known or done; for example, an accident arising from ignorance of traffic laws" (CCC §1736). In this case, ignorance is voluntary, as Aquinas explains, "either directly, as when a man wishes of set purpose to be ignorant of certain things that he may sin the more freely; or indirectly, as when a man, through stress of work or other occupations, neglects to acquire the knowledge which would restrain him from sin. For such like negligence renders the ignorance itself voluntary and sinful, provided it be about matters one is bound and able to know. Consequently, this ignorance does not altogether excuse him from sin." In addition, the *Catechism* adds, "No one is deemed to be ignorant of the principles of the moral law, which are written in the conscience of every man" (CCC §1860).

As the *Catechism* puts it, "Feigned ignorance and hardness of heart do not diminish, but rather increase, the voluntary character of a sin" (CCC §1859). In addition, "ignorance of Christ and his Gospel, bad example given by others, enslavement to one's passions, assertions of a mistaken notion of autonomy of conscience, rejection of the Church's authority and her teaching, lack of conversion and of charity: these can be at the source of errors of judgment in moral conduct" (CCC §1792). This, too, is Aquinas's view when he speaks about how the failure to understand a moral precept may be caused "by passion, or evil habit, or an evil disposition" (ST I-II, q. 94, a. 4). Indeed, Aquinas identifies five ways in which that may be the case: passion, evil habit, and evil disposition of nature, vicious custom, and evil persuasion. J. Budziszewski succinctly explains Aquinas's view:

> *Corruption of reason by passion:* Momentarily blinded by grief and rage, I unjustly strike the bearer of the news that my wife is deep in adultery with another man. *Corruption of reason by evil habit:* little by little I get into the habit of using pornography or cutting corners on my taxes. At first my conscience bothers me, but eventually I can see nothing wrong with my behavior.... Although I am still capable of restraint, it is more difficult for me than it might be for someone else. *Corruption of reason by evil disposition of nature:* a defect in one of my chromosomes predisposes me to violence, abuse of alcohol or homosexual acts. Although I am still capable of restraint, it is more difficult for me than it might be for someone else. *Corruption of reason by vicious custom:* I have grown up among people who do not regard bribery as wrong, and so I take it for granted. *Corruption of reason by evil persuasion:* I use electronic tricks to make free long-distance telephone calls, justifying my behavior by the theory that I am merely exploiting the exploiters.[142]

None of these factors figures in Francis's account in *Amoris Laetitia*, nor in the account of Coccopalmerio, et al., regarding civil marriage, divorced and civilly remarried, or cohabitation. There is also no mention made of the reasoning that led them to hold these false beliefs, for example, reflecting negligent reasoning, ideological rationalization, or wishful thinking.[143] Although he draws on the Church's solid body of reflection concerning mitigating factors and situations, he overlooks the corresponding body of reflections concerning whether the ignorance is voluntary or not, invincible or vincible, and hence a result of ethical value-blindness. As Josef Seifert describes the latter, "Often ethical value-blindness is rooted in evil acts and attitudes and the subject is responsible for his blindness such that he even a worse sinner than the one who clearly knows his sin and recognizes his guilt."[144]

The Law of Gradualness vs the Gradualness of the Law

Fifth, appealing to the purport of the distinction between objective morality and subjective morality, Francis holds that "For this reason, a negative judgment about an objective situation does not imply a judgment about the imputability or culpability of the person involved." (AL §302). In other words, it is conceivable that an individual could be in "irregular situations" of adultery, homosexual acts, and so forth, living objectively in serious sin, but subjectively in the state of grace, and hence without sin. In this context, I would like now to consider the role of conscience in morally problematic situations. These are "consciences of the faithful," says Francis, "who very often respond as best they can to the Gospel amid their limitations, and are capable of carrying out their own discernment in complex situations. We have been called to form consciences, not to replace them" (AL §37). These are acts of individual conscience—which Francis says are under the influence of mitigating factors—that "do not objectively embody our [the Church's] understanding of marriage" (AL §303). Of course, in this connection, we must appeal to the law of gradualness, which, according to Francis, gradualness is not in the law itself, but rather in "the prudential exercise of free acts on the parts of subjects who are not in a position to understand, appreciate, or fully carry out the objective demands of the law" (AL §295). The following diagram may help us to understand the difference between the "law of gradualness" and the "gradualness of the law."[145]

The Law of Gradualness **The Gradualness of Law**

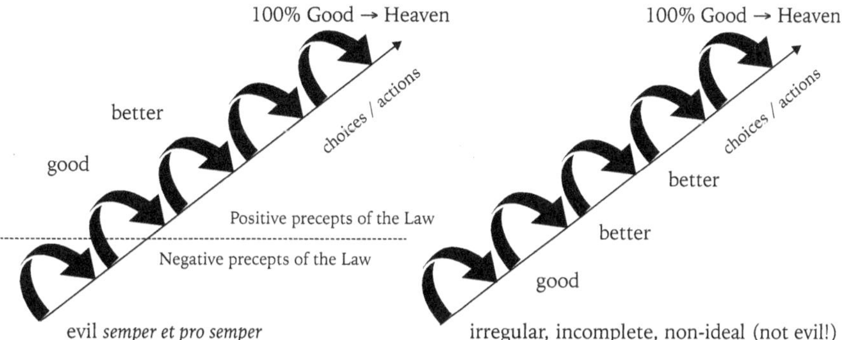

I have already examined above with some skepticism Francis's claim that having trouble understanding and appreciating a moral precept in itself is sufficient to render a person blameless, but also the circumstances under which he is unable to carry out fully the objective demands of the law because whatever he does he cannot avoid sin.

Rather than return to those matters, let's assume for the sake of following Francis's argument where it logically leads, that an individual is acting with judgments of conscience, by virtue of being subjectively blameless for doing the wrong thing, objectively speaking. Says Francis, "because of forms of conditioning and mitigating factors, it is possible that in an objective situation of sin—which may not be subjectively culpable, or fully culpable—a person can be living in God's grace, can love, and can also grow in the life of grace and charity, while receiving the Church's help to this end" (AL §305). He struggles to make judgments of conscience given the limits of his situation, finding "possible ways of responding to God and growing in the midst of limits." He recognizes that the "given situation [he is in] does not correspond objectively to the overall demands of the Gospel."

However, conscience is about more than rule following and, accordingly, the acknowledgement that an individual's judgment of conscience itself is in tension with the objective exemplar, or moral norm, objectively speaking. He "can also recognize with sincerity and honesty what for now is the most generous response which can be given to God, and come to see with a certain moral security that it is what God himself is asking amid the concrete complexity of one's limits, while yet not fully the objective ideal." What is the nature of the limiting conditions an individual apprehends? Are they such that they are good elements open in principle to the overall demands of the Gospel?

The limits of the concrete situation are a mixed bag of good and bad elements. For example, the good elements[146] of a cohabiting couple[147] are that they, says Francis, "lovingly care for each other, serve the community in which they live and work, have attained a noteworthy stability through a public bond—and is characterized by deep affection, responsibility toward the children, and the ability to overcome trials." Yet this couple is purportedly subjectively blameless although engaged in fornication, which objectively speaking is contrary to the moral teachings of the Church and hence to the overall demands of the Gospel.[148]

Still, according to Francis in *Amoris Laetitia* §303—which is perhaps the most contentious passage in this document—one's conscience sometimes "can also recognize with sincerity and honesty" that acting contrary to an objective moral norm, the objective ideal of marriage, is "what God himself is asking amid the concrete complexity of one's limits,"[149] because one's judgment of conscience "discerns" that an act which one is, here and now, choosing—though knowing that it violates a moral rule prohibiting fornication—"for now is the most generous response which can be given to God."[150]

Also, appealing again to the law of gradualness, conscience's discernment of what "God himself is asking amid the concrete complexity of one's limits" is said to be dynamic: it "must remain ever open to new stages of growth and new decisions which can enable the ideal to be more fully realized" (AL §303). Yet, one must also ask whether Francis implies that judgments of conscience are such that "there can be degrees of disorder that an individual knowingly, deliberately, and indeed, with moral rectitude, allows into his life, since this is the 'most generous response' he can make in pursuit of the ideal," as Flannery & Berg decidedly put it.[151] Is Francis suggesting here that under those circumstances sexual intimacy is morally permissible, a subjectively good choice, for the sake of maintaining a faithful "invalid marriage" so that the children do not suffer? I think his moral logic of pastoral reasoning implies an affirmative response to that question.

If so, then gradualness—*contra* Francis—has been inserted into the law itself "as if there were different degrees or forms of precept in God's law for different individuals and situations," as John Paul II puts it (FC §34). Looking back now to the situation of moral perplexity, or moral dilemma, we can now appreciate why Josef Seifert asked in view of this situation: "If only one case of an intrinsically immoral act can be permitted and even willed by God, must this not apply to all acts considered 'intrinsically wrong.' If it is true that God can want an adulterous couple to live in adultery, should then not also the commandment 'Do not commit adultery" be reformulated: 'If in your situation adultery is not the lesser evil, do not commit it! If it is, continue living in it'?[152]

In *Veritatis Splendor*, John Paul is concerned with conscience and truth, with the aim of clarifying why the proposal of some kind of double status of moral truth is mistaken.[153]

> Beyond the doctrinal and abstract level, one would have to acknowledge the priority of a certain more concrete existential consideration. The latter, by taking account of circumstances and the situation, could legitimately be the basis of certain exceptions to the general rule and thus permit one to do in practice and in good conscience what is qualified as intrinsically evil by the moral law. A separation, or even an opposition, is thus established in some cases between the teaching of the precept, which is valid in general, and the norm of the individual conscience, which would in fact make the final decision about what is good and what is evil. On this basis, an attempt is made to legitimize so-called "pastoral" solutions contrary to the teaching of the Magisterium, and to justify a "creative" hermeneutic according to which the moral conscience is in no way obliged, in every case, by a particular negative precept. (VS §56).[154]

In the next section, I examine Blase Cardinal Cupich's claim that following Francis's line of thought means urging that room has to be made "for the consciences of the faithful, who very often respond as best they can to the Gospel amid their limitations," which means that in some situations their conscientious judgments are justifiably made in opposition to the demands of the objective moral law. "We have been called to form consciences, not to replace them" (AL §37). This means that we should not impose rules on peoples' consciences without considering their struggles.

Judgments of Conscience in Conflict with Moral Law

Consider now one example of the role of conscience rejected by John Paul

II, but apparently embraced by Francis. In his 9 February 2018 address at the Von Hügel Institute, St. Edmund Campion College, Cambridge University, Cardinal Blase Cupich claimed that at the heart of the so-called "new hermeneutic" of Chapter 8 of Pope Francis's *Amoris Laetitia* is the role of conscience for discerning what God is asking of me *here and now*.[155]

In one sense, of course, there is nothing disturbing about focusing on the situation of the person-specific role of conscience. John Henry Newman also observed that "conscience is not a judgment upon any speculative truth, any abstract doctrine but bears immediately on conduct, on something to be done or not done." Newman adds, citing Thomas Aquinas, "'Conscience', says St. Thomas, 'is the practical judgment or dictate of reason, by which we judge what *hic et nunc* is to be done as being good, or to be avoided as evil.'"

For Thomas and Newman, then, the particular judgment of conscience about the morality of given acts is about doing good and avoiding evil.

Unlike Thomas and Newman, however, Cardinal Cupich distinguishes conscience's role in this sense from conscience's ability to grasp objective moral truths. He interprets conscience as an *oracle* in which the situation and person-specific judgments of conscience are equated with the voice of God:[156] "Their decisions of conscience represent God's personal guidance for the particularities of their lives. In other words, the voice of conscience—the voice of God—or... what Newman called 'the aboriginal Vicar of Christ', could very well affirm the *necessity of living at some distance* [here and now] from the Church's understanding of the [moral] ideal" (emphasis added).

Therefore, the individual's subjective conscience hears God telling him that he is justified in doing that which is inconsistent with what is objectively right and avoiding what is objectively wrong. According to Cupich, then, conscience justifiably retains the final word in opposition to the objective truth. Despite his protest, Cupich's "new hermeneutic" regarding pastoral reasoning is a version of situation ethics, or of the gradualness of the law.

The Cardinal is, furthermore, wrong about Newman's account of conscience. For Newman, although he refers to conscience as the voice of God, conscience is an organ, not an oracle. Like perception, memory, reasoning, and human testimony, conscience involves a way of forming beliefs and evaluating them. Conscience, explains Newman, is "a principle planted within us, before we have had any training, though such training and experience is necessary for its strength, growth, and due formation."

Newman adds, likening conscience to other ways of forming beliefs and evaluating them, conscience is "a constituent element of the mind, as our perception of other ideas may be, as our powers of reasoning, as our sense of order and the beautiful, and our other intellectual endowments." Significantly, he concludes, "as Catholics consider it," conscience is "the internal witness of both the existence and the law of God."

In this light, we can see why Newman rejects conscience as "the right of self-will." "Conscience has rights because it has duties." In other words, conscience cannot "ignore a Lawgiver and Judge, [as if it were] independent of... obligations."

This conclusion brings us to Cardinal Cupich's claim that this "new hermeneutic" has fully embraced the "understanding of conscience found in Vatican II's *Gaudium et spes* §16." "Conscience is the most secret core and sanctuary of a man. There he is alone with God, Whose voice echoes in his depths." Here, too, Cupich wrongly interprets conscience not only as an oracle rather than an organ, but he also wrongly asserts that an individual is justified in doing that which is inconsistent with what is objectively right and avoiding what is objectively wrong.

But Cupich couldn't be more wrong not only about *Gaudium et spes* §16, in particular, but also the role of universally binding moral norms—the natural law—in Vatican Council II.

Like Newman, *Gaudium et spes* §16 understands conscience to be "the internal witness of both the existence and the law of God." It states: "In the depths of his conscience, man detects a law which he does not impose upon himself, but which holds him to obedience. Always summoning him to love good and avoid evil, the voice of conscience when necessary speaks to his heart: do this, shun that. For man has in his heart a law written by God; to obey it is the very dignity of man; according to it he will be judged."

Similarly, we read in *Dignitatis Humanae* §3 that "the highest norm of human life is God's divine law—eternal, objective, and universal." In addition, "Wherefore every man has the duty, and therefore the right, to seek the truth... in order that he may with prudence form for himself right and true judgments of conscience."

Gaudium et spes §79 focuses on "the permanent binding force of universal natural law and its all-embracing principles [see GS §27]. *Man's conscience itself gives ever more emphatic voice to these principles. Therefore, actions which deliberately conflict with these same principles... cannot excuse those who yield to them*" (emphasis added). Vatican II is emphatically contrary to Cardinal Cupich's account of conscience.

Moreover, subordinate to God's divine, eternal, objective, and universal law that summons man to "love and to do what is good and avoid evil," is Vatican II's true norm for guiding human choices and actions." In *Gaudium et spes* §35 we read that this norm "is that in accord with the divine plan and will, *human activity should harmonize with the genuine good of the human race,* and allow men as individuals and as members of society to pursue their total vocation and fulfill it" (emphasis added).

Pace Cardinal Cupich, by any fair reading, there is no justification in Newman or in Vatican II for removing the universally binding validity of particular norms in specific judgments of conscience.

Aquinas, Natural Law, and Concrete Action

One final claim of Francis remains to be considered. "It is reductive simply to consider whether or not an individual's actions correspond to a general law or rule, because that is not enough to discern and ensure full fidelity to God in the concrete life of a human being" (AL §304). It is precisely here that Francis issues a plea to incorporate Aquinas into the practice of pastoral discernment. Why? Well, pastoral discernment is no longer merely about recognizing that mitigating factors may sometimes diminish subjective culpability for disobeying the moral law against adultery. However, in appealing to Aquinas, Francis seems to be saying that the general law itself may not apply in every particular situation.[157] So, based on Aquinas's teaching, is Francis suggesting that there may be particular cases where the moral law prohibiting adultery is inapplicable?

> I earnestly ask that we always recall a teaching of Saint Thomas Aquinas and learn to incorporate it in our pastoral discernment: "Although there is necessity in the general principles, the more we descend to matters of detail, the more frequently we encounter defects... In matters of action, truth or practical rectitude is not the same for all, as to matters of detail, but only as to the general principles; and where there is the same rectitude in matters of detail, it is not equally known to all... The principle will be found to fail, according as we descend further into detail" [ST I-II, q. 94, a.4].

Francis proceeds by way of conclusion:

> It is true that general rules set forth a good which can never be disregarded or neglected, but in their formulation they cannot provide absolutely for all particular situations. At the same time, it must be said that, precisely for that reason, what is part of a practical discernment in particular circumstances cannot be elevated to the level of a rule. That would not only lead to an intolerable casuistry, but would endanger the very values which must be preserved with special care.

For clarity's sake, as well as for our assessment of Francis's appeal to the argument of *Summa Theologiae* I-II, q. 94, a. 4, it is important to note that Francis does not attend to or even mention Aquinas's distinction between negative moral norms that hold *semper et ad semper* and affirmative moral norms—prima facie obligations—that hold *semper sed non ad semper*.[158] Whereas the latter norms oblige always but not for every occasion, and hence they have presumptive validity, the former exclude actions that are evil in themselves and cannot under any circumstance become good; they are exceptionless moral norms, or moral absolutes.[159] The language employed by Aquinas here corresponding to this distinction is that between "common principles" [general principles] and "proper conclusions." As Flannery & Berg explain, "[Aquinas] considers the lower principles as conclusions (or sometimes 'quasi conclusions' [ST I-II, q. 94, a. 4; q. 97, a. 4, ad 3] of the common principles. In any cases, it is clear that the proper conclusions are not 'matters of detail'. They are propositions, sometimes spoken of by Thomas as principles and sometimes as conclusions, sometimes as precepts."[160] The import of this reading of Aquinas is that the contrast in *Summa Theologiae* I-II, q. 94, a. 4, "is not between 'general principles' and concrete moral situations to which the 'general principles' supposedly cannot be applied, but between common principles and proper principles." In other words, the contrast is between negative precepts and positive precepts, moral absolutes and prima facie obligations, between those that apply in all cases and those that apply in most cases, with exceptions. Flannery & Berg explain:

> What sometimes happens is that a proper principle "is found not to hit the mark" (*invenitur deficere*). This never happens with a common principle (such as "do not steal"). A proper principle, however, such as "return deposits to their owner" can fail to hit the mark—but only in the sense that, when it was originally formulated, the lawmaker wisely did not mention explicitly the many situations that would make it not applicable. But they are there implicitly in the law, since it is presupposed in law that all the exceptions cannot be mentioned and, indeed, ought not to be mentioned—although they are there "in the intention of the lawmaker." When the man who owns the weapon given to another in trust returns and... asks for his weapon back, the other person is not obliged to give it to him—because not returning that deposit is already in the law (because it was in the intention of the lawmaker). In such a case, the proper principle as *formulated* misses the mark.[161]

Therefore, according to Aquinas, on the one hand, the negative moral norm regarding adultery is such that there are no exceptions to the moral precept that adultery is wrong, always and everywhere, in every circumstance. So, since marriage involves an unconditional promise to be faithful until death do us part, such that it is permanent, there are no conditions under which it would be right to leave one's spouse, marry someone else, and have sexual intercourse. In that case, one would commit adultery. On the other hand, a moral precept that has *prima facie*, or presumptive, validity is such that there may be good reason to permit an exception rendering it inapplicable in this particular case. To take an example from Aquinas: I have a presumptive obligation to return someone's property to him, say, his car keys, that he has put in my safe keeping. "Goods entrusted to another must be restored to their owner." However, suppose this individual gets drunk. Under that circumstance, it would be morally permissible not to return his keys to him because of the danger he poses to himself and others if he drives his car. In short, there may be certain exceptions regarding the affirmative norm that one should return what one has borrowed, entrusted with for safekeeping. This makes it clear that what Aquinas has in mind here are affirmative norms that oblige always but not on every occasion, and not negative norms (moral absolutes) that hold *semper et ad semper*, excluding acts that are evil in themselves and cannot become good.[162]

Francis misses this understanding in his appeal to Aquinas.[163] He overlooks the distinction between common principles and proper principles, and hence he thinks that the application of general principles is indeterminate depending upon "pastoral" or "practical discernment" because "in their formulation they [general principles] cannot provide absolutely for all particular situations" (AL §304). However, this is not Aquinas's position. "Thomas's position is rather that, also below the level of common principles, there are principles that, given the appropriate circumstances, are quite determinate but that, in other (inappropriate) circumstances, must be applied (or not applied) according to the mind of the legislator. When the legislator decrees that deposits must be returned, he, even by so doing, knows that there will be situations in which it would be irrational—and so contrary to his intention—to apply the precept. A prudent interpreter of the precept will immediately recognize such circumstances for what they are."[164]

Francis's appeal to Aquinas to justify the inapplicability of moral norms can be squared neither with Aquinas' understanding in ST I-II, q. 94, a. 4, nor with the Church's teaching that some moral norms are absolute by virtue of being exceptionless.[165] Notwithstanding Francis's insistence that general principles "can never be disregarded," his appeal to Aquinas encourages us in particular situations to do just that. Francis never uses the term "moral absolute" or "intrinsically evil act"[166] because the concept of a moral absolute, in his moral logic, is replaced by ideals or goals to be achieved. In addition, since Francis overlooks the distinction between moral absolutes and prima facie obligations, common principles and proper principles, negative precepts and positive precepts, his reasoning implies that a specific and exceptionless moral norm may be inapplicable in particular cases.

No wonder the second dubia of the "dubia" Cardinals[167] raised a doubt as to whether one still needs to regard as valid the teaching of *Veritatis Splendor* §79, where the reality of moral absolutes, or exceptionless moral norms, is reaffirmed.

> Reason attests that there are objects of the human act which are by their nature "incapable of being ordered" to God, because they radically contradict the good of the person made in his image. These are the acts which, in the Church's moral tradition, have been termed "intrinsically evil" (*intrinsece malum*): they are such *always and per se*, in other words, on account of their very object, and quite apart from the ulterior intentions of the one acting and the circumstances. Consequently, without in the least denying the influence on morality exercised by circumstances and especially by intentions, the Church teaches that "there exist acts which *per se* and in them-

> selves, independently of circumstances, are always seriously wrong by reason of their object." (VS §79)

In conclusion, Francis urged us that *Amoris Laetitia* should be "treated with a hermeneutic of the Church, always in continuity (without ruptures), yet always maturing." I agree with this principle of interpretation. I have now shown that Chapter 8 of *Amoris Laetitia* represents a rupture with the Church's tradition in its logic of pastoral reasoning and discernment; it is because Francis's reasoning leads to the conclusion that a person's mitigating circumstances are such that he is not bound in his situation by a specific moral precept excluding an intrinsically evil act, such as the moral absolute excluding adultery. He is simply doing the best that he can in light of his limits, rendering him incapable of keeping the commandments.[168] This conclusion is inconsistent not only with Aquinas, such that, as Flannery & Berg rightly state, "Aquinas ought never to have been cited in support of the ideas put forward in that part of AL §304," but also with the pastoral strategy of *Veritatis Splendor* §§102-104. In the latter case, it is inconsistent in two ways. First, John Paul II orders man's possibilities not to the limits of the situation but to the mystery of Christ's redemption.

> *Only in the mystery of Christ's Redemption do we discover the "concrete" possibilities of man....* But what are the "concrete possibilities of man"? And of *which* man are we speaking? Of man *dominated* by lust or of man *redeemed* by Christ? This is what is at stake: the *reality* of Christ's redemption. *Christ has redeemed us!* This means that he has given us the possibility of realizing *the entire* truth of our being; he has set our freedom free from the *domination* of concupiscence. And if redeemed man still sins, this is not due to an imperfection of Christ's redemptive act, but to man's will not to avail himself of the grace which flows from that act. God's command is of course proportioned to man's capabilities; but to the capabilities of the man to whom the Holy Spirit has been given; of the man who, though he has fallen into sin, can always obtain pardon and enjoy the presence of the Holy Spirit." (VS §103)

John Paul II is articulating in this above passage Trent's *Decree on Justification* §1836: "No one should say that the observance of God's commandments is impossible for the man justified and constituted in grace" (see also canon 18, Denzinger §1568). He adds, "Keeping God's law in particular situations can be difficult, extremely difficult, but it is never impossible. This is the constant teaching of the Church's tradition, and was expressed by the Council of Trent."

In short, the Church's teaching at the Council of Trent, reiterated by John Paul II in *Veritatis Splendor*, definitively excludes the very claim that Pope Francis makes in *Amoris Laetitia*, namely, that it is not always possible in certain situations to keep the commandments by God's grace (2

Cor 12:9). John Paul rejects such a claim. He says, "Even in the most difficult situations man must respect the norm of morality so that he can be obedient to God's holy commandment and consistent with his own dignity as a person. Certainly, maintaining a harmony between freedom and truth occasionally demands uncommon sacrifices, and must be won at a high price: it can even involve martyrdom. But, as universal and daily experience demonstrates, man is tempted to break that harmony: 'I do not do what I want, but I do the very thing I hate... I do not do the good I want, but the evil I do not want' (Rom 7:15, 19)." Of course, adds John Paul, "In this context, appropriate allowance is made both for *God's mercy* towards the sinner who converts and for the *understanding of human weakness*. Such understanding never means compromising and falsifying the standard of good and evil in order to adapt it to particular circumstances. It is quite human for the sinner to acknowledge his weakness and to ask mercy for his failings; what is unacceptable is the attitude of one who makes his own weakness the criterion of the truth about the good, so that he can feel self-justified, without even the need to have recourse to God and his mercy." And when we fail to do so we have the Lord's promise: "If we confess our sins, He is faithful and just to forgive us our sins and to cleanse us from all unrighteousness" (1 John 1:9).

Finally, Flannery & Berg are correct: "Sound pastoral discernment will embrace such true, exceptionless moral principles and endeavor to find a way, consistent with God's mercy and justice, of explaining their application even to particular situations that call for personal asceticism and sacrifice."[169] This pastoral strategy is consistent with 2 Cor 12:9, "Jesus said [in response to St. Paul's prayer], 'My grace is sufficient for you, for my power is made perfect in weakness.'" However, not with the claim of those who say that the Church's teaching on marriage is, according to Kasper, "too hard for the 'ordinary Christian' to follow," and hence that the moral law may be adapted to a person's situational possibilities.[170] This position inserts gradualness into the moral law itself—"as if there were in divine law various levels or forms of precept for various persons and conditions."[171] *Pace* Kasper, Francis's position cannot be justified by reference to Aquinas who allegedly thought, "'someone may possess grace and charity, yet not be able to exercise any one of the virtues well'" (AL §301).[172] Francis refers to two works of Aquinas to explain his position that an individual may find himself in a concrete situation where he is forced to choose between two moral evils; he cannot act differently and choose otherwise without further sin: ST I-II, q. 65, art. 3 ad 2; De Malo, q. 2, art. 2.

Regarding the second reference, Flannery & Berg state, "It is difficult to find anything in this article having to do with people who have infused virtues but cannot exercise them well."[173] As to the first reference, it is one thing to claim—legitimately—that people acting in accordance with the virtues can experience difficulty; another to claim that they are less obliged to act in accordance with them.[174] Yes, regarding the experience of difficulty, it is important to understand that being in a "state of grace...

can coexist with a *difficulty* in actively exercising a virtue."[175] Being justified in Christ does not exempt believers from the lifelong struggle against sinful tendencies. Francis rightly holds that "The Christian life is a constant battle" (GE §158). This is different from claiming—as Francis seems to be suggesting about Aquinas—"the state of grace can coexist with an *act* that is gravely contrary to a virtue (a mortal sin)."[176] Bonino explains why Francis may not appeal to Aquinas to justify his view. "Whatever otherwise may be the case concerning the question of a possible coexistence between, on the one hand, the life of grace, and, on the other hand, voluntary acts that objectively are of a gravely sinful nature (such as adulterous sexual relations) but that may not be mortal sins due to subjective conditioning, this is not directly what the thesis of St. Thomas intends."[177] *Pace* Francis, here, too, he cannot say that he "follows the classical doctrine of St. Thomas Aquinas."

Appendix

Throughout his pontificate Pope Francis has consistently taught—even if his teaching has not been in the limelight compared to his teaching on environmental issues—the conjugal view of marriage—marriage as the two-in-one-flesh union between a man and a woman. Suffice it here to give a sample of statements that confirm his unequivocal support for this view. For example, in his trip to the Philippines in early 2015 Pope Francis said: "The family is also threatened by growing efforts on the part of some to redefine the very institution of marriage, by relativism, by the culture of the ephemeral, by a lack of openness to life. Our world needs good and strong families to overcome these threats! The Philippines needs holy and loving families to protect the beauty and truth of the family in God's plan and to be a support and example for other families. Every threat to the family is a threat to society itself. The future of humanity, as Saint John Paul II often said, passes through the family [cf. FC §85].... Be sanctuaries of respect for life, proclaiming the sacredness of every human life from conception to natural death. What a gift this would be to society, if every Christian family lived fully its noble vocation!"[178] Also, in his homily at the Mass at the Cathedral of the Immaculate Conception, Manila, 16 January 2015, he urged the faithful, "Proclaim the beauty and truth of the Christian message to a society which is tempted by confusing presentations of sexuality, marriage and the family." The pope continues: "As you know, these realities are increasingly under attack from powerful forces which threaten to disfigure God's plan for creation and betray the very values which have inspired and shaped all that is best in your culture."[179] Here are some other examples.

In Francis's "Opening Speech to the Humanum Conference," an International Ecumenical and Interreligious Conference on Traditional Marriage, 17-19 November 2014, he defends the complementarity of man and woman in marriage and family life. "It is fitting that you have gathered here in this international colloquium to explore the complementarity of man and woman. This complementarity is at the root of marriage and family.... Children have a right to grow up in a family with a father and a mother capable of creating a suitable environment for the child's development and emotional maturity."[180]

In this connection, it is important to emphasize that Pope Francis's anthropology underscores sexual complementarity of man and woman. In his address to the Plenary Assembly of the Pontifical Council for Culture, 7 February 2015, he said: "The first theme [of this assembly] is: Between equality and difference: seeking a balance. This aspect should not be approached ideologically, because the 'lens' of ideology impedes one from seeing reality well. The equality and difference of women—like men—are perceived better from the perspective of 'with', of relationship, than 'against.' For some time, we have left behind us, at least in Western societies, the model of the social subordination of women to men, a secular model which, however, has never been spent of all its negative effects,' Francis noted. 'We have also overcome a second model, that of mere equality, applied mechanically, and of absolute equality. A new paradigm was configured, that of reciprocity and in equivalence and in difference. The man-woman relationship, therefore, should recognize that both are necessary in that they possess, yes, an identical nature, but with their own modality.'"[181] In another example, Francis asks, "What is marriage? It is a true and authentic vocation, as are the priesthood and the religious life. Two Christians who marry have recognized the call of the Lord in their own love story, the vocation to form one flesh and one life from two, male and female."[182] Another example is found in Francis's General Audience of 2 April 2014: "So God created mankind in his own image, in the image of God he created them; male and female he created them.... That is why a man leaves his father and mother and is united to his wife, and they become one flesh". "The image of God is a married couple, man and woman, not only man, not only woman, but rather both. This is the image of God: love, God's alliance with us is represented in the alliance between man and woman."[183] Still another: "The first setting in which faith enlightens the human city is the family. I think first and foremost of the stable union of man and woman in marriage. This union is born of their love, as a sign and presence of God's own love, and of the acknowledgment and acceptance of the goodness of sexual differentiation, whereby spouses can become one flesh [cf. Gen 2:24] and are enabled to give birth to a new life, a manifestation of the Creator's goodness, wisdom and loving plan" (LF, §52). Again, *Evangelii Gaudium*:

> The family is experiencing a profound cultural crisis, as are all communities and social bonds. In the case of the family, the weakening of these bonds is particularly serious because the family is the fundamental cell of society, where we learn to live with others despite our differences and to belong to one another; it is also the place where parents pass on the faith to their children. Marriage now

> tends to be viewed as a form of mere emotional satisfaction that can be constructed in any way or modified at will. But the indispensible contribution of marriage to society transcends the feelings and momentary needs of the couple. As the French bishops have taught, it is not born 'of loving sentiment, ephemeral by definition, but from the depth of the obligation assumed by the spouses who accept to enter a total communion of life' [Conférence Des Évêques De France, Conseil Famille et Société, *Élargir le mariage aux personnes de même sexe? Ouvrons le débat!* (28 September 2012)]. (EG §66)

In this passage, Francis is criticizing the conception of marriage that S. Girgis, R. Anderson, and R. George call the "revisionist view" and which they critically examine and contrast with the conjugal view (Francis's own teaching).[184] A more philosophical defense of conjugal marriage is given by Robert George and Patrick Lee.[185] Furthermore, Pope Francis, in a question and answer time with Schoenstatt Movement, the international Marian movement, Pope Francis warned that the sacrament of marriage has been reduced to a mere association, and urged participants to be witnesses in a secular world. "The family is being hit, the family is being struck and the family is being bastardized," the Pope told those in attendance at the audience on 25 October 2014. He warned against the common view in society that "you can call everything family, right?" "What is being proposed is not marriage, it's an association. But it's not marriage! It's necessary to say these things very clearly and we have to say it!" Pope Francis stressed and lamented that there are so many "new forms" of unions which are "totally destructive and limiting the greatness of the love of marriage."[186]

Given Jorge Mario Bergoglio's integral involvement in the writing of the Aparecida document, we may cite it as support for his views. "Among the premises that weaken and undermine family life, we find the ideology of gender, according to which each everyone can choose his or her sexual orientation, without taking into account the differences set to them by human nature. This has led to legislative changes that gravely injure the dignity of marriage, respect for the right to life, and the identity of the family" (§40). "We bless God for having created the human being man and woman, although today some would seek to confuse this truth: 'God created man in his image; in the divine image he created him; male and female he created them' [Gen 1:27]. It is part of human nature that man and woman seek their reciprocity and complementarity in one another" (§116). Finally, his support for the view that family life is grounded in the conjugal view of marriage goes back to 27 July 2010. He affirmed in a letter to the Argentinean Bishops' Conference "the need to ensure the right of children to have a father and a mother for their upbringing and education.... This is not merely a question of terminology or formal conventions of a private relationship. Rather, it is a natural anthropological bond.... Marriage precedes the state: it is the foundation for the family and for a cell within society, predating any legislation, and even predating the Church itself. Therefore, the approval of a law in favor of same-sex marriage would mean a very real and grave step backward from an anthropological point of view."[187]

NOTES

1. John Paul II, "Discorso Di Giovanni Paolo II Ai Partecipanti Al Congresso Internazionale Di Teologia Morale," §1.
2. Benedict XVI, "La pastorale del matrimonio deve fondarsi sulla verità."
3. Romano Guardini, *Wahrheit des Denkens und Wahrheit des Tuns*, ed. J. Messerschmid, 3d ed. (Paderborn, 1980), 85; as cited by Joseph Ratzinger in "Pluralism as a Problem for Church and Theology," 92n20.
4. Bishop Johan Bonny, Roger Burggraeve, *Mag ik? Sorry, Dank je, Vrijmoedige dialoog over relaties, huwelijk en gezin* (Lannoo, 2016). See my article review, "Belgium bishop co-authors book in support of pre-marital sex, same-sex relations."
5. David Schoenmaekers, "Kardinal De Kesel vindt seksualiteitsbeleving bij holebi's aanvaardbaar."
6. So, too, GS §48. See the Appendix to this chapter for a sampling of statements from Pope Francis showing his unequivocal support for conjugal marriage as the two-in-one-flesh union of a man and a woman.
7. Pope Francis, with Dominique Wolton, *A Future of Faith, The Path of Change in Politics and Society*, 225.
8. Josef Seifert correctly states, "Throughout the entire world, many voices have responded to the post-synodal apostolic exhortation *Amoris Laetitia* with joy and praise for the latest document by Pope Francis. And its text contains no doubt many beautiful thoughts and deep truths that lift up the reader's mind to the beauty and happiness of true love, glorify God and delight the reader. In particular, the text exudes the merciful love of God and of the Pope for all persons in all situations of economic or moral poverty and of material and spiritual wealth, of sin and of virtue. The text contains treasures of wisdom." ("*Amoris Laetitia*: Joy, Sadness and Hopes," 168-69).
9. John Paul II already called for a human ecology in his 1991 Encyclical *Centesimus Annus*, §38.
10. Benedict XVI, too, calls for a moral and human ecology in his address to the Bundestag, 22 September 2011. He had earlier made this point in an Address to the Roman Curia, 22 December 2008. Furthermore, Benedict stated regarding so-called "gender theory" in a 2012 "Address of his Holiness Benedict XVI on the Occasion of Christmas Greetings to the Roman Curia."
11. The recent Evangelical Protestant declaration, the Nashville Statement, may best be seen as a contribution—whatever its limitations—to the promotion of an integral human ecology. A context for discussing the Nashville Statement is the Salzburg Declaration (SD). In Salzburg, Austria, 6 September 2015, a historic ecumenical Congress organized by the (Protestant) *International Christian Network* (*Internationale Konferenz Bekennender Gemeinschaften*) met to consider current cultural threats to the human person and his created nature, and a plan for responding to them. This document is called the Salzburg Declaration: "Current Threats to Human Creatureliness and Their Overcoming: Life According to the Creator's Will." The participants expressed concern that while the ecology of the environment is well developed the same cannot be said for the "ecology of man." It is in the light of the call for an integral ecology of man that we should understand and appreciate the Nashville Statement. See my article, "The Nashville Statement is part of

an ecumenical 'ecology of man.'"

12. John Paul II, *Man and Woman He Created Them: A Theology of the Body.*

13. See Francis, *Amoris Laetitia* §297, "Here I am not speaking only of the divorced and remarried, but of everyone, in whatever [irregular] situation they find themselves." For example, Blase Cardinal Cupich has drawn out the implications of the logic of pastoral reasoning and discernment to homosexual relations (DeBernardo, "Cupich: Synod Would Have Gained from Hearing from Lesbian and Gay Couples"). This logic was already evident in the extraordinary and ordinary synods on the family, 2014-2015, and it is reflected in *Amoris Laetitia.*

14. Pope Francis, "Preface to Stephen Walford, *Pope Francis, The Family and Divorce,*" xi-xii.

15. Similarly, in a recent book of interviews, Francis says, "To understand *Amoris Laetitia* you need to read it all the way from the beginning to the end. Start with the first chapter, and then go on to the second and so on... and reflect. And read what was said in the Synod" (*Open to God, Open to the World,* Pope Francis with Antonio Spadaro, 142).

16. Stephen Walford does not consider any of the critics of Chapter 8 of *Amoris Laetitia,* such as the late Germain Grisez, John Finnis, Josef Seifert, Robert Spaemann or the so-called "dubia" cardinals, such as the late Cardinal Carlo Caffara, to have raised one single legitimate point of criticism, or even a question of clarification. It seems that is because they do not understand Francis's work, or are blinded by their own presuppositions. Furthermore, he regards them all as "dissenters of the papal magisterium" who have "manufactured confusion" (Walford, Pope Francis, *The Family and Divorce,* xviii, xx). Representative of defenders of Chapter 8 of Francis's *Amoris Laetitia* is the claim that his critics do not understand him and hence not a legitimate question is raised of this chapter. See Massimo Borghesi, who falls into this camp, *The Mind of Pope Francis, Jorge Mario Bergoglio's Intellectual Journey,* 259-66.

17. This second hermeneutical principle obviously involves a reference to the significant address of Pope Benedict XVI, in his now famous 2005 Christmas address to the Roman Curia, where he called the hermeneutics of Vatican II "the 'hermeneutic of reform', of renewal in the continuity of the one subject-Church which the Lord has given to us. She is a subject which increases in time and develops, yet always remaining the same, the one subject of the journeying People of God."

18. Gerhard Cardinal Müller, "Development, or Corruption?"

19. Flannery and Berg, "*Amoris Laetitia,* Pastoral Discernment, and Thomas Aquinas," 87.

20. As I made clear in Chapter 1, it is not clear in Francis's hermeneutics of renewal exactly *what* is consolidated, expanded upon, and developed because he pays no attention to the intrinsic bond between mediating dogmas and the cognitive/propositional content of divine revelation. Given the historically conditioned formulations of dogma, with their possible correction, modification, and complementation, how is the historicity of dogma reconciled with the permanence of its meaning and truth. The original context makes clear that Vincent is referring to dogmas of the Christian religion to which this law of development applies. But Francis is referring to the Gospel message, the revealed truth, the substance of the deposit of the faith, to which this law applies. Now, although this passage of Vincent is cited several times by Francis, this question is never really answered. Pope Francis, *Laudato Si',* Encyclical Letter, 2015, §121. Endnote 98 explicitly refers to the *Commonitorium Primum,* 23.3, §29, of Vincent of Lérins. "Address of Pope Francis to the Community of the Pontifical Gregorian University, together with Members of the Pontifical Biblical Institute and the Pontifical Oriental Institute." Again, "Address of the Holy Father, Incontro Con I Rappresentanti del V Convegno Nazionale Della Chiesa Italiana," 10 November 2015. Most recently, he refers to it again in a book of interviews, *Open to God, Open to the World,* Pope Francis with Antonio Spadaro, SJ, 51.

21. Actually, hermeneutics means the theory and practice of interpretation. As Jens Zimmermann puts it, "The word 'hermeneutics' comes from the ancient Greek language (*hermeneuein* = to utter, to explain, to translate), and was first used by thinkers who discussed how divine messages or mental ideas are expressed in human language. The

ancient Greek philosopher Plato (427-347 BCE), for example, used the word *hermeneutics* in dealing with poets as 'hermeneutics of the divine', and his student Aristotle (384-322 BCE) wrote the first extant treatise on hermeneutics, in which he showed how spoken and written words were expressions of inner thoughts. Thus, from its very first appearance, the term *hermeneuein*, along with its later Latin equivalent 'interpretari', was associated with the task of understanding some kind of spoken or written communication" (*Hermeneutics, A Very Short Introduction* [Oxford: Oxford University Press, 2015). So, hermeneutics doesn't mean growth, but it may involve development by way of a clarifying interpretation, not mutability; progress, not change.

22. Pope Francis, with Dominique Wolton, *A Future of Faith, The Path of Change in Politics and Society*, 224.

23. See Francis, "Preface for Stephen Walford, *Pope Francis, The Family and Divorce*." Similarly, in *Open to God, Open to the World*, Francis says, "I want to repeat clearly that the morality of *Amoris Laetitia* is Thomist, the morality of the great Thomas" (142).

24. In the following sections, I am drawing on my book, *"In the Beginning": A Theology of the Body*, Chapter 5.

25. John Paul II, *Man and Woman He Created Them*, 3.3.

26. Ibid., 4.1.

27. On this point, see De Lubac, *Catholicism: Christ and the Common Destiny of Man*, 313-14.

28. Jacques Maritain, *Clairvoyance de Rome*, 222 (italics added), *"There is one error that consists in ignoring the distinction between nature and grace. There is another that consists in ignoring their union,"* as cited in De Lubac, "Apologetics and Theology," *Theological Fragments*, 91-104, and this citation at 103, note 28.

29. This theological understanding of the relation between nature, sin and grace is fundamental to John Paul II's *Theology of the Body*.

30. De Lubac, *A Brief Catechesis on Nature & Grace*, 81-82.

31. Joseph Ratzinger, *The Spirit of the Liturgy*, 24, 34.

32. The Rev. Thomas G. Guarino, *Foundations of Systematic Theology*, 20.

33. I owe this succinct way of formulating the various possibilities of relating nature, sin and grace to Albert Wolters, "What is to be done? Toward a neo-Calvinist Agenda." For an introduction to his thinking, see *Creation Regained*. For my own analysis of these various possibilities with respect to a Catholic theology of culture, see *Slitting the Sycamore: Christ and Culture in the New Evangelization*. Especially influential not only in my own thinking but also that of Wolter's on the relation between nature and grace are the writings of Dutch neo-Calvinist philosopher Herman Dooyeweerd (1894-1977). For a brief introduction to his thinking, see *In the Twilight of Western Thought: Studies in the Pretended Autonomy of Philosophical Thought*.

34. I am drawing here on Chapter 5 of my book, *"In the Beginning" A Theology of the Body*, 206-13.

35. See Matthias Joseph Scheeben, *Nature and Grace*, 308.

36. John Henry Newman, *Apologia Pro Vita Sua*, 222.

37. Robert Sokolowski, *The God of Faith & Reason, Foundations of Christian Theology*, 72.

38. E.L. Mascall, *The Openness of Being, Natural Theology Today*, 151, italics added.

39. Ibid., 153. These two maxims are derived from St. Thomas Aquinas, *Summa Theologiae*, I, q. 1, art. 8 ad 2, and I, q.2. art. 2 ad 1, respectively.

40. Pontifical Council for Culture, *Towards Pastoral Approach to Culture*, §6. The quotation inside this quotation is from John Paul II, "Homily of the Enthronement Mass."

41. Mascall, *The Openness of Being*, 153.

42. Ibid.

43. Cessario, *Christian Faith & The Theological Life*, 28.

44. Mascall, *The Openness of Being*, 150.

45. Pontifical Council for Justice and Peace, *Compendium of the Social Doctrine of the Church*, §109.

46. St. Augustine, *The City of God*, Book XIV, Chapter XI, http://www.ccel.org/ccel/schaff/npnf102.iv.XIV.11.html.

47. All the quotations in this paragraph, except the quotation from St. Augustine's *The City of God*, are from the *Catechism of the Catholic Church* §§1603, 1606-1609, 1614-1615.

48. Gilson, *Christianity and Philosophy*, 21, 24, and 111, respectively.

49. The quote within this quote is from Paul VI, *Evangelii Nuntiandi* §18. Paul VI then adds, "The purpose of evangelization is therefore precisely this interior change, and if it had to be expressed in one sentence the best way of stating it would be to say that the Church evangelizes when she seeks to convert, solely through the divine power of the message she proclaims, both the personal and collective consciences of people, the activities in which they engage, and the lives and concrete milieu which are theirs."

50. John Paul II, *Man and Woman He Created Them*, 99.7.

51. Ibid., 49.4.

52. This teaching is explicitly embraced by Benedict XVI, e.g., "Address of his Holiness Benedict XVI on the Occasion of Christmas Greetings to the Roman Curia"; and by Pope Francis, particularly in *Amoris Laetitia* §56, §§74-75, and *Laudato Si'* §155.

53. Patrick Lee and Robert George, "Sex and the Body," in *Body-Self Dualism in Contemporary Ethics and Politics*, 176-217. See also, William E. May, *Catholic Sexual Ethics*.

54. Lee and George, "Sex and the Body," 107.

55. John Paul II, *Letter to Families*, §19.

56. Wojtyla, "The Problem of Catholic Sexual Ethics," 287.

57. John Finnis, "Personal Integrity, Sexual Morality and Responsible Parenthood," at 177.

58. Wojtyla, "The Problem of Catholic Sexual Ethics," 289.

59. John Paul II develops the moral and anthropological significance of the unity of the human person as body and soul in *Veritatis Splendor*, §§46-50.

60. Joseph Ratzinger, *Eschatology, Death and Eternal Life*, 179-81. Ratzinger is persuaded that Aquinas' philosophical understanding of the "formula *anima forma corporis*: the soul is the form of the body" embodies a "complete transformation of Aristotelianism." He writes, "Thomas' twofold affirmation that the spirit is at once something personal and also the 'form' of matter would simply have been unthinkable for Aristotle.... And so we come at last to a really tremendous idea: the human spirit is so utterly one with the body that the term 'form' can be used of the body and retain its proper meaning. Conversely, the form of the body is spirit, and this is what makes the human being a person.... What seemed philosophically impossible has thus been achieved.... The soul belongs to the body as 'form', but that which is the form of the body is still spirit. It makes man a person and opens him to immortality. Compared with all the conceptions of the soul available in antiquity, this notion of the soul is quite novel. It is a product of Christian faith, and of the exigencies of faith for human thought" (Ibid., 148-49).

61. Wojtyla, *The Acting Person*, 11.

62. Ibid., 203-204.

63. John Paul II, *Man and Woman He Created Them*, 9.4; also note 18, and 12.5.

64. Wojtyla, *The Acting Person*, 205.

65. Herman Dooyeweerd, *A New Critique of Theoretical Thought*, Vol. III, 89. This, too, is the view of Reformed philosopher, Herman Dooyeweerd's philosophical anthropology, *Reformation and Scholasticism in Philosophy*, Volume Three, *Philosophy of Nature and Philosophical*

Anthropology, Part II, chapters 1-3: "[T]he human spirit cannot carry out any real acts outside its temporal corporal individuality-structure. For that reason, we said: it is the *individual human being* in the integral unity of 'body' and 'soul' who accomplishes the acts. The full person as a totality is the subject of the act.... In the acts, the 'soul' is actually operative in the entire enkaptic structure of the body, and only in the body does the soul have the capacity to do so, insofar as the acts are included in the temporal order of the body. In other words, we can take the 'acts' neither to be purely 'corporal' nor purely 'spiritual.' They are *both* inseparably connected and precisely for that reason they bear a *typically human* character. Only the act-structure in its *fundamental dependence upon the spirit* stamps the body as human" (162-63).

66. J. Budziszewski, *On The Meaning of Sex*, 28.

67. Eberhard Schockenhoff, *Natural Law & Human Dignity, Universal Ethics in an Historical World*, 208.

68. John Paul II, *Man and Woman He Created Them*, 7.2.

69. Schockenhoff, *Natural Law & Human Dignity*, 208.

70. Ibid., 208.

71. John Finnis, "Personal Integrity, Sexual Morality and Responsible Parenthood," 177.

72. John F. Crosby, "The Estrangement of Persons from their Bodies," 130-31.

73. Patrick Lee, "The Human Body and Sexuality in the Teaching of Pope John Paul II," 114.

74. Eberhard Schockenhoff, "A Consistent Ethic of Life (with a Few Blemishes)" 249.

75. Ibid.

76. Ibid.

77. Luijpen, *Existential Phenomenology*, 187-88.

78. Ibid., 313-14, note 64.

79. Ibid., 187-88.

80. John Paul II, *Man and Woman He Created Them*, 15.5. Cf. Francis, *Amoris Laetitia* §150.

81. Ibid., 15.2.

82. Müller, *The Cardinal Müller Report*, 147.

83. John Paul II, *Man and Woman He Created Them*, 15.2. "Such a doctrine revives, in new forms, certain ancient errors which have always been opposed by the Church, inasmuch as they reduce the human person to a 'spiritual' and purely formal freedom. This reduction misunderstands the moral meaning of the body and of kinds of behavior involving it [cf. 1 Cor 6:19]. Saint Paul declares that 'the immoral, idolaters, adulterers, sexual perverts, thieves, the greedy, drunkards, revilers, robbers' are excluded from the Kingdom of God [cf. 1 Cor 6:9]. This condemnation—repeated by the Council of Trent—lists as 'mortal sins' or 'immoral practices' certain specific kinds of behavior the willful acceptance of which prevents believers from sharing in the inheritance promised to them."

84. John Paul II, *Man and Woman He Created Them*, 7.2.

85. Ibid., 103.3.4.5.

86. Wojtyla, *Love and Responsibility*, 293.

87. For example, *Remaining in the Truth of Christ, Marriage and Communion in the Catholic Church*, Edited by Robert Dodaro, O.S.A.; *Eleven Cardinals Speak on Marriage and the Family*, Edited by Winfried Aymans; *The Gospel of the Family*, Juan José Pérez-Soba and Stephan Kampowski; and *Christ's New Homeland—Africa, Contribution to the Synod on the Family by African Pastors*, Translated by Michael J. Miller.

88. Inés San Martín, "Cardinal calls pope's family text 'development' in Church doctrine."

89. Fr. Raymond J. De Souza, "'Amoris Laetitia,' The Holy Spirit and the Synod of Surprises."

90. Richard Gaillardetz, "Francis wishes to release Vatican II's bold vision from Captivity"; emphasis added. Gaillardetz develops this notion of pastoral-oriented doctrinal development in his book, *An Unfinished Council, Vatican II, Pope Francis, and the Renewal of Catholicism.* I already critically discussed Gaillardetz's pastoral-oriented notion of doctrinal development in Chapter 1. It is not faithful to Vatican II's own Lérinian hermeneutics of renewal; rather, he holds an instrumentalist view of doctrine, in which doctrines are neither absolute truths nor objectively true affirmations; in fact, doctrines do not make assertions about objective reality at all.

91. Recent critics of Pope Francis's Apostolic Exhortation *Amoris Laetitia* (AL) have used either a "scatter gun" approach that hits everything in sight or a sniper's rifle aiming with accuracy at a specific target. The former leads to a hysterical approach to *Amoris Laetitia,* assuming that Pope Francis has given up everything; the latter approach is more tempered, raising serious questions, especially regarding the moral logic evident in certain paragraphs in Chapter 8. The former approach is irresponsible, but the latter is not.

92. *Pace* Borghesi, *The Mind of Pope Francis,* 260. In some cases, it is obvious that the writer has not read *Amoris Laetitia.* For example, Andrew Brown, "The War Against Pope Francis," *The Guardian,* 27 October 2017, "The document [*Amoris Laetitia*], written by Francis, is a summary of the current debate over divorce, and it is in this footnote that he makes an apparently mild assertion that divorced and remarried couples may sometimes receive communion."

93. Ross Douthat, *To Change the Church,* 82-93.

94. Cardinal Cupich, "'Not our Policy' to deny Communion to People in Same-Sex Marriages."

95. Ibid.

96. It is not surprising that Francis holds this view since he holds, "There is no white or black; there is white, black, gray, and then all the many shades of gray.... Life itself is gray; it is a journey in search of something toward which we cannot be rigid but, as society, proudly multicolored" (*God is Young,* 58).

97. Kevin L. Flannery, S.J. & Thomas V. Berg write, "The words "unmerited, unconditional and gratuitous" are taken from Francis's homily on 15 February 2015, to the then newly created Cardinals (*Acta Apostolicae Sedis* 107 [2015]: 258). A note makes reference to 1 Cor 13. The words are said in reference to charity, not mercy, although the immediately preceding paragraph speaks of mercy, mentioning "the repentant prodigal son." The sentence in AL is followed by an exclamatory affirmation that "no one can be condemned forever, because that is not the logic of the Gospel!" [This claim occurs earlier in this paragraph as well: 'The way of the Church is not to condemn anyone forever.'] One can only speculate about the Pope's meaning here. A charitable interpretation would say that he is referring to some kind of perpetual 'condemnation' during one's life (the possibility of eternal condemnation after death being a matter of revealed truth; the Church cannot withdraw Christ's offer of forgiveness to the repentant sinner" ("*Amoris Laetitia,* Pastoral Discernment, and Thomas Aquinas," 85n5). This, too, is Gerhard Cardinal Müller's interpretation: "Even when it is said 'that no one can be condemned forever' this must be understood from the point of view of care, that never surrenders, for the eternal salvation of a sinner rather than as a categorical denial of the possibility of an eternal condemnation which, however, presupposes voluntary obstinacy in sin" ("Communion to the remarried, Müller, 'There can be mitigating factors in guilt.") It is also the reading of Walford, *Pope Francis, The Family and Divorce,* 64n6. Not unreasonably, the late Germain Grisez and John Finnis asked for clarification on this very point because it implies universalism, namely, that all men are saved. In their Letter to Pope Francis, "The Misuse of *Amoris Laetitia* to Support Errors Against the Catholic Faith," they cite the following references to *Amoris Laetitia*: "since by virtue of Christ's redemptive act and God's "indulgent love" (AL 62), every human person will inherit eternal life and none will end in hell (see AL 117, 297, 310, 325; also see Encyclical *Laudato Sí,* 83 and 243). For a refutation of that implication from these assertions of Pope Francis, see 23-30 of the Letter. To the best of my knowledge, there are only two times in his six-year pontificate where Francis states that there is a limit to God's mercy, such that he says that Jesus rejects man. "Je-

sus 'is good and merciful', but he is also 'just'. So beware of rejecting him: 'If you close the door of your heart from within, He cannot open it, because He is very respectful of our heart'. And to 'those who reject Jesus, Jesus waits, he will give a second chance, perhaps a third, a fourth, a fifth... But in the end, he will be the one to reject you'. For Pope Francis the idea that 'in the end, Jesus forgives everything' works only to a certain point." (Salvatore Cernuzio, "The Pope, 'Beware of rejecting Jesus: He is good, merciful, he waits, but in the end, it is He who rejects.") See also, Glatz, "God's wrath is just as great as his mercy, Pope warns."

98. For a meticulous analysis of the concept and examples of possible "irregular situations," see Josef Seifert, "*Amoris Laetitia*, Joy, Sadness and Hopes."

99. This, too, is the position of Benedict XVI, "[P]astoral care must not be understood as if it were somehow in conflict with the law. Rather, one should begin by assuming that the fundamental point of encounter between the law and pastoral care is love for the truth: truth is never something purely abstract, but 'a real part of the human and Christian journey of every member of the faithful' [*Propositio* 40]," *Sacramentum Caritas*.

100. Francis, "God makes us His Children and His Brothers and Sisters, not Members of an Agency," in *Only Love Can Save*, 91-95, and at 93. In a statement that I have always found extremely baffling "Religion has the right to express its opinion in the service of the people, but God in creation has set us free: it is not possible to interfere spiritually in the life of a person" (*A Big Heart Open to God*, 33). It is not at all clear what this means here. Elsewhere, in *On Heaven and Earth*, Francis gives us some perspective on what he might mean. "The religious minister... does not have the right to force anything on anyone's private life. If God, in creation, runs the risk of making us free, who am I to get involved? We condemn spiritual harassment that takes place when a minister imposes directive, conduct, and demands in such a way that it takes away the freedom of the other person. God left the freedom to sin in our hands. One has to speak very clearly about values, limits, commandments, but spiritual and pastoral harassment is not allowed" (114).

101. In Chapter 1, I considered Francis's problematic dismissal of the notion of abstract truth, his reluctance to speak of "absolute" truth, which I suggest has something to do with the absence of the notion of moral absolutes in Chapter 8 of *Amoris Laetitia*, and his theologico-pastoral epistemology and its attending principle prioritizing realities over ideas.

102. Francis, "Homily of his Holiness Pope Francis, Holy Chrism Mass." See Fr. Gerald Murray, "Of Truth and Idols."

103. Bergoglio, "The Importance of Academic Formation," 143.

104. I understand that it is a common practice to refer to all human beings as "children of God," but this is theologically erroneous. Yes, all men are created in the image of God (see Gen 1:27). God is the "father" of all because he is the Creator of the human family (Eph 3:14-15). Man—male and female—was fashioned in his very image (Gen 1:26-27), and he exercises sovereignty over all. But being a son or daughter of God is an adopted status (Gal 4:4-7) by virtue of Christian Baptism. In Jesus' conversation with Nicodemus, he tells him "you *must* be born again" (John 3:7), and St. Paul wrote, "not by works of righteousness which we have done, but according to His mercy He saved us, through the washing of regeneration and renewing of the Holy Spirit" (Titus 3:5). The reborn child of God is called to "be renewed in the spirit of [his] mind, and that [he] put on the new man which was created according to God, in true righteousness and holiness" (Eph 4:23-24). As Cessario astutely notes (*Christian Faith & The Theological Life*, 28-29), overlooking this distinction "threatens to confuse God's creative presence to the human creature with the realization of the same person's call to beatitude. The danger here is the risk of emphasizing the pervasive and inclusive character of divine grace in a way that practically eliminates the need for a real grace of justification—one that effectively transforms an impious person into a holy one. But the New Testament makes it exceedingly difficult to glide over the fact that the justification won by the blood of Christ really involves a movement from our being 'by nature children of wrath, like everyone else' to our being 'alive together with Christ—by grace you have been saved'" (Eph. 2:3, 5).

105. Francis, "Homily of his Holiness Pope Francis, Holy Chrism Mass."

106. Os Guiness, *Time for Truth: Living Free in a World of Lies, Hype, & Spin.*

107. Inspired by Pope Francis, Johannes zu Eltz, Catholic Dean of the city of Frankfurt am Main, in the preface of the German edition of James Martin, SJ, *Building a Bridge*, Zu Eltz says, "The steps which James Martin mentions in his book are important for the church in Germany, as well. To me, the next step for the church is to accept and appreciate the relationships of homosexual couples and to give them the opportunity to be blessed in a liturgical service. Put simply, the question is whether the church is able to learn that good things happen in those relationships; that homosexual couples who cannot celebrate the Sacrament of Matrimony (civil same sex marriage was established by law in Germany in 2017) by their companionship give birth to moral goods for themselves and for others: love, loyalty, commitment, fecundity, chastity. If this is true, then there is the possibility to confirm these goods and to ask for God's providence and guidance for this couple. That is what we call a blessing." For my refutation of the proposal to bless same-sex couples, see the Conclusion.

108. Similarly, Gerhard Cardinal Müller correctly writes, "Even when some constitutive elements of marriage are found in cohabitations that resemble marriage, however, the sinful transgression against other constitutive elements of marriage and against marriage as a whole, is not good. Contradiction with goodness can never become part of it, or the beginning of a journey towards the fulfillment of God's holy and sanctifying will" ("Communion to the remarried, 'There can be mitigating factors in guilt.'") Stephen Walford completely overlooks this problem with Francis's pastoral strategy, *Pope Francis, The Family and Divorce*, 131. Elsewhere Müller says, "This principle ["seeds of the Word"] does not legitimize immoral relationships, however, because the seeds of the Word do not abide in sinful situations such as cohabitation without marriage and other types of sexual unions. In these situations, despite the fact that it might seem otherwise, there can be no authentic dynamic of love but, rather, only a serious obstacle to the ability to grow in humanity" (*The Cardinal Müller Report*, 53). Inexplicably, Müller overlooks that this point is precisely what Francis affirms, see "Communion to the remarried."

109. Francis, *A Big Heart Open to God*, 35. The Congregation for the Doctrine of the Faith during the pontificate of John Paul II takes a completely different approach to Jesus' pastoral strategy in the 1989 commentary, "The moral norm of *Humanae Vitae* and pastoral duty." "The Gospels bear witness to the fact that truth and mercy unite to form the single and undivided attitude of the Lord Jesus. His pastoral attitude is revealed in an outstandingly clear and typical example in the word which Jesus addresses to the woman who was a sinner: "Has no one condemned you?... Neither do I condemn you, go, and do not sin again" (John 8:10-11). Calling good and evil by their right names, Jesus does not falsify moral truth, but bears witness to it in an unmistakable way, and in offering his merciful love to the woman who had sinned and repented, he leads her back to the truth and to salvation. Thus love and pastoral concern towards couples in difficulty can never (*if one means to offer them real help*) be separated from the truth, and can never evade or dilute the duty of calling good and evil by their right names. As was well said by Paul VI in his Encyclical, 'it is an outstanding manifestation of charity towards souls to omit nothing from the saving doctrine of Christ' (HV §29)."

110. But not in *The Name of God is Mercy*. See Chapter 3 of this book.

111. Francis does not always overlook the hermeneutical value of sin in explaining human reality. "Nor can we overlook the social degeneration brought about by sin, as, for example, when human beings tyrannize nature, selfishly and even brutally ravaging it. This leads to the desertification of the earth (cf. Gen 3:17-19) and those social and economic imbalances denounced by the prophets, beginning with Elijah (cf. 1 Kgs 21) and culminating in Jesus' own words against injustice [cf. Luke 12:13; 16:1-31]" (AL §26).

112. Karl Rahner, *Theological Investigations*, XIII, 90.

113. Stephen Walford presents a straw man when he says that those who reject the moral logic in the pastoral reasoning and discernment of *Amoris Laetitia*, Chapter 8, are "guided simply by a manual of prohibitions [rather than] the centrality of our relationship to

the merciful Christ" ("The Magisterium of Pope Francis: His Predecessors Come to His Defense." Similarly, he claims to enlist Ratzinger on his side by citing his statement, "As judge, Christ is not a cold legalist" ("Amoris Laetitia: The Questions that Really Need Answers").

114. Indeed, Francis insists now and again in response to the charge that his view of mercy is sentimental and distorts the Gospel, as we saw in Chapter 2, that "mercy does not exclude justice and truth" (ibid.). But he is more concerned that "we [not] put so many conditions on mercy that we empty it of its concrete meaning and real significance. That is the worst way of watering down the Gospel." Francis's approach is inclusion in the ecclesial community first; conversion second. For example, he welcomes cohabiting couples into the Church without any conditions, such as repentance. See on cohabitation, Francis, "Address of His Holiness Pope Francis to Participants in the Course on the Marriage Process." This approach has come to be known as the Zacchaeus paradigm. It is prominent in the work of James Martin, SJ, and San Diego Bishop Robert McElroy. For the former, see his "How parishes can welcome L.G.B.T. Catholics." For the latter, see his "Speech at the 2018 Assembly of the Association of US Catholic Priests." For a critique of their approach, see Leroy Huizenga, "Abusing Zacchaeus."

115. On cohabitation, see Francis, "Address of His Holiness Pope Francis to Participants in the Course on the Marriage Process": "At the same time, reach out in the Gospel way by meeting and welcoming young people who prefer to live together without being married. On the spiritual and moral level, they are among the poor and the little ones, towards whom the Church, following in the footsteps of her Master and Lord, seeks to be a mother who does not abandon but draws near and takes care of them."

116. This approach is contrary to St. Paul in 1 Cor 5:6-11, "Do you not know that a little leaven leavens the whole lump? Therefore, purge out the old leaven, that you may be a new lump, since you truly are unleavened. For indeed Christ, our Passover, was sacrificed for us. Therefore, let us keep the feast, not with old leaven, nor with the leaven of malice and wickedness, but with the unleavened bread of sincerity and truth. I wrote to you in my epistle not to keep company with sexually immoral people. Yet I certainly did not mean with the sexually immoral people of this world, or with the covetous, or extortioners, or idolaters, since then you would need to go out of the world. But now I have written to you not to keep company with anyone named a brother, who is sexually immoral, or covetous, or an idolater, or a reviler, or a drunkard, or an extortioner—not even to eat with such a person."

117. See note 109. Most recently, we find that caricature, not to say distortion, of John Paul II's view of the relationship of doctrine and pastoral approach, between mercy and truth, the Church as Teacher and as Mother (see RP §34; VS §§95-105), or in Thomas Knieps-Port Le Roi's own words, "church as a fortress of truth" and as a "field hospital," to be such that it stems from overlooking John Paul's emphasis on the "coexistence and mutual influence of two equally important [complementary] principles [of mercy and truth] ("Preserving and Perpetuating the Heritage of Pope John Paul II," at 514).

118. *Contra* Fastiggi & Goldstein, "Does Amoris Laetitia 303 Really Undermine Catholic Moral Teaching?" John Paul II "Reconciliation in the sacrament of Penance which would open the way to the Eucharist, can only be granted to those who, repenting of having broken the sign of the Covenant and of fidelity to Christ, are sincerely ready to undertake a way of life that is no longer in contradiction to the indissolubility of marriage. This means, in practice, that when, for serious reasons, such as for example the children's upbringing, a man and a woman cannot satisfy the obligation to separate, they 'take on themselves the duty to live in complete continence, that is, by abstinence from the acts proper to married couples'" (FC §84). This is also his position in *Reconciliatio et Paenitentia* §34, and Benedict XVI's position in *Sacramentum Caritatis* §29.

119. For accuracy's sake, the Second Vatican Council's text, GS §51, is not addressing the case of the divorced and civilly remarried abstaining from sexual intimacy; rather this text is addressing married couples: "where the intimacy of married life is broken off, its faithfulness can sometimes be imperiled and its quality of fruitfulness ruined, for then the upbringing of the children and the courage to accept new ones are both endangered."

Hence, Francis' claim is not supported by *Gaudium et Spes*.

120. Gerhard Cardinal Müller, "Development, or Corruption?" For a critique of Walford's defense of the moral justification of ongoing sexual relations in the union of civilly remarried divorcees, see Dan Hitchens, "Against Inevitable Adultery."

121. Douthat, *To Change the Church*, 96.

122. Ibid., 98. Since Stephen Walford does not think that a legitimate question can be raised here, he blindly and insouciantly defends a morally permissible choice that is made under a lesser-of-two-evils calculus. See Walford, "Amoris Laetitia: The Questions That Really Needs Answers."

123. On Spadaro's approval of cohabitation, following the lead of Pope Francis as well as the 2015 Synod on the Family, see Spadaro, "The welcoming of those young people who prefer to live together without getting married." For a critique of this approach, see Maureen Mullarkey, "Cohabitation & Mother Church."

124. Francesco Cardinal Coccopalmerio, *A Commentary on Chapter Eight of Amoris Laetitia*.

125. Víctor Manuel Fernández, "El capítulo VIII de Amoris Laetitia: lo que queda después de la tormenta," 449-68. For an English-language summary of this article, see Austin Ivereigh,"Papal confidante says 'Amoris' critics locked in 'death-trap' logic." For a critique of Archbishop Fernandez's claims, see Raymond J. de Souza, "Papal Adviser Undermines Magisterium 'in a Discreet Way.'"

126. Kasper, in particular, was asked, in an interview with the Catholic magazine *Commonweal*, "So, just to be clear, when you talk about a divorced and remarried Catholic not being able to fulfill the rigorist's requirements without incurring a new guilt, what would he or she be guilty of? The breakup of the second family. If there are children, you cannot do it. If you're engaged to a new partner, you've given your word, and so it's not possible" (Boudway et al, "An Interview with Cardinal Walter Kasper.")

127. Cardinal Cupich, "'Not our Policy' to deny Communion to People in Same-Sex Marriages."

128. Serge-Thomas Bonino, O.P., "Saint Thomas Aquinas in the Apostolic Exhortation *Amoris Laetitia*," 510.

129. Thomas Aquinas, *Summa Theologiae*, I-II, q. 19, a. 6, ad 3. See also, Flannery and Berg, "*Amoris Laetitia*, Pastoral Discernment, and Thomas Aquinas," 92-93. Thomas's solution—but not Francis's—is the solution of the Pontifical Council for the Family, "Vademecum for Confessors Concerning some Aspects of the Morality of Conjugal Life," §9: "The pastoral 'law of gradualness', not to be confused with the 'gradualness of the law' which would tend to diminish the demands it places on us, consists of requiring a *decisive break* with sin together with a *progressive path* towards total union with the will of God and with his loving demands" [Cf. FC §34]."

130. Coccopalmerio, *A Commentary on Chapter Eight of Amoris Laetitia*, 15-29.

131. Ibid., 19.

132. Ibid., 20 and 25.71-83.

133. Coccopalmerio would even give "absolution" to such an individual in the confessional. In a 1 March 2017, interview, he said, "To the one who says, 'I'm in grave sin, but I don't want to change' [absolution is not possible]. When someone comes to confess and says to you, 'I committed this sin. I want to change, but I know that I am not capable of changing, but I want to change', what do you do? Do you send him away? No, you absolve him." (Edward Pentin, "Cardinal Coccopalmerio Explains His Positions on Catholics in Irregular Unions.")

134. For the sake of accuracy, furthermore, John Paul II is not speaking in *Familaris Consortio* §34 about the inherent values of marital permanence and indissolubility but rather about the Church's teaching on the responsible transmission of life. Furthermore, the Council states: "This council realizes that certain modern conditions often keep couples from arranging their married lives harmoniously, and that they find themselves in cir-

cumstances where at least temporarily the size of their families should not be increased. As a result, the faithful exercise of love and the full intimacy of their lives is hard to maintain. But where the intimacy of married life is broken off, its faithfulness can sometimes be imperiled and its quality of fruitfulness ruined, for then the upbringing of the children and the courage to accept new ones are both endangered. To these problems there are those who presume to offer dishonorable solutions indeed; they do not recoil even from the taking of life. But the Church issues the reminder that a true contradiction cannot exist between the divine laws pertaining to the transmission of life and those pertaining to authentic conjugal love." (GS §51)

135. Flannery and Berg, "*Amoris Laetitia*, Pastoral Discernment, and Thomas Aquinas," 93.

136. John Paul II, "Homily at the Close of the Fifth Synod of Bishops" §11. The problem is in the way that Francis conceives the unity of teaching and practice. He there affirms unity as "certainly necessary in the Church, but this does not preclude various ways of interpreting some aspects of that teaching or drawing consequences from it" (AL §3).

137. John Paul II, "Homily at the Close of the Fifth Synod of Bishops," which is not available in English on the Vatican website.

138. Ibid., §7.

139. Coccopalmerio, *A Commentary on Chapter Eight of Amoris Laetitia*, 16.

140. Aquinas, *De malo*, q. 3, a. 8, as quoted in Flannery and Berg, "*Amoris Laetitia*, Pastoral Discernment, and Thomas Aquinas," 90.

141. Karl Rahner, SJ, "The Appeal to Conscience," at 50.

142. J. Budziszewski, *Written on the Heart: The Case for Natural Law*, 63-64.

143. In addition to a "rejection of values concerning the family and marriage," Francis mentions, chiefly, economic causes, such as "being opposed to anything institutional or definitive; it can also be done while awaiting more security in life (a steady job and steady income).... [Thus] celebrating a marriage is considered too expensive in the social circumstances. As a result, material poverty drives people into de facto unions" (*Amoris Laetitia* §294).

144. Josef Seifert, "Amoris Laetitia, Joy, Sadness and Hopes," *Aemaet* Wissenschaftliche Zeitschrift für Philosophie und Theologie, Bd. 5, Nr. 2 (2016): 160-249.

145. I owe this diagram to Branislav Kuljovsky, "The Law of Gradualness or the Gradualness of Law? A Critical Analysis of *Amoris Laetitia*," at 57.

146. Writes Francis, "Entering into pastoral dialogue with these persons is needed to distinguish elements in their lives that can lead to a greater openness to the Gospel of marriage in its fullness. In this pastoral discernment, there is a need to 'identify elements that can foster evangelization and human and spiritual growth" (AL §293). He adds, "By thinking that everything is black and white, we sometimes close off the way of grace and of growth" (AL §305).

147. Coccopalmerio said in a 2014 interview that the Church must "emphasize" the "positive realities" that he said are present in homosexual relationships. "If I meet a homosexual couple, I notice immediately that their relationship is illicit: the doctrine says this, which I reaffirm with absolute certainty. However, if I stop at the doctrine, I do not look anymore at the persons. But if I see that the two persons truly love each other, do acts of charity to those in need, for example... then I can also say that, although the relationship remains illicit, positive elements also emerge in the two persons. Instead of closing our eyes to such positive realities, I emphasize them. It is to be objective and objectively recognize the positive of a certain relationship, of itself illicit," he said in a 2014 interview with *Rossoporpora*" (Pete Baklinski, "Cardinal linked to Vatican gay orgy emphasized 'positive elements' in gay lifestyle."). This is a fundamentally flawed pastoral strategy. See my objections in note 109, and in Chapter 3.

148. On cohabitation, see the "Address of His Holiness Pope Francis to Participants in the Course on the Marriage Process": "At the same time, reach out in the Gospel way by

meeting and welcoming young people who prefer to live together without being married. On the spiritual and moral level, they are among the poor and the little ones, towards whom the Church, following in the footsteps of her Master and Lord, seeks to be a mother who does not abandon but draws near and takes care of them." This approach runs the serious risk of separating the Church as Mother from the Church as Teacher, of separating the pastoral from the doctrinal. Where is the illuminating truth expressed in the moral norm prohibiting fornication (CCC §2353), and all its consequences that offend the dignity of marriage, family, and weakening the sense of fidelity (CCC §2390)? Why don't we hear: "The sexual act must take place exclusively within marriage. Outside of marriage it always constitutes a grave sin and excludes one from sacramental communion?" Francis pastoral strategy is expressed in the following passage from *Amoris Laetitia* §78: "The light of Christ enlightens every person [cf. John 1:9; GS, 22]. Seeing things with the eyes of Christ inspires the Church's pastoral care for the faithful who are living together, or are only married civilly, or are divorced and remarried. Following this divine pedagogy, the Church turns with love to those who participate in her life in an imperfect manner: she seeks the grace of conversion for them; she encourages them to do good, to take loving care of each other and to serve the community in which they live and work... When a couple in an irregular union attains a noteworthy stability through a public bond—and is characterized by deep affection, responsibility towards the children and the ability to overcome trials—this can be seen as an opportunity, where possible, to lead them to celebrate the sacrament of Matrimony." As I argued in Chapter 3, Francis theologically justifies the good or constructive elements in these situations by employing the concept of the "*semina Verbi*," or "seeds of the Word," in order to find goodness or positive elements in these relationships, suggesting that these relationships *qua* relationships are imperfect forms, partial and analogous, and hence incomplete realizations of conjugal marriage, ordered to the good of an exclusive and permanent relationship. However, this approach—and the one in this passage where the Light of Christ is central—cannot do justice to the teaching of the *Catechism* because it does not take seriously the reality of sin and man's resistance to the light of Christ. Francis ignores that the human reception of that light is open to resistance and hence to distortion, misinterpretation, and rejection. John 1:9 describes light in its fullness and universality, but not every individual is in fact enlightened by the light. *Pace* Francis, therefore, the Word does not illuminate all human beings because they *resist* the light. Consider John 1:5, 10. "And the light shines in the darkness and the darkness has not understood it." "He was in the world, and the world was made through Him, and the world did not know Him." Both of these verses speak of the negative reaction of the world to the coming of the light. Where is this resistance to the Light in Francis's pedagogy?

149. Reminiscent of Pope Pius XII's description of "situation ethics: "Such judgments of conscience, however contrary they may seem at first sight to divine precepts, would be valid before God, because, they say, in the eyes of God a seriously formed conscience takes precedence over 'precept' and 'law'" ("Soyez les Bienvenues," Address to the Participants in the Congress of the World Federation of Catholic Young Women, §6).

150. Francis writes in *Amoris Laetitia* §305, "Discernment must help to find possible ways of responding to God and growing in the midst of limits. By thinking that everything is black and white, we sometimes close off the way of grace and of growth, and discourage paths of sanctification which give glory to God. Let us remember that 'a small step, in the midst of great human limitations, can be more pleasing to God than a life which appears outwardly in order, but moves through the day without confronting great difficulties' [EG §44]. The practical pastoral care of ministers and of communities must not fail to embrace this reality."

151. Flannery and Berg, "*Amoris Laetitia*, Pastoral Discernment, and Thomas Aquinas," 95.

152. Josef Seifert, "Does Pure Logic Threaten to Destroy the Entire Moral Doctrine of the Church." Similarly, Douthat, *To Change the Church*, 97.

153. I am aware that Francis denies that his reflection on "a specific discernment may lead people to think that the Church maintains a double standard" (AL §300). Notwithstanding his denial, that is precisely what his reflections imply.

154. John Paul then proceeds in VS §§57–61 to show how these views are at odds with Scripture and Tradition.

155. Blase Cardinal Cupich, "Pope Francis' Revolution of Mercy: Amoris Laetitia as a New Paradigm of Catholicity."

156. One may grant Fastiggi's claim that "Pope Francis does not consider conscience 'a faculty for autonomously deciding about good and evil' [fifth dubium of the five Cardinals]. Instead, he sees conscience as rooted in 'the living God' who helps to free us from the imprisonment of ourselves." Agreed. However, this clarification does not free us from understanding conscience as an oracle rather than an organ; plus, it is not clear in Francis—even when he sees conscience as rooted in the living God—that conscience is "the internal witness of both the existence and the law of God" (Newman). On this last point, Grisez & Finnis have rightly written regarding *Gaudium et Spes* §16, "But the Latin (for which alone the Fathers [of Vatican II] voted) unambiguously means 'the voice of this law' (In imo conscientiae legem homo detegit, quam ipse sibi non dat, sed cui obedire debet, et cuius vox, semper ad bonum amandum et faciendum ac malum vitandum eum advocans, ubi oportet auribus cordis sonat: fac hoc, illud devita.); the usual Italian and French translations (and even more closely and clearly the Spanish and German) sufficiently confirm this, and include nothing meaning or suggesting "voice of conscience."

157. *Contra* Archbishop Fernandez, "El capítulo VIII de Amoris Laetitia: lo que queda después de la tormenta," 454: "It is the formulation of the norm that cannot cover everything, not the norm in itself."

158. *Contra* Archbishop Fernandez, "El capítulo VIII de Amoris Laetitia: lo que queda después de la tormenta," 454-56. Also, *contra* Walford, *Pope Francis, The Family and Divorce*, 60, 92-93.

159. ST, IIa-IIae, q. 33, a.2. See also *Super Sent.* lib. 1 d. 48 q. 1 a. 2 ad 5; lib. 2 d. 40 q. 1 a. 2 co.; Super Sent., lib. 2 d. 36 q. 1 a. 5 ad 2. Numerous texts by Aquinas apply, moreover, these negative moral norms that hold semper et ad semper to the case of adultery: *Quodlibet* IX, q. 7 a. 2 co.; *Sententia Ethic.*, lib. 2 l. 7 n. 11; *De malo*, q. 15 a. 2 ad 6; *Super Sent.*, lib. 4 d. 33 q. 1 a. 3 qc. 3 co., ST, Suppl. q. 65, a. 5 co. but also to the case of rape, murder of innocents, lying, giving false testimony, etc.: ST, IIª-IIae q. 64 a. 6 co.; ST, IIª-IIae q. 64 a. 5 co.; ST, IIª-IIae q. 66 a. 5 co.; ST, IIª-IIae q. 70 a. 4 co.; ST, IIª-IIae q. 110 a. 3 co. I am grateful to my colleague, the Belgian Thomist, Jörgen Vijgen for these references to Aquinas's many works. See also, Bonino, "Saint Thomas Aquinas in the Apostolic Exhortation *Amoris Laetitia*," 513-19.

160. Flannery and Berg, "*Amoris Laetitia*, Pastoral Discernment, and Thomas Aquinas," 98-99.

161. Ibid., 99-100. See also, Flannery's article on the International Theological Commission, *In Search of a Universal Ethics: A New Look at Natural Law* (2009), which Francis appeals to in order to justify the indeterminacy of general principles when applied to particular actions: "Determinacy in Natural Law," *Nova et Vetera*, Vol. 9, No. 3 (2011) 763-73.

162. The distinction between negative norms and positive norms, moral absolutes and prima facie obligations, plays a fundamental role in John Paul II"s encyclical *Veritatis Splendor*: "The *negative precepts* of the natural law are universally valid. They oblige each and every individual, always and in every circumstance. It is a matter of prohibitions which forbid a given action *semper et pro semper*, without exception, because the choice of this kind of behaviour is in no case compatible with the goodness of the will of the acting person, with his vocation to life with God and to communion with his neighbour. It is prohibited — to everyone and in every case — to violate these precepts. They oblige everyone, regardless of the cost, never to offend in anyone, beginning with oneself, the personal dignity common to all" (VS §52). See also: "In the case of the positive moral precepts, prudence always has the task of verifying that they apply in a specific situation, for example, in view of other duties which may be more important or urgent. But the negative moral precepts, those prohibiting certain concrete actions or kinds of behaviour as intrinsically evil, do not allow for any legitimate exception. They do not leave room, in any morally acceptable way, for the "creativity" of any contrary determination what-

soever. Once the moral species of an action prohibited by a universal rule is concretely recognized, the only morally good act is that of obeying the moral law and of refraining from the action which it forbids" (VS §67).

163. *Pace* Borghesi, *The Mind of Pope Francis*, 263-65.

164. Flannery and Berg, "*Amoris Laetitia*, Pastoral Discernment, and Thomas Aquinas," 100-101.

165. Given the limits of this chapter, I cannot examine Flannery's thesis, namely, "Around the time of the Second Vatican Council, one begins to encounter in the writings of certain Catholic scholars the idea that the general precepts of the natural law are all well and good, but they cannot speak in a determinate way to particular situations and to particular acts that a person might perform" ("Determinacy in Natural Law," 763-64). Francis is under the influence of these scholars, as is evident from his view of the natural law and concrete action.

166. *Pace* Walford, *Pope Francis, The Family and Divorce*, 96.

167. Edward Pentin, "Full Text and Explanatory Notes of Cardinals' Questions on 'Amoris Laetitia.'" Emeritus Pope Benedict has recently written that the abandonment of moral absolutes—exceptionless moral norms—is one of the chief causes of the collapse of Catholic moral theology that rendered the Church defenseless against the sexual revolution and its impact on the culture and the Church. He states, "In the end, it was chiefly the hypothesis that morality was to be exclusively determined by the purposes of human action that prevailed. While the old phrase 'the end justifies the means' was not confirmed in this crude form, its way of thinking had become definitive. Consequently, there could no longer be anything that constituted an absolute good, any more than anything fundamentally evil; (there could be) only relative value judgments. There no longer was the (absolute) good, but only the relatively better, contingent on the moment and on circumstances." Benedict adds, "Pope John Paul II, who knew very well the situation of moral theology and followed it closely, commissioned work on an encyclical that would set these things right again. It was published under the title *Veritatis splendor* on August 6, 1993, and it triggered vehement backlashes on the part of moral theologians. Before it, the *Catechism of the Catholic Church* already had persuasively presented, in a systematic fashion, morality as proclaimed by the Church."

168. See Walford, *Pope Francis, The Family and Divorce*, 131, "Pope Francis has nevertheless taught that 'moral security' can be had when certain circumstances don't allow for the full objective ideal to be realized. In essence, this means that even if the sinfulness of an act remains, God will take into account our intentions, and the other factors that affect a decision made in good conscience."

169. Flannery and Berg, "*Amoris Laetitia*, Pastoral Discernment, and Thomas Aquinas," 110.

170. I have in mind here Walter Cardinal Kasper. In an interview with the Catholic magazine Commonweal, he said regarding the divorce and civilly remarried and the reception of communion: "But I would say that people must do what is possible in their situation. We cannot as human beings always do the ideal, the best. We must do the best possible in a given situation" (https://www.commonwealmagazine.org/interview-cardinal-walter-kasper). This, too, is the position of Stephen Walford, "In relation to St. John Paul II's requirement to live as brother and sister, that is an ideal that realism tells us is not always possible" ("Open Letter to the Four Dubia Cardinals").

171. Grisez, *Christian Moral Principles*, 687.

172. Aquinas is also cited in EG §171 to make the same point.

173. Flannery and Berg, "*Amoris Laetitia*, Pastoral Discernment, and Thomas Aquinas," 91n13.

174. Ibid.

175. Bonino, "Saint Thomas Aquinas in the Apostolic Exhortation *Amoris Laetitia*," 513.

176. Ibid.

177. Ibid.
178. Francis, "Address of His Holiness Pope Francis in Meeting with Families in Manila."
179. Francis X. Rocca, "Pope, in Philippines, says same-sex marriage threatens family."
180. Francis, "Pope Francis's Opening Address to Humanum Conference."
181. Idem, "Address to the Plenary Assembly of the Pontifical Council for Culture."
182. Idem, "Meeting with the Young People of Umbria."
183. Idem, "General Audience." St. Peter's Square, 2 April 2014.
184. Girgis, Sherif et al. *What is Marriage? Man and Woman, A Defense*.
185. Robert George and Patrick Lee, *Conjugal Union, What Marriage is and Why it Matters*.
186. Elise Harris, "'What is being proposed is not marriage'—Pope calls for defense of family."
187. Pope Francis, *Only Love Can Save Us*, Marriage, 127-29, and 127-28.

5

An Integral Hermeneutics of Life

> We really must return to the core, to the essential or, in other words: the central problem of our times is the absence of God and therefore, the Christian's primary duty is to bear witness to the living God. It seems to me that before we offer all those moralisms, before we fulfill all those duties that we have we must bear witness to the core of our faith and do it forcefully and clearly. We must render the reality of the living God present in our faith, in our hope and in our charity. If, today, there is a problem of morality, of the moral recomposition of society, I think it is the fruit of the absence of God in our thinking, in our lives. And, in more concrete terms, it is the fruit of the absence of God.—Joseph Ratzinger[1]

Throughout the span of his pontificate, Pope Francis has not managed to outrun the confusion that was caused by his pronouncement that "The church's pastoral ministry cannot be obsessed with the transmission of a disjointed multitude of [moral] doctrines to be imposed insistently" (EG §34).[2] Referring to these doctrines as "secondary aspects" of the Christian life because they allegedly do not in themselves convey the heart of Christ's message, Francis has unintentionally conveyed the impression that he lacks an integral hermeneutics of life—of life in Christ and morality. This chapter is devoted to presenting that hermeneutics from his writings while criticizing the ways that Francis has infelicitously expressed himself.

Believing in Joy

"And here is the first word that I wish to say to you: *joy!*"[3] Like the Angel of the Lord announcing to the Shepherds, Pope Francis, too, exclaims, "I Bring You News of Great Joy" (Luke 2:10). Why the emphasis on believing in joy in Pope Francis's writings, even his pre-papal writings? From his first Palm Sunday homily to his 2013 Apostolic Exhortation, *Evangelii Gaudium* (*Joy of the Gospel*), and most recently to his 2016 Apostolic Exhortation, *Gaudete et Exsultate* (*Rejoice and Be Glad*), a major theme runs throughout them that is well expressed in the opening lines of the first exhortation. "The joy of the gospel fills the hearts and lives of all who encounter Jesus. Those who accept his offer of salvation are set free from sin, sorrow, inner emptiness and loneliness. With Christ joy is constantly born anew." (EG §1) But why does Pope Francis emphasize joy rather than some other fruit of knowing Christ? Of course it is a biblically founded emphasis. We read Jesus proclaiming a Gospel of Joy: "I have said these things [about abiding in the love of the Father when we keep his commandments] so that my joy may be in you and that your joy may be complete" (John 15:11; see also John 17:13). Thus, Jesus, too, speaks of believing in joy.

Still, why emphasize believing in joy rather than faith, hope and charity? Well, clearly Francis picks up a theme to which Pope Paul VI devoted his 1975 Apostolic Exhortation, *Gaudete in Domino* ("On Christian Joy"). Of all the previous popes in recent history, Paul VI is a mentor of Francis who has shaped his mind and heart, citing him in his writings most frequently.[4] Yet, what is the significance of taking believing in joy as a starting point, right now, at this time in the history of our culture? Well, of course, Francis would say that we're trying to present "the very heart of the Gospel which gives it meaning, beauty and attractiveness" (EG §34). Referring to catechesis, he says, "Every form of catechesis would do well to attend to the 'way of beauty' (via pulchritudinis). Proclaiming Christ means showing that to believe in and to follow him is not only something right and true, but also something beautiful, capable of filling life with new splendor and profound joy, even in the midst of difficulties" (EG §167). Although profoundly true, we need to probe a little more deeply with the help of the then Jorge Bergoglio who rightly sees a connection between a deafness on man's part to the Gospel of Joy and the crisis of meaning in our culture.[5]

What is Man?

Although man is a religious being, it seems evident that this "'intimate and vital bond of man to God' [GS §19,1] can be forgotten, overlooked, or even explicitly rejected by man" (CCC §28). In this light, we can understand Bergoglio's fascination with Reinhold Niebuhr's statement: "Nothing is so incredible as an answer to an unasked question." Picking up this insight, Bergoglio urges us to consider that man ignores or suppresses the great questions that keep alive a possible receptivity to the Gospel of Joy: "Why is there pain, why death, why evil? Why is life worth living? What is the ultimate meaning of reality, of existence? What sense does it make to work, love, become involved in the world? Who am I? Where did I come from? Where am I going? These are great and primary questions that young people ask, and adults too—and not only believers but everyone, atheists and agnostics alike. Sooner or later, especially in the situations at the very edge of existence, in the face of great grief or great love, in the experience of educating one's children or of working at a job that apparently makes no sense, these questions inevitably rise to the surface. They cannot be uprooted."[6]

And yet, the challenge of our culture is that we are distracted by the completing and conflicting voices ("the supermarket culture") making it difficult to express these existential questions. "Offers are made to everyone to hush the clamoring of their hearts." Bergoglio adds, "This is the challenge." That is, "Faced with the torpor of life, with this tranquility offered at a low cost by the supermarket culture (even if in a wide assortment of ways), the challenge consists in asking ourselves the real questions about human meaning, of our existence, and in answering these questions." He continues: "But if we wish to answer questions that we do not dare to answer, do not know how to answer, or cannot formulate, we fall into absurdity." In other words, we cease to be what we are. But how do we make some sense of these questions "that are hidden or buried, that are perhaps almost dying but that nevertheless exist?"[7] More than this Bergoglio doesn't actually say about the crisis of meaning in our culture and the question of joy, but I think his immediate papal predecessor suggests the answer to this question.

Christianity is Life-Affirming

More than thirty years ago, the future Pope Benedict XVI, then Joseph Cardinal Ratzinger, gave the answer to this question by suggesting one reason more than any other why so many unbelievers are put off from the Christian faith. "The most telling refutation of what Christianity claims to be," wrote Ratzinger, is "this feeling that Christianity is opposed to joy, this impression of punctiliousness [showing great attention to correct behavior] and unhappiness." Furthermore, he adds, Christians are perceived to be obsessed with the "fourth [parental authority] and sixth commandments [sexual morality] that the resultant complex with regard to authority and purity renders the individual so incapable of free self-development that his selflessness degenerates into a loss of self and a denial of love, and his faith leads, not to freedom but to rigidity and an absence of freedom."[8] Of course, this alleged malady is our culture's distorted vision of the Christian life.

This distorted vision of Christianity is found in thinkers, such as Friedrich Nietzsche, who attacked Christianity, not as a doctrinal system with truth claims, but rather as a way of living. Nietzsche wrote: "Up to the present the assault against Christianity has not only been fainthearted, it has been wide of the mark. So long as Christian *ethics* are not felt to be a *capital crime against life*, their defenders will have the game in their hand. The problem of the "truth" of Christianity—the existence of its God or the historicity of its legend, to say nothing of its astronomy and its natural science—is in itself a very subsidiary problem so long as the value of Christian ethics goes unquestioned."[9] According to Nietzsche and others, such as Albert Camus, the concept of value that informs Christian ethics is fundamentally anti-life, rather than life-affirming or life-fulfilling. These critics of Christianity seem to think that Christianity holds that "life in this world is nothing but a means to reach heaven."[10] In other words, "nothing one does in this life contributes directly to human fulfillment: the only human fulfillment is in enjoyment of God in heaven." Hence, "life in this world is only a means to reach heaven, and that heaven is an entirely other-worldly goal."[11] Is it any wonder that Camus expressed his revolt against this other-worldliness, parodying the words of Christ, "'My kingdom is not of this world,' with the statement '*Notre royaume est de ce monde*—our kingdom is of this world.'"[12] Ratzinger concludes regarding the anti-life worldview that is taken to be core Christianity, "it is surely a more likely explanation of why people leave the Church than are any of the [intellectual challenges or] problems the faith may pose today."[13]

Yet, Ratzinger quickly responds by stating that the dangers for the culture today seem to be not scrupulosity ("moralism") but laxity, not legalism but antinomianism ("lawlessness"), not a lack of freedom but license ("anything goes"), since, he correctly notes, "there are no longer any forbidden trees" (with an allusion to Gen 3:1-7). We seem to be living in a time when there are "those who call evil good, and good evil; who put darkness for light, and light for darkness; who put bitter for sweet, and sweet for bitter!" (Is 5:20). In this biblical light, Ratzinger asks whether mankind has become any healthier. Those who have eyes to see must conclude that it seems not. Thus, he observes, "morality," wrongly understood as a straightjacket, on the one hand, "and immorality," on the other, "seem to enslave man, to make him joyless and empty. Is there, in the last analysis, no hope for him?"

Ratzinger proceeds to ask more specifically: "What makes a man joyful? What robs him of joy? What puts him at odds with himself? What opens him to himself and to others?" The approach that Ratzinger takes to answering these questions is similar to Bergoglio's analysis briefly sketched above. That is, a man must come to terms with his own existence, accepting himself, rather than being at odds with who he is, in short, self-affirmation. Ratzinger makes clear that he is not talking about egoism: the theory of human nature affirming that one's own self is, or ought to be, the motivation or goal of all of one's actions. He insists that egoism is not the same as true self-acceptance or self-affirmation. Says Ratzinger, "The former must be overcome; the latter must be discovered." Unfortunately, however, Christians have all too often confused "egoism" with the call to self-acceptance, self-affirmation, and hence they wrongly assumed, argues Ratzinger, that to root out egoism is at the same time "exorcizing the affirmation of self." In reaction to this confusion, egoism has sought "to avenge such a betrayal [of oneself] by becoming all the more rampant—this, ultimately, is the root of what the French have labeled the *maladie catholique*." This so-called malady can be easily understood in light of the points Nietzsche and Camus made above in revolt against an "other-worldly" view of Christianity. On this view, says Ratzinger, "one who wants to live only on the supernatural level and to the exclusion of self will be, in the end, without a self but not, for that reason, selfless."[14]

The Key to Joy

So the key to answering the question of joy is as follows: "the root of man's joy is the harmony that he enjoys with himself. He lives in this affirmation." But, adds Ratzinger, "how does one go about affirming, assenting to, one's *I*?" Intriguingly, he continues, "We cannot do so by our own efforts alone. Of ourselves we cannot come to terms with ourselves. Our *I* becomes acceptable to us only if it has first become acceptable to another *I*. We can love ourselves only if we have first been loved by someone else." In other words, the source of authentic self-love begins with someone else who not only says to you, "It is good that you exist," but also shows you the truth of that assertion with an "act of the entire being that we call love." "For it is the way of love to will the other's existence and, at the same time, to bring that existence forth again." But this act of loving the other for himself, of affirming him in his own self-existence, raises the question of truth. "Is it true, then, when someone says to me: 'It is good that you exist'? Is it really good? Is it not possible that that person's love, which wills my existence, is just a tragic error? If the love that gives me courage to exist is not based on truth, then I must, in the end, come to curse the love that deceives me, that maintains in existence something that were better destroyed."[15]

Ratzinger then takes an interesting turn in his argument by claiming that the question of my own existence, of being at one with myself, "actually raises the question of the whole universe." "Is it good that anything at all exists? Is the world good? How many persons today would dare to affirm this question from the heart—to believe it is good that they exist? That is the source of the anxiety and despair that incessantly affects mankind." And the latter cannot be resolved by love alone. Love is not all you need! Indeed, "only when truth and love are in harmony can man know joy. For it is truth that makes man free."[16] Here we come to the truth of the Gospel: The Yes of Jesus Christ.[17] "The truth is that only in the mystery of the incarnate Word does the mystery of man take on light" (GS §22).[18] Ratzinger elaborates:

> The content of the Christian *evangelium* reads: God finds man so important that he himself has suffered for man. The Cross, which was for Nietzsche the most detestable expression of the negative character of the Christian religion, is in truth the center of the *evangelium*, the glad tidings: "It is good that you exist"—no, "It is necessary that you exist." The Cross is the approbation of our existence, not in words, but in an act so completely radical that it caused God to become flesh and pierced this flesh to the quick; that, to God, it was worth the death of his incarnate Son. One who is so loved that the other identified his life with this love and no longer desires to live if he is deprived of it; one who is loved even unto death—such a one knows that he is truly loved. But if God so loved us,

> then we are loved in truth. Then love is truth, and truth is love. Then life is worth living. This is the *evangelium*. This is why, even as the message of the Cross, it is glad tidings for one who believes; the only glad tidings that destroy the ambiguity of all other joys and make them worthy to be joy. Christianity is, by its very nature, joy—the ability to be joyful... "Rejoice!" with which it begins expresses its whole nature.[19]

Pace Nietzsche and Camus, then, Christianity is life-affirming: the grace of the Cross neither destroys fallen human nature nor leaves it untouched but, rather, renews and transforms it from within, bringing about nature's fulfillment by ordering it to its proper ends.

Ratzinger leaves us with the question, "What can the Church do, what ought she to do, that we may truly experience the joy of the *evangelium*?"[20] In response to this question, Pope Francis proclaims the Gospel of Jesus Christ not only to the "desolation and anguish born of a complacent yet covetous heart, the feverish pursuit of frivolous pleasures, and a blunted conscience." But the Gospel is proclaimed anew also to those who are trapped in a mere theology of condemnation, telling others merely what is false and what they may not do, turning, Francis says, "Christian morality [into] a form of stoicism, or self-denial, or merely... a catalogue of sins and faults." These people look like those "who have just come back from a funeral!" How, then, are we to live a dignified, fulfilled, and yes, a joyful life?

Christian Joy—A Gift of the Holy Spirit

Francis's answer to this question echoes the words of the epigraph to Paul VI's *Gaudete in Domino*: "Rejoice in the Lord always; the Lord is near to all who call upon him in truth" (Phil 4:4; Ps 145:18). Man has been created by God and for God to exist in an intimate and vital bond of fellowship. This means that he has been made with the capacity of knowing and loving God. As Pope Paul wrote, "God disposes the mind and heart of His creatures to meet joy, at the same time as truth." Still, sin has savagely wounded man such that this capacity or disposition has been severely disoriented. "Man set himself against God and sought to find fulfillment apart from God," the Second Vatican Council states. The council adds, "For sin has diminished man, blocking his path to fulfillment" (GS §13).

The Gospel proclamation is that this wounded condition is not God's will for us. Instead, says Francis, we become fully human when... we let God bring us beyond ourselves in order to attain the fullest truth of our being." The source of this fulfillment flows "from the infinite love of God, who has revealed himself to us in Jesus Christ." It is in knowing and loving Christ that we find joy. What, then, is joy?

"Entering into the joy of the Lord" is one of several expressions the New Testament uses to describe the beatitude to which God calls man. This believing in joy is a fruit of the indwelling of the Holy Spirit in our life.

Thus, spiritual joy is a gift of God's grace, a sign of the abiding presence of Christ, of a fundamental peace that man truly enters into by knowing and loving God, by turning away from sin, and by embracing the redemptive purpose of the cross. Francis states, "The Gospel, radiant with the glory of Christ's cross, constantly invites us to rejoice." He then asks, "Why should we not also enter into this great stream of joy?" Of course "Without doubt 'flesh and blood' [Matt 16:17] are incapable of this. But Revelation can open up this possibility and grace can bring about this return."

Put differently, this fundamental peace is about human flourishing in all its dimensions: first and foremost in and with our relationship to God, but then with our fellow human beings, to nature, and, last but not least, an interior flourishing that flows from self-knowledge. As Pope Francis puts it, "The sign of this unity and reconciliation of all things in him is peace. Christ 'is our peace' (Eph 2:14)... 'by making peace through the blood of his cross' (Col 1:20)." Indeed, he adds, "The Cross is the 'final battle' of Jesus: in the cross is to be found the definitive victory."[21]

Furthermore, since essential to human flourishing is our relationship with God, the transforming power of the Gospel impels us to communicate the truth about God and humanity to the world, urging us to respond to the God of love and mercy who saves us in and through Christ's cross, "to see God in others and to go forth from ourselves to seek the good of others." But to seek *the* good of others can only mean first and foremost that man be fully revealed to himself in relation to God. "The truth is that only in the mystery of the incarnate Word does the mystery of man take on light.... Christ... by the revelation of the mystery of the Father and His love, fully reveals man to himself and makes his supreme calling clear," the Second Vatican Council stated (GS §22). Our joy in the Lord—in Christ who is the *Way, the Truth, and the Life*—should then generate missionary enthusiasm.[22]

Mission and Vocation

When the joy of the Lord takes root in our life, then we are impelled by that joy to share the truth of the gospel with others. We do so because the Gospel is *the* truth of human existence. Thus, "The Gospel joy which enlivens the community of disciples is a missionary joy." In this conviction, Francis is echoing Benedict XVI, who writes: "*Discipleship* and *mission* are like the two sides of a single coin: when the disciple is in love with Christ, he cannot stop proclaiming to the world that only in him do we find salvation [cf. Acts 4:12]. In effect, the disciple knows that without Christ there is no light, no hope, no love, no future."[23] Furthermore, Francis adds, "Every Christian is challenged, here and now, to be actively engaged in evangelization; indeed, anyone who has truly experienced God's saving love... is a missionary to the extent that he or she has encountered the love of God in Christ Jesus: we longer say that we are 'disciples' and missionaries', but rather that we are always 'missionary disciples.'" Moreover, "When the Church summons Christians to take up the task of evangelization, she is simply pointing to the source of authentic personal fulfillment."

Indeed, the Gospel is the source of personal fulfillment for all men. Indeed, in this light we can understand the missionary nature of man and hence the Church's missional hermeneutic. Francis writes: "My mission of being in the heart of the people is not just a part of my life or a badge I can take off; it is not an 'extra' or just another moment in life. Instead, it is something I cannot uproot from my being without destroying my very self. *I am a mission* on this earth; that is the reason why I am here in this world." Alternatively put, Francis speaks of the Lord giving us our mission and, consequently, establishing our being. In Christ, I am missionary by nature and not just in a merely functional sense. "Rather he does it with the power of his Spirit, in such a way that we belong to the mission and our very identity is indelibly marked by it."[24] Do we know who we are? Have we responded in our life to the challenge of a missionary spirituality, to be actively engaged in evangelization?

When we respond in faith to the calling that we have received in Christ we come to understand that the Lord has sent us into spiritual combat, to engage for Christ's sake in the renewal of the whole of life, including the spectrum of culture. "What is at stake in this war?" Francis responds to this question that he has posed. At stake in this spiritual warfare against sin and the Devil, says Francis, is nothing less than "war waged against the enemy of human nature," which is sin, that separates us from God, "by the friend of human nature, the Lord Jesus, who wants to win us for God and to recapitulate in himself all that is good in creation, in order to offer it to the Father, to the praise of his glory."[25] To be fit for spiritual warfare we need to put on the whole armor of God, says St. Paul, in order to resist temptation and stand our ground in the Lord (Eph 6:10-13). "The people of God is an 'army corps,' the Christian life is combat." Francis adds, "And God's most powerful weapon is the Cross."[26] It is with the Cross of Jesus Christ that sin, death and the Devil suffered defeat once and for all. "True joy is forged," concludes Francis, "in the cross."[27]

The Hierarchy of Truths

In a 2006 interview of Pope Benedict XVI, he was asked by Vatican Radio why he never spoke of same-sex marriage, abortion, or contraception at the recent meeting in Valencia of the World Meeting of Families. Sound familiar? Critics of Pope Francis have often raised a similar objection. Benedict's answer is in line with Francis's own perspective. He said, "Christianity, Catholicism, is not a [mere] collection of prohibitions: it is a positive option.... We have heard so much about what is not allowed that now it is time to say: we have a positive idea to offer, that man and woman are made for each other, that the scale of sexuality, eros, agape, indicates the level of love and it is in this way that marriage develops, first of all as a joyful and blessing-filled encounter between a man and a woman, and then, the family, which guarantees continuity among generations and through which generations are reconciled to each other and even cultures can meet. So, firstly it is important to stress what we want. Secondly, we can also see why we do not want something. I believe we need to see and reflect on the fact that it's not a Catholic invention that man and woman are made for each other, so that humanity can go on living: all cultures know this [fact]."[28] The Church's moral teaching is an integral part of her evangelizing mission to proclaim the meaning, beauty and attractiveness of the Gospel.

Yet, Pope Francis reminds us of the risk of distorting or reducing the Gospel message "to some of its secondary aspects." He explains, "In this way certain issues which are part of the Church's moral teaching are taken out of context which gives them their meaning." And here he identifies what he takes to be the "biggest problem is when the message we preach" is "identified with those secondary aspects which, important as they are, do not in and of themselves convey the heart of Christ's message" (EG §34). This was not the first time Pope Francis made this point about some truths being more fundamental than others, and hence that we must take care not to reduce the Gospel to some of its secondary aspects, which he seemed to be suggesting had to do with Catholic moral teachings about abortion, same-sex marriage, contraception, and sexual morality.[29] Of course, the pope made clear that he affirmed these teachings, but that it was "not necessary to talk about these issues all the time."

Unfortunately, since making that point early in his papacy, Francis has held to it since most of the time he leaves these teachings in the shadows. And when he does bring them into the light, as he did in his recent apostolic exhortation *Gaudete et Exsultate*, his approach reminds many people of the "seamless garment" approach to life issues. "Our defense of the innocent unborn, for example, needs to be clear, firm and passionate, for at stake is the dignity of a human life, which is always sacred and demands love for each person, regardless of his or her stage of development. *Equally sacred*, however, are the lives of the poor, those already born, the destitute, the abandoned and the underprivileged, the vulnerable infirm and elderly exposed to covert euthanasia, the victims of human trafficking, new forms of slavery, and every form of rejection." (GE §101, emphasis added). Of course, the principle of human life's dignity is universal, since human life—in all its stages and conditions—was created in the image of God, belonging to the human family, and having moral and legal standing. Notwithstanding the importance of this enlarged pro-life vision, the right to life—and thus of the unborn child—should be prioritized as the foundation for all other rights, in the sense that it is foundational to all other rights, and hence abortion is more important in the scheme of things than these other life issues.[30] Intriguingly, Francis himself says, similarly, "The right to life is the *first human right*. Abortion is killing someone that cannot defend him or herself."[31] Nevertheless, that statement is not typical of him. Elsewhere, Francis has given a more developed justification of his typical position. He says,

> The dogmatic and moral teachings of the church are not all equivalent. The church's pastoral ministry cannot be

> obsessed with the transmission of a disjointed multitude of doctrines to be imposed insistently. Proclamation in a missionary style focuses on the essentials, on the necessary things: this is also what fascinates and attracts more, what makes the heart burn, as it did for the disciples at Emmaus. We have to find a new balance; otherwise, even the moral edifice of the Church is likely to fall like a house of cards, losing the freshness and fragrance of the gospel. The proposal of the gospel must be more simple, profound, radiant. It is from this proposition that the moral consequences then flow.[32]

It would not be an overstatement to suggest that Pope Francis's use of the word "obsession" in reference to an evangelical ministry dealing with the moral teachings of the Church on sexual morality unsettled many Catholics. Janet E. Smith, for one, wrote: "My reason for being unsettled is that it would not be a complete distortion to say that I have been 'obsessed' with the issues of abortion, contraception, and homosexuality for nearly all of my professional life. I prefer the terms 'dedicated' or 'committed,' of course, but whatever word is appropriate, I have long thought that helping people understand why abortion, contraception, and homosexual acts are not in accord with God's plans for human happiness is a very effective way of drawing people closer to the Lord and to the Church, and thus, more or less, most of my adult life, I have been evangelizing in this way."[33] Furthermore, what concerned others, like R.R. Reno, the Editor of the ecumenical journal *First Things*, is that words like "obsession" and phrases like "small things, in small-minded rules,"[34] and others phrases, evoke "the standard playbook of progressive reform," in particular, "by Catholics who would like the Church to change her teachings on many issues."[35]

So you can imagine that some people took away from what the pope was saying that abortion, contraception and homosexuality were small things, rules of small-minded people, "legalists," expressing an "exaggerated doctrinal security," and who have locked themselves up in this box, with the faith becoming an "ideology,"[36] and hence have forgotten the most important thing, the "first proclamation: Christ has saved you."[37] We have met these themes of legalism, ideology, etc., in earlier chapters of this book, and so I will not repeat here my criticisms. Clearly, there is a way to say what Francis has in mind about the relationship of the Gospel and moral issues, and indeed, Joseph Cardinal Ratzinger had already said it in an address to the Waldensian community, Rome, in 1993, which is the epigraph to this chapter.

Respectfully, I think it is fair to say that Francis expressed himself in his interview[38] in a most infelicitous manner. It seems to reflect a one-sidedness that is not present elsewhere.[39] For instance, there is no one-sidedness in his 2013 address to the Leadership of CELAM.[40] But I do say one-sidedness because Pope Francis, of course, supports the Church's teaching on abortion as a violation of the humanity of the unborn. Elsewhere he writes,

> Among the vulnerable for whom the Church wishes to care with particular love and concern are unborn children, the most defenseless and innocent among us. Nowadays efforts are made to deny them their human dignity and to do with them whatever one pleases, taking their lives and passing laws preventing anyone from standing in the way of this. Frequently, as a way of ridiculing the Church's effort to defend their lives, attempts are made to present her position as ideological, obscurantist and conservative. Yet this defense of unborn life is closely linked to the defense of each and every other human right. It involves the conviction that a human being is always sacred and inviolable, in any situation and at every stage of development. Human beings are ends in themselves and never a means of resolving other problems. Once this conviction disappears, so do solid and lasting foundations for the defense of human rights, which would always be subject to the passing whims of the powers that be. Reason alone is sufficient to recognize the inviolable value of each single human life, but if we also look at the issue from the standpoint of faith, every violation of the personal dignity of the human being cries out in vengeance to God and is an offence against the creator of the individual. (EG §§213-14)

Francis makes several points here that are integral to a Catholic ontological anthropology. A human being has an inviolable right to life by virtue of his humanity. Indeed, being human is the ground of all human rights, and thus he prioritizes the right to life as the foundation of human dignity. Hence, if we deny unborn *human* life the right to life we remove our humanity as the foundation of *all* rights. Furthermore, the human person is an end in himself, never a mere means to an end, existing as a being of his own, for his own sake, unique and unrepeatable, a whole of his own and hence never a mere part of any totality. We can then understand why the pope says that a human being is "never a means of resolving other problems." Francis continues: "Precisely because this [ontological anthropology] involves the *internal consistency* of our message about the value of the human person, the Church cannot be expected to change her position on this question. I want to be completely honest in this regard. This is not something subject to alleged reforms or 'modernizations.' *It is not 'progressive' to try to resolve problems by eliminating a human life.*" (EG §214, emphasis added)[41]

Undoubtedly, Pope Francis is wholeheartedly committed to the Gospel of Life as integral to the evangelizing mission of the Church.[42] In fact, most recently in his address to the Italian Association of Catholic Doctors, he is admirably clear in affirming the "Gospel of Life." The Vatican

Insider reported the Pope's words: "Fidelity to the Gospel of life and respect for life as a gift from God sometimes require choices that are courageous and go against the current, which in particular circumstances, may become points of conscientious objection." "The dominant thinking sometimes suggests a 'false compassion,' that which retains that it is: helpful to women to promote abortion; an act of dignity to obtain euthanasia; a scientific breakthrough to 'produce' a child and to consider it to be a right rather than a gift to welcome; or to use human lives as guinea pigs presumably to save others," the Pope said in his speech. Instead, he pointed out, "the compassion of the Gospel is that which accompanies in times of need, that is, the compassion of the Good Samaritan, who 'sees,' 'has compassion,' approaches and provides concrete help." "Human life is always sacred and always 'of quality.' There is no human life that is more sacred than another, as there is no human life qualitatively more significant than another, only by virtue of resources, rights, great social and economic opportunities." Francis underlined that human life "is always sacred, valuable, and inviolable."[43] Indeed, in his 2015 Message for the World Day of the Sick, the pope underscores the same point about human life by unmasking, as he pointedly says, "the lie that lurks behind certain phrases which so insist on the importance of 'quality of life' that they make people think that lives affected by grave illness are not worth living!" Furthermore, Francis adds regarding this "great lie," that "even when illness, loneliness and inability make it hard for us to reach out to others, the experience of suffering can become a privileged means of transmitting grace." Thus, "people immersed in the mystery of suffering and pain, when they accept these in faith, can themselves become living witnesses of a faith capable of embracing suffering, even without being able to understand its full meaning."[44]

Most recently, Pope Francis gave an address to the European Parliament. He spoke to the EU about promoting a culture of inalienable human rights, grounded in the nature of man, central to human dignity, and rejecting a "throwaway culture" in which the value of human life is denied, the value of "the terminally ill, the elderly who are abandoned and uncared for, and children who are killed in the womb."[45]

A More Balanced Perspective

Still, why didn't Francis take aim in this interview[46] at the doctrinal minimalist, those who separate faith from beliefs, pitting faith against dogma, understanding the latter as the Catholic faith's doctrinal trappings, who thus blunt the "doctrinal edges" of the faith by setting love against doctrine, who are religious subjectivist[47] or relativists, and who reduce the Catholic faith to simply being a "good person"?[48] And what about moral laxity of those Catholics who have prominent positions in public life who cause scandal[49] by promoting support for abortion rights, same-sex marriage, and health insurance coverage for contraception, sterilization, and abortifacients? In a recent homily given by Pope Francis at Santa Marta, he says that Christians must never cause scandal. Scandal, he said, "is to proclaim and profess a way of life—'I am a Christian'—and then live like a pagan, who does not believe in anything. This gives scandal 'because there is no witness,' while 'the faith is professed'—Pope Francis reiterated—'by the way you live your life.'" Francis continues:

> When a Christian man or a Christian woman, who goes to church, is part of the parish, does not live in this way, they cause scandal. How often have we heard men and women say: "I do not go to church because it is better to be honest at home and not go to church like that man or woman who then do this, this, this..." Scandal destroys, it destroys the faith! And that is why Jesus is so strong: "Beware! Watch out!" It would do us good to repeat this today: "Be on your guard!" All of us are capable of causing scandal.[50]

Again, what about self-professed Catholic organizations such as *Call to Action*,[51] *Catholics for Choice*, whose mission statement says: "We are part of the great majority of the faithful in the Catholic church who disagrees with the dictates of the Vatican on matters related to sex, marriage, family life and motherhood."[52] In this connection, consider also the *Pfarrer-Initiative* with its initial plea for disobedience (2011), followed up by a plea for a credible church—both supporting changes in Church teaching regarding marriage, sexual morality, the divorce and civilly remarried, celibacy, and so forth.[53] In general, consider the recent Quinnipiac University poll on American Catholic attitudes regarding a range of issues, including abortion and same-sex marriage.

> The poll findings on abortion are consistent with previous surveys. Catholic attitudes were fairly similar to the rest of the population. Thirty-nine percent of all respondents—and 42 percent of self-identified Catholics—felt abortion should be illegal in either "all" or "most" cases. However, there was a substantial difference in the opinions among Catholics who attended Mass on a weekly basis and those who did not. According to the survey, 61 percent of Catholics who attend Mass on a weekly basis thought abortion should be either mostly or entirely illegal. Only 29 percent of Catholics who attend Mass less often felt this way. The results on same-sex marriage were unsettling. The poll found that Catholic attitudes were again consistent with the rest of the population. Fifty-six percent of all respondents—and 60 percent of Catholics—support same-sex marriage. However, what

> was disappointing was that a majority of Catholics (53 percent) who attend Mass weekly support same-sex marriage. Interestingly, adherents of other faiths who attend church on a weekly basis were much less likely to support same-sex marriage. Among all faith traditions—only 34 percent of weekly church attendees support same-sex marriage.[54]

If anything, the problem that the Church faces is not obsession with respect to the moral issues of abortion, contraception, and same-sex marriage, or legalism,[55] and doctrinal certainty, but rather laxity, not to say outright rejection of the Church's teaching on these matters. I think some Catholics would like to hear Pope Francis on those who—as St. Paul wrote—do "not endure sound doctrine," live "according to their own desires, because they have itching ears," and hence "they will turn their ears away from the truth" (2 Tim 4:3-4).

Once Again, Hierarchy of Truths

Now, many Catholics understand the moral issues Francis referred to as "secondary"—because they allegedly do not in themselves convey the heart of Christ's message—to be actually integral to the Gospel of Life. They were committed to the vision of *Evangelium Vitae,* the 1995 Encyclical Letter of John Paul II. "The Gospel of life is at the heart of Jesus' message." (EV Introduction). They were unsettled by Pope Francis's remarks, but I think there is a way to make sense of what he was trying to say in that interview by turning to his Apostolic Exhortation, *Evangelli gaudium,* where he appeals to the notion of the "hierarchy of truths" to make the following point. In the interview, he said: "the dogmatic and moral teachings of the church are not all equivalent."[56] I presume the pope was implicitly thinking here of that notion, but does not actually say so. As it stands, this manner of expressing the idea that there is an order of importance or hierarchy of truths such that some truths have ultimate importance whereas others only relative importance may lead to an attitude of *indifference* regarding those truths lower in importance. Of course, Pope Francis rejects that interpretation as an "ideological error" (GE §§101-102) because the hierarchy of truths does not mean imply indifference to those truths lower in the hierarchy. However, it is precisely that interpretation which "unsettled Catholics" took Francis to be suggesting. Be that as it may, in *Evangelii Gaudium,* he explicitly appeals to the hierarchy of truths and suggests an accurate, even if not a fully worked-out, interpretation of it. He writes:

> All revealed truths derive from the same divine source and are to be believed with the same divine faith, yet some of them are important for giving direct expression to the heart of the Gospel. In this basic core, what shines forth is the beauty of the saving love of God made man-

> ifest in Jesus Christ who died and rose from the dead. In this sense, the Second Vatican Council explained, "in Catholic doctrine there exists an order or a 'hierarchy' of truths, since they vary in their relation to the foundation of the Christian faith." This holds true as much for the dogmas of faith as for the whole corpus of the Church's teaching, including her moral teaching. (EG §36)

Significantly, I think the first sentence in the above quoted paragraph makes clear that the pope echoes the 1973 CDF document, *Mysterium ecclesiae*: "all dogmas, since they are revealed, must be believed with the same divine faith" (ME §4). Hence, "no truth may be denied" (EG §39). That means no moral truth either regarding abortion, contraception, homosexuality, and conjugal marriage. Yet, Francis also says that the hierarchy or order of truths exists by virtue of their varying relationship to the foundation of the faith suggesting then that a hierarchy of truths exists. This, too, is affirmed by *Mysterium ecclesiae*: "This hierarchy means that some dogmas are founded on other dogmas which are the principal ones, and are illuminated by these latter" (ME §4). But how then should we understand those teachings ranking lower in importance without sliding into indifference?

Clearly, the following statement from the pope makes clear that Francis has no intention of treating the hierarchy in a "quantitative" fashion as if reduction of Christian truth to its essential content is the point of the hierarchy. The pope was in danger of being interpreted as if he were suggesting—which he clearly was not if one considers his remarks with other things he says elsewhere and that I have been citing in this chapter—this interpretation in his interview, leaving us with the idea that the hierarchy of truth is about separating nonnegotiable teaching from optional or, worse, negotiable teachings of the Church. But I suggest that the pope aims to bring an integral perspective to bear upon the whole body of truths—dogmatic and moral—by considering the question of their interconnectedness with the central truths of the Christian faith.[57] As he says, "The integrity of the Gospel message must not be deformed. What is more, each truth is better understood when related to the harmonious totality of the Christian message; in this context all of the truths are important and illumine one another" (EG §39). On the one hand, all the truths of the Church's teaching must be held with the same divine faith. On the other hand, and this is where Francis confuses his listeners, that does *not* mean that they all bear an equivalent relationship to those truths that are central to the foundation of the faith.

Still, they nonetheless bear a relationship such that those truths lower in rank in the hierarchy are *illuminated* by those that are higher in the order of truths. If the fundamental truths of the Catholic faith are not illuminating those truths lower in rank in the hierarchy, then the latter moral truths are "disjointed" because they have lost "the freshness and fragrance of the gospel." In short, it then becomes unclear that these teachings are "the moral consequences" that "flow" from the gospel.[58] The pope applies this general interpretation of the hierarchy of truth to the Church's moral teaching. In terms of the former, we can say that "all revealed truths derive from the same divine source and [hence] are to be believed with the same divine faith."[59] But in terms of the latter we can say that some truths are more fundamental and more important than others because they "give direct expression to the heart of the Gospel." And yet, we must not lose sight of the point that those truths lower in importance also give expression to the Gospel and hence must be illuminated by those higher in importance. When we lose sight of that relationship the lower ranking truths lose their sense of "radiating forcefully and attractively... with the fragrance of the Gospel." At his clearest, the pope explains:

> When preaching is faithful to the Gospel, the centrality of certain truth is evident and it becomes clear that Christian morality is not a form of stoicism, or self-denial, or merely a practical philosophy of catalogue of sins and faults. Before all else, the Gospel invites us to respond to the God of love who saves us, to see God in others and to go forth from ourselves to seek the good of others. Under no circumstances can this invitation be obscure! All of the [moral] virtues are at the service of this response to love. If this invitation does not radiate forcefully and attractively, the edifice of the Church's moral teaching risks becoming a house of cards, and this is our greatest risk. It would mean that it is not the Gospel which is being preached, but certain doctrinal or moral points based on specific ideological options. The message will run the risk of losing its freshness and will cease to have "the fragrance of the Gospel" (EG §39).

Briefly, let me illustrate what Francis has in mind here with a brief discussion of the "Gospel of Life." The Aparecida Document that resulted from CELAM's Fifth General Conference in 2007, and which the then Archbishop Bergoglio was an integral contributor, takes as one of its reference points the following thesis: "John Paul II's encyclical 'Gospel of Life' sheds light on the great value of human life, which we must safeguard, and for which we continually praise God."[60] That Pope Francis takes this document to be important is evident from a letter of 17 April 2013 that he wrote to the Argentine Assembly of Bishops directing them to implement the Aparecida Document. He said, "These are the guidelines we need for this time in history."[61] With that thesis as our starting-point, I turn to a brief reflection of the "Gospel of Life."

Evangelium Vitae

"John Paul II states the key thesis of *Evangelium Vitae*: "*We are witnessing the emergence of a new culture... whose content and character are often in conflict with the Gospel and the dignity of the human person.*"[62] Western culture is failing because its Christian roots are eroding. This failing culture has reached its lowest point in the emerging *culture of death*, which is antithetical to what John Paul II also calls the *culture of life*. There are four specific roots of the culture of death: individual autonomy; a debased notion of freedom detached from objective truth; the eclipse of the sense of God and, in consequence, of the human person; and the darkening of human conscience, indeed, moral blindness, resulting in a confusion between good and evil in the individual and in society. In short, the Church is engaged in a battle for the soul of Western culture. What is the consequence of this conclusion for the Church? What ought *we* to do in engaging this failing culture?

In response, John Paul II has provided us with an all-embracive "plan of action" involving the whole Church in the whole spectrum of life and in the whole culture.[63] We are called to be the people of God at the *service of life*. We need to bring the gospel of Jesus to the heart of every man and woman. There is a deep spiritual hunger in every human heart "for fullness of life and truth" (SE §56). In no uncertain terms, Pope John Paul II boldly proclaims the truth of the gospel: "Jesus Christ is the answer to the question that is every human life."[64] *"No demand... is more urgent than the 'new evangelization' needed to satisfy the spiritual hunger of our times."*[65] Pope Francis echoes this demand:

> But there is also a deeper hunger, the hunger for a happiness that only God can satisfy, the hunger for dignity. There is neither real promotion of the common good nor real human development when there is ignorance of the fundamental pillars that govern a nation, its non-material goods: *life*, which is a gift of God, a value always to be protected and promoted; the *family*, the foundation of coexistence and a remedy against social fragmentation; *integral education*, which cannot be reduced to the mere transmission of information for purposes of generating profit; *health*, which must seek the integral well-being of the person, including the spiritual dimension, essential for human balance and healthy coexistence; *security*, in the conviction that violence can be overcome only by changing human hearts.[66]

Most important for its overall approach to culture, however, the Church must include each one of the typical answers, but now only as aspects of its total approach, to the enduring question of how Christ relates to culture. The *culture* that embodies the *gospel of life* is *opposed* to the *culture of death*—abortion, infanticide, physician-assisted suicide, euthanasia, cloning, along with issues regarding bioethics, sexual ethics, marriage, and family life (SE §148-49). Christians are not only called to be *against* these practices but also to be agents of Christ-centered cultural *renewal*. The Church must evangelize, indeed, transform not only individuals but also cultural institutions and broader societal structures that support and promote the *gospel of life*. God's people are called to be in service to life by *building a new culture of human life.*

At the core of the new evangelization is the good news that *human life is a good, a gift of God*: Man is made in the image of God (Gen 1:26), and who is the crown of creation given dominion over all of creation (Gen 1:28), possessing human dignity, and incomparable value. Man's image was marred, indeed, savagely wounded by sin but God is rich in mercy (Eph 2:4) and thus man's image is "restored, renewed, and brought to perfection" in and through the redemptive incarnation of the eternal Son of God, Jesus Christ. John Paul says: "All who commit themselves to following Christ are given the fullness of life... God's plan for human beings is this: that they should be 'conformed to the image of his Son' [Rom 8:29]." Furthermore: "The dignity of [human] life is linked not only to its beginning, to the fact that it comes from God, but also to its final end, to its destiny of fellowship with God in knowledge and love of him." Thus, *"The Gospel of God's love for man, the Gospel of the dignity of the person and the Gospel of life are a single and indivisible Gospel."*[67] Pope Francis, of course, is committed to this vision of the human person:

> The original dignity of every man and woman is therefore inalienable and inaccessible to any power or ideology. Unfortunately, in our own time, one so rich in achievements and hopes, there are many powers and forces that end up producing a culture of waste; and this tends to become the common mentality. The victims of this culture are precisely the weakest and most fragile human beings—the unborn, the poorest, the sick and elderly, the seriously handicapped, *et al.*—who are in danger of being "thrown away," expelled from a system that must be efficient at all costs. In fact, this false model of man and society implements a practical atheism by rejecting the Word of God, which says: "Let us make man in our image, after our likeness" [cf. Gen 1:26].[68]

In order to be fully equipped as God's people to be at the service of life, this "single and indivisible Gospel" must be taught and lived from the outset in the life of the family. Indeed, the family has a decisive and irreplaceable role to play in building a culture of life. Children must be raised by their parents with the understanding that *procreation* is about receiving, not possessing, the divine *gift of human life*. Human life is not only a *gift*, however, it is also a *task*. That is, they must learn that in receiving this gift they have a corresponding responsibility to affirm and protect human life as a good. They do this by making choices that show respect for others, not only by respecting their rights, but also, indeed chiefly, by the sincere *gift of self* that is shown in being hospitable, in engaging in dialogue, in generous service, in bearing each other's burdens, and in expressing solidarity with others. At the root of this self-giving is the divine commandment *to love, respect, and promote life*, especially but not only where life is weak and defenseless but also where life is challenged by hardship, sickness or rejection, and suffering.[69] "Human life is sacred and inviolable at every stage and in every situation; it is an indivisible good."[70] This, too, needless to say, is the teaching of Pope Francis who unreservedly embraces the priority of the Church's Magisterium for the Gospel of Life[71]:

> A widespread mentality of the useful, the "culture of waste" that today enslaves the hearts and minds of so many, comes at a very high cost: it asks for the elimination of human beings, especially if they are physically or socially weaker. Our response to this mentality is a decisive and unreserved "yes" to life. "The first right of the human person is his life. He has other goods and some are more precious, but this one is fundamental—the condition of all the others" (Congregation for the Doctrine of the Faith, *Declaration on procured abortion*, 18 November 1974, §11). Things have a price and can be sold, but people have a dignity; they are worth more than things and are above price. So often we find ourselves in situations where we see that what is valued the least is life. That is why concern for human life in its totality has become in recent years a real priority for the Church's Magisterium, especially for the most defenseless; i.e., the disabled, the sick, the newborn, children, the elderly, those whose lives are most defenseless.[72]
>
> "Unfortunately, what is thrown away is not only food and dispensable objects, but often human beings themselves, who are discarded as 'unnecessary.' For example, it is frightful even to think there are children, victims of abortion, who will never see the light of day; children being used as soldiers, abused and killed in armed conflicts; and children being bought and sold in that terrible form of modern slavery which is human trafficking, which is a crime against humanity."[73]

The truths of this single and indivisible gospel of life must be taught thereafter *"in catechesis, in the various forms of preaching, in personal dialogue, and in all educational activity."* Yet, there is more: the gospel of life should be culturally embodied. As John Paul II constantly urged, "A faith that does not become culture is a faith not fully accepted, not entirely thought out, not faithfully lived."[74] To that end, we must support and express solidarity with agencies and centers of service to life such as hospitals, clinics, and convalescent homes by emphasizing the intrinsic and undeniable *moral dimension* of their responsibility. In particular, to be actively pro-life for the common good of society requires Christian health-care professionals—doctors, nurses, pharmacists, administrators, and chaplains—to bear witness to the gospel of life in their respective areas of responsibility. The apostolate of the laity "is exercised... when they endeavor to have the Gospel spirit permeate and improve the temporal order, going about it in a way that bears clear witness to Christ and helps forward the salvation of men. Characteristic of the lay state is a life led in the midst of the world and of secular affairs, and hence laymen are called by God to make of their apostolate, through the vigor of their Christian spirit, a leaven in the world" *(AA §2)*. This apostolate is particularly important today given the current temptation of health-care professionals "to become manipulators of life, or even agents of death." This temptation may be resisted by recovering the meaning of the *Hippocratic Oath*, "which requires every doctor to commit himself to absolute respect for human life and its sacredness" (EV §§88-89). Pope Francis has made a similar appeal:

> Although, by their very nature, healthcare professions are at the service of life, they are sometimes induced to disregard life itself. Yet, as the Encyclical *Caritas in Veritate* [of Benedict XVI] reminds us: "Openness to life is at the center of true development." There is no true development without this openness to life. "If personal and social sensitivity towards the acceptance of a new life is lost, then other forms of acceptance that are valuable for society also wither away. The acceptance of life strengthens moral fibre and makes people capable of mutual help" (§28). This paradoxical situation may be seen in the fact that, while persons are being accorded new rights—at times even presumed rights—life itself is not always protected as a primary value and primordial right of every human being. The final aim of the doctor's action is always the defense and promotion of life.[75]

Furthermore, Christians involved in the political, social, and civic arenas of cultural life are also responsible for implementing the gospel of life by "shaping society and developing cultural, economic, political, and legislative projects that, with respect for all and in keeping with democratic principles will contribute to the building of a society in which the dignity of each person is recognized and protected and the lives of all are defended and enhanced" (EV §90). Moreover, Christian scholars—philosophers, theologians, indeed all those intellectuals engaged in the study of man—at work in institutions of higher education, centers, institutes, and committees addressing bioethical questions are also obligated by virtue of their calling in Christ to contribute to building a new culture of life. Summarily stated, Pope Francis concludes our brief discussion of *Evangelium Vitae*:

> The third aspect is a mandate: *be witnesses and diffusers of the "culture of life."* Your being Catholic entails a greater responsibility: first of all to yourselves, through a commitment consistent with your Christian vocation; and then to contemporary culture, by contributing to recognizing the transcendent dimension of human life, the imprint of God's creative work, from the first moment of its concep-

> tion. This is a task of the new evangelization that often requires going against the tide and paying for it personally. The Lord is also counting on you to spread the "gospel of life." Within this perspective, hospital departments of gynecology are privileged places of witness and evangelization, for wherever the Church becomes "the bearer of the presence of God", there, too, she becomes the "instrument of the true humanization of man and the world" (Congregation for the Doctrine of the Faith, *Doctrinal Note on Some Aspects of Evangelization*, §9). By fostering an awareness that the human person in his frailty stands at the center of all medical and healthcare work, the healthcare facility becomes "a place in which the relationship of treatment is not a profession"—your relationship of treatment is not a profession—"but a mission; where the charity of the Good Samaritan is the first seat of learning and the face of suffering man is the Christ's own Face" [Benedict XVI, "Address at the Catholic University of the Sacred Heart," 3 May 2012].

The Moral Life in Christ

Thus, there remains to ask about the place of morality in regard to living out our life in the joy of the Lord.[76] The *Catechism of the Catholic Church* teaches that "the way of Christ 'leads to life'; a contrary way 'leads to destruction.'" One may easily see this two-fold way of living in St. Paul's *Letter to the Galatians*: "walking in the Spirit" versus "walking in the flesh" (Gal 5:16-25). This Pauline context is the one in which we should see "the importance of moral decisions for our salvation." Francis echoes this antithesis: "The objective context in which we can pose this [moral] question is the life and death battle between the Two Standards. Cardinal Martini speaks of 'two opposing life projects' (life and death, progress or degradation of human existence). Two battle plans with no room for a no-man's-land of 'more or less. Only the law of contraries applies: either one or the other."[77] In this context, we must not think of authentic self-fulfillment in opposition to the demands of the moral life in Christ—moral precepts to respect our parents; the prohibition of adultery, homosexual practice, stealing, lying, murder, and so much more; virtues such as wisdom, justice, temperance, fortitude; and basic goods of human flourishing, such as human life, marriage and family, knowledge, and others. These are all demands expressing moral truths that are not of our own making but that are inherent to realizing the general purpose of human life. The dynamic of grace that disposes Christians to live the moral life in a relationship with God are the theological virtues of faith, hope, and charity. They are "the foundations of Christian moral activity; they animate it and give it its special character."

In sum, we are called by the Gospel to make moral choices that are worthy of the calling that we have received and embraced in Christ. We have become a new creation in Christ (2 Cor 5:17) and hence as the French Dominican moral theologian, Ceslaus Spicq, once put it, "elevated to this divine condition [means that we] must adopt moral actions to conform to [our] new dignity."[78] Thus, we cannot separate the moral choices that we make from knowing and loving God. "We should not be deceived.... Do you not know that the unrighteous will not inherit the kingdom of God?" (1 Cor 6:9). Thus, we must consider the moral life with respect to the general purpose of human life as a whole, namely, what man was made for. Pope Francis puts it this way: we must relate the Church's moral teaching to the "harmonious totality of the Christian message; in this context all of the [moral] truths illumine one another. When preaching is faithful to the Gospel, the centrality of certain truths is evident and it becomes clear that Christian morality is not a form of stoicism, or self-denial, or... a catalogue of sins and faults." The moral life in Christ is not a form of stoicism because we are not gritting our teeth when we choose to do the right thing; we know that doing the right thing is about authentic self-fulfillment. It is not just about cataloging sins and faults—although it is important to know what actions are sinful—but firstly about the central commandment of love: loving the Lord above all things, with our whole mind, soul and strength, and loving our neighbor as ourselves.

Thus, at one and the same time and inseparably, the moral life is, in light of man's final end, about a loving union with God. Our final end is to become co-lovers with God, entering by grace into the eternal exchange of love of the mystery of God himself, Trinitarian communion: Father, Son, and Holy Spirit. This love is God's own love flooding our hearts through the Holy Spirit given to us through faith in Jesus Christ (Rom 5:5; 8:9). Hence the moral life is relational in this way. The moral life is about happiness, indeed, about entering into the joy of the Lord, that is, about the deliberate ordering, by God's grace, of our moral actions to God, to eternal life.

NOTES

1. Joseph Cardinal Ratzinger, "Dialogue on the Papacy and Ecumenism between the Prefect of the Congregation for the Doctrine of the Faith and Rome's Waldensian Community."

2. See also, Pope Francis, *A Big Heart Open to God, A Conversation with Pope Francis*, 34.

3. Pope Francis, Homily, Palm Sunday, 24 March 2013, in *New Beginning, New Hope*, 10. See also, idem, "Believing in Joy," *Open Mind, Faithful Heart*, 12-18, for Bergoglio's reflections on other scriptural passages on joy, such as 1 John 1:4; John 15:11; and John 17:13.

4. Consider in this connection, Pope Francis, *In Him Alone is Our Hope, The Heart of the Church according to Pope Francis*. In this book, consisting of a Ignatian retreat the then-Cardinal Jorge Mario Bergoglio gave to the bishops of Spain during Holy Week 2012, the most cited work is Paul VI, *Evangelii nuntiandi*—besides, of course, the *Spiritual Exercises of St. Ignatius Loyola*.

5. Jorge Mario Bergoglio, "For Man," at 80-83. This essay is Bergoglio's presentation for the Spanish translation of Luigi Giussani, *The Religious Sense*, Translated by John Zucci (Montreal/Kingston: McGill-Queen's University Press, 1997).
6. Bergoglio, "For Man," 82.
7. Ibid., 82-83.
8. Joseph Ratzinger, *Principles of Catholic Theology*, 75-80, and at 76-77. This view of Ratzinger, now Pope Emeritus Benedict XVI, has remained unchanged almost thirty-five years later in *Without Roots: The West, Relativism, Christianity, Islam*, 124-26.
9. Cited in Henri de Lubac, S.J., *The Drama of Atheist Humanism*, 115.
10. Germain Grisez, *The Way of the Lord Jesus*, Vol. 1, Christian Moral Principles, 807.
11. Ibid.
12. Cited in Ratzinger, *Principles of Catholic Theology*, 76.
13. Ratzinger, *Principles of Catholic Theology*, 76.
14. Ibid., 79.
15. Ibid., 80.
16. Ibid.
17. 2 Cor 1:18-20: "But as God is faithful, our word to you was not Yes and No. For the Son of God, Jesus Christ, who was preached among you by us... was not Yes and No, but in Him was Yes. For all the promises of God in Him are Yes, and in Him Amen, to the glory of God through us."
18. See also, Joseph Ratzinger, *The Yes of Jesus Christ*.
19. Ratzinger, *Principles of Catholic Theology*, 81.
20. Ibid., 82.
21. Bergoglio, "The Courage of the Cross," in *Open Mind, Faithful Heart*, 64.
22. Bergoglio, "Believing in Joy," in *Open Mind, Faithful Heart*, 13.
23. Pope Benedict XVI, "Inaugural Session of the Fifth General Conference of the Bishops of Latin America and the Caribbean," §3.
24. Jorge Mario Bergoglio, *In Him Alone is Our Hope*, 20.
25. Ibid., 69.
26. Ibid., 109.
27. Ibid., 90. See also, "Joy and Perseverance," in *Open Mind, Faithful Heart*, 19.
28. Pope Benedict XVI Interviewed by German Reporters, "Interview of the Holy Father Benedict XVI in Preparation for the Upcoming Visit to Bavaria." In an address to the bishops of Switzerland, Benedict said: "If we let ourselves be drawn into these discussions [about moral issues], the Church is then identified with certain commandments or prohibitions; we give the impression that we are moralists with a few somewhat antiquated convictions, and not even a hint of the true greatness of the faith appears. I therefore consider it essential always to highlight the greatness of our faith—a commitment from which we must not allow such situations to divert us." ("Address of his Holiness Benedict XVI at the Conclusion of the Meeting with the Bishops of Switzerland").
29. Pope Francis, *A Big Heart Open to God*, 34. In his recent book of interviews with Dominique Wolton, *Pope Francis; A Future of Faith*, Francis states, "The least serious sins are the sins of the flesh... on the sins of sexuality.... That's what I've already talked to you about: what I call 'below-the-waist' morality. The more serious sins are elsewhere" (173).
30. Prioritizing the right to life of the unborn is, *contra* Archbishop Vincenzo Paglia, not an "abstraction." Abortion denies the humanity of the flesh and blood concrete reality of preborn human life ("What did Pope Francis mean when he said the unborn and the

poor are equally sacred?"). Such a claim is inconsistent with Pope Francis's recent denunciation of abortion as "what the Nazis did but only with 'white gloves.'" http://www.latimes.com/world/europe/la-fg-pope-abortion-20180617-story.html.

31. Cardinal Bergoglio with Rabbi Abraham Skorka in the book of dialogues, *On Heaven and Earth*, 107.

32. Pope Francis, *A Big Heart Open to God*, 34-35.

33. Janet Smith, "Are We Obsessed?"

34. Pope Francis, *A Big Heart Open to God*, 31.

35. R.R. Reno, "Francis, Our Jesuit Pope."

36. In my article, "Pope Francis and Ideology," I give an account of Pope Francis's treatment of the meaning of the concept of ideology and of its use by him in ideological explanations.

37. Pope Francis, *A Big Heart Open to God*, 31, 50.

38. Ibid.

39. For instance, Pope Francis, EG §§213-14.

40. Francis, "Address to the Leadership of the Episcopal Conferences of Latin America."

41. Here Pope Francis is crystal clear about the wrongness of abortion. But then he raises a question that he leaves unanswered about crisis pregnancies. He says: "On the other hand, it is also true that we have done little to adequately accompany women in very difficult situations, where abortion appears as a quick solution to their profound anguish, especially when the life developing within them is the result of rape or a situation of extreme poverty. Who can remain unmoved before such painful situations?" In respect of this concluding remark, Hadley Arkes correctly notes, "Nothing the Pope says here [§214] offers permission for aborting the child in these circumstances. But given what he has famously said about holding back from casting judgments, will we be surprised if people read his silence here as offering a tacit forgiveness in advance for the abortions that would dissolve the problem? Francis surely knows that these cases have caused the most strain in explaining the position of the Church. This is the place where teaching is needed. He might have called back his earlier words and said, 'I understand the grief of people who have to endure great suffering, yet slowly but surely we all have to let the joy of faith slowly revive as a quiet yet firm trust, even amid the greatest distress.' But he chose to remain silent on the matter, even after he had raised the question" (Hadley Arkes, "Francis, The Writer Unbound"). And yet, most recently Pope Francis has said in his address to the Italian Association of Large Families, Vatican City, 28 December 2014 (italics added): "Dear parents, I am grateful to you for the example of love towards life, that you preserve from conception to natural end, *despite all the difficulties and burdens of life*, and that unfortunately, the public institutions do not always help you" (Francis, "Pope Francis' Address to the Italian Association of Large Families"). Arkes's fear is, however, materialized in Leonardo Boff who didn't remain silent on the matter raised by Pope Francis: *Francis of Rome & Francis of Assisi, A New Springtime for the Church*, 111-12.

42. See most recently: Deborah Castellano Lubov, "'Abortion and Euthanasia Are Extremely Grave Evils Which Contradict Spirit of Life,' Condemns Pope Francis." For a compilation of twenty-two texts of Pope Francis since the Extraordinary Synod of October 2014 on abortion, euthanasia, divorce, marriage, contraception, homosexuality, see Sandro Magister, http://chiesa.espresso.repubblica.it/articolo/1351008?eng=y

43. Francis, "Address of His Holiness Pope Francis to... the Italian Catholic Physicians' Association." See also Pope Francis, "Urbi et Orbi Message, Christmas 2014": "My thoughts turn to all those children today who are killed and ill-treated, be they infants killed in the womb, deprived of that generous love of their parents and then buried in the egoism of a culture that does not love life."

44. "The Pope says that 'quality of life' is a lie."

45. Francis, "Address to the European Parliament."

46. Pope Francis, *A Big Heart Open to God.*

47. Pope Francis does indeed reject "religious subjectivism," a reductionist ideology that he calls "psychologizing." He means thereby an "elitist hermeneutics which ultimately reduces the 'encounter with Jesus Christ' and its development to a process of growing self-awareness. It is ordinarily to be found in spirituality courses, spiritual retreats, etc. It ends up being an immanent, self-centered approach. It has nothing to do with transcendence and consequently, with missionary spirit" (Pope Francis's address to the Leadership of CELAM). This religious subjectivism has expressed itself in the project of sexual liberation. On this latter development, see James Kalb, "Sex and the Religion of Me," in *First Things*, December 2014, 39-43.

48. Baggett, "Another Legacy of Vatican II," 50.

49. "Scandal is an attitude or behavior which leads another to do evil. The person who gives scandal becomes his neighbor's tempter. He damages virtue and integrity; he may even draw his brother into spiritual death. Scandal is a grave offense if by deed or omission another is deliberately led into a grave offense" (CCC §2284).

50. Pope Francis quoted in Junno Arocho Esteves, "Pope's Morning Homily: 'Scandal Destroys Faith!'"

51. See the website of Call to Action: http://cta-usa.org/faq/

52. Catholics for Choice website: http://www.catholicsforchoice.org/about-us/about-our-work/.

53. http://www.pfarrer-initiative.at/prot1_engl.pdf. Consider also the recent (2 March 2019) "Offener Brief an [Cardinal] Marx: Theologen fordern Reformen" regarding changes in the Church's teaching on sexual morality, particularly, homosexuality, women's ordination, and compulsory celibacy for the priesthood. Online: https://www.katholisch.de/aktuelles/aktuelle-artikel/offener-brief-an-marx-theologen-fordern-reformen.

54. Michael J. New, "Quinnipiac University Releases Poll on Catholic Attitudes Toward Abortion and Same-Sex Marriage." For the source of this summary, see Quinnipiac University National Poll, http://www.quinnipiac.edu/news-and-events/quinnipiac-university-poll/national/release-detail?ReleaseID=1961.

55. I treated the question of legalism and the Gospel in Chapter 3.

56. Pope Francis, *A Big Heart Open to God*, 34.

57. This integral perspective is missed by, for instance, Gerard O'Connell, "Call to Conversion." Also missed, most recently, by Archbishop Vincenzo Paglia, in his remarks on Francis's "seamless garment" approach to all of life issues (Cindy Wooden, "What did Pope Francis mean when he said the unborn and the poor are equally sacred?").

58. Pope Francis, *A Big Heart Open to God*, 34.

59. The point that Francis is making here requires some clarification on different levels of magisterial teaching. I discussed this matter briefly in the Preface. Helpful in this respect is the "Doctrinal Commentary on the Concluding Formula of the *Professio fidei*," by the Congregation for the Doctrine of the Faith. On the one hand, dogmas of divine and Catholic faith that require the assent of theological faith are such because "the Church proposes [them] as divinely and formally revealed and, as such, as irreformable." "These doctrines are contained in the word of God, written or handed down, and defined with a solemn judgment as divinely revealed truths either by the Roman Pontiff when he speaks 'ex cathedra,' or by the College of Bishops gathered in council, or infallibly proposed for belief by the ordinary and universal Magisterium." On the other hand, there are "all those teachings belonging to the dogmatic or moral area, which are necessary for faithfully keeping and expounding the deposit of faith, even if they have not been proposed by the Magisterium of the Church as formally revealed." Such doctrines can be defined solemnly by the Roman Pontiff when he speaks 'ex cathedra' or by the College of Bishops gathered in council, or they can be taught infallibly by the ordinary and universal Magisterium of the Church as a 'sententia definitive tenenda' [cf. LG §25]. Every believer, therefore, is required to give firm and definitive assent to these truths, based on faith in

the Holy Spirit's assistance to the Church's Magisterium, and on the Catholic doctrine of the infallibility of the Magisterium in these matters. Whoever denies these truths would be in a position of rejecting a truth of Catholic doctrine and would therefore no longer be in full communion with the Catholic Church" (§11).

60. Fifth General Conference of the Bishops of Latin America and the Caribbean, Aparecida, 13-31 May 2007, *Concluding Document*, no. 106.

61. Francis, "Carta del Papa Francisco a la 105° AP de la CEA." Pope Francis wrote: "Les expreso un deseo: Me gustaría que los trabajos de la Asamblea tengan como marco referencial al Documento de Aparecida y 'Navega mar adentro'. *Allí están las orientaciones que necesitamos para este momento de la historia*" (emphasis added).

62. John Paul II, *Ecclesia in Europa*, 2003 Post-Synodal Apostolic Exhortation, §§7, 9. I develop the implications of John Paul II's argument for developing a culture of life in my book, *Slitting the Sycamore, Christ and Culture in New Evangelization*.

63. John Paul II, *Springtime of Evangelization*, 59, 76. See also, EV §§19-24.

64. Ibid., 44, 58, 85.

65. Ibid., 148.

66. Pope Francis, "Address to the Community of Varginha." See also his 2016, "Address of His Holiness Pope Francis to Participants in the ... Assembly of the Pontifical Academy for Life." See also his 2017 address to the same group; and his 2018 address.

67. John Paul II, EV, §2, but also, §§32-36, and 38.

68. Pope Francis, "Address of Pope Francis to a Delegation from the Dignitatis Humanae Institute."

69. In his homily for the Holy Mass of "Evangelium Vitae" Day, Sunday, 16 June 2013, Pope Francis proclaimed the Gospel: "God is the Living One, the Merciful One; Jesus brings us the life of God; the Holy Spirit gives and keeps us in our new life as true sons and daughters of God. But all too often, as we know from experience, people do not choose life, they do not accept the 'Gospel of Life' but let themselves be led by ideologies and ways of thinking that block life, that do not respect life, because they are dictated by selfishness, self-interest, profit, power and pleasure, and not by love, by concern for the good of others. It is the eternal dream of wanting to build the city of man without God, without God's life and love—a new Tower of Babel. It is the idea that rejecting God, the message of Christ, the Gospel of Life, will somehow lead to freedom, to complete human fulfillment. As a result, the Living God is replaced by fleeting human idols which offer the intoxication of a flash of freedom, but in the end bring new forms of slavery and death. The wisdom of the Psalmist says: 'The precepts of the Lord are right, rejoicing the heart; the commandment of the Lord is pure, enlightening the eyes' [Ps 19:8]. Let us always remember: the Lord is the Living One, he is merciful. The Lord is the Living One, he is merciful" (§3).

70. John Paul II, *Evangelium Vitae*, §§92-93, 96, and 52, 4, and for this quote at §87.

71. LaVonne Neff reviewed Pope Francis's book, *The Church of Mercy*, and concluded that "Francis, who speaks often and passionately about issues of social justice, says not one word about abortion, euthanasia, or human sexuality" (*Christian Century*, 9 July 2014, 36-37). Two comments deserve to be made here. First, Neff is not a very careful reader of Francis. As I have argued in the text of this chapter, Francis speaks of the "culture of waste," "the "throwaway culture," which is a "common mentality that infects everyone. Human life, the person, is no longer seen as a primary value to be respected and safeguarded, especially if that person is poor or disabled or not yet useful, *like the unborn child*, or is no longer of any use, like the elderly person" (113; see also 60). Admittedly, it is not front and center here in this book, but that he says "not one word" is simply not true. Second, one can only wonder why the editors of this collection of homilies, addresses, and so forth didn't see fit to incorporate some of the addresses that I have cited in the text that abundantly demonstrate Pope Francis's commitment to the culture of life versus a culture of waste or a throwaway culture, which clearly is a continuation of

the previous two pontificates' commitment to the Gospel of Life. Was there tendentiousness in their selection? Were they trying to promote the narrative that this pope is not obsessed with the Gospel of Life?

72. Francis, "Address of Holy Father Francis to... the International Federation of Catholic Medical Associations." The paradox to which Francis is referring is fully analyzed in EV, §§18-19. Francis also says in the same address: "Every child who, rather than being born, is condemned unjustly to being aborted, bears the face of Jesus Christ, bears the face of the Lord, who even before he was born, and then just after birth, experienced the world's rejection. And every elderly person... even if he is ill or at the end of his days, bears the face of Christ. They cannot be discarded, as the 'culture of waste' suggests!"

73. Francis, "Address of His Holiness Pope Francis to the Members of the Diplomatic Corps Accredited to the Holy See."

74. John Paul II, cited in *Towards a Pastoral Approach to Culture,* Pontifical Council for Culture, §1.

75. Francis, "Address of Holy Father Francis to... the International Federation of Catholic Medical Associations."

76. In Chapter 3, I addressed the question of the relationship between the law and the Gospel.

77. Bergoglio, *In Him Alone is Our Hope,* 71. Indeed, this approach to the Christian life and hence to the moral choices that we make, has its roots in the *Didache*'s teaching that "There are two ways, one of life and one of death! and there is a great difference between the two ways." The *Didache* (=Teaching) is a brief early Christian treatise, which probably originated in the first or second century. Online: http://www.paracletepress.com/didache.html.

78. Ceslaus Spicq, O.P., *Charity and Liberty... in the New Testament,* 5.

6

The One Church, the Many Churches

I appeal to you, brothers, by the name of our Lord Jesus Christ, that all of you agree, and that there be no divisions among you, but that you be united in the same mind and the same judgment. (1 Cor 1:10)

The very mystery of the church invites, rather compels us, to ask about the perspective ahead for the difficult way of estrangement and rapprochement, of dialogue, contact, controversy, and for the ecumenical striving to overcome the divisions of the church.... Our thoughts about the future of the church must come out of tensions in the present, tensions that must creatively produce watchfulness, prayer, faith, and commitment, love for *truth* and unity, love for *unity* and truth—G. C. Berkouwer[1]

As Christians we cannot humble ourselves deeply enough over the schisms and discord that have existed all through the centuries in the church of Christ. It is a sin against God, in conflict with Christ's [high-priestly] prayer [for unity; John 17:21], and caused by the darkness of our minds and the lovelessness of our hearts.... [Christ] reigns... over the divisions and schisms of his church on earth. And his prayer for unity was not born of unfamiliarity with its history nor from his inability to govern it. In and through the discord and dissension, that prayer is daily heard and is led to its complete fulfillment.... Christ, who prayed for it [unity], is also the One—and he alone—who can bring it about. His prayer is the guarantee that it already exists in him and that in due time, accomplished by him, it will also be manifest in all believers.—Herman Bavinck[2]

"Ecumenical" must not mean concealing truth so as not to displease others. What is true must be said openly and without concealment; full truth is part of full love. "Ecumenical" must mean that we cease seeing others as mere adversaries against whom we must defend ourselves. We have pursued such a course long enough. "Ecumenical" means that we must try to recognize as brothers, with whom we can speak and from whom we can also learn, those who do not share out views. "Ecumenical" must mean that we give proper attention to the truth which another has, and to another's serious Christian concern in a matter in which he differs from us, or even errs. "Ecumenical" means to consider the whole, and not to single out some partial aspect that calls for condemnation or correction. "Ecumenical" means that we present the inner totality of our faith in order to make known to our separated brothers that Catholicism clearly contains all that is truly Christian. "Ecumenical" and "Catholic" in their very etymology say the same thing. Therefore, to be a Catholic is not to become entangled in separatism, but to be open to the fullness of Christianity. —Joseph Ratzinger[3]

If we are to speak to each other, we should know how each partner of the conversation appears to himself. It is antecedently thinkable that the partner in dialogue is in error in his self-evaluation but it is unthinkable that the intercourse would be fruitful if we did not take such self-evaluation into account.—Gustav Weigel, S.J.[4]

Ecumenical dialogue and research provides a uniquely privileged and potentially productive field for collaboration between Catholic theologians and those of other Christian traditions. *In such work, issues of faith, meaning [truth] and language are deeply pondered.* As they work to promote mutual understanding on issues that have been contentious between their traditions, perhaps for many centuries, theologians act as ambassadors for their communities in the holy task of seeking the reconciliation and unity of Christians, so that the world may believe [cf. John 17:21]. That ambassadorial task requires particular adherence to the criteria outlined here on the part of Catholic participants, so that the manifold gifts that the Catholic tradition contains can truly be offered in the *"exchange of gift"* that ecumenical dialogue and collaboration more widely always in some sense is.[5]

Walter Cardinal Kasper wrote early in the pontificate of Pope Francis that the latter's approach to ecumenism[6] is nothing new, everything of the Church's teaching is affirmed, and hence an ecumenism of conviction is still fundamental. The difference is that the unity of faith is lived out in a really new way, that is, in a style that uniquely characterizes Francis's Petrine ministry.[7] "Francesco è un Papa dell'incontro e un promotore ecumenico dell'incontro."[8] Francis is a pope who engages in encounter with others and promotes a culture of encounter through friendship and dialogue.[9] "An authentic [theological] dialogue is," says Pope Francis, "in every case, an encounter between persons with a name, a face, a past, and not merely a meeting of ideas."[10] In this respect, Massimo Faggioli is correct that Francis's ecumenical encounters are contextual and existential.[11]

Receptive Ecumenism

As the then Cardinal Ratzinger says about ecumenism, "Ecumenism is primarily an underlying attitude, a way of living Christianity. It is not a particular sector alongside other sectors. The desire for unity, the commitment to unity belongs to the structure of the same act of faith."[12] Of course, as is evident from his ecumenical practice, Pope Francis agrees with Ratzinger that ecumenism is a way of living the Christian faith, and hence ecumenism is not merely an afterthought about theological dialogue. It is inherent to the Church's self-understanding. There is, of course, no either/or here in Francis's understanding and practice of ecumenism as if he were asking us to choose between an ecumenism of friendship and an ecumenism of conviction,[13] or between the visible and invisible aspects of the one reality that is the Church.[14] As I plan to make clear, Francis practices, and hence urges us to practice, a dynamic process of "reconciled diversity" in which we walk together in the baptismal unity of Trinitarian communion—spiritual ecumenism, says Pope Francis—while at the same time engaged in ecumenical dialogue seeking full visible communion by means of the authentic ecumenism that is a gift at the service of truth, requiring "a continual path of deepening comprehension."[15] Clearly, then, Francis has not chosen between these two ways of practicing ecumenism. A recent example is found in his address to the Delegation of German Evangelical Lutheran Churches.

> The common goal of full and visible unity of Christians sometimes seems to recede in the distance when the dialog itself raises different interpretations of the nature of the Church and unity between Christians. Despite these outstanding issues, we must not give up, but rather need to focus on the next possible step. Let us not forget that we are taking a path of friendship, mutual respect, and theological research, a path that allows us to look hopefully to the future. I am pleased that the Commission responsible for the bilateral dialogues between the German Bishops' Conference and the Evangelical Lutheran Church of Germany is about to complete its work on the theme of "God and the dignity of man." Highly relevant

> are the issues that affect the dignity of the human person at the beginning and at the end of her life, as well as those of family, marriage and sexuality—issues that must not be ignored or neglected just because you don't want to jeopardize the ecumenical consensus that you have reached so far.[16]

Two other important examples make it abundantly clear that Pope Francis is not asking us to choose between an ecumenism of friendship and an ecumenism of conviction.[17] The first example is of the recent meeting with a Delegation of Old Catholic Bishops of the Union of Utrecht. In the last half century of ecumenical dialogue, says Francis, "Convergences and consensus have been found, and differences have been better identified and set in new contexts." He adds, however, "While we rejoice whenever we take steps towards a stronger communion in faith and life, we are also saddened when we recognize that in the course of time new disagreements between us have emerged. The theological and ecclesiological questions that arose during our separation are now more difficult to overcome due to the increasing distance between us on matters of ministry and ethical discernment."[18] These new disagreements that have complicated the ecumenical journey are found especially in new anthropological and ethical questions arising from issues in sexual morality.[19]

The second example is the Common Declaration signed by Pope Francis and the Ecumenical Patriarch Bartholomew. Notice that Pope Francis does not hold that full communion has been reached, but that we are making the journey towards full communion.

> To this end, the theological dialogue undertaken by the Joint International Commission offers a fundamental contribution to the search for full communion among Catholics and Orthodox. Throughout the subsequent times of Popes John Paul II and Benedict XVI, and Patriarch Dimitrios, the progress of our theological encounters has been substantial. Today we express heartfelt appreciation for the achievements to date, as well as for the current endeavors. This is no mere theoretical exercise, but an exercise in truth and love that demands an ever deeper knowledge of each other's traditions in order to understand them and to learn from them. Thus we affirm once again that the theological dialogue does not seek a theological lowest common denominator on which to reach a compromise, but is rather about deepening one's grasp of the whole truth that Christ has given to his Church, a truth that we never cease to understand better as we follow the Holy Spirit's promptings. Hence, we affirm together that our faithfulness to the Lord demands fraternal encounter and true dialogue. Such a common pursuit does not lead us away from the truth; rather, through an

> *exchange of gifts*, through the guidance of the Holy Spirit, it will lead us into all truth [cf. John 16:13].

Francis's ecumenical practice is, then, done in continuity with and hence radical dependency on the founding documents of Catholic ecumenism, Vatican II, *Unitatis Redintegratio*,[20] as well as the reiteration and development of the Church's irrevocable commitment to and a deepened theological reflection on ecumenism in John Paul II's *Ut unum sint*. Francis hasn't forgotten the ecumenical work of Joseph Ratzinger/Benedict XVI and Cardinal Kasper.[21] We must also not forget the fruit of the bilateral ecumenical dialogue of the last half century of the Pontifical Council for Promoting Christian Unity, most recently headed by the now President Emeritus Kasper. Indeed, Francis early on his pontificate "assures [us] that, "in continuity with my predecessors, it is my first intention to pursue the path of ecumenical dialogue."[22] On another early occasion he reminds us that the work of his predecessors, St. John XXIII, St. John Paul II, and St. Paul VI, "enabled ecumenical dialogue to become an essential dimension of the ministry of the Bishop of Rome." Indeed, this is so much that "today the Petrine ministry cannot be fully understood without this openness to dialogue with all believers in Christ. We can say also that the journey of ecumenism has allowed us to come to a deeper understanding of the ministry of the Successor of Peter, and we must be confident that it will continue to do so in the future."[23]

Arguably, there is a certain optimism expressed by Francis, but questioned by others, regarding the extent of agreement reached, for one, via the bilateral ecumenical dialogues between the Catholic Church and the Reformed, Lutherans, Anglicans, and Methodists. Cardinal Kasper's analysis of these dialogues gives us a more tempered judgment.[24] For another, Francis overstates the extent of agreement regarding the *Joint Declaration on the Doctrine of Justification*.[25]

In this chapter, I shall first discuss the relationship between an ecumenism of friendship and the dynamics of spiritual ecumenism. In the second place, I will develop Francis's claim that "the most suitable instrument for recovering a culture of encounter is awakening the capacity for dialogue."[26] I will follow this point with a third: an extended reflection on the ecumenical implications of the mark of the Church, *credo unam ecclesiam*, and in this connection also consider the question of unity and diversity in the One Church, the Catholic Church. I will then turn to a brief discussion of the relationship between receptive ecumenism and truth. Finally, I consider Pope Francis's appeal to the "hierarchy of truths" as a way of "progressing decidedly towards common expressions of proclamation, service and witness" (EG §246).

Ecumenical Dialogue

The Roman Catholic Church, according to John Paul II, holds that "full [visible] communion of course [would] have to come about through the acceptance of the whole truth into which the Holy Spirit guides Christ's disciples." Thus the Church's vision of visible unity "takes account of all the demands of revealed truth." Therefore, she seeks to avoid all forms of reductionism or facile agreement, false irenicism, indifference to the Church's teaching, and common-denominator ecumenicity. John Paul II correctly writes, "Love for the truth is the deepest dimension of any authentic quest for full communion between Christians." In other words, he adds, "The unity willed by God can be attained only by the adherence of all to the content of revealed faith in its entirety. In matters of faith, compromise is in contradiction with God who is Truth. In the Body of Christ, 'the way, and the truth, and the life' (John 14:6), who would consider legitimate a reconciliation brought about at the expense of the truth?... A 'being together' which betrayed the truth would thus be opposed both to the nature of God who offers his communion and to the need for truth found in the depths of every human heart." In short, "Authentic ecumenism is a gift at the service of truth" (UUS §§36, 79,18, and 38). These are some of the presuppositions of an ecumenism of conviction.

But an ecumenism of encounter, existential and contextual, such as practiced by Pope Francis is also important; indeed, such an encounter is deepened in an ecumenism of friendship and is itself the fruit of spiritual ecumenism. In this context, I shall say something, albeit briefly, about the nature and purpose of dialogue as expressed in UUS §§21-40. Most important, an interior conversion of the heart, indeed, repentance, is required as a precondition for engaging in ecumenical dialogue. Why this summons to conversion? "*Christian unity is possible,*" says John Paul, "provided that we are humbly conscious of having sinned against unity and are convinced of our need for conversion" (UUS §34, see also UUS §82). In this light, we can understand why an examination of conscience is required for authentic dialogue; confessing our sins, repentance, putting ourselves, by God's grace, in that "interior space where Christ, the source of the Church's unity, can effectively act, with all the power of his Spirit, the Paraclete" (UUS §35). Pope Francis has recently added his own words to this call for interior conversion. "In a spirit of mutual forgiveness and humble repentance, we need now to strengthen our desire for reconciliation. The path towards unity begins with a change of heart, an interior conversion [cf. UR §4]. It is a spiritual journey from encounter to friendship, from friendship to brotherhood, from brotherhood to communion. Along the way, change is inevitable. We must always be willing to listen to and follow the promptings of the Holy Spirit who leads us into all truth."[27]

The journey of ecumenical dialogue is thus an ongoing "dialogue of conversion," *on both sides*, trusting in the reconciling power of the truth that is Christ, to overcome the obstacles to unity. This, too, is Pope Francis's view.[28] The ground motive of this dialogue for reconciliation is "*common prayer with our brothers and sisters who seek unity in Christ and in His Church*" (UUS §24). "Prayer is the 'soul' of the ecumenical renewal and of the yearning for unity," adds John Paul II. In short, it is the basis and support for *everything the [Second Vatican Ecumenical] Council defines as 'dialogue'*" (UUS

§28). Indeed, prayer is the heart of spiritual ecumenism.

Sometimes dialogue is made more difficult, indeed, impossible, when our words, judgments, and actions manifest a failure to deal with each other with understanding, truthfully and fairly. "When undertaking dialogue, *each side must presuppose in the other a desire for reconciliation, for unity in truth*" (UUS §29). In this connection, Bergoglio's point is important that dialogue "means not only *hearing* but recovering the ability to *listen*."[29] He links this ability to listen with receptive ecumenism. Francis writes: "It is not just about being better informed about others, but rather about reaping what the Spirit has sown in them, which is also meant to be a gift for us.... Through an exchange of gifts, the Spirit can lead us ever more fully into truth and goodness" (EG §246). Furthermore, dialogue must be deepened in order to engage the other person in a relationship of mutual trust and acceptance as a fellow Christian, responsive to him in Christian love. "We must never forget that we are pilgrims journeying alongside one another. This means that we must have sincere trust in our fellow pilgrims, putting aside all suspicion or mistrust, and turn our gaze to what we are all seeking: the radiant peace of God's face" (EG §244). A necessary sign of this encounter is that we have passed from "antagonism and conflict to a situation where each party recognizes the other as a *partner*" (UUS §41).[30] "You shall love your neighbor as yourself" (Gal 5:14), and in St. Paul's words, "especially those who are of the household of faith" (Gal 6:10).

Clearly, the Church regards non-Catholic Christians as belonging, however imperfectly, to the household of faith, and hence she speaks of them as "separated brethren." Notwithstanding their separation, they are still brethren, brothers and sisters in the Lord Jesus Christ. Thus: we must speak the truth in love (Eph 4:15). "With non-Catholic Christians," the Congregation for the Doctrine of the Faith adds, "Catholics must enter into a respectful dialogue of charity and truth, a dialogue which is not only an exchange of ideas, but also of gifts, in order that the fullness of the means of salvation can be offered to one's partners in dialogue. In this way, they are led to an ever deeper conversion in Christ."[31] In short, the ecumenism of conversion embodies the conviction that "dialogue is not simply an exchange of ideas. In some way it is always an 'exchange of gifts'" (UUS §28), indeed a "dialogue of love" (UUS §47). This is receptive ecumenism at its best. Francis stresses that receptive ecumenism is not driven by the desire to be better informed about others, "but rather about reaping what the Spirit has sown in them, which is also meant to be a gift for us.... Through an exchange of gifts, the Spirit can lead us ever more fully into truth and goodness" (EG §246).[32]

In the report of the second phase of the ecumenical conversations between the World Alliance of Reformed Churches and the Pontifical Council for Promoting Christian Unity (1984-1990), three contemporary Reformed and Evangelical attitudes toward the Roman Catholic Church are distinguished: "There are within the Reformed [and Evangelical] family those whose attitude to the Roman Catholic Church remains essentially negative: [1] some because they remain to be convinced that the modern developments of the Roman Catholic Church has really addressed the issues of the Reformation, and [2] others because they have been largely untouched by the ecumenical exchanges of recent times and have therefore not been challenged or encouraged to reconsider their traditional stance. But this is only one part of the picture. [3] Others in the Reformed [and Evangelical] tradition have sought to engage in a fresh constructive and critical evaluation both of the contemporary teaching and practice of the Roman Catholic Church and of the classical controverted issues."[33] How do those who belong to positions [1] and [2] make the transition to position [3]? Making that transition is a precondition for engaging in receptive ecumenism for only then will "we really believe in the abundantly free working of the Holy Spirit [such that] we can learn so much from one another!" (EG §246). In particular, what reasons motivated them to make that transition? In the next section of this chapter, I will consider a possible answer to this question in the realm of ecclesiology and ecclesiological epistemology.

Credo in unam ecclesiam

This section examines two fundamental ecclesiological questions in light of the confession "*credo in unam ecclesiam*," which is one of the marks of the Church—indeed, it has first place in the list of marks: one, holy, catholic, and apostolic—in the Nicene-Constantinopolitan Creed (A.D. 381). This confession can mean two things. First, it can mean that there is only one Church, not many churches, and this oneness then refers to the *unicity* of the one and only Church in which many individual churches are united in Trinitarian communion, the unity of the Father, and of the Son, and of the Holy Spirit. Second, it can mean that the Church possesses inner unity, meaning thereby as Walter Cardinal Kasper explains, "being undivided, and thus the identity of the Church with itself and the unanimity in the Church."[34] Now I shall examine the unicity of the Church and her inner unity by addressing two questions: "*What* is the Church? But also: *Where* is the Church and where is she realized in her fullness?"[35] These questions will be considered in light of the ecclesiology of the Dutch master of dogmatic and ecumenical theology, G.C. Berkouwer (1903-1996),[36] and Walter Kasper (1933-), the Roman Catholic theologian, cardinal, and the former President of the Pontifical Council for Promoting Christian Unity (2001-2010).

First, I consider the views of Berkouwer and Kasper on the unicity and hence unity of the Church as well as the concrete place where the Church is realized in all her fullness. Especially important in making their views clear is understanding the distinctions they make between unity and uniformity,[37] division and diversity, and complementary and contradictory differences in ecclesiological epistemology. Second, Catholic teaching holds that "[j]ust as in Jesus Christ, God has taken form not in any general humanity, but by becoming concretely 'this' man Jesus of Nazareth, it is analogously true that the fullness of salvation revealed in Jesus Christ is also present in a concrete visible form"[38] in the Catholic Church. This scandal of ecclesiological particularity in *this* concrete Church "provokes opposition in other churches and church communities."[39] In sum, the main aim of this section is to provide an answer to the question regarding ecclesial unity and diversity within the one Church of Jesus Christ.[40] Let me set up this ecclesiological question with some of Pope Francis's remarks on unity and diversity in an ecclesial sense.

In his "Address to the Pentecostal Community in Caserta," 29 July 2014, Francis rightly distinguishes "unity" and "uniformity." He often repeats the refrain: "true unity in the richness of diversity" with an appeal to the notion of "reconciled diversity"[41] and appeals to an image to explain that notion. He says, "We think of the polyhedron: the polyhedron is a unity, but with all different parts; each one has its peculiarity, its charism. This is unity in diversity. It is on this path that we, Christians, do what we call with the theological name of ecumenism. We try to have this *diversity become more harmonized by the Holy Spirit and become unity*."[42] Francis does not explain here how diversity, or difference, differs from division. He does not explain how this unity and diversity relate, that is, how unity becomes more harmonized and hence exhibited in and through diversity. Is he suggesting that diversity is to be valued in and of itself? However, if so, this would lead to ecclesiological relativism—which is contrary to Catholic ecclesiology. Elsewhere, he carefully distinguishes "diversity" and "division." He says, "The Holy Spirit is the Spirit of unity, which is not the same thing as uniformity. Only the Holy Spirit is able to kindle diversity, multiplicity and, at the same time, bring about unity. When we try to create diversity, but are closed within our own particular and exclusive ways of seeing things, we create division. When we try to create unity through our own human designs, we end up with uniformity and homogenization. If we let ourselves be led by the Spirit, however, richness, variety and diversity will never create conflict, because the Spirit spurs us to experience variety in the communion of the Church."[43]

Clearly, the pope has in mind bringing the unity of the Church to expression in and through the diversity. Some have appealed to the notion of "reconciled diversity" *à la* Oscar Cullman to explain Pope Francis's suggestive remarks.[44] According to Kasper, "With this formula [of unity through diversity] Francis means more than mutual recognition of the existing churches. He proceeds from the principle that the whole is placed over the part and, therefore, it is not only the sum of the parts or their combination" (EG §§234-37). Says Francis, "the whole is greater than the part, but it is also greater than the sum of its parts" (EG §235). This is one of Francis's first principles.[45] Therefore, according to Francis, the Church is greater than any one ecclesial community, but it is also greater than the sum of all these communities. What, then, is the Church, and is it coterminous with the Catholic Church, according to Francis? Francis does not say. In light of normative Catholic ecclesiology, this is a point of weakness in his ecclesiology. What we can discern is that he gives a great deal of room to the diversity and the individual character of the different churches. His model of unity is not that of a sphere "where every point is equidistant from the center, and there are no differences between them. Instead, it is the polyhedron [that is, three-dimensional body with many angles and surfaces], which reflects the convergence of all its parts, each of which preserves its distinctiveness" and seeks "to gather in this polyhedron the best of each" (EG §236). Kasper adds, "[The model of the polyhedron] replaces the model of concentric circles, often used on the Catholic side, and it makes possible a unity that preserves the distinctiveness of the different churches without, however, obscuring the identity of the whole. This image enables a mutual, ecumenical process of learning and a complementary relationship that is mutually enriching (EG §246). That is harmony, as created by the Spirit of God."[46] But this model of unity and diversity does not help us to distinguish diversity and division. Interestingly, Kasper himself uses the model of concentric circles in his book, *Katholische Kirche*.[47] Regarding this harmony, Francis explains, "This is not to opt for a kind of syncretism, or for the absorption of one into the other, but rather for a resolution which takes place on a higher place and preserves what is valid and useful on both sides" (EG §228). From what transcendent standpoint does Francis hope to see ecclesial unity and diversity within the one Church, the Catholic Church? He does not say, and hence he, unintentionally, leaves us with the impression of being an ecclesiological relativist or pluralist.

In my judgment, Ratzinger has a better grasp of reconciled diversity, indeed an excellent grasp of Cullman here, and hence of what Pope Francis, and, I would add, Kasper have in mind.

> I have found very helpful the formula that Oscar Cullman recently injected into the [ecumenical] debate: unity through multiplicity, through diversity. Certainly, division is harmful, especially when it leads to enmity and an impoverishment of Christian witness. But if the position of hostility is slowly removed from the division, and if, through mutual acceptance, diversity leads no longer to mere impoverishment but rather to a new wealth of listening and understanding, then during the transition to unity division can become a *felix culpa*, a happy fault, even before it is completely healed.... Along the path marked out by Cullman, therefore, we should first try to find unity *through* diversity, in other words, to accept what is fruitful in our divisions, to detoxify them, and to welcome the positive things that come precisely from diversity—of course, in the hope that in the end the division will cease to be division at all and will just be 'polarity' without contradiction. But any attempt to reach this final stage too directly in a hasty and hectic do-it-yourself rush only deepens the division instead of healing it.[48]

However, Ratzinger understands that the unity of the Church is not a human construction but a divine reality received as a gift; indeed, unity is both a gift and a task. That is why he can say, "the true Church is a concrete reality, an existing reality, *even now.*" Put differently, it is about catholicity in a concrete form. The Church is a *concretum universal*. Walter Cardinal Kasper explains:

> Just as in Jesus Christ God has taken form not in any general humanity, but by becoming "this" man Jesus of Nazareth, it is analogously true that the fullness of salvation revealed in Jesus Christ is also present in the Church in a concrete, visible form. Thus, the Catholic Church is convinced that in it—which means in the church in communion with the successor of Peter and the bishops who are in communion with him—the Church of Jesus Christ is historically realized in a concrete, visible form, so that the Church of Jesus Christ subsists in it—in other words, it has its concrete form of existence.

This constitutive feature of Catholic ecclesial identity, as correctly underscored by Kasper, does not imply that others outside the Church are not Christians or, adds Ratzinger, "dispute the fact that their communities have an ecclesial character." They do not exist in an ecclesial vacuum. True, they exist in real communion with *the* Church, the Catholic Church, but they are "true particular churches" (DI §17) only in some *analogous* sense since they remain in "imperfect communion" with that Church (UR §3). The Council describes these "true particular churches" as "positive ecclesial entities" (as Ratzinger phrases it), and, in addition, says Ratzinger, since "uniformity and unity are not identical," this means that "a real multiplicity of Churches must be made alive again within the framework of Catholic unity." It is this teaching that is missing from Francis's ecclesiological reflections.

Summarily stated, the then Cardinal Ratzinger put the question regarding the unity and pluriformity of the one Church this way:

> [The] Catholic tradition, as Vatican II newly formulated it, is not determined by the notion that all existing "churchdoms" are only fragments of a true church that exists nowhere and that one would have to try to create by assembling these pieces: such an idea would render the Church purely into a work of man. Also, the Second Vatican Council specifically states that the only Church of Christ "subsists in the Catholic Church, which is governed by the successor of Peter and by the bishops in communion with him" [LG 8]. As we know, this "subsists" replace the earlier "is" (the only Church "is" the Catholic Church) because there are also many true Christians and much that is truly Christian outside the [visible boundaries of the] Church. However, the latter insight and recognition, which lies at the very founda-

> tion of Catholic ecumenism, does not mean that, from now on, a Catholic would have to view the "true Church" only as a utopian idea that may ensue in the end of days: the true Church is reality, an existing reality, even now, without having to deny that others are Christian or to dispute the fact that their communities have an ecclesial character.... However, that unity of the one Church that already exists indestructibly is a guarantee for us that this greater unity will happen someday.[49]

Clearly, the Church regards non-Catholic Christians, by virtue of our one common baptism, as belonging, however imperfectly, to the household of faith, i.e., the Catholic Church, and hence she speaks of them as "separated brethren," brothers and sisters in the Lord Jesus Christ. Indeed, the Church expresses its identity as the one Church of Jesus Christ by establishing a relationship of dialogue with these churches. Dialogue means that we all learn from each other and do not dismiss each other out of hand. We must still speak the truth, in love (Eph 4:15), however, in our search to realize a fuller unity, namely, the fullest communion that includes unity in the faith, in the sacraments and in church ministry (LG §14; UR §2). Full visible communion is the goal of ecumenical dialogue.

The Second Vatican Council made a courageous step forward toward the unity of all Christians, according to Ratzinger. Indeed, the movement towards ecumenism, Ratzinger explains, "is the genuinely ecclesiological breakthrough of the Council," and, significantly, is an important illustration of the hermeneutics of continuity and renewal, and hence that development is organic and homogeneous. In other words, the Council found a way within "the logic of Catholicism for the ecclesial character of non-Catholic communities... without detriment to Catholic identity." Constitutive of Catholic ecclesial identity is that the Church of Jesus Christ is a *single* reality. Ratzinger adds, "this one and only Church, which is at once spiritual and earthly, is so concrete that she can be called by name." That is, she is "constituted and organized in this world as a society," and "subsists in the Catholic Church, which is governed by the successor of Peter and the bishops in union with that successor." "This declaration of the Second Vatican Council," states *Mysterium Ecclesiae*, a 1973 intervention of the Congregation for the Doctrine of the Faith, "is illustrated by the same Council's statement that 'it is through Christ's Catholic Church alone, which is the general means of salvation, that the fullness of the means of salvation can be obtained' [UR §3], and that same Catholic Church 'has been endowed with all divinely revealed truth and with all the means of grace' [§4], with which Christ wished to enhance His messianic community" (ME §1).

And yet, the Church must heed Jesus Christ's call to unity. In the words of John Paul II put it, "How is it possible to remain divided, if we have been 'buried' through Baptism in the Lord's death, in the very act by which God, through the death of his Son, has broken down the walls of division?" "With non-Catholic Christians," the Congregation for the Doctrine of the Faith states, "Catholics must enter into a respectful dialogue of charity and truth, a dialogue which is not only an exchange of ideas, but also of gifts, [indeed, a dialogue of love], in order that the fullness of the means of salvation can be offered to one's partners in dialogue. In this way, they are led to an ever deeper conversion in Christ" (UUS §§28, 47; LG §14; UR §2). This is receptive ecumenism at its best. It is the fruit of an ecumenism of encounter and spiritual friendship.

In light of Ratzinger's prescriptions in which a distinction is implied between division and diversity, I bring Berkouwer into ecumenical dialogue with Kasper in order to show that we can have "polarity" without contradiction.[50]

Unicity and Inner Unity of the Church

In Chapters 2 and 3 of Vol. 1 of his 1970 dogmatic study, *De Kerk*, Berkouwer reflects on the Church's confession, "*credo in unam ecclesiam*," on both the unicity of the Church and her inner unity, the division among Christians, disunity in the church, which has its origin in sin, as well as the difference between ecclesial diversity and division. Berkouwer develops an ecclesiology in which the unicity and inner unity of the Church, given the Church's pluriformity, is not shifted into the future or into an *ecclesia invisibilis*, a purely Platonic entity, as it were, with the latter seeking "to make everything dependent on the already present, but hidden, unity of the invisible church."[51] He is persuaded that the New Testament teaches that there is only one Church, not many churches, and this Church is the concrete, visible Church, here and now, rather than a prospective future reality.

For Berkouwer, the Church's unity as unicity, that is, the one and only Church, is the foundation of the inner unity of the Church. He says, "We have in mind the reference to the unity between Father and Son: 'that they may all be one; even as thou, Father, art in me, and I in thee, that they also may be in us, so that the world may believe that thou hast sent me' (John 17:21). Unity cannot be indicated more deeply than in this analogy."[52] Thus, according to Berkouwer, "the being of the Church, as willed by God, implies unity."[53] He adds, "Our conviction that the plural for 'church' is an inner contradiction is confirmed by the numerous characterizations of the Church of Christ in the whole of the New Testament: the one people of God, the temple of the Holy Spirit, the building of God, the flock of the good Shepherd. These images indicate in various ways the one reality of the church."[54] Therefore: "unity belongs essentially to the Church's being: the expression 'one church' is really a pleonasm."[55] He concludes that in light of the Fourth Gospel's reference to Jesus rounding up the scattered sheep, "Nothing else than one flock and one Shepherd (John 10:16) is conceivable." Hence, "The Church may forget neither the harvest nor the Shepherd of the sheep, for the Shepherd is known and recognized in the one flock. The picture of the Shepherd shows us Christ's unique work of gathering, which brings and holds the flock together."[56] He adds, "The unity is unquestionably clear: the Church is the household of God (1 Tim 3:15), the temple of God (1 Pet 2:9f.), the one flock of the one Shepherd (John 10:16). All such characterizations make any thought of the plural simply ridiculous."[57] So there cannot be many churches. Still, Berkouwer distinguishes between unity and uniformity, urging us to recognize not only ecclesial pluriformity but at the same time the calling to unity within the unicity of the one Church, the one fellowship.[58] He explains:

> The extreme concentration and responsibility of the Church's whole life does not require a forced, unattractive uniformity (in place of "pluriformity"). The Lord of the church who is the Shepherd of the flock, knows all the sheep—in all variation, in need and threat, and in the dangers of doubt and temptation. In only one thing are they "uniform": he cares for them all, in their individuality, their history, their problems, their time, their cares, their new tasks, their gifts, and their lacks. this care makes room for an unexpected, enriching pluriformity, which is manifold and inexhaustible.... Yet this pluriformity is possible only within the one fellowship, within which the possibilities of all times, lands, and circumstances are unlimited. Because the many questions today are so different and complicated, there cannot be uniformity in all solutions. But "pluralism" in various provisional solutions is subject to "necessity" as the decisive aspect of the good Shepherd's messianic life-work. The necessity was related to a new reality, to deep fellowship in him: "I have other sheep, that are not of this fold; I must bring them also, and they will heed my voice. So there shall be one flock, one shepherd" (John 10:16). Whoever abstracts in this pluralism even for an instant from the necessity of Christ's bringing the others [into the fold] must despair of unity and fellowship in the church, since there is so much variation in the many problems that face the church.[59]

Furthermore, we need to make clear that "pluriformity" is not the same thing as ecclesiastical relativism or pluralism. As Kasper explains, "It would be an anachronism to read into the New Testament the situation of today, which history produced, of separated denominational churches existing side by side. In the eyes of Paul, such a coexistence and pluralism of different denominational churches would be a totally unbearable idea."[60] Denominationalism would affect Christ himself by leaving us with a divided Christ. But given that the Church has *one* Lord, *one*

Mediator, and *one* Savior we cannot "replace the singular with a plural for the Church."[61] The reality of many separated churches would also leave us with a contradicting pluralism, or a confessional relativism,[62] meaning thereby a pluriformity that tolerates contradictions such that we can be indifferent to claims that purport to be equally valid. Says Kasper rightly, "Sooner or later, this causes new divisions or leads to indifference and relativism in the question of truth."[63] Rather, there exists a plurality of churches in the one and only Church, which Kasper calls a "complementary *communio*-unity." This concept anticipates the import of distinguishing division from diversity in one's ecclesiological epistemology. More about this epistemology below.

Kasper, like Berkouwer, also turns to John's gospel account for justifying the Church's unicity. He also justifies the Church's unicity in accordance with the confession of one Lord, one Mediator between God and man, one Savior (Acts 4:12; Eph 4:5; 1 Tim 2:5). Also significant for justifying unicity is that we are baptized in the one Spirit into the one body of Christ. "The body is a unit, though it is made up of many parts; and though all its parts are many, they form one body. So it is with Christ. For we were all baptized by one Spirit into one body" (1 Cor 12:12-13; see also Gal 3:28). Furthermore, the basis of the Church's unicity "is the one God who gathers his people and unites them in Jesus Christ in the Holy Spirit. Ultimately, the Church is one in the unity of the Father, and of the Son, and of the Holy Spirit."[64] Moreover, regarding the Church's inner unity, it is Christ who unites the Church in "one faith and one Spirit, and formed it in one Spirit into one body of many parts. The inner unity has its foundation in one Holy Spirit through one baptism (1 Cor 12:13) and participation in the one Eucharistic bread (1 Cor 10:17). Paul can even say we are 'one' in Jesus Christ (Gal 3:28; Col 3:11). In short, the Church *is* one in Jesus Christ. Again and again Paul calls for unity and unanimity in the Church. He believes: 'there is one body, one Spirit, just as one hope is the goal of your calling by God. There is one Lord, one faith, one baptism, and one God and Father of all' (Eph 4:4f)."[65]

In short, this inner unity or union with Christ in the Spirit refers to the reality of fellowship, of *communio*-unity. And this fellowship with Christ is not a mystical reality, says Berkouwer, as if that is the essence of the Church's *communio*. That would lose sight of "a penetrating, indissoluble connection with the concrete life of the Church on earth, directed to a unique 'representation' of Christ's work of salvation and of His fullness."[66] Rather, adds Berkouwer, "Fellowship arises here among those in whose midst He dwells and is present, fellowship in unity and concord, in knowledge, faith, and love. His nearness excludes 'schism' in the body. It is not a secondary result, but is due to the nature of His being Lord and Redeemer. The Church is gathered around Him and is assigned to testify to her common faith (Titus 1:4) and to our common salvation (Jude 3). In this light the fiery, passionate character of the admonition [to unity] is understandable, because an attack on fellowship signifies a violation of the mystery of Christ through a dark resistance, in which the Spirit is grieved (Eph 4:30) and the fellowship of the Spirit is obscured [cf. Phil 2:1; 2 Cor 13:14]."[67] Kasper adds to our understanding of this inner unity, this *communio*-unity, by drawing on the image of Trinitarian unity. We noted above that Berkouwer refers to Jesus' speaking of unity in terms of the unity between Father and Son. Adds Kasper, "a unity of reciprocal being in each other." Accordingly, relationality is constitutive for God himself because "God is one but not solitary" (CCC §254). He explains, "Trinitarian doctrine conceives the unity in God as the unity of the one God in three persons and as their reciprocal existing in each other." This unity is a unity of being, relationship, and love. "The relational unity in love should be the paradigm of unity in the Church. Just as three persons subsists in the one God, so the unity of the Church does not exclude but includes diversity. Hence, Vatican II spoke of unity as *communio* after the prime image of the Trinitarian unity [LG §4; UR §2]."[68]

Of course neither Berkouwer nor Kasper are blind to the reality of a divided Church. Hence, in view of that division, unity is both a *gift* and a *task*, an indicative and an imperative, with the former preceding the latter; with the latter being an admonition to restore unity among a divided Church, heeding Jesus' ecumenical imperative in his prayer that all should be one (John 17:21). Berkouwer says, "The problematic of unity and division affects the *credo* from the beginning on. There is no other Church than the earthly Church—in Corinth, in Philippi, in Smyrna, or in any other part of the world. As a result, whoever speaks confessionally about the unity of the Church must give account of what is in full view, namely, the Church in her disunity."[69] Yes, there is division among Christians, disunity in the one church, but this division is the fruit of human sin, and such disunity is sharply placed "under the criticism of the gospel."[70] Adds Berkouwer, "the disunity of the Church stands under God's criticism!"[71] Still, division and diversity or pluriformity are not the same thing. Significantly, pluriformity is not just another name for division; for unlike division it is positive.

How then do Berkouwer and Kasper give an account of unity in legitimate diversity and diversity within unity? Geoffrey Wainwright helpfully gives us a sense of ecclesial diversity.[72] Wainwright's typology is summed up by William Henn.[73]

1. First is the third-century view of Cyprian (d. 258), which completely identifies the unique, true Church of Christ with one's own church, in such a way that the rites celebrated in other communities have no validity whatsoever.

2. Another view would hold, with Calvin, that communities other than one's own may contain "traces of the church" (*vestigia ecclesiae*), though not the fullness of what God intended for the Christian community. Wainwright signals the recent Catholic teaching that the Church of Christ "subsists" in the Catholic Church as a current example of this view.

3. A further ecclesiology is assigned especially to the Lutheran reform. While not abandoning the view that the Church is a visible institution, emphasis is placed upon the Church as an event, which occurs whenever

the gospel is purely preached and the sacraments administered according to the gospel.

4. A fourth ecclesiological type is the "branch" theory characteristic of some theologians of the Anglican tradition. The one and only Church of Christ has various branches.

5. Wainwright's fifth type is called a more "subjective" ecclesiology and is associated with Protestant pietism of the 17th and 18th centuries. Christianity is a religion of the heart and the one Church is comprised of true believers everywhere, all who have a warm relationship with Christ and thus enjoy a certain union of affection with one another.

6. A sixth vision of "church" is associated with the great Protestant missions of the 18th and 19th centuries and is called an evangelistic model. It practices "open communion," emphasizing the inviting character of the gospel and the welcoming nature of the Church.

7. Wainwright's final type is associated with the Life and Work Movement and reflects the slogan "service unites." This pragmatic or secular approach holds that those who collaborate together in the cause of justice and peace are in fellowship with one another.

Berkouwer and Kasper's dialogue is best understood in light of one and two above. Furthermore, neither of them turn to a conception of unity in terms of the branch theory or a federation conception of the church in order to account for unity in legitimate diversity. As Lesslie Newbigin once wrote, and Berkouwer and Kasper agree, "the disastrous error of the idea of federation is that it offers us reunion without repentance."[74] There is diversity, but it is "the pluriformity of the church" and not a "plurality of churches."[75] Berkouwer's ecclesiology "seeks to examine the concrete, visible church, and does so by placing her in the light of pluriformity."[76] He explains, "One must definitely ask what we are to think of the undeniable 'plural' that dominates our speech, particularly in light of the self-evident singular."[77] Thus, there must be another way to do justice to the pluriformity of the one church, of unity and diversity, and diversity within unity, and it is here that Berkouwer brings into this discussion Abraham Kuyper's ecclesiastical epistemology.[78] This will remind us of Ratzinger's reflections on ecclesial unity and diversity as one of "polarity" without contradiction.

Kuyperian Ecclesiastical Epistemology: Truth and Its Formulations

Ecclesiastical epistemology deals with "the [perennial] problem of the relationship between truth and its human expression.... This is the problem of variable, historically defined thought forms in different eras when all kinds of philosophical notions have played a definite role. What is the relationship between unchanging truth and theological formulations and doctrinal choices?"[79] Francis's Lérinian conception[80] should be able to appreciate the ecumenical significance of this way of formulating an ecclesiastical epistemology in order to account for the distinction between unity and uniformity, division and difference. As Francis says, "In the Church there legitimately coexist different ways of interpreting many aspects of doctrine and Christian life; in their variety, they 'help to express more clearly the immense riches of God's word' [EG §40]" (GE §43). Similarly, but more explicitly, Kuyper's ecclesiastical epistemology attempts to make intelligible ecclesial diversity or pluriformity. Says Berkouwer, "Kuyper was dealing with a real problem, and he definitely touched on present-day problems when he asked whether varying interpretation as such already breaks fellowship with respect to the reality to which varying understanding is directed."[81]

The first principle of this epistemology is epistemic perspectivalism, namely, that "our knowledge of the truth is always imperfect and inadequate."[82] In other words, perspectivalism recognizes "subjectivity in the understanding of truth."[83] The acceptance of perspectivalism is a result of recognizing that "absolute or objective truth, which Kuyper affirmed," cannot "appear in unity of form and content."[84] Kuyper makes clear his rejection of the claim that "truth, which of necessity must be absolute, was also bound to maintain this absolute character in the unity of form and expression."[85] In Kuyper's view, "the truth of God was too rich and the great salvation in Christ too aboundingly precious, by reason of the Divine character exhibited in both, for them to be able to reach their full expression in one human form." Of course Kuyper understood "that theology as such could not dismiss the problem of how this multiformity was to be brought into harmony with the unity of the body of Christ."[86] Berkouwer explains Kuyper's view regarding the distinction between truth and its formulations, "Even though 'objective' truth is one, the 'subjective' application and confession must differ." "Revelation... is not an 'objective truth' suspended above human life. Consequently, Kuyper characterizes opposition to pluriformity as a form of dualism that does not allow the gospel to penetrate the fabric of life.... All of this is concentrated in Kuyper's conception of the [epistemic] distance between 'absolute' truth and what we men assimilate of it in our subjective perception."[87]

Clearly, for Kuyper, it is not that divine truth recedes behind various perspectives; truth itself is not plural, but our understanding of truth is.[88] Says Berkouwer, "Certainly, revelation is one, and truth in Christ is one; but when Christ is formed in believers, the law of development and subjectivity comes into operation along the way of a meaningful pluriformity."[89]

Berkouwer insists with some justification that a concern for perspectival pluriformity, such as in Kuyper's ecclesiastical epistemology, should not be mistakenly understood as relativism or subjectivism about truth.[90] But one must make clear that inadequacy of expression does not mean inexpressibility of truth, even divine truth. Kasper rightly remarks, "This modern principle of subjectivity must not be confused with the subjectivism which gives absolute importance to single, individual needs, concerns, perspectives, and so forth, thus making these the measure of all things. The principle of subjectivity makes no such particularist claim. Its claim is an entirely universal one. It postulates that in any given (and ultimately unique) subjective decision, the truth is at stake."[91]

It must also not be understood as a plea for ecclesiological relativism, meaning thereby that there are many concrete churches, or even that Kuyper was oblivious to disunity and division in the Church as the fruit of sin. Regarding the first point, Berkouwer explains: "Kuyper's anti-dualism in itself is irrefutable; revelation is fully intended to be understood and known, to enter into human conceptions, experiences, feelings, knowledge, and understanding. This 'entrance into' does not cast shadows on revelation; nevertheless, the Church must be aware of the incompleteness in all her speaking and confessing." In other words, Kuyper's anti-dualism does not imply that inadequacy of expression means, according to Kuyper, inexpressibility of divine truth. Still, Kuyper's distinction between truth and its formulations rests upon a more particular epistemological presupposition, namely, that all formulations of the truth are inadequate. Such formulations can never be adequate because they can never be exhaustive expressions of the truth. In other words, Berkouwer adds, "the issue is not about challenging revealed truth, but about recognizing the 'limitation' or 'incompleteness' of our knowledge... that is only sketched even in the most worthwhile formulation."[92] There is always more to say about the reality of faith. In short, "this has everything to do with inexhaustibility of the truth of the gospel."[93] As Francis puts it, "In fact such variety serves to bring out and develop different facets of the inexhaustible riches of the Gospel" (EG §40).

Unquestionably true, but Berkouwer leaves unanswered the question, as does Francis, how, say, Nicaea's or Chalcedon's formulations consist of statements that describe reality entirely truthfully even if inadequately?[94] In other words, his and hence Kuyper's ecclesiastical epistemology, in their attempts to legitimize ecclesial diversity, must answer the question in what sense dogmatic formulations or creedal statements are determinately true— actually corresponding to reality, bearing some determinative relation to truth itself[95]—but also how "every formula in which the faith is expressed can in principle be surpassed while still retaining its truth." To answer this question one must show that it doesn't follow from the true claim that doctrinal statements are historically conditioned and limited, indeed, inadequate, that this must result in their not being wholly true. As Karl Rahner correctly states, "they are an '*adequatio intellectus et rei*,' insofar as they state absolutely nothing which is false."[96] So the new linguistic formulation or expression can vary, as long as they mediate the same judgment about objective reality. What is more, adds Rahner, "a more complete and more perfect statement does not falsify the one it supersedes."[97] All of this requires treatment that I cannot give here. For now, let me just note that Kuyper fails to show a relationship between language and reality in respect of truth. Kasper is right: "When the thinking subject takes the centre of the stage, there is a danger that any objective truth—and even more a dogmatic truth of general validity—will seem to many people to be beyond reach. For them the centre is not the faith of the church but their own religious experience."[98] Rather, the relationship between dogmatic formulations and reality determines the truth status of the dogma. Consider, for example, the creeds of Nicaea and Chalcedon. Is what they assert and hence make judgments about, for example, the Trinity and the person and natures (human and divine) of Christ, true to reality? In other words, do they have truth-conveying status, meaning thereby that what is asserted in them is ontologically true? And what about linguistically articulated doctrine, judgments expressive of propositional truth, supporting the conclusive and abiding assertions of revelation and doctrine, and logically sustaining the affirmations of Christian belief, their universality, continuity, and material identity? Divine truth may be expressed incompletely and inadequately, but neither falsely nor indeterminately. Just because we do not know everything that there is to know about a particular divine truth it does not follow that what we do know is not determinately true in these doctrinal formulations.

Regarding Berkouwer's second point that justifying ecclesial diversity does not justify ecclesiastical relativism or pluralism, "Yet the decisive question arises precisely at this point. Must the so greatly varied subjectivity inevitably lead to the pluriformity of the Church (in the sense of many concrete churches)? Convinced that this question must be answered in the negative, we want to point out that a different conclusion can be derived from the variations in subjectivity and the plural assimilation of new, modern information than the conclusion that Kuyper drew from history: precisely when plurality becomes more visible than ever before, the call to unity and fellowship gains more force!" In other words, adds Berkouwer, "The stress on inadequacy and incompleteness does not legitimize the Church's pluriformity [in the sense of ecclesiological relativism], but rejects it because of the necessity of unity. In New Testament times, when the 'spread' of subjectivity had also become a reality, it was subjected to the discipline of unity in Christ. Imperfection is recognized, but it is taken up in the call—in antithesis to the individualizing of our knowledge—to understand the love of Christ 'with all the saints' (Eph 3:17). There is simply no road from the incompleteness that has its place within the framework of love (1 Cor 13; Eph 3:17) to a pluriformity whose form is division, disunity, and contradiction."[99]

Kuyper was already criticized by his contemporary,[100] Catholic theologian, Theodore Bensdorp, who argued that Kuyper never made clear how mutually contradictory creedal statements could nevertheless be the formulations of the same revealed truth, according to the same meaning and same judgment.[101] He criticized Kuyper of ultra-subjectivism. I agree with Berkouwer that "it would be erroneous to interpret this concern [for plurality and pluralism] as relativism or subjectivism." He adds, "rather, in the plurality it is necessary to grope for that which truly binds and unites."[102] Berkouwer elaborates: "That harmony [between various dogmatic formulations] had always been presumed, virtually self-evidently, to be an implication of the mystery of the truth '*eodem sensu eademque sen-*

tentia.' Now, however, attention is captivated primarily by the historical-factual process that does not transcend the times, but is entangled with them in all sorts of ways. It cannot be denied that one encounters the undeniable fact of the situated setting of the various pronouncements made by the Church in any given era."[103] How then, exactly, is a single and unitary revelation homogeneously expressed, keeping the same meaning and the same judgment, given the undeniable fact "of time-conditioning, one can even say: of historicity."[104] Says Berkouwer, "All the problems of more recent interpretation of dogma are connected very closely to this search for continuity.... Thus, the question of the nature of continuity has to be faced."[105]

One might say that Kuyper's ecclesiastical epistemology, in its most favorable light, is after a commensurable pluralism, to use a term coined by the American Catholic dogmatic theologian Thomas Guarino—allowing for legitimate pluralism and authentic diversity within a fundamental unity of truth. But neither Kuyper nor Berkouwer succeeded in giving coherent expression to a commensurable pluralism. Still, Berkouwer is correct that "the rise of a stronger sense of plurality coincides with new openness for the ecumenical problematic."[106] In my judgment, Vatican Council II was successful precisely where Kuyper and Berkouwer failed, despite the fact that Berkouwer recognized the hermeneutics of Vatican II's ecumenical significance almost a half-century back. In the fourth epigraph to this chapter, the International Theological Commission rightly stated that issues of faith, meaning, truth, and language are deeply pondered in order to promote mutual understanding on issues that have been contentious between the traditions of Catholicism and Protestantism.

Vatican II and Lérinian Hermeneutics

The ecclesiastical epistemology implied by Vatican II's Lérinian hermeneutics[107] helps us to address the issue of how to distinguish unity from uniformity, division from diversity, conflicting from complementary formulations of the truths of faith. Turning now to Kasper, who stands in the line of this hermeneutics, he, too, like Berkouwer, recognizes the ecumenical significance of the distinction between unchanging truth and theological formulations and doctrinal choices.[108] He explains: "The dogmatic decisions always take place in a specific historical situation, they use historical human language and ways of expression and are insofar historically conditioned. It pertains also to the historicity that dogmas can subsequently be deepened and complemented, obviously always in the same sense and the same meaning ['*eodem sensu eademque sententia*']. In other words, there is growth and progress in understanding the faith. However, within all this historical conditionality they express something that is valid and binding for all times."[109]

Hence, Kasper is drawing here a distinction between truth and its formulations in dogma, between form and content, content and context, propositions and sentences, such as was suggested by John XXIII in his opening address to Vatican II, *Gaudet Mater Ecclesia*: "The deposit or the truths of faith, contained in our sacred teaching, are one thing, while the mode in which they are enunciated, keeping the same meaning and the same judgment [*'eodem sensu eademque sententia'*], is another thing."[110] In my view, because of the connection between meaning and truth such that what is meant is judged to be true to reality, the most fitting translation is "keeping the same meaning and the same judgment." Briefly, the pope's statement raised the question of the continuity or material identity of Christian truth over the course of time. The Council's Lerinian legacy distinguishes between propositions and sentences. Propositions—contents of thought that are true or false, expressible in various languages, but more than mere words, expressing possible, and if true, actual states of affairs—do not vary as the language in which they are expressed varies (propositions are not linguistic entities). The subordinate clause in this passage is part of a larger passage from Vatican I, *Dei Filius* (Denzinger §3020), and this passage is itself from the *Commonitorium primum* 23.3 of Vincent of Lérins: "Therefore, let there be growth and abundant progress in understanding, knowledge, and wisdom, in each and all, in individuals and in the whole Church, at all times and in the progress of ages, but only with the proper limits, i.e., *within the same dogma, the same meaning, the same judgment*." Significantly, normative Catholicism has been Lérinian on this very point since Vatican I, through Vatican II and post-conciliar interpretations of doctrine—and hence anti-historicist or relativist.

Vincent already saw this clearly in the early fifth century—doctrine can develop, but cannot change its fundamental meaning and truth, i.e., the realistic meaning embedded in the dogmas, creeds, and confessions themselves. In short, the Lerinian legacy of Vatican II is that of commensurable pluralism—allowing for legitimate pluralism and authentic diversity within a fundamental unity of truth. Commensurable pluralism is, arguably, presupposed, even if not fully worked out, in post-conciliar interpretations of dogma/doctrine. Commensurable pluralism can (a) account for the need for new dogmatic formulations; (b) explain why propositions of dogmas/doctrines are unchangeable, irreformable, or definitive; and (c) justify the distinction between content/context, form/content, message and the medium.

Given the distinction between truth and its formulations, we can now see the import of the distinction between unity and uniformity, division and diversity, and complementary and conflicting formulations in ecclesiastical epistemology. Vatican II does not require "uniformity" in four distinct and specific areas of the Church's life: theology, spirituality, liturgical forms, and discipline. *Unitatis Redintegratio* states:

> All in the Church must preserve unity in essentials. But let all, according to the gifts they have received enjoy a proper freedom, in their various forms of spiritual life and discipline, in their different liturgical rites, and even in their theological *elaborations* of revealed truth. In all things let charity prevail. If they are true to this course

> of action, they will be giving ever better *expression* to the authentic catholicity and apostolicity of the Church. On the other hand, Catholics must gladly acknowledge and esteem the truly Christian endowments from our common heritage which are to be found among our separated brethren. It is right and salutary to recognize the riches of Christ and virtuous works in the lives of others who are bearing witness to Christ, sometimes even to the shedding of their blood. For God is always wonderful in His works and worthy of all praise. Nor should we forget that anything wrought by the grace of the Holy Spirit in the hearts of our separated brethren can be a help to our own edification. Whatever is truly Christian is never contrary to what genuinely belongs to the faith; indeed, it can always bring a deeper realization of the mystery of Christ and the Church. (UR §4, emphasis added)

It is significant that Vatican II refers, in particular, to "the differences in theological *expression* of doctrine" (emphasis added). In other words, different theological traditions "have developed differently their understanding and confession of God's truth. It is hardly surprising, then, if from time to time one tradition has come nearer to a full *appreciation* of some aspects of a mystery of revelation than the other, or has *expressed* it to better advantage. In such cases, these various theological *expressions* are to be considered often as mutually *complementary* rather than *conflicting*.... Thus they promote the right ordering of Christian life and, indeed, pave the way to a full vision of Christian truth" (UR §17, emphasis added). Expanding on the distinction between complementary and conflicting, consider the more exacting distinction that Yves Congar draws between contrast (*Gegensatz*) and contradiction (*Widerspruch*).[111] Says Congar, "The *Gegensätze* are contrasted positions which express different aspects of reality. When they are held in the living unity of the church which embraces them, each one is corrected by at least a potential openness to the complementary aspect. They interpenetrate in such a way that they have a mutual relationship. These are diversities in unity."[112] But "there is the danger that what are contrasts"—in short, as John Paul II puts it, "two different ways of looking at the same reality" (UUS §39)—might become contradictions."[113] John Paul explains:

> In dialogue, one inevitably comes up against the problem of the different formulations whereby doctrine is expressed in the various Churches and Ecclesial Communities. This has more than one consequence for the work of ecumenism. In the first place, with regard to doctrinal formulations which differ from those normally in use in the community to which one belongs, it is certainly right to determine whether the words involved say the same thing.... In this regard, ecumenical dialogue, which

> prompts the parties involved to question each other, to understand each other and to explain their positions to each other, makes surprising discoveries possible. Intolerant polemics and controversies have made incompatible assertions out of what was really the result of two different ways of looking at the same reality. Nowadays we need to find the formula which, by capturing the reality in its entirety, will enable us to move beyond partial readings and eliminate false interpretations. One of the advantages of ecumenism is that it helps Christian Communities to discover the unfathomable riches of the truth. Here too, everything that the Spirit brings about in "others" can serve for the building up of all Communities and in a certain sense instruct them in the mystery of Christ. Authentic ecumenism is a gift at the service of truth. (UUS §38)

Furthermore, contradictions fall out of unity with the whole tradition of faith and hence break the unity of the Church. A proposition and its negation cannot both be true (nor both false) at the same time. What for one is true, for another is false. Congar rightly rejects a dialectical notion of truth à la Schelling and Hegel in which unity is restored by reconciling contradictions among themselves.[114] Yes, unity may be restored when "false oppositions turn into authentic contrasts in the church."[115] This is what Thomas Guarino rightly calls "'commensurable' pluralism, i.e., different systems cannot hold positions that are fundamentally contradictory." He adds, they "must be commensurable with the fundamental creedal and doctrinal affirmations of faith. These affirmations are patient of reconceptualization, but always adhering to the '*eodem sensu eademque sententia*.'"[116]

But there are limits to pluralism: false oppositions may in fact be genuine contradictions. Commensurable pluralism is precisely what Kasper also defends as unity in variety. He explains: "Here we have to distinguish variety from mere multiplicity, and pluriformity from a pluralism of opposing and therefore irreconcilable standpoints. The pluralism of opposing and irreconcilable standpoints is a sign of disintegration, meaninglessness and the incapacity for synthesis. But variety is an expression of richness, and the abundance which is so immense that it cannot be reduced to any single concept, or uttered in any single statement."[117]

Moreover, the receptive ecumenist understands that "the condemnation of an error should not cast a shadow over what is valuable in its insights." Congar concludes, "A condemnation should not damage the development of these insights or of these demands with respect to what is true about them."[118] It is precisely Congar's approach—distinguishing between contrast and contradiction, and if the latter, learning from its insights, questions, and so forth, that helps us to understand receptive ecumenism. The latter means that ecumenical "Dialogue is not simply an exchange of ideas. In some way it is always an 'exchange of gifts'.... Dialogue does not extend exclusively to matters of doctrine but engages the whole person; it is also a dialogue of love" (UUS §§28, 47).

In this connection, I shall distinguish three dimensions in the work of ecumenism following the Congregation for the Doctrine of the Faith in its "Doctrinal Note on some Aspects of Evangelization." This Doctrinal Note states:

> Above all, there is [1] listening, as a fundamental condition for any dialogue, then, [2] theological discussion, in which, by seeking to understand the beliefs, traditions and convictions of others, agreement can be found, at times hidden under disagreement. Inseparably united with this is another essential [3] dimension of the ecumenical commitment: witness and proclamation of elements which are not particular traditions or theological subtleties, but which belong rather to the Tradition of the faith itself.[119]

In the first instance, then, listening means letting your ecumenical interlocutor speak for himself as a partner, allowing him to formulate his position in his own terms. Furthermore, inseparably united with listening is the necessity of theological discussion, of comparing and contrasting different theological viewpoints, and of critically examining disagreements that are obstacles to full visible unity with the Church, and hence dialogue—with the two dimensions of listening and theological discussion—as a means for resolving doctrinal disagreements and determining whether the beliefs of our ecumenical interlocutor are true or false in light of the authoritative sources of the faith (UUS §35). Hence, ecumenical apologetics is also a dimension of theological discussion.

Finally, again following the recent doctrinal note regarding some aspects of evangelization, there is the third dimension of witness and proclamation, and it flows from the Catholic conviction that the entire fullness of the means of salvation is present in the Catholic Church. "Everywhere and always, each Catholic has the right and the duty to give the witness and the full proclamation of his faith. With non-Catholic Christians, Catholics must enter into a respectful dialogue of charity and truth, a dialogue which is not only an exchange of ideas, but also of gifts, in order that the fullness of the means of salvation can be offered to one's partners in dialogue. In this way, they are led to an ever deeper conversion to Christ."[120] As I understand the doctrinal note, it urges us to distinguish the proclamation of the truths that belong to the Tradition of the faith itself (e.g., "Eucharistic Presence, Eucharistic Unity, and Eucharistic Sacrifice"), from those elements of particular philosophical and theological traditions, say Aristotelian Thomism, (concepts of substance/accidents), which are used to give expression to these truths in various theological formulations.

The main point of this section on Vatican II's Lérinian hermeneutics is to show that the ecumenical council held for the continuity of the Catholic faith "*in eodem sensu eademque sententia*" with the prior tradition. This, too, is the case with respect to its fundamental ecclesiology and the meaning of "*subsistit in.*"

"Subsistit in": The Church as *concretum universale*

I turn now to the second ecclesiological question posed by Kasper, "*Where* is the Church and where is she realized in her fullness?"[121] Let us be clear that the difference between Berkouwer and Kasper hinges on their answer to this question, rather than over the unicity and inner unity of the Church. This second question was addressed by Vatican II in *Lumen Gentium* §8. Says Kasper, "The Council declared that the one and only Church of Jesus Christ subsists in (*subsistit in*) the Catholic Church. In other words, the one Church is concretely present and remained to be concretely found in the church which is in communion with the bishop of Rome and in the communion of bishops among themselves."[122] For brevity's sake, rather than considering Kasper's worked-out account of the meaning of "subsists in" found in *Katholische Kirche* (234-38 [159-62]), I will turn to his summary statement in his 2004 address at the Conference on the 40th Anniversary of the promulgation of the Conciliar Decree, *Unitatis Redintegratio*. In this address, Cardinal Kasper gives an account, in part III, of the meaning of "*Subsistit in*"—meaning thereby an expression used to characterize the unicity of an historically concrete ecclesiology.[123]

> The concept "*subsistit in,*" according to the intention of the Theological Commission of the Council, means: the church of Christ Jesus has its concrete location in the Catholic Church; it is there that it is found. It is not a purely Platonic entity or a prospective future reality, it exists in a concrete historical form, it is located in the Catholic Church. Understood in this sense "*subsistit in*" encompasses the essential thrust of the "*est.*" But it no longer formulates the self-concept [self-image] of the Catholic Church in "splendid isolation," but also takes account of churches and ecclesial communities in which the one church of Jesus Christ is effectively present [UUS, 11], but which are not in full communion with it. In formulating its own identity, the Catholic Church at the same time establishes a relationship of dialogue with these churches and ecclesial communities. Accordingly, it is a misunderstanding of "*subsistit in*" to make it the basis of an ecclesiological pluralism or relativism which implies that the one church of Christ Jesus subsists in many churches, and thus the Catholic Church is merely one among many other churches. Such theories of ecclesiological pluralism contradict the self-concept which the Catholic Church—like the Orthodox Churches, incidentally—has always had of itself and which the Second Vatican Council also

> wished to maintain. The Catholic Church continues to claim, as it always has, to be the true church of Christ Jesus, in which the entire fullness of the means of salvation are present [UR, 3; UUS, 14], but it now sees itself in a context of dialogue with the other churches and ecclesial communities. It does not propound any new doctrine but establishes a new outlook, abandons triumphalism and formulates its traditional self-concept in a realistic, historically concrete—one could even say, humble—manner. The Council is aware that the church is on a journey through history towards a concrete historical realization of what its most profound essence "is" ["*est*"].[124]

Kasper makes several important points here. First, the unicity of the Church is characterized by an historically concrete ecclesiology because it is an existing reality, even now, having a concrete historical form in the Catholic Church, rather than being a purely Platonic entity or a prospective future reality. Second, the first principle of Catholic ecclesiology is retained, namely, that the Catholic Church is the most fully and rightly ordered expression of the Body of Christ, but also that there are elements or vestiges of the true Church outside the visible boundaries of the Church (LG §8, UR §3). Berkouwer rightly notes, "The elements of the Church in other churches, hence, are not seen as 'dead remnants' of the past; rather, their positive significance as a means in the hand of the Holy Spirit is stressed."[125] Indeed, says *Unitatis Redintegratio*, "These most certainly can truly engender a life of grace in ways that vary according to the condition of each Church or Community. These liturgical actions must be regarded as capable of giving access to the community of salvation" (UR §3). In other words, they are "by no means deprived of significance and importance in the mystery of salvation. For the Spirit of Christ has not refrained from using them as means of salvation which derive their efficacy from the very fullness of grace and truth entrusted to the Church."

Still, what Berkouwer sees here as a "radical change in the Roman Catholic judgment of other churches"[126] does not mean that she has either relativized—in the sense of ecclesiological pluralism[127]—or taken back her first principle of ecclesiology—the entire fullness of the means of salvation are present. "The other churches—in spite of their relatedness to Christ and the Holy Spirit—still do not partake in this concrete, institutional condensation and centralization of fullness."[128] Although the aspect of fullness continues to play a constitutive role in Catholic ecclesiology, it is now the case that it no longer means all or nothing, Kasper rightly states.[129]

To the extent that these elements or vestiges are present with varying degrees in these other churches, the Church of Jesus Christ, which is realized *per se* and *per essentiam* in the Catholic Church, is efficaciously present in these particular churches, meaning thereby that they participate *formaliter et substantialiter* in Christ's Church. Berkouwer agrees with this interpretation of Vatican II. "Since the relationship between churches is not simply a question of confession or denial of the truth, the problem arises as to degrees of [unity and] catholicity in the understanding of God's truth." Significantly then, "'Fullness' is not always contrasted to emptiness,' but also to incompleteness and partiality."[130]

Kasper summarily states, "The Council thus advocates a graded concept of Church according to which the non-Catholic churches and ecclesial communities participate in a graded way in the unity and catholicity of the Catholic Church."[131] Hence, the following dilemma must be avoided in reflecting on the meaning of "subsists in":

- *either* correctly affirming that the Church of Christ fully and totally subsists alone in its own right in the Catholic Church, because the entire fullness of the means of salvation and of unity, which is not found in any other church, is present in her; and then implausibly denying that Orthodoxy and the historic churches of the Reformation are churches in any real sense whatsoever, such that there exists an ecclesial wasteland or emptiness outside the Church's visible boundaries.[132]
- *or* rightly affirming that they are churches in some sense, in a lesser or greater degree to the extent that there exists ecclesial elements of truth and sanctification in them, but then wrongly accepting ecclesiological relativism or pluralism—meaning thereby that the one Church of Christ Jesus subsists in many churches, with the Catholic Church being merely one among many churches.[133]

Thomas Guarino instructively assists us in avoiding this dilemma by drawing on the concepts of analogy and participation, of primary and secondary analogates.[134] He argues, "In Vatican II's understanding, there exists full but not exhaustive identity between the church of Christ and the Catholic Church. The point is crucial lest some think that Christ's church is a Platonic idea, not fully realized in any one denomination. But that is the thinking neither of [Gerard] Philips nor of Vatican II. As Philips plainly states, the church of Christ is 'fully present' in the Catholic Church. Other churches participate—truly, intensively, and substantially—in Christ's church to a greater or lesser extent. To invoke again the traditional terms, the Catholic Church is the *per se* realization of Christ's church—but not exhaustively so. Other churches are the church of Christ by participation, *per participationem*."[135]

In short, the Catholic Church is the primary analogate of the church of Christ and the other churches, ecclesial communities, by virtue of their participation in that church, which is shown by the elements of truth and sanctification realized in them to a greater or lesser extent, are the secondary analogates. Concludes Guarino, "Vatican II's accent on the analogical similarity of other churches to Catholicism is one of the council's most significant theological fruits. It has given rise to a vibrant ecumenical spirit within the Catholic Church."[136] Analogical and participatory thinking helps us to give an account of unity and diversity within the One Church.

Proselytism, Evangelization, "Ecumenism of Return"

In a 2016 interview arranged by Fr. Antonio Spadaro, S.J., the editor of *La Civiltà Cattolica*, prior to the trip to Sweden for an ecumenical gathering anticipating the 500th anniversary of the Reformation, Pope Francis expressed something that he has voiced several times during his pontificate: "to proselytize in the ecclesial field is a sin." He added: "Proselytism is a sinful attitude." In a recent address to the Pontifical Council for Promoting Christian Unity, he repeats this point, saying that "proselytism is poisonous to the path of ecumenism." And even more recently, in his prepared address for his visit to Roma Tre University, he repeated this point, although more generally, namely, that in witnessing to the Christian faith, he did "not wish to engage in proselytism." This is strong language and deserves careful attention, because many think the pope is saying that the Catholic Church should no longer evangelize other Christians; in particular, many think that he is an ecclesiological relativist or pluralist. However, since the Church rejects ecclesiological relativism, it is difficult to understand Francis's negative attitude toward evangelization in the "ecclesial field," in the pope's phrase, of ecumenical dialogue.

Unfortunately, Francis did not define what he means by proselytizing, and did not distinguish it from evangelizing.[137] However, since his 2013 Apostolic Exhortation, *Evangelii Gaudium*, clearly regards the Church called by the Lord Jesus to evangelize, given her missionary nature, there is a difference here to be drawn. Francis, however, simply states that proselytism as such is a sin or poisonous. But he doesn't tell us why. Nor does he distinguish between unethical and ethical means of proselytizing. It helps to turn to a document produced by a working group organized by the Catholic Church and the World Council of Churches.[138] The group formulated some basic points about what would constitute improper "proselytizing" in an ecumenical context:

1. Unfair criticism or caricaturing of the doctrines, beliefs, and practices of another church without attempting to understand or enter into dialogue on those issues.
2. Presenting one's church or confession as "the true church" and its teachings as "the right faith" and the only way to salvation.
3. Portraying one's own church as having high moral and spiritual status over against the perceived weaknesses and problems of other churches.
4. Offering humanitarian aid or educational opportunities as an inducement to join another church.
5. Using political, economic, cultural, and ethnic pressure or historical arguments to win others to one's own church.
6. Taking advantage of lack of education or Christian instruction, which makes people vulnerable to changing their church allegiance.
7. Using physical violence or moral and psychological pressure to induce people to change their church affiliation.
8. Exploiting people's loneliness, illness, distress or even disillusionment with their own church in order to "convert" them.

Pared down for present purposes, only the second point raises fundamental ecclesiological questions (the rest may be accepted as unethical means, without any real theological difficulty). The ecclesiological question has to do with ecclesial unity and diversity in the one and only Church of Jesus Christ, the Catholic Church.

In his address to the Pontifical Council, Pope Francis reiterates the teaching of Vatican II, and of his two illustrious predecessors, John Paul II and Benedict XVI, namely, "Dialogue is not simply an exchange of ideas. In some way it is always an 'exchange of gifts.'... a dialogue of love" (UUS §§28, 47). Furthermore, he also repeats the statement of Pope Benedict XVI who, at an ecumenical meeting during his 2005 Apostolic Journey to Cologne on the occasion of the 20th World Youth Day, said, "unity does not mean what could be called an ecumenism of return: that is, to deny and to reject one's own faith history. Absolutely not! It does not mean uniformity in all expressions of theology and spirituality, in liturgical forms and in discipline."[139]

How should we understand the rejection of what is called here an "ecumenism of return"? As my colleague Daniel Keating describes it, "The model of 'return' positions the Catholic Church like the sun surrounded by so many planets who have spun off, and who are called to simply 'return' to the body from which they came."[140] Is Benedict XVI suggesting that the Catholic Church should no longer understand herself as the one true Church? Is he implying that there are many ecclesial expressions of the one Church that Christ founded, all being part of the one Church, and hence that the Church of Jesus Christ also subsists in these other churches and ecclesial communities? In other words, is Benedict XVI affirming ecclesiological relativism or pluralism?

The answer to this question is "no." In the Catholic Church alone is given the fullness of all means of salvation. The Church of Jesus Christ does not subsist in other churches and ecclesial communities, but only subsists in an undetachable and lasting way in the Catholic Church. Therefore, the essential unity of the Church is already present in it. But unity is a gift and a task; the latter precisely because of the division among Christians. Furthermore, as Vatican II's *Lumen Gentium* §8 affirms, there are elements of truth and sanctification existing outside the visible boundaries of the Church, and these do not exist in an ecclesial vacuum but rather in ecclesial communities: the written Word of God, the life of grace, faith, hope, and love, and other gifts of the Holy Spirit and visible elements of sanctification and truth, such as the sacrament of baptism. To the extent that these elements are present, the Church of Jesus Christ is efficaciously present in these particular churches to a lesser or greater degree. But the presence of these elements of sanctification and truth also means, as Berkouwer correctly states when describing the teaching of Vatican II, "'Fullness' is not always contrasted to 'emptiness', but also to incompleteness and partiality." Catholicity, then, like unity, stands in the light of gift and task.

Still, note well that Benedict XVI distinguishes in his ecumenical speech between "unity" and "uniformity." In making this distinction, Benedict is following Vatican II by not requiring "uniformity" in four distinct and specific areas of the Church's life: theology, spirituality, liturgical forms, and discipline. He is referring here to *Unitatis Redintegratio*: "All in the Church must preserve unity in essentials. But let all, according to the gifts they have received enjoy a proper freedom, in their various forms of spiritual life and discipline, in their different liturgical rites, and even in their theological elaborations of revealed truth. In all things let charity prevail. If they are true to this course of action, they will be giving ever better expression to the authentic catholicity and apostolicity of the Church" (UR §4; emphasis added).

It is significant that Vatican II refers, in particular, to "the differences in theological *expression* of doctrine" (UR §17; emphasis added). In other words, different theological traditions "have developed differently their understanding and confession of God's truth. It is hardly surprising, then, if from time to time one tradition has come nearer to a full *appreciation* of some aspects of a mystery of revelation than the other, or has *expressed* it to better advantage. In such cases, these various theological *expressions* are to be considered often as mutually complementary rather than conflicting" (UR §17; emphasis added). I think this claim about the legitimacy of diverse theological expression and articulation is at the root of the rejection of the notion of an ecumenism of return.

I think it would also be helpful to change the model/metaphor of the relationship of the Catholic Church to our separated brethren from "return" to "pilgrimage and journey." Keating here again is helpful.

> The language we find in the Church's documents on ecumenism, however, uses the metaphor of a common pilgrimage and journey that we are all on together. The Catholic Church cannot renounce her fundamental convictions while on this journey, but we recognize that we are all traveling together, and that as we go together we seek to draw closer in unity, hoping and working for the day when full unity will be attained. I also draw strongly on Ratzinger's comments about the requirement for "intermediate steps" on the road to full unity—the practice of ecumenism is principally these intermediate steps that both express and advance the unity we have. An ecumenism of return [1] has little or no place for the idea of intermediate steps; [2] nor does it put positive value on the expressions of unity that allow us even now to cooperate in common prayer, action, and mission for bringing the kingdom to the world. The pilgrimage model allows for all this and so better represents what ecumenism is intended to be.[141]

Thus, in rejecting the notion of an ecumenism of return, Benedict is *not* implying that there are many churches and hence urging the acceptance of ecclesiological pluralism or relativism, that is, with the Catholic Church being merely one among many churches. Rather, he means that we can no longer speak of a simple "return" to the Church as an ecumenical demand for non-Catholics when that is taken to mean, as the French Catholic ecclesiologist Yves Congar rightly states, "absorption or annexation by the Catholic Church, as if they themselves had no contribution to make to us as full and as 'catholic' a realization as possible of Christianity." In other words, our separated brethren have a real contribution to make to the fuller realization of the Church's unity and catholicity, and hence to the fullness of understanding and living of Catholic truth.

As Vatican II stated, they may come nearer to a fuller theological appreciation and expressions of some aspects of revealed truths, and "these various theological expressions are to be considered often as mutually complementary rather than conflicting." To use the term coined by the American Catholic dogmatic theologian, Thomas Guarino, this position may best be called "commensurable pluralism." As John Paul II puts it:

> In dialogue, one inevitably comes up against the problem of the different formulations whereby doctrine is expressed in the various Churches and Ecclesial Communities. This has more than one consequence for the work of ecumenism. In the first place, with regard to doctrinal formulations which differ from those normally in use in the community to which one belongs, it is certainly right to determine whether the words involved say the same thing.... In this regard, ecumenical dialogue, which prompts the parties involved to question each other, to understand each other and to explain their positions to each other, makes surprising discoveries possible. Intolerant polemics and controversies have made incompatible assertions out of what was really the result of two different ways of looking at the same reality. Nowadays we need to find the formula which, by capturing the reality in its entirety, will enable us to move beyond partial readings and eliminate false interpretations. (UUS §38)

Furthermore, adds Congar, "A Catholic ecumenism cannot forget that the church of Christ and of the apostles *exists*. Therefore, the point of departure for Catholic ecumenism is this [already] existing church, and its goal is to strengthen within the church the sources of catholicity that it seeks to integrate and to respect all their *legitimate* differences." In short, the unity of the Church is a complex notion; it is both *gift* and *task*, both indicative and imperative. Disunity is, thus, ultimately a failure to recognize the full measure of the one body of Christ, of that "*of the Catholic Church*," and as Congar adds, "in this sense it would not be *another* church, that is, an ecclesial body other than the Catholic Church, the Church of Christ and of the apostles."

In conclusion, there are three dimensions in ecumenical dialogue, namely, "above all, there is [1] listening, as a fundamental condition for any dialogue, then, [2] theological discussion, in which, by seeking to understand the beliefs, traditions and convictions of others, agreement can be found, at times hidden under disagreement." This second dimension includes ecumenical apologetics. Such apologetics and receptive ecumenism are not at odds. It is best illustrated in a book such as Matthew Levering's *Mary's Bodily Assumption*.

Accordingly, we may conclude with Berkouwer, who shares the heart of the ecumenical calling: "The very mystery of the Church invites, rather compels us, to ask about the perspective ahead for the difficult way of estrangement and rapprochement, of dialogue, contact, controversy, and for the ecumenical striving to overcome the divisions of the Church." Furthermore, he adds, "Our thoughts about the future of the church must come out of tensions in the present, tensions that must creatively produce watchfulness, prayer, faith and commitment, love for *truth* and unity, love for *unity* and truth." Love for the truth is the dynamic behind any authentic quest for unity between Christians, and the love for unity— "our fellowship is with the Father and with his Son Jesus Christ" (1 John 1:3)—for acceptance, reconciliation, and communion, is a desire for unity in the truth of faith and doctrine. Clearly, Berkouwer does not play truth and unity against one another, and, for that matter, neither does the Catholic Church.

Moreover, "Inseparably united with this is another essential dimension of the ecumenical commitment: [3] witness and proclamation of elements which are not particular traditions or theological subtleties, but which belong rather to the Tradition of the faith itself." This third dimension flows from the Catholic conviction that the entire fullness of the means of salvation is present in the Catholic Church. "In this connection," the Congregation adds, "it needs also to be recalled that if a non-Catholic Christian, for reasons of conscience and having been convinced of Catholic truth, asks to enter into the full communion of the Catholic Church, this is to be respected as the work of the Holy Spirit and as an expression of freedom of conscience and of religion. In such a case, it would not be a question of proselytism in the negative sense that has been attributed to this term." This is the essential difference between negative and positive proselytism, the latter—as the Church clearly teaches—being an integral aspect of evangelization, and so this is beyond ecumenical dialogue, that we are called always to bear "witness" to one another of the faith that is in us. We do this as brethren who recognize the Pauline mandate to overcome that which divides us. "I appeal to you, brothers, by the name of our Lord Jesus Christ, that all of you agree, and that there be no divisions among you, but that you be united in the same mind and the same judgment (1 Cor 1:10).

Unity, Catholicity, and Fullness

Both unity and catholicity are already an existing reality, a concrete embodiment, given in the Catholic Church, but they are also dynamic realities because "In the fullness that the Church received, she is directed toward fullness."[142] Hence, unity as well as catholicity are both gifts and tasks. Regarding the former, "unity is flawed because of the divisions. The ecumenical dialogue is to heal these wounds. Through it the imperfect unity is to be brought to full unity. This dialogue is not only an exchange of ideas but also of gifts."[143] The latter is again a reference to receptive ecumenism. In other words, different theological traditions "have developed differently their understanding and confession of God's truth. It is hardly surprising, then, if from time to time one tradition has come nearer to a full *appreciation* of some aspects of a mystery of revelation than the other, or has *expressed* it to better advantage. In such cases, these various theological *expressions* are to be considered often as mutually *complementary* rather than *conflicting*.... Thus they promote the right ordering of Christian life and, indeed, pave the way to a full vision of Christian truth" (UR §17; emphasis added). Thus, these traditions of other churches and ecclesial communities have a contribution to make—through integrating and respecting all their *legitimate* differences—to the Catholic Church bringing about a fuller and hence more perfect—that is, catholic—realization as possible of the Church. In other words, our separated brethren have a real contribution to make to the fuller realization of the Church's unity and catholicity, and hence to the fullness of understanding and living of Catholic truth. There is a connection to be made between unity, catholicity, and fullness. In sum, says Kasper,

> In contrast to the model of mutual recognition of equal churches, this results in an ecumenical understanding of catholicity in concentric circles and a graded participation in [unity and] catholicity. Whereas according to the previous model all churches are a part of the one catholic Church, the Catholic Church (similarly the Orthodox churches) teaches that, in it, the [unity and] catholicity is given in a way of concrete shape (subsists), that other churches already participate in this to different degrees and should on the way of ecumenical exchange participate in it ever more.[144]

In the Catholic Church alone is given the fullness of all means of salvation. Berkouwer's reflections on "fullness in Christ"[145] and the Church's participation in that fullness, having been entrusted to the Church in all its fullness, and in its concrete form, are very helpful for gaining a proper perspective on this ecclesiastical sticking point for Protestants in general. Regarding Jesus Christ, he is full of grace and truth (John 1:14), full of the Holy Spirit (Luke 4:1), with the fullness of God pleased to dwell in him (Col 1:19), and "in him the whole fullness of deity dwells bodily" (Col 2:9). Now, in what way is the Church related to the fullness of Christ and the fullness of God? Berkouwer explains: "The purpose of the knowledge of Christ is to be filled with all the fullness of God [Eph 3:18f.]; and in the unity of faith and knowledge, everything is directed to mature manhood, to the measure of the stature of the fullness of Christ [Eph 4:13]."[146] Admittedly, adds Berkouwer, "the sentences relating fullness to the Church are difficult to understand, but one cannot deny that we are offered an outlook on fullness and richness. Only if one honors, not minimizes, the Church's 'riches' and fullness, does one get a correct view of Paul's understanding of the Church. And whoever hesitates to do that should consider a statement that appears to be a simple fact: 'you have come to fullness of life in Him, Who is the head of all rule and authority' (Col 2:10)."[147]

Significantly, "fullness and fulfillment" are a gift to the Church's being, entailing a task as well since this gift does "not describe a tensionless 'being', as if the Church had already achieved the final purpose of all her ways; rather they appear in living and relevant connection with her concrete life on earth." Thus, Berkouwer rightly says, "In the fullness that the Church received, she is directed toward fullness. That is the fantastic dynamic characterizing Paul's view of the Church, and through it he wants to make the Church rest in Christ's self-sufficient work."[148] Furthermore, we cannot abstract the fullness that the Church received from Christ and his all-sufficient work from the calling to preserve this relatedness to him. Christology is not assimilated into the ecclesiology as if we are left with a deistic conception of the Church, meaning thereby that she is "left to her own, independent existence, as if her acquisition of fullness meant that she could find and go her own way." What Berkouwer calls the "correlative language of the Scriptures" must be attended to so that we might see the Church in the light of the fullness of Christ. "Therefore, the Church, after receiving this fullness, must set her mind on and seek many things [Col 3:1f.]; and from the fullness, the whole life becomes visible in a radical, utterly concrete admonition [Col. 3: 5f.; cf. Eph 4:17ff]."[149]

In this connection, the limits of this chapter will only allow me to give one brief example to illustrate that dynamic correlation between Christ and the Church, and hence between fullness and fulfillment.[150] *Lumen Gentium* §8 states about the Church that she "is at one and the same time holy and always in need of being purified (*sancta simul et semper purificanda*), and incessantly pursues the path of penance and renewal." In *Unitatis Redintegratio* §6 the Council states that the Church is called "to continual reformation" (*ad hance perennem reformationem*). Furthermore, several other paragraphs of *Lumen Gentium* makes clear that purification, renewal, indeed, reformation of the Church is the work of the Holy Spirit. "The Spirit guides the Church into the fullness of truth.... By the power of the gospel He makes the Church grow, perpetually renews her [*Ecclesiae eamque perpetuo renovat*], and leads her to perfect unity with her Spouse" (LG §4). In *Lumen Gentium* §7, the Church is subject to her Head, Christ "[i]n order that we may be unceasingly renewed in Him [*Ut autem in illo incessanter renovemur*]... so that she may grow and reach all the fulfillment of God." It is said about the Church in *Lumen Gentium* §9, "that moved by the Holy Spirit she may never cease to renew herself [seipsam renovare non desinat], until through the cross she arrives at the light which knows no setting." Finally, *Lumen Gentium* §12 states that the gifts of the Spirit among

Christ's faithful "renders them fit and ready to undertake the various tasks and offices which help the renewal and upbuilding of the Church [*pro renovation et aedificantione ecclesiae*]."

The Second Vatican Council focused not only on the dynamics of the hermeneutics of reform and renewal in the life of the Church but also on the development in her understanding of the truth. This is evident in the Vatican II decree on ecumenism, *Unitatis Redintegratio* §§4, 6: "All [Catholics] are led to examine their own faithfulness to Christ's will for the Church and accordingly to undertake with vigor the task of renewal and reform.... Christ summons the Church to continual reformation as she sojourns here on earth.... Thus if, in various times and circumstances, there have been deficiencies... in the way that Church teaching has been formulated—to be carefully distinguished from the deposit of faith itself—these can and should be set right at the opportune moment." Elsewhere in the Dogmatic Constitution on divine revelation, *Dei Verbum* we read: "For there is a growth in the understanding of the realities and the words [of divine revelation] which have been handed down.... For as the centuries succeed one another, the Church constantly moves forward toward the fullness of divine truth until the words of God reach their complete fulfillment in her" (DV §§8-9). Pope Benedict XVI, in his now famous 2005 Christmas address to the Roman Curia, called this hermeneutics of Vatican II "the 'hermeneutic of reform,' of renewal in the continuity of the one subject-Church which the Lord has given to us. She is a subject which increases in time and develops, yet always remaining the same, the one subject of the journeying People of God."[151] I have argued elsewhere in my recent book, *Revelation, History, and Truth: A Hermeneutics of Dogma*, particularly in Chapter 1, that a hermeneutics of creative retrieval, in short, of *ressourcement*,[152] is at the heart of the Second Vatican Council's Lérinian hermeneutics.[153]

In sum, I have given an answer to the fundamental ecclesiological question regarding ecclesial unity and diversity within the one Church of Jesus Christ. I have sought to be faithful to the Church's teaching regarding the unicity and inner unity of the Church, distinguishing between unity and uniformity, between division and diversity, and complementary and contradictory differences in ecclesiological epistemology. I have brought into ecumenical conversation the ecclesiology of Catholic and Reformed theologians, Kasper and Berkouwer.

Hierarchy of Truths, Encore

In *Evangelii Gaudium*, Pope Francis remarks in several paragraphs on the nature of ecumenical dialogue (§§244-46). In this final section, revisiting the notion of hierarchy of truths,[154] I would like to take as my starting point in discussing an ecumenism of conviction the remark that he makes regarding the ecumenical significance of this notion. Francis says, "If we concentrate on the convictions we share, and if we keep in mind the principle of the hierarchy of truths, we will be able to progress decidedly towards common expressions of proclamation, service and witness" (EG §246). Given the nature of his exhortation, Francis leaves unexplained how we are to understand the ecumenical significance of this notion. Still, he had elaborated on this notion earlier in Evangelii Gaudium:

> All revealed truths derive from the same divine source and are to be believed with the same faith, yet some of them are more important for giving direct expression to the heart of the Gospel. In this basic core, what shines forth is the beauty of the saving love of God made manifest in Jesus Christ who died and rose from the dead. In this sense, the Second Vatican Council explained, "in Catholic doctrine there exists an order or a 'hierarchy' of truths, since they vary in their relation to the foundation of the Christian faith" [UR §11]. This holds true as much for the dogmas of faith as for the whole corpus of the Church's teaching, including her moral teaching. (EG §36)

The claim here is that there is an ordered priority among the revealed truths of the faith, differing in their relationship to the foundation of the Christian faith. *Pace* Gaillardetz, I see no reason to be troubled by the 1973 CDF formulation of the hierarchy of truths that "some dogmas are founded on other dogmas which are the principal ones, and are illuminated by these latter." The whole passage in which this statement occurs is this: "It is true that there exists an order, as it were a hierarchy, of the Church's dogmas, as a result of their varying relationship to the foundation of the faith. This hierarchy means that some dogmas are founded on other dogmas which are the principal ones, and are illuminated by these latter. But all dogmas, since they are revealed, must be believed with the same divine faith" (ME §4). He claims, "The council introduced a crucial distinction between the content of divine revelation, understood as God's self-communication in Christ by the power of the Spirit, and those church doctrines which, in varying degrees, mediate that content."[155] However, that is not accurate. The council states, "When comparing doctrines with one another, they should remember that in Catholic doctrine there exists a 'hierarchy' of truths, since they vary in their relation to the fundamental Christian faith." The fundamental or foundation of the Christian faith is "the triune God, One and Three, and in the incarnate Son of God, our Redeemer and Lord" (UR §12). Gaillardetz is inhibited from seeing that the comparison is between divinely revealed propositions because he plays off against each other God's self-revelation and propositional revelation. However, revelation is both personal and propositional. I discussed this matter in the Introduction, and so I will not return to it here.

For now, I propose to explain the ecumenical significance of the notion "hierarchy of truths—with a little ecumenical help from the great Reformed master of dogmatic and ecumenical theology, Berkouwer, who has already played a significant role in my discussion of ecclesiology.

Pope Francis, then, joins the chorus of voices, which include luminaries like G. C. Berkouwer,[156] Oscar Cullmann, and Karl Rahner,[157] regarding the Roman Catholic Church's bold, new approach to ecumenism in Vatican II's *Unitatis Redintegratio* ("Decree on Ecumenism"), which represents a significant breakthrough, especially in view of one of its key principles, namely, the "hierarchy of truths." This stated principle regarding the hierarchy of truths was not only unexpected but also, says Berkouwer in his second Vatican II book, *Retrospective of the Council*, "a highly remarkable viewpoint brought in direct connection with the ecumenical problematic."[158]

> The way and method in which the Catholic faith is expressed should never become an obstacle to dialogue with our brethren. It is, of course, essential that the doctrine should be clearly presented in its entirety. Nothing is so foreign to the spirit of ecumenism as a false irenicism, in which the purity of Catholic doctrine suffers loss and its genuine and certain meaning is clouded. At the same time, the Catholic faith must be explained more profoundly and precisely, in such a way and in such terms as our separated brethren can also really understand. Moreover, in ecumenical dialogue, Catholic theologians standing fast by the teaching of the Church and investigating the divine mysteries with the separated brethren must proceed with love for the truth, with charity, and with humility. When comparing doctrines with one another, they should remember that in Catholic doctrine there exists a "hierarchy" of truths, since they vary in their relation to the fundamental Christian faith. Thus the way will be opened by which through fraternal rivalry all will be stirred to a deeper understanding and a clearer presentation of the unfathomable riches of Christ. (UR §11)[159]

In this paragraph, two matters must be highlighted. First, there is an order of priority or hierarchy among truths resulting from their different relation to the foundation of the Christian faith ("faith in the triune God, One and Three, and in the incarnate Son of God, our Redeemer and Lord" [UR §12]). Second, attending to this hierarchy of revealed truths helps us to understand better what unites and divides Christians in matters of doctrine. Two points need to be emphasized if we are to understand properly what is meant by a "hierarchy of truths," namely the nature of the order of priority and that there is no quantitative reductionism in this hierarchy. Let me briefly explain each of these points.[160]

Regarding point one, Christian truths are seen in relationship not only to each other but chiefly in respect of the central truths of the Christian faith. The nature of this relation is such, Rahner rightly states, that "one can first of all quite properly say that it consists of the fundamental truths of faith, those truths, therefore, on which everything else is based and which themselves are not actually derived from other truths."[161] Following Rahner, let's call this an "'objective' hierarchy of truth."[162] Thus, the Immaculate Conception of Mary and papal infallibility derive their justification from foundational truths such as the Trinity and the Incarnation. For example, "the dogma of Mary's Immaculate Conception, which may not be isolated from what the Council of Ephesus declares about Mary, the Mother of God, presupposes before it can be properly grasped in a true life of faith, the dogma of grace to which it is linked and which in its turn necessarily rests upon the redemptive incarnation of the Word."[163] The upshot of the objective hierarchy of truths is that any truth of divine revelation—the entire hierarchy—must be connected to the foundations of the Christian faith.

Regarding point two, exactly how attention to the hierarchy of truths helps us to have a better estimate of what divides Christians is unclear. Berkouwer notes, "It is not enough to merely gauge the meaning and scope of this expression. It is undoubtedly flabbergasting that this 'concentration' (on the fundamentals) that pretty much occupies all churches today is unexpectedly set forth in a conciliar decree and that this did not elicit more opposition despite its 'strangeness.'"[164] Indeed, that lack of clarity led to misunderstanding the hierarchy of truths in a "quantitative" fashion as if a reduction of Christianity to its essential content was the point of the hierarchy. In this regard, the "hierarchy of truths" is taken to ranking truths in the order of their importance such that there was a reduction of some truths to ultimate importance and others to relative importance.[165]

Consequently, so it was said, we may adopt an attitude of indifference regarding those truths lower in importance in that hierarchy with respect to the foundation of our faith, say, the Assumption of Mary. In other words, the latter could no longer remain a church-dividing issue because of its low rank—non-fundamental truths—in regard to the foundation of faith and hence the fundamental revealed truths at its base. This interpretation of the hierarchy is evident in the following passage. "A hierarchy of truths implies that an ecumenical consensus need not take place in every detail but, rather, on the more basic and fundamental truths of Christianity."[166]

But this interpretation of the hierarchy of truths is mistaken, as Berkouwer himself notes, because it breeds theological indifference. "Hierarchy is the very opposite of indifferentism."[167] Thus, the hierarchy of truths is not about separating nonnegotiable teaching from optional teachings of the Church. Rather, it brings an integral perspective to bear upon the whole body of truths by considering the question of their interconnectedness with the central mystery of Christ and the Trinity. Berkouwer explains: "In the first place, embedded in this expression in the decree is the question of the connection that binds together the 'elements' of doctrine, and above all the 'nexus' with Christ as the foundation, and of the variation in the connection with this foundation." Furthermore, adds Berkouwer, "The background of the hierarchy of truths lies in the perception that in the doctrine of the Church one can speak about the *center*, about the fundamental mystery of salvation, and also about the fact that not everything that the Church teaches can be called *central* in the same sense and without nuance."[168] In other words, the fundamental issue of the hierarchy is the question regarding the relation of all revealed truths to the foundation of the Christian faith—the Christological concentration, as Berkouwer and others have called it.[169]

This conclusion shouldn't lead us to overlook the legitimate sense in which some truths are weightier than others. Most important, the last consideration is a material principle—Christological concentration—that is, a principle of interpretation, not a selective principle.[170] As Walter Kasper explains: "It may even be—and has indeed often been in the history of the Church—that fundamental principles have been resolved on the basis of relatively peripheral questions. At the Council of Ephesus in 431, for example, the true incarnation of God was discussed on the basis of the title 'Godbearer' (*Theotokos*). The so-called peripheral truths should therefore not be treated with indifference."[171]

Furthermore, this mistaken interpretation implies an opposition between the hierarchy of truths of Vatican II's "Decree on Ecumenism" and Pius XI's 1928 Encyclical *Mortalium Animos*. "In the encyclical '*Mortalium animos*' the distinction between '*capita fundamentalia*' and '*capita non-fundamentalia*' is rejected. The value of this kind of distinction was opposed with the question of whether God had not revealed all truths, thus without nuancing them."[172] In his own words, Pius XI wrote:

> In connection with things which must be believed, it is nowise licit to use that distinction which some have seen fit to introduce between those articles of faith which are *fundamental* and those which are not fundamental, as they say, as if the former are to be accepted by all, while the latter may be left to the free assent of the faithful: for supernatural virtue of faith has a formal cause, namely, the authority of God revealing, and this is patient of no such distinction. For this reason it is that all who are truly Christ's believe, for example, the Conception of the Mother of God without stain of original sin with the same faith as they believe the mystery of the August Trinity, and the Incarnation of our Lord just as they do the infallible teaching authority of the Roman Pontiff, according to the senses in which it was defined by the Ecumenical Council of the Vatican. Are these truths not equally certain, or equally to be believed, because the Church has solemnly sanctioned and defined them, some in one age and some in another, even in those times immediately before our own? Has not God revealed them all? (MA §9)

Pius's point is, essentially, that all revealed truths must be held with the same divine faith because they are revealed and the Church infallibly declares them to be true. This very point was made by Archbishop Andrea

Pangrazio of Gorizia (Italy) to the council in its discussion of the schema of ecumenism, November 1963, when he introduced the principle of the "hierarchy of truths."[173] Still, Cardinal Pangrazio did not fail to add that some of these truths are more important than others. More important, in what sense?

We can get at that sense by following a distinction first drawn by Herbert Mühlen between a "doctrine's content from the authority with which it is proposed." Alternatively put, in the words of Thomas Guarino, "the distinction is between *centrality* to the foundation of the faith as opposed to the *certainty* with which the Church teaches it." In this regard, dogmas, such as the Immaculate Conception (1854) and Mary's Assumption (1950), may be very high in certainty but "relatively low with regard to the central truths of the Christian faith."[174] So, some revealed truths may be important because they provide the foundation to non-foundational teaching; in that regard they are central to the Christian faith. Yes, as *Mysterium Ecclesiae* reiterates, "all dogmas, since they are revealed, must be believed with the same divine faith." But what kind of ecumenical importance does this emphasis leave us with? Are we back to Pius XI, unable to make a distinction "between the act of faith by which a Christian believes in the Incarnation and that of the infallible papal magisterium [?]"[175] I don't think so. Congar's respectful criticism of *Mortalium Animos* is apt in this instance:

> While valid on its own level, Pius XI's criticism does not quite accord with reality. It is somewhat one-sided. Faith can be considered from two perspectives, either from that of its content, the objects to which it relates—I would say the *quod*—or from that of the formal motive, that is to say, what motivates us to believe—one might say the *quo*. ... From this point of view it is clear that the mystery of the holy Trinity is more fundamental and more important for the nature of Christianity than that of the Immaculate Conception, and the mystery of the incarnation more fundamental and more important than the infallibility of the papal *magisterium*![176]

Thus, we can hold on to Pius's point without forfeiting the distinction between foundational and non-foundational teachings. We may do so by focusing on the distinction between the certainty with which the Church teaches, the *quo* or formal authority infallibly declaring this or that dogma, and the centrality of content, the *quod* or material content of a doctrine. In terms of the former, we can now say that all revealed truths are equal; but in terms of the latter we can say that some truths are more fundamental and more important than others. In this sense, then, there is no inconsistency between *Unitatis Redintegratio* and *Mortalium Animos*.

What, then, are the practical implications of the idea of a 'hierarchy of truths' in an approach to ecumenical dialogue where significant theological differences remain between Reformed and Catholic Christians in their advancement of unity in truth?[177] The most important implication is that the hierarchy of truths is essential for discerning the extent of agreement between us regarding the foundations of faith as well as the basic differences that remain on particular questions. Properly understood, using the 'hierarchy' also illustrates the revealed truths that vary in importance, depending on their closeness to that foundation. These so-called peripheral truths, such as the four Marian dogmas, are not negotiable, and hence we are not indifferent to them. Still, the question arises as to how exactly we deal with these differences in ecumenical conversation when for the Church they remain church-dividing issues. This, too, is Berkouwer's question:

> The question can come up, then, of whether believers, Catholic and non-Catholic, cannot find one another in confessing the *central* doctrines and of whether a marked difference in "weight" and importance does not exist within the circle of the Church's doctrines, for example, between the doctrines of the seven sacraments and the hierarchical structure of the church, and the doctrine of the incarnation as the central, major mystery of the faith. In this way, exclusive attention to the *ranking order* is placed ahead of the *breadth* of doctrine; and ranking order of doctrine is not fixed arbitrarily, but from the perspective of proximity to the center. One could ask the question of whether the idea of a hierarchy of truths in the Roman Catholic system of doctrine is not a huge risk ... now that this 'ranking order' will need to be subjected to the judgment of other churches in connection with their 'proximity' and believing connection to Christ as the foundation.[178]

Berkouwer doesn't mention what risk he has in mind. But one can surmise from everything else he says that the risk is that the "hierarchy of truths" is misused in such a way that those truths, so-called peripheral ones, having less weight in the hierarchy, will somehow be treated with indifference. We may counter this misuse in ecumenical dialogue by keeping our focus on the relation of a stated teaching to the foundation, of proximity to the center, showing the sense in which it derives its justification from that foundation.

In this regard, Berkouwer's student, the late Canadian Reformed ecumenist, George Vandervelde rightly notes: "the discussion of differences must remain open and move toward greater agreement concerning the core of faith." He adds, "Precisely such a notion as the 'hierarchy of truths' can help maintain the ecumenical dynamic in the face of differences. This notion can break through a static fixation of 'basic differences' by constantly forcing dialogue partners to the unity that is to be found in the 'foundation of faith,' while at the same time opening up the possibility of articulating the confessional expression of that unity."[179] Putting into practice Vandervelde's ecumenical proposal requires that the Catholic ecumenist be clear that the Church rejects ecclesiological relativism ("all churches are basically the same"), false irenicism (a false conciliatory approach), doctrinal indifferentism ("doctrine divides"), a common denominator ecumenism ("mere Christianity"), and last but not least, ecumenical dialogue when it is understood as a negotiating or cognitive bargaining of doctrines ("these doctrines are non-negotiable as opposed to more peripheral aspects of Catholic teaching").

Of course, in order to move beyond a static fixation of basic differences, Catholic ecumenical dialogue requires that we "understand the outlook of our separated brethren," as the Decree on Ecumenism states. "Study is absolutely required for this, and should be pursued with fidelity to truth and in a spirit of good will. When they are properly prepared for this study, Catholics need to acquire a more adequate understanding of the distinctive doctrines of our separated brethren" (UR §9). Maintaining the ecumenical dynamic requires that we understand and practice authentic ecumenism as a gift of God's grace that is at the service of truth (UUS §39). It requires a receptive ecumenism in which we understand that ecumenical "Dialogue is not simply an exchange of ideas. In some way it is always an 'exchange of gifts'" (UUS §28). This is the legacy of Vatican II that John Paul II and Benedict XVI embraced, and, despite the lack of clarity in Pope Francis's thought—he sounds like an ecclesiological relativist—on the question of ecclesial unity and diversity in the One Church, the Catholic Church, it is also his legacy.

NOTES

1. *Vatikaans Concilie en de Nieuwe Theologie*, 249-50. The phrase "nieuwe theologie" (literally "new theology") in the Dutch title of the book is a clear reference to the *nouvelle théologie* of Henri de Lubac, Yves Congar, et al. That reference is lost in the English translation, which speaks of "New Catholicism." The Dutch historian of the Reformation and Reformed theologian Heiko Oberman (1930–2001) describes Berkouwer's book on Vatican II as "breathtakingly important" (*Evangelische Theologie*, v. 28, 1968: 388).
2. *Gereformeerde Dogmatiek* 4, 316.
3. Joseph Ratzinger, *Theological Highlights of Vatican II*, 45-46.
4. *Catholic Theology in Dialogue*, 76.
5. International Theological Commission, *Theology Today: Perspectives, Principles, and Criteria*.
6. The phrase "receptive ecumenism" was coined by Paul Murray, Dean and Director of the Centre for Catholic Studies, University of Durham, UK. It means: The essential principle behind Receptive Ecumenism is that the primary ecumenical responsibility is to ask not 'What do the other traditions first need to learn from us?' but 'What do we need to learn from them?' The assumption is that if all were asking this question seriously and acting upon it then all would be moving in ways that would both deepen our authentic respective identities and draw us into more intimate relationship" (https://www.dur.ac.uk/theology.religion/ccs/projects/receptiveecumenism/).
7. In his preface to the work by Riccardo Burigana, *Un cuore solo. Papa Francesco e l'unità della chiesa* (Milano: Edizioni Terra Santa, 2014).

8. Walter Cardinal Kasper, "Ecumenismo, i passi di Papa Francesco."

9. Jorge Cardinal Bergoglio, "Building a Culture of Encounter," Speech at the Twelfth Day of Social Pastoral Care, Buenos Aires, 19 September 2009, in Francis, Encountering Christ: Homilies, Letters, and Addresses of Cardinal Jorge Bergoglio, 136-39. Although this speech is not specifically about ecumenical dialogue, it certainly has a bearing on that dialogue.

10. Francis, "Address at the Divine Liturgy, Patriarchal Church of St. George in Istanbul."

11. Faggioli, "Ecumenism in Pope Francis," in *Pope Francis, Evangelii Gaudium and the Renewal of the Church*, at 162, 167.

12. Joseph Cardinal Ratzinger, "Dialogue on the Papacy and Ecumenism between the Prefect of the Congregation for the Doctrine of the Faith and Rome's Waldensian Community."

13. In 2014, the pope denied the Swiss bishops' the opportunity of uniting with Protestants at the Lord's Supper because it comes, he said, at the cost of denying the truth of Eucharist faith. Online: http://www.katholisch.de/de/katholisch/themen/kirche_2/141201_papst_gegen_gemeinsames_abendmahl.php. Since then the discussion regarding Protestants receiving communion, particularly the spouses of Catholic individuals, has changed this denial into a possibility via a pastoral approach. The limits of this chapter prohibit discussion of this pastoral approach inspired by the logic of pastoral reasoning in Chapter 8 of *Amoris Laetitia*.

14. Helpful here is Sean Corkery, "Interpreting 'subsistit in' today." By contrast, Fr. Thomas Rossica's address ("New Directions in Ecumenical and Inter-faith relations in the Mind & Heart of Pope Francis") to the USCCB Committee on Ecumenical and Interreligious Affairs November 2014 meeting is not helpful at all in clarifying the relationship between an ecumenism of friendship and an ecumenism of conviction. Online: http://vaticaninsider.lastampa.it/en/documents/detail/articolo/ecumenismo-ecumenism-ecumenismo-37469/.

15. Jorge Mario Bergoglio, *Education for Choosing Life*, 57.

16. Francis, "Address of His Holiness Pope Francis to a Delegation of the Evangelical Lutheran Church of Germany."

17. Another example would be Pope Francis, "Address at the Divine Liturgy, Patriarchal Church of St. George in Istanbul."

18. Pope Francis, "Greeting of His Holiness Pope Francis to a Delegation of the Old Catholic Bishops' Conference of the Union of Utrecht." In his letter commemorating the fiftieth anniversary of the "Decree on Ecumenism" (Unitatis Redintegratio), Vatican Radio reported that Pope Francis said that in the last half century "Earlier hostility and indifference that caused such deep wounds between Christians, the Pope says, have given way to a process of healing that allows us to welcome others as brothers and sisters, united in our common baptism. This changed mentality, he says, must penetrate ever more deeply into the theological teachings and pastoral practice of dioceses, institutes of consecrated life, associations and ecclesial movements. At the same time, he adds, this anniversary offers an opportunity to give thanks to God that we can now appreciate all that is good and true within the life of the different Christian communities. Pope Francis thanks all those who, over the past half century, have pioneered this process of reconciliation and he mentions the important role that ecumenical translations of the Bible have played in developing closer cooperation among Christians." Yet, since authentic ecumenism is a gift at the service of truth, then, "as we give thanks," the Pope says, "we must also recognize continuing divisions and new ethical issues which are complicating our journey towards unity in Christ. Rather than being resigned to the difficulties, he says, we must continue to trust in God who plants seeds of love in the hearts of all Christians."

19. Francis "Letter of His Holiness Pope Francis to Participants in the Plenary Assembly of the Pontifical Council for Promoting Christian Unity for the 50th Anniversary of the Decree 'Unitatis Redintegratio.'"

20. In Pope Francis's 2014 visit to Turkey: "By happy coincidence, my visit falls a few days after the fiftieth anniversary of the promulgation of *Unitatis Redintegratio*, the Second Vatican Council's Decree on Christian Unity. This is a fundamental document which opened new avenues for encounter between Catholics and their brothers and sisters of other Churches and ecclesial communities. In particular, in that Decree the Catholic Church acknowledges that the Orthodox Churches 'possess true sacraments, above all—by apostolic succession—the priesthood and the Eucharist, whereby they are still joined to us in closest intimacy' [§15]. The Decree goes on to state that in order to guard faithfully the fullness of the Christian tradition and to bring to fulfillment the reconciliation of Eastern and Western Christians, it is of the greatest importance to preserve and support the rich patrimony of the Eastern Churches. This regards not only their liturgical and spiritual traditions, but also their canonical disciplines, sanctioned as they are by the Fathers and by Councils, which regulate the lives of these Churches [cf. §§15-16]." (Francis, "Address at the Divine Liturgy, Patriarchal Church of St. George in Istanbul.")
21. For example, Joseph Ratzinger, *Church, Ecumenism, & Politics, New Endeavors in Ecclesiology*, Part Two, Ecumenical Problems, 69-138. Walter Cardinal Kasper, *Harvesting the Fruits: Basic Aspects of Christian Faith in Ecumenical Dialogue*. See also, Jared Wicks, S.J., "The Ecumenical Imperative in Catholic Theology and Life."
22. Francis, "Address of the Holy Father Pope Francis to Representatives of the Churches and Ecclesial Communities and of the Different Religions."
23. Francis, "Homily of Pope Francis at the Celebration of Vespers on the Solemnity of the Conversion of St. Paul the Apostle."
24. Kasper, *Harvesting the Fruits, Basic Aspects of Christian Faith in Ecumenical Dialogue.*
25. Lutheran World Federation and the Catholic Church, *Joint Declaration on the Doctrine of Justification*. Questions remained even after reaching some agreement.
26. Bergoglio, "Building a Culture of Encounter," 138. In this emphasis on dialogue, Pope Francis stands in continuity with Pope Paul VI who in August 1964, in the midst of Vatican II, issued the encyclical *Ecclesiam suam*. Pope Paul identifies dialogue as the governing theme in his ecclesiology, the Church's apostolic mission and calling. Francis, of course, is also following Pope John Paul II who, in *Ut unum sint*, viewed dialogue "as an indispensable step along the path toward human self-realization, the self-realization both of each individual and of every human community." John Paul adds, dialogue is a profoundly human act "rooted in the nature and dignity of the human person," and "involving the human subject in his or her entirety." Significantly, "Dialogue is not simply an exchange of ideas. In some way it is always an 'exchange of gifts'" (§28). Pope Benedict XVI also identified dialogue as a "duty... to continue towards this goal [of unity]... in order to deepen the common theological, liturgical and spiritual patrimony; with reciprocal knowledge, with the ecumenical formation of the new generation and, especially, with conversion of heart and with prayer" ("Homily of his Holiness Benedict XVI at the Liturgy of Vespers for the Conclusion of the Week of Prayer for Christian Unity").
27. Francis, "Greeting of His Holiness Pope Francis to a Delegation of the Old Catholic Bishops' Conference of the Union of Utrecht."
28. Elise Harris, "'Conversion is a prerequisite to ecumenism,' Pope Francis says."
29. Bergoglio, "Building a Culture of Encounter," 138.
30. We hear a clear echo of John Paul's point in Pope Francis's homily concluding the week of Christian Unity at the Basilica of St. Paul Outside the Walls, Rome: "So many past controversies between Christians can be overcome when we put aside all polemical or apologetic approaches, and seek instead to grasp more fully what unites us, namely, our call to share in the mystery of the Father's love revealed to us by the Son through the Holy Spirit." Christian unity "will not be the fruit of subtle theoretical discussions in which each party tries to convince the other of the soundness of their opinions. The Son of man will come and find us engaged in an argument," the Pope warned. Instead, "we need to realize that, to plumb the depths of the mystery of God, we need one another, we need to encounter one another and to challenge one another under the guidance of

the Holy Spirit, who harmonizes diversities and overcomes conflicts" ("Homily of Pope Francis at the Celebration of Vespers on the Solemnity of the Conversion of St. Paul the Apostle," 2015). See also, Pope Francis, "We must never forget that we are pilgrims journeying alongside one another. This means that we must have sincere trust in our fellow pilgrims, putting aside al suspicion or mistrust, and turn our gaze to what we are all seeking: the radiant peace of God's face" (EG §244).

31. "Doctrinal Note on Some Aspects of Evangelization," 3 December 2007, Section IV.

32. See also, *A Big Heart Open to God*, "In ecumenical relations it is important not only to know each other better, but also to recognize what the Spirit has sown in the other as a gift for us" (39).

33. William G. Rusch et al. eds. "Towards a Common Understanding of the Church," in *Deepening Communion*, 179-229, and at 187.

34. Walter Cardinal Kasper, *Katholische Kirche: Wesen, Wirklichkeit, Sendung*; ET: *The Catholic Church*, 152.

35. Idem, *Harvesting the Fruits*, 153.

36. G.C. Berkouwer, *De Kerk*, Vol. I, *Eenheid en Katholiciteit*; Vol. II, *Apostoliciteit en Heiligheid*. ET of both volumes: *The Church*. For an in-depth study of Berkouwer's ecumenical theology and his decades-long engagement with Catholicism, see my *Berkouwer and Catholicism: Disputed Questions*.

37. Francis repeatedly underscores this distinction. See Hannah Brockhaus, "Unity is not the same as uniformity, Pope Francis says."

38. Kasper, *Katholische Kirche*, 261 [179]. See also, Kasper, *Harvesting the Fruits*, 154.

39. Ibid., 233 [158].

40. Given the limits of this chapter, I will not respond to this opposition that is expressed in the charge, for example, that the Catholic Church's ecclesiology has the tendency to "assimilate Christology into ecclesiology," or make "the church... constitutive of the Son's identities as are the Father and the Spirit" (Kevin Vanhoozer, *Biblical Authority After Babel*, 152). Objections like this have been around for a while. The great American Presbyterian theologian, B. B. Warfield (1851-1921) raised this charge in his 1915 study, *The Plan of Salvation*, Chapter 3, Sacerdotalism, 48-65. For example, "[The Church] does not, of course, supersede the work of Christ.... But in the present dispensation, the Church, in large measure, has taken over the work of Christ. It is in a real sense, a reincarnation of Christ to the end of the continuation and completion of his redemptive mission" (50). Again, "In one word, the Church in this [Roman] system is conceived to be Jesus Christ himself in his earthly form, and it is therefore substituted for him as the proximate object of the faith of Christians" (51). And again, "It is to the Church rather than to Christ or to the grace of God that the salvation of men is immediately ascribed" (52). Gregg Allison, too, raises a similar objection. He is deeply distressed by the tendency in Catholic theology of substituting "'the church in the place of its absent Lord'" (Michael Horton cited by Allison, *Roman Catholic Theology & Practice: An Evangelical Assessment*, 65). Similarly, Leonardo De Chirico, *Evangelical Theological Perspectives on post-Vatican II Roman Catholicism*. Vol. 19, Religions and Discourse. I have criticized elsewhere De Chirico's hermeneutics of Catholicism, namely, in my article review of Allison's book, which is uncritically dependent on De Chirico's assessment of Catholicism. See my article review, "A Catholic Assessment of Gregg Allison's Critique of the 'Hermeneutics of Catholicism.'"

41. Francis, "The Church a unity of diversities, Pope tells Brazil's bishops"; idem, "Homily on Apostolic Journey of His Holiness Pope Francis to Turkey."

42. Idem, "Pope's Address to Pentecostal Community in Caserta."

43. Idem, "Homily on Apostolic Journey of his Holiness Pope Francis to Turkey."

44. Francis himself appeals to the notion of "reconciled diversity' (EG §230). See O. Cullmann, *L'unité par la diversité*.

45. There are four first principles: time is greater than space, unity prevails over conflict, realities are more important than ideas, the whole is greater than the part (EG §§222-37).

46. Kasper, *Pope Francis' Revolution of Tenderness and Love*, Translated by William Madges, 57.

47. Idem, *Katholische Kirche*, 264 [181].

48. Cardinal Ratzinger, "On the Progress of Ecumenism," in *Church, Ecumenism, & Politics*, 130-38, and 135-36.

49. "Luther and the Unity of the Churches," (1983), *Church, Ecumenism, & Politics*, 118-20.

50. Ratzinger's formulation here of unity and diversity is under the influence of Guardini and Möhler.

51. Berkouwer, *De Kerk*, Vol. I, 61 [51].

52. Ibid., 56-57 [48].

53. Ibid., 32 [30].

54. Ibid., 94 [77].

55. Ibid., 33 [30].

56. Ibid., 59 [50].

57. Ibid., 47 [42]. See also, John Williamson Nevin, "Catholic Unity," (1844), in *The Anxious Bench*, Second Edition, edited by Augustine Thompson, O.P. (Eugene, Ore.: Wipf and Stock Publishers), "The unity of the Church is a cardinal truth, in the Christian system. It is involved in the conception of the Christian salvation itself. To renounce it, or lose sight of it, is to make shipwreck of the gospel, to the same extent. There is no room here for individualism or particularism, as such.... Christ cannot be divided.... We are not Christians, each one by himself and for himself, but we become such through the Church" (7).

58. Berkouwer, *De Kerk*, Vol. I, 93 [75-76].

59. Ibid., 93 [75-76].

60. Kasper, *Katholische Kirche*, 226 [153].

61. Berkouwer, *De Kerk*, Vol. I, 47 [41].

62. Ibid., 82.

63. Kasper, *Katholische Kirche*, 263 [181].

64. Ibid., 225 [153].

65. Ibid., 227 [154].

66. Berkouwer, *De Kerk*, Vol. I, 107 [88].

67. Ibid., 109 [90].

68. Kasper, *Katholische Kirche*, 227-28 [154].

69. Berkouwer, *De Kerk*, Vol. I, 32 [29].

70. Ibid., 36 [33]. This, too, is the view of Vatican II's *Unitatis Redintegratio* §1: "Such division openly contradicts the will of Christ, scandalizes the world, and damages the holy cause of preaching the Gospel to every creature."

71. Ibid., 64 [54].

72. Geoffrey Wainwright, "Church," in N. Lossky et al., ed., *Dictionary of the Ecumenical Movement*, (Geneva: 2002), 176-86.

73. William Henn, "The Church."

74. Lesslie Newbigin, *The Household of God, Lectures on the Nature of the Church*, 17. See also UR §7, "There can be no ecumenism worthy of the name without a change of heart." John Paul II explains what this change of heart entails, "Christians cannot underestimate the

burden of *long-standing misgivings* inherited from the past, and of mutual *misunderstandings* and *prejudices. Complacency, indifference and insufficient knowledge of one another* often make this situation worse [UR §4]. Consequently, the commitment to ecumenism must be based upon the conversion of hearts and upon prayer, which will also lead to the *necessary purification of past memories*. With the grace of the Holy Spirit, the Lord's disciples, inspired by love, by the power of the truth and by a sincere desire for mutual forgiveness and reconciliation, are called to *re-examine together their painful past* and the hurt which that past regrettably continues to provoke even today. All together, they are invited by the ever fresh power of the Gospel to acknowledge with sincere and total objectivity the mistakes made and the contingent factors at work at the origins of their deplorable divisions. *What is needed is a calm, clear-sighted and truthful vision of things*, a vision enlivened by divine mercy and capable of freeing people's minds and of inspiring in everyone a renewed willingness, precisely with a view to proclaiming the Gospel to the men and women of every people and nation." (UUS §2).

75. Berkouwer, *De Kerk*, Vol. I, 61 [51]. Newbigin concurs, "Any serious reading of the New Testament must surely make [the fact] inescapable, that to speak of a plurality of churches, is strictly absurd; that we can only do so in so far as we have ceased to understand by the word 'church' what the New Testament means by it" (*The Household of God*, 17).

76. Ibid.

77. Ibid., 59-60 [50].

78. Berkouwer, *De Kerk*, Vol. I, 65-76 [55-63].

79. Berkouwer, *Nieuwe Perspectieven in de Controvers: Rome-Reformatie*, 18 (my translation).

80. For this conception, see the Introduction.

81. Berkouwer, *De Kerk*, I, 73 [61]. Berkouwer is drawing mainly from Abraham Kuyper (1837-1920), *Principles of Sacred Theology*, particularly §104, Development of Multiformity [Pluriformity], 658-68. In the Dutch original this is a three-volume work. The English translation contains the first fifty-three pages of Vol. I of the original, and the entirety of Vol. II (*Encyclopaedie der Heilige Godgeleerdheid*. Tweede Deel). Berkouwer also occasionally draws from Vol. III [*Gemene Gratie* "Common Grace"], particularly 232-38. Until recently, available in English translation from these volumes are selections; see *Abraham Kuyper: A Centennial Reader*, "Common Grace," 165-201. Now the entire three volumes are available in English translation by the Acton Institute. For another discussion of Kuyper's theory of multiformity, see Richard J. Mouw, "True Church and True Christians: Some Reflections on Calvinist Discernment," in *The Challenges of Cultural Discipleship: Essays in the Line of Abraham Kuyper*.

82. Berkouwer, *De Kerk*, Vol. I, 70 [58].

83. Ibid., 73 [60].

84. Ibid., 67 [56]. Like Kuyper, Herman Bavinck also claims, "No one claims that content and expression, essence and form, are in complete correspondence and coincide. The dogma that the church confesses and the dogmatician develops is not identical with the absolute truth of God itself" (*Gereformeerde Dogmatiek*, I, 7 [32–33]).

85. Kuyper, *Principles of Sacred Theology*, 664.

86. Ibid.

87. Berkouwer, *De Kerk*, Vol. I, 69 [57-58].

88. Kuyper, *Lectures on Calvinism*, 14: A positive assessment of ecclesial multiformity gradually led to an appreciation for "national difference of morals, differences of disposition and of emotions, [and] different degrees in depth of life and insight, [which] necessarily resulted in emphasizing first one, and then another side of the same truth."

89. Kuyper, *Gemene Gratie* III, 237, "The objective truth remains one, but its appropriation, application and confession must differ, even as the color of the light differs according to the glass in which it is refracted" (my translation). Berkouwer compares Abraham Kuyper and Karl Rahner: "Neither Kuyper nor Rahner postulates that truth is not one,

but they touch each other with respect to the limited, and therefore varied, understanding of truth." Still, Berkouwer is right: "From the nature of the case, there are profound problems here, both for Rahner in connection with the old tradition of the infallible confession of the Church and for Kuyper in connection with pluriformity in confessions" (Berkouwer, *De Kerk*, I, 69-70, 74 [58, 60-61]. See also, Kuyper, *Principles of Sacred Theology*, 170, "organically connected multiformity." Regarding Rome, Kuyper says, "However much Rome has insisted upon uniformity, it has never been able to establish it, and in the end she has adopted the system of giving to each expression of the multiformity a place in the organic harmony of her great hierarchy" (Ibid).

90. Berkouwer, *De Kerk*, I, 73 [60].

91. Kasper, "The Church as the Place of Truth," at 141.

92. G.C. Berkouwer, "Vragen Rondom De Belijdenis," at 6, and also 10, 22, 25–26, 35–36 (my translation).

93. Ibid., 5.

94. For an examination of Berkouwer's theological epistemology and its corresponding hermeneutics of dogmas, creeds and confessions, see Echeverria, *Berkouwer and Catholicism*, 20-109, 394-413.

95. Kasper, "The Church as the Place of Truth," 135.

96. Karl Rahner, S.J., "The Development of Dogma," at 44.

97. Idem, "*Mysterium Ecclesiae*," in *Theological Investigations*, Vol. XVII.

98. Kasper, "The Church as the Place of Truth," 141.

99. Berkouwer, *De Kerk*, I 75 [62]. Furthermore, on this view, according to Ratzinger, "then no Church could claim to possess definitively binding teaching authority, and in this way institutional relativism will lead to doctrinal relativism." "If belief in 'the body' of the Church is taken away," he adds, "the Church's concrete claims regarding the content of faith disappear along with her bodiliness" ("*Deus Locutus Est Nobis In Filio: Some reflections on Subjectivity, Christology, and the Church*," 13-30, and 26-27).

100. The Dutch neo-Calvinist tradition also engaged in *aggiornamento*. Berkouwer writes, "Herman Dooyeweerd criticizes Abraham Kuyper's 'metaphysical doctrine of the Logos' and his failure to extricate himself from the scholastic, Aristotelian tradition, but agrees fully with Kuyper's "basic religious conception," a conception which, according to Dooyeweerd, must now be developed more consistently than Kuyper himself succeeded in doing. Herman Bavinck talks of the need for theology to relate itself to the 'mind and spirit of the era in which it speaks' (Bavinck, *Modernisme en Orthodoxie*, 1911, 35). Kuyper wanted to bring Reformed theology into contact with 'human consciousness as it had developed at the end of the nineteenth century,' and he spoke of bringing one's confession awareness to the 'level of the modern consciousness,' *Encyclopaedie*, I, 1908, Foreword, and II, 532. Kuyper frequently talked of the need for bringing the forms of orthodoxy into harmony with the thought forms of modern times" (*Vatikaans Concilie en Nieuwe Theologie*, 63n 9, 64n 10[59n 2]). See also, Berkouwer, *Nieuwe Perspectieven*, 15. For Dooyeweerd's critical essay on Kuyper, see "Kuyper's Wetenschapsleer." *Philosophia Reformata* 4, 1939: 193–232.

101. Berkouwer, *De Kerk*, I, 70-71, but missing from the English translation. Brief summary of Bensdorp's objections in the English translation, *The Church*, 60n35, "Bensdorp asked how flatly contradictory confessions can both be 'forms' of one revealed truth. How can there be harmony in the contradictions? Kuyper replied that he did not mean to say that in the doctrine of the Lord's supper, for instance, both transubstantiation and consubstantiation are true. But there is a certain 'harmony' in the sense that 'the mystical fellowship with Christ is partaken of in the sacrament; however, the way that that fellowship comes about cannot be expressed by us in an adequate form.' The differing formulations are attempts to understand the same mystical reality."

102. Ibid., 73 [60].

103. Idem, *Nabetrachting op het Concilie*, 52.

104. Ibid.

105. Idem, *De Kerk*, I, 236-37 [190-91]. All of Chapter Seven, "The Continuity of the Church" in *De Kerk*, I, deserves a careful examination for getting at Berkouwer's hermeneutics of dogma, creeds, and confessions.

106. Ibid., 73 [60].

107. On Lérinian hermeneutics, see Eduardo Echeverria, *Revelation, History, and Truth: A Hermeneutics of Dogma*.

108. Kasper, "The Continuing Challenge of the Second Vatican Council: The Hermeneutics of the Conciliar Statements," 166-76.

109. Idem, *Katholische Kirche*, 376 [264].

110. "Est enim aliud ipsum depositum Fidei, seu veritates, quae veneranda doctrina nostra continentur, aliud modus, quo eaedem enuntiantur, eodem tamen sensu eademque sententia," Ioannes XXIII, "Allocutio habita d. 11 oct. 1962, in initio Concilii," *Acta Apostolicae Sedis* (1962), 792. Denzinger, §3020. For a commentary on this text of John XXIII, see Chapter 1, note 35.

111. Yves Congar, O.P., *True and False Reform in the Church*, 205–208. The distinction originates with Johann Adam Möhler (1796-1838), and "Cardinal [Charles] Journet has felicitously rendered [these distinctions] by the words contrast and contradiction" (as cited in Congar, *True and False Reform in the Church*, 205). See Johann Adam Möhler, *Unity in the Church, Or the Principle of Catholicism*, Chapter 4, "Unity in Diversity," 166-205.

112. Congar, *Diversity and Communion*, 151.

113. Idem, *True and False Reform in the Church*, 206. As I have argued in my book, *Revelation, History, and Truth: A Hermeneutics of Dogma*, "Vanhoozer's hermeneutics of creative retrieval dovetails with that of Vatican II's Lérinian hermeneutics" (xvi). Vanhoozer misses out completely on this point in his book, *Biblical Authority after Babel*. That he doesn't understand Vatican II's Lérinian hermeneutics and its impact on post-Vatican II theology is clear from his implied criticism of Catholicism in the following: "Catholics [should be reminded] that the specific formulations of their magisterial traditions, while definitive for them, are not exhaustive.... There are other ways of expressing the same theological truth. Works need to be done to outline the possibilities for diverse formulations of essential theological truths, as well as the limits of diversity" ("Epilogue," in *Evangelicals and Catholics Together at Twenty, Vital Statements on Contested Topics*, at 169-70). Yes, other ways that are complementary, not conflicting; contrasting, not contradictory.

114. Referring to J. R.Geiselmann's study, *Johann Adam Möhler, Die Einheit der Kirche und die Wiedervereinigung der Konfessionen* (Vienna, 1940), Congar says: "Geiselmann clearly shows that by his distinction between the *Gegensätze* (contrasts within and essential to the church) and the *Widerspräche* (extrinsic and accidental contradictions), Möhler distanced himself both from Schelling (who succeeded his professor, Drey) and from Hegel. Möhler was able to avoid making development depend upon oppositions extrinsic to the church (heresies)" (*True and False Reform in the Church*, 206).

115. Congar, *Diversity and Communion*, 151.

116. Guarino, *Revelation and Truth, Unity and Plurality in Contemporary Theology*, 37.

117. Kasper, "The Church as the Place of Truth," 144.

118. Congar, *True and False Reform in the Church*, 210.

119. Congregation for the Doctrine of the Faith, "Doctrinal Note on Some Aspects of Evangelization." §12. See also Kevin Vanhoozer, "The spiritual discipline of ecumenical dialogue involves patient listening, sympathetic understanding, and a willingness to probe the deeper concerns that often lead our traditions to read Scripture with different emphases and interpret the Great Tradition along different lines. This discipline allows us to come to a deeper understanding of one another's traditions—and our own" ("Epi-

logue," in *Evangelicals and Catholics Together at Twenty*, 168).

120. Congregation for the Doctrine of the Faith, "Doctrinal Note on Some Aspects of Evangelization," §12.

121. Kasper, *Harvesting the Fruits*, 153.

122. Idem, *Katholische Kirche*, 234 [159].

123. See also, Joseph Ratzinger, "The Ecclesiology of the Constitution *Lumen Gentium*," 148.

124. Kasper, "The Decree on Ecumenism—Read Anew After Forty Years."

125. Berkouwer, *De Kerk*, Vol. I, 84 [69].

126. Ibid., 138 [114].

127. Given his conviction regarding the unicity of the Church, Berkouwer, too, seeks to avoid ecclesiological relativism. He says (*De Kerk*, Vol. I, 89 [72]), "If this recognition of positive traces of the Church in other churches is not to result in [ecclesiological] relativism, how is one to think concretely of the [Church's] relation to other churches?" Kasper rightly notes that most Protestant churches are advocates of ecclesiastical relativism in "that all churches are part of the one Church of Jesus Christ and thus the one Church was more or less the sum of all churches." This position is incompatible with the first principle of Catholic ecclesiology. Furthermore, it entails a contradicting pluralism: "As these churches and ecclesial communities contradict each other in many respects, such a unity would be a sum of contradictions that could not last" (Kasper, *Katholische Kirche*, 236 [161]).

128. Berkouwer, *De Kerk*, Vol. I, 138 [114-115].

129. Kasper, *Katholische Kirche*, 235 [160].

130. Berkouwer, *De Kerk*, Vol. I, 145 [120].

131. Kasper, *Katholische Kirche*, 235 [160].

132. *Lumen Gentium* §8; *Unitatis Redintegratio* §§3-4; *Ut Unum Sint*, §14; *Dominus Iesus* §16, "With the expression subsistit in, the Second Vatican Council sought to harmonize two doctrinal statements: on the one hand, that the Church of Christ, despite the divisions which exist among Christians, continues to exist fully only in the Catholic Church, and on the other hand, that 'outside of her structure, many elements can be found of sanctification and truth', that is, in those Churches and ecclesial communities which are not yet in full communion with the Catholic Church."

133. LG §8; UR §§3-4, 20-21, 23. For helping me to formulate this dilemma, I am grateful to Thomas Guarino, Seton Hall University.

134. Guarino, *The Disputed Teachings of Vatican II*, 25-29.

135. Ibid., 95.

136. Ibid., 96.

137. In his book of interviews, *Pope Francis, A Future of Faith*, he still doesn't define proselytism (20) and its difference from evangelization (26).

138. Catholic Church, et al.,"The Challenge of Proselytism and the Calling to Common Witness."

139. Benedict XVI, *God's Revolution, World Youth Day and Other Cologne Talks*, 85.

140. Personal email, 12 September 2018.

141. Ibid.

142. Berkouwer, *De Kerk*, Vol. I, 135-136 [113].

143. Kasper, *Katholische Kirche*, 236 [160].

144. Ibid., 264 [181].

145. Berkouwer, *De Kerk*, Vol. I, 135-139 [112-115].

146. Ibid., 134 [112].

147. Ibid., 134 [112].

148. Ibid., 135-36 [113].

149. Ibid., 137 [114].

150. Peter De Mey, "Church Renewal and Reform in the Documents of Vatican II," *The Jurist* 71 (2011) 369-400 is helpful.

151. Benedict XVI, "Address of his Holiness Benedict XVI to the Roman Curia offering them his Christmas greetings."

152. Regarding the term *ressourcement* Gabriel Flynn writes, "The word *ressourcement* was coined by the poet and social critic Charles Péguy (1873–1914).... The liturgical changes inaugurated by Pope Pius X (1835–1914) were also an inspiration for *ressourcement*" ("A Renaissance in Twentieth-Century Catholic Theology," at 327).

153. Vanhoozer denies in his recent book, *Biblical Authority after Babel*, that Catholicism as such can embrace a hermeneutics of creative retrieval. He approvingly cites the claims of Robert McAfee Brown who insists that Catholic ecclesiology and its corresponding notion of the Church's teaching authority is such that its position is "'incompatible with the notion that the church is *semper reformanda*, always to be reformed'" (*Spirit of Protestantism* [Oxford: Oxford University Press, 1965], 167, cited in *Biblical Authority After Babel*, 222). In my discussion of the hermeneutics of Vatican II in Chapter 1 of my book, I show that Vanhoozer is not only mistaken about this claim, but also that his hermeneutics of creative retrieval dovetails with that of Vatican II's Lérinian hermeneutics.

154. I already considered in Chapter 5 Francis's appeal to this notion in an earlier paragraph of EG, §36.

155. Gaillardetz, "The 'Francis Moment': A New Kairos for Catholic Ecclesiology."

156. For Berkouwer's reflections on the ecumenical significance of the hierarchy of truths, see *Nabetrachting op het Concilie*, 106–111

157. Oscar Cullmann maintained that "this text sets forth for all time *a completely new concept of ecumenism*—new at any rate from the Catholic point of view" ("Comments on the Decree on Ecumenism"). Berkouwer cites Cullmann as having said about the hierarchy of truths, "perhaps one of the most promising among all the texts of the council, although curiously so little is said about it" ("vieleicht eine der meistversprechenden unter allen Texten des Konzils, obwohl merkwurdigerweise so wenig von ihr gesprochen wird" (Berkouwer, *Nabetrachting op het Concilie*, 102n78). Rahner similarly wrote regarding the "hierarchy of truths" that this notion was "of fundamental importance for the contemporary situation of faith and one of the really great acts of the Council" ("von fundamentaler Wichtigkeit auch fur die gesamte Glaubenssituation der Gegenwart" and "eine der wirklichen Grosztaten des Konzils" (also cited in Berkouwer).

158. Berkouwer, *Nabetrachting op het Concilie*, 102. If anything Cullmann went further than Berkouwer, calling this statement "the most revolutionary to be found, not only in the *Schema de oecumenismo* but in any of the schemas of the present Council" ("Comments," 94).

159. For a helpful account of the Decree on Ecumenism, *Unitatis Redintegratio*, see Charles Morerod, O.P., 311–41. For an account of the historical origin of the term "hierarchy of truths" before Vatican II and twenty years afterwards, see William Henn, O.F.M. Cap., "The Hierarchy of Truths Twenty Years Later"; idem, "The Hierarchy of Truths," in *Dictionary of Fundamental Theology*, 425–27; Thomas G. Guarino, *Revelation and Truth, Unity and Plurality in Contemporary Theology*, 138–61; Congar, *Diversity and Communion*, 107–133; Karl Rahner, "A Hierarchy of Truths," 162–67; idem, "The Notion of Hierarchy of Truths—An Ecumenical Interpretation."

160. In the following, I draw on Echeverria, *Berkouwer and Catholicism*, 101-108. See also, Echeverria, "Hierarchy of Truths Revisited."

161. Rahner, "A Hierarchy of Truths," 164. See also, Congregation for the Doctrine of the

Faith, *Mysterium Ecclesiae*, §4.

162. Rahner, "A Hierarchy of Truths," 165.

163. Secretariat for Christian Unity, 15 August 1970, "Reflections and Suggestions concerning Ecumenical Dialogue," paragraph IV, 4b; as cited in Congar, *Diversity and Communion*, 128.

164. Berkouwer, *Nabetrachting op het Concilie*, 103.

165. Helpful in formulating this point is George Vandervelde, "*BEM [Baptism, Eucharist, and Ministry]* and the 'Hierarchy of Truths': A Vatican Contribution to the Reception Process," at 79. This article deals with what some consider to be perhaps the most important documents ever produced by the World Council of Churches, *Baptism, Eucharist and Ministry* (Lima, 1982).

166. James C. Livingston, et al., *Modern Christian Thought, The Twentieth Century*, 246–47.

167. Berkouwer, *Nabetrachting op het Concilie*, 108.

168. Ibid., 103.

169. Berkouwer, *Nabetrachting op het Concilie*, 102, 106, respectively. See also, Walter Kasper, *An Introduction to Christian Faith*, section entitled "Concentration rather than reduction," 99–104.

170. Kasper, *Introduction to Christian Faith*, 103.

171. Ibid., 103-104.

172. Berkouwer, *Nabetrachting op het Concilie*, 101.

173. As cited in Morerod, "The Decree on Ecumenism," 322–23.

174. Guarino, *Revelation and Truth*, 142–43.

175. Ibid., 147.

176. Congar, *Diversity and Communion*, 119. For Congar's discussion of types of one-sidedness, see *True and False Reform in the Church*, 208–13.

177. Berkouwer, *Nabetrachting op het Concilie*, 108.

178. Ibid., 104.

179. Vandervelde, "*BEM* and the 'Hierarchy of Truths,'" 83–84.

7

The Dialogue of Religions and the Question of Truth

"There is salvation in no one else [but Jesus], for there is no other name under heaven given among men by which we must be saved," said Peter to the rulers and the elders of the people of Israel [Acts 4:12]. Can this absolute claim still be maintained today? How does it relate to the search for peace among religions and cultures?... The Catholic Christian could only, in all humility, put the question that Martin Buber once formulated to an atheist: but what if it is true? Thus it becomes apparent that, beyond all particular questions, the real problem lies in the question about truth. Can truth be recognized? Or, is the question about truth simply inappropriate in the realm of religion and belief? But what meaning does belief then have, what positive meaning does religion have, if it cannot be connected with truth?
—Joseph Cardinal Ratzinger[1]

Dialogue is a means of seeking after truth and sharing it with others. For truth is light, newness, and strength. The Catholic Church holds that "Truth, however, is to be sought after in a manner proper to the dignity of the human person and his social nature. The inquiry is to be free, carried on with the aid of teaching or instruction, communication and dialogue, in the course of which men explain to one another the truth they have discovered, or think they have discovered, in order thus to assist one another in the quest for truth. Moreover, as the truth is discovered, it is by a personal assent that men are to adhere to it." —John Paul II[2]

[I]t is clear that the discussion about the truth claim of the religions cannot be a marginal or partial aspect of theology. The respectful confrontation with this truth claim must play a role in the center of the daily work of theology; it must be an integral part of it.[3]

Leaving Behind Absolutism and Relativism?

In this chapter, I deal with the question of truth, in particular, of the truth of Christianity, of its central claims, religious disagreement and incompatible truth claims. This question must be distinguished from the question of salvation.[4] Pope Francis's thought is the centerpiece of my analysis.

In his 1964 Encyclical, *Ecclesiam Suam*, Pope Paul VI stipulates that one of the proper characteristics of dialogue is clarity. He explains:

> Clarity before all else; the dialogue demands that what is said should be intelligible. We can think of it as a kind of thought transfusion. It is an invitation to the exercise and development of the highest spiritual and mental powers a man possesses. This fact alone would suffice to make such dialogue rank among the greatest manifestations of human activity and culture. In order to satisfy this first requirement, all of us who feel the spur of the apostolate should examine closely the kind of speech we use. (ES §81)

Respectfully, throughout this book I have shown that clarity is precisely one of the virtues lacking in Francis's writings, homilies, and the like. Clarity is also missing from his remarks about the dialogue of religions. But not only his writings. For example, many of us have been eager to forget the video[5] where Pope Francis urges a dialogue among the religions present—Jewish, Christian, Muslim, and Buddhist. Of course, I think we can honor the pope's well-meaning motives here for dialogue, namely, encouraging the "maintaining of good fellowship among the nations" (1 Pet 2:12), and if possible, "as far as depends on one, to live at peace with all men" (Rom 12:18).[6] Still, that video leaves the impression of a leveling out of the fundamental differences between these religions, suggesting a muting of the primary call to evangelize and proclaim the Gospel, and leaving out the question not only of truth in general, but also of religious disagreement and conflicting truth claims among the religions in particular.[7]

Yes, Francis does not supplant evangelization with interreligious dialogue (RM §9), however central the latter is to his theology, but expresses the conviction, "In this dialogue [of religions], ever friendly and sincere, attention must always be paid to the essential bond between dialogue and proclamation, which leads the Church to maintain and intensify her relationship with non-Christians.... Evangelization and interreligious dialogue, far from being opposed, mutually support and nourish one another" (EG §251). How exactly do they mutually influence each other is far from clear. Still, what is sufficiently clear is that in this dialogue Francis rejects neutrality,[8] indifferentism,[9] easy compromise, and the practice of facile irenicism,[10] although one might be excused for thinking that the video is a prime example of easy reconciliation, and syncretism.[11] On the one hand, to be fair to Francis, he says, we cannot "say 'yes' to everything in order to avoid problems, for this would be a way of deceiving others and denying them *the good* [emphasis added] which we have been given to share generously with others." What is "the good" to which he is referring? He does not say here, but one can surmise from *Evangelii Gaudium* that it is the good of the Gospel of Jesus Christ, the good to which we are called to bear witness to all men (EG §§40-45). "Proclaiming Christ means showing that to believe in and to follow him is not only something right and true, but also something beautiful, capable of filling life with new splendor and profound joy even in the midst of difficulties. Every expression of true beauty can thus be acknowledged as a path leading to an encounter with the Lord Jesus. This has nothing to do with fostering an aesthetic relativism which would downplay the inseparable bond between truth, goodness and beauty, but rather a renewed esteem for beauty as a means of touching the human heart and enabling the truth and goodness of the Risen Christ to radiate within it" (EG §167).

On the other hand, we cannot "ignore greater values [of justice, peace, integrity of creation] of which [we] are not the masters." Therefore, he adds, "True openness [in dialogue] involves remaining steadfast in one's deepest convictions, clear and joyful in one's own identity, while at the same being 'open to understanding those of the other party' and 'knowing that dialogue can enrich each side' [RM §56]" (EG §251).

The two requirements here for interreligious dialogue are maintaining one's own identity and uniqueness, on the one hand, and knowledge of the other, on the other hand.[12] Francis's emphasis is always on maintaining the uniqueness and identity of being a Christian while seeing a positive value to the differences of religions. Thus, as Christians, we can bring firm commitments to the interreligious dialogue table. That is important because it seems to distinguish Francis's approach from the pluralist assumption that meaningful dialogue precludes a commitment to the definitive truth of Christianity.[13] In Sri Lanka, addressing an audience on interreligious dialogue, Francis repeats his understanding of dialogue:

> Dialogue... is essential if we are to know, understand and respect one another. But, as experience has shown, for such dialogue and encounter to be effective, it must be grounded in a full and forthright presentation of our respective convictions. Certainly, such dialogue will accentuate how varied our beliefs, traditions and practices are. But if we are honest in presenting our convictions, we will be able to see more clearly what we hold in common. New avenues will be opened for mutual esteem, cooperation and indeed friendship.[14]

Summarily stated, says Francis, "To dialogue means to believe that the 'other' has something worthwhile to say, and to entertain his or her point of view and perspective."

Significantly, however, Francis also writes, but now with a certain qualification, "Engaging in dialogue does not mean renouncing our own ideas and traditions, *but the [renouncing of the] claim that they alone are valid or absolute*."[15] His disclaimer, withdrawing the validity or absoluteness of

Christian beliefs, sounds like relativism. Is Francis claiming that the truth claims of all religions are equally valid or absolute? What does that even mean?

Consider Cardinal Kasper's reflections on what it means to claim absoluteness for Christianity. It can mean two things: one, "God has revealed himself in an unsurpassable way in Jesus Christ"; two, "the claim of the Church to be in possession of the absolute truth." The first is constitutive of Christianity, and hence cannot be given up. Says Kasper, "the second is problematic." He explains, "In the actual sense, God alone is absolute and God is not possessed by anyone. Concerning the testimony of the Church, one must not overlook its historical dimension. In other words, one must distinguish between the claim of revelation itself and its historical mediation through the Church."[16] This objection sounds like Francis.

In response to Kasper's second point, he is inconsistent with his own hermeneutics of dogma. He stands in the line of what I have called Lérinian hermeneutics, which recognizes the significance of the distinction between unchanging truth and theological formulations and doctrinal choices.[17] Kasper explains: "The dogmatic decisions always take place in a specific historical situation, they use historical human language and ways of expression and are insofar historically conditioned. It pertains also to the historicity that dogmas can subsequently be deepened and complemented, obviously always in the same sense and the same meaning [*'eodem sensu eademque sententia'*]. In other words, there is growth and progress in understanding the faith. However, within all this historical conditionality they express something that is valid and binding for all times."[18] Furthermore,

> As such, [dogmatic] decisions are true, they are also irreformable, for what is true today will also be true tomorrow and cannot be wrong tomorrow. Thus, the dogma testifies within history the truth, which transcends all historical conditioning, of the truth that appeared eschatologically definitely in Jesus Christ and of God's unconditional love. Such a decision puts an end to all dialectics [taking back any determinate assertion that has just been made with its opposite]. Therefore, it is not legitimized through subsequent reception in the Church. Still, such decisions are interpreted in a subsequent process of reception and are integrated into the whole of the faith and life of the Church.[20]

Thus, Kasper's objection to speaking of the absoluteness of Christianity does not stand because history, on the one hand, and unchanging and absolute truth on the other, are not mutually exclusive in Lérinian hermeneutics, to which he subscribes.[20]

Where does that leave the matter of incompatible truth claims among the religions? Is Francis a relativist about truth? According to the then Joseph Ratzinger, "In the relativist meaning, [to dialogue] means to put one's own position, i.e., one's faith, on the same level as the convictions of others without recognizing in principle more truth in it than that which is attributed to the opinion of the others. Only if I suppose in principle that the other can be as right, or more right than I, can an authentic dialogue take place. According to this concept, dialogue must be an exchange between positions which have fundamentally the same rank and therefore are mutually relative."[21] Similarly, elsewhere Francis writes urging *"us to give up only the pretension that they [our beliefs] are unique and absolute."*[22] What does it, then, mean to deny that Christianity is in itself unique and absolute and hence the one true religion? Most importantly, with the denial of the unique and absolute status of the Christian faith is Francis implicitly denying the fullness and completeness of God's revelatory presence in Jesus Christ such that God is present in Jesus in a unique, absolute, and unparalleled way? Is Francis denying that claim? Certainly not explicitly,[23] but the denial of Christological orthodoxy is implied. He does not seem to realize the implication of denying the uniqueness and absoluteness of Christian beliefs.

In this connection, is Francis suggesting, like Edward Schillebeeckx, "that we can, may and must say that there is more religious truth in all the religions together than in one particular religion, and that this also applies to Christianity[?]"[24] We know that Francis rejects syncretism, meaning thereby, in the words of Schillebeeckx, "Christianity can never arrive at one synthesis, but only enter into dialogue, in a conversation of two religions which cannot be reduced to either of them."[25]

Consider here the difference between ontological and epistemological complementarity.[26] The former is rejected by *Dominus Iesus*. "Therefore, the theory of the limited, incomplete, or imperfect character of the revelation of Jesus Christ, which would be complementary to that found in other religions, is contrary to the Church's faith.... Such a position is in radical contradiction with the... statements of Catholic faith according to which the full and complete revelation of the salvific mystery of God is given in Jesus Christ" (DI §6). So, ontological complementarity is ruled out by the teaching of the Church because of Christological orthodoxy.

However, what about epistemological complementarity? Briefly, let us look at how the term complementarity is used in *Unitatis Redintegratio*. In §17, the Council refers to the legitimate diversity of theological expressions of doctrine. This way of speaking alludes to a distinction between dogmatic truth and its formulations, between form and content, content and context, propositions and sentences, such as was suggested by John XXIII in his opening address to Vatican II, *Gaudet Mater Ecclesia*: "The deposit or the truths of faith, contained in our sacred teaching, are one thing, while the mode in which they are enunciated, keeping the same meaning and the same judgment ['*eodem sensu eademque sententia*'], is another thing."[27] In my view, because of the connection between meaning and truth such that what is meant is judged to be true to reality, the most fitting translation is "keeping the same meaning and the same judgment." The subordinate clause in this passage is part of a larger passage from Vatican I, *Dei Filius* (Denzinger §3020), which is also cited by Leo XIII in his 1899 Encyclical, *Testem Benevolentiae Nostrae*, and this passage is itself from the *Commonitorium primum* 23.3 of Vincent of Lérins: "Therefore, let there be growth and abundant progress in understanding, knowledge, and wisdom, in each and all, in individuals and in the whole Church, at all times and in the progress of ages, but only with the proper limits, i.e., *within the same dogma, the same meaning, the same judgment*." (*in eodem scilicet dogmate, eodem sensu eademque sententia*). In this context, we can understand what the Council says, "It is hardly surprising, then, if from time to time one tradition has come nearer to a full appreciation of some aspects of a mystery of revelation than the other, or has expressed it to better advantage. In such cases, these various theological expressions are to be considered often as *mutually complementary* rather than conflicting" (emphasis added)." The condition for epistemological complementarity is that the alternative formulation or expression is within the boundaries of the dogma, according to the same meaning and same judgment; otherwise it is conflicting or a competing truth claim. In other words, the new linguistic formulations or expressions can vary, but only as long as they mediate the same judgment about objective reality.

However, it is unclear whether Jesuit theologian Francis Clooney understands this point. He says, regarding *Dominus Iesus*,

> *Dominus Iesus* answers some questions [about Christology] very clearly, but it seems not even to imagine how true interreligious learning might change not the Creed but how we hear and profess the Creed, which we are likely to keep reciting, in the same words, into the far future. Thinking may upset us but does not diminish our faith. The declaration [*Dominus Iesus*] seems not to consider how a clear and honest affirmation of Christ is not less vigorous and firm, even if we have noticed religious diversity as a fact of life that is not about to go away any time soon, even as we live in a world where claims about truth do not substitute for the work of actually showing to seekers what is true. Even if we suppose, in faith, that Jesus is Lord, we who live among people of many faith are the ones who need to show what that Lordship means, among people who respect each other's religions deeply. *Dominus Iesus* is a help, a boundary marker, but not itself the meaning of Christ amid diversity.[28]

Clooney runs together several claims in this passage, which need distinguishing. Yes, thinking may deepen our understanding of the Catholic faith because theology is the disciplined exploration of the content of revelation. Yes, making truth claims about Christ does not substitute for helping others to come to knowledge of the truth. Yes, we must give an account of the sense in which Christ is Lord (Phil 2:11), the Way, the Truth, and the Life (John 14:6), preeminent in all things, for all the fullness of God dwells in Him, the concentration point of God's reconciling work (Col 1:15-20), in respect of the plurality of religions. *Pace* Clooney, *Dominus Iesus* asserts the meaning and truth of Christ amid religious diversity.

> Not infrequently it is proposed that theology should avoid the use of terms like "unicity," "universality," and "absoluteness," which give the impression of excessive emphasis on the significance and value of the salvific event of Jesus Christ in relation to other religions. In reality, however, such language is simply being faithful to revelation.... From the beginning, the community of believers has recognized in Jesus a salvific value such that he alone, as Son of God made man, crucified and risen, by the mission received from the Father and in the power of the Holy Spirit, bestows revelation [cf. Matt 11:27] and divine life [cf. John 1:12; 5:25-26; 17:2] to all humanity and to every person. In this sense, one can and must say that Jesus Christ has a significance and a value for the human race and its history, which are unique and singular, proper to him alone, exclusive, universal, and absolute. Jesus is, in fact, the Word of God made man for the salvation of all. (DI §15)

> Therefore, the theory of the limited, incomplete, or imperfect character of the revelation of Jesus Christ, which would be complementary to that found in other religions, is contrary to the Church's faith. Such a position would claim to be based on the notion that the truth about God cannot be grasped and manifested in its globality and completeness by any historical religion, neither by Christianity nor by Jesus Christ. (DI §6)

And *Dominus Iesus* reflects the assertion of *Gaudium et Spes*:

> The truth is that only in the mystery of the incarnate Word does the mystery of man take on light. For Adam, the first man, was a figure of Him Who was to come, namely Christ the Lord. Christ, the final Adam, by the revelation of the mystery of the Father and His love, fully reveals man to man himself and makes his supreme calling clear. It is not surprising, then, that in Him all the aforementioned truths find their root and attain their crown. (GS §22)

Furthermore, what these statements of *Dominus Iesus* assert is the truth about reality. Yes, they are, in a sense, boundary markers, but that is not because they are merely linguistic stipulations or guardrails; rather, chiefly, they are such because they assert truths about objective reality. The only way interreligious learning would not change the assertions of the Creed, and how we hear and profess it, is if the alternative formulations kept the same meaning and the same judgment (*eodem sensu eademque sententia*). This is why the question of competing truth claims is unavoidable.

Back to the distinction between ontological and epistemological complementarity, admittedly the Council applied the category of epistemological complementarity to the relation between Catholicism and other Christian traditions. However, I see no reason why in principle it cannot be applied to non-Christian traditions as well. Thus, this complementarity may pertain to non-Christian religions who may deepen our understanding of dogmatic truth. Paul Griffiths rightly says,

> The claim *the revelation of God in Christ is complete* (which must be said) is not the same as and does not imply the claim *the truth about God explicitly known and taught by the Church is complete*. Likewise, to say that the subject of the church's teaching is the complete revelation of God in Christ (which must be said, and is right) is not to say that what the church teaches is co-extensive with that complete revelation (which, if said, would at the very least anticipate the eschaton a little too eagerly.[29]

I agree with Griffiths' plea for epistemological complementarity so long as we attend explicitly to the principle of *Lérinian* hermeneutics, namely, alternative expressions or formulations of dogma are legitimate, but only within the proper limits, i.e., within the same dogma, the same meaning, the same judgment" (*in eodem scilicet dogmate, eodem sensu eademque sententia*).[30]

Francis overlooks this distinction between ontological and epistemological complementarity. Therefore, he seems concerned that making the claim that Christianity is unique and absolute entails that there cannot be any grasp of truth or goodness in other religions. If that is his concern, then he is mistaken because to hold that Christianity is the one true religion does not entail the view "that *all* of the claims of all other religions are false."[31] It only means that those claims of other religions are false that are logically incompatible with the central truth claims of Christianity. Furthermore, to claim that Christianity is absolutely true entails the idea of logically exclusive beliefs. Earlier in Chapter 1, I argued that this claim about renouncing the absoluteness of, say, the central truth-claims of Christianity is confusing. If *p* is true, then –*p* must be false, and hence anyone who holds –*p* must be wrong. We live in culture where people claim that there are no true propositions; but if there are no true propositions, then there are no false ones either. There are just differences and no one is wrong. This is relativism about truth.

If I am not mistaken, then Francis's renunciation that the central truth claims of Christianity are valid and absolute implies the dismissal of the claim that Christianity alone is the one true religion. Is there any other way to interpret this renunciation? If so, I do not see it. As I have said earlier, Francis's position suggests that he wants to leave behind both absolutism and relativism in religious matters.[32] My interpretation is borne out by virtue of Francis not raising the question of religious disagreement and conflicting truth claims. This is not surprising given his dismissal of abstract truth, i.e., propositional truth, skepticism about absolute truth, and his theologico-pastoral epistemology, with its attending principle that realities are greater than ideas.[33] Does this mean that he rules out the question of truth?

Not exactly; ruled out is the claim that one has a monopoly of the truth.[34] Says Francis, "The theologian who is satisfied with his complete and conclusive thought is mediocre. The good theologian and philosopher has an open thought, that is, an incomplete thought, always open to the *maius* of God and of the truth."[35] Elsewhere he says in a similar vein, "The truth of God is inexhaustible, it is an ocean from which we barely see the shore. It is something that we are beginning to discover in these times: not to enslave ourselves to an almost paranoid defense of *our truth* (if I *have* it, he doesn't *have* it; if he can *have* it, then I don't *have* it)."[36] However, *pace* Francis, we can know truth determinately, even if not exhaustively; inadequacy of expression does not mean inexpressibility of truth. Of course, Francis must recognize that he makes truth claims, and hence that the central truth claims of Christianity conflict with the truth claims of other religions.

This conclusion dovetails with the proposal of *Dialogue and Proclamation* and its call for interreligious apologetics.[37] "An open and positive approach to other religious traditions cannot overlook the *contradictions* that may exist between them and Christian revelation. It must, where necessary, recognize that there is *incompatibility* between some fundamental elements of the Christian religion and some aspects of such traditions."[38] Furthermore, in this connection Ratzinger rightly insists, "Anyone who sees in the religions of the world only reprehensible superstition is wrong; but also anyone who wants only to give a positive evaluation of all religions, and who has suddenly forgotten the criticism of religions that has been burned into our souls not only by Feurbach and Marx but also by such great theologians as Karl Barth and Bonhoeffer, is equally wrong."[39] Francis overlooks both these points, but particularly the matter of conflicting truth claims, emphasizing, "It is a matter of being more attentive to the genuineness of the good, the beautiful and the true that is accomplished, than to the name and provenance of those who do it."[40] It follows from Francis's point—valid in itself—that the Christian should accept truth and goodness wherever it appears among fallen human beings, even among unbelievers. Overlooked by Francis is that the grasp of truth in that context may be incomplete, inadequate, even distorted. This is not a point overlooked by Ratzinger.

In this connection, Ratzinger makes an important qualification here completely overlooked by Francis. "I must always look for what is positive in the other's beliefs—and in this way he becomes a help to me in searching for the truth."[41] However, adds, Ratzinger, "the critical element... may not be missing; in fact, it is needed." In particular, "Religion can fall sick, it can become something destructive. *It can and should lead us to truth, but it can also cut men off from truth.* The criticism of religion found in the Old Testament is still very relevant today."[42] This is a common theme in Ratzinger's writings on the dialogue of religions. And it is completely absent in Francis's practical approach to other religions. Thus, although Francis does distinguish in principle between evangelization and inter-religious dialogue, in fact his practical approach fosters—I think it is fair to say—a religious indifferentism.[43]

Years later as Benedict XVI he makes a relevant and important point on the 50th anniversary of the opening of Vatican II regarding the reception of *Nostra Aetate*. "In the process of active reception [of *Nostra Aetate*], a weakness in this otherwise extraordinary text has gradually emerged: it speaks of religion solely in a positive way and it disregards the sick and distorted forms of religion which, from the historical and theological viewpoints, are of far-reaching importance; for this reason the Christian faith, from the outset, adopted a critical stance towards religion, both internally and externally."[44] Still, the Spirit of God is the sole foundation of all that is true, and hence we honor him by accepting that truth. *All truth is God's truth.*[45]

In light of the point made in *Dialogue and Proclamation*, let us turn to consider briefly where Francis stands in respect of six basic approaches to religious disagreement and truth:

1. There is sufficient reason to conclude that all religions are false; there is no religion whose central claims are true.
2. One particular religion (e.g., Christianity) can be shown to be true or rationally preferable to others.
3. Although it is not possible to show that one religion is true or rationally preferable to others, it nevertheless can be reasonable for a religious believer (e.g., Christian) to regard one's own religion as true.
4. Disagreement between religions undermines the claims of any single religion to distinctive truth; the most reasonable perspective is to suspend judgments and remain agnostic.
5. Each religion can be regarded as "true" and "effective" for its own adherents, but there is no objective or tradition-transcending sense in which we speak of religious truth.
6. There are strong reasons for believing that, in spite of clear disagreements among them, the major religions are all "in touch" with the same ultimate divine reality. No single religion can legitimately claim to be superior to others in terms of truth or soteriological effectiveness.[46]

How would Francis stand with respect to these approaches? I think it is fair to say that Francis never addresses the question as such of religious disagreement and conflicting truth claims through appeal to reason and argument. Still, I am certain that he would dismiss outright approaches 1 and 4, atheism and agnosticism. I have been arguing that Francis seems to leave behind both absolutism and relativism in the matter of the dialogue of religion. However, I have also argued that this position is indefensible. Francis affirms that the message of the Gospel is a universal message for all men, that "Christ is the 'eternal Gospel' [Rev 14:6]" (EG §11) Francis holds the Gospel to be true. Is it difficult to see how he could leave behind both absolutism and relativism? Hence, how he could overlook the matter of conflicting truth claims. Rather than addressing these questions, his approach is practical because he is interested in maintaining the uniqueness and identity of being a Christian while seeing a positive value to the differences of religions.

Thus, it is difficult to say for which of the other four approaches he would opt. The classical Catholic approach is option 2. Option 3 is a more contemporary approach. One strand of this approach is a *deontic* concept of epistemic justification, which involves the root idea that there is a set of noetic obligations that apply to our cognitive acts; on this view the individual is justified in believing that *p* provided he does not violate these obligations. Another strand is *epistemic relativism*—the idea that justified belief is dependent on epistemic context, with the criteria of epistemic justification being inseparable from particular intellectual and cultural traditions in which they embody them. Thus, on this approach, one can be justified in holding a belief to be true. However, in order for this position not to slide into a relativism about truth, a distinction must be drawn between justification and truth, with the former being relative but not truth itself. The failure to distinguish what I am justified in holding to be true from truth itself slides into option 5 that expresses religious relativism. Religious pluralism[47] is option 6 because—in the words of Dominican theologian Edward Schillebeeckx—it "produces the danger that Christianity may be seen as a special historical form of an unchangeable, supra-historical, metaphysical and religious nucleus, of which all religions are simply chance expressions."[48] In short, on this option, religious diversity is God's will.[49]

I will turn now to discuss briefly the views of three Catholics on the question of religious diversity, truth, and God's will, starting with John Paul II, then Joseph Ratzinger/Benedict XVI, followed up by Edward Schillebeeckx, OP. I will then conclude this chapter with a defense of the necessity of interreligious apologetics, which I consider a lacuna in contemporary interreligious dialogue.

The Full Meaning of the Assisi Meeting

We need a clear context to understand the interreligious meeting of Pope Francis in Assisi two years ago, 20 September 2016, which commemorated the 30th anniversary of the Meeting of Prayer for Peace, held first by John Paul II on 27 October 1986. Such meetings generate confusion in an already confused culture, where most people have embraced a pluralistic theology of religions: i.e., all religions are the same, equally vehicles of salvation, equally true and good, and as such where religious diversity is taken to be part of the will of God. However, this understanding of religious pluralism or relativism (see options 5 and 6 above) is not the Church's teaching. This is clear in the *Catechism of the Catholic Church*, John Paul II's 1990 Encyclical *Redemptoris Missio*, as well as the 2000 Congregation for the Doctrine of the Faith document, *Dominus Iesus*.[50] It is also clear in the opening address of John Paul II in his pastoral visit to Perugia and Assisi for the World Day of Prayer. "The fact that we have come here does not imply any intention of seeking a religious consensus among ourselves or of negotiating our faith convictions. Neither does it mean that religions can be reconciled at the level of a common commitment in an earthly project that would surpass them all. Nor is it a concession to relativism in religious beliefs, because every human being must sincerely follow his or her upright conscience with the intention of seeking and obeying the truth."[51] However, here, I will let John Paul II speak for himself on the meaning of Assisi in the context of considering his view of religious diversity and the will of God. He does so in his 1986, "Christmas Address to the Roman Curia."[52]

John Paul distinguishes the orders of creation, the fall into sin, and redemption in Jesus Christ. The order of creation is the ground of the universality of man's very identity as God's image bearer as well as the unity of the divine origin of all members of the human family. Man is stamped in his created nature with the dynamic of desiring God because of being created by him and for him. Thus, all men have a radical unity because they have one single origin and goal.

The order of redemption finds its concentration point in Jesus Christ, the Word made flesh, says John Paul, quoting *Nostra Aetate* §2: "Indeed, she [the Church] proclaims, and ever must proclaim Christ "the way, the truth, and the life" (John 14:6), in whom men find the fullness of their religious life, and in whom God has reconciled all things to himself." This order grounds the universal scope of the atoning work of Christ. In his infinite, all-embracing love, God desires the salvation of all men in Christ (1 Tim 2:4-6). Still, although it is profoundly true that "all men are called to salvation by the grace of God" (LG §13), there is a basic difference between "offer" and "call,' on the one hand, and actuality of reception on the other.[53]

Someone may remark that the context in which this passage cited above occurs is crucial for understanding the Church's position on the positive character of the other religions. "The Catholic Church rejects nothing that is true and holy in these religions. She regards with sincere reverence those ways of conduct and of life, those precepts and teachings which, though differing in many aspects from the ones she holds and sets forth, nonetheless often reflect a ray of that Truth which enlightens all men." This commonly cited passage from *Nostra Aetate* §2, which speaks of those things in other religions that are "true and holy" and reflecting a "ray of that Truth, which enlightens all human beings," is misinterpreted by many contemporary Catholic theologians because they ignore that the human reception of that light is open to resistance and hence to distortion, misinterpretation, and rejection (see John 1:9-11). For one, Australian Catholic theologian, Gerald O'Collins comments, "Even if the text included no explicit [biblical] reference, it obviously echoed the language of the

Johannine prologue about the Word being 'the light of human beings' (John 1:4), 'the true light that enlightens everyone' (John 1:9)." Elsewhere he says, "This article of *Nostra Aetate* does not expressly state that Christ is both universal Revealer and universal Savior, but what it says amounts to that. How can he 'illuminate' all human beings without conveying to them something of God's self-revelation and hence also the offer of salvation?"[54] Again, he says: "The *light* of revelation brings the *life* of salvation, and vice versa."[55] However, here, too, O'Collins ignores that the human reception of that light is open to resistance and hence to distortion, misinterpretation, and rejection.[56] Thus the *offer* of salvation, or being *called* to salvation by God's grace (LG §13), is one thing, and the actuality of reception is another. But O'Collins assumes that the response to that light is positive, paying absolutely no attention to the difference between the offer, or calling, and its efficacy and finality.

Reformed biblical theologian Herman Ridderbos rightly notes that John 1:9 "describes light in its fullness and universality." But, he adds, "It does not say that every individual is in fact enlightened by the light."[57] *Pace* O'Collins, therefore, the Word does not illuminate all human beings because they *resist* the light. Consider John 1:5, 10. "And the light shines in the darkness and the darkness has not understood it." "He was in the world, and the world was made through Him, and the world did not know Him." Both of these verses speak "of the negative reaction of the world to the coming of the light." Methodist biblical theologian, Ben Witherington, III, explains: "The darkness the author talks about is... a spiritual darkness that involves not only ignorance of the truth but also moral darkness and fallenness, which leads one to reject the light and life even when they are offered. Thus our author wishes to stress the ultimate irony of this all. The creatures reject their own creator when they reject the Son of God."[58] Catholic biblical theologian Rudolph Schnackenberg agrees:

> The Logos was not just the fundamental and universal principle of light in the divine plan: he also illumined the existence and way of man from within the historical reality of man's environment or "world." "He was in the world," so close to men that they could reach him and cleave to him for their salvation; but the "world," that is, humanity installed in its earthly, historical home, "did not know him." This is the brutal and shattering fact, which the hymn signals in a few short words, and re-iterates more poignantly in the following verse (v. 11). Thus the hymn pursues, of set purpose, the thought of the second strophe, the relationship of the Logos to mankind, but depicts the tragic breach in the historical course of the relationship.[59]

In sum, says Ridderbos insightfully:

> All this means, then, that what is said about the Logos in vss. 1-4 is directly applied to what one can call the great content of this Gospel, that is, to Christ's appearance as the light of the world in its confrontation with the darkness (cf. 8:12; 3:19f.; 9:5; 12:35, all passages in which the core concept of 1:4, 5 [and 10] return). For that reason it is not permissible to end the first cycle of ideas, the Word in the beginning and so on, at vs. 4. All the imperfect verbs in vss. 1-4 that describe the preexistence and essence of the Word that was antecedent to all existence and experience have their point and meaning in that they reveal the grand background of the actual situation of proclamation in which the Evangelist and the Christian community know themselves to be: "The light shines in the darkness, and the darkness has not understood it."[60]

Furthermore, the purpose of the Gospel According to John was "to trace the gospel story to its final and deepest origins and so—taking up the conflict between what he will refer to over and over as darkness and lies versus truth and light—to point out at the outset the important range of what he is about to narrate and the grounds on which he will call people to believe that Jesus is the Christ, the Son of God (John 20:31)."[61] O'Collins overlooks that the human reception of that light is open to resistance and hence to distortion, misinterpretation, and rejection. Put differently, he overlooks the place of sin that is at the root of man's resistance. He is not the only contemporary Catholic theologian who overlooks this matter. Jesuit theologian Francis X. Clooney does as well. He claims that Christ is not relativized in *Nostra Aetate* §2; indeed, he is the concentration point and hence the source of truth and goodness in other religions, and hence Christ opens us to whatever is true, good, and holy in them. He interprets this to mean, "Christ is the way, truth, and life validates rather than diminishes the truth and holiness of the religions."[62] But this is a half-truth; it completely overlooks that the human reception of that Christological light is open to resistance and hence to distortion, misinterpretation, and rejection, and hence he overlooks the place not only of philosophical reason but also of sin that is at the root of man's resistance.

However, John Paul II overlooks neither. With respect to the former, he holds, "The Church knows that the 'treasures of wisdom and knowledge are hidden in Christ' [cf. Col 2:3], and therefore insists on the development of philosophical inquiry to prevent the obstruction of the path that leads to the recognition of the mystery" (FR §50). With respect to the latter, he does not overlook the root of man's resistance. In between the orders of divine creation and redemption is the order of the fall into sin. In this context John Paul locates "religious differences" because they do not "derive from the design of God." He says, "If it is the order of unity that goes back to creation and redemption and is therefore, in this sense, 'divine', such differences—and even religious divergences—go back to a 'human fact', and must be overcome in progress towards the realization of the mighty plan of [salvific] unity which dominates the creation."[63] Therefore, the plurality of religions belongs to the order of the fall into sin and hence needs removal. It belongs to this order because it reflects the human reception of that "offer," "call," and "grace" such that man is open to resistance and hence to distorting, misinterpreting, and rejecting God's revelation in creation and redemption in Christ. John Paul says, these differences reveal "the limitations, the evolutions and the falls of the human spirit which is undermined by the spirit of evil in history (LG §16)." He adds, these religious differences are such that they "are diverse and mutually incompatible," so much so that "one can also feel that their divisions are insuperable."[64]

Yes, religious diversity, according to John Paul, may also be regarded in a positive light because the Church does not hold that non-Christian religions are completely false in all the claims they make, but only in those that are logically incompatible with Christian truth claims. So, as Vatican II says in *Nostra Aetate* §2, "The Catholic Church rejects nothing that is true and holy in these religions." Elsewhere John Paul says, "The universal unity based on the event of creation and redemption cannot fail to leave a trace in the lived reality of people, even when they belong to different religions. For this reason, the Council invited the Church to discover and respect the seeds of the Word present in such religions [cf. AG §11], and affirmed that all those who have not yet received the Gospel are 'orientated' toward the supreme unity of the People of God."[65] At the same time the Church unequivocally affirms "the duty of the Church's preaching to proclaim the cross of Christ as the sign of God's all-embracing love and as the fountain from which every grace flows" (NA §4). "This means," John Paul explains, "that the Church is called to work with all her energies (evangelization, prayer, dialogue) so that the wounds and divisions of men—which separate them from their Origin and Goal, and make them hostile to one another—may be healed..., consolidated, and raised up" in accordance with the salvific plan of God in Jesus Christ."[66]

Of course, interreligious dialogue is integral to carrying out this task of evangelization, according to John Paul. This is evident from his papal magisterium of twenty-seven years. In the compendium of documents on interreligious dialogue, John Paul II has some 800 paragraphs expressing his commitment to interreligious dialogue. Typical of John Paul is the following statements: "However, the Church's commitment to dialogue with non-Christians in no way alters her essential mission of evangelization."[67] "Just as interreligious dialogue is one element in *the mission of the Church, the proclamation of God's saving work in our Lord Jesus Christ is another*. Christ's followers must carry out his mandate to make disciples of all nations, to baptize and to teach the observance of the commandments (cf. Matt 28:19-20)."[68] Again, "Interreligious dialogue at its deepest level is always a *dialogue of salvation*, because it seeks to discover, clarify, and understand better the signs of the age-long dialogue which God maintains with mankind. From the Christian's point of view, it presupposes the desire to make Jesus Christ better known, recognized, and loved, but it requires that this proclamation should be carried out in the Gospel spirit of understanding and peace."[69]

Furthermore, at the heart of dialogue is the quest for truth itself.[70] According to John Paul, "*the Church is committed to pursuing a dialogue of truth and love* with all humanity, and in a special way with... the followers of other religions."[71] In other words, the deepest purpose of dialogue is "seeking after truth and sharing it with others. For truth is light, newness, and strength."[72] Therefore, in the quest for truth, according to the then Secretariat for Dialogue with Non-believers, "dialogue does not necessarily exclude other forms of contact, such as, among others, apologetics, confrontation, and discussion."[73] In other words, although not the whole story about interreligious relations, the latter should include apologetics, particularly when we deal with conflicting truth claims. Intellectual confrontation and critical discussion regarding metaphysical, anthropological, and epistemological commitments that inform and shape the various religions. None of these religions has a neutral standpoint with respect to ultimate commitments. Hence, interactions between the participants of religious communities are intellectually obligated to argue for the truth of what they take themselves to hold to be true. This brings us to "reasoned argument in defense of what one takes to be true against views that one takes to be false—against, that is, potential or actual challengers to one's own beliefs."[74] We will return to these other forms of contact in the concluding section of this chapter when I make a case for the necessity of interreligious apologetics.

For now, I conclude with my discussion of John Paul II's theology of religions. The deep structure "of the created unity of the human race, and of the unity of the salvific work of Christ," says John Paul, as well as the positive elements within non-Christian religions, expresses "that all those who have not yet received the Gospel are 'orientated' [LG §16] toward the supreme unity of the people of God." By virtue of the "real and objective value of this 'orientation,'" there is a basis, not only for dialogue but also evangelization.[75] For evangelization because these religious people belong to God's people in potentiality, as only a "possibility," according to Aquinas, "not a reality. This possibility is rooted in the "power of Christ, which is sufficient [but not efficacious] for the salvation of the whole human race."[76]

Lastly, by *Nostra Aetate*'s lights, Assisi was called to encourage the "maintaining of good fellowship among the nations" (1 Pet 2:12), and, if possible, as far as depends on one, to live at peace with all men" (Rom 12:18).

I turn now to discuss briefly the view of Joseph Ratzinger/Benedict XVI on the question of religious diversity, truth, and God's will.

A Genuinely Dialogical but Also Critical Encounter

Joseph Ratzinger takes a very different stance that Francis regarding the question: "What, in concrete terms, is Christianity's position in the dialogue of religions?" In a gem of an essay, "The Dialogue of the Religions and the Relationship between Judaism and Christianity,"[77] an abridged version that is more fully worked out in *Truth and Tolerance*,[78] Ratzinger denies dialogue should supplant evangelization, but also, while maintaining the integrity of dialogue, sublates[79] it into the necessity of the quest for truth and justification of a religious commitment.

The claim that missionary activity should cease entails the denial of truth. This leaves us, Ratzinger says, with the idea that dialogue is a matter "of making one another better Christians, Jews, Moslems, Hindus, or Buddhists." He pronounces an emphatic "No" to that claim: "For this would be nothing other than total lack of conviction; under the pretext of affirming one another in our best points, we would, in fact, be failing to take ourselves (or others) seriously; we would be finally renouncing truth."[80]

So how does Ratzinger account for what not only unites us, more or less, but also makes possible a genuinely dialogical, but also critical, encounter, given the separation and contradictory affirmations between the religions, "On what basis can one even begin to look for this unity?"[81]

He delineates three approaches to the question of unity in diversity: mystical, theistic, and pragmatic.[82] *The pragmatic approach*, which affirms the primacy of orthopraxy ("right practice") over orthodoxy, arises from a skepticism engendered by endless disputes about rational justification and the truth of religion. Renouncing truth and conviction, unity in religious diversity is sought in orthopraxis serving ethical values that promote peace, justice, and the protection of creation. "The religions could all keep their formulas, forms, and ritual, but everything should be geared to this *right practice*."[83] Ratzinger affirms these ends as such but opposes cutting short the rational debate about the truth of religion. He also opposes advancing a "religiously motivated moralism" about the goals that best serve these ends. Why?

He says the "religions have no *a priori* knowledge" of the means to attain these ends. There is a "pluralism of paths" here rather than only one right path. Argument is needed to select and support which is the best path. Ratzinger, then, argues that the pragmatic approach to unity in religious diversity perverts religion "into an ideological dictatorship with a totalitarian passion." Think here of the religiously motivated moralism of some global warming advocates. Thus: "Religion cannot be forced into the service of practical-political objectives; the latter would become an idol; man, making God the slave of his plans, would degrade both God and himself."[84] Unity cannot be found in orthopraxy.

The mystical approach hopes to find unity in religious diversity at the level of mystical experience. An absolute value is attributed to an unnamable experience that is also ineffable and beyond all concepts. Unity is promoted here "by withdrawing all affirmative propositions (which means those claiming to be composed of truths)." A strongly negative or apophatic theology drives this approach so "no [determinate] claims are made as to knowledge of the divine." On this view, the claims of diverse religions are penultimate, and hence it "does not matter whether the divine is conceived in personal or non-personal terms." Adds Ratzinger, "The God who speaks [and hears] and the silent depth of being are, it is suggested, only two different ways of conceiving the ineffable that lies beyond all concepts."[85] But ineffability is incoherent. Here is the gist of Ratzinger's critique:

> Is this view really "more pious," and, above all, is it more true? Let us ask, in practical terms, What does it change? What happens in terms of our faith and prayer? First of all, if personal and impersonal concepts of God are equal, interchangeable, then prayer becomes merely a fiction, since if God is not a God who sees and hears, if he does not recognize me and stand over against me, then prayer is going out into the void. It is then merely a form of self-recollection, of conversing with myself, not a dialogue. It may be a preparation for the absolute, a deliberate foray out of the separation of the self into the infinite being with which I am myself at the deepest level to be identified and into which I wish to be absorbed. But it has no point of reference that sets me a standard and from which I may in any sense expect a response. And further: if I can leave behind the belief in God as a "person," as one possible conception side by side with the impersonal one, then not only is this God not a God who perceives me, hears me, speaks to me (a Logos)—then he certainly has no will of his own.[86]

The central problem with this approach to the "Religious Ultimate," derives from insisting that this "Ultimate" transcends all concepts, personal or nonpersonal conceptions. If so, then it cannot provide an explanation of religious diversity; it cannot be causally responsible for the religious experiences of the different religions, and, most significantly, since there is no will of God, says Ratzinger, "neither, then, is there any ultimate distinction between good and evil."[87] Furthermore, it does not stand up to reality, and hence the question of unity cannot be resolved by this approach. The variety of religions makes profoundly contradictory and irreconcilable claims. Not all religions can then be true. Hence, they cannot be saying the same thing, making the same truth claims; so the question concerning conflicting truth is unavoidable and one cannot run around it with this approach.

This brings us to the *Christian theistic approach* (I leave Judaism aside). God is there and He is not silent. God's self-revelation in the history of salvation is realized in words and deeds. For instance, "Christ died is the deed; Christ died for our sins is the divinely given word of interpretation that makes the act revelatory," as the late Evangelical theologian, G.E. Ladd puts it. Hence, concurs Ratzinger: "faith in God cannot dispense with a [revealed] truth whose [determinate] substance can be articulated." Yes, the Christian faith has a mystical and apophatic and even an eschatological aspect such that, e.g., the dogmas of Trinity and the person of Christ are determinately true but also "invite us to an infinite journey to a God who is always infinitely greater." Vatican Council I put a heavy accent on dogmatic apophasis and hence, does not easily forget the ineffable and infinite mystery of God. The Council claimed that we see as in a mirror darkly (1 Cor 13:12)! Apophaticism is, arguably, at the heart of the analogy of being: "For between creator and creature no similitude can be expressed without implying a greater dissimilitude."[88] This apophaticism is reiterated at Vatican I: "For divine mysteries by their very nature so exceed the created intellect that, even when they have been communicated in revelation and received by faith, they remain covered by the veil of faith itself and shrouded, as it were, in darkness as long as in this mortal life 'we are away from the Lord; for we walk by faith and not by sight' [Cor 5:6-7]." In short, we can know something truly without knowing it exhaustively.[89]

Thus: "God becomes concrete, tangible in history [in the Incarnation]. He approaches men in bodily form. But this very God, become graspable, is utterly mysterious." So, the revealed truth regarding the mystery of the Incarnation, although determinate, "both conceals and reveals himself," the God-Logos.

How, then, does the proclamation of the Gospel involve dialogue? In Ratzinger's view, the "theistic, incarnational model brings us farther than the mystical and the pragmatic." On the one hand, revealed truth is accessible in faith. Still, God has not left himself without witness through general revelation, elements of which are found in the variety of religions (Rom 1:20, 2:14-16; Acts 14:17), albeit distorted, misinterpreted, and rejected. On the other hand, general revelation not only reveals common ground, a unity we already share in varying degrees, among the religions, but also these fragments may deepen our understanding of the Christian faith "through dialogue, allowing us to acknowledge its mystery and infinity."

However, dialogue *per se* is worthless, says Ratzinger, without "aiming at conviction, at finding the truth." This fundamental point is missing from Francis's view of dialogue and hence it is a lacuna in his thought. This claim needs development. I turn now to Benedict XVI's view of interreligious dialogue.[90]

In my view, Benedict XVI provides much-needed clarity about interreligious dialogue and its goals, especially the goal of truth-seeking and the concomitant justification of one's religious commitment. I have briefly discussed above Joseph Ratzinger's view of the dialogue of the religions. Although he was committed to dialogical relations among the religions, Benedict explicitly excludes religious relativism, indifferentism, and syncretism from his understanding. He, accordingly, sees this relation as a truth-seeking enterprise rather than just about "learning to accept the [religious] other in his otherness and the otherness of his thinking,"[91] as he puts it. Furthermore, following St. John Paul II (in his encyclical *Redempto-*

ris Missio), he rejects the supplanting of evangelization with interreligious dialogue, and, therefore, prioritizes the call of Jesus (John 1:39)—"Come and see!"—of proclamation and evangelization. Also rejected by Benedict is the claim that "it is possible for a believer to think that religions are all variations on a single theme." He explains:

> No, there is one reality of the living God, who has spoken, and there is *one* God, *one* incarnate God, thus *one* word of God, that is truly God's word. But there is religious experience, with a certain *human light from creation* [emphasis added], and therefore it is necessary and possible to enter into dialogue, and thus to become open to one another and to open everyone to the peace of God, the peace of all his sons and daughters, the peace of his entire family.[92]

However, Benedict does not claim to possess a full grasp of the "interlinked realities of the unicity of God's revelation, the unicity of the one God incarnate in Christ, and the multiplicity of religions, by which we seek peace and also hearts that are open to the light of the Holy Spirit, who illumines and leads to Christ."[93] Still, like *Lumen Gentium* §16, what he does understand is that notwithstanding this light of creation referred to in the above passage, "Often men, deceived by the Evil One, have become vain in their reasonings and have exchanged the truth of God for a lie, serving the creature rather than the Creator."

Furthermore, according to Benedict, a dialogical relation among the religions is multi-dimensional. First, it is about learning to co-exist, about being together, that is, about peace and justice, "shared responsibility for society, for the state, for humanity." To achieve that end, Benedict affirms the necessity of a dialogue among the religions. Second, although a hermeneutic of justice and peace is a guiding principle of this dialogical relation, says Benedict, it "is bound to pass beyond the purely pragmatic to an ethical quest for the values that come before everything." He adds, "In this way what began as a purely practical dialogue becomes a quest for the right way to live as a human being."

For Benedict, the starting point of the dialogue has two generally accepted rules for interreligious dialogue so that we "learn to accept the other in his otherness and the otherness of his thinking." The first is that: "Dialogue does not aim at conversion, but at understanding. In this respect it differs from evangelization, from mission; accordingly, both parties to the dialogue remain consciously within their identity, which the dialogue does not place in question either for themselves or for the other." Specifically, he means that at this point no explicit attention is given to answering the question: "Why am I a Christian, and not a Buddhist, Hindu, Moslem, Jew, and so forth?" Eventually, however, this crucial question must be addressed, especially given the cultural dominance in our time of a pluralistic and relativistic ethos that rejects any particular religion as uniquely and absolutely true.

In other words, as Benedict puts it, the justification and truth of "fundamental [religious] choices themselves are not under discussion." To rise to that level of discussion, which we must, would involve what Paul Griffiths calls the "necessity of inter-religious apologetics" ("NOIA" principle). Still, he says, "the search for an answer to a specific question becomes a process in which, through listening to the other, both sides can obtain purification and enrichment. In the process, this search can also mean taking common steps towards the one truth, even if the fundamental choices remain unaltered. If both sides set out from a hermeneutic of justice and peace, the fundamental difference will not disappear, but a deeper closeness will emerge nevertheless."[94]

Benedict accepts these two rules that guide interreligious dialogue, but he thinks them too "superficial" (his word) because they exclude the question of truth and justification as well as evangelization. A dialogical relation operates in the realm of pre-evangelization because it "does not aim at conversion, but at better mutual understanding." "But all the same," Benedict adds, "the search for knowledge and understanding always has to involve drawing closer to the truth." Otherwise, merely accepting fundamental differences, in short, one's religious identity, says Benedict, "effectively blocks the path to truth." The fundamental religious choices would consequently appear arbitrary, as having nothing to do with rationality and the truth about reality, particularly "with the possibility that religion has to do with truth." Significantly, Benedict fills in the lacunae of Francis's approach because Benedict urges us to consider that we must be interested in more than just maintaining the uniqueness and identity of being a Christian while seeing a positive value to the differences of religions.

Hence, Benedict affirms a third principle, that "Both sides in this piece-by-piece approach to truth are therefore on the path that leads forward and towards greater commonality, brought about by the oneness of the truth." One might add to the above-formulated rules the realist presuppositions of a theory of knowledge: truth exists, and we can know it, and be justified in our claims to know.

> Religious belief presupposes truth. The one who believes is the one who seeks truth and lives by it. Although the medium by which we understand the discovery and communication of truth differs in part from religion to religion, we should not be deterred in our efforts to bear witness to truth's power. Together we can proclaim that God exists and can be known, that the earth is his creation, that we are his creatures, and that he calls every man and woman to a way of life that respects his design for the world. Friends, if we believe we have a criterion of judgment and discernment that is divine in origin and intended for all humanity, then we cannot tire of bringing that knowledge to bear on civic life. *Truth should be offered to all* [emphasis added]; it serves all members of society. It sheds light on the foundation of morality and ethics,

> and suffuses reason with the strength to reach beyond its own limitations in order to give expression to our deepest common aspirations. Far from threatening the tolerance of differences or cultural plurality, truth makes consensus possible and keeps public debate rational, honest and accountable, and opens the gateway to peace. Fostering the will to be obedient to the truth in fact broadens our concept of reason and its scope of application, and makes possible the genuine dialogue of cultures and religions so urgently needed today.[95]

Yes, Benedict urges us to broaden our concept of rationality so that we might engage in rational debate about the metaphysical, epistemological, and anthropological commitments that inform our respective religious views. Still, I argued in Chapter 4 about the noetic influences of sin. The individual's "natural mind" is none other than what the Sacred Scriptures call the vanity of the "carnal mind" (Col 2:18), the "futility of one's thinking," a "darkened understanding" (Eph 4:17-18), indeed, a "gnoseological concupiscence,"[96] in which the intellect is apostate from Christ by declaring itself sovereign "due to the hardening of one's heart." In this connection, we can understand Benedict's perspective:

> Each one of us here also knows, however, that God's voice is heard less clearly today, and reason itself has in so many instances become deaf to the divine. Yet that "void" is not one of silence. Indeed, it is the din of egotistical demands, empty promises and false hopes that so often invades the very space in which God seeks us. Can we then make spaces—oases of peace and profound reflection—where God's voice can be heard anew, where his truth can be discovered within the universality of reason, where every individual, regardless of dwelling, or ethnic group, or political hue, or religious belief, can be respected as a person, as a fellow human being? In an age of instant access to information and social tendencies that engender a kind of monoculture, deep reflection against the backdrop of God's presence will embolden reason, stimulate creative genius, facilitate critical appreciation of cultural practices and uphold the universal value of religious belief.[97]

Against the background of man being both a truth-seeker and a trust-twister, we can see why this third principle is then fundamental to dialogue, "The broader purpose of dialogue is to discover the truth. What is the origin and destiny of mankind? What are good and evil? What awaits us at the end of our earthly existence?... We are living in an age when these questions are too often marginalized. Yet they can never be erased from the human heart." Then Benedict presses a critical point: "Confronted with these deeper questions concerning the origin and destiny of mankind, Christianity proposes Jesus of Nazareth. He, we believe, is the eternal *Logos* who became flesh in order to reconcile man to God and reveal the underlying reason of all things. It is he whom we bring to the forum of interreligious dialogue. The ardent desire to follow in his footsteps spurs Christians to open their minds and hearts in dialogue (cf. Luke 10:25-37; John 4:7-26). Benedict reminds us of what we have forgotten to "listen attentively to the voice of truth." He adds, "In this way, our dialogue will not stop at identifying a common set of values, but go on to probe their ultimate foundation. We have no reason to fear, for the truth unveils for us the essential relationship between the world and God."

Furthermore, given the necessity of interreligious apologetics, this also presupposes two precepts of would-be knowers, namely, knowing the truth, and avoiding error. Moreover, summarizing his Christian theory of knowledge as it pertains to the truth-seeker, Benedict concludes, "Christ, who is the truth, has taken us by the hand, and we know that his hand is holding us securely on the path of our quest for knowledge. Being inwardly held by the hand of Christ makes us free and keeps us safe: free—because if we are held by him, we can enter openly and fearlessly into any dialogue; safe—because he does not let go of us, unless we cut ourselves off from him. At one with him, we stand in the light of truth."

Finally, this process of searching for the truth eventually brings us in our dialogical relation to evangelizing a truth-seeker, and turning him from his truth-twisting ways. This seeker is "listening and following behind Jesus, which is not yet discipleship, but rather a holy curiosity, a movement of seeking." Then, adds Benedict, "Jesus turns round, approaches them and asks: 'What do you seek?' They respond with a further question, which demonstrates the openness of their expectation, their readiness to take new steps."

In short, this process is "effective in situations where man is listening in readiness for God to draw near, where man is inwardly searching and thus on the way towards the Lord.... As he walks with Jesus, he is led to the place where Jesus lives, to the community of the Church, which is his body. That means entering into the journeying community of catechumens, a community of both learning and living, in which our eyes are opened as we walk."

Benedict XVI's theology of inter-religious dialogue, therefore, does not stop at the necessary recognition of the other, but also encourages the dialogical relation to remain on the path of seeking and finding the truth in Christ and His Church.

Once Again, Beyond Absolutism and Relativism—This Time, Schillebeeckx

The Flemish Dominican Theologian, Edward Schillebeeckx (1914-2009) also aims to move beyond both absolutism and relativism regarding the matter of religions. I argued earlier, in this chapter, that this, too, is implied by Francis's claims. The central claims of the Christian faith neither are exclusively true such that the claims of other religions are false, and hence superior; nor are the claims of religions relatively true such that they are only valid for those who hold them to be true. Looking back to the six basic approaches to religious disagreement and truth I described earlier, Schillebeeckx rejects the first option because he does not hold that all religions are equally wrong. He also rejects option 5 because all religions are not equally relative; although no one religion is the true religion it would be a "cheap form of tolerance" to suspend the question of truth. Schillebeeckx asks, "Is Christianity the one true religion, or is it (in a milder version) a better religion that all the rest?"[98] On the one hand, Schillebeeckx holds, "No single religion exhausts the question of truth."[99] On the other hand, "we can, may and must say that there is more religious truth in all the religions together than in one particular religion, and that this also applies to Christianity."[100]

Still, as I shall explain below, according to Schillebeeckx, the definitive answer to the question of truth "can only be eschatological." Furthermore, like Francis, Schillebeeckx also aims at maintaining the uniqueness and identity of being a Christian while seeing a positive value to the differences of religions. He affirms, "The expression of the uniqueness of Jesus Christ on the one hand without discrimination against other religions but on the other hand without falling into 'religious indifferentism', suggesting that all religions are equal."[101] Like Francis, Schillebeeckx claims that this approach does not overlook the question of truth. Rather, "[T] he truth here is that no one has a monopoly of the truth and that no one can ask for the fullness of God's riches for himself or herself alone."[102] Nonetheless, despite the similarities between Francis and Schillebeeckx, the latter, but not the former, draws out the implications of this position for Christology.

For one, he claims that Christianity does not withdraw its claim to universality, which is "Jesus' message of universal liberation." Schillebeeckx explains:

> The universality of Christian salvation is an *offer* of salvation from God to all men and women... an offer of salvation with the aim of actually realizing salvation and liberation for all, in freedom, through a praxis in accordance with the gospel, in the steps of Jesus. The salvation that is founded in Christ as a promise for all becomes universal, not through the mediation of an abstract, universal idea, but by the power of its cognitive, critical and liberating character in and through a consistent praxis of the kingdom of God. So this is not a purely speculative, theoretical universality, but a universality which can be realized in the fragmentary forms of our history only through the spreading of the story of Jesus confessed by Christians as the Christ, and through Christian praxis.[103]

It would take us too far afield here to examine Schillebeeckx's soteriology. Looking back to the universality of the Gospel's message of liberation, however, Schillebeeckx does withdraw "its exclusivist and inclusivist claim to absoluteness."[104] The former because Christ is not the sole, full and sufficient cause of our salvation, and hence Christianity is not the one true religion; the latter because the good that is found in other religions is not only good because already present and fulfilled in an eminent way in Christianity itself. Inclusivism is mistaken. "Here 'Christian values' are discovered in other religions, but by the same token these are deprived of their own identity."[105]

For another, Schillebeeckx's attempt to get beyond absolutism and relativism has Christological implications, denying Christological orthodoxy's assertion regarding the fullness and completeness of God's revelatory presence in Jesus Christ such that God is present in Jesus in a unique, absolute, and unparalleled way because in Jesus the Word became flesh (DI §5). What are the three great Christological truths of Christological orthodoxy?[106]

> 1. It is *truly God the Son* who is man. Here the emphasis is focused upon the full divinity of the Son.
>
> 2. It is *truly* man that God the Son is. Here the emphasis is focused upon the full and complete humanity.
>
> 3. The Son of God *truly* is man. Here the emphasis is focused upon the ontological union between the person of the Son and his humanity—that is, Jesus must be one being or reality, and the one being or reality that Jesus is the Son of God *existing* as man.

Rather, Schillebeeckx embraces not only ontological complementarity because there is an "open" rather than a "closed" "identification which Jesus himself gives of God."[107] "Open" because the "revelation of God in Jesus... in no way means that God absolutizes a historical particularity (even Jesus of Nazareth)."[108] God's revelation in Jesus is a historically limited particularity, meaning thereby that this revelation is incomplete and imperfect. Jesus is unique and universal but not absolute. "Here we are confronted with the difficult, almost paradoxical idea on the one hand of Jesus' particular, indescribably special relationship with God, and, on the other hand, with the fact that as a historical phenomenon he is a 'contingent event' which cannot exclude or deny other ways to God."[109] When asked whether, in his view, Jesus is God, Schillebeeckx provides an indirect answer to this question.

> However, what Jesus did so that others began to experience decisive salvation in him, salvation from God, ultimately raises the question: Who is he, that he was able to do such things? If he passes on to us a new attitude to God and his kingdom, it is obvious that people should ask: What is his relationship to God and—by way of the

> answer to this question—what is God's relationship to him?[110]

Jesus' personal relationship to God defines his humanity in its depth. In what sense? For human beings, it means that we are creatures and inescapably so. But Jesus' relationship to God is more than this status as creature. "It is already evident from the New Testament, on the one hand that God can only be defined from and in terms of the human life of Jesus, and on the other hand that as a man in his full humanity Jesus can only be defined in terms of his unique relationship with God and man.... According to the New Testament, God belongs in a very special and unparalleled way to the definition of what and who the man Jesus is."[111] This claim about the unique and unparalleled sense in which God belongs to who Jesus is still does not say that Jesus is God or that God is this man Jesus. In fact, Schillebeeckx explains that the "humanity of Jesus is an essential pointer to God." In other words, he adds, "the real significance of Jesus lies in this way in which he points from himself to God, whom he called Creator and Father. For Christian belief Jesus is therefore the decisive and definitive revelation of God."[112] However, this claim about God's revelation in Jesus does not affirm the three Christological truths stated above. Jesus is the revelation of the true God because "God revealed himself in Jesus in and through the non-divine form of Jesus' humanity"[113]; in other words, "God is (or acts) in Jesus Christ,"[114] and hence is only present in Jesus, but is not God himself.

Schillebeeckx's claim entails that Jesus is not fully and truly God, and God is not fully and truly Jesus. There seems to be "two subjects in Jesus, God and Jesus the human being."[115] In what sense, then, is God present in Jesus if God does not take upon himself full solidarity with the humanity of Jesus? Schillebeeckx asks "If he mediates a new relationship to God and his kingdom to us, it is natural to ask: what is his relationship to God? And what is God's relationship to him?"[116] Is the crucified Jesus God himself? Says Schillebeeckx, "Jesus has an abiding and constitutive significance for the approach of the Kingdom of God and thus for the comprehensive healing of human beings and making them whole."[117] As Roch Kereszty describes views like that of Schillebeeckx, "It is not God himself who became the subject of a full human experience including our purest joys and greatest burdens, our sufferings and our death. God did not die for us in Jesus; only Jesus the human being died who was joined to God by God's unique presence in him."[118]

Furthermore, Schillebeeckx adds, "We learn from the revelation of God in Jesus that no individual historical particularity can be said to be absolute, *and that therefore through the relativity present in Jesus anyone can encounter God even outside Jesus*, especially in our worldly history and in the many religions which have arisen in it."[119] Therefore, Schillebeeckx holds—unlike John Paul II—that "the pluralism of religions is [not] a matter of fact" but rather a "matter of principle,"[120] and hence "the multiplicity of religions is not an evil which needs to be removed, but rather a wealth which is to be welcomed and enjoyed by all."[121] Therefore, Schillebeeckx seeks, contrary to *Dominus Iesus*, "to justify religious pluralism, not only *de facto* but also *de iure* (or *in principle*)."[122] This is ontological complementarity, and it rest on the presupposition denying that Jesus is truly and fully God, and vice-versa. Furthermore, "The risen Jesus of Nazareth also continues to point to God beyond himself. One could say: God points via Jesus Christ in the Spirit to himself as creator and redeemer, as a God of men and women, of *all* men and women. God is absolute, but no single religion is absolute."[123] Denying this, Schillebeeckx claims, implies the claim that regards all religions other than Christianity as "nothingness." He continues, "This then seems essentially to conflict with the deepest sense of all Christological councils and confessions and ultimately with the very being of God as absolute freedom. In this view, Jesus' humanity is reduced to a docetic pseudo-humanity, while on the other hand the identity of all non-Christian religions is trivialized."[124] Schillebeeckx refuses to say that Jesus is God or that God is this man Jesus, not only because he holds that Jesus' true human existence is undermined, but also "absolutizing" Jesus' historical particularity implies that there is no good or truth in other religions. However, is he right?

Schillebeeckx repeats several times that Jesus' true human existence, his contingent, historical, limited particularity, isn't affirmed if he is absolutized. Consequently, the deepest sense of all Christological councils and confessions, which reject docetic pseudo-humanity, is lost. But the Christological orthodoxy stated above need not be interpreted in this way. The Son of God is fully and truly divine and fully and truly man. He became man "substantially uniting to his very person (hypostasis), through the power of the Holy Spirit, a human nature so that he, in his very person, actually came to exist as a man.... The Holy Spirit simultaneously brought into being a human nature and substantially brought into being a human nature and substantially united it to the person of the Son so that Son actually came to exist as man. Traditionally, this type of union came to be termed 'the hypostatic union.'"[125] Such interpretations of Christological councils and confessions, argues Kereszty, reflect a "misunderstanding of the hypostatic union as if that admitted only a human nature or essence in Jesus, but no human existence." Kereszty adds, "God, by his own infinite act of being, assumes Jesus as an actual human being into personal union with him." Jesus *is* the Son of God existing *as a man*. "This, Jesus must be God, but at the same time a true human being."[126]

There is another point to consider, namely, Schillebeeckx's claim that affirming the three Christological truths stated above "introduces a reduction in which God is absorbed into Christ: in that case his saving presence in nature and history, outside Jesus, in God's great word of creation, in in practice denied."[127] However, the Christological councils and confessions do not entail a Christological monistic conception of revelation: Christ alone reveals God in an absolutely exclusive sense. G.C. Berkouwer rightly raises the pivotal question: "whether we have the right to simply conclude from the exclusive salvation in Christ to the exclusive revelation in Christ."[128] The brief answer here to this question is "no" because a distinction must be drawn between general and special revelation.[129]

What is the distinction between the two modes of revelation, namely, general and special revelation? Briefly, general revelation is God's revelation of himself to all men in and through the works of creation. Regarding this revelation, God reveals himself to all men at all times and all places such that men, in principle, may know something of God's existence, of his attributes, and his moral law (Rom 1:20; 2:14-15).[130] This is the revelation that Schillebeeckx refers to in the above quotation. This "revelation is not limited to certain people, places, or times, but is truly general."[131] It is ubiquitous because "it comes to us through conditions [created realities and conscience] that are present at all times and places."[132] Thus, in principle, all have access to some knowledge of God via his general revelation. By contrast, according to *Dei Verbum* §2, special revelation is about God revealing himself specially in and through salvation history, a history that runs through the events and people of Israel, culminating in the concentration point of that history in Jesus Christ who is the mediator and fullness of all revelation. This revelation is historical, verbal, and salvific. Jointly constitutive of God's special revelation are its inseparably connected words (verbal revelation) and deeds, intrinsically bound to each other because neither is complete without the other; the historical realities of redemption are inseparably connected to God's verbal communication of truth in order that we may, as Catholic theologian Francis Martin puts it, "participate more fully in the *realities* mediated by the words."[133] In other words, a core presupposition of the concept of revelation in *Dei Verbum* §2 is that "without God's acts the words would be empty, without His word the acts would be blind,"[134] as was admirably stated by Reformed theologian Geerhardus Vos. Moreover, special revelation, by contrast with general revelation, "is spatiotemporally limited—it comes to us through historical events at special times and places and then through the testimony of others about these events."[135] Thus, here too Schillebeeckx is mistaken that the orthodox interpretation of the Christological councils and creeds entails a monistic concept of revelation.

The Necessity of Interreligious Apologetics

This chapter has dealt with Pope Francis's views on the dialogue of religions and his failure to raise the question of truth. I have argued that this question must be raised in view of the competing truth claims among the religions. After exposing the flaws in Francis's approach to the dialogue and his aim of getting beyond absolutism and relativism, I turned to John Paul II and Benedict XVI, both of whom raise the question of truth in the context of the dynamics of dialogue. Benedict, in particular, understands that we have to justify why one is a Christian and not something else. In the concluding section of this chapter, I turn now briefly to discuss Schillebeeckx's view on justification and truth. Schillebeeckx draws on the reflections of the German philosophical theologian, Wolfhart Pannenberg (1928-2014) and hence he too will be a crucial part of my discussion.

This topic on justification and truth is crucial for understanding the nature and necessity of interreligious apologetics that I have been hinting at throughout this chapter in view of the matter of competing truth claims. The question of truth and justification is missing in Francis's dialogue of religions, but not in his predecessors, John Paul II and Benedict XVI, not in the documents of the Pontifical Council for Interreligious Dialogue, for example, *Dialogue in Truth and Charity*, and not in Schillebeeckx. In particular, Schillebeeckx does not think that all religions are equal; that is a "cheap form of tolerance." Francis, too, rejects relativism. "Relativism wounds people too: all things seem equal, all things appear the same" (NGM §§15-16). Still, he never raises the question of meaning and truth. Thus, to his credit, Schillebeeckx raises not only the question of meaning and truth but also suggests criteria for exercising the epistemic responsibility of making judgments about religious claims. After a brief discussion of Schillebeeckx, I conclude, in light of my analysis, with a plea for interreligious apologetics.

Schillebeeckx makes several remarks about the nature of truth. For one, he affirms the idea of *universal* truth. However, truth-in-itself, meaning thereby "absolute" truth does not exist, according to Schillebeeckx, because a subject (knower) always mediates truth historically.[136] Still, Schillebeeckx does not hold truths to be valid only for the individual who affirm them, and hence only in that historical content, not capable of being proposed to others. Indeed, Schillebeeckx holds, "The universality of Christian faith means that the Christian community of faith is an open community.... However, universality—which in Greek is 'catholicity—means that the Christian faith is open (critically) to all, to every people and to every culture. 'Universal' means that which is equally valid for all."[137] What is the ground of that universality?

Let us recall the distinction I made in Chapter 1 between the conditions under which I affirm something to be true and the conditions that make something true. My knowing that something is true is not what makes it true; objective reality does that. A proposition is true if and only if the state of affairs to which it refers is the case; otherwise, it is false.[138] Presupposing that distinction allows one to see that there is no opposition here between asserting that *p* is true *simpliciter*—what *p* says is the case, actually is the case, valid for everyone—and acknowledging the conditions under which I know that *p*. Now, although Schillebeeckx alludes to reality, he focuses on the epistemic conditions of justification rather than the truth conditions that make something true. "Reality is expressed only by subjects who experience it, so that truth does not just have a primary relationship to reality, but also a relationship to subjects."[139] I agree with this in light of the distinction drawn above. However, Schillebeeckx renders the epistemic criteria of consensus the ground of universality. Yes, truth is ordered by reality, he says, but it "is also ordered by a universal consensus, if it is in fact to be called universal, i.e., the truth."[140] Now, although Schillebeeckx follows Wolfhart Pannenberg on meaning and truth, he overlooks Pannenberg's critique of a pure consensus theory of truth.

Pannenberg reasserts objective reality as "a critical principle preventing pure conventionalism."[141] He seems to reject the identification of truth and warranted assertion via consensus as implausible because our most justified beliefs might yet be false. Pannenberg explains,

> Nevertheless, since it is possible only for *subjects* to learn about facts, interpersonal agreement retains a predominance in decisions about the truth of statements. Since interpersonal consensus is [however] only one aspect of the general harmony of all the factors of experience, that is, of the coherence of experience,... a conventionally accepted view may be rejected if it is irreconcilable with the content of an individual's experience.[142]

The reference in the concluding sentence to the content of an individual's experience refers to the object of that experience that is mediated by propositions that assert something to be the case. This forms the basis for the correspondence theory of truth. On that theory, a proposition is true if and only if what that proposition asserts is in fact the case about objective reality; otherwise, the proposition is false. Yes, according to Pannenberg, "the correspondence of statements with the facts cannot be determined without reference to the judgments of others."[143] Again, there is no opposition here between asserting that *p* is true *simpliciter*—what *p* says is the case, actually is the case, valid for everyone—and acknowledging the conditions under which the subject knows that *p*. Consider the following example as an illustration of the distinction between truth and justification:

> In the eighteenth century, chemists such as Georg Ernest Stahl and Joseph Priestley held that when something burns, it loses a substance called "phlogiston." Later, after the researches of Antoine Lavoisier, chemists came to reject the phlogiston theory in favor of the theory that combustion involves not the loss of something, but the gain of something, namely, oxygen. Before Lavoisier, the most informed chemists in the world all believed the phlogiston theory; very likely they were *justified* in doing so; perhaps evidence for the phlogiston theory was so strong that they would have been unreasonable if they had not believed it. But Lavoisier acquired new evidence, which justified rejecting the phlogiston theory and believing the oxidation theory instead.[144]

Now, what this suggests is that epistemic justification and truth require different treatment. To say that Stahl and Priestley were justified in their view and Lavoisier was justified in rejecting it, is not the same as saying that the "phlogiston theory was 'true for Stahl [and Priestley], but not true for Lavoisier. It is one thing for a person to be justified in holding a belief, and a very different thing for the belief to be true."[145] Hence, even if justification is relative to epistemic context, say, via universal consensus, that does not mean the truth of a given belief is relative. One may be an epistemic relativist without being a relativist about truth. Justification may be lost, but not truth. Truth hinges not on justification but on the world, reality. This is the position of philosophical realism about truth. John Paul II holds this position. He writes in respect of a philosophy of knowledge that can be of service to the Gospel is one that affirms the "human capacity to *know the truth*," that is, "to come to a knowledge which can reach objective truth by means of the *correspondence between thing and intellect (adaequatio rei et intellectus)*" (FR §82).

As Francis Schüssler Fiorenza explains: "This definition, originating with Aristotle, has come down to us through Isaac ben Israeli and Thomas Aquinas." He elaborates "*Veritas est adequatio (convenientia, correspondentia) intellectus et rei.*" "Truth is the adequation, (the coming together or correspondence) of understanding and reality."[146]

Both Schillebeeckx and Pannenberg rightly distinguish meaning and truth, but these two may not be separated because after identifying what an assertion means, its truth claims need examination. How do we distinguish?[147] Consider Berkouwer's insistence here is, then, that to grasp the meaning of a dogma we must understand its historical context. He is right that it is surely simplistic to ignore the historical context in understanding "the various terms, concepts, images, and propositions that the Church has used to confess its faith." He is also surely right that the meaning of dogmas is not always immediately transparent. For example, there exist unclear terms "in the Christological and Trinitarian controversies, such words as consubstantial, hypostasis, person, nature, and many others. The terms often evoked misunderstandings, and different interpretations of them created conflict of opinion."[148] Still, argues Schillebeeckx, siding with Pannenberg, "the question of truth is not ultimately related to the question of 'meaning' and 'significance' simply by way of being a purely external addition."[149] I take this to mean that we are not simply interested in the conditions under which these statements were originally asserted, but rather particularly with "what is asserted in them, the theological truth-content."[150] Thus, Pannenberg, "The fact that the experienced particular meaning has objects as its contents naturally does not mean that the meaning asserted is correct." Bernard Lonergan is right that "meaning of its nature is related to what is meant, and what is meant may or may not correspond to what is in fact so [or is the case]." "If it corresponds," Lonergan adds, "the meaning is true. If it does not correspond, the meaning is false."[151] This is philosophical realism about truth. So, Germain Grisez is also right that "if the propositions signified by certain expressions were true," say, the Chalcedonian formula of faith regarding the relationship between the two natures in the unity of the divine person, "subsequent variations in the meaning of the expressions do not affect the truth of the propositions, but only the ability of the expressions to communicate truth without interpretation." In short, adds Grisez, "If this proposition is true, it will be true always and everywhere."[152] For example, if the assertions of the Apostles' Creed, as Colin Gunton correctly notes, "were once true, they are always true."[153]

Finally, according to Pannenberg, and Schillebeeckx who sides with him, is truth the whole, the all-encompassing totality of truth, making truth of its very nature a matter of coherence such that a statement of truth is determinately true only when meaning and truth coincide in that totality? If the latter, the truth status of dogmatic formulations is such that truth cannot be known now in a determinate way. Rather, only changeable approximations to—or anticipation of—the whole truth can be had, which to a certain extent distort or alter it. Says Pannenberg, "This is so even when the limitations of the semantic horizon of the utterances are shown to be the source of their untruth, in that every assertion claims to possess the truth about its object and by doing so within a limited horizon of meaning sets itself in opposition to the totality of truth." Why opposition to the whole truth?

Divine truth may be expressed incompletely and inadequately, but neither falsely nor indeterminately. Just because we do not know everything—the whole truth—that there is to know about a particular divine truth it does not follow that what we do know is not determinately true in these doctrinal formulations but only approximations of that truth. Furthermore, Rahner is correct: "They are an *'adequatio intellectus et rei'*, insofar as they state absolutely nothing which is false. Anyone who wants to call them 'half false' because they do not state everything about the whole of the truth of the matter in question would eventually abolish the distinction between truth and falsehood."[154] So the new linguistic formulation or expression can vary, as long as they mediate the same judgment. What is more, adds Rahner, "a more complete and more perfect statement does not falsify the one it supersedes." (ME §11). The content of the concepts informing the propositions that God is triune, and that the Second Person of the Trinity is God Incarnate, is meaning invariant, is fixed and hence determinate, and that meaning does not change precisely because it is true to reality, to an objective state of affairs.

On the view that seems to be Pannenberg's and Schillebeeckx's position, "every assertion, and to a correspondingly greater degree every outline of systematic networks of meaning which integrates perceived meaning and makes interpersonal agreement possible, anticipates truth." Pannenberg adds, "This element of anticipation is expressed in the very *form* of an assertion, in that as an assertion the proposition claims to be true while at the same time laying itself open to refutation."[155]

This epistemological position is inconsistent with Vatican I and II, the CDF document *Mysterium Ecclesiae*, the International Theological Commission document, *The Interpretation of Dogma*, and John Paul II's *Fides et Ratio*. All these documents subscribe to the claim of Lérinian hermeneutics that we can know determinately the true and unchanging meaning of dogmas. I discussed this hermeneutics in Chapter 1, so I will not repeat my arguments again. The affirmations of faith do have a determinable content of truth in respect of their correspondence to reality. Without that contact with reality, it is difficult to avoid dogmatic relativism and the corruption of "the concept of the Church's infallibility relative to the truth to be taught or held in a determinate way" (ME §5). This epistemological position is compatible with the claim, as Guarino notes, "that every statement requires further thought and elucidation, that every assertion is open to reconceptualization and reformulation, and that no statement comprehensively exhausts truth, much less divine truth."[156] In other words, the distinction between the permanent meaning and truth of dogmas and their historically conditioned formulations, which can be subject to correction, modification, and complementary restatement, accommodates the aspect of "anticipation" Pannenberg is referring to, but without denying that we can know determinately the true and unchanging meaning of dogmas.

We noted earlier in this chapter, according to Ratzinger, dialogue *per se* is worthless without "aiming at conviction, at finding the truth." Pope Francis, like Benedict XVI, accepts that the starting point of the dialogue is governed by two generally accepted rules for interreligious dialogue. In Benedict's words, the first rule is, "learn to accept the other in his otherness and the otherness of his thinking." The second rule is, "Dialogue does not aim at conversion, but at understanding. In this respect it differs from evangelization, from mission; accordingly, both parties to the dialogue remain consciously within their identity, which the dialogue does not place in question either for themselves or for the other." In other words, as Benedict puts it, the justification and truth of "fundamental [religious] choices themselves are not under discussion." Specifically, Benedict means that at this point no explicit attention is given to answering the question: "Why am I a Christian, and not a Buddhist, Hindu, Moslem, Jew, and so forth?" Eventually, however, this crucial question must be addressed. These two rules must be surpassed, particularly since the dialogue of religions must include an acknowledgment of the incompatible truth claims of the religions. Hence, Benedict rightly thinks these two rules too "superficial" (his word) because they exclude the question of truth as well as evangelization.

Interreligious apologetics is necessary because we need to give an answer to the above question. We are called as Christians to be ready to give reasons for the hope that is in us (1 Peter 3:15). This will require engaging in both negative and positive apologetics. The former refutes objections to the Christian faith from the side of other religions; the latter give reasons for being a Christian. Paul Griffiths states, "Where negative apologetics is defensive, positive apologetics is offensive. Where negative apologetics mans the barricade, positive apologetic takes the battle to the enemy's camp."[157] Summarily stated:

> If representative intellectuals belonging to some specific religious community come to judge at a particular time that some or all of their own doctrine-expressing sentences are incompatible with some alien religious claims(s), then they should feel obliged to engage in both positive and negative apologetics vis-à-vis these alien religious claim(s) and their promulgators.[158]

Truth matters. Francis's emphasis is always on maintaining the uniqueness and identity of being a Christian while seeing a positive value to the differences of religions. I have argued in this chapter for the insufficiency of this approach because it ignores the question of incompatible truth claims. I have also argued that Francis's attempt to get beyond absolutism and relativism in matters of religion is unsuccessful, indeed, that the very attempt is misguided. Truth matters. Hence, the justification of our religious commitment and the claims one holds to be true must be justified. Otherwise, merely accepting fundamental differences, in short, one's religious identity, says Benedict, "effectively blocks the path to truth." The fundamental religious choices would consequently appear arbitrary, as having nothing to do with rationality and the truth about reality, particularly "with the possibility that religion has to do with truth." Hence, truth matters.

NOTES

1. Joseph Cardinal Ratzinger, *Truth and Tolerance, Christian Belief and World Religions*, 9.
2. John Paul II, "To Representatives of the Various Religions of India," §509.
3. International Theological Commission, *Christianity and the World Religions*, §102.
4. Netland rightly says, "There is no logical connection between the assertion that Christianity is the true religion and any particular view of the extent of salvation." *Christianity & Religious Diversity*, 182. I have discussed the question of salvation in three separate articles: "Vatican II and the Religions," "*Ad* Father O'Collins," and "The Salvation of Non-Christians? Reflections on Vatican II's *Gaudium et Spes* §22, *Lumen Gentium* §16, Gerald O'Collins, S.J., and St. John Paul II."
5. Francis, "Video of 6 January 2016."
6. Francis, "Message of His Holiness Pope Francis to Mark the Opening of the Interreligious Meeting of Prayer For Peace."
7. "Religions, if they do not pursue ways of peace, deny themselves. They can only build bridges, in the name of the One who does not tire of joining Heaven and earth. Our differences should not therefore put us against each other: the heart of those who truly believe exhorts to open, always and everywhere, ways of communion." Do all the religions call upon the same One? Of course not! The disagreements between the religions are muted not least because Francis emphasizes that despite all our differences what we have in common is that we are all children of God; this way of speaking of all men threatens practically to eliminate the need for a real grace of justification won by the Passion of Christ. "The first work of the grace of the Holy Spirit is *conversion* effecting justification in accordance with Jesus' proclamation at the beginning of the Gospel: 'Repent, for the kingdom of heaven is at hand'" [CCC §1989].For my main theological objection to speaking of all men as children of God, see Chapter 4, note 104. Francis on occasion says, more accurately, that what binds us all together is that "we were created in the image and likeness of God" (Address of Pope Francis to the Plenary Session, Pontifical Council for Promoting the New Evangelization, 14 October 2013).
8. "Address of His Holiness Pope Francis to Representatives of Different Religions." Says Francis, 28 November 2013, "We do not impose anything, we do not use any deceitful strategy to attract faithful, rather we witness with joy, with simplicity what we believe in and what we are. In fact, an encounter in which each one puts to one side what he believes in, pretending to give up what is dearest to him, would certainly not be a genuine

relation. In such a case, one could speak of a false fraternity" ("Pope's Address to Plenary Assembly of the Pontifical Council for Interreligious Dialogue").

9. "[The] mentality of indifferentism [is] 'characterized by a religious relativism which leads to the belief that "one religion is as good as another" [John Paul II, Encyclical Letter *Redemptoris Missio*, §36].' (*Dominus Iesus* §22)."

10. Pontifical Council for Interreligious Dialogue defines "irenicism" as "an inordinate attempt to make peace at all costs by eliminating difference," and this "'is ultimately nothing more than skepticism about the power and content of the Word of God which we preach'" (*Dialogue in Truth and Charity*, §48).

11. Pontifical Council for Interreligious Dialogue defines "syncretism" as "a blending of elements, especially doctrines and practices of different religions" (*Dialogue in Truth and Charity*, §47).

12. See *Evangelii Gaudium* §250, and also, Jean-Louis Cardinal Tauran, "Interreligious Dialogue and the New Evangelization," Pontifical Council for Interreligious Dialogue, http://pcinterreligious.org/interreligious-dialogue-and-the-new-evangelization_139.html.

13. See Gerald R. McDermott and Harold A. Netland, *A Trinitarian Theology of Religions, An Evangelical Proposal*, for a critique of this understanding of dialogue, 277-83.

14. Full text of Pope Francis's address on interfaith dialogue: "Pope's Address at Interreligious Meeting in Colombo, Sri Lanka." His approach reminds me of the interreligious vision of Francis Clooney. "Yes, we must adhere deeply to our Christian faith, in its fullness; yes, we must avoid watering things down, and must steer clear of relativism. But it is also true that our deep faith commitment to Christ need not translate into disrespect for the beliefs and practices of others" (Francis X. Clooney, SJ, *Learning Interreligiously, In The Text, In The World*, 247).

15. "Message of Pope Francis for the 48th World Communications Day." So, too, Jacques Dupuis, SJ, *Toward a Christian Theology of Religious Pluralism*, 294, citing Wesley Ariarajah in support of his own view, "'However true our own experience, however convinced we are about a faith-claim, it has to be given as a claim of faith and not as truth in the absolute sense.'"

16. Kasper, *The Catholic Church, Nature, Reality and Mission*, 318.

17. Idem, "The Continuing Challenge of the Second Vatican Council: The Hermeneutics of the Conciliar Statements."

18. Idem, *The Catholic Church*, 264.

19. Ibid.

20. See Chapter 1 of this book.

21. Address of Joseph Cardinal Ratzinger, "Relativism: The Central Problem for Faith Today."

22. Francis, *The People Wish to See Jesus*, 68.

23. Pope Francis on 16 February 2018, approved the CDF Letter, *Placuit Deo*, On Certain Aspects of Christian Salvation, that uphold the traditional teaching on salvation, including "the confession of the Christian faith, which proclaims Jesus as the only Savior of the whole human person and of all humanity (cf. Acts 4:12; Rom 3:23-24; 1 Tim 2:4-5; Tit 2:11-15) [*Dominus Iesus* §§5-8]."

24. Edward Schillebeeckx, OP, *Mensen als verhaal van God*, 185. ET, 166.

25. Ibid., 200; ET, 181.

26. See Paul J. Griffiths, "On *Dominus Iesus*, Complementarity Can Be Claimed," 22-24.

27. "Est enim aliud ipsum depositum Fidei, seu veritates, quae veneranda doctrina nostra continentur, aliud modus, quo eaedem enuntiantur, eodem tamen sensu eademque sententia," Ioannes XXIII, "Allocutio habita d. 11 oct. 1962, in initio Concilii," *Acta*

Apostolicae Sedis (1962), 792. Denzinger, §3020. For a commentary on this text of John XXIII, see Chapter 1, note 36.

28. Clooney, *Learning Interreligiously*, 280.
29. Griffiths, "On *Dominus Iesus*, Complementarity Can Be Claimed," 23-24.
30. I discuss *Lérinian* hermeneutics extensively in Chapter 1, and its application to ecumenism in Chapter 6.
31. Netland, *Christianity & Religious Diversity*, 180.
32. Francis's approach to leave behind both absolutism and relativism is reminiscent of the approach of Schillebeeckx, *Mensen als verhaal van God*, 178-204; ET, 159-86. More on Schillebeeckx in the text.
33. See Chapter 1 of this book where these claims of Francis are critically discussed.
34. Bergoglio, *Education for Choosing Life*, 56-57.
35. "Address of Pope Francis to the Community of the Pontifical Gregorian University."
36. Francis, *The People Wish to See Jesus*, 68.
37. On the legitimacy and, indeed, necessity of interreligious apologetics, see Paul Griffiths, *An Apology for Apologetics: A Study in the Logic of Interreligious Dialogue*; idem, "Why We Need Interreligious Polemics." See also, Glenn B. Siniscalchi, "Conciliar Apologetics and Interreligious Dialogue"; McDermott and Netland, *A Trinitarian Theology of Religions*, 283-92. I address the question of the necessity of interreligious apologetics in the concluding section of this chapter.
38. *Dialogue and Proclamation*, §31.
39. Ratzinger, *Truth and Tolerance*, 65-66.
40. CNA/EWTN News, "Pope: Be Open to the Good Wherever it comes from."
41. Joseph Cardinal Ratzinger, *Many Religions—One Covenant*, 110.
42. Ibid., 110-11, emphasis added.
43. For example, in his recent trip to Morocco Francis stressed inter-religious dialogue with Moslems, rejecting proselytism (which he once again does not define), and hence evangelizing with the aim of conversion. On the one hand, one could understand Francis' emphasis as a prudential judgment given that Islam is the religion of Morocco, with its penal code prohibiting undermining Islam or proselytizing. On the other hand, if my analysis in chapter 1 and in this chapter of Francis's views is correct, then it seems that his emphasis is a judgment derived from principle rather than from prudence. O'Connell, "In Morocco Pope Francis explains what it means to be Christian in a majority Muslim land."
44. Benedict XVI, "Reflections of His Holiness Benedict XVI Published for the First Time on the Occasion of the 50th Anniversary of the Opening of the Second Vatican Council." This exclusively positive approach also informs Gerald O'Collins' approach to the Sacred Scriptures resulting in his treatment of just the "positive" passages in them and not the "negative" ones critical of non-biblical religions. I agree with Paul J. Griffiths's judgment of O'Collins' earlier book *Salvation for All* that the latter "jettisons some essential elements of the scriptural witness" because his biblical hermeneutic "shows a deep desire to avoid looking at and commenting upon the fact that some among the prophets and founders [of other religions] may have been agents of absence, advocates of lack, entrepreneurs of evil" ("Review Symposium," at 135-36). This judgment applies to another of O'Collins' works, *The Second Vatican Council on Other Religions*. We find in O'Collins' work an echo of Jacques Dupuis' book, *Toward a Christian Theology of Religious Pluralism*. Dupuis acknowledges "the Old Testament's unambiguous condemnation of idolatrous practices among the nations and the inanity, or even the inexistence, of the false gods they venerate... as... an unequivocal basis for a negative theological evaluation of the traditions concerned.... In the new situation, however, which today's search for mutual comprehension and openness to dialogue have created, it seems fair for a theological

account of the Bible's evaluation of the religions of the nations to allow such positive elements to stand out as are liable to provide in a new context a valid foundation for a more generous theological evaluation of the other religious traditions of the world. An attempt is made here to bring forward some of the biblical data capable of providing a valid basis for such a positive evaluation" (30). Joseph Ratzinger argues that there is a "sharp criticism of false gods... in evidence and that is alive in the tradition of the [Old Testament] prophets from the very beginning," and hence "a decided rejection" (*Truth and Tolerance*, 20-21). In his 1968 *Introduction to Christianity* (139), he argues that there is a parallel "between the philosophers' criticism of the myths in Greece and the prophets' criticism of the gods in Israel." In short, "the prophetic and Wisdom literature cultivated [the] demythologization of the divine powers in favor of the one and only God."

45. Both St. Thomas Aquinas (1225–1274) and, centuries later, the Protestant reformer John Calvin (1509–1564) held similar views on this score. Aquinas wrote, "Although some minds are enwrapped in darkness, that is, deprived of clear and meaningful knowledge, yet there is no human mind in such darkness as not to participate in some of the divine light... because all that is true by whomsoever it is uttered, comes from the Holy Spirit." I found this passage by Aquinas in John Paul II, "Method and Doctrine of St. Thomas in Dialogue with Modern Culture," in *The Whole Truth about Man*, 268–69. Similarly, Calvin wrote: "If we regard the Spirit of God as the sole fountain of truth, we shall neither reject the truth itself, nor despise it wherever it shall appear, unless we wish to dishonor the Spirit of God" (*Institutes of the Christian Religion*, ed. John T. McNeill [Philadelphia: Westminster, 1960], 2.2.15.273–74).

46. Netland, *Christianity & Religious Diversity*, 140-41.

47. Ibid., 141n8, "The term 'religious pluralism' is employed in different ways. Sociologists often use it in a descriptive sense as a synonym for religious diversity. Others take it to mean a more or less positive attitude toward religious diversity, without carefully defining what this includes. I use it to refer to the view that the major religions are all valid religions in that they are roughly equally true and equally effective as appropriate responses to the one religious ultimate."

48. Schillebeeckx, *Mensen als verhaal van God*, 198; ET: 180.

49. Pope Francis seemed to accept that religious diversity is willed by God in a joint statement he signed with Ahmed el-Tayeb, Grand Imam of al-Azhar, during an interreligious meeting in Abu Dhabi. (Mary Rezac, "Pope Francis signs peace declaration on 'Human Fraternity' with Grand Imam") However, he clarified his position during the ad limina visit to Rome of the bishops of Kazakhstan and Central Asia: "The Pope explicitly stated that Bishop Schneider could share the contents of their exchange on this point. 'You can say that the phrase in question on the diversity of religions means the permissive will of God', he told the assembled bishops, who come from predominantly Muslim regions" (Diane Montagna, "Bishop Schneider wins clarification on 'diversity of religions' from Pope Francis, brands abuse summit a 'failure'").

50. "Not infrequently it is proposed that theology should avoid the use of terms like 'unicity', 'universality', and 'absoluteness', which give the impression of excessive emphasis on the significance and value of the salvific event of Jesus Christ in relation to other religions. In reality, however, such language is simply being faithful to revelation, since it represents a development of the sources of the faith themselves. From the beginning, the community of believers has recognized in Jesus a salvific value such that he alone, as Son of God made man, crucified and risen, by the mission received from the Father and in the power of the Holy Spirit, bestows revelation (cf. Matt 11:27) and divine life (cf. John 1:12; 5:25-26; 17:2) to all humanity and to every person. In this sense, one can and must say that Jesus Christ has a significance and a value for the human race and its history, which are unique and singular, proper to him alone, *exclusive, universal, and absolute*. Jesus is, in fact, the Word of God made man for the salvation of all" (DI §15, emphasis added).

51. Pope John Paul II, "Address of John Paul II to the Representatives of the Christian Churches and Ecclesial Communities Gathered in Assisi for the World Day of Prayer," §2.

52. "To the Roman Curia," in *Interreligious Dialogue*, §§562-73. The English translation is available online, "Pope's Christmas Address To Roman Curia."

53. According to the Catechism, "Jesus, the Son of God, freely suffered death for us in complete and free submission to the will of God, his Father. By his death he has conquered death, and so opened the possibility of salvation to all men" (CCC §1019). Yet, Trent says, "even though 'Christ died for all' [2 Cor 5:15], still not all do receive the benefit of His death, but those only to whom the merit of His passion is imparted" (Denzinger, §1523). Says Aquinas, Christ is "the propitiation for our sins, efficaciously for some, but sufficiently for all, because the price of his blood is sufficient for the salvation of all; but it has its effect only in the elect" (Aquinas, *Commentary on St. Paul's Epistle to Timothy, Titus, and Philemon*, 1:2:6). See also, Aquinas, *Summa Theologiae* III, q. 48, a. 2, "And therefore Christ's Passion was not only a sufficient but a superabundant atonement for the sins of the human race; according to 1 John 2:2: 'He is the propitiation for our sins: and not for ours only, but also for those of the whole world.'"

54. O'Collins, *The Second Vatican Council, Message and Meaning*, 116, and also 56, 122.

55. Ibid., 13.

56. International Theological Commission, *Christianity and the World Religions*, §91, "But although God has been able to enlighten men in different ways, we are never guaranteed that these lights will be properly welcomed and interpreted by those to whom they are given. Only in Jesus do we have the guarantee of the full welcoming of the will of God the Father."

57. Herman Ridderbos, *The Gospel of John, A Theological Commentary*, 43. So, too. Francis Martin and William M. Wrights IV, *The Gospel of John*, on vv. 10-11, "The Light, which was in the world, is the divine Word through which the world was made. However, the world preferred to ignore the Light: the world did not know him. As St. Paul writes in Rom 1:18, human beings, despite the witness to God in creation, 'in their wickedness suppress the truth'" (36). See also William Grossouw, *Revelation and Redemption, An Introduction to the Theology of St. John*, "This is the great event [Incarnation] in history which St. John contemplates with respectful astonishment and loving gratitude: the plenitude of divine Lie and Light has come forth from the bosom of the divinity... and has appeared among us in the person of Jesus Christ." O'Collins, of course, heartily affirms this truth. Missing from his account is man's resistant response to the Light. That is, "Almost as great is the tremendous and incomprehensible tragedy of the world: 'the world knew him not', for from the very beginning the darkness has been opposed to the Light (1:5 ff.). John rears his concept of the world on a great antithesis; his history is a drama. The darkness consists in the denial and overthrow of divine revelation. Just as the Light is the manifestation of the divine truth, so the darkness is a futile but terrible attempt to blot out the operation of the Light. The stage of this struggle is the spirit of man. With painful bewilderment St. John observes that the majority of men shun the Light. The world did not receive Him (1:5) and His own rejected Him (1:11). Men have loved the darkness rather the Light (3:19)" (29-30). One sees nothing of this struggle in O'Collins' theology of religions.

58. Ben Witherington, III, *John's Wisdom: A Commentary on the Fourth Gospel*, 55.

59. Rudolph Schnackenburg, *The Gospel According to St John*, Volume One, 255-56,

60. Ridderbos, *The Gospel of John*, 40. Schnackenburg agrees: "Man is called on to make his own active decision (of faith), but that he did not 'lay hold' of it when it was within his grasp" (*Gospel According to St John*, 246).

61. Ibid. For the same flawed exegesis, see Jacques Dupuis, SJ, "The Pangs of a Process," in *Do Not Stifle the Spirit, Conversations with Jacques Dupuis*, 178-80. See also, Dupuis, *Toward a Christian Theology of Religious Pluralism*, 288.

62. Francis X. Clooney, SJ, "Interreligious Learning in a Changing Church: From Paul VI to Francis," *Irish Theological Quarterly* 2017, Vol 82 (4) 269-283.

63. John Paul II, "To the Roman Curia," §566.

64. Ibid.

65. Ibid., §568.

66. Ibid., §567.

67. "To the Bishops of Sri Lanka," in *Interreligious Dialogue*, §642.

68. "To the Plenary Session of the Secretariat for Non-Christians," in *Interreligious Dialogue*, §587.

69. "To the Pontifical Council for Interreligious Dialogue," in *Interreligious Dialogue*, §779. See also, "To the Representatives of the Various Religions of Tanzania," *Interreligious Dialogue*, §688.

70. "To the Representatives of the Various Religions of Indonesia," in *Interreligious Dialogue*, §659.

71. Ibid., §685.

72. Ibid., §509.

73. Franziskus Cardinal König, Secretariat for Dialogue with Non-believers, "Dialogue with Nonbelievers," §1.

74. Paul J. Griffiths, "Why We Need Interreligious Polemics." See also, idem, *An Apology for Apologetics, A Study in the Logic of Interreligious Dialogue*. I'll return in the last section of this chapter to Griffiths' defense of NOIA—the necessity of interreligious apologetics.

75. John Paul II, "To the Roman Curia," §568.

76. Thomas Aquinas, *Summa Theologiae*, 3, q. 8, a. 3; q. 48, a. 2. See also, Aquinas, *Commentary on Timothy, Titus and Philemon*, 1, q. 2, a. 6.

77. Ratzinger, *Many Religions—One Covenant*, 89-113.

78. Idem, *Truth and Tolerance, Christian Belief and World Religions*.

79. Lonergan, *Method in Theology*; I adapt Lonergan's understanding of sublation. The quest for truth and justification sublates dialogue in the sense of going beyond it, sets up a new principle, directs it to a new goal but, so far from dwarfing it, preserves it and brings it to a far fuller fruition.

80. Ratzinger, *Many Religions—One Covenant*, 111-12.

81. Ibid., 94.

82. Ibid., 94-96.

83. Ibid., 96.

84. Ibid., 101-2.

85. Ibid., 98.

86. Ratzinger, *Truth and Tolerance*, 103.

87. Ibid. For a critique of ineffability that dovetails with Ratzinger's, see Netland, *Christianity & Religious Diversity*, 160-63.

88. Denzinger §806.

89. Ibid., §3016.

90. Unless otherwise indicated, the quote in the following paragraphs derive from "Address of His Holiness Benedict XVI On the Occasion of Christmas Greetings to the Roman Curia," 21 December 2012.

91. Benedict XVI, "Address of His Holiness Benedict XVI On the Occasion of Christmas Greetings to the Roman Curia."

92. Idem, "Address of His Holiness Pope Benedict XVI, Meeting with the Parish Priests and the Clergy of Rome."

93. Ibid.

94. Idem, "Address of His Holiness Benedict XVI on the Occasion of Christmas Greetings to the Roman Curia."

95. Idem, "Address of His Holiness Benedict XVI, Meeting with Organizations for Interreligious Dialogue."

96. Karl Rahner, *Theological Investigations*, XIII, 90.

97. Benedict XVI, "Address of His Holiness Benedict XVI, Meeting with Organizations for Interreligious Dialogue."

98. Schillebeeckx, *Mensen als Verhaal van God*, 183; ET: 164.

99. Ibid., 181; ET: 162.

100. Ibid., 185; ET: 166.

101. Ibid., 121; ET: 102.

102. Ibid., 186; ET: 167.

103. Ibid., 195; ET: 176.

104. Ibid., 180; ET: 161.

105. Ibid., 182; ET: 163.

106. Thomas G. Weinandy, O.F.M. Cap., Jesus the Christ, 54, 79. See also, Bernard Lonergan, SJ, Collected Works of Bernard Lonergan, Vol. 7, *The Ontological and Psychological Constitution of Christ*, 109: "The gist of the dogma [of the Incarnation] is this: one and the same is both truly God and truly man; that, the one person of the divine Word subsists in two natures, divine and human; and since the person must not be divided so as to have one person who is divine and another who is human, the union is said to be in the person, in contradiction to the opinion of the Nestorians; on the other hand, since the two natures are not to be merged so that a single nature somehow results from the two, the union is said to be on the basis of the person, in contradiction to the opinion of the Monophysites."

107. Schillebeeckx, *Mensen als Verhaal van God*, 199; ET: 180.

108. Ibid., 184; ET: 165.

109. Schillebeeckx, *On Christian Faith, The Spiritual, Ethical, and Political Dimensions*, 3.

110. Idem, *Interim Report on the books, Jesus & Christ*, 141.

111. Ibid., 141. See also, idem, *Mensen als Verhaal van God*, 140; ET: 121.

112. Idem, *Interim Report*, 142.

113. Idem, *Mensen als Verhaal van God*, 143; ET: 124.

114. Raniero Cantalamessa, *Jesus Christ, The Holy One of God*, 126.

115. Roch A. Kereszty, *Jesus Christ, Fundamentals of Christology*, 346.

116. Schillebeeckx, *Mensen als Verhaal van God*, 140, ET: 121.

117. Ibid., ET: 121.

118. Kereszty, *Jesus Christ, Fundamentals of Christology*, 346.

119. Schillebeeckx, *Mensen als Verhaal van God*, 184-85; ET: 165-66, emphasis added.

120. Ibid., 184; ET: 164.

121. Ibid., 187; ET: 167. See also, "That is no way to deny that the historical plurality of religions which in principle is not to be removed is inwardly nurtured and supported by a unity which cannot be made an explicit theme within our history and cannot be practiced: i.e. the unity of God (the trinitarian God confessed by Christians) in so far as this transcendent unity is reflected in the immanent family likenesses between these religions and allows us to give the one name "religion" to all these different religious

phenomena" (167). This claim regarding "unity" is unclear given that Schillebeeckx later says, "Christianity may [not] be seen as a special historical form of an unchangeable, supra-historical, metaphysical and religious nucleus, of which all religions are simply chance expressions" (180).

122. *Dominus Iesus* §4, "The Church's constant missionary proclamation is endangered today by relativistic theories that seek to justify religious pluralism, not only *de facto* but also *de iure* (or *in principle*)."

123. Schillebeeckx, *Mensen als Verhaal van God*, 184-85; ET: 165-66, emphasis added.

124. Ibid., 184; ET: 165.

125. Weinandy, *Jesus the Christ*, 74.

126. Kereszty, *Jesus Christ, Fundamentals of Christology*, 346n14.

127. Schillebeeckx, *Mensen als Verhaal van God*, 184; ET: 124.

128. Berkouwer, *General Revelation*, 93.

129. I discuss this question extensively in my book, *Berkouwer and Catholicism*, 110-272.

130. International Theological Commission, 1997, *Christianity and the World Religions*, §90: "God has given himself to be known and continues to give himself to be known by men in many ways: through the works of creation (cf. Wis 13:5; Rom 1:19-20), through the judgments of conscience (cf. Rom 2:14-15), etc."

131. Jeroen de Ridder and René van Woudenberg, "Referring to, Believing in, and Worshipping the Same God: A Reformed View," at 47.

132. Ibid., 50.

133. Fr. Francis Martin, "Some Directions in Catholic Biblical Theology," In *Out of Egypt, Biblical Theology and Biblical Interpretation*, at 67-68.

134. As Geerhardus Vos says in his address, "The Idea of Biblical Theology as a Science and as a Theological Discipline," Inaugural address as Professor of Biblical Theology, Princeton Theological Seminary, delivered at the First Presbyterian Church, Princeton on May 8, 1894. Reprinted in Richard B. Gaffin Jr. *Redemptive History and Biblical Interpretation: The Shorter Writings of Geerhardus Vos* (Phillipsburg, N.J.: Presbyterian and Reformed, 1980), 3-24.

135. De Ridder and Van Woudenberg, "Referring to, Believing in, and Worshipping the Same God: A Reformed View," 50.

136. Schillebeeckx, *Mensen als Verhaal van God*, 191; ET: 173.

137. Ibid., 187; ET: 169.

138. See William P. Alston, *A Realist Conception of Truth* (Ithaca, N.Y.: Cornell University Press, 1996), 5.

139. Schillebeeckx, *Mensen als Verhaal van God*, 193; ET: 173.

140. Ibid., 192; ET: 173.

141. Wolfhart Pannenberg, *Theology and the Philosophy of Science*, 220.

142. Ibid.

143. Ibid., 219.

144. Allen Wood, "Relativism," 4.

145. Ibid.

146. Fiorenza, *Foundational Theology*, 272–73. The quote within the quote from Aquinas is from the English translation of the *Summa Contra Gentiles, On the Truth of the Catholic Faith*, vol. 1, 59.

147. I draw here on some material from Eduardo J. Echeverria, *Berkouwer and Catholicism, Disputed Questions*, 65–81.

148. Berkouwer, *Vatikaans Concilie en Nieuwe Theologie*, 85 [74]. So, Pannenberg, "To this extent it is an intrinsic part of the hermeneutical consideration of the composite meanings of linguistic utterances to investigate their truth" (Pannenberg, *Theology and the Philosophy of Science*, 220).

149. Schillebeeckx, *Mensen als Verhaal van God*, 192; ET: 173. See also, Pannenberg, *Theology and the Philosophy of Science*, 220.

150. Paul Helm, *Faith, Form, and Fashion, Classical Reformed Theology and its Postmodern Critics*, 176.

151. Bernard Lonergan, "The Dehellenization of Dogma," in *A Second Collection*, at 14.

152. Germain Grisez, *The Way of the Lord Jesus, Christian Moral Principles*, vol. 1, 172; idem, "On Interpreting Dogmas." *Communio: International Catholic Review* 17 (1990): 120–26.

153. Colin E. Gunton, *A Brief Theology of Revelation: The 1993 Warfield Lectures*, 13–14.

154. Rahner, "The Development of Dogma," 44. Hans Küng, "Why are Dogmatic Pronouncements So Difficult to Make Today?", 207: "Every proposition can, as far as the verbal formulation goes, be true and false, according to how it is aimed, situated, intended."

155. Pannenberg, *Theology and the Philosophy of Science*, 220.

156. Thomas Guarino, *Foundations of Systematic Theology*, 139 n. 59; see also, 100 n. 20. See also, Interpretation of Dogma, "It is true that dogmas are historical creations in the sense that their meaning 'depends in part on the power of expression the language used had at a particular point in history and in particular circumstances'. Later definitions preserve and ratify the earlier ones, and also explain their meanings, mostly in the case of new questions or in the case of error, and so make them alive to the benefit of the Church. This does not mean that infallibility can be reduced to a frozen truth. Dogmatic formulations do not define truth in an undetermined, changing or approximative fashion, much less do they transform or maim it. Truth must be kept to a determined form."

157. Griffiths, *An Apology for Apologetics*, 14.

158. Ibid., 3.

8

The Crisis of the Church

The root of this evil [sexual abuse] is not clericalism, whatever that might be, but rejection of the truth and moral licentiousness. The corruption of doctrine always brings with it, and manifests itself in, the corruption of morals. This grave sin without remorse against the holiness of the Church is the result of the relativization of the Church's dogmatic foundations.—Gerhard Cardinal Müller[1]

Despite an elaborate *Catechism*, Rome exhibits a dogmatic timidity—which some see as a studied pose that provides cover for more mischievous developments. —Carl Trueman[2]

A church which takes the course of adaptation will not be able to work in a missionary way.—Robert Spaemann[3]

In this concluding chapter, I develop a response to the current crisis of the Church by arguing that this crisis is as such doctrinal, moral, and ecclesial—in particular, regarding the latter it pertains to the epistemological significance of the *sensus fidei fidelium* and the corresponding notion of synodality in the life of the Church.[4] Therefore, in light of this crisis, Vatican II enjoins, "All [Catholics] are led to examine their own faithfulness to Christ's will for the Church and accordingly to undertake with vigor the task of renewal and reform" (UR §4). The whole Church, laity and hierarchy together, engages in this task and it is more than ever needed now. In this conclusion, I will say something about each of these aspects needing renewal and reform. The motives for renewal and reform are well stated in the epigraphs to this chapter, doctrinal timidity, indeed, the relativizing of the Church's dogmatic foundations manifests itself in the corruption of morals, in particular, now sexual morality.[5]

Pope Francis takes the position that clericalism is at the root of the sexual abuse crisis in the Church.[6] However, Archbishop Carlo Mario Viganò disagrees, "to claim the crisis itself to be clericalism, is pure sophistry. It is to pretend that a means, an instrument, is in fact the main motive." What then is the root of the crisis?

The crisis is not about pedophilia—any adult who is sexually attracted to prepubescent children. Kenneth Woodward rightly states, "According to the John Jay Report, only about 5 percent of cases of clerical sex abuse in the past seventy years involved prepubescent children." Rather, he adds, the abusers fit "the clinical profile of an ephebophile—that is, someone who is sexually attracted to postpubescent minors, typically between the ages of twelve and eighteen." Furthermore, Woodward continues,

> [I]t is true that eight out of ten reported abuses by priests over the past seventy years were cases of males abusing other males. What accounts for this? In part it can be explained by the fact that in the fifteen years or so between the late 1960s and the early '80s, when most of the abuse took place, male adolescents were more readily available to priests in Catholic schools and seminaries than female adolescents. An even better though still incomplete explanation is that men who discover that they are sexually attracted to pre- or post-pubescent males are naturally drawn to occupations like the priesthood—and teaching and coaching and scouting—because of the trust accorded the members of these occupations, as well as the access to boys all these occupations provide.[7]

He then concludes, "One cannot deny that homosexuality has played a role in the abuse scandals and their cover-up, and to dismiss this aspect as homophobia one would have to be either blind or dishonest." This conclusion dovetails with Archbishop Viganò explanation:

> This is a crisis due to the scourge of homosexuality, in its agents, in its motives, in its resistance to reform. It is no exaggeration to say that homosexuality has become a plague in the clergy, and it can only be eradicated with spiritual weapons. It is an enormous hypocrisy to condemn the abuse, claim to weep for the victims, and yet refuse to denounce the root cause of so much sexual abuse: homosexuality. It is hypocrisy to refuse to acknowledge that this scourge is due to a serious crisis in the spiritual life of the clergy and to fail to take the steps necessary to remedy it. Unquestionably, there exist philandering clergy, and unquestionably, they too damage their own souls, the souls of those whom they corrupt, and the Church at large. But these violations of priestly celibacy are usually confined to the individuals immediately involved. Philandering clergy usually do not recruit other philanderers, nor work to promote them, nor cover-up their misdeeds —whereas the evidence for homosexual collusion, with its deep roots that are so difficult to eradicate, is overwhelming. It is well established that homosexual predators exploit clerical privilege to their advantage.[8]

In order to deal with the sexual abuse crisis in the Church, therefore, we need to engage in renewal and reform in the areas of doctrinal, moral, and ecclesial issues. I now turn to justify the project of renewal and reform in light of Vatican II's Lérinian hermeneutics, a hermeneutics that is central to this book's arguments.

Ressourcement and *Aggiornamento*

In Chapter 1, I made a case for Vatican II's Lérinian hermeneutics. This is, arguably, a form of retrieval theology, meaning thereby a "mode or style of theological discernment that looks back [to authoritative sources of faith, Scripture and Tradition] in order to move forward."[9] As Evangelical theologian, Kevin Vanhoozer correctly states, "*Ressourcement* describes a return to authoritative sources for the sake of revitalizing the present." He adds, "*To retrieve is to look back creatively in order to move forward faithfully.*"[10] Vatican II expressed its commitment to retrieval theology, to *ressourcement*.

> Every renewal of the Church is essentially grounded in an increase of fidelity to her own calling.... Christ summons the Church to continual reformation as she sojourns here on earth. The Church is always in need of this, in so far as she is an institution of men here on earth. Thus if, in various times and circumstances, there have been deficiencies in moral conduct or in church discipline, or even in the way that church teaching has been [doctrinally] formulated—to be carefully distinguished from the deposit of faith itself—these can and should be set right at the opportune moment. (UR §6)

Particularly important in this task of retrieval, of *ressourcement*, is the "learning Church," *Ecclesia discens*, which is distinct from the *Ecclesia docens*, the "teaching Church." Yet, these are aspects of the same Church.

In this connection, an expression of the "learning Church" is the *sensus fidei fidelium*—the sense of faith of the faithful, of those who share in the faith of the Church as a believing subject—of the whole Church, laity and hierarchy together, are instruments of the Church's living Tradition. They bear "responsibility for and [are] mediators in history [of] the revelation which is contained in the Holy Scriptures and in the living apostolic Tradition. The Second Vatican Council stated that the latter form 'a single sacred deposit of the word of God' which is 'entrusted to the Church', that is, 'the entire holy people, united to its pastors' [DV §10]. The council clearly taught that the faithful are not merely passive recipients of what the hierarchy teaches and theologians explain; rather, they are living and active subjects within the Church. In this context, it underscored the vital role played by all believers in the articulation and development of the faith: 'the Tradition that comes from the apostles makes progress in the Church, with the help of the Holy Spirit'" (SF §67). The notion of the *sensus fidei* is especially important not only in overcoming the separation between the learning Church and the teaching Church but also it is "a vital aspect of theological epistemology in Catholicism."[11] Francis appreciates the former but is not as clear about the latter.

Regarding the former, he says correctly, "The *sensus fidei* prevents rigid separation between 'Ecclesia" (Church) and the Church teaching, and learning (Ecclesia docens, discerns), since even the Flock has an 'instinct' to discern *new* ways that the Lord is revealing to the Church."[12] This spiritual instinct of faith is an active capacity, a personal aptitude, indeed, more exactly, a set of dispositions, shaped by ecclesial, spiritual, and ethical factors (SF §88), for discerning the truth of faith. In particular, this active capacity for spiritual discernment enables the believer, within the communion of the Church, to recognize the Lord and proclaim his Word. To qualify, as Francis does, this spiritual capacity as an instinct for discerning "new" ways that the Lord is revealing to the Church is a distraction from properly understanding the retrospective and prospective aspects of the *sensus fidei* of the believing subject in the life of the Church. The International Theological Commission expresses correctly how these aspects function in that life.

> [T]he *sensus fidei* needs to be viewed within the context of history, a history in which the Holy Spirit makes each day a day to hear the voice of the Lord afresh [cf. Heb 3:7-15]. The Good News of the life, death and resurrection of Jesus Christ is transmitted to the Church as a whole through the living apostolic Tradition, of which the Scriptures are the authoritative written witness. Hence, by the grace of the Holy Spirit, who reminds the Church of all that Jesus said and did [cf. John 14:26], believers rely on the Scriptures and on the continuing apostolic Tradition in their life of faith and in the exercise of the *sensus fidei*. (SF §68)

However, since, as Vanhoozer states, "*ressourcement* describes a return to authoritative sources for the sake of revitalizing the present," the Commission continues, "faith and the *sensus fidei* are not only anchored in the past; they are also orientated towards the future. The communion of believers is a historical reality: 'built upon the foundation of the apostles and the prophets, with Christ Jesus himself as the cornerstone,' it 'grows into a holy temple in the Lord' (Eph 2:20-21), in the power of the Holy Spirit, who guides the Church 'into all the truth' and declares to believers already now 'the things that are to come' [John 16:13], so that, especially in the Eucharist, the Church anticipates the return of the Lord and the coming of his kingdom [cf. 1 Cor 11:26]" (SF §69).

On the other hand, the *sensus fidei fidelium* has an essential role to play in reading the "sign of the times," and hence in moving faithfully forward in the present context. This involves "*aggiornamento*," the meaning of which is best captured in Vatican II's *Gaudium et Spes*:

> To carry out such a task, the Church has always had the

> duty of scrutinizing the signs of the times and of interpreting them in the light of the Gospel. Thus, in language intelligible to each generation, she can respond to the perennial questions which men ask about this present life and the life to come, and about the relationship of the one to the other. We must therefore recognize and understand the world in which we live, its explanations, its longings, and its often dramatic characteristics. (GS §4)

Significantly, as Oscar Cullman rightly stressed, "*aggiornamento* should be a consequence, not a starting point,"[13] of renewal, of *ressourcement*. Indeed, he adds, *aggiornamento* should not be understood as an "*isolated motive* for renewal."[14] Respectfully, it is not clear to me that Francis consistently grasps this point. For example, in his opening address to the recent synod on the youth, Francis emphasizes that a "listening Church" is about dialogue, that is, dialogue in which we listen to each other before we present a mutually honest, transparent, and constructive critique of each other's views: "The first fruit of dialogue is that everyone is open to newness, to change their opinion thanks to what they have heard from others." He adds, "Let us feel free to welcome and understand others and therefore to change our convictions and positions: this is a sign of great human and spiritual maturity." This "openness" is so important to Francis that he takes it to be a "sign of a Church that really listens, that allows herself to be questioned by the experiences of those she meets, and who does not always have a ready-made answer." Indeed, "The accumulation of human experiences throughout history is the most precious and trustworthy treasure that one generation inherits from another." There is something right about urging us read the "sign of the times" by listening discerningly to what others are saying about the new circumstances that confronts them, the contemporary challenges, and so forth (SF §70). But what is missing in Francis's call for *aggiornamento* is the normative reference point of interpreting the "signs of the times" in light of the divine Word, and "to discern how they may enable revealed truth itself to be 'more deeply penetrated, better understood and more deeply presented' [GS §44]" (SF §70).

The second key goal of Vatican II is *aggiornamento*, meaning—according to John XXIII —"looking at the present times which have introduced new conditions and new forms of life, and have opened new avenues for the Catholic apostolate." Francis's description of a "listening Church" along with its characteristic practices of listening, openness, experience, change, etc., are features of *aggiornamento*. But in John XXIII this is not an isolated motive for renewal, which it seems to be in Francis's opening synod address. Francis urges us not to forget about divine revelation because it "enlightens and gives meaning to history and to our existence." An orthodox Christian obviously could not think otherwise. Still, absent from Francis's address is any reference not only to the nature of divine revelation, of the revelation that is contained in the Holy Scriptures and in the living apostolic Tradition, but also the central role of the Church's teaching in her ongoing life.

Therefore, in the interplay between *ressourcement* and *aggiornamento*, the former has normative priority. This faithful movement forward cannot be done without affirming the normativity of the "letter" of the texts, of the literal sense of Vatican II documents, as the point of reference of Catholic theology and life, and in particular, of *ressourcement*. We turn now to discuss briefly each area of the Church's crisis.

History, Unchanging Truth, and Vatican II.

The threefold crisis is doctrinal, moral, and ecclesial. Some Catholics have correctly identified the relativization of doctrine as a contributing factor to this crisis. Against this relativizing, I now argue that faithful Catholics are obliged to give an irrevocable adherence of faith to truth not only contained in divine Revelation but also to those truths, which the Church's Magisterium proposed in a definitive way, having a necessary connection with revelation (CCC §88). "Faith is the theological virtue by which we believe in God and believe all that he has said and revealed to us, and that Holy Church proposes for our belief, because he is truth itself" (CCC §1814).[15] Faith involves both the *fides qua creditur*—the faith *with which* one believes—and the *fides quae creditur*—the faith *which* one believes.[16] Minimally, therefore, faith involves belief, and to have a belief means that one is intellectually committed to the whole truth that God has revealed.[17] Furthermore, faith involves holding certain beliefs to be true, explains Thomas Aquinas, because "belief is called assent, and it can only be about a proposition, in which truth or falsity is found" (ST II-II, q. 1, a.2, ad. 2). Thus, reality is what is known by a true affirmation.[18]

Moreover, the *fides quae creditur* is the objective content of truth that has been unpacked and developed in the creeds and confessions of the Church, dogmas, doctrinal definitions, and canons. As Pelikan rightly sees, "underlying the creedal and conciliar definitions of orthodoxy from the beginning have been three shared presuppositions: first, that there is a straight line... from the Gospels to the Creed; consequently, second, that the true doctrine being confessed by the councils and creeds of the church is identical with what the New Testament calls the 'faith which was once for all delivered to the saints' [Jude 3]; and therefore, third, that continuity with that faith is the essence of orthodoxy, and discontinuity with it the essence of heresy."[19]

Although Pelikan does not develop the points he rightly makes here with respect to the question of the nature of continuity that binds together the revealed Word of God to the true doctrines asserted by the creeds and confessions and hence to the essence of orthodoxy, that question has to be faced. But not here.[20] Here, I will simply presuppose the traditional notions of truth and language—a realist notion—because, arguably, it best explains the material identity of Christian truth over the course of time. In other words, it explains the nature of continuity—the intrinsic bond between mediating doctrines and divine revelation—presupposed by Pelikan's presuppositions. Lonergan explains:

> Dogma emerges from the revealed Word of God, carried forward by the tradition of the Church; it does so, however, only to the extent that, prescinding from all other riches [of language] contained in that word of God, one concentrates on it precisely *as true*.... Secondly, if one separates the word from the truth, if one rejects propositional truth in favor of some other kind of truth, then one is not attending to the Word of God as true... [Thirdly,] it is not enough to attend to the Word of God as true, if one has a false conception of the relationship between truth and reality. Reality is known through true judgment.... What in fact corresponds to the word as true is that which is [the case]. [Fourthly,] it was the Word of God, considered precisely as true, that led from the gospels to the dogmas.... There is a bond that unites them [and] that bond is the word as true.[21]

Against this background, it would be helpful to have an overall specification of the characteristics of dogma: "It is *(a)* an expression of the truth of revelation *(b)* in the form of a judgment (proposition) that is *(c)* the infallible expression of faith and therefore *(d)* binding in conscience; each dogma *(e)* arises on account of a specific historical problem."[22]

Now, we can understand why the Church teaches, "there is an organic connection between our spiritual life and the dogmas." What is the nature of that connection?[23] Dogmas are normative statements of beliefs. Hence: "Dogmas are lights along the path of faith; they illuminate it and make it secure. Conversely, if our life is upright, our intellect and heart will be open to welcome the light shed by our dogmas of faith" (CCC §89). Now, given Francis's relentless criticism against what he calls a "hostile inflexibility" regarding doctrine,[24] "doctrinal rigidity,"[25] against those he speaks of as Pharisaic stone-throwers who embody a merciless rigorism,[26] an "ahistorical fundamentalism" (CCC §231), he seems to have created the impression—whatever his intention was—that he is against dogma, or at least has a lesser regard for it than is expressed by the Church. Whatever his intention, Francis treats dogmas "as noble but irrelevant monuments from the past. To echo Thomas Mann, they are like deserted houses, still impressive but uninhabited."[27] He seems to think that behind the appeal to dogmas as normative statements of Christian beliefs is traditionalism—which is the "dead faith of the living." If so, he is mistaken. Appeals to the dogmatic faith of tradition is an appeal to the "living faith of the dead."[28] To recover a sense of the truth of dogmas as normative statements of belief and their relation to life, as "guides and incentives for living,"[29] the task of renewal and reform requires us to address some fundamental questions regarding the Second Vatican Council.

In 1985, on the twentieth anniversary of the close of Vatican II, John Paul II convened an extraordinary assembly of the Synod of Bishops with the aim of encouraging a deeper reception and implementation of the Council. The Synod set forth, in the document *A Message to the People of God and The Final Report*, a proper framework for interpreting the conciliar texts. In particular, six hermeneutical principles for sound interpretation of these texts were set forth.

All would-be interpreters of Vatican II, who make claims about what the Council actually teaches, should adhere to these principles. These hermeneutical principles are important, particularly in our time, since we seem to be living in an ecclesial culture where some are suffering from amnesia about the invaluable contributions of John Paul II and Benedict XVI to the authoritative interpretation of Vatican II.

Now, I will briefly explain the principles postulated by the 1985 synod for interpreting Vatican II texts:

1. The theological interpretation of the Conciliar doctrine must show attention to all the documents, in themselves and in their close interrelationship, in such a way that the integral meaning of the Council's affirmations—often very complex—might be understood and expressed.
2. The four "constitutions" of the Council (those on liturgy, the Church, revelation, and the Church in the modern world) are the hermeneutical key to the other documents—namely, the Council's nine decrees and three declarations.
3. The pastoral import of the documents ought not to be separated from, or set in opposition to, their doctrinal content.
4. No opposition may be made between the spirit and the letter of Vatican II.
5. The Council must be interpreted in continuity with the great tradition of the Church, including earlier councils. The Church is one and the same throughout all the councils.
6. Vatican II should be accepted as illuminating the problems of our own day.

The hermeneutical norm of the first and second principles is twofold: one, *intratextuality*, meaning thereby interpreting the meaning of a particular passage within the context of the whole document; and two, *intertextuality*, meaning thereby interpreting any specific document in the context of the whole body of documents, particularly attending to the authoritative priority of the constitutions. The third principle states the unity and interdependence of the doctrinal and pastoral dimensions of the council documents. It is particularly this third principle that is in jeopardy today of being sidelined, even if not openly rejected.

The fourth principle pertains to the relationship between the "spirit" of Vatican II and its "texts," that is, the "letter." The former refers to the deep motivating force of the Council to revitalize the Church, biblical interpretation, and theology, by way of *ressourcement* and *aggiornamento*.

This principle is a segue to the sixth principle, namely, Vatican II illuminates contemporary problems.

The fifth principle is also particularly important today given the "development" that some claim to find in the pastoral orientation of *Amoris*

Laetitia. As Gerhard Cardinal Müller, for one, has stressed, the unclear passages in chapter eight of Pope Francis's post-synodal Apostolic Exhortation (§§295-308) must be interpreted in continuity with the great tradition of the Church, including the documents of Vatican II, as well as earlier encyclicals, such as John Paul II's *Veritatis Splendor*.[30] Pope Francis has also stressed this as a hermeneutical principle for interpreting *Amoris Laetitia*, but we saw good reason for questioning that Chapter 8 actually satisfied this principle.

Yes, *Amoris Laetitia* §§38-58 reaffirms or confirms definitive doctrine infallibly taught regarding marriage and family by the ordinary universal Magisterium of the Church. Much of what Francis says in those paragraphs formally attests to truth already possessed and infallibly transmitted by the Church.

However, that is not the case with respect to the possibility of opening up Communion to the divorced and civilly remarried, as some episcopal conferences throughout the world have claimed, and to cohabiting couples, and same-sex couples, as some bishops, archbishops, and cardinals have proposed.[31]

To discern whether this possibility is a legitimate or an illegitimate development must be decided, as always, in light of ecclesial warrants, such as Holy Scripture, Church councils, creeds and confessions, theological doctors of the Church, Christian faithful (*sensus fidei*), and the past normative exercise of the Magisterium.

Without those sources, there is no sure and stable guide to Catholic truth.

Now, if we are to take seriously the fifth hermeneutical principle stated above, we must address, albeit briefly, one of the most contentious questions in the reception of the documents of the Second Vatican Council, namely, the relationship between unchangeable and absolute truth, on the one hand, and the human expression of that truth in a variety of historically-conditioned forms of thought, on the other. In short: Given that they did not fall from heaven, how do we maintain the enduring validity of the statements of truth asserted in confessions, creeds, and dogmas, and, yes, the documents of Vatican II, while acknowledging their historical conditioning? The answers given to this question of unchanging truth and history reflect conflicting interpretations of Vatican II and its work-product, its sixteen documents.

Pope Benedict XVI identified two basic ways of interpreting the Vatican II documents: a difference that is at the root of the conflict over interpreting Vatican II. Are the Council's documents justifiably interpreted as being in discontinuity and rupture with the Church's living Tradition? Ironically, Neo-Modernists and Neo-Traditionalists both agree with this way of reading the documents; the former are "boosters" and the latter "knockers" of Vatican II.

Alternatively, should these documents be interpreted as being in continuity with the truths long asserted by the Church, even as we recognize that the Council was engaged in a creative retrieval of the authoritative sources of faith—Scripture and Tradition—so that Catholicism might move forward faithfully into the future, itself renewed so that it could convert the world as it is today?

This distinction between two ways of reading Vatican II's documents is not a magician's wand capable of answering every burning question about the proper interpretation of Vatican II. But perhaps an answer comes from within Vatican II itself. I argued in Chapter 1 that the Council's own framework of interpretation—its own approach to the question of truth and history—is inspired by such *nouveaux théologiens* as Yves Congar (1904-1995), Henri de Lubac (1896-1991), which seems to have been recognized by John Paul II and Benedict XVI. Congar, de Lubac, John Paul II (the pope who created both men cardinals), and Benedict XVI represent a creative retrieval of the authoritative sources, of reform and renewal in continuity with the Church's living Tradition.

In this connection, it is worth noting that Pope John XXIII invoked the distinction between truth and its historically conditioned formulations in his opening address at Vatican II, *Gaudet Mater Ecclesia* [Mother Church Rejoices]. That address has been read by many as a clear indication that the Pope wanted the considerations begun by the nouveaux théologiens to be given continued study. As he said in *Gaudet Mater Ecclesia*, "What is needed is that this certain and unchangeable doctrine, to which loyal submission is due, be investigated and presented in the way demanded by our times. For the deposit of faith, the truths contained in our sacred teaching, are one thing, while the mode in which they are expressed, but with the same meaning and the same judgment ['*eodem sensu eademque sententia*'], is another thing."[32]

The subordinate clause, which I have cited in its Latin original, is part of a larger passage from Vatican I's Dogmatic Constitution on Faith and Reason, *Dei Filius*, which is also cited by Leo XIII in his 1899 Encyclical, *Testem benevolentiae Nostrae*; and this formula is itself taken from the *Commonitórium primum* 23 of Vincent of Lérins: "Therefore, let there be growth and abundant progress in understanding, knowledge, and wisdom, in each and all, in individuals and in the whole Church, at all times and in the progress of ages, but only within the proper limits, i.e., within the same dogma, the same meaning, the same judgment" (*in eodem scilicet dogmate, eodem sensu eademque sententia*).[33]

According to this "Lérinian" interpretation of dogma (and of Vatican II), linguistic formulations or expressions of truth can vary in our attempt to deepen our understanding, as long as they maintain the same meaning and mediate the same judgment of truth.

The documents of Vatican II are, however interpreted in another way, which I will call Neo-Traditionalism. The Neo-Traditionalists are anti-Modernists to the degree that they do not acknowledge that theological Modernism had actually identified a real problem in upholding the permanence of meaning and truth. Therefore, the Neo-Traditionalists absolutize continuity of dogmatic truth without displaying any appreciation for the historical nature of those truths' human expression. As Jaroslav Pelikan describes the position that I am calling Neo-Traditionalism: "Tradition without history has homogenized all the stages of development into one statically defined truth."[34]

Now the contention of the *nouveaux théologiens*, and arguably, of John XXIII and of the Council itself is that, despite the untenable solutions of the Modernists, Modernism had been onto something of importance for the future of the Church. As the Dominican theologian Aidan Nichols put it succinctly, "though Modernism had been a false answer, it had set a real question" and the question is about the relationship between abiding, permanent truth and its historically conditioned formulation. The false answer of the Modernism problem was rooted in their sense that the basic presupposition of the hermeneutics of continuity-in-renewal was no longer self-evident—"within the same dogma, the same meaning, the same judgment" (*in eodem scilicet dogmate, eodem sensu eademque sententia*).

Truth's expressions are historically conditioned; they are never absolute, in the sense of wholly adequate and irreplaceable. The *nouveaux théologiens* acknowledge that point; hence their distinction between unchanging truth and its formulations. Where the Modernists and *nouveaux théologiens* differ is over the claim that inadequacy of expression implies inexpressibility of divine truth; hence, unlike the *nouveaux théologiens*, the Modernist reduces truth to its changing historical and linguistic expressions. To quote Pelikan again, "history without tradition has produced a historicism that relativized the development of Christian doctrine in such a way as to make the distinction between authentic growth and cancerous aberration seem completely arbitrary."[35]

Thanks to a fixation on the historical-factual process, and the corresponding idea that truth-claims do not transcend the times but are entangled with the historical process in all sorts of ways, a Neo-Modernism has surfaced in the so-called *"new paradigm,"* or *"pastorality of doctrine"* approach of Richard Gaillardetz and Christoph Theobald, SJ.

Theobald, for example, collapses the distinction between the substance of the deposit of faith and its formulation into a historical context, without attending to the "Lérinian" subordinate clause—*eodem sensu eademque sententia*—while also dismissing the notion that unchanging truths and their formulations may be distinguished within the deposit of faith. And Theobald does not hesitate to draw a dramatic conclusion: the substance of the deposit of faith as a whole is "subject to continual reinterpretation [and re-contextualization] according to the situation of those to whom it is transmitted." This "pastorality of doctrine" approach, of which one can hear echoes not only in some interventions at Synod-2018, but also in the writings of Pope Francis, as I argued in Chapter 1, is a Neo-Modernism *because* it expresses merely an instrumentalist view of doctrine, in which doctrines are not absolute truths, or objectively true affirmations about state of affairs; in fact, doctrines do not make assertions about objective reality at all.

Given Francis's dismissal of the notion of abstract truth, his skepticism about absolute truth and his theologico-pastoral epistemology with its attendant principle that realities are greater than ideas, his affinity for the "pastorality of doctrine" approach is not surprising. This Neo-Modernism forfeits the distinction between faith (*fides quae*) and its content in statements of truth, propositions whose truth-status bear a relation to objective reality. Rather, for the Neo-Modernists, the content of faith is always derived from faith's experience of God. So that content is only a product of theological reflection upon this faith, with doctrines mediating that experience in secondary formulations. In sum: there are no revealed truths.

The Lérinian way of interpreting Vatican II acknowledges that the various pronouncements made by the Church in any given era reflect the historical setting and situation of the moment. Berkouwer is right, "All the problems of more recent interpretation of dogma are connected very closely to this search for continuity.... Thus, the question of the nature of continuity has to be faced." How, then, exactly, is a single and unitary revelation of revealed truths homogeneously expressed, according to the same meaning and the same judgment, given the undeniable fact of historical conditioning? Berkouwer identifies the chief question, but unfortunately leaves it unanswered.

Yves Congar, on the other hand, has argued that the distinction between the permanent meaning and truth of dogmas and their historically conditioned formulations, which can be subject to correction, modification, and complementary restatement, summarizes the meaning of the Second Vatican Council. Here we find the crucial difference between not only the *nouvelle théologie* and *modernism and the Neo Modernism of the* "pastorality of doctrine" approach, but between the *nouvelle théologie* and Neo-Traditionalism. Modernism, Congar wrote, identified the theological problem posed by "variations in the representations and the intellectual construction of the affirmations of faith." The *nouvelle théologie* solved this problem, he argued, by "distinguishing between an invariant of affirmations, and the variable usage of technical notions to translate essential truth in historic contexts differing culturally and philosophically." Given this distinction, the Church can avoid the trap of dogmatic relativism, into which the Modernists and now the neo-Modernists (with their "new paradigm") have fallen. The Lérinian way of interpreting Vatican II stands firmly against relativism about truth, and firmly for truth's permanence.

Christian Anthropology and Sexual Ethics

Pope Francis makes a point about inculturation, diversity, and inclusion in *Amoris Laetitia* that has proven most troubling for maintaining the catholicity and unity of the Church, leaving us with "local-option Catholicism," as Weigel calls it.[36] He adds, "Local-option Catholicism is a prescription for utter incoherence." Francis states:

> I would make it clear that not all discussions of doctrinal, moral or pastoral issues need to be settled by interven-

> tions of the magisterium. Unity of teaching and practice is certainly necessary in the Church, but this does not preclude various ways of interpreting some aspects of that teaching or drawing certain consequences from it. This will always be the case as the Spirit guides us towards the entire truth [cf. John 16:13], until he leads us fully into the mystery of Christ and enables us to see all things as he does. Each country or region, moreover, can seek solutions better suited to its culture and sensitive to its traditions and local needs. For "cultures are in fact quite diverse and every general principle... needs to be inculturated, if it is to be respected and applied." (AL §3)

The last two sentences of this passage has given bishops, archbishops, yes, even cardinals of the Church license to accommodate, and, worse, in some instances even to reject the Church's Christian anthropology and normative sexual morality—embodied in the *Catechism of the Catholic Church*, Part III, Article 6, The Sixth Commandment (§§2331-2400). This "local-option Catholicism" is about "differing (and perhaps even conflicting) theologies and pastoral practices."[37] This emphasis on the nature and limits of inculturation is stressed at the Conclusion of the Synod of Bishops on the Family 2015,

> And—apart from dogmatic questions clearly defined by the Church's Magisterium—we have also seen that what seems normal for a bishop on one continent, is considered strange and almost scandalous—almost!—for a bishop from another; what is considered a violation of a right in one society is an evident and inviolable rule in another; what for some is freedom of conscience is for others simply confusion. Cultures are in fact quite diverse, and every general principle—as I said, dogmatic questions clearly defined by the Church's magisterium—every general principle needs to be inculturated, if it is to be respected and applied. The 1985 Synod, which celebrated the twentieth anniversary of the conclusion of the Second Vatican Council, spoke of *inculturation* as 'the intimate transformation of authentic cultural values through their integration in Christianity, and the taking root of Christianity in the various human cultures.' *Inculturation* does not weaken true values, but demonstrates their true strength and authenticity, since they adapt without changing; indeed they quietly and gradually transform the different cultures."[38]

It is not clear why Francis limits inculturation, namely, that inculturation does not pertain to dogma clearly defined by the Magisterium. Ambiguous teaching on this matter is a source of consternation regarding Chapter 8 of *Amoris Laetitia*. This exhortation doesn't question the dogma that marriage is indissoluble. Yet, Francis's moral logic of pastoral reasoning is such that it renders under certain circumstances morally justified the choice of civilly remarried divorcees. They may stay in this union for the time being for the sake of the family and they are acting with moral rectitude even if they engage in sexual activity. Furthermore, this limitation is in tension with the claim that "cultures are in fact quite diverse and every general principle... needs to be inculturated, if it is to be respected and applied." In particular, the license offered in *Amoris Laetitia* §3, and which has been exercised by several members of the episcopacy, has fractured the unity of the Church encouraging doctrinal division and moral discord. I am not just thinking here of the statements from various episcopal conferences (Belgian, Polish, German, Argentinian, Philippine, et al) on communion for civilly remarried divorces that contradict each other.[39] There are other examples of those exercising the option of local-Catholicism to decide for some form of liturgical blessing for homosexual couples. Consider also the recent announcement of Cardinal Marx, the president of the German bishops' conference, of a "binding synodal process" (code word for local-option Catholicism) during which discussion of the Church's sexual ethic will take place.[40] According to Marx, the Church has yet to understand fully "the intimate personal significance of sexuality in modern day culture." "The Church needs synodal progress," he asserted. "Pope Francis encourages this." Furthermore, consider the recent pronouncement of Bishop Olivier Ribadeau-Dumas, the secretary general of the French Bishops' Conference, who affirmed that homosexual relationships are morally legitimate since they manifest the love of God.[41]

One wonders how, in view of that license for the option of local-Catholicism, Francis can maintain the unity of the Church, "not only *cum Petro*, but also *sub Petro*"—which is, according to Francis himself, "a guarantee of unity"? He explains: the Pope

> "who is called upon to pronounce as 'pastor and teacher of all Christians', not based on his personal convictions but as a supreme witness of '*totius fides Ecclesiae*' (the faith of the whole Church), of the guarantor of obedience and the conformity of the Church to the will of God, to the Gospel of Christ and to the Tradition of the Church.... In fact, the Pope, by the will of the Lord, is 'the perpetual and visible source and foundation of the unity both of the bishops as much as of the multitude of the faithful.' To this is connected the concept of '*ierarchia communio*' (hierarchical communio) used by Vatican II: the Bishops being united with the Bishop of Rome by the bond of episcopal communio (*cum Petro*) and at the same time hierarchically subjected to him as head of the college (*sub Petro*)."[42]

This is Catholic teaching but it is at odds not only with the license granted by Pope Francis in *Amoris Laetitia* §3, but also with the idea of a synodal Church—a listening, dialogical, and discerning Church and the corresponding idea of the *sensus fidei fidelium*—when that idea is regarded as a model for the Church's life in general.[43] Both synodality and *sensus fidei* have been misunderstood and misinterpreted by turning them into the true sources of authority in the Church. For one thing, the concept of synodality is "theologically nebulous, susceptible of manipulation, and in tension with the teaching of Vatican II on the role of bishops in the Church."[44] For another, Dominican theologian Thomas Petri rightly notes, "Some commenters seem to reduce the *sensus fidei* to the mere expression of any individual or group's 'personal experience.' This is an impoverishment of what the *sensus fidei* actually is and runs the risk, in my view, of exalting human experience to be a font of revelation co-equal with scripture and tradition." Similarly, theologian Jessica Murdoch says, "A wrong understanding of synodality flattens the divinely instituted hierarchical order into a majoritarian mass. The collective wisdom and perspective of the bishops, and of others in the Church, can certainly be an important tool, but it has definite limits," she added. In other words, "No measure of synodal discussion, debate or voting can replace the true sources of authority in the Church. Those sources, Murdoch said, are divine revelation and the unbroken magisterium handed down by the Church together with, and guarded by, the authority of the pope."[45]

Yet, this is precisely how some interpret Francis's claim, "The Synod of Bishops is the convergence point of this dynamic of listening [to the *sensus fidei fidelium*] conducted at all levels of church life. The synodal process starts by listening to the people, who 'even participate in the prophetic office of Christ' [LG §12], according to a principle dear to the Church of the first millennium: '*Quod omnes tangit ab omnibus tractari debet*' [what concerns all needs to be debated by all]." He adds, "It is a mutual listening in which everyone has something to learn. Faithful people, the College of Bishops, the Bishop of Rome: we are one in listening to others; and all are listening to the Holy Spirit, the 'Spirit of truth' (John 14:17), to know what the Spirit 'is saying to the Churches' (Rev 2:7)."[46] Several questions arise here.

Who are the *sensus fidelium*? Surely, Nichols is right, "[It] cannot include people who practice their faith irregularly, or people not sharing the already defined faith of the Church."[47] As Janet Smith asks regarding this last question, "Is being a *baptized* Catholic sufficient to qualify as one of the faithful? Does one need to be a *practicing* Catholic? Does one need to *believe* the central *dogmas* of the Faith? Are there any other qualifying criteria?"[48]

What exactly is the *sensus fidei*? And by virtue of what ecclesial warrants providing an objective anchor does one discern that they are listening to the Holy Spirit, the Spirit of truth, rather than just popular opinion, or the prejudices of the *Zeitgeist*? We read in Col 2:8: "Beware lest any man spoil you through philosophy and vain deceit, after the tradition of men, after the rudiments of the world, and not after Christ." The *sensus fidei fidelium* is not self-authenticating. It must be formed and exercised in relation to the objective revelation granted in Christ, that is, "the life, death and resurrection of Jesus Christ [that] is transmitted to the Church as a whole through the living apostolic Tradition, of which the Scriptures are the authoritative written witness. Hence, by the grace of the Holy Spirit, who reminds the Church of all that Jesus said and did [cf. John 14:26], believers rely on the Scriptures and on the continuing apostolic Tradition in their life of faith and in the exercise of the *sensus fidei*" (SF §68). Consequently, detached from or elevated above this revelation, it loses its criterion and corrective and opens the door to all sorts of arbitrariness, and heresy. In order to avoid opening that door we must insist on holding Word and Spirit fast together. I return to all these questions below.

Furthermore, can we discern what they are saying to us by questionnaires? Even if not entirely, Francis assumes so. "Certainly, a consultation like this [two-phase synod on the family] would never be able to hear the entire *sensus fidei* [*fidelium*] (sense of the faith [of the faithful]). But how would we ever be able to speak about the family without engaging families, listening to their joys and their hopes, their sorrows and their anguish? Through the answers to the two questionnaires sent to the particular Churches, we had the opportunity to at least hear some of the people on those issues that closely affect them and about which they have much to say."[49]

If one stops here to take this aspect of synodality—a listening and dialogical Church—as an end in itself rather than as an instrument in the service of the Church's life,[50] the risk is run of turning the Church's whole life into a series of discussions about the content of Christianity and of ways of realizing it. Intentionally or not, this is the way that some have understood Francis's push for a synodal Church. For this reason, I doubt whether synodality can be seen as "a constitutive dimension of the Church." It is difficult to see that "synodality gives us the more appropriate interpretive framework to understand the hierarchical ministry."[51] Doesn't that make the normative content of Christianity open-ended such that the constant discussion of Christian themes comes to be considered the content of Christianity itself? Is this the view that precipitated the unraveling in the coherence of Church life, worship and thinking, that is, in the words of Carl Braaten, "a free fall into doctrinal normlessness and liturgical adventurism?"[52] The Australian Archbishop, Dominican Anthony Fisher, who participated in the recent 2018 Synod of Bishops on Youth was asked in an interview whether he thought that there's a danger with these synods, particularly the notion of a synodal Church, that they can be vehicles for heterodoxy. He answered,

> Yes, a real danger. This is not the way to make doctrine. If you are preparing a Vatican document on a topic, you get a group of highly qualified theologians or experts in that area to do drafts and redrafts. You get others to critique it. You ultimately bring it to the bishops of the CDF. The pope may contribute at various stages along the way,

> and, finally, it is his approval that gives the document real authority. It all takes time—in my experience, usually several years — before a document is mature enough for publication as the faith of the Church. But in this synod, we were writing doctrine, as it were, on the run—with respect to synodality, in less than a week.[53]

In this connection, I think Ratzinger was correct when he said ten years after Vatican II that in this approach of synodality lies the failure to recognize the true meaning of Christianity: "The real content of Christianity is not the discussion of its Christian content and of ways of realizing it: the content of Christianity is the community of Word, sacrament and love of neighbor to which justice and truth bear a fundamental relationship. The dream of making one's whole life a series of discussions... also exercised an influence on the Church under the label of the conciliar idea."[54]

Thankfully, Francis moves beyond understanding the Church as merely a listening and dialogical Church to calling the Synod Fathers, the bishops, to "act as true stewards, interpreters and witnesses of the faith of the whole Church, [and] who must be able to carefully distinguish [the faith of the Church] from that which flows from frequently changing public opinion."[55] Thus, Pope Francis does not hold that the opinions of the faithful are self-authenticating and hence may be identified with the *sensus fidei*. Says Francis, "And, of course, we must be very careful not to think that this *infallibilitas* of all the faithful I am talking about in the light of Vatican II is a form of populism. No; it is the experience of 'holy mother the hierarchical church,' as St. Ignatius called it, the church as the people of God, pastors and people together. The church is the totality of God's people." As Aquinas correctly states, "For it is possible for a believer to have a false opinion through a human conjecture, but it is quite impossible for a false opinion to be the outcome of faith" (ST II-II, q. 1, a. 3, ad 3).

Yet, this claim stands at odds with the license for local-option Catholicism he grants at the start of *Amoris Laetitia* and elsewhere which has provided a warrant for the actions of some in the Church.

For example, Bishop Johan Bonny of Antwerp, Belgium, accepts the culturally dominant sexual morality of our time, in particular its affirmation of pre-marital sex and hence cohabitation, contraceptive sex, and same-sex relations. He and his co-author, Roger Burggraeve, accept this morality because not only is it the way things are socially, but also the Church's teaching no longer reflects what Christians experience as sin. They also attempt to provide a moral as well as theological justification of these practices, going so far as to make a plea for ecclesial rites of blessing for cohabiting and same-sex couples.[56] For another, Josef Cardinal De Kesel, Archbishop of Brussels-Malines, Belgium, urges the acceptance of the sexual life of homosexuals, yet rejects same-sex marriage—he is an ecclesial positivist—but accepts the possibility of a public prayer or thanksgiving in church for a same-sex relation, where honesty, constancy, and faithfulness are central."[57] Both these men stop short of supporting same-sex marriage because they claim that, according to Church law, marriage is the union of a man and a woman. Still, they are ecclesial positivists or conventionalist because they give as the only reason for rejecting same-sex marriage the fact that "Church law" says so. This positivism is similar to one thinking that human beings have rights because the state or society says so.

In fact, the Church holds that marriage is a two-in-one-flesh union between a man and woman because that judgment is true to an objective reality, according to the order of creation. The Catholic tradition is the supporter of Christian realism: marriage is grounded in the order of creation, of an independently existing reality, and therefore has an objective structure judged by the Church to be the case or the way things really are. Ecclesial positivism vs. Christian realism—this is one of the points of confusion.

For still another, the German archbishop, Cardinal Marx, refers to Pope Francis's "fundamental orientation" for the Church to take "the situation of the individual… their life-story, their biography… their relationships" more seriously and accompany them, as individuals."[58] This reflects the passage quoted above. In some cultural contexts, the pressing issues are not only of the divorced and civilly remarried, but also of homosexual couples, cohabitation; while Francis makes clear in *Amoris Laetitia* the overriding importance of inclusion. They must be met where they are, in order to "avoid judgments which do not take into account the complexity of various situations' (AL §296). It is about pastoral care of people in so-called "irregular situations," which are morally problematic, employing the troubling logic of pastoral reasoning that I discussed in Chapter 4. Although he is not promoting a general ecclesial solution and hence a general public blessing for same-sex relations, nevertheless, he says, "the decision [whether or not to bless a same-sex couple] should be made 'on the ground, and the individual under pastoral care.'"[59]

Another German, this time Johannes zu Eltz, the Catholic Dean of the city of Frankfurt am Main, is engaged in the pastoral care of homosexuals. He says, "the question is whether the church is able to learn that good things happen in those relationships; that homosexual couples who cannot celebrate the Sacrament of Matrimony (civil same sex marriage was established by law in Germany in 2017) by their companionship give birth to moral goods for themselves and for others: love, loyalty, commitment, fecundity, chastity. If this is true, then there is the possibility to confirm these goods and to ask for God's providence and guidance for this couple. That is what we call a blessing." Furthermore, he adds, if giving these same-sex couples a blessing is possible, then it must be a public act rather than just the private act of an open-minded pastor. He says, "Liturgy is a public office of the church. Therefore, it is no viable way if some priests respond individually to the request for a blessing by offering a private celebration. I noticed that homosexual Catholics are quite sensitive about that. They know the difference between a blessing by an open-minded pastor, who feels not restricted by rules of the canon law, and the blessing of the Church. This is the reason why we have to try hard to convince the bishop and to seek the consent of the whole diocese."[60]

We find similar reasoning made by Bishop Franz-Josef Bode of Osnabrück, the deputy chairman of the German Bishops' Conference. "We have to ask ourselves how we should deal with people who tie this knot. Some of them are active in the church. So how are we going to accompany them with pastoral care and in the liturgy?" Bode asked. "We could think about giving them a blessing." He, too, adds, "I'm not for 'marriage for all,' but if two homosexuals enter a same-sex relationship, if they want to take responsibility for each other, then I can bless this mutual responsibility," he said. "This is valuable and praiseworthy, even if this bond is not in complete agreement with the church."[61]

Both these men are ecclesial positivists and hence they are confused about the ontological status of marriage as an objective state of affairs. We are currently awash in ecclesial positivism in the culture of the Church. I think that Pope Francis has contributed to this confusion because the place of the moral law—both the moral law in revelation and the moral laws grounded in the order of creation that we can know by reason—in his teaching is subdued, in the background, and unclear.[62] However, there is another problem to deal with here.

They speak of "blessing" homosexual couples.[63] Since God is the source and end of all blessings, the question regarding the particularity of God's will and purpose in creating man as male and female arises here (Gen 1:27).[64] This creation receives the judgment of goodness by God, which is his blessing. The Church has always understood same-sex sex to be inconsistent with Scripture, tradition, and natural law reasoning that teaches marriage to be an intrinsically male-female union. Hence, this one-flesh union is not just posited by ecclesiastical law. Jesus was no positivist or conventionalist. Rather, he calls us back to the law of creation (Mark 10:6-7) that grounds an inextricable nexus of permanence, twoness, and sexual differentiation for marriage. John Paul II rightly notes, "Law must therefore be considered an expression of divine wisdom: by submitting to the law, freedom submits to the truth of creation" (VS §41). In particular, marriage is such that it requires sexual difference, the bodily-sexual act, as a foundational prerequisite, indeed, as *intrinsic* to a one-flesh union of man and woman. "So then they are no longer two but one flesh." (Mark 10:8) "Basing itself on Sacred Scripture, which presents homosexual acts as acts of grave depravity, tradition has always declared that 'homosexual acts are intrinsically disordered.' They are contrary to the natural law. They close the sexual act to the gift of life. They do not proceed from a genuine affective and sexual complementarity. Under no circumstances can they be approved." (CCC §2357). Given this constant teaching of the Church, how can a place of blessing, private or public, be found for a homosexual couple within the context of the Church? How can a homosexual couple find a pathway to receive Communion in that circumstance, as some—e.g. Blase Cardinal Cupich—suggest?[65] How can they not be living in mortal sin? Radner is right, "As we know, where these latter [same-sex couplings] are mentioned in Scripture and tradition, they are rejected precisely in the context of fruitfulness that upholds the scriptural claims about and character of blessing (e.g., Lev 18-19, Rom 1)."[66]

Helpfully, Radner probes more deeply. Suppose we grant the point that there are "goods" as such in these relationships—"love," "commitment," "fidelity," "mutuality." However, we must not treat them as *neutral* goods abstracted from the practice of particular sexual behavior, which the Church unequivocally rejects, and from the larger culture of homosexuality, as well as the worldview underpinning the interpretation of these goods. Once relocated in that interpretive context, these "goods" are not "conformable to the gospel in its integrity, let alone in its fullness," that is, "the fullness of God's truth in Christ Jesus."[67]

There are others, such as the American Bishop Robert McElroy[68] and the Jesuit James Martin[69] who implicitly presuppose that "same-sex" attraction, homosexual attraction, is good from the order of creation. That is, a homosexual *qua* homosexual is "wonderfully made" (Ps 139), as Martin suggests in asking a homosexual to reflect on himself in light of that psalm. In this connection, it follows that he holds it to be legitimate to ground human identity in homosexual orientation, which encompasses an individual's personal and social identity. How does Fr. Martin justify the legitimacy of this self-description—indeed, insisting on it? The only criterion that he suggests that legitimizes it is individual experience. Individual experience becomes a supreme court of appeal for adjudicating the gospel, the teachings of the Church. This leads him to the conclusion that a person's homosexuality is a creational given rather than being in itself inherently disordered, a sign of brokenness, an expression of man's fallen condition.

But this emphasis on experience ignores the distinction between the normative order of creation and the order of the fall, followed by the order of redemption. In the words of Dominican theologian Aidan Nichols, "It is not experience we should trust but the transmutation of experience by Scripture and Tradition."[70] In this connection, one would then take as normative the truth that God made man, our created nature, as male and female for each other (Gen 1:27), and that this nature is savagely wounded by sin, broken, but, thanks be to God, it is redeemed in Christ through his atoning work. Hence, homosexual practice is morally unacceptable, because not only are such sexual acts not open to life but also they cannot realize unity, because sexual differentiation is a fundamental prerequisite for the two-in-one-flesh union between a man and a woman. As Robert Reilly puts it, "only a unitive act can be generative, and only a generative act can be unitive—in that only it makes two 'one flesh.'"[71]

These men and others in the Catholic Church have capitulated to the sexual revolution. They have retreated from anything resembling clarity about sexual morality. Some of them do not explicitly challenge the Church's sexual morality, but appeal to pastoral practice to render it inapplicable—hence, the troubling consequences of *Amoris Laetitia*, particularly Chapter 8. Rusty Reno rightly notes, "These capitulations have obscured the Gospel and wounded the Church.... [They] confer legitimacy on the sexual revolution and undercut resistance."[72] Reno explains:

> Catholicism and other forms of establishment Christianity in the West tend to take the form of bourgeois religion. That term denotes the fusion of church culture with the moral consensus held by the good, respectable people who set the tone for society as a whole. In the aftermath of the sexual revolution, that consensus shifted. For a long time now it has been socially acceptable to divorce and contracept. Soon thereafter it was OK to cohabitate, and then the good and responsible people who run things adopted an affirmative attitude toward gay sex. During all this, the same consensus became hostile to those who say otherwise. It became "cruel," "hateful," and "bigoted" to call something wrong that the bourgeois consensus now deems right. In this way, the good and responsible people did not just accommodate themselves to the sexual revolution; they took ownership of it. Amid this change, most Catholic bishops and priests have been disoriented.... Given the inconvenience of the Catholic commitment to moral truth, the approach has been to remain silent. Insofar as bishops and cardinals have spoken about sex, it has almost always been to qualify and soften the Church's moral voice. The strategy was one of careful retreat. The enduring hope has been to find a way to moderate the obvious clash between what the Church teaches and the bourgeois consensus about sex.[73]

Does Pope Francis want to make this retreat more explicit? Does he want to sign a peace treaty with the sexual revolution, as Reno suggests? Whatever his intentions on this score, it is clear that the moral logic of pastoral reasoning in Chapter 8 of *Amoris Laetitia* has contributed to this retreat and hence lack of clarity regarding sexual morality.

How might we as Catholics who are of one mind with the Church's normative teaching respond to this moral crisis? The Final Document of the recent Synod of Bishops on the Youth states in §150: "There are questions concerning the body, affectivity and sexuality which require a deepened anthropological, theological and pastoral elaboration, to be carried out in the most appropriate ways and at the most appropriate levels, from the local to the universal."[74] We need a normative Christian anthropology and corresponding sexual ethics that integrates personalism and natural law ethics—such as we find in the work of Karol Wojtyla/John Paul II. His work is particularly important in light of the unfounded charge recently made by Cardinal Marx that "the significance of sexuality to personhood has not yet received sufficient attention from the Church."[75] Marx is not the only member of the hierarchy to make such an unfounded charge. In fact, both are criticizing a "straw man." I refer here to the Pastoral Letter of Bishop Johan Bonny (Antwerp, Belgium) who suggests that post-conciliar Catholic moral theology has been monolithic in approach, resistant to "the human intellect's multifaceted search for truth and goodness," and hence closed to the "complementarity of theological models."[76] He claims that the "personalist school [was] consigned to the corner as suspicious and to be avoided." I criticized Bonny in the first edition of this work. *Pace* Bonny, Karol Wojtyla/John Paul II sought to integrate personalism, existential/hermeneutic phenomenology, and Thomism, particularly natural law ethics, in his philosophical and theological work.[77] In short, as George Weigel correctly remarks, John Paul II offers the Church and the wider culture a "richly personalistic explanation of the Church's ethic of human love."[78]

The troubling sentences in Pope Francis's AL §3 and his concluding address to the Synod of Bishops, which I cited at the beginning of this section, suggesting what pastoral application means raises the specter of the option of local Catholicism and all that this option entails, namely, the breakdown of the Church's unity not only but especially regarding sexual morality, as I have tried to argue above. I will sketch Wojtyla's explanation in the next four sections.[79]

How Do We Love Responsibly?

In a 2006 interview, Pope Benedict XVI was asked by Vatican Radio why he never spoke of same-sex marriage, abortion, or contraception at the recent meeting in Valencia of the World Meeting of Families. Benedict's answer sets the tone and perspective for this section of the chapter. He said,

> Christianity, Catholicism, is not [firstly] a collection of prohibitions: it is a positive option.... We have heard so much about what is not allowed that now it is time to say: we have a positive idea to offer, that man and woman are made for each other [Gen 1:27; 2:24], that the scale of sexuality, eros, agape, indicates the level of love and it is in this way that marriage develops, first of all as a joyful and blessing-filled encounter between a man and a woman, and then, the family, which guarantees continuity among generations and through which generations are reconciled to each other and even cultures can meet. So, firstly it is important to stress what we want. Secondly, we can also see why we don't want something. I believe we need to see and reflect on the fact that it's not a Catholic invention that man and woman are made for each other [Gen 1:27; 2:24], so that humanity can go on living: all cultures know this [fact]."[80]

Of course, that does not mean that we should not be concerned about the prevalence of divorce, contraception, promiscuity, social acceptance of homosexuality, widespread use of pornography, cohabitation, etc. For example, although contraception is mentioned here as one in a list of several concerns, it is actually at the root of the crisis resulting from the sexual revolution. Contraception changed the sex act itself by separating sex and babies. In the contraceptive morality, the sexual act became a self-sterilizing act, and once the idea took hold in our culture that there is nothing intrinsically wrong with contraceptive sex, there was no longer any reason to deny homosexual sex that by its very nature is sterile.[81] This understanding of the root-significance of contraception is not just a Catholic view, or, for that matter, a Christian view.

Anthony Giddens, for one, identifies contraception as the creation of what he called "*plastic sexuality*." It "severed [the sexual act] from its age-old integration with reproduction, kinship and the generations, [and this] was the precondition of the sexual revolution of the past decades."[82] Sex became what Giddens calls a "pure relationship," that is, "a social relation... entered into for its own sake, for what can be derived by each person from a sustained association with another; and which is continued only in so far as it is thought by both parties to deliver enough satisfactions for each individual to stay within it."[83] As Elizabeth Anscombe noted, "If you can turn intercourse into something other than the reproductive *type* of act... then why, if you can change it, should it be restricted to the married?"[84] Or to heterosexuals? One of the consequences of this change is that it also transformed our attitude to children, in particular, children became extrinsically related to sex. Furthermore, transforming the sex act by separating it from procreation through contraception resulted in the contraceptive mentality that justified abortion; children were not intrinsically related to the sexual act, and hence they were disposable consequences if unwanted. Giddens writes: "Sexuality came into being as part of a progressive differentiation of sex from the exigencies of reproduction. With the further elaboration of reproductive technologies, that differentiation has today become complete." Children became a man-made product rather than a gift, a fruit of the conjugal act. "Now that conception can be artificially produced, rather than only artificially inhibited, sexuality is at last fully autonomous. Reproduction can occur in the absence of sexual activity; this is a final 'liberation' for sexuality, which thence can become wholly a quality of individuals and their transactions with one another."[85]

Moreover, Giddens also shows that this transformation led to considering gender/sex apart from the body's natural determinations, a sexually differentiated body, even to the extent of dissolving the meaning of the masculine/feminine difference, and hence resulting in the "moral insignificance of sexual difference."[86] As Giddens maintains: "the changes now affecting sexuality are indeed revolutionary, and in a very profound way."[87]

Finally, contraception also transformed the relationship between men and women. In particular, wrote Harvey Cox, "Sex becomes one of the items of leisure activity that the knowledgeable consumer of leisure handles with his characteristic skill and detachment. The girl becomes a desirable—indeed an indispensable—'Playboy accessory.'" On this view, "sex must be contained, at all costs, within the entertainment-recreation area.... [This view] is basically anti-sexual. [It] dilutes and dissipates authentic sexuality by reducing it to an accessory, by keeping it at a safe distance."[88] Last but not least, Paul VI wrote: "Another effect that gives cause for alarm [from the use of contraception] is that a man who grows accustomed to the use of contraceptive methods may forget the reverence due to a woman, and, disregarding her physical and emotional equilibrium, reduce her to being a mere instrument for the satisfaction of his own desires, no longer considering her as his partner whom he should surround with care and affection" (HV §17).

Consequently, human sexuality cannot be reduced to a mere source of pleasure, but is something of deeper importance because how we live our sexual lives has a deep impact on our relationship with God, on our capacity to love other persons, the stability of marriage and family life, which includes the good of children, and each person's internal harmony and well-being. In short, sex has a moral center that cannot be eradicated.[89]

We find the same tone and message in *Familiaris Consortio*, the 1981 Post-Synodal Apostolic Exhortation of St. John Paul II: "God created man in His own image and likeness: calling him to existence *through love*, He called him at the same time *for love*.... Love is therefore the fundamental and innate vocation of every human being." In particular, he says, "God inscribed in the humanity of man and woman the vocation, and thus the capacity and responsibility, *of love* and communion" (FC §11). One might say that being created in and for love, man in his freedom is unintelligible without love. For the Christian faith, love is the supreme value and goal (end) not only of the sexual relationship but of *all* personal relationships, whether sexual, in the whole of their bodily life, or otherwise. Indeed, morality itself is fulfilled when it becomes true love of God and of man.

In this light, we must consider the reality of the human person in the order of love. Why? Because the "person finds in love the greatest fullness of his being, of his objective existence. Love is such action, such an act, which most fully develops the existence of the person. Of course this has to be true love. What does true love mean?" (LR, 66). Since man—male and female—is created in and for love, accordingly, sexual ethics is, too, unintelligible without love. Hence, this crucial point about finding in love the greatest fullness of his being must also be applied to love between a man and a woman. "In this field also, true love perfects the being of the person and develops his existence. False love, on the other hand, causes quite contrary effects. False love is a love that either turns to an apparent good or—as usually happens—turns to some true good, but in a way that does not correspond to the nature of the good, in a way contrary to it. At times this happens to be the love between a man and a woman either in its assumptions or—even despite (apparently) good assumptions—in its particular manifestations, in its realizations. False love is, in fact, evil love" (LR, 66).

Sexual ethics,[90] then, appeals to the most elementary and undeniable moral truths and to the most fundamental values or goods to which the human person is ordered. For instance, the transcendent and objective value of the human person. Karol Wojtyla explains, "Such a good is the person, and the moral truth most clearly connected to the world of persons in particular is the 'commandment to love'—for love is the good proper to the world of persons. And therefore the most fundamental grasp of sexual morality is to grasp it on the basis of 'love and responsibility.'"[91] In other words, there exists responsibility in love, that is, responsibility for the person, for the person's true good.

> The human person, who is the most perfect being in the visible world, also, therefore, has the highest value. The value of the person is, in turn, the basis of the norm that should govern actions that have a person as their object. This norm may be called *personalistic* to distinguish it from other norms, which are based on the various natures of beings lower than the human being—nonpersonal natures.... All norms, including the personalistic norm, as based on the essences, or natures, or beings, are expressions of the order that governs the world. This order is intelligible to reason, to the person. Consequently, only the person is a *particeps legis aeternae et conscia legis naturae,* which means that the person is conscious of the normative force that flows from the essences, or natures, of all beings. In particular, the person is conscious of the normative force that flows from humanity, and this humanity in its individual form always appears as a person.[92]

Love separated from responsibility is a denial of itself, and, as a rule, is always egoism. "The more the sense of responsibility for the person, the more true love there is." (LR, 113). Wojtyla explains:

> For the choice of a person is a process in which the sexual value cannot play a role of the only motive or even—in the ultimate analysis of this act of the will—the primary motive. This would contradict the very notion of the "choice of a person." If the only, or least, the primary motive of this choice were the sexual value itself, then we would not be able to speak of choosing a person, but only of choosing the other sex connected with some "man" or even with some "body that is a possible object of use." It is clear that if we are to speak of choosing a person, the primary [although not the only] motive must be the very value of the person.... And only then, when each of them [choosing a woman by a man or a man by a woman] in this way, is the act of choice interiorly mature and complete. For only then is the proper integration of the object accomplished in it: the object of choice—the person—was grasped in his whole truth. (LR, 114-15)

Therefore, sexual ethics is concerned with an "introduction of love into [sexual] love" (LR, xviii). The love that is being introduced is an expression of the central commandment of love— "You should love the Lord, your God, with all your heart, with all your soul, and with all your mind. This is the greatest and the first commandment. The second is like it:

You shall love your neighbor as yourself. The whole law and the prophets depend on these two commandments" (Matt 22:36-40). The central commandment of love demands from us the responsibility that we love our neighbor. Indeed, the command is about responsible love for persons because the person is a good towards which the only proper and adequate response is love. "For if Jesus Christ commanded us to love those beings who are persons, then love is the proper form of relating to persons; it is the form of behavior for which we should strive when our behavior has a person as its object, since this form is demanded by that person's essence, or nature" (LR, 289).

In this light, we must consider the reality of the human person in the order of love. The commandment to love and the attendant object of this love is the person. In other words, "Love persons." This love is grounded in the personalist principle and this principle negatively formulated demands: "the person is a kind of good that is incompatible with using, which may not be treated as an object of use and, in this sense, as a means to an end." In short, "Love is a union of persons," and this means-end relation with the end being pleasure, reflects a subjectivism, indeed, adds Wojtyla, "an egoism that is most rapacious, using another person for one's own sake, for one's 'maximum pleasure'" (LR, 23). A positive formulation of this principle states that the person is a kind of good to which only love constitutes the proper response. "And this positive content of the personalistic norm is precisely what the commandment to love brings out" (Ibid.). Furthermore, since love is a union of persons, of male and female, Wojtyla explains, "love... is the distinct opposite of using the person in the role of a means to an end" (LR, 12). The personalistic norm is grounded in the value of the person rather than in the value of pleasure, and hence "the person cannot be subordinated to pleasure; he cannot serve as a means to the end which is pleasure" (Ibid.). Therefore, Wojtyla explains, "The affirmation of the value of the person as such is contained in the essence of love. [In other words,] the love of the person must consist in affirming his supra-material and supra-consumer (supra-utilitarian) value.... Therefore, we must seek the proper solutions for sexual morality within the scope of the personalistic norm if these solutions are to be Christian. They must be based on the commandment to love" (LR, 26-28).

Why? Because the "person finds in love the greatest fullness of his being, of his objective existence. Love is such action, such an act, which most fully develops the existence of the person. Of course this has to be true love. What does true love mean?" (LR, 66). Since man—male and female—is created in and for love, accordingly, sexual ethics is, too, unintelligible without love. Hence, this crucial point about finding in love the greatest fullness of his being must also be applied to love between a man and a woman. "In this field also, true love perfects the being of the person and develops his existence. False love, on the other hand, causes quite contrary effects. False love is a love that either turns to an apparent good or—as usually happens—turns to some true good, but in a way that does not correspond to the nature of the good, in a way contrary to it. At times this happens to be the love between a man and a woman either in its assumptions or—even despite (apparently) good assumptions—in its particular manifestations, in its realizations. False love is, in fact, evil love" (LR, 66).

In the second case, love refers to sexual love, and hence to sexual ethics. In this connection, "What is this thing called [sexual] love?" The crucial question that needs to be answered is what *specifies* sexual love as such; what makes it different from parental or filial or fraternal or friendly love? Put differently, the question is: "What is the intrinsic purpose of sexuality?" Or, to put the question more theologically, "Why did God create human beings sexual?" For now, we can say briefly, according to Benedict Ashley, that "what specifies sexual love is that humanity was created male and female with a drive to sexual union precisely in view of the *family* community through which only the expansion, continuity, and education of the human species can be attained." Indeed, adds Ashley, "The Bible does see the survival of the species as the *fundamental* purpose without which the very existence of the sexual differentiation of humanity into male and female would be unintelligible."[93] There are four presuppositions that are foundational to this sexual ethics.[94]

Four Foundational Presuppositions to Sexual Ethics

In Wojtyla's Introduction to the Second Polish Edition (1965) of *Love and Responsibility*, he identifies the primary authoritative sources that provide "an impetus for philosophical reflections concerning sexual problems." "That superior source is the Gospel together with its extension, the teaching of the Church. This source fostered reflections, whereas experience provides facts for confrontation with doctrine. The Gospel contains relatively few texts that speak directly about sexual and conjugal ethics, for example Matthew 5:27-28, Matthew 19:1-13, Mark 10:1-12, Luke 20:27-35, John 8:1-11, 1 Corinthians 7 (the entire chapter), and Ephesians 5:22-33, not to mention extremely significant texts in the Old Testament, especially in Genesis [1:27, 2:24]." Then Wojtyla states the crucial hermeneutical principle of canonical criticism, attending to the unity and content of all of Scripture (see Dei Verbum §12). "All the above mentioned passages organically inhere in the whole of the Gospel and must be in this whole as in their essential context. Read in this way, they give an incentive for philosophical reflection"(LR, xxvii). This incentive gives rise to four foundational presuppositions to sexual ethics, according to Wojtyla.

First, there is a distinctive sexual ethics rather than just a general ethics governing inter-personal relationships. If there is only a general ethics, sometimes called the "responsible-relational" (H. Richard Niebuhr)[95] position, moral norms that prohibit lying, deception, and exploitation are sufficient to render sexual acts morally good. This is how Margaret Farley describes the norms for what she calls sexual justice: refusal to do unjust harm, free consent, mutuality, equality, commitment, fruitfulness, and social justice.[96]

Whatever its undeniable merits—surely all interpersonal relationships should be free of deception, noncoercive, and nonexploitative—this ethics leaves us without a specific *sexual* ethics. The question here that needs attention is: what is the proper end of our sexual powers and their relationship to the nature of marriage? Aren't there "special moral responsibilities that flow from concern for the human goods [the interpersonal unity that is marital communion and its natural fulfillment in procreation] toward which sexuality itself is ordered [?]."[97] In other words, there can only be special moral responsibilities if sexual acts are uniquely distinct from other bodily acts because they are ordered to real human goods—the natural meanings and ends of man's sexual powers: union and procreation—that are intrinsic aspects of the well-being and fulfillment of human persons.

Patrick Lee rightly states, "It seems that there is something special about sex, and it seems that we can be aware of this point whether we accept revelation or not. For example, it seems clear to most people that a punch in the nose is far less serious than rape, although both involve violence. And it seems that this can be true only if sexual acts have some feature or features making them significantly different from other bodily acts."[98] What then is it about sexual acts that make them different from other bodily acts? And if they are uniquely distinct, because they are ordered by their very nature to marital communion and procreation, marital love and children, in short, to the unitive and procreative ends of sexuality, doesn't that mean that there is a distinctive sexual ethics?

Second, one of the central reasons why a distinctive sexual ethics is denied by many is that there is no room, on their view, for a moral law, grounded in the one human nature, willed by God, and known as the natural law (CV §59). The reason for the rejection of a moral law derives from the view that the meaning of the body is no longer rooted in the very nature of man as an embodied person, male or female; this nature possessing a creational teleology ordering the body-soul person to the sexual "other" and hence to procreation and union.[99] Put differently, this view seems to be denying that there are meanings and ends embedded in the human sexual design that is grounded in the order of creation (GS §48). In other words, since sex is merely a biological category ("interesting external equipment") and gender is a socially and culturally constructed category, this view entails the rejection of the historic Church teaching, indeed of Vatican II, that "the principles of the moral order... spring from human nature itself" (DH §14).

In contrast to this view, Benedict XVI argues that there is an ecology of man, language and order of nature. Benedict says, "Man too has a nature that he must respect and that he cannot manipulate at will. Man is not merely self-creating freedom. Man does not create himself. He is intellect and will, but he is also nature, and his will is rightly ordered if he respects his nature, listens to it and accepts himself for who he is, as one who did not create himself. In this way, and in no other, is true human freedom fulfilled."[100] In short, this fundamental anthropology rejects the dualism between person and nature, as well as freedom and nature. Unsurprisingly, this too is the view of John Paul II, "And since the human person cannot be reduced to a freedom which is self-designing, but entails a particular spiritual and bodily structure, the primordial moral requirement of loving and respecting the person as an end [in the medium of its unity as body and soul] and never as a mere means also implies, by its very nature, respect for certain fundamental goods [toward which sexuality itself is ordered], without which one would fall into relativism and arbitrariness" (VS §48). In sum, one might conclude that in addition to the denial of a distinctive sexual ethics, the problem with contemporary thinking about human sexuality is that "it flouts the embedded principles and the inbuilt meanings of the human sexual design," or as *Gaudium et spes* §51 puts it: "objective criteria... drawn from the nature of the human person and human action."

Third, a key to understanding Catholic sexual ethics is the truth that the human person is bodily.[101] This view rejects a dualistic view of the human person—"dualistic in the sense of viewing the self as something which *has* or *inhabits* a body, rather than being a living, bodily entity."[102] But if the "human person is essentially a bodily being, a unity of body and soul, and that therefore the masculinity or femininity of the human being is internal to his or her personhood (rather than just interesting external 'equipment')," as John Paul II has argued, then it seems likely that this view does not do justice to the embodiment of human persons as man and woman and hence to sexual differences between them. By assuming the insignificance of sexual difference for making a sexual act morally right, this view fails to grasp the unified totality that is the body-person and hence the human meaning of the body, especially but not only for sexual acts (VS §50). A Christian sexual ethics must properly express the intrinsic place of the body in interpersonal unity rather than holding the body to remain extrinsic to personhood.

Fourth, a rehabilitation of the "culture of the person" is necessary because the objective good of the person constitutes the essential core of all human culture. To promote that culture requires a whole nexus of fundamental goods that together determine marriage and family life. Marriage is grounded in God's purpose for creation. It is the two-in-one-flesh union of a man and a woman, with conjugal love being the integrating principle of the whole communion of marriage and family life. *Gaudium et spes* §50 stated it this way: "Marriage and conjugal love are by their nature ordained toward the begetting and educating of children. Children are really the supreme gift of marriage." I shall return to the question of what is the proper end of our sexual powers and their relationship to the nature of marriage when I consider the issue of why giving oneself in sexual intercourse to the other is fully justified only in marriage. "Marriage corresponds to the truth of love and mutually safeguards the dignity of person, only if both a man and a woman perform it [sexual intercourse] as spouses, as husband and wife" (LR, 293).

Returning to the Love-Ethic

Returning now to this love-ethic, there is more to say about its nature. For one, it is not opposed to universally valid moral precepts. Consider the Bible. Well, yes, concrete commands, such as, "Anyone who curses his father or mother must be put to death" (Exod 21:17), are culturally conditioned. However, this concrete command is an *application* of a primary commandment that is absolute and universal: "Honor your father and your mother" (Exod 20:12).[103] Helpful here in distinguishing between commandments that are still valid from those that are not, is Lewis Smedes' distinction between "primary commandments" and "concrete commandments." The former cover specific areas of life, such as human existence, property, communication, marriage, family. The latter demand or prohibit a specific act. Christians appeal to God's prohibition against same-sex relations in Lev 18:22 ("You shall not have intercourse with a man as you would with a woman. It is an abomination."), but ignore the punishment of death for same-sex relations in Lev 20:13. Lev 18:22 overlaps with the order of creation. There is scriptural warrant in the sixth commandment, which is a primary commandment, for rejecting adultery as wrong (Exod 20:14), but the concrete commandment that the punishment for committing adultery is death (see Lev 20:10) is no longer valid. The fourth commandment tells us that we should honor our parents (Exod 20:12), but Exod 21:17 says that we should execute a son who swears at his father. Christians readily cite scriptural warrant for parental authority but none accept execution as a punishment for disrespecting parents.

Furthermore, at the root of each and every command is the "foundational commandment" that covers all of life, namely, the central commandment of Love: We are called to love God completely and to love our neighbor as we love ourselves.[104] All the biblical commands are not culturally conditioned such that there are no universally valid and permanent moral precepts. For example, the biblical commandments against incest, bestiality (Exod 22:19), adultery (Exod 20:14), child sacrifice, prostitution (Lev 19:29; Deut 23:17-18), and rape (Deut 22:25-29), are absolute and universally valid. It is never morally acceptable to oppress the poor, commit idolatry (Exod 20:4; Deut 13:6-11),[105] or bribery (Exod 23:8; 2 Chron 19:7). Bearing false witness against one's neighbor (Exod 23:1-2) is also always wrong.[106]

In short, ethics has a normative character; it has a *deontological* basis,[107] involving, then, a morality of duty, making judgments about duty in respect of the question: what ought I to do? What is good and what is evil in human acts and why? This love-ethic is also *axiological*[108] because duty possesses "deontic dynamism,"[109] that is, duty "always arises in strict connection with the deeper, ontic reality of the person: 'to be good or evil.' Man is 'good or evil' through his acts—he is, or rather 'becomes' such because the act itself not so much 'is' as each time 'becomes.' Duty—not as an abstraction but as a reality—always enters into just that dynamic structure.... Moral duty is dynamically connected with moral good and evil—and that this connection is both strict and exclusive. *Duty* arises 'because of' good or evil; it is always a *specific actualization of the spiritual potentiality of a person in action*; that actualization comes out 'for good' and 'against' evil."[110] Furthermore, this love-ethics is also *praxiological* because "*a man, as a man, becomes good or evil through the act*." This is, therefore, a reality that is thoroughly anthropological and personalistic. In sum, "the metaphysical aspect is present in the entire experience of morality, which is an experience of being and becoming good or evil through one or another act.... [T]he subject itself, the 'I'—the person, becomes morally good or evil. The person becomes morally good or evil through an act which is morally good or evil. Both '*becoming*' and '*being*' are *metaphysical categories* which define and express being—in this case, man as being: a one which is, which becomes, and which becomes in and through action."[111] Therefore, "Only on an ontological (anthropological) ground thus understood can the interpretation of morality as a reality given in experience also have an *axiological* character. For it is about good or evil—and those are [objective] values."[112]

Moreover, "moral values are an actual reality: in the act, in the activity of a person, in which a man becomes good or evil. The ontological aspect of axiology is more fundamental than the gnosiological [epistemic] aspect. The interpretation of morality must uncover afresh both of those aspects and in proper proportion. The experience of morality shows that the cognition of the moral values 'good' or 'evil,' in one sense, *precedes* the realization of them in action. In another sense, the cognition *follows* that realization."[113] In short, the values of good and evil are transcendent realities, and, therefore, morality then contains a peculiar union of axiology, deontology, praxeology, and ontology of man.

For now, let me emphasize that the commandment to love rests on not only a personalistic axiology but also the personalistic principle and norm. On the one hand, the love of the person must consist in affirming his supra-utilitarian value; on the other hand, the personalistic norm enjoins us to relate to beings that are persons by responsibly loving them. Says Karol Wojtyla, "As a principle formulated negatively, this norm states that the person is a kind of good that is incompatible with using, which may not be treated as an object of use and, in this sense, as a means to an end. Hand in hand with this goes the positive formulation of the personalistic norm: the person is a kind of good to which only love constitutes the proper and fully-mature relation. And this positive content of the personalistic norm is precisely what the commandment to love brings out" (LR, 25). Accordingly, we must seek the proper understanding of sexual ethics within the scope of the personalistic norm, if this ethics is to be Christian. The fundamental anthropology of the human person presupposed by a Christian sexual ethics is necessary when addressing the question of why the normative context for sexual relations is marriage, and anything outside that moral context falls short of the personalistic norm.[114]

What is the Christian anthropology informing the personalistic norm? What is that norm? Says Karol Wojtyla, "As a principle formulated negatively, this norm states that the person is a kind of good that is incompatible with using, which may not be treated as an object of use and, in this sense, as a means to an end. Hand in hand with this goes the positive formulation of the personalistic norm: the person is a kind of good to which only love constitutes the proper and fully-mature relation. And this positive content of the personalistic norm is precisely what the commandment to love brings out" (LR, 25). In short, adds Wojtyla, the personalistic norm is "the *principle of loving the person*, i.e., treating the person in a way corresponding to the being he is" (LR, 195). Accordingly, we must seek the proper answer to the question as to why marriage is the appropriate framework for the union of a man and a woman in which full sexual intercourse is realized within the scope of the personalistic norm.

As to the Christian anthropology, the objective world to which human beings belong consists of persons, a woman and a man, and things. Although animals are not merely things, for the latter are deprived of reason, but also of life, being inanimate objects, we cannot speak convincingly of an "animal person." Says Karol Wojtyla, "Instead, one speaks about animal individuals, regarding them simply as specimens of a given animal species. And such a description suffices. Yet, it is not sufficient to speak of man as an individual—a rational moral agent, a person of intrinsic moral worth—of the species *Homo sapiens*." Furthermore, Wojtyla adds, "the word 'person' has been coined in order to stress that man cannot be reduced wholly to what is contained in the concept of a 'specimen of the species', but has in himself something more, some particular fullness and perfection of being." He explains:

> The most proximate and the more proper reason for this is the fact that man possesses reason, that he is a rational being, which by no means can be stated about any other being of the visible world, for in none of them do we encounter any trace of conceptual thinking.... The fact that the person is an individual of a rational nature—that is, an individual to whose nature reason belongs—makes the person at the same time the only subject of its kind among the whole world of beings.... [T]he person as a subject differs from even the most perfect animals by his *interiority* and a specific life, which is concentrated in it, i.e., an interior life.... Man has a fundamentally different nature from animals. His nature includes the power of self-determination based on reflection and manifested in the fact that while acting, man chooses what he wants to do. This power is called free will. Thanks to the fact that man—a person—possesses free will, he is a person. A second characteristic property of the person remains closely linked to this distinctive feature of his. The Latin of philosophers grasped this property in the statement that the person is *alteri incommunicabilis*—nontransferable, incommunicable.... This nontransferability or incommunicability of the person is most closely linked with his

> interiority, with self-determination, with free will. No one else can will in my stead—and precisely in this I am *incommunicabilis*. I am and should be self-reliant in my actions. (LR, 4, 6)

In this light, I turn now to marriage, which is an inter-personal and a social matter, monogamous and indissoluble, requiring sexual differentiation, because it is only this institution based on the presuppositions of the personalistic norm that "is able to ensure the truly personal character of the union between two persons. The social constitution of the family is good when it enables and supports precisely this character of marriage" (LR, 202). We need a brief biblical perspective of marriage before going on to argue the claim that it is only in marriage that a man and a woman are justified to engage in sexual intercourse.[115]

In Matt 19:3-8, the words of Jesus Christ refer back to the Genesis texts of 1:27 and 2:24. "They are seminal texts, ones that the biblical and post-biblical traditions take very seriously. They are, Christians should believe, true, and true in a deep way."[116] "Back-to-creation" is the *leitmotif* in Jesus' teaching. In his own teaching regarding marital monogamy, indissolubility, and sexual differentiation (Mark 10:6-9; Matt 19:4-6), creation texts in Genesis 1-2 have foundational importance, in particular Gen 1:27 and 2:24: "Male and female he created them" and "for this reason... a man will be joined to his wife and the two will become one flesh." These texts are absolutely normative for conjugal ethics, indeed, for sexual ethics. Jesus unites into an inextricable nexus the concepts of permanence, twoness, and sexual complementarity. Yes, Gen 2:24 is about the permanence of marriage; it is also about the exclusivity of the relationship: "twoness"; but it also about the fundamental prerequisite of complementary sexual differentiation for effecting the "two-in-one-flesh" union of man and woman. "So then they are no longer two but one flesh" (Mark 10:8). Indeed, as Alexander Pruss rightly notes, "the text [Gen 2:24] is a seminal scriptural text on the nature of human sexuality."[117] For Jesus bi-unitary sexuality is the foundation upon which bi-unitary marriage—a two-in-one-flesh union of a man and a woman—in particular and sexual ethics in general is based.

Marriage is an objective structure of creation in which the male-female prerequisite—a bodily-sexual, emotional, intellectual, and spiritual union—of the "twoness" of the sexes, ordained by God "in the beginning," is necessary for the reality of becoming "one flesh" in marriage, a conjugal union that is naturally fulfilled in procreation and rearing children. In an abundantly clear manner, Dutch Calvinist philosopher Herman Dooyeweerd, for one, holds that "marriage is... intrinsically qualified as a moral community of love for the duration of the common life-span of two persons of different sex." The moral aspect of this love relationship (its qualifying or leading function), shows an individuality type that "refers back to... the organic life-aspect of the conjugal relation, namely, the lasting sexual biotic bond between husband and wife." Dooyeweerd adds, "According to its two radical functions (the moral and biotic functions) the marriage community can be described as a community of moral life-long love between husband and wife based on a relatively durable organic sexual bond."[118] Strictly speaking, "The moral individuality-type of the conjugal love-community is typically founded in the sexual-biotic function of marriage."[119] According to Dooyeweerd's social ontology, complementary sexual differentiation is a necessary condition for marriage in order to effect the "one flesh" union of marriage. Thus, marriage is a moral community founded in a one-flesh union of sexually complementary persons that is ordered to mutual love and procreation with its irreducible identity being inherently and exclusively heterosexual. In short, marriage is the only kind of union whose essential feature is founded in organic bodily-sexual unity so that it can only exist between opposite-sex individuals.

Along with many contemporary Catholic thinkers, such as the late Germain Grisez, John Finnis, Robert George, Patrick Lee, John Paul II,[120] et al., Dooyeweerd argues that the internal structural principle of the marital love-communion, the ethical aspect of this love-community being its qualifying function, may not be detached from, in Dooyeweerd's words, "its biotic foundation in the organic difference between the sexes."[121] In other words, Dooyeweerd upholds the conjugal view of marriage in which two people who unite in marriage, must, in addition to other things, unite organically, meaning thereby in the bodily-sexual dimension of their being—marriage's founding function (in Dooyeweerd's terms).[122]

What justifies, then, the sexual intercourse between a man and a woman? Its justification occurs not only with respect to society because of the ordinary consequence of sexual intercourse, namely, babies, but also with respect to the persons involved. Let me be clear that the claim that marriage is the normative setting for sexual intercourse proceeds not only from the legal-social order or a religious order that is "external" to the person and his love. Rather, "marriage proceeds from the very 'interiority' of this love, for the shape of the reciprocal self-giving of a man and a woman."

Wojtyla elaborates, "If we consider this concrete issue [of justifying sexual intercourse] in its whole truth, which means in complete objective reality as well, then we must acknowledge that sexual intercourse can be honest and honorable only as a conjugal act. Outside of marriage, and thus also before marriage, sexual intercourse is always an abuse of the 'law of the gift', it is... treating the person as a means of use." In conclusion,

> When they give themselves to each other in sexual intercourse, such self-giving is fully justified; it corresponds to the truth of love and mutually safeguards the dignity of the person, only if both a man and a woman perform it as spouses, as husband and wife. Otherwise, an abuse of the "law of the gift" takes place. Marriage is not only a social and religious discernment of the whole rectitude of being and action of persons, of men and women, but, above all, it is *a discernment of this rectitude in persons*, in a woman and

> a man, in the essential meaning of the action of sexual intercourse for both of them. (LR, 292-93)

As Wojtyla explains,

> The significance of the institution of marriage lies in this, that it justified the fact of sexual intercourse between a given couple, Y and X, within the whole of social life. This is important not only with regard to the consequences of this fact... but also with regard to the persons themselves taking part in it. This is also important with regard to the moral qualification of their love, as their love demands some orienting toward other people, toward a more proximate society and a society at large.... The facts of sexual intercourse between a man and a woman demand the institution of marriage as their natural setting, for the institution legitimates these facts above all in the consciousness of the very persons partaking in sexual intercourse.... Marriage as an institution is indispensable to justify the fact of conjugal relations between a man and a woman, first of all regarding themselves, but also regarding society. (LR, 203, 206)

Finally, then, I end this section on Christian anthropology and sexual ethics with the teaching of John Paul II. It is the best response the Church has to the sexual revolution. This teaching should have been at the center of the discussion in the recent Synod on Youth when the question regarding sexual morality was raised. Rather than just listening to the young people, the Church should have been teaching. This is what it should have taught.

> The only "place" in which this self-giving in its whole truth is made possible is marriage, the covenant of conjugal love freely and consciously chosen, whereby man and woman accept the intimate community of life and love willed by God Himself which only in this light manifests its true meaning. The institution of marriage is not an undue interference by society or authority, nor the extrinsic imposition of a form. Rather it is an interior requirement of the covenant of conjugal love which is publicly affirmed as unique and exclusive, in order to live in complete fidelity to the plan of God, the Creator. A person's freedom, far from being restricted by this fidelity, is secured against every form of subjectivism or relativism and is made a sharer in creative Wisdom. (FC §11)

One reason why this teaching is not considered at the recent Synod is that the ecclesial crisis of the Church is reflected in the dualism between the listening or learning Church and the Church as teacher. In one final section, I briefly discuss this dualism and urge the Church to return to the mutual influence and co-existence of the Church, Mother and Teacher. (CCC §2030-40, 2044-47).

The Learning Church and the Teaching Church

A central feature of Pope Francis's ecclesiological vision is his call for a "listening Church," which is a variation of the "learning Church," *Ecclesia discens*. This aspect of the Church is distinguished from the *Ecclesia docens*, the "teaching Church."[123] In order to learn, the Church has to listen in its totality as the People of God, laity and hierarchy together, to the authoritative sources of Christian revelation—Scripture and Tradition—so that Catholicism might move forward faithfully into the future, itself renewed so that it could convert the world as it is today. The notion of the *sensus fidei* is especially important in overcoming the separation between the learning Church and the teaching Church. The International Theological Commission explains the importance of the *sensus fidei*.

> The importance of the *sensus fidei* in the life of the Church was strongly emphasized by the Second Vatican Council. Banishing the caricature of an active hierarchy and a passive laity, and in particular the notion of a strict separation between the teaching Church (*Ecclesia docens*) and the learning Church (*Ecclesia discens*), the council taught that all the baptized participate in their own proper way in the three offices of Christ as prophet, priest and king. In particular, it taught that Christ fulfills his prophetic office not only by means of the hierarchy but also via the laity. (SF §4)

Vatican II taught that every Christian is called to be a witness to the faith and to that extent a teacher. For the prophetic office of Christ is fulfilled "not only through the hierarchy who teach in his name and by his power, but also through the laity whom he constitutes his witnesses and equips with a sense of the faith (*sensus fidei*) and a grace of speech precisely so that the power of the gospel may shine forth in the daily life of family and society" (LG §35). Still, from the truth that every Christian is called to be a witness to the faith and to that extent a teacher some have concluded that certain *parity* exists in regard to the teaching function of both the *sensus fidelium* and the magisterium. But no such parity is posited by *Lumen Gentium*, the Dogmatic Constitution on the Church of Vatican II. A more adequate view of that constitution is given by Yves Congar.

> When... all infallibility in the Church is expressly referred to the working of the Holy Spirit, which Jesus promised should enable his Church to live in the truth, then the prospect widens out. In that case, each [hierarchy and faithful] is acted on in view of an infallibility (finally one) according to his place in the body, receiving the infallibility that belongs to him in function of the infallibility of the

> total organism, rather as each of man's various powers receives its part and pertinent energy from the soul. The episcopal body, heir to the apostolic body, has the help of the Holy Spirit lest it err in discharging its teaching office; it forms a college in whose midst, like Peter amidst the other apostles, the Bishop of Rome, Peter's heir and successor, has the help of carrying out his part as the final criterion of unity and orthodoxy; the faithful people has the help of the Holy Spirit to be faithful people, that is, to cleave to God with a living faith in him, *but a faith whose objective determinations are, in accordance with the divine economy, brought to the people by the teaching of its hierarchs.*[124]

I return below to the question of the relationship between the *sensus fidei* and the magisterium. For now, let me say, as I noted earlier in this chapter, that Pope Francis has argued, "A synodal church is a listening church."[125] It is also a dialogical Church. Corresponding to this idea of listening and dialogue is the idea of the *sensus fidei fidelium*, the active capacity of the faith of the Christian believer to engage in spiritual discernment.

> Fr. Hugo Rahner used to say that Jesuits have to be able to discern both in the field of God and in that of the devil. I think discernment gives us this ability, this sense of the supernatural: the sense of the divine and of the diabolic in the moments of human life and in history. We need to ask to know both the intentions of the Lord and those of the enemy of human nature and his deceptions.[126]

Francis sees spiritual discernment as an effective remedy for engaging in spiritual warfare. What is discernment's grounding in the New Testament? For example, "And this I pray, that your love [in Christ] may abound still more and more in knowledge and all *discernment*, that you may approve the things that are excellent." (Phil 1:10-11). Among the gifts of the Holy Spirit, one is given the gift of "prophecy, to another *discernment* of spirits" (1 Cor 12:10); "But solid food belongs to those who are of full age [spiritually mature], that is, those who by reason of use have their senses exercised to *discern* both good and evil" (Heb 5:14); "Do not judge according to appearance, but judge with righteous *judgment*" (John 7:24); "By all means use your *judgment*, and hold on to whatever is good. Steer clear of evil in any form." (1 Thess 5:21-22). Lastly, in the Old Testament, we read, "the *discerning* heart seeks knowledge." (Prov 15:14). Clearly, the drift of these passages suggests that the biblical sense of discernment or judgment means exercising a proper discrimination in light of the revelation contained in the Holy Scriptures and in the living apostolic Tradition to understand where we are in the flow of the culture, with all its challenges and opportunities.

This capacity for spiritual discernment is an expression of the *sensus fidei fidelium*. Francis says,

> "The people [of God] itself constitute a subject. And the

> church is the people of God on the journey through history, with joys and sorrows. Thinking with the church, therefore, is my way of being a part of this people. And all the faithful, considered as a whole, are infallible in matters of belief, and the people display this *infallibilitas in credendo*, this infallibility in believing, through a supernatural sense of the faith [*sensus fidei*] of all the people walking together [cf. Lumen Gentium §12]. This is what I understand today as the 'thinking with the church' [*sentire cum ecclesiae*] of which St. Ignatius speaks. When the dialogue among the people and the bishops and the pope goes down this road and is genuine, then it is assisted by the Holy Spirit. So this thinking with the church does not concern theologians only."[127]

Several questions arise here about the nature of the *sensus fidei*, under what conditions is it authentically exercised in discerning the truth of faith, and the ecclesial warrants appealed to for that discernment. But it would be best to cite the text of *Lumen Gentium* to which Francis is referring here.

> The holy people of God shares also in Christ's prophetic office; it spreads abroad a living witness to Him, especially by means of a life of faith and charity and by offering to God a sacrifice of praise, the tribute of lips which give praise to His name [cf. Heb 13:15]. *The entire body of the faithful*, anointed as they are by the Holy One [cf. John 2:20, 27], cannot err in matters of belief. They manifest this special property by means of the whole peoples' supernatural discernment [*sensus fidei*] in matters of faith when "from the Bishops down to the last of the lay faithful" (LG §8) they show universal agreement [*universalem suum consensum*] in matters of faith and morals. That discernment in matters of faith [*sensus fidei*] is aroused and sustained by the Spirit of truth. It is exercised under the guidance of the sacred teaching authority, in faithful and respectful obedience to which the people of God accepts that which is not just the word of men but truly the Word of God [cf. 1 Thess 2:13]. Through it, the people of God adheres unwaveringly to the faith given once and for all to the saints [cf. Jude 3], penetrates it more deeply with right thinking, and applies it more fully in its life. (LG §12)

For one thing, what is the *sensus fidei*? In what sense, if any, is the *sensus fidei* an authentic theological source? Why does it have any authority in establishing Church teaching? What are the limits of its authority? Regarding the first question, I said earlier following ITC that the *sensus fidei* is a "set of dispositions, influence by ecclesial, spiritual, and ethical factors" (SF §88). Consider now the succinct definition of the concept of *sensus fidei* given in a joint statement of the Anglican-Roman Catholic International Theological Commission: "In every Christian who is seeking to be faithful to Christ and is fully incorporated into the life of the Church, there is a *sensus fidei*. This *sensus fidei* may be described as an active capacity for spiritual discernment, an intuition that is formed by worshipping and living in communion as a faithful member of the Church."[128] This active capacity of the faithful for spiritual discernment, as Geiselmann puts it, "a special Christian tact or flair, a deep and sure feeling which guides and directs into all truth, a deep inner sense,"[129] is generally more acute in proportion to a Christian's personal faith and holiness. Therefore, a fundamental disposition for authentic participation in the *sensus fidei fidelium* is "active participation in the life of the Church." The *sensus fidei fidelium* is "a vital aspect of theological epistemology in Catholicism"[130] ITC states,

> Participation in the life of the Church means constant prayer [cf. 1Thess 5:17], active participation in the liturgy, especially the Eucharist, regular reception of the sacrament of reconciliation, discernment and exercise of gifts and charisms received from the Holy Spirit, and active engagement in the Church's mission and in her *diakonia*. It presumes an acceptance of the Church's teaching on matters of faith and morals, a willingness to follow the commands of God, and courage both to correct one's brothers and sisters, and also to accept correction oneself. (SF §89)

This passage, in part, conveys the meaning of *sentire cum ecclesia*, that is, "to feel, sense and perceive in harmony with the Church. This is required not just of theologians, but of all the faithful; it unites all the members of the people of God as they make their pilgrim journey. It is the key to their 'walking together'" (SF §90). There is another disposition needed for authentic participation in the sensus fidei fidelium, namely, listening to the Word of God.

> Authentic participation in the *sensus fidei* relies necessarily on a profound and attentive listening to the word of God. Because the Bible is the original testimony of the word of God, which is handed down from generation to generation in the community of faith [cf. LG §12; DV §8], coherence to Scripture and Tradition is the main indicator of such listening. The *sensus fidei* is the appreciation of the faith by which the people of God "receives not the mere word of men, but truly the word of God" [LG §12, with reference to 1 Thess 2:13].

The first and second dispositions for authentic participation in the *sensus fidei fidelium* can be considered *principia cognoscendi externum*. There is another *principium*: "acceptance of the proper role of reason in relation to faith." In other words, "Faith and reason belong together [cf. Fides et Ratio]. Jesus taught that God is to be loved not only 'with all your heart, and with all your soul,... and with all your strength', but also 'with all your mind [*nous*]' (Mark 12:30). Because there is only one God, there is only one truth, recognized from different [and complementary] points of view and in different ways by faith and by reason, respectively. Faith purifies reason and widens its scope, and reason purifies faith and clarifies its coherence [cf. ITC, Theology Today, §§63, 64, 84]". (see FR §§56, 76).

Significantly, there is still another *principium cognoscendi externum* for authentic participation in the *sensus fidei fidelium*, namely, "attentiveness to the magisterium of the Church, and a willingness to listen to the teaching of the pastors of the Church, as an act of freedom and deeply held conviction" (SF §97). For my purpose here, the most important thing in the passage of *Lumen Gentium* §12 would be ignored if we simply emphasize that the laity itself is, for theologians, a source of teaching authority; an authentic source for discerning what is and what is not compatible with the biblical revelation. Rather, most important is that their sense of the faith is *not* in isolation, however, from the "*guidance of the sacred teaching authority (magisterium)*." This means that only the laity who understand and concretely lives what the Church teaches is a reliable interpreter of the faith. As John Paul II puts it, "In the community of the faithful—which must always maintain Catholic unity with the Bishops and the Apostolic See—there are great insights of faith. The Holy Spirit is active in enlightening the minds of the faithful with his truth, and in inflaming their hearts with his love. But these insights of faith and this *sensus fidelium* are not independent of the magisterium of the Church, which is an instrument of the same Holy Spirit and is assisted by him. *It is only when the faithful have been nourished by the Word of God, faithfully transmitted in its purity and integrity, that their own charisms are fully operative and fruitful.*"[131]

Accordingly, an independent status should not be ascribed to the sense of faithful, "isolating it from the enduring testimony of the successors of the apostles in the Church. The 'sense' always remains linked to the witness borne by the apostolic ministry and is an organic part of the testimony of the Church as a whole."[132] Therefore, "As Newman said: 'the gift of discerning, discriminating, defining, promulgating, and enforcing any portion of that tradition resides solely in the *Ecclesia docens*'. Thus, judgement regarding the authenticity of the *sensus fidelium* belongs ultimately not to the faithful themselves nor to theology but to the magisterium. Nevertheless, as already emphasized, the faith which it serves is the faith of the Church, which lives in all of the faithful, so it is always within the communion life of the Church that the magisterium exercises its essential ministry of oversight" (SF §77).

The magisterium of the Church is ultimately charged with determining what the normative substance of Christian believing is, that is, authentic Catholic teaching, because "decisive authority is located in the power of the keys, given to Peter by Christ the Lord himself."[133] Christ's lay faithful, while they do teach, do not do so in virtue of apostolic authority; the hierarchy alone teaches with such authority, expounding and maintaining the continuity and consistency of Christian belief, indeed, of the deposit of faith by way of authoritative judgment. In contrast, the laity "teach in virtue of the faith within, through all the activities of life and mind that it stimulates and develops," says Congar. "More exactly still," Congar adds, "all the richness of the deposit confided to the Church that can be revealed to a life of active faith objectively ruled and supervised by the apostolic hierarchy—it is through that that the faithful teach."[134] This conclusion brings us back to the question regarding the nature of the *sensus fidei*.

For one thing, the *sensus fidei* is embedded in and flows from the theological virtue of faith. For another, being a gift of God's grace, theological faith is that "which enables one to adhere personally to the Truth," and it is for that reason that the *sensus fidei* "cannot err." Furthermore, "This personal faith is also the faith of the Church since God has given guardianship of the Word to the Church. Consequently, what the believer believes is what the Church believes. The '*sensus fidei*' implies then by its nature a profound agreement of spirit and heart with the Church, '*sentire cum Ecclesia*'" (DV §35). What is, then, the nature of this infallibility, of a sure grasp of the truth, when faith is "believing in God and believing all that he has said and revealed to us, and that Holy Church proposes for our belief[?]" (CCC §1814). Nichols answers this question admirably well. "The gift of teaching Christian truth without deceiving is a useless gift unless it is matched by some sort of reciprocal gift of believing, some gift of infallibly receiving infallible teaching among the laity.... Thus, infallibility, or a sure grasp on the gospel message, is a characteristic of the entire Church, laity and clergy together, though it is differentiated in various ways as between the episcopate on the one hand and the [lay] faithful on the other."[135] This brings us to another question. What then is the *nature* of this active capacity, Christian tact or flair, for spiritually discerning what is compatible with the revelation of the Gospel and what is not?

Janet Smith nicely answers this question and she is guided by the Thomistic idea of the virtue of prudence. She explains,

> Prudence is that virtue or *habitus* possessed by the person who has authentic and reliable knowledge of the reality to which some moral precept applies, as well as, of course, an understanding and acceptance of the precept as well. The understanding of the precept is not the understanding of the philosopher or the expert; it is the understanding that can be described as the acceptance of the truth of the precept as corresponding to the truth of reality. Aquinas's concept of connaturality is applicable here; as an analogy we might speak of the horse trainer who knows horses so well that he can judge quickly when a horse is ill or out of sorts and knows how to remedy its condition; or the connoisseur of wine who can identify to what region and year a wine belongs. These individuals know a great deal about horses and wines generally and also of horses and wines in particular. The person who possesses prudence is one who has lived a virtuous life and has extensive knowledge of the realm of life in which he must make

> his moral judgment. The faithful spouse needs not only to know that adultery is wrong, but [also] must know what presents a temptation to infidelity for him or herself, and also have the virtues to avoid or extricate one's self from such situations. Connaturality is also reliable in matters of faith, but requires knowledge both of general principles and experience of relevant lived realities. [For example] That the bishops consulted the faithful about Mary's Immaculate Conception makes sense only if they believed that the faithful had an intimate knowledge of Mary acquired, one supposes, through having acquired a knowledge of Mary's role in [the history of] salvation, most likely through instruction and through prayerful practice of Marian devotions.[136]

Smith's analysis of the virtue is, by analogy, helpful in grasping the nature and function of the *sensus fidei*. The *sensus fidei* is embedded in and hence flows from the supernatural virtue of faith. This theological virtue is a gift of God's grace establishing in one a permanent disposition "by which we believe in God and believe all that he has said and revealed to us, and the Holy Church proposes for our belief" (CCC §1814). As Smith suggests, the concept of connaturality is also applicable in matters of faith because that virtue establishes, by virtue of connaturality, "a particular and profound form of knowledge, between the believing subject and the authentic object of faith" (SF §§49-50). Pope Francis provides a useful summary of the import of connaturality: "As part of his mysterious love for humanity, God furnishes the totality of the faithful with an instinct of faith—*sensus fidei*—which helps them to discern what is truly of God. The presence of the Spirit gives Christians a certain connaturality with divine realities, and a wisdom which enables them to grasp those realities intuitively, even when they lack the wherewithal to give them precise expression" (EG §119). Congar admirably explains the relationship between the believing subject and the authentic object of faith:

> [T]here is a gift of God (of the Holy Spirit) which relates to the twofold reality, objective and subjective, of faith (*fides quae creditur; fides qua creditur*), which is given to the hierarchy and the whole body of the faithful together... and which ensures an indefectible faith to the Church. This gift, we say, relates to the objective reality of faith, that is, the deposit of notions *and of realities* which constitute tradition; correlatively, it relates to subjective reality, that is, to the grace of faith in the *fidelis*, or religious subject, the quasi-instinctive ability that faith has to see and adhere to its object (at least within certain limits).[137]

As we can see from Congar's description in the above passage, the *sensus fidei* includes two related realities. On the one hand, the *sensus fidei* is a quality of religious subjectivity (*fides qua creditur*), the faith by which one believes. The supernatural gift of God's grace is infused in the subject with faith, love, and the gifts of the Holy Spirit (wisdom, understanding, counsel, fortitude, knowledge, piety, and fear of the Lord [CCC §1831]), conferring on that subject the active capacity for spiritual discernment between the truth of faith and its denial. On the other hand, Congar speaks of that objective reality of faith that the religious subject holds to be true, to which objective content of truth is what the faithful assent, believe and confess (*fides quae creditur*), namely, the faith with which one believes and that can be known objectively.

Thus far, I have been using interchangeably *sensus fidei* and *sensus fidelium*. Pié-Ninot helpfully explains that the second of these two notions—namely, the *fides quae creditur*—underwent development and was then regarded as the *sensus fidelium*. Therefore, there is a distinction to be made between *sensus fidei* and *sensus fidelium*; the terms are not exactly equivalent. What, then, is the difference? The Anglican-Roman Catholic International Commission (ARCIC) answers this question. It states, "when this capacity [*sensus fidei*] is exercised in concert by the body of the faithful we may speak of the exercise of the *sensus fidelium*." In other words, "The exercise of the *sensus fidei* by each member of the Church contributes to the formation of the *sensus fidelium* through which the Church as a whole remains faithful to Christ."[138] The difference here is that the notion of universality was added to the assent involved in the *fides quae creditur*. This, says Pié-Ninot, "refers to the situation in which the entire body of believers, 'from the bishops down to the last member of the laity'... maintain the same faith. It is in this situation, Vatican II asserts, that the whole people of God cannot err." Adds Pié-Ninot,

> An assertion of this infallibility is legitimate, then, when the content of the proposition under consideration fulfills the following four conditions: [1] when it is a matter of universal consent, [2] when it refers to revelation, [3] when it is a work of the Holy Spirit, and [4] when it is recognized by the magisterium (cf. DV, 8, 10; LG, 12, 25).[139]

Synodality in and of itself is a feeding ground for doctrinal normlessness. But also the *sensus fidei* contributes to that normlessness when considered in isolation from the Magisterium. It is the task of the magisterium to "guarantee the Church's unity in the truth of the Lord." *Donum Veritatis*, the 1990 Instruction on the Ecclesial Vocation of the Theologian, makes this point abundantly clear. Therefore, it is worthy of being cited at some length:

> Dissent sometimes also appeals to a kind of sociological argument which holds that the opinion of a large number of Christians would be a direct and adequate expression of the "supernatural sense of the faith." Actually, the opinions of the faithful cannot be purely and simply identified with the "*sensus fidei*." The sense of the faith is a property of theological faith; and, as God's gift which en-

> ables one to adhere personally to the Truth, it cannot err. This personal faith is also the faith of the Church since God has given guardianship of the Word to the Church. The "*sensus fidei*" implies then by its nature a profound agreement of spirit and heart with the Church, "*sentire cum Ecclesia*." Although theological faith as such then cannot err, the believer can still have erroneous opinions since all his thoughts do not spring from faith. Not all the ideas which circulate among the People of God are compatible with the faith. This is all the more so given that people can be swayed by a public opinion influenced by modern communications media. Not without reason did the Second Vatican Council emphasize the indissoluble bond between the "*sensus fidei*" and the guidance of God's People by the magisterium of the Pastors. These two realities cannot be separated. Magisterial interventions serve to guarantee the Church's unity in the truth of the Lord. They aid her to "abide in the truth" in the face of the arbitrary character of changeable opinions and are an expression of obedience to the Word of God. (DV §35)

How, then, does the *sensus fidelium* display, as Pope Francis suggested in line with Vatican II, infallibility in matters of believing, infallible *in credendo*? Francis did not answer that question. Congar does and his answer is consistent with *Lumen Gentium* §12: "The loving and believing Church is infallible only when it listens to the teaching Church and this partakes of *the teaching Church's infallibility*; again: the loving and believing Church is infallible through the animation received from the Holy Spirit in her quality as loving and believing Church, which implies organic reference and submission to the magisterium. In the first case, the Holy Spirit makes the hierarchy infallible, and the hierarchy, by subjecting the faithful to itself, communicates the benefits of *its* infallibility to them; in the second case, the Holy Spirit makes the Church, as a whole and as such, infallible, and in her each organic part according to what it is—the whole body in order that it may believe and live, the apostolic and magisterial hierarchy in order that it may transmit the apostolical deposit to the body and declare its authentic meaning."[140]

If we are to work towards resolving the crisis in the Church, not only the doctrinal and moral crises, but also the ecclesial one, especially as it pertains to the *sensus fidei fidelium*, we shall need, first, to attend to the hermeneutical principles propounded by the 1985 Extraordinary Synod of Bishops; second, retrieve and develop the Christian anthropology and sexual ethics developed by Karol Wojtyla/John Paul II; and third, be articulate as to how the *sensus fidei* is a vital aspect of theological epistemology in Catholicism.

NOTES

1. Gerhard Cardinal Müller, "Corruption of doctrine always brings with it corruption of morals." See also, his extensive "Interview with Dr. Maike Hickson." For an account of the present Church crisis and the contribution of Francis' papacy to this crisis, see Douglas Farrow, "The Conversion of the Papacy and the Present Church Crisis." For a comprehensive account of the crisis, see Philip F. Lawler, *The Smoke of Satan*.
2. Carl Trueman, "The Reformation We Need."
3. Msgr. Hans Feichtinger, "German Bishops Use Abuse Crisis to Promote Dissent." See also, Martin Mosebach, "Remembering Robert Spaemann."
4. My discussion of the *sensus fidelium* is indebted not only to Janet Smith and Yves Congar, but also to Dominican theologian, Aidan Nichols, *Shape of Catholic Theology*, 221-31.
5. See Emeritus Pope Bendict XVI, "The Church and the sexual abuse crisis." Benedict gives an account of the threefold character of this crisis: doctrinal (absence of God), moral (loss of moral absolutes rendering the Church indefensible against the impact of the sexual revolution in the culture and the Church), and ecclesial (the denial of the Church's moral authority).
6. Francis, "Letter of His Holiness Pope Francis to the People of God". See also Synod18 – Documento finale e Votazioni del Documento finale del Sinodo dei Vescovi al Santo Padre Francesco (27 ottobre 2018), which defines clericalism as "an elitist and exclusive vision of vocation, which interprets the ministry received as a power to be exercised rather than a free and generous service."
7. Kenneth L. Woodward, "Double Lives, The Peril of Clerical Hypocrisy." Kenneth Woodward was for thirty-eight years religion editor of Newsweek. The Swiss Auxiliary Bishop of Church, Marian Eleganti, rightly states, "No one denies that clericalism plays a role, but nevertheless it is in the Church proven that the abusers are mainly homosexual. The silencing of this fact is an additional form of cover-up.... With all respect toward people with a homosexual inclination who do not commit any sexual assaults, it does not help to close the eyes in front of the facts when dealing with sexual assaults. Without full transparency and truthfulness, there will be no credible investigation, nor any effective prevention." Online: https://de.catholicnewsagency.com/story/eleganti-krise-der-kirche-muss-schonungslos-aufgeklart-werden-3552. Matthew E. Bunson, "Is Catholic Clergy Sex Abuse Related to Homosexual Priests?" an interview with sociologist Father Paul Sullins, whose new study documents a strong linkage between the incidence of abuse and homosexuality in the priesthood and in seminaries.
8. Archbishop Viganò's Third Testimony, https://www.scribd.com/document/391175546/Archbishop-Vigano-s-Third-Testimony.
9. Buschart and Eilers, *Theology as Retrieval: Receiving the Past, Renewing the Church*, 12.
10. Vanhoozer, *Biblical Authority After Babel*, 23, and 24.
11. Nichols, *The Shape of Catholic Theology*, 223.
12. Francis, "Pope Calls for a 'Listening Church.'"
13. Oscar Cullman, "Have Expectations Been Fulfilled?" at 57.
14. Ibid., 58.
15. See also §150, "Faith is first of all a personal adherence of man to God. At the same time, and inseparably, it is a *free assent to the whole truth that God has revealed.*"
16. Nichols, *The Shape of Catholic Theology*, 15-16.

17. I say minimally because "The creed does not only involve giving one's assent to a body of abstract truths; rather, when it is recited the whole of life is drawn into a journey toward full communion with the living God. We can say that in the creed believers are invited to enter into the mystery which they profess and to be transformed by it" (LF §45). This encyclical is co-authored with Benedict XVI, and hence this balanced statement reflects Benedict's thought (§7).

18. Lonergan, "The Origins of Christian Realism (1961)."

19. Jaroslav Pelikan, *Credo, Historical and Theological Guide to Creeds and Confessions*, 9.

20. I have dealt in-depth with this question regarding the nature of continuity in my book, *Berkouwer and Catholicism, Disputed Questions*, 20-109, and more recently in *Revelation, History and Truth*, 1-47.

21. Lonergan, *The Way to Nicea*, 8-10.

22. Wolfgang Beinert, "Dogma/Dogmatic Statement," entry in *Handbook of Catholic Theology*, at 187.

23. If Francis's thought was truly dialectical, that is, thinking in terms of oppositions, polarities, rather than contradictions, it would show itself here. So, notwithstanding Massimo Borghesi's insistence that "dialectical polarity" is at the core of Bergoglio/Pope Francis's thought, meaning thereby that he thinks in terms of the opposition of contraries, not contradictions, there is no evidence in his thought of dialectical thinking on this question of the relation between dogmas, which are normative statements of belief, and life (see *The Mind of Pope Francis*, Chapters 1, 6, 9, 12-13, 19, and Chapters 2 and 3).

24. Francis, "Pope Francis's Address to the Synod Fathers."

25. In an address of 18 February 2009, "The Importance of Academic Formation," *Only Love Can Save Us*, 139-49, and at 145. In a recent book of interviews, *God is Young*, Francis says, "A person who turns to extremes and tends toward rigidity is a fearful person. He hides behind rigidity as a defense. Behind and under every rigidity there is always an unresolved problem and also, perhaps, an illness" (59-60). This criticism that "rigidity" is a sickness or illness is fairly typical for Pope Francis. See Pentin, "Pope Francis: Rigid People Are Sick." This criticism is *ad hominem* rather than engaging the question of the truth-status dogmatic formulations.

26. There is a steady drumbeat of this charge throughout Francis's pontificate. I cite only a couple of instances here. Francis, *Amoris Laetitia* §37, which is citing from "Concluding Address of the Fourteenth Ordinary General Assembly of the Synod of Bishops," 13. See also, AL §305 where he repeats the charge of Pharisaic stone-thrower but adds, "This would bespeak the closed heart of one used to hiding behind the Church's teachings, 'sitting on the chair of Moses and judging at times with superiority and superficiality difficult cases and wounded families.'" In addition, most recently, he lambasts, once again, the doctors of the law, "In a word, Pope Francis continued, the Pharisees and doctors of the Law were rigid people, not disposed to change. 'But always, under or behind rigidity, there are problems, grave problems', the Pope said. We intend to have the appearance of being a good Christian; we intend to appear a certain way, we put make-up on our souls. However, Pope Francis said, behind these appearances, 'there are problems. Jesus is not there. The spirit of the world is there'" ("Pope at Mass: Be careful around rigid Christians.")

27. As cited in Gerald O'Collins, SJ, *The Case Against Dogma*, xi.

28. The contrast between "traditionalism" and "tradition" is made by Jaroslav Pelikan, *The Christian Tradition*, I, The Emergence of the Catholic Tradition (100-600), 9.

29. M.E. Williams, "Dogma," *New Catholic Encyclopedia*, Vol. 4, 948, as cited in O'Collins, *The Case Against Dogma*, xii.

30. See Chapter 4 for an extensive analysis of Chapter 8 of *Amoris Laetitia*.

31. See the next section of this chapter.

32. John XXIII, "*Gaudet Mater Ecclesia*," Opening speech at Vatican II, 11 October 1962. "Est

enim aliud ipsum depositum Fidei, seu veritates, quae veneranda doctrina nostra continentur, aliud modus, quo eaedem enuntiantur, eodem tamen sensu eademque sententia," Ioannes XXIII, "Allocutio habita d. 11 oct. 1962, in initio Concilii," *Acta Apostolicae Sedis* (1962): 792.

33. *The Commonitory of Vincent of Lérins*, Chapter 23, §28.

34. Pelikan, *The Christian Tradition*, I, 9.

35. Ibid.

36. George Weigel, "Concluding Unscientific Postscripts [On the XVth General Assembly of the Synod of Bishops]."

37. Ibid.

38. Francis, "Concluding Address of the Fourteenth Ordinary General Assembly of the Synod of Bishops."

39. Pentin, "'Doctrinal Anarchy' as Bishops' Conflicting Positions on Amoris Laetitia Show."

40. Reinhard Cardinal Marx. "Bischöfe beschließen 'synodalen Weg' zu Sexualmoral und Zölibat." See George Weigel, "An Open Letter to Cardinal Reinhard Marx."

41. Bishop Olivier Ribadeau-Dumas, "Qui nous fera voir le bonheur?" See also the English excerpt.

42. Francis, "Pope calls for a 'Listening Church.'"

43. I am objecting to the idea of synodality that has led to the fracturing of the Church's unity. I am open to the positive development of this idea. See the International Theological Commission document for the development of the idea of "Synodality in the Life and Mission of the Church."

44. George Weigel, "Concluding Unscientific Postscripts." Similarly, Anglican theologian Ephraim Radner in "Whose Synodality? (First Things, 7 November 2018) worries that "synodality" may become, as it has in Anglicanism, a "code-word for moral permissiveness and cultural accommodation."

45. Catholic News Agency. "What is 'synodality'? Experts explain." See also Edward Pentin, "Draft of Final Document Thrusts Synodality to the Fore."

46. Francis, "Pope calls for a 'Listening Church.'"

47. Nichols, *Shape of Catholic Theology*, 229-30.

48. Janet E. Smith, "The *Sensus Fidelium* and *Humanae Vitae*," at 279.

49. Francis, "Pope calls for a 'Listening Church.'"

50. See Joseph Cardinal Ratzinger, *Principles of Catholic Theology*, 374.

51. Francis, "Pope calls for a 'Listening Church.'"

52. Braaten, *Mother Church: Ecclesiology and Ecumenism*, 92.

53. Pentin, "Synod Reflections From Down Under: Interview With Archbishop Anthony Fisher."

54. Ratzinger, *Principles of Catholic Theology*, 374. For my critique of this idea, especially as developed by Giuseppe Alberigo of the Bologna School, see my book, *Revelation, History, and Truth*, 4-14.

55. Francis, "Pope calls for a 'Listening Church.'"

56. See *Mag ik? Sorry, Dank je, Vrijmoedige dialoog over relaties, huwelijk en gezin*, on pre-marital sex and cohabitation (33-36, 41-46, 48-50, 63, 70), contraceptive sex (108-110), and same-sex relations (62, 137, 143-45, 148-49, 151, 153, 155-57, 161, 169, 174). On Christian experience being the final standard as to what they experience as sin, see 41-42, 84, and on justifying ecclesial rites for cohabiting and same-sex couples, see 52, 54-55, 163-64.

57. David Schoenmaekers, "Kardinaal De Kesel vindt seksualiteitsbeleving bij holebi's aanvaardbaar." 'Holebi' is the Dutch acronym for LGBT.

58. Anian Christoph Wimmer, "Cardinal Marx endorses blessing ceremonies for same-sex couples."

59. Dwight Longenecker, "Does Cardinal Marx see a Way to Bless Gay Unions or Not?"

60. Eltz, Johannes zu. "Johannes zu Eltz on building bridges and celebrating the Eucharist with L.G.B.T. Catholics."

61. Tom Heneghan, "German bishops grapple with blessings for gay marriage."

62. I have extensively discussed this matter regarding the place of the moral law in the Christian life in Chapter 3.

63. Ephraim Radner, "Blessing: A Scriptural and Theological Reflection." I am indebted to Radner for his reflections,

64. I have dealt with marriage's nature in Chapter 4.

65. Westen and Baklinski. "Archbishop Cupich lays out pathway for gay couples to receive Communion at Vatican press scrum."

66. Radner, "Blessing," 24. I discuss other reasons why the Catholic moral tradition rejects same-sex relations in Chapter 4, the section on the two-in-one flesh bodily unity.

67. Ibid., 26.

68. Robert McElroy, "Attacks on Father James Martin expose a cancer within the U.S. Catholic Church.".

69. James Martin, SJ, *Building a Bridge: How the Catholic Church and the LGBT Community can Enter into a Relationship of Respect, Compassion, and Sensitivity*. See my article review of his work, "Fr. James Martin, 'bridges', and the triumph of the therapeutic mentality."

70. Nichols, *Christendom Awake: On Reenergizing the Church in Culture*.

71. Robert Reilly, *Making Gay Okay*.

72. R.R. Reno, "Catholic Capitulation on Marriage."

73. Idem, "Liberal Tradition, Yes; Liberal Ideology, No."

74. "Synod18 – Documento finale e Votazioni del Documento finale del Sinodo dei Vescovi al Santo Padre Francesco": "Esistono questioni relative al corpo, all'affettività e alla sessualità che hanno bisogno di una più approfondita elaborazione antropologica, teologica e pastorale, da realizzare nelle modalità e ai livelli più convenienti, da quelli locali a quello universale."

75. Wimmer, Anian Christoph. "German bishops announce 'synodal process' on celibacy, sexual morality."

76. Bishop Johan Bonny, "Synod on the Family: Expectations of a Diocesan Bishop."

77. For instance, in addition to *Love and Responsibility* and *Man and Woman He Created Them: A Theology of the Body*, consider his philosophical magnum opus, *The Acting Person*; idem., "Subjectivity and the Irreducible in Man," and *Person and Community, Selected Essays*.

78. George Weigel, "An Open Letter to Cardinal Reinhard Marx."

79. I have sketched a Christian anthropology in greater detail in the first part of Chapter 4.

80. Benedict XVI, "Interview of the Holy Father Benedict XVI in Preparation for the Upcoming Visit to Bavaria."

81. Joseph Cardinal Ratzinger, with Vittorio Messori, *The Ratzinger Report*, on the section, "Against 'trivialized' sex," where the same argument is made. See also, Walter Cardinal Brandmüller in "Gomorrah in the 21st Century. The Appeal of a Cardinal and Church Historian."

82. Anthony Giddens, *The Transformation of Intimacy, Sexuality, Love & Eroticism in Modern So-*

cieties, 27.

83. Ibid., 58.

84. Elizabeth Anscombe, "Contraception and Chastity," tells us what she means by a reproductive type of sex act, "I don't mean of course that every act is reproductive any more than every acorn leads to an oak-tree but it's the reproductive type of act."

85. Giddens, *The Transformation of Intimacy*, 27.

86. Christopher C. Roberts, *Creation & Covenant, The Significance of Sexual Difference in the Moral Theology of Marriage*, 186.

87. Giddens, *The Transformation of Intimacy*, 3.

88. Harvey Cox, *The Secular City*, 201, 204. See also, Mark Regnerus, *Cheap Sex: The Transformation of Men, Marriage, and Monogamy*.

89. Thomas Joseph White, *The Light of Christ, An Introduction to Catholicism*, 239.

90. On sexual ethics, Karol Wojtyla, "The Problem of Catholic Sexual Ethics, Reflections and Postulates," 279-99.

91. Idem, *Love and Responsibility*, "Author's Introduction to the First Polish Edition (1960)," xxii.

92. Idem, "The Problem of Catholic Sexual Ethics," 287.

93. Benedict M. Ashley, OP, *Living the Truth in Love, A Biblical Introduction to Moral Theology*, 429, and 215, respectively. This, too, is the teaching of the *Catechism of the Catholic Church* §§2331-36.

94. Wojtyla states, "To justify the norms of morality means to give reasons for their rightness. In performing this task, moral theologians should have before their eyes, as far as possible, the complete theoretical vision of reality contained in revelation, especially those elements of its that are indispensable for justifying the respective normative judgments, Normative judgments are based on value judgments, which, in turn, presupposes theoretical knowledge of the reality evaluated" ("The Problem of Catholic Sexual Ethics," 280).

95. Ronald Lawler, O.F.M. Cap., Joseph Boyle, Jr., & William May, *Catholic Sexual Ethics*, 14.

96. Farley, *Just Love*, 231: "Sex should not be used in ways that exploit, objectify, or dominate; rape, violence, and harmful uses of power in sexual relationships are ruled out; freedom, wholeness, intimacy, pleasure are values to be affirmed in relationships marked by mutuality, equality, and some form of commitment; sexual relations like other profound interpersonal relations can and ought to be fruitful both within and beyond the relationship; the affections of desire and love that bring about and sustain sexual relationships are all in all genuinely to affirm both lover and beloved."

97. William E. May, et al., *Catholic Sexual Ethics*, 14.

98. Patrick Lee, "The Human Body and Sexuality in the Teaching of Pope John Paul II," 108.

99. Levering, "Knowing What is 'Natural'," 135.

100. Benedict XVI, "Address of his Holiness Benedict XVI on the Occasion of Christmas Greetings to the Roman Curia": "According to this philosophy, sex is no longer a given element of nature, that man has to accept and personally make sense of: it is a social role that we choose for ourselves, while in the past it was chosen for us by society. The profound falsehood of this theory and of the anthropological revolution contained within it is obvious. People dispute the idea that they have a nature, given by their bodily identity, that serves as a defining element of the human being. They deny their nature and decide that it is not something previously given to them, but that they make it for themselves. According to the biblical creation account, being created by God as male and female pertains to the essence of the human creature. This duality is an essential aspect of what being human is all about, as ordained by God. This very duality as something previously given is what is now disputed. The words of the creation account: "male and female he

created them" [Gen 1:27] no longer apply. No, what applies now is this: it was not God who created them male and female—hitherto society did this, now we decide for ourselves. Man and woman as created realities, as the nature of the human being, no longer exist. Man calls his nature into question. From now on he is merely spirit and will. The manipulation of nature, which we deplore today where our environment is concerned, now becomes man's fundamental choice where he himself is concerned. From now on there is only the abstract human being, who chooses for himself what his nature is to be. Man and woman in their created state as complementary versions of what it means to be human are disputed. But if there is no pre-ordained duality of man and woman in creation, then neither is the family any longer a reality established by creation. Likewise, the child has lost the place he had occupied hitherto and the dignity pertaining to him. Bernheim shows that now, perforce, from being a subject of rights, the child has become an object to which people have a right and which they have a right to obtain. When the freedom to be creative becomes the freedom to create oneself, then necessarily the Maker himself is denied and ultimately man too is stripped of his dignity as a creature of God, as the image of God at the core of his being. The defense of the family is about man himself. And it becomes clear that when God is denied, human dignity also disappears. Whoever defends God is defending man."

101. Lee and George, "Sex and the Body." See also, William E. May, *Catholic Sexual Ethics.*

102. Ibid., 107.

103. On these distinctions, see Lewis Smedes' *Mere Morality*, especially chapter 1. Smedes develops these distinctions more fully in his paper, "The Bible and Ethics," portions of which are published in the first and last chapters of *Mere Morality*.

104. Helpful in understanding the central commandment of Love is David E. Holwerda, "Jesus and the Law: A Question of Fulfillment," 122-45.

105. Of course here, too, we have an instance of a concrete command ("Whoever sacrifices to any god other than the LORD must be destroyed" [Exod 22:20]) which is an application of a primary commandment from the Decalogue (Exod 20:1-6). The concrete command is contextually conditioned but not the primary command on which it is based.

106. Robert A.J. Gagnon, "Are there universally valid sex precepts? A Critique of Walter Wink's View on the Bible and Homosexuality."

107. The word "deontology" comes from the Greek roots *deon*, which means duty, and *logos*, which means science, discourse, reasoning. Thus, deontology is the "science of duty."

108. Axiology from Greek *axios*, "worthy," and *logos*, "science." Axiology is a theory of objective value, which is the philosophical study of goodness. In this light, a personalistic axiology is about the objective good or value of the person.

109. Wojtyla, *Man in the Field of Responsibility*, 45, 57.

110. Ibid., 16-17.

111. Ibid., 17, 21-22.

112. Ibid., 18.

113. Ibid., 24.

114. Erich Fromm, *The Art of Loving*, 7, "*Any theory of love must begin with a theory of man, of human existence.*" The italics are in the original.

115. See Chapter 4 where I present the Catholic teaching on marriage along with the Appendix that contains Pope Francis's consistent teaching on marriage as a two-in-one-flesh union of a man and a woman.

116. Alexander Pruss, *One Body, An Essay in Christian Sexual Ethics*, 155.

117. Ibid.

118. Herman Dooyeweerd, *A Christian Theory of Social Institutions*, 87.

119. Idem, "Sociology of Law and Its Philosophical Foundations," 83.

120. John Paul II, *Man and Woman He Created Them: A Theology of the Body*. Dutch translation: *Theologie van het Lichaam*.

121. Herman Dooyeweerd, *A New Critique of Theoretical Thought*, Part II, §4, 320.

122. Robert R. Reilly, *Making Gay Okay*, 36: Robert Reilly correctly puts it, "only a unitive act can be generative, and only a generative act can be unitive—in that only it makes two 'one flesh'." In my judgment, for brevity, the single, best philosophical defense of conjugal marriage is Girgis et al, *What Is Marriage? Man and Woman: A Defense*.

123. I discussed in Chapter 3 the risk that Francis's pastoral approach runs of separating the "listening Church" and the "teaching Church."

124. Congar, *Lay People in the Church*, 290; emphasis added.

125. Francis, "Pope Calls for a 'Listening Church.'"

126. Francis, "I believe the Lord wants a change in the Church: A private dialogue with the Jesuits in the Baltics."

127. Francis, *A Big Heart Open to God*, 25-26.

128. The Anglican Roman Catholic International commission, *The Gift of Authority*, §29.

129. Geiselmann, *The Meaning of Tradition*, 20.

130. Nichols, *The Shape of Catholic Theology*, 221-31.

131. John Paul II's address during the *ad limina* visit of the bishops of India, May 1979. This, too, is the view of the International Theological Commission, "The magisterium also judges with authority whether opinions which are present among the people of God, and which may seem to be the *sensus fidelium*, actually correspond to the truth of the Tradition received from the Apostles. (SF, §77).

132. Geiselmann, *The Meaning of Tradition*, 20.

133. Nichols, *The Shape of Catholic Theology*, 257.

134. Congar, *Lay People in the Church*, 293.

135. Nichols, *The Shape of Catholic Theology*, 223.

136. Smith, "The *Sensus Fidelium* and *Humanae Vitae*," 282.

137. Congar, *Lay People in the Church*, 288.

138. ARCIC, *The Gift of Authority*, §29.

139. Salvador Pié-Ninot, "Sensus Fidei," 992-93. Pié-Ninot explains the biblical roots of the *sensus fidei*: "An effort to base the *sensus fidei* theologically finds in the NT clear testimonials to the reality of an organ of faith, in each of the baptized, as well as in the entire church. Thus, in various texts, we read of 'the mind of Christ' (1 Cor 2:16), 'spiritual insight' (Col 1:9), and 'innermost vision' (lit. 'enlightened eyes of the heart,' Eph 1:18; cf. John 14:17, 16:13; Phil 1:9; etc.). On this basis, patristic and theological tradition frequently speaks of the 'eyes of the heart', 'the eyes of the spirit', or the 'eyes of faith'. Suffice it to recall Augustine's expression: *Habet namque fides oculos suos* ("*After all, faith has its eyes*," *Epist*. 120.2.8); as well as the words of Aquinas: *Per lumen fidei vident esse credenda* ("Through the light of faith, they see that these [things] are to be believed," ST 2-2, q. 1, a. 5, ad 1) and *occulata fide* with reference to Jesus' resurrection ("by a faith endowed with eyes," ST 3, q. 55, a. 2, ad 1)" (993).

140. Congar, *Lay People in the Church*, 290-91. There is an important qualification by the International Theological Commission: "There are occasions, however, when the reception of magisterial teaching by the faithful meets with difficulty and resistance, and appropriate action on both sides is required in such situations. The faithful must reflect on the teaching that has been given, making every effort to understand and accept it. Resistance, as a matter of principle, to the teaching of the magisterium is incompatible with the authentic *sensus fidei*. The magisterium must likewise reflect on the teaching that has been given and consider whether it needs clarification or reformulation in order

to communicate more effectively the essential message. These mutual efforts in times of difficulty themselves express the communion that is essential to the life of the Church, and likewise a yearning for the grace of the Spirit who guides the Church 'into all the truth' [John 16:13]" (SF, §80).

Works Cited

Allison, Gregg R. *Roman Catholic Theology & Practice: An Evangelical Assessment*. (Wheaton, Ill.: Crossway, 2014).

Alston, William P. *A Realist Conception of Truth*. (Ithaca, N.Y.: Cornell University Press, 1996).

Aquinas, Thomas. *Commentary on St. Paul's Epistle to Timothy, Titus, and Philemon*, Translated Chrysostom Baer, O. Praem. (South Bend, Ind.: St. Augustine's Press, 2008).

— *Disputed Questions on Truth*. (Chicago: Henry Regnery, 1952).

— *Summa Contra Gentiles*, Translated, with an Introduction and Notes, by Charles J. O'Neil (Notre Dame/London: University of Notre Dame Press, 1975).

— *Summa Contra Gentiles, On the Truth of the Catholic Faith*, vol. 1. (Garden City, N.Y.: Doubleday, 1955).

— *Summa Theologiae*.

Anglican Roman Catholic International Commission (ARCIC), *The Gift of Authority*. (London: Catholic Truth Society, 1999). Online: http://www.vatican.va/roman_curia/pontifical_councils/chrstuni/documents/rc_pc_chrstuni_doc_12051999_gift-of-autority_en.html.

Anscombe, Elizabeth. *Contraception and Chastity*. 1972. http://www.orthodoxytoday.org/articles/AnscombeChastity.php.

Arkes, Hadley. "Francis, The Writer Unbound," *The Catholic Thing*, 3 December 2013. https://www.thecatholicthing.org/2013/12/03/francis-the-writer-unbound/.

Arocho Esteves, Junno. "Pope's Morning Homily: 'Scandal Destroys Faith!'" *Zenit*, 10 November 2014. https://zenit.org/articles/pope-s-morning-homily-scandal-destroys-faith/.

Ashley OP, Benedict M. *Living the Truth in Love, A Biblical Introduction to Moral Theology* (New York: Alba House, 1996).

Aymans, Winfried, ed. *Eleven Cardinals Speak on Marriage and the Family*. (San Francisco: Ignatius Press, 2015).

Baggett, Jerome P. "Another Legacy of Vatican II: Cultural Dilemmas among American Catholics." *From Vatican II to Pope Francis*. 47-52.

Baklinski, Pete. "Cardinal linked to Vatican gay orgy emphasized 'positive elements' in gay lifestyle." *Life Site News*, 6 July 2017. https://www.lifesitenews.com/news/vatican-cardinal-in-charge-of-gay-orgy-priest-emphasized-positive-elements.

Balthasar, Hans Urs von. *Love Alone is Credible*. (San Francisco: Ignatius Press, 2004 [1963]).

Bavinck, Herman. *Gereformeerde Dogmatiek* 4, Zesde Onveranderde Druk (Kampen: J.H. Kok, 1876 [1901], ET: *Reformed Dogmatics* Vol. 4, Translated John Vriend, General Editor, John Bolt (Grand Rapids, MI: Baker Academic, 2008).

— *Gereformeerde Dogmatiek*, I (Kampen: J.H. Kok, 1895); ET: *Reformed Dogmatics, Prolegomena*, I, Translated by John Vriend, editor John Bolt (Grand Rapids, MI: Baker Academic, 2003).

Beinert, Wolfgang. "Dogma/Dogmatic Statement," entry in *Handbook of Catholic Theology*, edited by Wolfgang Beinert and F.S. Fiorenza (New York: Crossroad, 1995), 185–88.

Benedict XVI, Emeritus Pope. "The Church and the sexual abuse crisis." *Catholic World Report*, 11 April 2019. https://www.catholicworldreport.com/2019/04/10/full-text-of-benedict-xvi-the-church-and-the-scandal-of-sexual-abuse/.

Benedict XVI, Pope. "Address of his Holiness Benedict XVI to the Roman Curia offering them his Christmas greetings." 22 December 2005. http://www.vatican.va/holy_father/benedict_xvi/speeches/2005/december/documents/hf_ben_xvi_spe_20051222_roman-curia_en.html.

— "Address of his Holiness Benedict XVI on the Occasion of Christmas Greetings to the Roman Curia," 21 December 2012. http://w2.vatican.va/content/benedict-xvi/en/speeches/2012/december/documents/hf_ben-xvi_spe_20121221_auguri-curia.html.

— "Address of his Holiness Benedict XVI at the Conclusion of the Meeting with the Bishops of Switzerland," 9 November 2006. http://w2.vatican.va/content/benedict-xvi/en/speeches/2006/november/documents/hf_ben-xvi_spe_20061109_concl-swiss-bishops.html.

— "Address of His Holiness Pope Benedict XVI, Meeting with Organizations for Interreligious Dialogue." *Auditorium of Notre Dame Center*, Jerusalem, 11 May 2009. https://www.catholicculture.org/culture/library/view.cfm?recnum=8944.

— "Address of His Holiness Pope Benedict XVI, Meeting with the Parish Priests and the Clergy of Rome," 14 February 2013. http://w2.vatican.va/content/benedict-xvi/en/speeches/2013/february/documents/hf_ben-xvi_spe_20130214_clero-roma.html.

— *Caritas in Veritate* (*On Integral Human Development in Charity and Truth*). encyclical, 29 June 2009. http://w2.vatican.va/content/benedict-xvi/en/encyclicals/documents/hf_ben-xvi_enc_20090629_caritas-in-veritate.html.

— *Deus Caritas Est* (*On Christian Love*). encyclical, 25 December 2005. http://w2.vatican.va/content/benedict-xvi/en/encyclicals/documents/hf_ben-xvi_enc_20051225_deus-caritas-est.html.

— *God's Revolution: World Youth Day and Other Cologne Talks*. (San Francisco, Ignatius Press, 2006).

— "Homily of his Holiness Benedict XVI at the Liturgy of Vespers for the Conclusion of the Week of Prayer for Christian Unity." 25 January 2011. http://w2.vatican.va/content/benedict-xvi/en/homilies/2011/documents/hf_ben-xvi_hom_20110125_week-prayer.html.

— "Inaugural Session of the Fifth General Conference of the Bishops of Latin America and the Caribbean." Shrine of Aparecida, 13 May 2007. http://w2.vatican.va/content/benedict-xvi/en/speeches/2007/may/documents/hf_ben-xvi_spe_20070513_conference-aparecida.html.

— *Jesus of Nazareth*, Vol. 1, From the Baptism in the Jordan to the Transfiguration. Translated by Adrian J. Walker (New York: Doubleday, 2007).

— "La pastorale del matrimonio deve fondarsi sulla verità," *Osservatore Romano*, 20 November 2011. https://cooperatores-veritatis.org/2011/11/30/la-pastorale-del-matrimonio-deve-fondarsi-sulla-verita/.

— "Interview of the Holy Father Benedict XVI in Preparation for the Upcoming Visit to Bavaria." 5 August 2006. http://w2.vatican.va/content/benedict-xvi/en/speeches/2006/august/documents/hf_ben-xvi_spe_20060805_intervista.html.

— "Reflections of His Holiness Benedict XVI Published for the First Time on the Occasion of the 50th Anniversary of the Opening of the Second Vatican Council," http://www.vatican.va/special/annus_fidei/documents/annus-fidei_bxvi_inedito-50-concilio_en.html.

— *Sacramentum Caritas*, Post-synodal Apostolic Exhortation, 22 February 2007. http://w2.vatican.va/content/benedict-xvi/en/apost_exhortations/documents/hf_ben-xvi_exh_20070222_sacramentum-caritatis.html.

Bergoglio, Cardinal Jorge Mario. *Education for Choosing Life*. Translation by Deborah Cole (San Francisco: Ignatius Press, 2014 [2005]).

— "For Man," translated by Susan Scott, in *A Generative Thought: An Introduction to the Work of Luigi Giussani*, edited by Elisa Bussi (Montreal/Kingston: McGill-Queen's University Press, 2003).

— *Only Love Can Save Us: Letters, Homilies, and Talks of Cardinal Jorge Bergoglio*. (Our Sunday Visitor, Inc., 2013).

Bergoglio, Jorge Mario and Abraham Skorka. *On Heaven and Earth*. trans. Alejandro Bermudez and Howard Goodman. Edited in Spanish by Diego F. Rosenberg (New York: Image, 2013).

Berkouwer, G. C. *De Kerk*, Vol. I, *Eenheid en Katholiciteit*. (Kampen: J. H. Kok, 1970); Vol. II, *Apostoliciteit en Heiligheid* (Kampen: J. H. Kok, 1972). Both volumes translated in one complete volume by James E. Davidson as *The Church* (Grand Rapids, Mich.: Eerdmans, 1976).

— *Divine Election*. Translated by Hugo Bekker (Grand Rapids, MI: Eerdmans, 1960).

— *General Revelation* (Grand Rapids, Mich.: Eerdmans, 1955).

— *Nabretrachting op het Concilie*. (Kampen: J. H. Kok, 1968).

— *Nieuwe Perspectieven in de Controvers: Rome-Reformatie*. Mededelingen der Koninklijke Nederlandse Akademie van Wetenschappen, afd. Letterkunde, Nieuwe Reeks, Deel 20, No. 1 (Amsterdam: N.V. Noord-Hollandsche UitgeversMaatschappij, 1957).

— *Sin*. Translated by Philip C. Holtrop (Grand Rapids, MI: Eerdmans, 1971).

— *Vatikaans Concilie en de Nieuwe Theologie*. (Kampen: J. H. Kok, 1964). Translated by Lewis B. Smedes as The Second Vatican Council and the New Catholicism (Grand Rapids, MI: Eerdmans, 1965).

— "Vragen Rondom De Belijdenis," *Gereformeerd Theologisch Tijdschrift* 63 (1963): 1–41.

— *The Work of Christ*. trans. Cornelius Lambregtse (Grand Rapids, MI: Eerdmans, 1965).

Blackburn, Simon. *The Oxford Dictionary of Philosophy*. (Oxford/New York: Oxford University Press, 1996).

Boff, Leonardo. *Francis of Rome & Francis of Assisi, A New Springtime for the Church*, Translated by Dinah Livingstone (Maryknoll, NY: Orbis Books, 2014).

Bonino O.P., Serge-Thomas. "Saint Thomas Aquinas in the Apostolic Exhortation Amoris Laetitia." *The Thomist* 80 (no. 4, October 2016): 499-519.

Bonny, Bishop Johan. "Synod on the Family: Expectations of a Diocesan Bishop." http://kerknet.be/admin/files/assets/subsites/4/documenten/SYNOD_ON_FAMILY_ENG.pdf..

Borghesi, Massimo. *The Mind of Pope Francis, Jorge Mario Bergoglio's Intellectual Journey*. trans. Barry Hudock (Collegeville, MN: Liturgical Press Academic, 2018).

Boudway, Matthew; and Grant Gallicho. "An Interview with Cardinal Walter Kasper." *Commonweal Magazine*, 7 May 2014. https://www.commonwealmagazine.org/interview-cardinal-walter-kasper.

Braaten, Carl. *Mother Church: Ecclesiology and Ecumenism* (Minneapolis: Fortress Press, 1998).

Brandmüller, Walter Cardinal. "Gomorrah in the 21st Century. The Appeal of a Cardinal and Church Historian," excerpts as translated by Matthew Sherry of article by Settimo Cielo in *L'Espresso*. http://magister.blogautore.espresso.repubblica.it/2018/11/05/gomorrah-in-the-21st-century-the-appeal-of-a-cardinal-and-church-historian/. For the entire article in Italian, "Omosessualità e abusi—Affrontare la crisi: le lezioni della storia," *Vatican Magazin*, November 2018. http://magister.blogautore.espresso.repubblica.it/2018/11/03/affrontare-la-crisi-le-lezioni-della-storia/.

Brockhaus, Hannah. "Unity is not the same as uniformity, Pope Francis says." *Catholic News Agency*, 10 November 2016. https://www.catholicnewsagency.com/news/unity-is-not-the-same-as-uniformity-pope-francis-says-34841.

Budziszewski, J. *Written on the Heart: The Case for Natural Law*. (Downers Grove, Ill: InterVarsity Press, 1997).

Bunson, Matthew E. "Is Catholic Clergy Sex Abuse Related to Homosexual Priests?," *National Catholic Register*, 2 November 2018. http://www.ncregister.com/daily-news/is-catholic-clergy-sex-abuse-related-to-homosexual-priests.

Buschart, W. David; and Eilers, Kent D. *Theology as Retrieval: Receiving the Past, Renewing the Church*. (Downers Grove, Ill.: IVP Academic, 2015).

Buttiglione, Rocco. "Here is the deviation in which Amoris Laetitia's critics fall." *La Stampa*, 20 November 2017. http://www.lastampa.it/2017/11/20/vaticaninsider/here-is-the-deviation-in-which-amoris-laetitias-critics-fall-9g1HyVV5sXCTGt9uc53prJ/pagina.html.

Cahill, Lisa Sowle. "Is Catholic Ethics Biblical?" Warren Lecture Series, in *Catholic Studies* 20, University of Tulsa, 1992.

Cantalamessa, Raniero. *Jesus Christ, The Holy One of God*, trans. Alan Neame (Collegeville, Minn.: The Liturgical Press, 1991).

Catholic Church and the World Council of Churches. "The Challenge of Proselytism and the Calling to Common Witness." https://berkleycenter.georgetown.edu/publications/the-challenge-of-proselytism-and-the-calling-to-common-witness.

Catholic News Agency. "What is 'synodality'? Experts explain." 25 October 2018. https://www.catholicnewsagency.com/news/what-is-synodality-experts-explain-60147.

Cernuzio, Salvatore. "The Pope, 'Beware of rejecting Jesus: He is good, merciful, he waits, but in the end, it is He who rejects." *Vatican Insider*, 6 November 2018. https://www.lastampa.it/2018/11/06/vaticaninsider/the-pope-beware-rejects-rejecting-jesus-he-is-good-merciful-he-waits-but-in-the-end-it-is-he-who-etODt1LILNiniWWZ9uCkZO/pagina.html.

Cessario O.P., Romanus. *Christian Faith & the Theological Life*. (Washington, DC: The Catholic University of America Press, 1996).

Chappin, S.J., Fr. Marcel. "Pope and Journalist, On a Recent Biography of Pope John XXIII," *Gregorianum* 67, 3 (1986): 517-531.

Clooney, S.J., Francis X. *Learning Interreligiously, In The Text, In The World* (Minneapolis, Minn.: Fortress Press, 2018).

CNA/EWTN News, "Pope: Be Open to the Good Wherever it comes from," *The Catholic World Report*, 30 September 2018. https://www.catholicworldreport.com/2018/09/30/pope-be-open-to-the-good-wherever-it-comes-from/.

Congar O.P. Yves, *Diversity and Communion*, Translated by John Bowden (London: SCM Press Ltd., 1984).

— *A History of Theology*. trans. Hunter Guthrie (Garden City, N.Y.: Doubleday, 1968).

— *Lay People in the Church*, Translated by Donald Attwater (Westminster, Md.: Newman Press, 1965).

— "Mercy: God's Supreme Attribute." in *The Revelation of God*. Translated by A. Manson and L.C. Sheppard (London: Darton, Longman & Todd Ltd.,1968 [1962]).

— *The Meaning of Tradition*. trans. A.N. Woodrow (San Francisco: Ignatius Press, 2004).

— *True and False Reform in the Church*. trans. Paul Philbert (Collegeville Minn., Liturgical Press, 2011).

Congregation for the Doctrine of the Faith. "Doctrinal Commentary on the Concluding Formula of the *Professio fidei*." 29 June 1998. http://www.vatican.va/roman_curia/congregations/cfaith/documents/rc_con_cfaith_doc_1998_professio-fidei_en.html.

— "Doctrinal Note on Some Aspects of Evangelization." 3 December 2007. http://www.vatican.va/roman_curia/congregations/cfaith/documents/rc_con_cfaith_doc_20071203_nota-evangelizzazione_en.html.

— *Dominus Iesus* (*On the Unicity and Salvific Universality of Jesus Christ and the Church*). 6 August 2000. http://www.vatican.va/roman_curia/congregations/cfaith/documents/rc_con_cfaith_doc_20000806_dominus-iesus_en.html.

— Instruction, *Donum Veritatis* (*On the Ecclesial Vocation of the Theologian*). 24 May 1990. http://www.vatican.va/roman_curia/congregations/cfaith/documents/rc_con_cfaith_doc_19900524_theologian-vocation_en.html.

— *Mysterium Ecclesiae* (*Declaration In Defense of the Catholic Doctrine on the Church Against Certain Errors of the Present Day*). 24 June 1973. http://www.vatican.va/roman_curia/congregations/cfaith/documents/rc_con_cfaith_doc_19730705_mysterium-ecclesiae_en.html.

Corkery, Sean. "Interpreting 'subsistit in' today," *Doctrine and Life* 64, No. 9 (November 2014), 11-22.

Cox, Harvey. *The Secular City* (New York: The MacMillan Press, 1965).

Craig, William Lane. *The Atonement* (Cambridge: Cambridge University Press, 2018).

Crisp, Oliver. "*Ad* Hector." *Journal of Analytic Theology*. Vol. 1, No. 1, May 2013, 133-39.

Cullmann, Oscar. "Comments on the Decree on Ecumenism," *The Ecumenical Review* 17 [April, 1965]: 93.

— "Have Expectations Been Fufilled?" in *Vatican II, The New Direction*. Essays Selected and Arranged by James D. Hester. (New York: Harper & Row, 1968), 54–63.

— *L'unité par la diversité*. (Paris, Cerf, 1986). German translation, *Einheit durch Vielfalt*. (Tübingen: Mohr, 1986).

Cupich, Blase Cardinal. "'Not our Policy' to deny Communion to People in Same-Sex Marriages." *Brown Pelican Society of Louisiana*, 9 October 2018. http://brownpelicanla.com/chicago-cardinal-cupich-not-our-policy-to-deny-communion-to-people-in-same-sex-marriages/.

— "Pope Francis' Revolution of Mercy: Amoris Laetitia as a New Paradigm of Catholicity." *Vatican Insider*, 9 February 2018. http://www.lastampa.it/2018/02/09/vaticaninsider/pope-francis-revolution-of-mercy-amoris-laetitia-as-a-new-paradigm-of-catholicity-skMox0lK-toX5szfKH6QgrL/pagina.html.

D'Ambrosio, Rocco. *Will Pope Francis Pull it Off? The Challenge of Church Reform*. trans. Barry Hudock. (Collegeville, MN: The Liturgical Press, 2016).

D'Antonio, William V.; Michael Dillon; and Mary L. Gautier. *American*

Catholics in Transition. (Lanham, MD: Rowman & Littlefield, 2013).

D'Costa, Gavin. *Vatican II: Catholic Doctrines on Jews & Muslims*. (Oxford: Oxford University Press, 2014).

De Chirico, Leonardo. *Evangelical Theological Perspectives on post-Vatican II Roman Catholicism*. (Bern: Peter Lang, 2003). Vol. 19, Religions and Discourse, Edited by James M.M. Francis.

de Lubac S.J., Henri. *The Drama of Atheist Humanism*, Translated by Edith M. Riley, et al (San Francisco: Ignatius Press, 1995 [1944]).

de Ridder, Jeroen, and René van Woudenberg, "Referring to, Believing in, and Worshipping the Same God: A Reformed View," *Faith and Philosophy* 31.1 (2014): 46–67.

de Souza, Raymond J. "'Amoris Laetitia,' the Holy Spirit and the Synod of Surprises." *National Catholic Register*, 8 April 2016. http://www.ncregister.com/daily-news/amoris-laetitia-the-holy-spirit-and-the-synod-of-surprises#.Vw43S4-cGUk.

— "Papal Adviser Undermines Magisterium 'in a Discreet Way.'" *National Catholic Register*, 24 August 2017. http://www.ncregister.com/daily-news/papal-adviser-undermines-magisterium-in-a-discreet-way.

DeBernardo, Francis. "Cupich: Synod Would Have Gained from Hearing from Lesbian and Gay Couples." *New Ways Ministry*, 17 October 2015. https://www.newwaysministry.org/2015/10/17/cupich-synod-would-have-gained-from-hearing-from-lesbian-and-gay-couples/.

Denzinger, Heinrich. *Compendium of Creeds, Definitions, and Declarations on Matters of Faith and Morals*. Latin-English, ed. Peter Hünermann, 43rd ed., English edition, eds. Robert Fastiggi and Anne Englund Nash. (San Francisco: Ignatius Press, 2012).

Dodaro O.S.A., Robert, ed. *Remaining in the Truth of Christ, Marriage and Communion in the Catholic Church*. (San Francisco: Ignatius Press, 2014).

Dooyeweerd, Herman. *A Christian Theory of Social Institutions*, translated by Magnus Verbrugge, Edited with an Introduction by John Witte, Jr. (La Jolla, Calif.: The Herman Dooyeweerd Foundation, 1986).

— *A New Critique of Theoretical Thought*, Vol. III, The Structures of Individuality of Temporal Reality. Translated by David H. Freeman et al. (Philadelphia: Presbyterian and Reformed Publishing Co., 1969 [1936]).

— *Reformation and Scholasticism in Philosophy*, Volume Three, Philosophy of Nature and Philosophical Anthropology. General editor: D.F.M. Strauss. Translated by Magnus Verbrugge and D.F.M. Strauss (Ancaster, ON: Paideia Press, 2011), Part II.

— "Sociology of Law and Its Philosophical Foundations," in *Essays in Legal, Social, and Political Philosophy* (Lewiston, N.Y.: Edwin Mellen, 1996).

Douma, Jochem. "Appendix: The Use of Scripture in Ethics," in *The Ten Commandments: Manual for the Christian Life*, translated by Nelson D. Kloosterman (Philipsburg, N.J.: Presbyterian & Reformed, 1996), 355-90.

Douthat, Ross. *To Change the Church: Pope Francis and the Future of Catholicism*. (New York: Simon & Schuster, 2018).

Dulles SJ, Avery Cardinal. *Magisterium, Teacher and Guardian of the Faith*.

(Naples: Sapientia Press, 2007).
— "Postmodernist Ecumenism," *Review of The Church in a Postliberal Age*, by George A. Lindbeck. First Things, October 2003.

Dupuis SJ, Jacques. "The Pangs of a Process," in *Do Not Stifle the Spirit, Conversations with Jacques Dupuis*, Gerard O'Connell, Preface by Gerald O'Collins, SJ (Maryknoll, N.Y.: Orbis Books, 2017).

Echeverria, Eduardo J. "Ad Father O'Collins," *Nova et Vetera*, Vol. 15, No. 4 (2017): 1251–79.

— "Belgium bishop co-authors book in support of pre-marital sex, same-sex relations," Review of Johan Bonny and Roger Burggraeve, *Mag ik? Sorry, Dank je, Vrijmoedige dialoog over relaties, huwelijk en gezin (May I? Sorry, Thank you: Open Dialogue about relationships, marriage and family)* [Lannoo, 2016]. *Catholic World Report*, 25 November 2016. https://www.catholicworldreport.com/2016/11/25/belgium-bishop-co-authors-book-in-support-of-pre-marital-sex-same-sex-relations/.

— *Berkouwer and Catholicism: Disputed Questions* (Leiden/Boston: Brill, 2013).

— "A Catholic Assessment of Gregg Allison's Critique of the 'Hermeneutics of Catholicism.'" *Called to Communion*, 17 August 2015. http://www.calledtocommunion.com/2015/08/a-catholic-assessment-of-gregg-allisons-critique-of-the-hermeneutics-of-catholicism/.

— "Dei Verbum and the Nature of Revelation," in *Josephinum Journal of Theology* 23, nos. 1 & 2 (2016): 250-80.

— "Fr. James Martin, 'bridges', and the triumph of the therapeutic mentality." *Catholic World Report*, 16 June 2017. https://www.catholicworldreport.com/2017/06/16/fr-james-martin-s-j-and-the-triumph-of-the-therapeutic-mentality/.

— "Hierarchy of Truths Revisited." *Acta Theologica* 2015 35 (2): 11-35.

— *"In the Beginning..." A Theology of the Body*. (Eugene, Ore.: Pickwick Publications, 2011).

— "The Nashville Statement is part of an ecumenical 'ecology of man.'" *Catholic World Report*, 3 September 2017. https://www.catholicworldreport.com/2017/09/03/the-nashville-statement-is-part-of-an-ecumenical-ecology-of-man/.

— "Pope Francis and Ideology," *Catholic World Report*, 13 January 2018. https://www.catholicworldreport.com/2018/01/13/pope-francis-and-ideology/.

— *Revelation, History, and Truth: A Hermeneutics of Dogma*. (New York: Peter Lang Publishing, 2018).

— "The Salvation of Non-Christians? Reflections on Vatican II's *Gaudium et Spes* 22, *Lumen Gentium* 16, Gerald O'Collins, S.J., and St. John Paul II," *Angelicum* 94 (2017) 93-194.

— "The Splendor of Truth in *Fides et Ratio*," in *Quaestiones Disputatae*, Vol. 9, No. 1 (Fall 2018): 49-78.

— *Slitting the Sycamore: Christ and Culture in the New Evangelization*. (Grand Rapid, Mich.: Action Institute, 2012).

— "The Synod's Interim Report: Ambiguity and Misinterpretation." *Crisis*

Magazine, 17 October 2014. https://www.crisismagazine.com/2014/synods-interim-report-ambiguity-misinterpretation.

— "Vatican II and the Religions," *Nova et Vetera* Vol. 13, No. 3 (2015): 837-73.

Eltz, Johannes zu. "Johannes zu Eltz on building bridges and celebrating the Eucharist with L.G.B.T. Catholics" Interview with Ulrich Sander, *America*, 10 October 2018. https://www.americamagazine.org/faith/2018/10/10/johannes-zu-eltz-building-bridges-and-celebrating-eucharist-lgbt-catholics.

Ernst, Harold E. "The Theological Notes and the Interpretation of Doctrine." *Theological Studies* 63 (2002): 813-25.

Faggioli, Massimo. "Ecumenism in Pope Francis," in *Pope Francis, Evangelii Gaudium and the Renewal of the Church*, edited by Duncan Dormor & Alana Harris (New York/Mahwah, NJ: Paulist Press, 2017), 161-89.

— *Pope Francis: Tradition in Transition*. (New York/Mahwah, NJ: Paulist Press, 2013).

— Farrow, Douglas. "The Conversion of the Papacy and the Present Church Crisis." *The Catholic World Report*, 10 November 2018. https://www.catholicworldreport.com/2018/11/10/the-conversion-of-the-papacy-and-the-present-church-crisis/?fbclid=IwAR1Wib4Aswlk2Msymo6gmqyKl5hfIZuS_IHkJQc6vCBtRcEQKRzJk4tFUaM.

Fastiggi, Robert; and Dawn Eden Goldstein, "Does Amoris Laetitia 303 Really Undermine Catholic Moral Teaching?" *Vatican Insider*, 26 September 2017. http://www.lastampa.it/2017/09/26/vaticaninsider/eng/documents/doesamoris-laetitia-really-undermine-catholic-moral-teaching-yom5rmEIfGPzsMDlS7o6eP/pagina.html.

Feichtinger, Msgr. Hans. "German Bishops Use Abuse Crisis to Promote Dissent." *Crisis Magazine*, 19 March 2019. https://www.crisismagazine.com/2019/german-bishops-use-abuse-crisis-to-promote-dissent.

Fernández, Víctor Manuel. "El capítulo VIII de Amoris Laetitia: lo que queda después de la tormenta," 449-68. http://documental.celam.org/medellin/index.php/medellin/article/viewFile/182/182.

Finnis, John and Germain Grisez. "The Misuse of Amoris Laetitia to Support Errors Against the Catholic Faith." (Notre Dame, Ind.: Online, 21 November 2016). http://www.twotlj.org/OW-MisuseAL.pdf.

Finnis, John. "Personal Integrity, Sexual Morality and Responsible Parenthood," in *Why Humanae Vitae was Right: A Reader*. Janet Smith ed. (San Francisco: Ignatius Press, 1993), 171-92.

Flynn, Gabriel. "A Renaissance in Twentieth-Century Catholic Theology." *Irish Theological Quarterly* 76 (2011): 323-38.

Forell, George Wolfgang. *History of Christian Ethics*, Vol. I: From the New Testament to Augustine. (Augsburg Pub. House, 1979).

Flannery SJ, Kevin L.; and Thomas V. Berg. "*Amoris Laetitia*, Pastoral Discernment, and Thomas Aquinas," in *Nova et Vetera*, Vol. 16, No. 1 [2018]: 81-111.

Francis, Pope. *A Big Heart Open to God: A Conversation with Pope Francis*.

(New York: HarperOne, 2013).
— "A Church of 'yes.'" morning meditation. 2 May 2013. http://w2.vatican.va/content/francesco/en/cotidie/2013/documents/papa-francesco-cotidie_20130502_church-of-yes.html.
— "Address at the Divine Liturgy, Patriarchal Church of St. George in Istanbul." 30 November 2014. http://w2.vatican.va/content/francesco/en/homilies/2014/documents/papa-francesco_20141130_divina-liturgia-turchia.html.
— "Address in Meetings with the Bishops of Asia, Shrine of Haemi." 17 August 2014. http://w2.vatican.va/content/francesco/en/speeches/2014/august/documents/papa-francesco_20140817_corea-vescovi-asia.html.
— "Address of His Holiness Pope Francis to a Delegation of the Evangelical Lutheran Church of Germany." 18 December 2014. http://w2.vatican.va/content/francesco/en/speeches/2014/december/documents/papa-francesco_20141218_chiesa-evangelica-luterana.html.
— "Address of His Holiness Pope Francis to Participants in the Course on the Marriage Process," 25 February 2018. http://w2.vatican.va/content/francesco/en/speeches/2017/february/documents/papa-francesco_20170225_corso-processo-matrimoniale.html.
— "Address of His Holiness Pope Francis to Participants in the Commemorative Conference of the Italian Catholic Physicians' Association on the Occasion of Its 70th Anniversary of Foundation." 15 November 2014. http://w2.vatican.va/content/francesco/en/speeches/2014/november/documents/papa-francesco_20141115_medici-cattolici-italiani.html.
— "Address of His Holiness Pope Francis to Participants in the General Assembly of the Pontifical Academy for Life." 5 October 2017. http://w2.vatican.va/content/francesco/en/speeches/2017/october/documents/papa-francesco_20171005_assemblea-pav.html.
— "Address of His Holiness Pope Francis to Participants in the Meeting Promoted by the Pontifical Council for Promoting the New Evangelization." 11 October 2017. http://w2.vatican.va/content/francesco/en/speeches/2017/october/documents/papa-francesco_20171011_convegno-nuova-evangelizzazione.html.
— "Address of His Holiness Pope Francis to Participants in the Plenary Assembly of the Pontifical Academy for Life." 3 March 2016. http://w2.vatican.va/content/francesco/en/speeches/2016/march/documents/papa-francesco_20160303_plenaria-accademia-vita.html.
— "Address of His Holiness Pope Francis to Participants in the Plenary Assembly of the Pontifical Academy for Life." 25 June 2018. http://w2.vatican.va/content/francesco/en/speeches/2018/june/documents/papa-francesco_20180625_accademia-provita.html.
— "Address of His Holiness Pope Francis to Representatives of Different Religions." 3 November 2016. http://w2.vatican.va/content/francesco/en/speeches/2016/november/documents/papa-francesco_20161103_udienza-interreligiosa.html..

— "Address of His Holiness Pope Francis to the Members of the Diplomatic Corps Accredited to the Holy See." 13 January 2014. http://w2.vatican.va/content/francesco/en/speeches/2014/january/documents/papa-francesco_20140113_corpo-diplomatico.html.

— "Address of Holy Father Francis to Participants in the Meeting Organized by the International Federation of Catholic Medical Associations." 20 September 2013. http://w2.vatican.va/content/francesco/en/speeches/2013/september/documents/papa-francesco_20130920_associazioni-medici-cattolici.html.

— "Address of the Holy Father, Meeting with the Participants in the Fifth Convention of the Italian Church." Cathedral of Santa Maria del Fiore, Florence. 10 November 2015. http://w2.vatican.va/content/francesco/en/speeches/2015/november/documents/papa-francesco_20151110_firenze-convegno-chiesa-italiana.html.

— "Address of Pope Francis to a Delegation from the Dignitatis Humanae Institute." 7 December 2013. http://w2.vatican.va/content/francesco/en/speeches/2013/december/documents/papa-francesco_20131207_istituto-dignitatis.html.

— "Address of Pope Francis to the Community of the Pontifical Gregorian University, together with Members of the Pontifical Biblical Institute and the Pontifical Oriental Institute." 10 April 2014. http://w2.vatican.va/content/francesco/en/speeches/2014/april/documents/papa-francesco_20140410_universita-consortium-gregorianum.html.

— "Address on the Feast of St. Stephen." St. Peter's Square. 26 December 2014. https://zenit.org/articles/on-the-feast-of-st-stephen--3/.

— "Address to the Community of Varginha." World Youth Day, Rio de Janeiro, 25 July 2013. http://w2.vatican.va/content/francesco/en/speeches/2013/july/documents/papa-francesco_20130725_gmg-comunita-varginha.html.

— "Address to the European Parliament." *Catholic Herald*, 25 November 2014. https://catholicherald.co.uk/news/2014/11/25/pope-franciss-address-to-the-european-parliament-in-full/.

— "Address to the Leadership of the Episcopal Conferences of Latin America." 28 July 2013. https://w2.vatican.va/content/francesco/en/speeches/2013/july/documents/papa-francesco_20130728_gmg-celam-rio.html.

— "Address to the Participants in the Plenary Assembly of the Pontifical Council for Interreligious Dialogue." Clementine Hall, 28 November 2013. http://w2.vatican.va/content/francesco/en/speeches/2013/november/documents/papa-francesco_20131128_pc-dialogo-interreligioso.html.

— "Address to the Plenary Assembly of the Pontifical Council for Culture." 7 February 2015. http://w2.vatican.va/content/francesco/en/speeches/2015/february/documents/papa-francesco_20150207_pontificio-consiglio-cultura.html.

— "Address of the Holy Father Pope Francis to Representatives of the

Churches and Ecclesial Communities and of the Different Religions." 20 March 2013. http://w2.vatican.va/content/francesco/en/speeches/2013/march/documents/papa-francesco_20130320_delegati-fraterni.html.

— "Address to the Plenary Session of the Congregation for the Doctrine of the Faith." 31 January 2014. http://www.catholicculture.org/culture/library/view.cfm?recnum=10439.

— *Amoris Laetitia* (*On Love in the Family*). post-synodal apostolic exhortation, 19 March 2016. http://w2.vatican.va/content/dam/francesco/pdf/apost_exhortations/documents/papa-francesco_esortazione-ap_20160319_amoris-laetitia_en.pdf.

— "An Infinite Horizon." morning meditation, 23 October 2014. http://w2.vatican.va/content/francesco/en/cotidie/2014/documents/papa-francesco-cotidie_20141023_an-infinite-horizon.html.

— "Carta del Papa Francisco a la 105° AP de la CEA." Vatican, 25 March 2013. http://www.celam.org/carta-del-papa-francisco-a-la-105o-ap-de-la-cea-667.html.

— Christus Vivit. Post-Synodal Apostolic Exhortation, 25 March 2019. http://w2.vatican.va/content/francesco/en/apost_exhortations/documents/papa-francesco_esortazione-ap_20190325_christus-vivit.html.

— "Concluding Address of the Fourteenth Ordinary General Assembly of the Synod of Bishops." 24 October 2015. Published in L'Osservatore Romano, 26-27 October 2015, 13. Online: http://w2.vatican.va/content/francesco/en/speeches/2015/october/documents/papa-francesco_20151024_sinodo-conclusione-lavori.html.

— "Discorso del Santo Padre Francesco Alla Comunità Accademica del Pontificio Istituto 'Giovanni Paolo II' Per Studi su Matrimonio E Famiglia," 26 October 2016. http://w2.vatican.va/content/francesco/it/speeches/2016/october/documents/papa-francesco_20161027_pontificio-istituto-gpii.html.

— "Doctrine and Ideology," 19 May 2017. Published in *L'Osservatore Romano*, n. 23, 9 June 2017. Online: http://w2.vatican.va/content/francesco/en/cotidie/2017/documents/papa-francesco-cotidie_20170519_doctrine-and-ideology.html.

— *Encountering Christ: Homilies, Letters, and Addresses of Cardinal Jorge Bergoglio*. (New Rochelle, NY: Scepter Publishers, 2013).

— *Evangelii Gaudium* (*The Joy of the Gospel*). apostolic exhortation, 24 November 2013. http://w2.vatican.va/content/francesco/en/apost_exhortations/documents/papa-francesco_esortazione-ap_20131124_evangelii-gaudium.html.

— *Gaudete et Exsultate* (*On the Call to Holiness in Today's World*). 19 March 2018. http://w2.vatican.va/content/francesco/en/apost_exhortations/documents/papa-francesco_esortazione-ap_20180319_gaudete-et-exsultate.html.

— "General Audience." St. Peter's Square, 2 April 2014. http://w2.vatican.

va/content/francesco/en/audiences/2014/documents/papa-francesco_20140402_udienza-generale.html.

— "General Audience, Wednesday of Holy Week, St. Peter's Square." 27 March 2013, in New Beginning, New Hope (Huntington, IN: Our Sunday Visitor, 2014), 15-20.

— *God is Young, A Conversation with Thomas Leoncini*. trans. Anne Milano Appel (New York: Random House, 2018).

— "Greeting of His Holiness Pope Francis to a Delegation of the Old Catholic Bishops' Conference of the Union of Utrecht." 30 October 2014. http://w2.vatican.va/content/francesco/en/speeches/2014/october/documents/papa-francesco_20141030_vescovi-veterocattolici.html.

— "Homily of His Holiness Pope Francis, Holy Chrism Mass." 29 March 2018. http://w2.vatican.va/content/francesco/en/homilies/2018/documents/papa-francesco_20180329_omelia-crisma.html.

— "Homily of Pope Francis at the Celebration of Vespers on the Solemnity of the Conversion of St. Paul the Apostle." 25 January 2014. http://w2.vatican.va/content/francesco/en/homilies/2014/documents/papa-francesco_20140125_vespri-conversione-san-paolo.html.

— "Homily of Pope Francis at the Celebration of Vespers on the Solemnity of the Conversion of St. Paul the Apostle." 25 January 2015. https://w2.vatican.va/content/francesco/en/homilies/2015/documents/papa-francesco_20150125_vespri-conversione-san-paolo.html.

— "Homily at Holy Mass for Peace and Reconciliation." Cathedral of Myeong-dong (Seoul) 18 August 2014. http://w2.vatican.va/content/francesco/en/homilies/2014/documents/papa-francesco_20140818_corea-omelia-pace-riconciliazione.html.

— "Homily at the Final Mass of the Synod." 28 October 2018. https://www.vaticannews.va/en/pope/news/2018-10/synod-youth-2018-final-mass-pope-francis-homily.html.

— "Homily on Apostolic Journey of His Holiness Pope Francis to Turkey." 29 November 2014. https://w2.vatican.va/content/francesco/en/homilies/2014/documents/papa-francesco_20141129_omelia-turchia.html.

— "'I believe the Lord wants a change in the Church': A private dialogue with the Jesuits in the Baltics." *La Civiltà Cattolica*, 17 October 2018. https://laciviltacattolica.com/i-believe-the-lord-wants-a-change-in-the-church-a-private-dialogue-with-the-jesuits-in-the-baltics/.

— *In Him Alone is Our Hope, The Heart of the Church according to Pope Francis*, Translated by Vincent Capuano, S.J., and Andrew Matt (New York: Magnificat, 2013).

— *Laudato Si'* (*On Care for Our Common Home*). encyclical, 24 May 2015. http://w2.vatican.va/content/francesco/en/encyclicals/documents/papa-francesco_20150524_enciclica-laudato-si.html.

— "Letter of His Holiness Pope Francis to Participants in the Plenary Assembly of the Pontifical Council for Promoting Christian Unity for the 50th Anniversary of the Decree 'Unitatis Redintegratio.'" 20 November 2014. http://w2.vatican.va/content/francesco/en/letters/2014/documents/papa-francesco_20141120_lettera-plenaria-unita-cristiani.html.

— "Letter of His Holiness Pope Francis to the People of God." Press Herald, 20 August 2018. https://www.pressherald.com/2018/08/20/read-the-letter-from-pope-francis-to-catholics-around-the-world/.

— "Letter to a Non-Believer." 4 September 2013. http://w2.vatican.va/content/francesco/en/letters/2013/documents/papa-francesco_20130911_eugenio-scalfari.html.

— "Letter to Cardinal Brandmüller." 19 November 2013. http://w2.vatican.va/content/francesco/la/letters/2013/documents/papa-francesco_20131119_brandmuller-450-chiusura-concilio-trento.html.

— *Lumen Fidei* (*The Light of Faith*). Encyclical, 29 June, 2013. http://w2.vatican.va/content/francesco/en/encyclicals/documents/papa-francesco_20130629_enciclica-lumen-fidei.html.

— "Meeting with the Young People of Umbria." 4 October 2013. http://w2.vatican.va/content/francesco/en/speeches/2013/october/documents/papa-francesco_20131004_giovani-assisi.html.

— "Message of His Holiness Pope Francis for the Thirty First World Youth Day 2016." 15 August 2015; as reported at Ignatian Solidarity Network: https://ignatiansolidarity.net/blog/2016/08/01/pope-francis-justice-mercy-must-go-together/.

— "Message of His Holiness Pope Francis to Mark the Opening of the Interreligious Meeting of Prayer For Peace "Bridges of Peace." 11 October 2018. http://w2.vatican.va/content/francesco/en/messages/pont-messages/2018/documents/papa-francesco_20181011_messaggio-incontropreghiera-bologna.html.

— "Message of Pope Francis for the 48th World Communications Day." 1 June 2014. http://w2.vatican.va/content/francesco/en/messages/communications/documents/papa-francesco_20140124_messaggio-comunicazioni-sociali.html.

— *Misericordiae Vultus* (*Bull of Indiction of the Extraordinary Jubilee of Mercy*). 11 April 2015. https://w2.vatican.va/content/francesco/en/apost_letters/documents/papa-francesco_bolla_20150411_misericordiae-vultus.html.

— *New Beginning, New Hope*. (Huntington, Ind.: Our Sunday Visitor, 2014).

— "On divorce/remarriage, Pope says keep justice and mercy together." homily at Santa Marta residence, 23 February 2017, as quoted online in *Crux*. https://cruxnow.com/vatican/2017/02/24/divorceremarriage-pope-says-keep-justice-mercy-together/.

— *Only Love Can Save Us: Letters, Homilies, and Talks of Cardinal Jorge Bergoglio*. (Our Sunday Visitor, Inc., 2013).

— *Open Mind, Faithful Heart*. Translated by Joseph V. Owens, S.J. (New York: Herder & Herder Book, 2013).

— *Our Father: Reflections on the Lord's Prayer*. (New York: Random House, 2017).

— "Playing with life is a sin against God." *Vatican Insider, La Stampa,* 15 November 2014. http://vaticaninsider.lastampa.it/en/the-vatican/detail/articolo/eutanasiaeuthanasiaeutanasia-medici-doctors-medico-37516/.
— "Pope at General Audience: 'Commandments are path to freedom.'" *Vatican News,* 20 June 2018. https://www.vaticannews.va/en/pope/news/2018-06/pope-general-audience-commandments-freedom.html.
— "Pope at Mass: Be careful around rigid Christians." Homily at Casa Santa Marta. *Vatican News,* 16 October 2018. https://www.vaticannews.va/en/pope-francis/mass-casa-santa-marta/2018-10/pope-francis-homily-daily-mass-be-careful-rigid-christians.html.
— "Pope at Mass: Gospel newness does not permit a double life." *Vatican News,* 10 September 2018. https://www.vaticannews.va/en/pope-francis/mass-casa-santa-marta/2018-09/pope-francis-homily-daily-mass-newness-gospel.html.
— "Pope at Mass: Love and justice are more important than attachment to the laws." *Vatican News,* 31 October 2014. http://www.catholiccincinnati.org/wp-content/uploads/2014/11/Pope-Francis.pdf.
— "Pope Calls for a 'Listening Church.'" *America,* 17 October 2015. https://www.americamagazine.org/content/all-things/pope-calls-listening-church.
— "Pope Continues Teachings on Ten Commandments." trans. Virginia Forrester, *Zenit*. 21 November 2018. https://zenit.org/articles/general-audience-pope-continues-teachings-on-ten-commandments/.
— "Pope Francis' Address to the Italian Association of Large Families." *Zenit,* 28 December 2014. http://www.zenit.org/en/articles/pope-francis-address-to-the-italian-association-of-large-families.
— "Pope Francis's Address to the Synod Fathers." *Vatican News,* 18 October 2014. http://w2.vatican.va/content/francesco/en/speeches/2014/october/documents/papa-francesco_20141018_conclusione-sinodo-dei-vescovi.html.
— "Pope Francis's Opening Address to Humanum Conference." *Catholic Herald,* 17 November 2014. http://www.catholicherald.co.uk/news/2014/11/17/full-text-pope-franciss-opening-address-to-humanum-conference/.
— "Pope Francis Message for World Mission Day 2018." *Zenit,* 21 October 2018. https://zenit.org/articles/pope-francis-message-for-world-mission-day-2018/.
— "Pope Supports 'Hermeneutic of Continuity' Approach to Vatican II in Letter." *Zenit,* 15 November 2013. https://zenit.org/articles/pope-supports-hermeneutic-of-continuity-approach-to-vatican-ii-in-letter/.
— "Pope Francis warns against those who judge [according to the Law] with closed hearts." https://ln54.blogspot.com/2016/04/pope-francis-warns-against-those-who.html.
— "Pope Tells Tribunal: Do Not Ensnare Salvation in the Constrictions of

Legalism." 24 January 2015. http://www.indcatholicnews.com/news.php?viewStory=26553.

— "Pope's Address at Interreligious Meeting in Colombo, Sri Lanka." *Zenit*, 13 January 2015. https://zenit.org/articles/pope-s-address-at-interreligious-meeting-in-colombo-sri-lanka/.

— "Pope's Address to Pentecostal Community in Caserta" *Call Me Jorge*, 28 July 2014. http://callmejorgebergoglio.blogspot.com/2014/07/francis-remarks-to-evangelicals-in.html.

— "Pope's Address to Plenary Assembly of the Pontifical Council for Interreligious Dialogue." *Zenit*, 28 November 2013. https://zenit.org/articles/pope-s-address-to-plenary-assembly-of-the-pontifical-council-for-interreligious-dialogue/.

— "Pope's Homily at Vespers on Eve of New Year [2015]." *Zenit*, 31 December 2014. http://www.zenit.org/en/articles/pope-s-homily-at-vespers-on-eve-of-new-year.

— "Pope's Morning Homily: While True Doctrine Unites, Ideology Divides." *Zenit*, 19 May 2017. https://zenit.org/articles/popes-morning-homily-while-true-doctrine-unites-ideology-divides/.

— "Preface for Stephen Walford, *Pope Francis, The Family and Divorce,*" [New York/Mahwah, NJ: Paulist Press, 2018]. *Vatican Insider*, 21 August 2018. http://www.lastampa.it/2018/08/21/vaticaninsider/amoris-laetitia-the-magisterial-hermeneutic-of-the-church-always-in-continuity-without-ruptures-yet-always-maturing-aId8FKxysgePZgiBbUMMbM/pagina.html. Also at *Crux*, 21 August 2018. https://cruxnow.com/vatican/2018/08/21/pope-no-rupture-in-amoris-which-is-rooted-in-classical-doctrine-of-aquinas/.

— "Santa Marta: Love with Small Gestures." *Zenit*, 20 September 2018. https://zenit.org/articles/santa-marta-love-with-small-gestures/.

— "Synod18 – Documento finale e Votazioni del Documento finale del Sinodo dei Vescovi al Santo Padre Francesco," 27 October 2018. http://press.vatican.va/content/salastampa/it/bollettino/pubblico/2018/10/27/0789/01722.html.

— "The Church a unity of diversities, Pope tells Brazil's bishops." *Catholic News Agency*, 27 July 2013. https://www.catholicnewsagency.com/news/the-church-a-unity-of-diversities-pope-tells-brazils-bishops.

— *The Church of Mercy*. (Chicago: Loyola Press, 2014).

— "The God of Surprises." morning meditation, *Vatican News*, 13 October 2014. http://w2.vatican.va/content/francesco/en/cotidie/2014/documents/papa-francesco-cotidie_20141013_the-god-of-surprises.html.

— *The Name of God is Mercy*. trans. Oonagh Stransky. (New York: Random House, 2016).

— *The People Wish to See Jesus: Reflections for Those Who Teach*. Translated by Michael O'Hearn (New York: Herder & Herder Book, 2014).

— "The Pope says that 'quality of life' is a lie." *Vatican Insider, La Stampa*, 30 December 2014. http://vaticaninsider.lastampa.it/en/the-vatican/detail/articolo/francesco-francis-francisco-malato-sick-enfermo-38307/.

— *Urbi et Orbi Message, Christmas 2014*. 25 December 2014. https://w2.vatican.va/content/francesco/en/messages/urbi/documents/papa-francesco_20141225_urbi-et-orbi-natale.html.

— *Veritatis Gaudium*, Apostolic Constitution. 8 December 2017. http://w2.vatican.va/content/francesco/en/apost_constitutions/documents/papa-francesco_costituzione-ap_20171208_veritatis-gaudium.html.

— "Video Message of His Holiness Pope Francis to Participants in an International Theological Congress Held at the Pontifical Catholic University of Argentina, Buenos Aires." 1-3 September 2015. https://w2.vatican.va/content/francesco/en/messages/pont-messages/2015/documents/papa-francesco_20150903_videomessaggio-teologia-buenos-aires.html.

— Video of 6 January 2016. https://www.youtube.com/watch?v=07dPzM5q43c.

Francis, Pope; with Antonio Spadaro SJ, *Open to God, Open to the World*. Translation by Shaun Whiteside. (New York: Bloomsbury Continuum, 2018).

Francis, Pope; with Dominique Wolton. *A Future of Faith: The Path of Change in Politics and Society*. Translation by Shaun Whiteside. (New York: St. Martin's Press, 2018).

Fromm, Erich. *The Art of Loving*, Introduction by Peter D. Kramer, 50th Anniversary Edition (New York: Harper, 2006 [1956]).

Frossard, André; and John Paul II, *"Be Not Afraid," Pope John Paul II Speaks Out on his Life, his Beliefs, and his Inspiring Vision for Humanity*, trans. J.R. Foster (New York: St. Martin's Press, 1984).

Gaffin Jr., Richard B. *Redemptive History and Biblical Interpretation: The Shorter Writings of Geerhardus Vos*. (Phillipsburg, N.J.: Presbyterian and Reformed, 1980), 3–24.

Gagnon, Robert A.J. "Are There Universally Valid Sex Precepts? A Critique of Walter Wink's View on the Bible and Homosexuality," *Horizons in Biblical Theology* 24 (2002): 72-125.

Gagnon, Robert A.J., and Dan O. Via. *Homosexuality and the Bible*. (Minneapolis: Fortress Press, 2003).

Gaillardetz, Richard R. *An Unfinished Council, Vatican II, Pope Francis, and the Renewal of Catholicism*. (Collegeville, Minn.: Liturgical Press, 2015).

— "The 'Francis Moment': A New Kairos for Catholic Ecclesiology," *CTSA Proceedings* 60 (2014): 63-80.

— "Francis wishes to release Vatican II's bold vision from Captivity." *National Catholic Reporter*, 25 September 2013.

Gallicho, Grant; and James F. Keenan SJ, eds. *Amoris Laetitia, A New Momentum for Moral Formation and Pastoral Practice*. (New York, Mahwah, NJ: Paulist Press, 2018), 115-21.

George Robert; and Patrick Lee. *Conjugal Union, What Marriage is and Why it Matters*. (New York: Cambridge University Press, 2014).

Giddens, Anthony. *The Transformation of Intimacy, Sexuality, Love & Eroticism in Modern Societies* (Stanford, CA: Stanford University Press, 1992).

Gilson, Etienne. *Christianity and Philosophy*. Translated by Ralph MacDonald. (Sheed & Ward, 1939 [1931]).

Girgis, Sherif; and Ryan T. Anderson and Robert P. George. *What is Marriage? Man and Woman, A Defense* (New York: Encounter Books, 2012).

Glatz, Carol "'Amoris Laetitia' is built on traditional Thomist morality, pope says." *Crux*, 28 September 2017. https://cruxnow.com/cns/2017/09/28/amoris-laetitia-built-traditional-thomist-morality-pope-says/.

— "God's wrath is just as great as his mercy, Pope warns." *Catholic Herald*, 28 February 2019. https://catholicherald.co.uk/news/2019/02/28/gods-wrath-is-just-as-great-as-his-mercy-pope-warns/.

Griffiths, Paul J. *An Apology for Apologetics: A Study in the Logic of Interreligious Dialogue* (Maryknoll, NY: Orbis Books, 1991).

— "On Dominus Iesus, Complementarity Can Be Claimed," in Learning from Other Faiths, edited by Hermann Häring, et al., Concilium (London: SCM Press, 2003/4), 22-24.

— "Review Symposium," *Horizons* Vol. 36, No. 1, Spring 2009: 121-42.

— "Why We Need Interreligious Polemics," *First Things*, June 1994. Online: http://www.firstthings.com/article/1994/06/why-we-needinterreligious-polemics.

Grisez, Germain. *The Way of the Lord Jesus*, Vol. 1, Christian Moral Principles. (Chicago, Ill.: Franciscan Herald Press, 1983). Online: http://www.twotlj.org/G-1-V-1.html.

Grossouw, William. *Revelation and Redemption, An Introduction to the Theology of St. John*, Translated and edited by Rev. Martin W. Schoenberg, O.S.C. (London: Geoffrey Chapman, 1965).

Guardini, Romano. *Vom Sinn der Kirche* (Mainz: Matthias Grünewalk Verlag, 1922). Translated by Ada Lane as *The Church and the Catholic*. (New York: Sheed & Ward, Inc., 1935).

Guarino, Thomas G. "Pope Francis Looks to St. Vincent of Lérins." *First Things*, 24 September 2013. http://www.firstthings.com/web-exclusives/2013/09/pope-francis-looks-to-st-vincent-of-lerins.

— *Revelation and Truth, Unity and Plurality in Contemporary Theology* (Scranton, Penn.: University of Scranton Press, 1993).

— *The Disputed Teachings of Vatican II: Continuity and Reversal in Catholic Doctrine*. (Grand Rapids, MI: Eerdmans, 2018).

— *Vincent of Lérins and the Development of Christian Doctrine*. (Grand Rapids, Mich.: Baker Academic, 2013).

Guiness, Os. *Time for Truth: Living Free in a World of Lies, Hype, & Spin*. (Baker Books, 2000).

Gunton, Colin E. *A Brief Theology of Revelation: The 1993 Warfield Lectures* (Edinburgh: T&T Clark, 1995).

Gutiérrez, Gustavo. *A Theology of Liberation*. 15th Edition, trans. Matthew J. O'Connell (Maryknoll, NY: Orbis Books, 1988 [1971]).

Harris, Elise. "'Conversion is a prerequisite to ecumenism', Pope Francis says." *Catholic News Agency*, 19 January 2017. https://www.catholicnewsagency.com/news/conversion-is-a-prerequisite-to-ecumenism-pope-francis-says-84165.

— "Pope Francis declares Holy Year for Mercy" *Catholic News Agency*, 13 March 2015. http://www.catholicnewsagency.com/news/pope-francis-declares-2016-to-be-a-jubilee-for-mercy-84325/.

— "'What is being proposed is not marriage'—Pope calls for defense of family." *Catholic News Agency*, 26 October 2014. http://www.catholicnewsagency.com/news/what-is-being-proposed-is-not-marriage-pope-calls-for-defense-of-family-12766/.

Heinbeck, Raeburne S. *Theology and Meaning, Critique of Metatheological Scepticism*. (London: George Allen and Unwin Ltd, 1969).

Helm, Paul. *Faith, Form, and Fashion, Classical Reformed Theology and its Postmodern Critics* (Eugene, Ore.: Cascade Books, 2014).

Henn O.F.M. Cap., William. "The Church," Lecture, 7 November 2014. http://www.oecumene.nl/files/Books/Overig/ALV_2014_Lecture_William_Henn/files/assets/common/downloads/Lecture_The_Church_by_William_Henn.pdf.

— "The Hierarchy of Truths," in *Dictionary of Fundamental Theology*, Edited by Rene Latourelle and Rino Fisichella, English-language edition edited by Rene Latourelle (New York: Crossroad, 1994), 425–27.

— "The Hierarchy of Truths Twenty Years Later," *Theological Studies* 48 (1987), 439–71.

Heneghan, Tom. "German bishops grapple with blessings for gay marriage." *America*, 24 January 2018. https://www.americamagazine.org/faith/2018/01/24/german-bishops-grapple-blessings-gay-marriage.

Hitchens, Dan. "Against Inevitable Adultery," *First Things*, 6 November 2018. https://www.firstthings.com/web-exclusives/2018/11/against-inevitable-adultery.

Holwerda, David E. "Jesus and the Law: A Question of Fulfillment," Chapter 5 in *Jesus and Israel, One or Two Covenants?* (Grand Rapids, Mich.: Eerdmans, 1995) 122-45.

Horton, Michael. *Christian Faith, A Systematic Theology for Pilgrims on the Way*. (Grand Rapids, MI: Zondervan, 2011).

— *Christless Christianity, The Alternative Gospel of the American Church*. (Grand Rapids, Mich.: Baker Books, 2008).

Huizenga, Leroy. "Abusing Zacchaeus." *Catholic World Report*, 30 August 2018. https://www.catholicworldreport.com/2018/08/30/abusing-zacchaeus/.

International Christian Network. "Current Threats to Human Creatureliness and Their Overcoming: Life According to the Creator's Will" (Salzburg Declaration). 6 September 2015. https://www.ikbg.net/pdf/Salzburger-Erklaerung-englisch.pdf.

International Theological Commission. *Christianity and the World Religions*. 1997. http://www.vatican.va/roman_curia/congregations/cfaith/cti_documents/rc_cti_1997_cristianesimo-religioni_en.html.

— *The Interpretation of Dogma*, 1989. http://www.vatican.va/roman_curia/congregations/cfaith/cti_documents/rc_cti_1989_interpretazionedogmi_en.html.

— *Sensus Fidei in the Life of the Church*. 10 June 2014. http://www.vatican.va/roman_curia/congregations/cfaith/cti_documents/rc_cti_20140610_sensus-fidei_en.html.

— "Synodality in the Life and Mission of the Church." 2 March 2018. http://www.vatican.va/roman_curia/congregations/cfaith/cti_documents/rc_cti_20180302_sinodalita_en.html.

— *Theology Today: Perspectives, Principles, and Criteria*. 29 November 2011. http://www.vatican.va/roman_curia/congregations/cfaith/cti_documents/rc_cti_doc_20111129_teologia-oggi_en.html.

Ivereigh, Austin. "Papal confidante says 'Amoris' critics locked in 'death-trap' logic," *Crux*, 21 August 2017. https://cruxnow.com/vatican/2017/08/21/papal-confidante-says-amoris-critics-locked-death-trap-logic/.

John Paul II, Pope. "Address of John Paul II to the Representatives of the Christian Churches and Ecclesial Communities Gathered in Assisi for the World Day of Prayer," 27 October 1986. https://w2.vatican.va/content/john-paul-ii/en/speeches/1986/october/documents/hf_jp-ii_spe_19861027_prayer-peace-assisi.html.

— *Dives in Misericordia* (*Rich in Mercy*). encyclical, 30 November 1980. http://w2.vatican.va/content/john-paul-ii/en/encyclicals/documents/hf_jp-ii_enc_30111980_dives-in-misericordia.html.

— *Centesimus Annus* (*On the Hundredth Anniversary of Rerum Novarum*). encyclical, 1 May 1991. http://w2.vatican.va/content/john-paul-ii/en/encyclicals/documents/hf_jp-ii_enc_01051991_centesimus-annus.html.

— "Discorso Di Giovanni Paolo II Ai Partecipanti Al Congresso Internazionale Di Teologia Morale." 10 April 1986. http://w2.vatican.va/content/john-paul-ii/it/speeches/1986/april/documents/hf_jp-ii_spe_19860410_teologia-morale.html.

— *Evangelium Vitae* (*On the Value and Inviolability of Human Life*). 25 March 1995. http://w2.vatican.va/content/john-paul-ii/en/encyclicals/documents/hf_jp-ii_enc_25031995_evangelium-vitae.html.

— *Familiaris consortio* (*On the Role of the Christian Family in the Modern World*) apostolic exhortation, 22 November 1981. http://w2.vatican.va/content/john-paul-ii/en/apost_exhortations/documents/hf_jp-ii_exh_19811122_familiaris-consortio.html.

— *Fides et ratio* (*On the Relationship Between Faith and Reason*). encyclical, 14 September 1998. http://w2.vatican.va/content/john-paul-ii/en/encyclicals/documents/hf_jp-ii_enc_14091998_fides-et-ratio.html.

— "Homily at the Close of the Fifth Synod of Bishops." 25 October 1980. https://w2.vatican.va/content/john-paul-ii/es/homilies/1980/documents/hf_jp-ii_hom_19801025_conclusione-sinodo.html. The homily is not available in English.

— *Man and Woman He Created Them: A Theology of the Body*, Translated by Michael Waldstein (Boston: Pauline, 2006 [1986]). Dutch translation: *Theologie van het Lichaam* ('s-Hertogenbosch: Betsaida Publishers,

2016).
— "Method and Doctrine of St. Thomas in Dialogue with Modern Culture," in *The Whole Truth about Man*, ed. with an intro. by James V. Schall, S.J. (Boston: Daughters of St. Paul, 1981).
— *Novo Millennio Ineunte* (*At the Close of the Great Jubilee of the Year 2000*). 6 January 2001. http://w2.vatican.va/content/john-paul-ii/en/apost_letters/2001/documents/hf_jp-ii_apl_20010106_novo-millennio-ineunte.html.
— *Person and Community, Selected Essays*, Translated by Theresa Sandok (New York: Lang, 1993).
— "Pope's Christmas Address To Roman Curia." 22 December 1986. http://www.ewtn.com/library/PAPALDOC/JP2XMSCU.htm.
— *Reconciliatio et Paenitentia* (*On Reconciliation and Penance in the Mission of the Church Today*). 2 December 1984. http://w2.vatican.va/content/john-paul-ii/en/apost_exhortations/documents/hf_jp-ii_exh_02121984_reconciliatio-et-paenitentia.html.
— *Redemptoris Missio*. encyclical. 7 December 1990. https://w2.vatican.va/content/john-paul-ii/en/encyclicals/documents/hf_jp-ii_enc_07121990_redemptoris-missio.html.
— *Springtime of Evangelization, The Complete Texts of the Holy Father's 1998 Ad Limina to the Bishops of the United States*, ed. and intro. Fr. Thomas D. Williams, L.C. (San Francisco: Ignatius Press, 1999).
— "Subjectivity and the Irreducible in Man," in *Analecta Husserliana* VII, 107-14 (Dordrecht: D. Reidel, 1978).
— "To Representatives of the Various Religions of India," Madrus, 5 February 1986, Section 4, in *Interreligious Dialogue, The Official Teaching of the Catholic Church from the Second Vatican Council to John Paul II (1963-2005)*, Edited by Francesco Gioia (Boston: Pauline Books & Media, 2006).
— *Ut Unum Sint* (*On commitment to Ecumenism*). encyclical, 25 May 1995. http://w2.vatican.va/content/john-paul-ii/en/encyclicals/documents/hf_jp-ii_enc_25051995_ut-unum-sint.html.
— *Veritatis Splendor* (*The Splendor of Truth*). encyclical, 6 August 1993. http://w2.vatican.va/content/john-paul-ii/en/encyclicals/documents/hf_jp-ii_enc_06081993_veritatis-splendor.html.
John XXIII, Pope. "Pope John's Opening Speech to the Council." in The Documents of Vatican II, General Editor, Walter M. Abbott, S.J., New York: Guild Press, 1966), 710-19.
Kaiser Jr., Walter C. *Mission in the Old Testament: Israel as a Light to the Nations*. (Grand Rapids, Mich.: Baker Academic, 2000 [2012]).
Kasper, Walter Cardinal. *An Introduction to Christian Faith* (New York: Paulist Press, 1980).
— "The Decree on Ecumenism—Read Anew After Forty Years." http://www.vatican.va/roman_curia/pontifical_councils/chrstuni/card-kasper-docs/rc_pc_chrstuni_doc_20041111_kasper-ecumenism_en.html.
— "Ecumenismo, i passi di Papa Francesco," *Avvenire*, 2 July 2014. https://

www.avvenire.it/agora/pagine/ecumenismo.

— *Harvesting the Fruits, Basic Aspects of Christian Faith in Ecumenical Dialogue.* (London: Bloomsbury Academic, 2009).

— *Katholische Kirche: Wesen, Wirklichkeit, Sendung* (Freiburg: Herder, 2011), 225; ET: *The Catholic Church: Nature, Reality and Mission*, translated by Thomas Hoebel, edited by R. David Nelson (London/New York: Bloomsbury T&T Clark, 2015).

— *Mercy, The Essence of the Gospel and the Key to Christian Life.* (New York/ Mahwah, NJ: Paulist Press, 2013).

— *Pope Francis' Revolution of Tenderness and Love*, Translated by William Madges (New York/Mahwah, NJ: Paulist Press, 2015).

— *The Catholic Church: Nature, Reality, and Mission.* trans. Thomas Hoebel, ed. R. David Nelson. Bloomsbury T&T Clark, 2015.

— *The Christian Understanding of Freedom and the History of Freedom in the Modern Era.* 1988 Père Marquette Lecture in Theology (Milwaukee, Wis.: Marquette University Press, 1988).

— "The Church as the Place of Truth," in *Theology and Church.* Translated by Margaret Kohl. (New York: Crossroad, 1989), 129-145.

— "The Continuing Challenge of the Second Vatican Council: The Hermeneutics of the Conciliar Statements," in *Theology and Church*, Translated by Margaret Kohl. (New York: Crossroad, 1989), 166-76.

— "The Timeliness of Speaking of God: Freedom and Communion as Basic Concepts of Theology." *Worship*, Vol. 83, no. 4 [July 2009]: 293-311.

Kereszty, Roch A. *Jesus Christ, Fundamentals of Christology*, Revised and Updated Edition (Staten Island, NY: Alba House, 2002).

Knieps-Port Le Roi, Thomas. "Preserving and Perpetuating the Heritage of Pope John Paul II." in *Ephemerides Theologicae Lovanienses* 94/3 (2018) 505-514.

Knudsen, Robert. "May we use the Term 'Theonomy'?" in *Roots and Branches, The Quest for Meaning and Truth in Modern Thought.* Edited by Donald Knudsen, With an Introduction by William Edgar (Grand Rapids, Mich.: Paideia Press, 2009), 80-98.

Komonchak, Fr. Joseph A. "Dealing with Diversity and Disagreement, Vatican II and Beyond." *Annual Catholic Common Ground Initiative Lecture 2003.* https://jakomonchak.files.wordpress.com/2015/04/jak-diversity-and-disagreement1.pdf.

König, Franziskus Cardinal. "Dialogue with Nonbelievers," 28 August 1968. *L'Osservatore Romano*, weekly Edition in English, 10 October 1968, 6. https://www.ewtn.com/library/CURIA/PCIDNONB.htm.

Köstenberger, Andreas J.; and Peter T. O'Brien. *Salvation to the Ends of the Earth, A Biblical Theology of Mission.* (Downers Grove, Ill.: InterVarsity Press, 2001).

Küng, Hans. "Why are Dogmatic Pronouncements So Difficult to Make Today?" in *The Council in Action, Reflections on the Second Vatican Council*, trans. Cecily Hastings (New York: Sheed and Ward, 1962).

Kuyper, Abraham. *Gemene Gratie* ("Common Grace"). Volumes I, II, III.

(Amsterdam: Höveker & Wormser; 1902, 1903, and 1904).
— *Lectures on Calvinism.* (Grand Rapids, Mich.: Eerdmans, 1931).
— *Principles of Sacred Theology*. Translated by J. Hendrik De Vries, Introduction by B.B. Warfield. (New York: Charles Scribner's Sons, 1898). In the Dutch original this is a three-volume work. The English translation contains the first fifty-three pages of Vol. I of the original, and the entirety of Vol. II (*Encyclopaedie der Heilige Godgeleerdheid*. Tweede Deel. Kampen: J.H. Kok, 1909). Now, the entire three volumes are available in English translation by the Acton Institute, Grand Rapids, Mich.
Ladd, George Eldon. *A Theology of the New Testament*. (Grand Rapids, MI: Eerdmans, 1974).
Lane, Anthony. "The Wrath of God as an Aspect of the Love of God." in *Nothing Greater, Nothing Better: Theological Essays on the Love of God*. edited Kevin J. Vanhoozer (Grand Rapids, Mich.: Eerdmans, 2001), 138-67.
Lawler, Michael G. *What Is and What Ought to Be: The Dialectic of Experience, Theology, and Church* (New York: Continuum, 2005).
Lawler, Philip F. "Reverence for the Law," in *Lost Shepherd, How Pope Francis is Misleading His Flock* (Washington, D.C.: Regnery Gateway, 2018).
— *The Smoke of Satan* (Charlotte, N.C.: Tan Books, 2018).
Lee, Patrick; and Robert P. George."Sex and the Body," in *Body-Self Dualism in Contemporary Ethics and Politics*. (Cambridge University Press, 2009), 176-217.
Leo XIII. *Tametsi Futura Prospicientibus* (*On Jesus Christ the Redeemer*). Encyclical, 1 November 1900. http://w2.vatican.va/content/leo-xiii/en/encyclicals/documents/hf_l-xiii_enc_01111900_tametsi-futura-prospicientibus.html.
— *Testem benevolentiae Nostrae*. Encyclical, 22 January 1899. http://www.papalencyclicals.net/Leo13/l13teste.htm.
Léon-Dufour, Xavier (Edited under the Direction of). *Dictionary of Biblical Theology*, Updated Second Edition, trans. under the direction of P. Joseph Cahill, S.J. (Boston: St. Paul Books & Media, 1995 [1962]).
Levering, Matthew. *An Introduction to Vatican II as an Ongoing Theological Event*. (Washington, D.C.: The Catholic University of America Press, 2017).
— *Mary's Bodily Assumption*. (Notre Dame, Ind.: University of Notre Dame Press, 2014).
Livingston, James C.; and Francis S. Fiorenza, et al., *Modern Christian Thought, The Twentieth Century* (Minneapolis: Fortress Press, 2006).
Lonergan SJ, Bernard J.F. *Collected Works of Bernard Lonergan*, Vol. 7, *The Ontological and Psychological Constitution of Christ*, trans. Michael G. Shields (Toronto: University of Toronto Press, 2005).
— "The Dehellenization of Dogma." in *A Second Collection*, 11–32. Edited by William F.J. Ryan, S.J. and Bernard J. Tyrrell, S.J. (Philadelphia: The Westminster Press, 1974).
— *Doctrinal Pluralism*. 1971 Pere Marquette Theology Lecture. (Milwaukee: Marquette University Press, 1971).
— *Method in Theology*. (New York: Herder and Herder, 1972).

— "The Origins of Christian Realism (1961)," in *Collected Works of Bernard Lonergan, Philosophical and Theological Papers 1958-1964*, edited by R.C. Croken, et al. (Toronto: University of Toronto Press, 1996), 80-93.

— "Pope John's Intention."

— *The Way to Nicea*, Translated by Conn O'Donovan (Philadelphia: The Westminster Press, 1976 [1964]).

Longenecker, Dwight. "Does Cardinal Marx see a Way to Bless Gay Unions or Not?" *Fr. Dwight Longenecker*, 4 February 2018. https://dwightlongenecker.com/does-cardinal-marx-see-a-way-to-bless-gay-unions-or-not/.

Loyola, St. Ignatius of. *The Spiritual Exercises of St. Ignatius Loyola*, Translated by Louis J. Puhl (Chicago: Loyola University Press, 1951).

Lutheran World Federation and the Catholic Church. *Joint Declaration on the Doctrine of Justification*. 31 October 1999. http://www.vatican.va/roman_curia/pontifical_councils/chrstuni/documents/rc_pc_chrstuni_doc_31101999_cath-luth-joint-declaration_en.html.

Magister, Sandro; with Rabbi Giuseppe Laras. "Catholic and Papal Anti-Judaism." *L'Espresso*, 13 March 2017. http://magister.blogautore.espresso.repubblica.it/2017/03/13/catholic-and-papal-anti-judaism-rabbi-laras-sounds-the-alarm/.

Maloney, Daniel P. "What Mercy is: A Review of Mercy." *First Things*. March 2015. https://www.firstthings.com/article/2015/03/what-mercy-is.

Maloney, Daniel P.; with Walter Cardinal Kasper. "Cardinal Kasper Responds to First Things Review of Mercy." *First Things*. 23 March 2015. https://www.firstthings.com/web-exclusives/2015/03/cardinal-kasper-responds-to-first-things-review-of-mercy.

Mansini, Guy F. "Dogma." in *Dictionary of Fundamental Theology*. eds. Rene Latourelle, et al. (New York: The Crossroad Publishing Company, 2000).

Maradiaga, Oscar Andres Cardinal Rodriguez. "The Meaning of Mercy: Reflection on a Central Theme of Pope Francis." Santa Clara University, 20 January 2015; as quoted online at *America Magazine*: http://www.americamagazine.org/content/dispatches/cardinal-rodriguez-mercy-divorce-homosexuality-unfree-free-market-and-limits.

Maritain, Jacques. *Moral Philosophy*. Translated and Edited by Joseph W. Evans, et al (New York: Charles Scribner's Sons, 1964).

— *The Living Thoughts of Saint Paul*. trans. Harry Lorin Binsse (London: Cassell, 1942).

Martin, Fr. Francis. "Some Directions in Catholic Biblical Theology," In *Out of Egypt, Biblical Theology and Biblical Interpretation*, Scripture and Hermeneutics Series, Vol. 5, eds. Craig Bartholomew, et al. (Grand Rapids, Mich.: Zondervan, 2004), 65-87.

Martin, Francis; and William M. Wrights IV, *The Gospel of John* (Grand Rapids, Mich.: Baker Academic, 2015).

Martin SJ, James. *Building a Bridge: How the Catholic Church and the LGBT Community can Enter into a Relationship of Respect, Compassion, and Sensitivity* (New York: HarperOne, 2017).

— "How parishes can welcome L.G.B.T. Catholics." *America Magazine*, 23 August 2018. https://www.americamagazine.org/faith/2018/08/23/father-james-martin-how-parishes-can-welcome-lgbt-catholics.

Marx, Reinhard Cardinal. "Bischöfe beschließen 'synodalen Weg' zu Sexualmoral und Zölibat" *Katholische*, 14 March 2019. https://www.katholisch.de/aktuelles/aktuelle-artikel/bischofe-beschlieen-synodalen-weg-zu-sexualmoral-und-zolibat.

McDermott, Gerald R., and Harold A. Netland, *A Trinitarian Theology of Religions, An Evangelical Proposal*. (Oxford/New York: Oxford University Press, 2014).

McElroy, Robert. "Attacks on Father James Martin expose a cancer within the U.S. Catholic Church." *America*, 18 September 2017. https://www.americamagazine.org/faith/2017/09/18/bishop-mcelroy-attacks-father-james-martin-expose-cancer-within-us-catholic-church.

— "Speech at the 2018 Assembly of the Association of US Catholic Priests" 28 June 2018. https://www.associationofcatholicpriests.ie/2018/06/pastoral-theology-for-a-post-modern-world/.

Miller, Michael J., trans. *Christ's New Homeland—Africa, Contribution to the Synod on the Family by African Pastors*. (San Francisco: Ignatius Press, 2015).

Möhler, Johann Adam. *Unity in the Church, Or the Principle of Catholicism*, Translated and Edited with an Introduction by Peter C. Erb (Washington, D.C.: Catholic University of America Press, 1996 [1825]).

Montagna, Diane. "Bishop Schneider wins clarification on 'diversity of religions' from Pope Francis, brands abuse summit a 'failure'" *LifeSite News*, 7 March 2019. https://www.lifesitenews.com/news/bishop-schneider-extracts-clarification-on-diversity-of-religions-from-pope-francis-brands-abuse-summit-a-failure.

Mosebach, Martin. "Remembering Robert Spaemann." *First Things*, 14 January 2019. https://www.firstthings.com/web-exclusives/2019/01/remembering-robert-spaemann.

Mouw, Richard J. "True Church and True Christians: Some Reflections on Calvinist Discernment," in *The Challenges of Cultural Discipleship: Essays in the Line of Abraham Kuyper*. (Grand Rapids, Mich.: Eerdmans, 2012), 159-70.

Mullarkey, Maureen. "Cohabitation & Mother Church." *Studio Matters*, 28 February 2017. http://studiomatters.com/cohabitation-mother-church

Müller, Gerhard Cardinal. "Communion to the remarried, Müller, 'There can be mitigating factors in guilt.'" *La Stampa*. 30 October 2017. http://www.lastampa.it/2017/10/30/vaticaninsider/communion-to-the-remarried-mller-there-can-be-mitigating-factors-in-guilt-OI0rK-5MajqAn9gHGQE1YbO/pagina.html.

— "Corruption of doctrine always brings with it corruption of morals," *Catholic World Report*, 19 September 2018. https://www.catholicworldreport.com/2018/09/19/cardinal-muller-corruption-of-doctrine-always-brings-with-it-the-corruption-of-morals/..

— "Development, or Corruption?" *First Things*. 20 February 2018. https://www.firstthings.com/web-exclusives/2018/02/development-or-corruption.

— Interview with Dr. Maike Hickson. *Life Site News*, 21 November 2018. https://www.lifesitenews.com/blogs/interview-cdl.-mueller-on-abuse-crisis-and-its-link-to-homosexuality-in-pri.

— *The Cardinal Müller Report*. (San Francisco: Ignatius Press, 2017).

Murray, J. *Redemption—Accomplished and Applied*. (Grand Rapids, Mich.: Eerdmans, 1955).

Murray, Fr. Gerald. "Of Truth and Idols." *The Catholic Thing*, 21 April 2018. https://www.thecatholicthing.org/2018/04/21/of-truth-and-idols/.

Netland, Harold A. "Can All Religions be True?" in *Christianity & Religious Diversity*. (Grand Rapids, MI: Baker Academic, 2015).

Neuhaus, Richard John. *The Naked Public Square: Religion and Democracy in America*. Second Edition. (Grand Rapids, Mich.: Eerdmans, 1988).

New, Michael J. "Quinnipiac University Releases Poll on Catholic Attitudes Toward Abortion and Same-Sex Marriage." *Catholic Vote*. http://www.catholicvote.org/quinnipac-releases-poll-on-catholic-attitudes-toward-abortion-and-same-sex-marriage/.

Newbigin, Lesslie. *The Household of God, Lectures on the Nature of the Church* (London: Paternoster Press, 1998 [1953]).

Nichols O.P., Aidan. *Christendom Awake: On Reenergizing the Church in Culture*. (Wm. B. Eerdmans, 1999).

— *Epiphany: A Theological Introduction to Catholicism* (Collegeville, Minn.: The Liturgical Press, 1995), 391-432.

— *From Newman to Congar: The Idea of Doctrinal Development from the Victorians to the Second Vatican Council*. (Edinburgh: T&T Clark, 1990).

— *The Shape of Catholic Theology*, (Collegeville, Minn.: Liturgical Press, 1991).

— "Thomism and the Nouvelle Theologie." The Thomist 64 (2000): 1-19.

Niebuhr, H. Richard. *The Kingdom of God in America*. (New York: Harper & Row, 1959 [1937]).

O'Collins SJ, Gerald. *The Case Against Dogma* (New York: Paulist Press, 1975).

— *The Second Vatican Council on Other Religions* (Oxford: Oxford University Press, 2013).

O'Connell, Gerard. "Call to Conversion." *America*, 8-15 December 2014. http://americamagazine.org/issue/call-conversion.

— "In Morocco Pope Francis explains what it means to be Christian in a majority Muslim land" *America*, 31 March 2019. https://www.americamagazine.org/faith/2019/03/31/morocco-pope-francis-explains-what-it-means-be-christian-majority-muslim-land.

O'Donovan, Oliver. *Resurrection and Moral Order*, Second Edition (Grand Rapids, Mich.: Eerdmans, 1994 [1986]).

Ocáriz, F., L.F. Mateo Seco, and J.A. Riestra. *The Mystery of Jesus Christ*. Translated by Michael Adams and James Gavigan. (Dublin, Ireland: Four Courts Press, 2011 [1991]).

Ott, Ludwig. *Fundamentals of Dogma*. trans. Patrick Lynch, ed. James Canon Bastible, New Edition Fully Revised and Updated, Robert Fastiggi (Baronius Press, 2018 [1952]).

Pannenberg, Wolfhart. *Theology and the Philosophy of Science*, trans. Francis McDonagh (Philadelphia: The Westminster Press, 1976).

Paul VI, Pope. *Ecclesiam Suam*, Encyclical, 6 August 1964. http://w2.vatican.va/content/paul-vi/en/encyclicals/documents/hf_p-vi_enc_06081964_ecclesiam.html.

— *Evangelii Nuntiandi*, 8 December 1975. http://w2.vatican.va/content/paul-vi/en/apost_exhortations/documents/hf_p-vi_exh_19751208_evangelii-nuntiandi.html.

— *Gaudete in Domino* (*On Christian Joy*). Apostolic Exhortation, 9 May 1975. http://www.vatican.va/holy_father/paul_vi/apost_exhortations/documents/hf_p-vi_exh_19750509_gaudete-in-domino_en.html.

— *Humanae Vitae* (*On the Regulation of Birth*). Encyclical, 25 July 1968. http://w2.vatican.va/content/paul-vi/en/encyclicals/documents/hf_p-vi_enc_25071968_humanae-vitae.html.

— *Paterna Cum Benevolentia*, Apostolic Exhortation, 8 December 1974. http://w2.vatican.va/content/paul-vi/it/apost_exhortations/documents/hf_p-vi_exh_19741208_paterna-cum-benevolentia.html.

Pelikan, Jaroslav. *The Christian Tradition*, I, The Emergence of the Catholic Tradition (100-600) (Chicago/London: The University of Chicago Press, 1971).

— *Credo, Historical and Theological Guide to Creeds and Confessions of Faith in the Christian Tradition*. (New Haven/London: Yale University Press, 2003).

Pentin, Edward. "Cardinal Coccopalmerio Explains His Positions on Catholics in Irregular Unions." *National Catholic Register*, 1 March 2017. https://www.ncregister.com/daily-news/cardinal-coccopalmerio-explains-his-positions-on-catholics-in-irregular-uni.

— "'Doctrinal Anarchy' as Bishops' Conflicting Positions on Amoris Laetitia Show." *National Catholic Register*, 17 June 2017. http://www.ncregister.com/blog/edward-pentin/doctrinal-anarchy-as-bishops-conflicting-positions-on-amoris-laetitia-.

— "Draft of Final Document Thrusts Synodality to the Fore," *National Catholic Register*, 25 October 2018, http://www.ncregister.com/blog/edward-pentin/final-draft-of-document-thrusts-the-issue-of-synodality-to-the-fore..

— "Full Text and Explanatory Notes of Cardinals' Questions on 'Amoris Laetitia.'" *National Catholic Register*, 14 November 2016. http://www.ncregister.com/blog/edward-pentin/full-text-and-explanatory-notes-of-cardinals-questions-on-amoris-laetitia

— "Pope Francis: Rigid People Are Sick." *National Catholic Register*. 24 October 2016. http://www.ncregister.com/blog/edward-pentin/pope-francis-rigidity-is-something-pathological.

— "Synod Reflections From Down Under: Interview With Archbishop Anthony Fisher." *National Catholic Register*, 1 November 2018. http://www.ncregister.com/daily-news/synod-reflections-from-down-under-interview-with-archbishop-anthony-fisher.

Pérez-Soba, Juan José; and Stephan Kampowski. *The Gospel of the Family*. Foreword by George Cardinal Pell. (San Francisco: Ignatius Press, 2014).

Pié-Ninot, Salvador. "Sensus Fidei," In *Dictionary of Fundamental Theology*, edited by Rene Latourelle and Rino Fisichella, 992-95 (New York: Crossroads, 1994).

Pinckaers, Servais. *The Sources of Christian Ethics*, trans. Mary Thomas Noble (Washington, D.C.: Catholic University of America Press, 1995).

Piper, John. "Final Judgment According to Works." blog, 6 February 1989. https://www.desiringgod.org/articles/final-judgment-according-to-works.

Pius X, Pope. *Pascendi Dominici Gregis*. Encyclical, 8 September 1907. http://w2.vatican.va/content/pius-x/en/encyclicals/documents/hf_p-x_enc_19070908_pascendi-dominici-gregis.html.

Pius XI, Pope. *Mortalium Animos*, Encyclical, 6 January 1928. http://www.vatican.va/holy_father/pius_xi/encyclicals/documents/hf_p-xi_enc_19280106_mortalium-animos_en.html.

Pius XII, Pope. *Haurietis Aquas* (*On Devotion to the Sacred Heart*). Encyclical Letter, 15 May 1956. http://w2.vatican.va/content/pius-xii/en/encyclicals/documents/hf_p-xii_enc_15051956_haurietis-aquas.html.

— "Soyez les Bienvenues," Address to the Participants in the Congress of the World Federation of Catholic Young Women, 18 April 1952. *Novus Ordo Watch*. https://novusordowatch.org/pius12-soyez-les-bienvenues/.

Pontifical Council for Culture. *Towards a Pastoral Approach to Culture*. Vatican City, 23 May 1999. http://www.vatican.va/roman_curia/pontifical_councils/cultr/documents/rc_pc_pc-cultr_doc_03061999_pastoral_en.html.

Pontifical Council for Interreligious Dialogue. *Dialogue and Proclamation*. Rome, 19 May 1991. http://www.vatican.va/roman_curia/pontifical_councils/interelg/documents/rc_pc_interelg_doc_19051991_dialogue-and-proclamatio_en.html.

— *Dialogue in Truth and Charity* (Libreria Editrice Vaticana, 2014).

— *Interreligious Dialogue and the New Evangelization*. http://pcinterreligious.org/interreligious-dialogue-and-the-new-evangelization_139.html.

Pontifical Council for Justice and Peace. *Compendium of the Social Doctrine of the Church*. Libreria Editrice Vaticana, 2004, Reprint April 2005. http://www.vatican.va/roman_curia/pontifical_councils/justpeace/documents/rc_pc_justpeace_doc_20060526_compendio-dott-soc_en.html.

Pronk, Pim. *Against Nature? Types of Moral Argumentation regarding Homosexuality*. (Grand Rapids, MI: Eerdmans, 1993).

Pruss, Alexander. *One Body, An Essay in Christian Sexual Ethics* (Notre Dame, Ind.: University of Notre Dame Press, 2013).

Radner, Ephraim. "Blessing: A Scriptural and Theological Reflection," *Pro Ecclesia* Vol. XIX, No. 1, Winter 2010: 7-27.

Rahner SJ, Karl. "The Appeal to Conscience," in *Nature and Grace, Dilemmas in the Modern Church*, trans. Dinah Wharton (New York: Sheed and Ward, 1964), 39-63.

— "The Development of Dogma," in *Theological Investigations*, Vol. I, Translated by Cornelius Ernst, O.P. (Baltimore, Md.: Helicon Press, 1961), 39–77.

— "A Hierarchy of Truths," *Theological Investigations*, Vol. XXI, Translated by Hugh M. Riley (New York: Crossroad, 1988), 162–67.

— "*Mysterium Ecclesiae*," in *Theological Investigations*, Vol. XVII, Translated by Margaret Kohl (New York: Crossroad, 1981), 151.

— "The Notion of Hierarchy of Truths—An Ecumenical Interpretation," in *Deepening Communion, International Ecumenical Documents with Roman Catholic Participation*, Edited by William G. Rusch et al., 561–71.

— *Theological Investigations*, Vol. XIII, trans. David Bourke. (New York: The Seabury Press, 1975).

Rahner, Karl; Herbert Vorgrimler. *Theological Dictionary*, Edited by Cornelius Ernst, O.P., Translated by Richard Strachan (New York: Herder and Herder, 1965).

Ratzinger, Joseph. *Introduction to Christianity*. trans. J.R. Foster (San Francisco: Ignatius, 1990 [1968]).

— *The Yes of Jesus Christ*. trans. Robert Nowell. (New York: Crossroad Publishing Co., 1991).

— *Theological Highlights of Vatican II*. Translated by Henry Traub, S.J., Gerard C. Thormann, and Werner Barzel. (New York: Paulist Press, 1966).

Ratzinger, Joseph Cardinal. *Church, Ecumenism, & Politics: New Endeavors in Ecclesiology*. (San Francisco: Ignatius Press, 2008 [1987]).

— "Commentary on Dogmatic Constitution on Divine Revelation." *Commentary on the Documents of Vatican II*, Volume III; General Editor, Herbert Vorgrimler. New York: Herder and Herder, 1969.

— "*Deus Locutus Est Nobis In Filio*: Some reflections on Subjectivity, Christology, and the Church," in *Proclaiming the Truth of Jesus Christ*. Papers from the Vallombrosa Meeting (Washington, D.C.: USCCB, 2000).

— "Dialogue on the Papacy and Ecumenism between the Prefect of the Congregation for the Doctrine of the Faith and Rome's Waldensian Community." 29 January 1993. http://www.stucom.nl/document/0141uk.pdf.

— *Donum Veritatis* (*On the Ecclesial Vocation of the Theologian*). 24 May 1990. http://www.vatican.va/roman_curia/congregations/cfaith/documents/rc_con_cfaith_doc_19900524_theologian-vocation_en.html.

— "The Ecclesiology of the Constitution *Lumen Gentium*," in *Pilgrim Fellowship of Faith, The Church as Communion*, Edited by Stephan Otto Horn and Vinzenz Pfnür, Translated by Henry Taylor (San Francisco: Ignatius Press, 2005), 123-52.

— *Many Religions—One Covenant, Israel, the Church and the World*. Translated by Graham Harrison. (San Francisco: Ignatius Press, 1999).

— *On the Way to Jesus Christ*. Translated by Michael J. Miller. (San Francisco: Ignatius Press, 2005).

— *Principles of Catholic Theology*, Translated by Sister Mary Francis McCarthy, S.N.D. (San Francisco: Ignatius Press, 1987 [1982]).
— "Relativism: The Central Problem for Faith Today," the *Doctrinal Commissions of the Bishops' Conferences of Latin America*, held in Guadalajara, Mexico, in May 1996. http://www.ewtn.com/library/curia/ratzrela.htm.
— "Searching for Peace: Tensions and Dangers." in *Values in a Time of Upheaval*. Translated by Brian McNeil (New York/San Francisco: Crossroad and Ignatius Press, 2006), 101-16.
— *The Nature and Mission of Theology*. (San Francisco: Ignatius Press, 1995).
— *Truth and Tolerance, Christian Belief and World Religions*, trans. Henry Taylor (San Francisco: Ignatius Press, 2004).
— *Without Roots: The West, Relativism, Christianity, Islam*. Translated by Michael F. Moore, Foreword by George Weigel (New York: Basic Books, 2006).
Ratzinger, Joseph Cardinal; with Vittorio Messori, *The Ratzinger Report, An Exclusive Interview on the State of the Church*, trans. Salvator Attanasio and Graham Harrison (San Francisco: Ignatius Press, 1985).
Regnerus, Mark. *Cheap Sex, The Transformation of Men, Marriage, and Monogamy* (Oxford: Oxford University Press, 2017).
Reilly, Robert R. *Making Gay Okay: How Rationalizing Homosexual Behavior is Changing Everything*, (San Francisco, Ignatius Press, 2014).
Reno, R. R. "Catholic Capitulation on Marriage." *First Things*, 3 November 2014. https://www.firstthings.com/web-exclusives/2014/11/catholic-capitulation-on-marriage.
— "Francis, Our Jesuit Pope." *First Things*, 23 September 2013. http://www.firstthings.com/web-exclusives/2013/09/francis-our-jesuit-pope.
— "Liberal Tradition, Yes; Liberal Ideology, No," *First Things*, December 2017. https://www.firstthings.com/article/2017/12/liberal-tradition-yes-liberal-ideology-no.
Rezac, Mary. "Pope Francis signs peace declaration on 'Human Fraternity' with Grand Imam" *Catholic Herald*, 5 February 2019. https://catholicherald.co.uk/news/2019/02/05/pope-signs-declaration-saying-god-wills-religions-pluralism-what-does-this-mean/.
Ribadeau-Dumas, Bishop Olivier. "Qui nous fera voir le bonheur?" *Devenir Un en Christ*, 7 October 2018. http://www.devenirunenchrist.net/qui-nous-fera-voir-le-bonheur-2018.html, excerpted in *Riposte Catholique*, 25 March 2019. https://www.riposte-catholique.fr/archives/150600. See also in English: "French bishops spokesman calls homosexual relationships 'something of God'" *LifeSite News*, 28 March 2019. https://www.lifesitenews.com/news/french-bishops-spokesman-calls-homosexual-relationships-something-of-god.
Ridderbos, Herman N. *The Gospel of John, A Theological Commentary*, Translated by John Vriend (Grand Rapids, Mich.: Eerdmans, 1997 [1987]).
— *Paul: An Outline of His Theology*, Translated by John Richard De Witt (Grand Rapids, Mich.: Eerdmans, 1975 [1966]).

— *The Epistle of Paul to the Churches of Galatia*. The New International Commentary on the New Testament. Translated by Henry Zylstra. (Grand Rapids, Mich.: Eerdmans, 1953).

Roberts, Christopher C. *Creation & Covenant, The Significance of Sexual Difference in the Moral Theology of Marriage* (New York: T&T Clark, New York, 2007).

Rocca, Francis X. "Pope, in Philippines, says same-sex marriage threatens family." *Catholic News Service*, 16 January 2015. https://cnsblog.wordpress.com/2015/01/16/pope-in-philippines-says-same-sex-marriage-threatens-family/.

Rosica CSB, Fr. Thomas. "The Ignatian Qualities of the Petrine Ministry of Pope Francis," *Salt & Light Media*, 31 July 2018. http://saltandlighttv.org/blogfeed/getpost.php?id=72516.

Royal, Robert. "First Reports—Part II." *The Catholic Thing*. 11 October 2018. https://www.thecatholicthing.org/2018/10/11/first-reports-part-ii/.

Rusch, William G.; and Jeffrey Gros, Editors. *Deepening Communion, International Ecumenical Documents with Roman Catholic Participation*. (Washington, D.C.: United States Catholic Conference, 1998).

San Martín, Inés. "Cardinal calls pope's family text 'development' in Church doctrine." *Crux*, 8 April 2016. http://www.cruxnow.com/church/2016/04/08/cardinal-calls-popes-family-text-a-development-in-church-doctrine/.

— "Pope Francis says priests must be taught to see shades of gray." Inés San Martín, *Crux*, 25 August 2016. https://cruxnow.com/world-youth-day-krakow/2016/08/25/pope-francis-says-priests-must-taught-see-shades-gray/.

Scaramuzzi, Iacopa. "The Pope on Amoris Laetitia's Comments: Respectable but Wrong." *Vatican Insider*. 28 September 2017. http://www.lastampa.it/2017/09/28/vaticaninsider/the-pope-on-amoris-laetitias-comments-respectable-but-wrong-fOM9GtHBSyp83Be3St2EVN/pagina.html.

Schillebeeckx O.P., Edward. *Interim Report on the books, Jesus & Christ*, trans. John Bowden (New York: Cross, 1981).

— *Mensen als verhaal van God*. (Baarn: Uitgeverij H. Nelissen, 1989). ET: *Church, The Human Story of God*, trans. John Bowden (New York: Crossroad Publishing Co., 1993).

— *On Christian Faith, The Spiritual, Ethical, and Political Dimensions*, trans. John Bowden (New York: Crossroads, 1987).

— "Towards a Catholic Use of Hermeneutics." *God the Future of Man*. (Sheed & Ward Ltd., 2012), 3-49.

Schmitz, Kenneth L. "St. Thomas and the Appeal to Experience." *Catholic Theological Society of America Proceedings* 47 (1992): 1-20.

Schnackenburg, Rudolph. *The Gospel According to St John*, Volume One, Introduction and Commentary on Chapters 1-4, Translated by Kevin Smyth (New York: Herder and Herder, 1968).

Schneiders, Sandra. *The Revelatory Text* (San Francisco: Harper, 1991).

Schockenhoff, Eberhard. "A Consistent Ethic of Life (with a Few Blemishes): Moral-Theological Remarks on Evangelium Vitae and on Some Protestant Questions About It," in *Ecumenical Ventures in Ethics*, hg. von R. Hütter/Th. Dieter, Grand Rapids, Mich./Cambridge U.K. 1998, 237-261.

Schoenmaekers, David. "Kardinaal De Kesel vindt seksualiteitsbeleving bij holebi's aanvaardbaar." *Zizo Online*, 2 May 2018. https://zizo-online.be/article/12971.

Schreiner, Thomas R. *40 Questions about Christians and Biblical Law*. (Grand Rapids, Mich.: Kregel Academic, 2010).

Schüssler Fiorenza, Francis. *Foundational Theology: Jesus and the Church*, 1984.

Seifert, Josef. "*Amoris Laetitia*: Joy, Sadness and Hopes." *Aemaet* Wissenschaftliche Zeitschrift für Philosophie und Theologie, Bd. 5, Nr. 2 (2016) 160-249; 2016. https://www.aemaet.de/wp-content/uploads/2018/09/Amoris-Laetitia-Joy-Sadness-and-Hopes.pdf.

— "Does Pure Logic Threaten to Destroy the Entire Moral Doctrine of the Church," *Aemaet* Wissenschaftliche Zeitschrift für Philosophie und Theologie, Bd. 6, Nr. 2 (2017).

Siniscalchi, Glenn B. "Conciliar Apologetics and Interreligious Dialogue," in *Retrieving Apologetics* (Eugene, Ore.: Pickwick Publications, 2016), 17-26.

Sirilla, Michael. "On the Moral Liceity of Publicly Correcting the Pope." *1P5*, 5 October 2017. https://onepeterfive.com/moral-liceity-publicly-correcting-pope/.

— "Superstition, Dissent, and Scandal? A Brief Defense of Fr. Thomas Weinandy." *Catholic World Report*. 5 November 2017. https://www.catholicworldreport.com/2017/11/05/superstition-dissent-and-scandal-a-brief-defense-of-fr-thomas-weinandy/.

Smedes, Lewis. *Mere Morality*. (Grand Rapids, MI: Eerdmans, 1983).

Smith, Christian, with Melinda Lundquist Denton. *Soul Searching: The Religious and Spiritual Lives of American Teenagers*. (New York: Oxford University Press, 2006).

Smith, Janet E. "Are We Obsessed?" *First Things*, 25 September 2013. http://www.firstthings.com/web-exclusives/2013/09/are-we-obsessed.

— "The Sensus Fidelium and Humanae Vitae," *Angelicum* 83 (2006): 271-97.

Spadaro SJ, Antonio. "The welcoming of those young people who prefer to live together without getting married." *CyberTeologia*. http://www.cyberteologia.it/2017/02/the-welcoming-of-those-young-people-who-prefer-to-live-together-without-getting-married/.

Spicq OP, Ceslaus. *Charity and Liberty... in the New Testament*, Translated by Francis V. Manning (Staten Island, NY: Alba House, 1965).

Stott, John R.W. *The Cross of Christ*. (Downers Grove, Ill.: IVP Books, 2006 [1986]).

Stout, Jeffrey. *Ethics After Babel*. (Boston: Beacon Press, 1988).

Taylor, Charles. *Varieties of Religion Today*. (Cambridge, Mass.: Harvard University Press, 2002).

Theobald S.J., Christoph. "The Courage to Anticipate the Future of the Church." in *The Future of the Church*. Edited by Thierry-Marie Courau, Stefanie Knauss and Enrico Galavotti, *Concilium* 2018/4, 13-22.

— "The Principle of Pastorality at Vatican II." in *The Legacy of Vatican II*. Edited by Massimo Faggioli and Andrea Vicini, S.J. (New York/Mahwah, N.J.: Paulist Press, 2015), 26-37.

— "The Theological Options of Vatican II: Seeking an 'Internal' Principle of Interpretation." in *Vatican II: A Forgotten Future*, edited by Alberto Melloni and Christoph Theobald, *Concilium* 2005/4, 87-107.

Tracy, David. "A Hermeneutics of Orthodoxy." in *Christian Orthodoxy*. edited by Felix Wilfred and Daniel F Pilario. *Concilium* 2014/2, 71-81.

Trueman, Carl R. "The Reformation We Need," *First Things*, 31 October 2018. Online: https://www.firstthings.com/web-exclusives/2018/10/the-reformation-we-need.

Turner, Philip. "An Unworkable Theology." *First Things*, June/July 2005, 10-12. Online: http://www.firstthings.com/article/2005/06/an-unworkable-theology.

Ureta, José Antonio. *Pope Francis's "Paradigm Shift": Continuity or Rupture in the Mission of the Church?* trans. José A. Schelini (Spring Grove, Penn.: The American Society for the Defense of Tradition, Family and Property, 2018), 151-63.

USCCB. *Catechism of the Catholic Church*. http://ccc.usccb.org/flipbooks/catechism/files/assets/basic-html/page-I.html.

Vandervelde, George. "*BEM [Baptism, Eucharist, and Ministry]* and the 'Hierarchy of Truths': A Vatican Contribution to the Reception Process," *Journal of Ecumenical Studies*, 25, 1 (Winter 1988): 74-84.

Vanhoozer, Kevin J. "The Atonement in Postmodernity." in *The Glory of the Atonement*. Edited by Charles E. Hill & Frank A. James III. (Downers Grove, Ill.: InterVarsity Press, 2004), 367-404.

— *Biblical Authority After Babel: retrieving the solas in the spirit of mere Protestant Christianity*. (Grand Rapids, Mich.: Brazos Press, 2016).

— "Epilogue," in *Evangelicals and Catholics Together at Twenty, Vital Statements on Contested Topics*, Edited by Timothy George and Thomas G. Guarino (Grand Rapids, Mich.: Brazos Press, 2015), 165-70.

VanHoye SJ, Rev. Albert. "The Apostle Paul as Moral Teacher and Guide," in *The Catholic Priest as Moral Teacher*. (San Francisco: Ignatius Press, 1990), 21-38.

Vatican Council I. *Dei Filius*. 24 April 1870. https://w2.vatican.va/content/pius-ix/la/documents/constitutio-dogmatica-dei-filius-24-aprilis-1870.html.

Vatican Council II. *Apostolicam Actuositatem* (*Decree on the Apostolate of the Laity*). 18 November 1965. http://www.vatican.va/archive/hist_councils/ii_vatican_council/documents/vat-ii_decree_19651118_apostolicam-actuositatem_en.html.

— *Dei Verbum*. Dogmatic Constitution on Divine Revelation. 18 November

1965. http://www.vatican.va/archive/hist_councils/ii_vatican_council/documents/vat-ii_const_19651118_dei-verbum_en.html.

— *Lumen Gentium*. Dogmatic Constitution on the Church. 21 November 1964. http://www.vatican.va/archive/hist_councils/ii_vatican_council/documents/vat-ii_const_19641121_lumen-gentium_en.html.

— *Gaudium et spes*. Pastoral Constitution on the Church. 7 December 1965. http://www.vatican.va/archive/hist_councils/ii_vatican_council/documents/vat-ii_cons_19651207_gaudium-et-spes_en.html.

— *Unitatis Redintegratio*. Decree on Ecumenism. 21 November 1964. http://www.vatican.va/archive/hist_councils/ii_vatican_council/documents/vat-ii_decree_19641121_unitatis-redintegratio_en.html.

Vos, Geerhardus. "The Idea of Biblical Theology as a Science and as a Theological Discipline" Inaugural address as Professor of Biblical Theology, Princeton Theological Seminary, delivered at the First Presbyterian Church, Princeton, 8 May 1894. Reprinted in Richard B. Gaffin Jr. *Redemptive History and Biblical Interpretation: The Shorter Writings of Geerhardus Vos*. Phillipsburg, N.J.: Presbyterian and Reformed, 1980.

Walford, Stephen. "Amoris Laetitia: The Questions that Really Need Answers," *La Stampa*, 27 March 2017, http://www.lastampa.it/2017/03/27/vaticaninsider/eng/documents/amoris-laetitia-the-questions-that-really-need-answers-ppy8l1yk7emPPR7TUYrjQN/pagina.html.

— "Open Letter to the Four Dubia Cardinals," *La Stampa*, 27 June 2017. https://www.lastampa.it/2017/06/27/vaticaninsider/open-letter-to-the-four-dubia-cardinals-nIsyPMFIjp2M5wjLZ1CHJO/pagina.html.

— *Pope Francis, The Family and Divorce*. Foreword by Cardinal Óscar Andrés Rodriguez Maradiaga. (New York/Mahwah, NJ: Paulist Press, 2018).

— "The Amoris Laetitia Dissenters, The Murky World of Distorting Facts, Creating False Arguments and Sowing Confusion." *La Stampa*, 4 January 2018. http://www.lastampa.it/2018/01/04/vaticaninsider/the-amoris-laetitia-dissenters-lGWxh795fjt5DHh7Wx74WP/pagina.html.

— "The Magisterium of Pope Francis: His Predecessors Come to His Defense," *La Stampa*, 7 February 2017, http://www.lastampa.it/2017/02/07/vaticaninsider/eng/the-vatican/the-magisterium-of-pope-francis-his-predecessors-come-to-his-defence-x5jzE4YtghvlnRvSvcolGM/pagina.html.

Waters, John. "Theological Deplorables," *First Things*, 4 October 2018. https://www.firstthings.com/web-exclusives/2018/10/theological-deplorables.

Weber, Jeremy. "Christian, What Do You Believe? Probably a Heresy About Jesus, Says Survey." *Christianity Today*, 16 October 2018. https://www.christianitytoday.com/news/2018/october/what-do-christians-believe-ligonier-state-theology-heresy.html.

Weigel, George. "An Open Letter to Cardinal Reinhard Marx." *First Things*, 27 March 2019. https://www.firstthings.com/web-exclusives/2019/03/an-open-letter-to-cardinal-reinhard-marx.

— "Concluding Unscientific Postscripts [On the XVth General Assembly of the Synod of Bishops]." *Catholic Herald*, 29 October 2018. http://catholicherald.co.uk/commentandblogs/2018/10/29/letters-from-the-synod-2018-the-final-letter/.

Weigel S.J., Gustav, *Catholic Theology in Dialogue* (New York: Harper & Brother, Publishers, 1960).

Weinandy O.F.M. Cap., Thomas. *Jesus the Christ*. (Huntington, Ind.: Our Sunday Visitor, Inc., 2003).

— "Letter to Pope Francis." *National Catholic Register*. 31 July 2017. http://www.ncregister.com/blog/edward-pentin/full-text-of-father-weinandys-letter-to-pope-francis.

Westen, John-Henry; and Pete Baklinski. "Archbishop Cupich lays out pathway for gay couples to receive Communion at Vatican press scrum." *Life Site News*, 16 October 2015. https://www.lifesitenews.com/news/archbishop-cupich-lays-out-pathway-for-gay-couples-to-receive-communion.

White, Thomas Joseph. *The Light of Christ, An Introduction to Catholicism*. (Washington, DC: Catholic University of America Press, 2017).

Wicks SJ, Jared. "A Catholic Theology Teacher Drawing on the Lutheran Legacy," in *Preaching and Teaching the Law and Gospel of God*, Edited by Carl E. Braaten (Delhi, NY: ALPB Books, 2013), 55-66.

— "The Ecumenical Imperative in Catholic Theology and Life," in *Ecumenical Trends* 42, No. 3 (March 2013): 1-4.

Wimmer, Anian Christoph. "Cardinal Marx endorses blessing ceremonies for same-sex couples." *Crux*, February 2018. https://cruxnow.com/global-church/2018/02/04/cardinal-marx-endorses-blessing-ceremonies-sex-couples.

— "German bishops announce 'synodal process' on celibacy, sexual morality." *Catholic Herald*, 15 March 2019. Online: https://catholicherald.co.uk/news/2019/03/15/cardinal-marx-announces-binding-synodal-process-on-celibacy-and-sexual-morality/.

Winfield, Nicole (Associated Press), "Pope Francis reaffirms primacy of conscience amid criticism of 'Amoris Laetitia.'" *America Magazine*, 11 November 2017. https://www.americamagazine.org/faith/2017/11/11/pope-francis-reaffirms-primacy-conscience-amid-criticism-amoris-laetitia.

Witherington, III, Ben. *John's Wisdom: A Commentary on the Fourth Gospel*. (Louisville, Ky.: Westminster John Knox Press, 1995).

Wojtyla, Karol. *The Acting Person*, Translated by Andrzej Potocki. Edited by Anna-Teresa Tymieniecka (Dordrecht: D. Reidel Publishing Company, 1979 [1969].

— *Love and Responsibility*, Translation, Endnotes, and Foreword by Grzegorz Ignatik, New Translation (Boston: Pauline Books & Media, 2013 [1960]).

— *Man in the Field of Responsibility*, Translation by Kenneth W. Kemp and Zuzanna Maślanka Kieroń, Introduction by Fr. Alfred Wierzbicki (South Bend, Ind.: St. Augustine's Press, 2011).

— *Person and Community: Selected Essays*, Translated by Theresa Sandok (New York: Lang, 1993).

— "The Problem of Catholic Sexual Ethics, Reflections and Postulates," in *Person and Community: Selected Essays*, translated by Theresa Sandok, OSM (New York: Peter Lang , 1993 [1965]).

— "Subjectivity and the Irreducible in Man," in *Analecta Husserliana* VII, 107-114 (Dordrecht: D. Reidel Publishing Company, 1978).

Wolters, Albert. *Creation Regained* (Grand Rapids, Mich.: Eerdmans, 1985).

Wood, Allen. "Relativism." https://www.csus.edu/indiv/e/eppersonm/phil002/documents/relativism_readings.pdf.

Wooden, Cindy. (*Catholic News Service*). "What did Pope Francis mean when he said the unborn and the poor are equally sacred?" *America*, 18 April 2018. https://www.americamagazine.org/faith/2018/04/18/what-did-pope-francis-mean-when-he-said-unborn-and-poor-are-equally-sacred.

Woodward, Kenneth L. "Double Lives, The Peril of Clerical Hypocrisy," *Commonweal*, 19 October 2018.

Yeago, David. "Grace and the Good Life: Why the God of the Gospel Cares How We Live," in *The Morally Divided Church*, edited by Michael Root & James J. Buckley (Eugene, Ore.: Cascade Books, 2012), 77-92.

Index

Absolute truth, 39-44, 300-309, 321-26
Absolutism/relativism, 301-3, 306, 321-26
Alberigo, Giuseppe, 60n13
Angeles, Peter, 103, 114n14
Antinomianism, 111-19, 135-37, 141, 147n16, 153n104, 220
Aparecida Document, 232
Aquinas, Thomas, 9, 12n30, 34-36, 123, 140-44, 154n131, 184, 186-87, 194-195, 198, 204n39, 211n129, 214n159, 335n53, 337n76, 346, 357
Amoris Laetitia, 122-23, 124, 157-174-176, 176-199
ARCIC, 379, 383
Ashley, Benedict, 146, 154n138, 367, 389n93
Assisi Meeting, 309-14
Baggett, Jerome P., 105n56
Balthasar, Hans Urs Von, 94, 97
Bavinck, Herman, 245, 177n45
Berg, Thomas, 190-91, 195, 197-98, 207n97
Berkouwer, G.C., 26-27, 69, 78, 105n46, 274, 277-79, 295n127, 329, 352
  on *credo unam ecclesiam*, 252, 257-61
  on ecclesiastical epistemology, 261-65
  on ecumenism, 245, 252, 257-60
  on hierarchy of truths, 280-87
  on *nouvelle théologie*, 26-28
Blackburn, Simon, 117, 148n43, 148n47
Bode, Franz-Josef, 359
Bodily unity, 167-173
Boff, Leonardo, 32n37, 63n48, 141n50
Bonhoeffer, Dietrich, 53, 64n67
Bonino, OP, Serge-Thomas, 150n64, 184, 199, 211n128
Bonny, Johan, Bishop, 155, 202n4, 357, 361-362, 387n56, 388n76
Borghesi, Massimo, 12n31, 67n162, 146n15, 215n163
Brandmüller, Walter Cardinal, 19
Braaten, Carl, 356
Budzizzewski, J., 188, 206n66
Buttiglione, Rocco, 150n65
Camus, Albert, 222
Catechism of the Catholic Church, 7, 11n22, 35, 38, 41, 49, 64n86, 74-74, 85, 96, 115, 119-123, 139, 157-158, 160, 185, 187-188
Cano, OP, Melchior, 1
Casuistry, 117
Central Commandment of Love, 112, 120, 139-140
Cessario, OP, Romanus. 34
Christ fulfillment of the law, 137-40, 144-46
Christian Anthropology, 352-76
Clairvaux, Bernard, 83
Clooney, Francis, 304-5, 312, 333n28, 336n62
Coccopalmerio, Cardinal Francesco, 184-85, 186-88, 211n130, 211n133, 212n139
Code of Canon Law, 8-9, 49
Cohabitation, 210n115, 213n148
Commandments, 113-14, 370
Commensurable pluralism, 3, 267-68, 276
Competing truth claims, 306-7, 308-9
Congar, Yves, 26-27, 62n41, 69, 267, 275-276, 285, 294n111, 352, 376-77, 382, 384, 391n140
Conscience, 190, 192-93
Contraception, 363-64
Council of Trent, 109-10, 116, 142
Crisp, Oliver, 10n6
Cullmann, Oscar, 253, 254, 296n157
Culpability, 185-87, 189
Cupich, Cardinal Blaise, 177, 181, 191-94, 207n94, 214n155, 373
D'Ambrosio, Rocco, 60n21, 184, 61n34
D'Costa, Gavin, 52, 65n112, 76
Decree on Justification, 86, 197
Deism, 80, 82
De Kesel, Josef Cardinal, 357, 388n57
De Lubac, Henri, 45, 63n45
De Mey, Peter, 295n150
Denzingertheologie, 32, 64n74
Dialogue and Proclamation, 307
Divine Acceptance, 78-80

Divine Redemption, 78-80
Doctrine, of Pastorality, 4, 21, 48-54, 175-76
Dogma, of Meaning, 347
Dominus Iesus, 303, 304-5, 335n50, 339n122
Donum Veritatis, 5-7
Douma, Joachim, 139, 153n117
Douthat, Ross, 149n56, 184-85, 207n93, 211n121
Dooyeweerd. Herman, 170, 204n33, 206n65, 373-74, 390n118, 391n121
Dulles, Avery, Cardinal, 52
Dupuis, SJ, Jacques, 333n15, 334n44, 336n61
Ecclesia discens, 343, 376
Ecclesia docens, 343, 376, 380
Ecclesial positivism, 155, 358
Ecclesial realism, 155, 159, 358
Ecclesial relativism, 272
Ecumenical Dialogue, 249-51, 276-77
Ecumenism of Return, 272
Eltz, Johannes zu, 358
Epistemological/Ontological Complementarity, 303-6
Essentialism, 51
Ethics,
Deontological, 370, 390n107
Axiological, 370, 390n108
Praxiological, 371
Personalistic norm, 371-72
Ethical Maximalism, 145
Evangelii gaudium, 22-25, 28-31, 225, 227, 230-32
Evangelium vitae, 133-38
Extraordinary Synod 1985, 348-49
Faggioli, Massimo, 59n3
Fastiggi, Robert, 149n49, 151n74, 210n118, 214n156
Fernandez, Victor Manuel, Archbishop, 184, 211n125, 214n157, 214n158
Finnis, John, 152n96, 205n57, 206n71
Flannery, Kevin, 190-91, 195, 197-98, 207n97
Forces of law, 76, 140
on compelling force, 142-44
on obliging force, 140-42
Francis, Pope,
on dialogue of religion, 299-302, 307
on ecumenism, 246-51
on faith, 33-39
on Gospel of Life, 226-28, 232-37, 242n69
on hierarchy of truths, 224-28, 230-32, 280-87
on Law and Gospel, 113, 116-17, 129
on legacy of Vatican II, 1-4, 17-21
on Lérinian legacy of Vatican II, 21-26, 28-34, 203n20
on marriage, 155-74, 199-202
on mercy and justice, 71-78, 82-83, 88-92
on pastoral reasoning, 199
on unity and diversity, 247, 253-54
on sensus fidei, 188-97
Freedom in Christ, 107, 111
Gagnon, Robert, 147n27, 154n129, 390n106
Gaillardetz, Richard, 17, 48, 50-51, 54-56, 175, 207n90, 281
Giddens, Anthony, 363-64, 389n82
Giussani, Luigi, 218-19
Goldstein, Dawn Eden, 151n74, 210n118
Gradualness of the Law, 125, 151n73, 151n75, 189-91
Grace and sin, 166-67
Griffiths, Paul, 306, 331, 333n26, 334n44, 337n74
Grisez, Germain, 53, 113, 147n23, 152n96, 239n10, 329, 340n152
Grillmeier, Aloys, 199, 208n71
Guardini, Romano, 81, 155, 202n3
Guarino, Thomas G., 11n10, 62n39, 66n136, 204n32, 265, 268, 272, 330-31
Guinness, Os, 179, 209n106
Gutiérrrez, Gustavo, 45, 65n116
Helm, Paul, 10, 27, 36n120, 340n150
Heinbeck, S. Raeburne, 65n101
Henn, William, 260-61, 291n73
Hermeneutics of continuity and reform, 17-21
Hierarchy of truths, 224-28, 230-32, 280-87
Horton, Michael, 73, 104n26, 105n52, 153n110
Ideology, 21-22, 45
of gender, 157
of Gnostic solution, 31-32
of Pelagianism, 73, 80
of psychologizing, 80-81, 241n47
Ignorance, Vincible/Invincible, 187-88
Inclusion, 97-102
Integral Hermeneutics, 228-30, 237-38
ITC, *Sensus Fidei in the Life of the Church*, 12n28, 12n29
John XXIII, Pope, 3, 25, 48, 50, 54, 62n35, 69, 103n6
John Paul II, St. Pope, 33, 39, 41, 46-48, 53-54, 56, 84-88, 90-93, 109, 113, 116, 118-19, 132-35, 145, 150n58, 151n75, 167-73, 179-80, 186, 191, 196-97, 232, 299
Kasper, Walter Cardinal, 70-71, 78, 82-83, 103n7, 103n12, 109, 198, 211n126, 215n170, 246, 249, 252-55, 257-61, 263, 265-69, 270-72, 278, 295n127, 301-2
Keating, Daniel, 274-75
Knieps-Port Le Roi, Thomas, 66n119, 210n117
Komonchak, Joseph, 81-82
Kukjovsky, Branislav, 212n145
Kuyper, Abraham, 262-65
Lane, Anthony, 81, 96n69

Laras, Giuseppe, 73
Law of Evangelization, 18-19, 23, 31, 45, 49
Law of gradualness, 125, 151n73, 151n75, 176-78, 189-91
Lawler, E., Philip, 146n8, 150n60
Leo XIII, 30n24
Legalism, 110-12, 119, 132
Levering, Matthew, 64n93, 389n99
Local-option Catholicism, 352-54, 362
  See also synodality, 354
Lonergan, Bernard,
  on meaning and truth, 37, 53-54, 347
  on pastoral, 48
Magister, Sandro, 240n42
Maloney, Daniel, 72, 103n18, 103n21
Marchetto, Agostino, 19-20
Maradiaga, Cardinal, 103n11
Maritain, Jacques, 109, 137, 153n112, 202n28
Martin, SJ, James, 388n69
Marx, Reinhard, Cardinal, 241n53, 354, 358, 387n40
McDermott, Gerald R., 333n13
Moralistic Therapeutic Deism, 80-83
Moral Absolutes, 123, 149n49, 149n50
Moral Ideals, 125, 151n74, 152n76
Moral Law, 110-13, 114-15, 138
Mortalium Animos, 170-72
Mühlen, Herbert, 285
Müller, Gerhard Cardinal, 36, 38-39, 152n81, 183, 206n82, 209n108, 211n120, 349, 355
Murray, John, 86
Mysterium Ecclesiae, 231, 256, 285
Nashville Statement, 202n11
Nature and grace, 160-66
Neff, LaVonne, 242n71
Neo-modernist, 26-27, 61n28, 67n151, 349, 351-52
  See also: doctrine, of pastorality
Neo-traditionalist, 349-50, 352
Netland, Harold, 65n99, 332n4, 33n13
Neutrality, 89
Neuhaus, Richard John, 99, 107n111
Newbigin, Lesslie, 264, 291n74
Newman, John Henry, 192-93
Nichols, OP, Aidan, 26, 56, 61n2558, 153n98
Niebuhr, H. Richard, 69, 87, 105n49, 381
Niebuhr, Reinhold, 218
Nietzsche, Friedrich, 219, 222
NOIA, 319, 321, 326-32, 334n37
Nostra Aetate, 310-12, 314
Nouvelle Théologie, 26-28, 351-52
Objective/Subjective Morality, 182-85
O'Brien, John, 50-51, 55
O'Collins, Gerald, 311-12, 332n4, 334n44, 336n57
O'Malley, John, 14-16, 28, 34
Ontological/Epistemological Complementarity, 303-6
Pannenberg, Wolfhart, 327-32
Paul VI, Pope, 218, 300
Pelikan, Jaroslav, 65n96, 346, 351, 386n19, 387n34
Pié-Ninot, Salvador, 383, 391n139
Piper, John, 95
Pius XI, Pope, 284
Pius XII, 213n149
Prima facie obligations, 123, 149n49
Pronk, Pim, 147n30
Propositional truth, 34-36, 43-44, 54
Proselytism, 272-73
Prudence, 381-82
Radner, Ephraim, 359-60, 388n63
Rahner, Karl, 52, 187, 263, 282, 330
Ratzinger, Joseph/Benedict XVI, Pope, 11n13, 19, 20-21, 27-28, 36-37, 51, 60n16, 70, 73-74, 82, 83, 86, 95, 98, 102n5, 104n28, 104n30, 119, 144, 299, 129-32, 152n82, 203n17, 205n60, 215n167315-321, 217, 219-23, 239n8, 239n28, 246, 247, 254-56, 299, 307-8, 314-16, 389n100
Realism, 54-58, 121, 346, 357
Receptive ecumenism, 1, 247, 251, 257, 268
Relativism, 97-101, 302-3
Relativism/absolutism, 301-3, 306, 321-26
Religious pluralism, 309-10, 313, 335n47, 335n49
Reno, R.R., 226, 240n35, 360-61, 388n72
Ressourcement/Aggiornamento, 343-46
Revelation, 57-58
Ribadeau-Dumas, Olivier, 354
Ridderbos, Herman, 75, 104n31, 113, 147n22, 311-12, 336n57, 336n60
Roberts, Christopher, 389n86
Rosica, Thomas, 10n1
Royal, Robert, ix-xi
Sacramental union, 173-74
Satisfaction, Justice, 76-77
Schillebeeckx, OP, Edward, 27, 62n36, 303, 321-26, 327, 334n32
Schnackenberg, Rudolph, 311
Seifert, Josef, 188-89, 191, 202n8, 208n98, 212n144, 213n152, 309
Sensus fidei, 344, 355, 356, 376, 378, 381-382-83
Sensus fidei fidelium, 343-44, 355, 356, 377, 379-80, 383-84
Sexual Ethics, 352, 362-69, 389n90
Skorka, Abraham, Rabbi, 24
Sirilla, Michael, 11n14, 11n17, 12n27
Smedes, Lewis, 115, 147n26, 147n32, 152n89
Smith, Christian, 105n54
Smith, Janet, v-vii,
Spadaro, SJ, Antonio, 149n49, 184, 211n123

Spaemann, Robert, 341
Spicq, Ceslaus, 238, 243n78
Stott, John, 76, 104n35, 104n40
Stout, Jeffrey, 43
Synodality, 8, 354, 356, 383, 387n43, n44
  See also local-option Catholicism, 352-53
Subsistit in, 270-72, 295n132
Sullivan, Francis, 8, 31n26, 179n82
Taylor, Charles, 81, 105n65
Theobald, SJ, Christoph, 11n11, 17, 49-50, 54, 61n35
Theological Notes, 7-9, 241n59
Theologico-Pastoral Epistemology, 44-46
Tracy, David, 51
Trueman, Carl, 355
Truth, 40-44, 51-52, 54-56, 58-59, 178-80, 299-332
Truth idolatry, 178-79
Truth and Mercy, 125-27, 180-82
Turner, Philip. 78-80
Unitatis Redintegratio, 249, 255, 271, 274-75
Ureta, José Antonio, 61n25, 61n27
Ut Unum Sint, 63n62, 249-51, 257
Vandervelde, George, 286-87, 297n165
Vanhoozer, Kevin, 70, 103n9, 296n153, 343
Van Hoye, Albert, 135, 153n103
Vatican I, 3, 25
Vatican II,
  interpretations of, 17, 21-26, 56
  on ecumenism, 246-87
Vincent of Lérins, 3, 25, 28-32
Viganò, Carlo, Mario, 341-43
Walford, Stephen, 11n15, 11n16, 62n37, 146n11, 149n49, 149n51, 202n16, 207n97, 210n113, 211n122, 215n166
Weigel, Gustav, 246, 362
Weinandy, Thomas, 12n34, 338n106
Wicks, Jared, 140-41, 153n122
Witherington, Ben III, 311
Wolters, Albert, 204n33
Wojtyla, Karel, 361, 362-69
Woodward, Kenneth, 342, 385
Wrath of God, 84-88
Yeago, David, 138, 153n115

Also by Eduardo Echeverria...

In Oceans Deep
Redemptive Suffering and the Crucified God

After the sudden death of his granddaughter, theologian Eduardo Echeverria explains why our suffering and death find their meaning when united to Christ. His faithful reasoning displays profound paths for healing broken hearts.

ISBN: 978-1-943901-07-4
Facebook@inOceansDeepBook

CPSIA information can be obtained
at www.ICGtesting.com
Printed in the USA
BVHW040529130320
574961BV00003B/49

9 781943 901111